THEM
DARK
DAYS

THEM
DARK
DAYS

*Slavery in the American
Rice Swamps*

William Dusinberre

New York   Oxford
OXFORD UNIVERSITY PRESS
1996

Oxford University Press

Oxford   New York
Athens   Auckland   Bangkok   Bombay
Calcutta   Cape Town   Dar es Salaam   Delhi
Florence   Hong Kong   Istanbul   Karachi
Kuala Lumpur   Madras   Madrid   Melbourne
Mexico City   Nairobi   Paris   Singapore
Taipei   Tokyo   Toronto

and associated companies in
Berlin   Ibadan

Copyright © 1996 by William Dusinberre

Published by Oxford University Press, Inc.
198 Madison Avenue, New York, New York 10016

Oxford is a registered trademark of Oxford University Press

Library of Congress Cataloging-in-Publication Data
Dusinberre, William, 1930–
Them dark days : slavery in the American rice swamps /
William Dusinberre.
p.   cm.
Includes bibliographical references (p.) and index.
ISBN 0-19-509021-7
1. Slavery—South Carolina—History—19th century.
2. Rice—South Carolina—History—19th century.
3. Plantation life—South Carolina—History—19th century.
4. South Carolina—History—1775–1865.
E445.S7D87   1996   306.3′62′09757—dc20   94-38350

For permission to quote from the following sources, the author and publisher extend their gratitude:

Malcolm Bell Jr., *Major Butler's Legacy* (Athens: University of Georgia Press, 1987), © 1987 University of Georgia Press.

James Clifton, ed., *Life and Labor on Argyle Island: Letters and Documents of a Savannah River Rice Plantation, 1833–1867* (Charlottesville: University Press of Virginia [for the Beehive Press], 1978), used by permission of the University Press of Virginia.

J. H. Easterby, ed., *The South Carolina Rice Plantation, as Revealed in the Papers of Robert F. W. Allston* (Chicago: University of Chicago Press, 1945), © 1945 by The University of Chicago.

Frances Anne Kemble, *Journal of a Residence on a Georgian Plantation* (1863; rpt. [ed. John A. Scott] New York, 1961), copyright © 1961 by Alfred A. Knopf, Inc.; quoted by permission of the publisher.

Elizabeth W. Allston Pringle, *Chronicles of "Chicora Wood"* (1922; rpt. Atlanta, Ga., 1976), quoted by permission of Dr. Richard I. Lowndes III.

9 8 7 6 5 4 3 2 1

Printed in the United States of America
on acid-free paper

To Juliet

Preface

Uncle Tom's Cabin and *Roots* are the most famous books about American slavery. Their popularity derives from diverse sources, for the theme of human slavery is a profound one, inspiring anger, revulsion, shame, compassion, and awe. The authors of these two books skillfully presented images of slavery congenial to millions of readers—or television viewers—in their respective eras. Harriet Beecher Stowe and Alex Haley, though inexpert as social historians, were each accomplished writers. Above all else, they managed to convey the experience of slavery through the lives of individual people.

The most influential histories of American slavery have shared all but one of these characteristics. Ulrich Phillips's *American Negro Slavery,* Kenneth Stampp's *Peculiar Institution,* and Eugene Genovese's *Roll, Jordan, Roll* all attempted—like *Uncle Tom's Cabin* and *Roots*—a comprehensive treatment of this great theme. Each spoke to its time. Phillips, writing in 1918 for a white audience both racist and reluctant to criticize the Southern gentry, claimed that slavery had helped to civilize "savage" Africans. Stampp's condemnation of slavery in 1956 coincided with the birth of the civil rights movement. Genovese's celebration in 1974 of the blacks' cultural resistance to slavery was an apt response to the black nationalist currents of that era. All three historians were, in their own ways, expert craftsmen, with Phillips bringing into the twentieth century the literary skills of a Victorian gentleman, Stampp writing with the suppressed passion of a liberal scholar, and Genovese shaping a brilliantly original view of his subject.

What each of these historians avoided was the temptation to individualize slavery. No characters stood forth from their books, as did Uncle Tom, Aunt Chloe, Augustine St. Clare, Kunta Kinte, Kizzy, and a host of others in *Uncle Tom's Cabin* and *Roots*. Ulrich Phillips came closest, for in his *Life and Labor in the Old South* (the sequel to *American Negro Slavery*) he dwelt—on one occasion for as long as a dozen pages—upon individual plantations. But he individualized planters and their regimes, not slaves; and, as I hope to indicate in the following pages, his prejudices almost wholly robbed him of insight into life on plantations like those of Charles Manigault and Pierce Butler.

One might question whether any work of nonfiction except a biography should try to portray—as novelists have always done—individual lives. No doubt the writer of fiction has an immense advantage over the historian, for every sort of invention is permitted the novelist within the limits of a loosely defined literary plausibility. Historians, by contrast, are tied to the factual record. When they exercise their imaginations to draw inferences, they must alert readers to the distinction between fact and interpretation. Yet this duty need not deter a historian from seeking to plumb individual lives so far as the evidence permits. The sources on nineteenth-century U.S. slavery are wonderfully rich—far more so than for any other country or epoch—and they permit us to gain a closer view of individual lives than is commonly known.

In undertaking a three-volume work on American slavery, I seek to capture the experiences of individual people—slaves, masters, observers—as far as the record allows. Firmly rooted in fact, the result may nevertheless have something of the effect of a nineteenth-century novel, for a general picture of slavery will emerge only from particular cases. I hope some individuals—like carpenter Jack Savage, his master Charles Manigault, and (on another plantation) the observer Frances Kemble—will become sufficiently distinct that a reader will apprehend slavery as they experienced it. Full acquaintance with people like these, and the plantations they knew, may make real what is for many of us only an abstract concept.

My central theme is evident from the title of this book. Those black people, born slaves, who later referred to the era of slavery as "them dark days" spoke truly. Slavery was even more horrific, I believe, than is generally acknowledged. The blacks were not "passive victims" of this institution because their responses were anything but passive; but their resistance was—and could not fail to be—only partially successful. Passive they were not, but injured parties they remained, as deeply marked by their experiences as were their masters, albeit in different ways.

If the later history of American blacks has diverged substantially from that of immigrant groups who came to the United States in the nineteenth and twentieth centuries, one explanation is self-evident. No other immigrant group was forcibly deported and subjected to hundreds of years of slavery, and to the vicious caste system which sprang up in the post–Civil War South as a natural consequence of slavery. Slavery was for many of the subjugated such a searing experience that generations would be required to efface its results. This, of course, does not imply that black people are culturally deprived: the lives of millions of black Americans prove the contrary. But it does imply that slavery has continued to shape twentieth-century life in the United States far more profoundly than most whites, and most blacks, wish to acknowledge.

When embarking on this project I had no idea it would grow beyond a single volume, but publication in installments now seems advisable because the record is so full. Richest of all are the sources on the rice plantations clustered in "low-country" South Carolina and Georgia, and the present volume is focused solely on them. The rice kingdom carried a weight in American history seldom suspected outside those two states. Here were concentrated many of the richest planters in the United States. Their perceived interests substantially shaped the policy of South Carolina. Although that state's premier role in the defense of slavery has always been clear, the central significance of rice to its political elite may have been obscured by the cotton boom which roared through the rest of the Deep South during the nineteenth century. As late as 1860, twelve of the perhaps seventeen largest slave masters in the United States were rice planters; and three-fifths of the families holding the most South Carolina slaves—twenty-one out of the thirty-five families which each held at least five hundred Carolina bondspeople—planted rice rather than cotton.

Slavery bore distinctive marks within the rice kingdom. Plantations there were larger than usual in the South, resembling Caribbean estates, and the region was peculiarly unhealthy for both blacks and (for somewhat different reasons) whites. The "task system" of the rice kingdom diverged from the "gang" labor experienced by most American slaves. The scarcity of white men willing to oversee rice plantations forced the planters to delegate unusually heavy managerial duties to enslaved "drivers." For all these reasons the rice kingdom needs to be examined separately from the cotton belt or the border states.

Yet, despite regional variations, slavery everywhere in the South had a common nature. The rice kingdom was an elder brother to the cotton kingdom, bearing a close family resemblance to its more famous kinsman; and what one finds in the character of the one illumines the other. The wealth of evidence on rice plantations and the political weight of the low country make the coastal swampland the best place to begin an investigation of slavery.

Unlike many books about the bondage of African-Americans, this one devotes substantial attention to white people: for slavery involved both blacks and whites, and cannot be understood unless both are considered. And this book contains—in addition to social history—a bit of political and even a snatch of economic history, because in the low country these different strands were so closely intertwined that none could be seen clearly without the others.

I hope no reader will be put off by the occasional appearance of numbers in the text. These are principally confined to a few pages of chapters 1, 3, 8, and 15, and can readily be skipped by anyone to whom figures are anathema. This book, based almost entirely on "literary" sources, is, I trust, nearly always easy to read, and I have resolutely relegated most numerical matter to appendixes (where specialists can check my estimates). But the Manigault and Butler records offer remarkable opportunities for exact statements about child mortality, while the manuscript census allows a clear definition of the place of rice grandees in South Carolina society; I hope readers will therefore permit me very occasionally to introduce a number into a work which principally aims to show the faces of individual human beings.

Specialists may ask three questions about this volume: Has it used enough black sources? Has it sufficiently emphasized the slaves' cultural resistance? Is the tone appropriate?

The best-known black sources on the low country are the interviews conducted by a white South Carolinian woman, Genevieve Chandler, in 1937–38; chapter 16 is based entirely upon them. But another black source is also available—the words of slaves reported in Frances Kemble's *Journal of a Residence on a Georgian Plantation*. In both records the testimony of blacks is reported by a white woman and must be taken with caution. Even a woman so sympathetic to the slaves as Kemble could not wholly win their confidence, as she herself often acknowledged. Yet they spoke to her from immediate experience, not through the mists which during the Great Depression divided the battered eighty-eight-year-old survivors from the remote days of their enslaved youth. To my ear the voices speaking to Kemble in 1839 sound—on some topics—even more authentic than those speaking to Genevieve Chandler nearly a century later. Thus, in devoting one whole section of the book to Kemble's record, I have sought to listen carefully to the testimony of black witnesses. Black sources on the cotton kingdom and on the border states are more abundant than on the rice kingdom, and in my second and third volumes I shall consider much more fully than has been possible here the words of African-Americans who were slaves.

Cultural resistance by rice workers against slavery has been admirably portrayed in Charles Joyner's *Down by the Riverside*. And Margaret Creel's book *"A Peculiar People"* sets forth a pioneering view of religion among the sea-island cotton slaves, which surely resembled closely that on the rice plantations. I do not seek here to dispute either Joyner's splendid assessment of the low-country slaves' religion, language and folk culture, nor Creel's valuable further discussion of low-country religion. I do aim, however, to complement Joyner's and Creel's work: to set their analyses of the slaves' culture within a wider context of health, discipline, privilege, and psychology, which I believe are not fully treated in their otherwise excellent books. If in so doing I have seemed to neglect cultural resistance, it is only because I take many of Joyner's and Creel's central theses as read; there is no need to repeat them here.

I hope the tone of my work avoids the triple perils of racialist bias, or liberal philanthropy, or indiscriminate praise. The last of these may perhaps be hardest to avoid, and my model in these matters has been Leslie Howard Owens's *This Species of Property*. In this exemplary study of American slavery, Owens, a black historian, has eschewed flattery of his own people. It may be harder for a white writer to get the tone right when discussing matters of immense emotional significance to both blacks and whites. If I have failed, I will not be the first or last writer to do so, and I can only say that I have tried to capture an appropriate tone.

The Civil War has gripped the American imagination as has no other event in its history. This is no accident, for the destruction of slavery (and the faltering subsequent effort to lay in its stead the foundations of an egalitarian society) was the most traumatic upheaval the country has witnessed. A social revolution, incomplete though it was, took place. It had to take place; for slavery was deeply rooted in American soil, and its effects upon slaves and masters were incalculable. To convey some sense of this alien way of life—which in its long-term consequences has shaped our world more than we would wish—is the object of this book.

The words of my title are those of Ben Horry, a freedman speaking to Genevieve Chandler in 1938. These three words were repeatedly used at that time by freedmen and women to epitomize their view of slavery. My spirit in telling the tale has been affected by that of Nathaniel Heyward's slaves. (Heyward, master of over two thousand bondsmen and women, was the greatest rice planter America has ever seen: his career is sketched in a few pages of chapter 2.) Heyward's admiration of Dutch methods of dike building and drainage had led him to name two of his rice plantations "Amsterdam" and "Rotterdam." His slaves, however, persisted in calling these two planta-tions "De Swamp" and "De Lower Swamp." This down-to-earth attitude accounts for my subtitle and hopefully informs the pages which follow.

Many people and institutions have contributed to this book. Foremost is James Clifton, whose edition of the Manigault papers was indispensable in demonstrating the richness of that source. J. H. Easterby's edition of the Allston papers, John Scott's edition of Frances Kemble's *Journal,* George Rogers's *History of Georgetown County,* and Malcolm Bell Jr.'s *Major But-ler's Legacy* have all proved immensely valuable. The patient, careful work which goes into books like these does not always receive full recognition, and I am delighted to record here my deep obligation to each of these scholars.

Eugene Genovese's originality, erudition, and humane spirit mark the great historian; and although my view of slavery differs from his at important points, his writings are constantly in my consciousness and have shaped no small number of my conclusions. I have often been persuaded by Orlando Patterson's formulations, and have attempted here to develop further his view of the constituent elements of slavery. The extent of my debt to Kenneth Stampp's pathbreaking work—perhaps the most important general study of the conditions to which American slaves were subjected—will be equally clear to every specialist.

My obligation to Charles Joyner is both professional and personal. His *Down by the Riverside* has deservedly been the most influential local history of American slavery ever published, and my work aims to pursue in a slightly different direction the path he has so fruitfully opened. His generosity was immense when I first did research in Carolina, and his magnanimity since then has meant more to me than I can say.

The following research libraries offered splendid working environments: the Southern Historical Collection at the University of North Carolina; the Perkins Library at Duke; the South Carolinian Library at the University of South Carolina; the South Carolina Historical Society, the Charleston Mu-seum, the Charleston Public Library, and the College of Charleston Library, all in Charleston; the Georgia Historical Society; the South Carolina Depart-ment of Archives and History; and my old friend, the Historical Society of

Pennsylvania. The individuals who helped me there were many, and I hope it will not seem invidious if I thank in particular Cam Alexander, Allen Stokes, Wylma Wates, John E. White, William Erwin Jr., and Tracy Bearden. The University of Cambridge and the University of Warwick libraries have year after year supplied indispensable support. Malcolm Bell Jr.'s generosity made possible the excellent organization of the Butler Papers at the Historical Society of Pennsylvania, for which every subsequent researcher will be greatly in his debt, as I am. I am very grateful to Ian Agnew, cartographer of the University of Cambridge's Department of Geography, for his expert drawing of my map.

The University of Warwick has contributed tremendously to this work. It has fully honored its early commitment to match the best study-leave policy in Britain, and its Research and Innovations Committee has munificently granted funding for research trips. Its history department has pioneered a kind of social history whose imprint will be visible, I hope, on each of the following pages. A more estimable, congenial, and generous-spirited group of colleagues could scarcely be imagined. And first-rate students there have contributed greatly to my thinking about American slavery. The British Academy has also most generously supported my research.

Among personal obligations, some of my greatest are to Professors Gwynne Lewis and Bernard Capp, Dr. Betty Wood, Dr. John Thompson, Dr. Joan Lane, and Dr. Maxine Berg; Dr. John Hammond Moore of Columbia, S.C.; Mr. Wesley Law of Savannah; Ann D. Harper and Mrs. J. S. Anderson of Charleston; Captain Sandy Vermont, Mr. Jamie W. Constance, and Mr. William Avant of Georgetown, S.C.; Professors Edward Countryman and Robert Bannister; Dr. Richard I. Lowndes III; Professors W. R. Brock and Peter Parish; and Mr. and Mrs. Robert Millar Craig. Each of these people has put herself or himself to immense trouble for my sake, and I am most grateful to them for their extraordinary kindness. Support from members of the University of Cambridge American History seminar has also meant a great deal to me over the years.

Oxford University Press has been wonderfully kind and helpful, and I wish to express my warmest thanks, especially to Sheldon Meyer, Karen Wolny, Andrew Albanese, Henry Krawitz, Joellyn Ausanka, and Susan Ecklund.

Two historians of very different bent, David Donald and Edward Thompson, have deeply marked my approach to the Carolina and Georgia low country. I would be very happy if the former should find that he has imparted at least something of his own rigorous standards to the following pages. And I greatly regret not having been able to show the work to Edward Thompson before his sad, untimely death.

Juliet Dusinberre has made my life rich beyond measure, and I hope a smidgen of her own bright spirit may have infused itself here.

University of Warwick W.D.
July 1995

Contents

IV   THE WIDER SCENE

I

GOWRIE:
A MANIGAULT
ESTATE

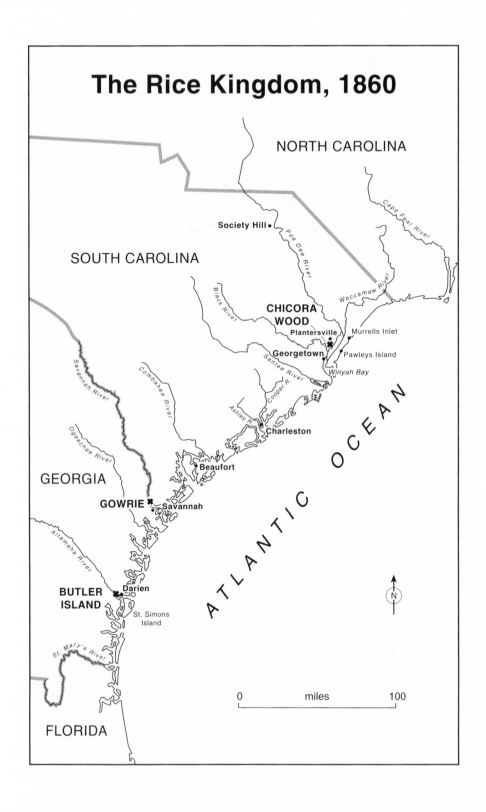

The Rice Kingdom, 1860

NORTH CAROLINA

SOUTH CAROLINA

GEORGIA

FLORIDA

ATLANTIC OCEAN

Cape Fear River

Society Hill •

Pee Dee River

Waccamaw River

CHICORA WOOD

Plantersville

Murrells Inlet

Georgetown

Pawleys Island

Winyah Bay

Black River

Santee River

Cooper R.

Ashley R.

Charleston

Savannah River

Combahee River

Ogeechee River

• Beaufort

GOWRIE ✕

• Savannah

Altamaha River

BUTLER ISLAND

• Darien

St. Simons Island

St. Mary's River

N

0   miles   100

1

Gentleman Capitalists

Perhaps nowhere in the world can individual slaves and their masters be better seen than at "Gowrie," a Georgia rice plantation eight miles upstream from Savannah. There—on an estate situated like a girdle across the waist of long, thin Argyle Island—Charles Manigault and his son Louis deployed about one hundred slaves in order to make themselves richer than Charles's older South Carolina plantation alone would have ensured. The characters of their slaves were diverse, and fear and the desire to get on with the holders of power led them to dissemble. The glimpse of a slave's countenance at Gowrie is therefore often enigmatic, as well as tantalizingly brief; yet dozens of individual faces are visible. Across the muddy waters of a century and a half, an event in the slaves' lives can sometimes be seen as clearly as—on December 24, 1864—Confederate soldiers retreating before General Sherman's army could view (across the turbid currents of "Savannah Back River") the flames consuming the wooden structure of Louis Manigault's beloved rice-pounding mill.

Prior to this denouement Charles Manigault—prosperous and methodical—had accumulated a treasure-house of historical records. He saved letters from his overseers, put his own ideas on paper, kept annual lists of his slaves, and taught his child Louis to do the same. The records are immensely rich, and anyone can read them, for many are published and easily accessible.[1] These sources also illuminate the lives of the masters, Charles and Louis Manigault, whose ideas and practices profoundly influenced their bondsmen and women. The regime the Manigaults sought to impose upon their slaves was an easily misunderstood, drastically altered variant of the system of great landed estates that had dominated England for centuries.

Born in 1795 during George Washington's presidency, Charles Manigault lived until well after the Civil War. In the 1850s, when his plantation records are most complete, he owned some 200 slaves, about the same number as Thomas Jefferson had possessed and not many fewer than George Washington himself. About 100 of Charles's slaves were at Gowrie, the rest at an older plantation in South Carolina and at a farm near Charleston. The Manigaults were leaders of society in that town. Charles's great-grandfather, Gabriel Manigault I, had been the richest colonial Charleston merchant and the owner of 491 slaves and nearly fifty thousand acres of land, including several valuable plantations.[2] Charles's grandfather, Peter Manigault, after being educated as a barrister in London, had three times been the Speaker of South Carolina's colonial assembly. Charles's father, Gabriel Manigault II, met his future wife (the daughter of a Carolinian Izard and a New York DeLancey) in Brussels; after they had lived some years in Charleston, they established a Northern residence near Philadelphia.

Charles Manigault, even more than his grandfather, Peter, and father, Gabriel II, was cosmopolitan: he spent nearly fourteen years abroad, and even when the family were in Charleston they customarily spoke French. Charles liked to boast that their slave butler had picked up an understanding of that language from listening to their dinner-table talk. Charles's family pride was evident in a letter he wrote from Charleston in 1857, urging his son Louis to make good use of the long evenings at Gowrie with Louis's new bride, the daughter of a Savannah doctor. She had been raised in Georgia; and although Charles himself did not bother with correct spelling, he seemed to feel that Georgia girls lived in outer darkness: "What a fine chance you have now (when all alone in the long evenings)," he exclaimed four weeks after Louis's wedding, "of giving your wife some lessons in French. It will be awkward if she dont understand our family Colloquial language. Whereas if she has a little iniciation from you, it will enable her to pick up a good deal from our Conversation."[3]

In 1790 Gabriel Manigault II (Charles's father) had owned nearly 200 slaves at a plantation named "Silk Hope," on the headwaters of the Cooper River forty miles inland from Charleston; but when he moved North in 1805, he sold it to his sister's husband, Nathaniel Heyward. This was early in Heyward's career as the largest slave master ever seen in the United States:[4] at Heyward's death he had acquired 2,340 slaves, seventeen rice plantations, and a couple of other plantations as well. Charles Manigault married one of Heyward's daughters (who was thus Charles's first cousin) when she was sixteen, and in 1827 Heyward gave them Silk Hope and 126 slaves as a present. This was a timely gift, for Charles—as a merchant in the East Indies between 1817 and 1823—had lost part of his own inheritance; and Silk Hope enabled him to restore his finances. The old plantation was not, however, hugely profitable, and after a few years Charles decided (against his father-in-law's strenuous opposition) to sell his stock in the Bank of the United States; and with that nearly fifteen thousand dollars, plus another five thousand dollars of ready cash, and by borrowing another twenty thousand dollars, he bought a newer Savannah River plantation and its 50 slaves. This was Gowrie. To work its 265 acres of rich rice lands[5] Charles immediately transferred 22 of the "primest" Silk Hope slaves; he soon moved many others as well.

Occasionally he took one of his children to Gowrie in winter—Louis had happy youthful memories of visits there when he was eleven and again when sixteen—but habitually Charles resided in Charleston from May until November each year; and from 1852 he spent most of the winter at neither Silk Hope nor Gowrie but at "Marshlands," a farm with a lovely mansion only seven miles from Charleston, also given him by Nathaniel Heyward. From here it was possible to get to Charleston for church or a dinner or an evening's entertainment and to return the same day. Journeys farther afield varied the family's routine; thus, in May 1846 they went abroad—partly to put Charles's fourteen-year-old daughter into a finishing school in Paris—and the family did not return from Europe until the autumn of 1848. By then Gowrie was paying well and Charles, burned by his early failures as a merchant, urged—with the zeal of a proselyte—the planter's life on young Carolinian gentlemen seeking to improve their fortunes.

So well satisfied with Gowrie was he that in December 1848 he nearly doubled his holding by the purchase of an adjacent plantation, which included an impressive three-story, all-brick, steam-powered thresher, the most resplendent on the Savannah River. He also bought fifty-two more slaves and moved another half dozen from Silk Hope to work the new land. He purchased another adjacent plantation in January 1854, bringing the total size of the enlarged Gowrie to exactly one square mile of rich rice lands.[6] He was thinking not only of his own finances but of establishing his sons—by now he had four of them and two daughters—and he soon made one of them (Louis) manager of Gowrie. He did not make King Lear's mistake of giving away his lands: Gowrie remained firmly in Charles's possession; but after Louis's marriage the young man received a quarter of the revenues for his managerial services, with the prospect of ownership when and if Charles ever died.

To manage a rice plantation was a highly skilled, risky undertaking. Like Charles, the son Louis only came to this work after two years of college, the completion of his education in a counting house, and a period of engaging in mercantile ventures. These took him to China in 1850 and to South America the next year, and by the time he settled down at Gowrie the two men's correspondence had a sophisticated air. "Mon Cher Louis," Charles usually addressed his son, while Louis loved to spice his own letters with a dash of Chinese pidgin English or of Chilean Spanish. Louis was insouciant; he looked on the brighter side of things, liked to spare his father's feelings, and thought of himself as comparable to a British aristocrat. The day after Christmas 1854, he wrote from Savannah (where he had come to survey the ruins left by what they supposed was a cholera epidemic),

> As Lord Raglan would say to the Duke of Newcastle, so Can I to You, viz.: that "it is now my painful duty to return You a list of the dead," and here they are in the order in which they died. —

Hester, Flora, Cain, George, Sam, Eve, Cuffy, Will, Amos, Ellen,
Rebecca,—Eleven from Cholera, and two Children viz.: Francis and Jane
not from Cholera.—In all Thirteen
names no longer on the Plantation Books.
    I have just returned from the ["cholera"] Camps. We are all well there
and every thing going on first rate. . . .[7]

Running a rice plantation sometimes did indeed resemble the conduct of a
deathly military operation. At other moments—as when floodwaters poured
down the Savannah River from Augusta, Georgia—the resemblance was nautical: all hatches were battened before the coming typhoon.[8] Annually the
parallel was purely mercantile, with the entrepreneur hastening his produce to
the Charleston market before the price should fall. Perennially the resemblance was industrial, for a large workforce was driven or cajoled each day
into labors that did not come spontaneously. Farmers' lore about weather and
soil was, of course, ubiquitous in the slave South, but on a rice plantation
calculations were complicated by the high tides at full moon and new moon
which facilitated—and the irregular winds which hindered—tidal irrigation.
Rice plantations had much in common with cotton, tobacco, and sugar plantations, but they were also sui generis.

There were marked economies of scale, and this was why the majority of
the South's truly rich antebellum slave masters derived their fortunes from
rice—not from cotton, tobacco, or sugar.[9] Rice culture in the Carolina and
Georgia low country, dead though it now is, once shaped the course of American history; for the rice planters set the tone of South Carolina society, and in
1860 South Carolina set in motion the spectacular suicide of the slave system.
Profits—gained or anticipated—from growing rice with slave labor contributed largely to this result. For a man like Charles Manigault the profits were
in no simple sense parasitic: like many another capitalistic entrepreneur,
Manigault risked large sums of money, and he might easily have lost his
investment—as he had done in his earlier mercantile ventures—if he had not
learned through hard experience a great deal about the business of making a
rice crop. No doubt the labor system was different from that of the North; the
ethos differed too, though not so much as one might suppose; and agriculture
inevitably differed from industry or commerce; yet Manigault's entrepreneurial activities at Gowrie resembled in complexity and uncertainty the most
advanced operations of a Northern capitalist.

That the parallel between planter capitalism and free-labor capitalism was
not always obvious was because no economist—not even Adam Smith or Karl
Marx—convincingly thought through the subject of slavery. The classical (and
sleep-inducing) division into three factors of production, "land," "labor," and
"capital," was wholly inappropriate for analyzing rice plantations. Potential
rice-growing "land"—a primordial swamp—was almost valueless until the
land was improved. Embankments must be thrown up to keep out the river;
great canals and ditches must be dug to move the water about for irrigation;
and the huge trees and luxuriant vines must be cleared, which for ages past

had made the swamp like a jungle. This massive capital investment in improving the value of the land did not fit the classical model of investing "capital" in machinery; instead, it took the form of investing (other people's) labor in moving quantities of mud from one place to another.[10] And if "land" was not an immutable factor of production, neither was "labor"—for the beauty of slavery from the investor's point of view was that it increased the supply of workers. Africans, who did not die quite as fast from malaria as Europeans did,[11] could be put to moving mud in the malarial swamps; and people who would not voluntarily have spent years moving mud (for every winter the embankments had to be repaired, and the canals and ditches cleared) could be forced to do so. Thus the two principal forms of capital investment by the rice planter were not in "capital," classically considered, but in (improved) "land" and (enslaved) "labor." That Charles Manigault also invested in "capital" in its narrow sense—in his excellent steam thresher and his beautiful tidal rice-pounding mill—merely completed his resemblance to a large-scale capitalist operator; but the capital he poured into slave labor, and into its capitalized forms—embankments, canals, and ditches ("land," in the economists' misleading terminology)—was the central element in his capitalist enterprise.

When late in the seventeenth century rice had been introduced to South Carolina, it was grown on dry land—and soon thereafter on inland swampland. Planters gradually discovered that (so long as slavery existed) they could do better by harnessing the ocean tides to their purposes. Salt water would kill the rice, but every large low-country river had a patch of about twenty miles where its water was not yet saline, yet where its level rose and fell several feet with each ocean tide. This water could be used to inundate a rice field at high tide, and several days or weeks later the water could be drained out at low tide. The fields were flooded three, four, or even five times a year—sometimes for only a few days, on other occasions for weeks at a stretch. These inundations and drainings served multiple purposes: they protected the newly planted seed rice from birds and from being scorched by the sun; and the floodings killed some weeds which flourished in hot, dry weather, while the drainings killed other weeds which had grown in the inundated fields. Thus they reduced the number of summer hoeings required to keep the weeds down and also furnished a dependable source of water so that the possibility of drought held few terrors during the summer months.

Against these advantages had to be set marked disadvantages. The embankments and ditches required repair in the wintertime, which meant for the slaves much more cold, wet, hard, unhealthy winter labor than was needed on cotton plantations. Estates like Gowrie, situated on the wonderfully fertile river islands, were periodically subject to "freshets" when a river flood might overflow the embankments, and almost everything would be underwater. At least ten times between 1833 and 1864 the whole plantation was flooded by freshets, hurricanes, or a freak combination of unusually high tides with a "northeaster" storm. And any number of other emergencies arose when breaks in the dikes must be hastily repaired, and when freshets or high tides (like those of September 1850 and August 1851) were only narrowly prevented from overflowing the embankments. The eleven-day flood which started on March 24, 1850, inundated the plantation "to the depth of 5 feet over the fields, leaving not a bank to be seen."[12] The slaves would huddle day after day in the pounding mill (on the plantation's highest ground), and when they finally returned to their houses everything would be covered with the river's muck. "The first [freshet] I saw, really scared me pretty well," Charles Manigault reminisced fifteen years later:

> I began to think that I had got myself into a pretty bad purchase, for when I had but just bought [Gowrie], down came one of the highest freshets covering nearly every floor then on the place, & even putting out the fire in the little room of the overseer's house, which I then inhabited, when "Mr. Potter" [a rich neighbor resident on the Georgia shore] sent his boat, & took me to his place.[13]

These unprogrammed floodings were probably a major source for the spread of those enteric diseases which doomed numbers of Savannah River slaves. From the Cape Fear River in North Carolina to the St. Mary's River (dividing Georgia from Florida) there were sixteen great rivers which—unlike the rivers flowing into the Gulf of Mexico—profited from ocean tides of at least four feet in magnitude; it was here that the rice kingdom burgeoned until consigned to a lingering death by the destruction of slavery.[14]

Before 1849 Gowrie comprised only 265 acres of rice land (plus 40 acres of woodland on a small adjacent island), but this was enough to occupy the labor of some seventy-five slaves. The land was divided into fifteen fields, each capable of separate flooding; and a system of canals and ditches brought water from Savannah Middle River into the plantation, and later let it drain into Savannah Back River. Great floodgates regulated the flow of river waters into the canals, and the cleverly constructed "trunks" were wooden sluices through which water could flow from the river or canals into the fields at high tide; and through which, when the mechanism was changed, the water could flow out again at low tide. When the harvest was finished, three fields were flooded again at every high tide, and this water supply was used (at low tide) to turn the covered waterwheel in the middle of the pounding mill. One of the many complexities of the system was that the annual pounding had to be completed early enough each spring that the three millponds could be drained and dried out before it was too late for them to be planted. For this reason Charles Manigault abandoned after 1838 his original practice of milling some of his neighbors' rice. By the time he had cleared the last four virgin fields, he was raising so much of his own rice that he could not afford to extend the period each winter when the three millponds were flooded.

A source of recurrent crisis was that the wooden floodgates and trunks constantly rotted, and the river persistently undermined the mud embankments.[15] Then a freshet, or even exceptionally high tides, could wreak havoc for weeks at a time, resulting in emergency demands on the slaves at all hours of the day and night. Thus, during the inundation of March 1850 the sub-merged banks were "much washed with a trunk blown up [i.e., dislodged with explosive force] causing an immense Break" in the embankment: it was "such a Break as I never saw before," Charles averred,

> Causing great delay & waste of labour in flatting dirt [moving it in a flatboat] &c. night & day—rebreaking, &c. &c. until the last of April. [A second break] occupied the whole Summer in five ineffectual attempts to stop it—principally from injudicious attempts, by which it remained open all Summer until December.[16]

What distressed Manigault was not the emergency demands on the slaves but the loss of the whole crop which had been planted in the seventy-eight acres of his best fields—the four newly cleared ones. The departure from Gowrie in December 1850 of the overseer Jesse Cooper, after only three years' service, probably resulted from Manigault's dissatisfaction with Cooper's failure effec-tually to repair the broken embankment, and thus to save nearly one-third of the year's crop.

Repeated crises with embankments and trunks explain Manigault's im-patience with the time-honored method of threshing rice by the hand flail. This process was so slow, and the threshing therefore occupied so much of the winter, that there was too little time to get the embankments repaired and the ditches cleared before the new planting season arrived. In a slave system one might have expected Manigault simply to import more slaves into Gowrie and carry on with the old labor-intensive threshing methods. But he observed that his slaves died at Gowrie with depressing frequency. This may have been the principal reason—along with his fascination for new technology—for his keen experiments with new threshing machinery. In 1846 he was the Savannah River's first purchaser of a new threshing apparatus which could be attached to the waterwheel of a pounding mill. He watched with sharp interest—firing advice and instruction to his overseer every fortnight—to see whether the machine would work; to determine how much it might speed the threshing; and to find whether the millponds furnished enough power to pound the rice at the same time the thresher was operating. The apparent success of the new machine filled Manigault with excitement such as one might expect in a capital-ist innovator anxious about losing both money and reputation. He assured his overseer after a favorable report:

> Already I feel great relief on the subject. For amongst other things I even feared the ridicule in case I should have added myself to the long list of failures in attempts at threshing machines. . . . The iron Beater of mine being the first of its great dimensions which has ever been made—my being the first to order such a one, & its triumphal performance, is really a source of pride as well as pleasure to me.[17]

Besides other skills, the overseer had to be able—with Stephen the slave miller and John Izard, the most capable slave artisan—to adjust the new machinery and devise alterations and repairs to improve its operation, after the return to Charleston of the white mechanic who had been sent by the manufacturer to install the machinery.

Further complications arose from the rush of work at harvest time, from mid-August until late October. All hands worked at high pressure to cut the mature rice before it became overripe, and Manigault sometimes sent five or even ten extra slaves from Silk Hope to augment Gowrie's workforce at this time of year.[18] Even so, it was necessary to spread out the planting of the rice over many weeks in the spring so that not too much would become ripe at any one time in the autumn. Each planting started a few days before high tide so that plenty of water would be available to flood each field for a week or two, as soon as it was planted. Manigault studied his almanac and pestered his overseers—or later his son Louis, when the latter assumed managerial duties— to ensure that they started planting soon enough each fortnight to take full advantage of the high tides. Even with these precautions, the pressure of work at harvest was so great that normally the rice had to be left stacked in the fields after being cut, and not until the cutting was finished in October did the slow, four-week[19] heavy labor begin of carrying rice to the barnyard for threshing.

The overseer's most critical moment arrived with the word from Augusta that a big freshet was on its way. Rumors raced from one plantation to the next, and the factor (the planter's urban business agent) was badgered for authoritative reports of the magnitude of the oncoming flood, which might take a week to reach Gowrie. If the river rose as much as twenty-three feet above low-water mark at Augusta (and if the Carolina swamps were already relatively full of water, so that they could not absorb the freshet's huge surplus), there was imminent peril that Gowrie would be inundated. And if the freshet threatened to overflow the banks, the harvest must be halted and all hands set to work carrying rice to the Mound—the highest point on the plantation, near the threshing yard—where it would be fairly safe, even if the whole plantation were flooded. But this would seriously delay cutting the remaining rice. If the danger of flooding had been exaggerated, or if—as sometimes happened—plantations farther north on the island were inundated but Gowrie was spared, financial disaster nevertheless would strike because the uncut rice, becoming overripe before it was finally harvested, would not fetch a good price in Charleston. If the overseer underestimated the size of a flood and went on cutting, leaving cut rice stacked in the fields, it might be swept into the river by the flood; if he was too cautious, and interrupted the cutting to carry rice to the Mound, the remaining rice might spoil. Either way, thousands of dollars would be lost. In this crisis an overseer would try to pass the buck to Charles Manigault in Charleston: the slave Hector—the chief boat hand—would be dispatched to Savannah with an urgent letter to put on the steamboat to Charleston; when the steamboat returned, Hector would be waiting for its arrival to hasten Manigault's reply into the overseer's hands.

The overseer had to exercise skilled judgment not only in speeding the annual milling; repairing and adjusting the thresher; planting at the right moment and outguessing the floods; but in myriad other ways as well. The turnover among overseers was rapid—Manigault employed fifteen[20] during a thirty-two-year period, none longer than seven and a half years—and despite every precaution in interviewing and securing good references, the employer knew that hiring a new overseer was a lottery. When Stephen Clark took charge of Gowrie in 1853, overseers at neighboring plantations were soon laughing to themselves at Clark's folly, for he was keeping the rice underwater longer than desirable, "watering to death this years crop";[21] and although the crop was large, its quality was low and Manigault nearly sacked his new overseer after the first year. Yet some of the Savannah River soil was so rich that a "wet culture" could be employed that was unsuitable elsewhere. By leaving the plants underwater longer than was customary, the manager could dispense with one or even two summer hoeings, and Manigault's relatively small labor force could cultivate the land better than otherwise.

An overseer's skill was further tested by the problem of "volunteer" rice. This rice grew not from the year's new seed but from grains left in the field the preceding year. Its quality was so low that any substantial admixture of volunteer rice in a barrel drastically reduced the market value of the whole barrel. How to eradicate volunteer rice from an infected field vexed Manigault and his overseers; and in their anxious efforts to purge the interloper they varied their plowing methods, changed their ways of disposing of stubble, and sometimes even planted cowpeas or sweet potatoes for a year in a valuable rice field.

One of Gowrie's innumerable crises arose in March 1858. The overseer for the two preceding years had seemed woefully unsatisfactory—he had produced a child by one of the slave women, but this was in Manigault's eyes the least of his offenses—and he had been sacked in December. Volunteer rice overran the plantation, infesting even its best-quality rice, which was normally set aside as seed for the next year's crop. The Manigaults therefore decided, instead of using Gowrie's own seed rice, to buy at highest prices some "Celebrated Georgetown seed" raised by the well-known rice planter Robert Allston (then governor of South Carolina). The seed rice was to be forwarded by schooner from Allston's pounding mill near Georgetown—sixty-five miles by sea northeast of Charleston—to that city, whence Charles Manigault would dispatch it in another schooner to his son Louis at Gowrie. Louis, just married, was spending a few months at Gowrie with his new bride—no doubt tutoring her in French—before they set off on an eight-month wedding trip to Europe. He waited impatiently for Allston's seed rice, but it did not come; and the fields must be planted. Every two or three days Charles sent him a bulletin: the schooner had been delayed at Georgetown; a flood impeded its progress up the Waccamaw River to Allston's mill; and so forth. Desperate, Louis bought the first third of his seed rice in Savannah and was pleased to get the first planting done on time. But he had been diddled, for—as a rival planter chortled with delight—this rice had been through a steam thresher, which damaged so many grains as to render it inferior for seed. Charles Manigault (learning through the indiscretion of his Charleston factor about the low quality of the seed rice sold to Louis) admonished his son to replant some of those fields after the second and third plantings (of other fields) had been completed.

But, meanwhile, where was Governor Allston's rice? Charles accosted Allston in Charleston, where the governor had just bought what some regarded as the finest dwelling in the city. The schooner with the delayed seed rice, Allston assured him, "is now looked for daily."[22] A week later the vessel still had not reached Charleston—adverse winds and so forth—and the famous seed rice was now in danger of not reaching Gowrie soon enough to plant before the impending high tides. Drawing on his long experience, Charles advised emergency measures: "Were I on the spot under the strong hope that the Vessel will reach Gowrie in a week at the farthest," he wrote anxiously,

> I would during the approaching high tides Put a full flow [inundation of irrigation water] on all the unplanted fields adjoining, or communicating with those fields you intend to plant & the Canals full also, and even take it on any of the planted fields whose young & recently planted Rice would not be injured by a flow of several days. This supply of water will give you a tolerable flow over the next planting [even after the high tides have receded]. Then draw off immediately from the other fields & canals (provided the tides then are running short) and the only difference this plan will make is that the next planting will not be so well Covered with water throughout each field & in every part of it as you would desire, and therefore require more Bird Minders [slaves equipped with noise makers or even with a gun to scare off the thousands of birds eager to eat the seed]—thats all. Mr Bryan's [the new overseer's] great experience will no doubt see this under our existing difficulties.[23]

Rice planting was thus an immensely complex business. Fraught with unexpected crises, it required long experience and depended on the managers' acquiring numerous and varied skills, and on their exercising fine judgment. It involved a large capital investment and demanded willingness to assume substantial financial risks. When things went well—if there was no hurricane like the one in September 1854 which swept two-thirds of Gowrie's crop into the sea, no freshet like the one in September 1852 which badly damaged that year's harvest, no Asiatic cholera epidemic—the profits could be wonderfully gratifying to the slave master.

How risky Charles Manigault's investment was at Gowrie is evident in its profit rate, which varied from minus 20 percent to plus 26 percent, depending on the death rate among the slaves, the size and quality of the harvest, and the price of rice at the moment it reached market. Manigault started miserably, diminishing his original investment by 6 percent in 1833 (because of a bad flood) and then losing no less than another 20 percent of his capital during the disastrous year of 1834, when Asiatic cholera decimated his slave force. "The first two or three years were very discouraging & embarrassing," he acknowledged many years later. Manigault's father-in-law, Nathaniel Heyward—the deportation of whose slaves from Silk Hope to Gowrie was a cardinal element in Manigault's enterprise—always disapproved of the venture at Gowrie. "A disastrous speculation on [Charles's] part," Heyward called it; and Manigault's self-esteem became deeply involved in his "long struggle of 14 years" (through 1846, when he wrote these words) to make a success of it.[24] The tension between the two men (resulting in several angry letters from Manigault to his father-in-law, which Heyward's son thought best to burn after the old man's death) arose partly because Manigault was deporting from Silk Hope to Gowrie—where many of them perished—dozens of slaves who legally were still chattels of his disapproving father-in-law.

Gowrie's profits for the three years from 1835 through 1837 enabled him to pay off over half of his original mortgage on the property, and even to buy a couple of "prime hands" to begin replacing those who had died in 1834. It was not until 1838, however, that Manigault could breathe a sigh of relief, for high prices and a good crop earned him 26 percent that year, the best profit rate he had ever achieved (see table 1, column g). And during the next nine years he never earned less than 9 percent, reaching a splendid 22 percent return in 1845. For the thirteen years from 1835 through 1847 his average profits were 15 percent a year—a rate few entrepreneurs would scorn, especially when extended over such a long period. Manigault then preached, in language any capitalist investor could understand, the virtues of rice planting. Having placed some of Gowrie's profits into other investments, he included the return from them in his calculations. Though his numbers cannot be taken at face value (for his estimates were inaccurate, and he assumed incautiously that his profits of the mid-1840s would be indefinitely repeated), his enthusiasm about entrepreneurial profits was unmistakable. "This plantation has in 14 years paid for itself twice," he effused to young Alfred Huger,

> and is going on to pay for itself a third time. . . . By placing only $20,000 down I have made that sum at the end of 14 Years establish an annual income of—say $12,000—besides $3000 income from investments made elsewhere—derived from the same plantation—, having thus by a little industry made a moderate sum [$20,000, in his misleading calculation] produce a steady income which it would require more than $200,000—placed at Legal Interest to yield.[25]

Manigault's taste for Gowrie's profits, and his wish to establish his sons in the business, led him to double the plantation's size the next year and to enlarge it even further in 1854. A series of devastating epidemics—measles, dysentery, and "cholera"—swept the plantation in 1848, 1850, 1852, 1853, and 1854; and these, added to chronic killers like malaria and pleurisy, carried off an astonishing number of slaves, making it seem surprising, to a modern eye, that the enterprise could have survived. Fifty-two babies were born between 1846 and 1854, but during those same years 144 bondsmen and women died: a huge net loss of 92 slaves. This, of course, played havoc with Gowrie's finances. The plantation could be kept going only by massive importations. Manigault deported some slaves from Silk Hope to Gowrie during these years and bought many more at slave auctions. Yet despite a capital loss of some $44,000 in dead slaves, Gowrie still averaged a 4 percent annual return from 1848 to 1854.[26]

Thereafter times improved. Misery abroad meant profits at home. Just as rice planters had prospered during the Napoleonic Wars and again during the

TABLE 1. Gowrie's Estimated Profits, 1833–60
(to nearest $100)

Year of crop	(a) Risk capital (at beginning of year)	(b) Gross revenues (on that crop)	(c) Recurrent expenses (attributable to that crop)	(d) Undistributed capital gain	(e) Capital loss of slaves	(f) Profits (b − c + d − e)	(g) Rate of profit (f/a)
1833	$32,000	$4,000	$4,200	—	$1,600	−$1,800	−6%
1834	30,200	7,200	3,300	—	10,000	−6,100	−20
1835	24,100	5,500	3,000	—	—	2,500	10
1836	26,600	7,400	2,800	—	—	4,600	17
1837	29,100	8,000	2,700	—	400	4,900	17
1838	42,000	13,400	2,300	—	—	11,100	26
1839	42,900	10,200	2,200	$1,000	2,000	7,000	16
1840	58,500	9,100	1,800	1,000	800	7,500	13
1841	58,700	7,300	1,800	1,000	1,200	5,300	9
1842	59,000	8,800	1,800	—	—	7,000	12
1843	61,500	10,000	1,800	—	—	8,200	13
1844	61,500	8,800	1,800	—	—	7,000	11

Year							
1845	62,500	15,300	1,800	—	—	13,500	12
1846	64,000	11,200	1,800	—	—	9,400	15
1847	64,000	9,700	1,800	—	—	7,900	12
1848	64,000	8,100	1,800	2,300	8,000	-1,700	-3
1849	105,000	14,000	3,500	2,000	1,000	11,800	11
1850	107,300	8,000	3,500	1,800	6,900	-400	-0
1851	103,400	13,600	4,100	1,700	2,000	9,300	9
1852	106,700	16,600	3,600	1,700	6,000	8,700	8
1853	110,400	16,900	3,600	1,700	6,500	8,500	8
1854	130,400	8,700	3,600	1,700	13,700	-6,900	-5
1855	118,400	20,900	3,500	1,700	4,100	15,000	13
1856	116,700	12,700	3,300	1,700	—	11,100	10
1857	132,600	13,000	4,900	2,100	—	10,200	8
1858	134,700	10,000	2,800	2,100	1,500	7,800	6
1859	135,800	13,600	3,700	2,100	—	12,000	9
1860	138,400	10,600	3,100	2,100	1,500	8,100	6
1861	138,500						
TOTAL		$302,600	$79,900	$26,000	$67,200	$181,500	—

Note: See appendix A for explanation and sources.

Mexican War, so the Crimean War pushed up prices again for the 1855 crop, and Gowrie earned a 13 percent return that year. The sum was $15,000, higher than ever before in Gowrie's history. Though no other crop of the 1850s was equally profitable, even a relatively bad year like 1857—when Charles Manigault eventually sacked his overseer for incompetence—yielded a profit of 8 percent (on an investment more than double that of the 1840s); and with revenues regularly this good or better, the vision of bonanza days spurred Louis to emulate his father. "As hope ever bears us onward," the younger man ruminated after the relatively poor 1856 harvest, "I try to forget the past, looking forward with brighter expectations for the Coming Season."[27] Charles spent over ninety-four thousand dollars[28] on Gowrie between 1848 and 1860, yet by 1860 the entrepreneur was once again in a happy situation, "now that I have paid up every debt for Land, and Negroes."[29]

Even the first three years of the Civil War did not end Gowrie's profitability. War had its usual effect of inflating the price of rice; and despite the hazards of the Yankee invasion of South Carolina's nearby sea islands in November 1861, Gowrie's gross revenues, after deducting wartime taxes, ranged from thirteen thousand dollars for the 1861 crop to twenty-eight thousand dollars (in inflated Confederate currency) for 1863.[30] The 1864 harvest, however, was seized on Christmas Eve by General Sherman's army, who after carrying off ten thousand bushels of rice burned the three-story brick thresher where the rice had been stored. By then every slave had boarded one of Gowrie's large flatboats and left the plantation for Savannah. The profits of this version of planter capitalism ceased suddenly, and forever.

Manigault's total investment in Gowrie—not counting profits he later plowed back into the plantation—was $49,500.[31] By 1861 he and Louis had magnified this sum into an estate probably worth about $266,000: not an inconsiderable return on the original investment.[32] Of this $266,000, Charles Manigault had paid his son some $17,000 for managerial services from 1852 through 1860, and the rest was all his own. It was not surprising, therefore, that he felt able to give Louis a princely cash gift in 1858 to finance a lavish wedding trip to Europe.[33]

How may one assess the growth of a capital investment of $49,500 into a fortune of some $266,000 by 1861? A fashion among economic historians is to allege that Charles Manigault's true "profit" rate was zero, and that rice planting was a shaky industry tottering even before the Civil War toward an untimely grave. This fashion began at least sixty years ago, when Lewis Gray mistakenly asserted that American rice production had declined during the 1850s.[34] But the correct figures indicate a gradual increase in production during the forty years before the Civil War.

In the light of these figures, and of Charles Manigault's obvious success in magnifying a $49,500 investment at Gowrie into a $266,000 fortune, a layperson might be mystified by any claim that Manigault was barking up the wrong tree, and that his profit rate was zero. The explanation lies in economists' efforts to redefine "profit" to mean something very different from what

Estimated Annual
American Rice Production,
1820–60 (millions of pounds
of "clean" rice)

1820–29	78
1830–39	88
1840–49	101
1850–60*	111

Note: See appendix E for sources.

*Omits the year 1854, when a September hurricane destroyed about 30 percent of the low-country crop.

a businessperson or a layperson would understand by the term. ("Profit," in this redefinition, would include only those earnings *over and above* the return an entrepreneur might have garnered from investing his capital in a fixed-rate bond. But economic historians have discovered no way of estimating the risks involved in fixed-rate investments, and indeed have sometimes appeared to forget those risks.)[35]

No nineteenth-century lender would have ignored the risks of a fixed-rate loan. Thus those individuals who lent Governor Robert Allston money at 7 percent fixed-rate interest in the late 1850s found, when his estate went bankrupt in 1868, that they could recover only about 25 percent of what they had lent him: the rest was down the drain. As there was in the nineteenth century no such thing as a risk-free, fixed-rate investment (and as one cannot readily quantify the risk in fixed-rate lending, because no one knows what proportion of fixed-rate loans were never repaid), surely the best procedure for historians is to use the conventional definition of "profit": the net return on those risky investments which did *not* promise fixed payments. Manigault invested in a rice plantation because, although he took a big risk in so doing, he thought his investment likely to yield better returns than any fixed-rate investment. Table 1 measures Manigault's successes and failures according to a conception of "profit" which he himself could have understood.

As rice plantations went, Gowrie—even after its acreage had been increased in 1849—was of only moderate size, and Manigault's pecuniary rewards should not be exaggerated. Certainly some mid-nineteenth-century entrepreneurs did even better than he. While his average annual profit rate of 15 percent from 1835 through 1847 is impressive, and his profits during the late 1850s (averaging almost 9 percent) were reasonably good, he had started badly in the early 1830s and had not done well financially from 1848 through 1854. The remarkable thing, perhaps, is that an enterprise resulting in the steady destruction of human "capital" (i.e., in a net death toll of twenty-nine slaves in 1833–34, and of another ninety-two slaves between 1846 and 1854) nevertheless produced substantial profits for the master. The dead slaves appear merely as "capital loss" in the cold accounting language of table 2; yet

TABLE 2. Estimated Capital Investment in Gowrie, 1833–60
(to nearest $100)

| Year of crop | (a) Risk capital at beginning of crop year (= f of preceding year) | Additional cash invested during year | | (c) Value of Silk Hope slaves deported to Gowrie | (d) Undistributed capital gain | (e) Capital loss of slaves | (f) Risk capital at end of crop year (a + b + c + d − e) |
		(b1) Repayment of debt	(b2) Other cash investment				
1833	$32,000	−$1,200	$1,000	—	—	$1,600	$30,200
1834	30,200	3,900	—	—	—	10,000	24,100
1835	24,100	2,500	—	—	—	—	26,600
1836	26,600	2,500	—	—	—	—	29,100
1837	29,100	5,300	2,100	$5,900	—	400	42,000
1838	42,000	900	—	—	—	—	42,900
1839	42,900	6,100	10,200	300	$1,000	2,000	58,500
1840	58,500	—	—	—	1,000	800	58,700
1841	58,700	—	—	500	1,000	1,200	59,000
1842	59,000	—	2,500	—	—	—	61,500
1843	61,500	—	—	—	—	—	61,500

Year							
1844	61,500	—	—	1,000	—	—	62,500
1845	62,500	—	—	1,500	—	—	64,000
1846	64,000	—	—	—	—	—	64,000
1847	64,000	—	—	—	—	—	64,000
1848	64,000	—	45,700	3,300	—	8,000	105,000
1849	105,000	—	—	1,000	2,300	1,000	107,300
1850	107,300	—	—	1,000	2,000	6,900	103,400
1851	103,400	—	1,000	2,500	1,800	2,000	106,700
1852	106,700	—	8,000	—	1,700	6,000	110,400
1853	110,400	—	24,800	—	1,700	6,500	130,400
1854	130,400	—	—	—	1,700	13,700	118,400
1855	118,400	—	700	—	1,700	4,100	116,700
1856	116,700	—	14,200	—	1,700	—	132,600
1857	132,600	—	—	—	2,100	—	134,700
1858	134,700	—	—	500	2,100	1,500	135,800
1859	135,800	—	500	—	2,100	—	138,400
1860	138,400	—	—	—	2,100	1,500	138,500
1861	138,500	—	-500	—	—	—	—
TOTAL	—	$20,000	$110,200	$17,500	$26,000	$67,200	

Note: See appendix A for sources.

despite this massive loss of $67,200 worth of slaves (column e), the value of Manigault's risk capital at Gowrie (column a) grew steadily from 1835.

This growth of Gowrie's value[36] was not the whole story. Until 1839 Charles Manigault had been obliged to plow all of his profits back into the business. (He built a house for himself to live in when he visited Gowrie; he paid off the original mortgage; he bought new slaves to replace those who died; and he began to clear and ditch seventy-eight virgin acres of his original purchase.) But by 1839 he began accumulating profits which he invested elsewhere—mainly in Charleston banks and insurance companies. This gave him the nest egg with which he could nearly double the size of Gowrie late in 1848, and buy new slaves with which to stock this new "East Hermitage" tract; and still have enough cash left over to meet emergencies (like those of the early 1850s), when he bought more slaves to take the places of those who died so fast. By the end of 1860 he had accumulated a surplus of $92,500, and his reinvestment of this surplus had earned him over the years perhaps another $35,300. This brought Gowrie's accumulated cash balance to some $127,800 (see table 3, column g). Gowrie's total worth to Charles Manigault by 1861 was therefore the $127,800 accumulated cash balance, plus the $138,500 capital value of the plantation and its slaves (see table 2, column a): a total of some $266,300.

The improvement in Gowrie's worth—from $49,500[37] to $266,300—may be compared with the return Manigault might have garnered from an alternative investment. One supposes that, in 1833, he might have discovered a different way of investing his capital, not so risky as a rice plantation, but not so risky either as Bank of United States stocks proved to be. If one presumes that he could have earned on average 3 percent a year from this alternative investment (taking into account bad years as well as good ones, and bad debts as well as good ones),[38] the value of this hypothetical investment would have grown by 1861 to $101,500.[39] The profit from this alternative investment is shown in the left-hand column, while Gowrie's *actual* profit is in the right-hand column:

	Hypothetical alternative investment at 3 percent	Actual investment in Gowrie
Value by 1861	$101,500	$266,300
Original Investment	49,500	49,500
Profit	$52,000	$216,800

Thus Manigault's actual profit from Gowrie was over four times as great as he might have earned from the hypothetical alternative. A hope that this would happen had led him to invest in Gowrie; and although no doubt he was disappointed that not all his entrepreneurial ambitions were fulfilled, he had grounds for self-satisfaction—so long as he could assume that investment in a slave plantation was a morally justified means of increasing his fortune.

The sums involved at Gowrie were huge by nineteenth-century standards.

Money then went a long way, as may be judged by examining the size of an overseer's salary. Overseeing a rice plantation was highly skilled, responsible work; it was also unhealthy—as illustrated by the fact that four of Manigault's fifteen overseers died while employed at Gowrie. But Manigault thought nothing of starting an inexperienced overseer on an annual wage of $250 (sweetened with a $50 tip at the end of the year, if the employer was satisfied with the overseer, and if the latter was willing to renew his contract for the following year). The median salary for Gowrie's overseers was $500, and Manigault paid only three of them more than $700 a year.[40] Yet he himself derived profits of at least $7,000 from Gowrie in every year after 1837 except four. Obviously, Manigault had invested in Gowrie in order to make money from his investment, just as any other capitalist would do.

Manigault's overseers understood that maximizing profits was their employer's goal. Thus in October 1852 Washington Skinner justified postponing the threshing—until all the cut rice had been moved from the field—with this argument: "The price of rice next Spring will be very high, and he that has the most rice at that time will make the most money." And when Asiatic cholera struck the Savannah River in 1849—leading to the evacuation of Gowrie's slaves to Dr. Pritchard's cholera camp—overseer Jesse Cooper took for granted that his employer's concern for the slaves' lives was principally economic: "Being fully aware that there must be considerable anxiety on your part in relation to your *interest* here," he assured Manigault, "I now for your satisfaction beg leave to state that we are all still in Camp."[41] Charles Manigault assessed an overseer's worth mainly in financial terms: "I have lost $4000 by his incapacity this year," he grumbled of Leonard Venters in 1856; and Manigault was clear that "making a crop" was a planter's principal concern. He took it as a matter of course that financial considerations, not sentiment, would determine whether or not other rice planters would sell their slaves. Despite Venters's "incapacity," Manigault had some cash to spare in December 1856 for buying slaves—he purchased twenty-one the next month—and he hoped poor crops near Georgetown, South Carolina, would throw slaves onto the market. Like any (relatively) moderate-sized businessman, he relished the financial discomfiture of his really big competitors. "There are complaints from all parts of [the rice crop's] falling short," he cheerily informed Louis, "near Georgetown in particular. Some of those big fellows there are Coming out at the Small end of the horn. I shall be ready to make a dash at any sale of first rate Negroes this winter & will go as far even as a purchase of $12,000 worth for Savh. River."[42]

Whether installing threshing machinery, calculating the profits of his investments, or planning to make a dash at Charleston's next slave auction, Charles Manigault regarded himself as a "man of business": a term he used with approbation. One of his sons, Dr. Gabriel Manigault, came back in the autumn of 1856 to the United States from a truly grand tour of the Old World, taking in Constantinople and Moscow as well as more usual places. Charles was annoyed that the young man did not notify his parents promptly of his safe arrival in New York. "A man of business," he complained mildly to Louis, "would perhaps have sent a Teligraphic [*sic*] despatch saying he had

TABLE 3. Gowrie's Estimated Cash Balance, 1833–60
(to nearest $100)

Year* of crop	(a) Debt (−) at beginning of year	(b) Interest on debt (paid at end of year)	(c) Cash return from year's crop	(d) Cash earmarked for immediate reinvestment (n.i. debt repayment)	(e) Repayment of debt (at end of year)	(f) Annual cash balance (c − d − e)	(g) Accumulated cash balance (at end of year)	(h) Earnings on previous year's accumulated cash balance (@3%)
1833	−$20,000	($1,400)	−$200	$1,000	−$1,200	—	−$21,200	—
1834	−21,200	(1,500)	3,900	—	3,900	—	−17,300	—
1835	−17,300	(1,200)	2,500	—	2,500	—	−14,800	—
1836	−14,800	(1,000)	4,600	2,100	2,500	—	−12,300	—
1837	−12,300	(900)	5,300	—	5,300	—	−7,000	—
1838	−7,000	(500)	11,100	10,200	900	—	−6,100	—
1839	−6,100	(400)	8,000	—	6,100	$1,900	1,900	—
1840	—	—	7,300	—	—	7,300	9,300	$100
1841	—	—	5,500	2,500	—	3,000	12,600	300
1842	—	—	7,000	—	—	7,000	20,000	400
1843	—	—	8,200	—	—	8,200	28,800	600
1844	—	—	7,000	—	—	7,000	36,700	900

Year						
1845	—	—	13,500	13,500	51,300	1,100
1846	—	—	9,400	9,400	62,200	1,500
1847	—	—	7,900	7,900	72,000	1,900
1848	—	45,700	6,300	−39,400	34,800	2,200
1849	—	—	10,500	10,500	46,300	1,000
1850	—	—	4,500	4,500	52,200	1,400
1851	—	1,000	9,500	8,500	62,300	1,600
1852	—	8,000	13,000	5,000	69,200	1,900
1853	—	24,800	13,300	−11,500	59,800	2,100
1854	—	—	5,100	5,100	66,700	1,800
1855	—	700	17,400	16,700	85,400	2,000
1856	—	14,200	9,400	−4,800	83,200	2,600
1857	—	—	8,100	8,100	93,800	2,500
1858	—	—	7,200	7,200	103,800	2,800
1859	—	500	9,900	9,400	116,300	3,100
1860	—	−500	7,500	8,000	127,800	3,500
TOTAL	$20,000	$110,200	$222,700	$92,500	$127,800	$35,300

Note: See appendix A for sources.

* Beginning in 1848, the financial year extends from April through April of the subsequent year.

returned." Like any good businessman, Charles employed rational calculation and assiduous attention to detail to achieve his purposes. Even at the age of sixty-six, he wrote to Louis that "your Rice Plantings the latter end of next month engross my constant thoughts." He showered the young man with advice on "open planting" (coating the seed rice beforehand in clay and then *not* covering it with earth after planting), and on the Savannah River's peculiar type of "water culture." Like many an acute businessman, he was capable of driving a hard bargain; indeed, some may have thought him a skinflint. He did not mind venturing large sums on buying slaves or a new threshing machine, but he resented expenditures which might prove superfluous. Thus in 1845 he declined the offer of paying a physician a fixed annual fee per slave, thinking he could economize by paying only for those doctor's visits which the overseer deemed indispensable; and the fees must be reasonable. This side of his character was encapsulated in instructions to Louis in 1858; tell the overseer, he requested, "that I wish particularly to get as soon as possible Dr. Dukes Bill for medical Attendance [on the slaves] last summer, & that my Continuance to request his services depends on the Moderation of his Charges."[43]

That Manigault's outlook was that of a planter capitalist did not preclude his allegiance to the ideals of the South Carolina gentry. The two mentalities were no more inconsistent with each other in Carolina than in England, where agricultural capitalism on great landed estates flourished cheek by jowl with an efflorescence of the gentry ideal. To be a gentleman was to possess wealth sufficient for "independence," so that one could live a cultivated and genteel life. The Manigaults lived well. At the Charleston house given them by Nathaniel Heyward—whose grounds were small compared with those at their country estate—they had such "a swarm of Negroes in our yard" that Charles once forbade Louis from bringing more than one house slave with him from Gowrie: there were already at Gibbes Street "3 Negro women . . . to say nothing of our 5 men servants, a girl, & 3 [slave] children." When Louis was still a bachelor in 1856 he spent the whole summer traveling in the North; his father, missing customary chats with him, did not mind the cost of having "a little Room 9 by 6 built by a partition in the corner of our dwelling under the piazza . . . for a smoking Room for you & I, in bad, or cold weather, & I have got some good Cigars since your departure." Louis's marriage the next year occasioned more extensive alterations, so that his bedroom at Gibbes Street would accommodate two. Charles Manigault, like Count Vronsky in *Anna Karenina,* had distinct priorities in settling his accounts. He claimed to be without funds to pay promptly a long-overdue bill for shingles for the big house at Gowrie, but this did not deter him from putting to work no less than twenty-four men (few of whom can have been his own unpaid slaves), making his own Charleston house ready for the bridal couple: "I have now at work," he notified Louis, "7 Carpenters, 6 Painters, 6 Lathers & Plasterers, & 2 men putting up a Chimney & marble mantle, besides Stepney working at the new stable, and Ben mixing mortar, & Jake hawling 2 loads of sand per day from the [Marshlands] Farm. . . . I will send you . . . 2 or 3 Doz. Madeira."[44]

The Manigaults shared the gentry's fondness for family portraits. Charles's own had been painted in 1817 by Sully; Louis's was accomplished in 1855; Fanny—Louis's new bride—must be painted in Paris on her wedding trip; and the new pictures required redisposition of those already occupying the walls. In 1859 Charles announced:

> We decided that the best place for Fannie's Portrait was to put it in the Summer Drawing Room where our family Picture hung for twenty years. We . . . hung near Fannie Mrs. J. Middleton [Charles's great-aunt], by Sully over the clock having reguilt [*sic*] her Frame. . . . Yours I have hung over the door in your bedroom, & put up several other Paintings in your room.

The Manigaults did *not* belong to the (rather indiscriminate) Jockey Club—which sponsored Charleston's big horse races in midwinter and a couple of massive balls; instead, their children attended the exclusive balls of the St. Cecilia Society, and sometimes there was one at home. A new painting could provide the occasion: "We had a famous Ball on Friday," Charles glowed, "which went off with great éclat. . . . All admired [Fanny's] Portrait very much."[45]

After Louis successfully attended Yale for two years, he interspersed a family tour to Europe, a year's mercantile apprenticeship, and his Far Eastern and Latin American mercantile ventures (financed by a gift[46] from his grandfather Nathaniel Heyward) with a young gentleman's luxurious life in Charleston. His translation by 1852 into a Savannah River planter was therefore not entirely easy. At Gowrie he decided to spend only a little time visiting genteel neighbors like his cousin Allan Izard, and he protested that he greatly preferred keeping his nose to the grindstone. Thus one Sunday the unforeseen arrival of a schooner to carry Gowrie's rice to the Charleston market conflicted with a social engagement with the Izards, and Louis expressed Chilean insouciance at the disruption of his social plans. "I have been kept here by this Schooner," he dutifully informed his father, "& I'd rather load a boat than pintar at a table. Caramba!" A few months earlier, visiting Gowrie's slaves at a "cholera" camp (to which survivors had been transferred to escape this plague), he claimed to have adapted well to his new role: "I like this kind of life very much, I feel prime & I dont think I shall return to Charleston to lead that idle life."[47] But a Savannah River planter's career did not, of course, prevent Louis from attending Charleston's Race Week and the attendant midwinter balls; and after a fortnight or so of these pleasures a steamer journey would bring him quickly back to Savannah to resume his plantation duties.

The gentry ideal of the Carolina low country was not confined to slave states: a handful of Northerners shared it, and it set the tone of British society. A Philadelphia gentleman, Sidney Fisher—more deeply attached than even the Manigaults to the vision of gentry life—articulated the gentry ideal to explain his dissatisfaction with his own circumstances. Fisher, brother of Philadelphia's leading investment banker, had inherited a large Maryland farm from his mother; but she honorably had by her will freed her slaves, greatly diminishing the value of his inheritance. Although Fisher was trained to be a lawyer, he preferred gentlemanly intellectual and cultural pursuits. He tried to supplement his modest rentier's income in Philadelphia by raising grain and peaches in Maryland; thinking the farm too unhealthy for permanent residence, however, he hired a series of farmers to manage it for him. He was an assiduous student, and wrote political articles and a significant book; he also gave an occasional historical oration and practiced law halfheartedly. He once even argued a case for the Reading Railroad before the U.S. Supreme Court, but the occasion was a failure; he yearned always for the life of a gentleman farmer. Farming, he felt—unlike the law—could be pursued at half steam, leaving a man enough leisure to cultivate himself. One cold January day in 1841, Fisher defined candidly the supposed advantages of being a gentleman farmer. "Read Gibbon & made notes all day & evening," he ruminated, contemplating his uncertain prospects.

> Money—money—what a magic is in the word. It is the talisman . . . which more than all gives a man to himself, gives him leisure & independence, the means of cultivating his mind, of improving his nature. . . . I have just enough to make me feel the advantages of wealth and the evils of poverty. . . . I have no work, no career in which I can engage with interest & pleasure. The Law—I have nothing to do, and to get something, must make sacrifices & do things from which my nature revolts. If I had a farm where I could live, then I could be usefully employed in a pursuit which accords with my taste. . . . Such a life would unite in just proportion, occupation & leisure, independence & ease, activity and retirement. If Mt. Harmon [Fisher's Maryland farm] was healthy I could lead a happy life and become rich.[48]

Restless in Philadelphia, Fisher envied the happy position of English gentleman farmers, enriching themselves by combining agricultural occupation and leisure, in just proportion. When Benjamin Disraeli set himself the task of defending "aristocracy" in Britain, he was not centrally concerned with hereditary titles: at the heart of the "aristocratic" system (in his view) were the great landed estates and the gentlemen—titled or otherwise—supported by those lands.[49] More than anywhere else in the United States, the Carolina and Georgia low country nourished a system of landed estates comparable to the British system, and this was no doubt a principal source for the Confederate sympathies permeating the upper reaches of British society during the American Civil War. When the Radical Republican leader Thaddeus Stevens declared that the Civil War pitted democracy against aristocracy, he was not merely indulging in rhetoric. If "aristocracy" be defined, in the Disraelian sense, as a system of great landed estates, the war was indeed antiaristocratic. The democratic revolution—which according to Alexis de Tocqueville swept America peaceably—in fact conquered the Carolina low country by force of arms.

Although the Manigaults and their associates created the closest analogue in the United States to the system of gentrified agricultural capitalism which had long flourished in Britain, there was of course a major difference. Land was scarce in Britain and concentrated in few hands, and a large population of essentially landless agricultural laborers was at hand to enrich the great land-owners. But land was hugely abundant in the American South: potential white agricultural laborers had for generations gone west, or disappeared into the nearby woods, rather than labor on someone else's estate. If one wished to recreate in North America the British system of agricultural capitalism, based on great estates run by gentleman farmers, the only way to do so was to coerce the laborers, and by far the most effective means was slavery. Slavery was not an economic system—it was not a "mode of production," as, for example, Marx believed; it was instead a system of domination and of social alienation which could be combined with any number of different economic systems.[50] In the Carolina and Georgia low country, slavery was the only means by which great agricultural estates could flourish. The quick decay of those estates after the Civil War showed that more than slavery had been at stake in that war: a vigorous system of large-scale agricultural capitalism had been dealt a crippling blow.

2

Manigaults and Heywards

In the first part of the nineteenth century—even after slavery had been put on the road to extinction in the North—a number of great Southern planters resided in Pennsylvania, New York, and Rhode Island, and married into the top stratum of Northern society. Charles Izard Manigault was an offshoot of this transsectional alliance, his maternal grandfather, Ralph Izard (who later became a U.S. senator from South Carolina), having married into New York's well-known DeLancey family (see genealogical table 4). Margaret Izard, the eldest child of this union, spent twelve impressionable early years in Europe,[1] and she wrote and spoke French as fluently as English. Unusually well educated, she implanted a French-speaking tradition so firmly into the family of her husband Gabriel Manigault II that their son Charles Manigault and their grandson Louis Manigault both cherished it. Margaret Izard Manigault regarded herself (through her DeLancey mother) as a Northern woman; and finding Charleston dull, she finally persuaded her husband to move to the North in 1805. The family soon acquired an estate north of Philadelphia. And from about 1809 until her death in 1824, Margaret established a free-thinking salon in Philadelphia itself—her winter residence there becoming (according to a contemporary) "the resort of all the [city's] intellectual and refined society. [The orthodox in Philadelphia considered her] to have had no very good influence on the religious sentiments of her *entourage*." Her son Charles Manigault further unsettled matters when, upon returning from South America in 1823, he introduced a "Spanish dance . . . , the first insinuation of the waltz into [Philadelphia's] precise society."[2] Margaret bequeathed to Charles, her favorite son, her library of French and English classics; and he inherited from her his cultivated tastes.[3]

TABLE 4. The Manigault Family

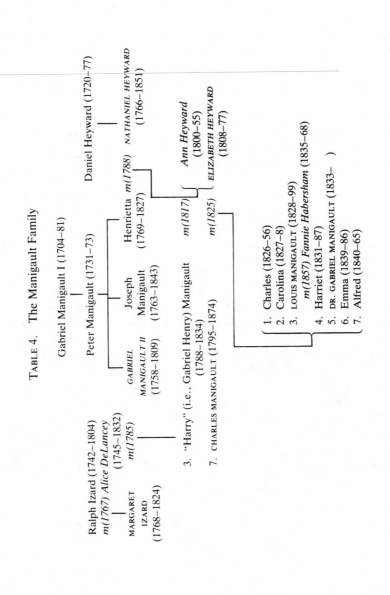

The boy Charles Manigault, raised in South Carolina, had been ten when the family moved to the North. After successfully attending the University of Pennsylvania for two years, Charles did a brief stint in the Pennsylvania militia during the War of 1812, then served an apprenticeship in a Philadelphia mercantile firm. He set off for the Far East at the age of twenty-two, taking money recently inherited from his father. Only after the failure of the Far Eastern venture did he decide—through his marriage to his first cousin Elizabeth Manigault Heyward—to reclaim his proud place among the South Carolina gentry.[4] A small fortune would better be augmented, he concluded, by a venture in rice planting, with slave labor, than by further mercantile speculation.

Charles Manigault could scarcely have failed to observe, from the example of his uncle (and soon his father-in-law) Nathaniel Heyward, that a well-managed capital investment in a rice plantation might be a splendid way of getting rich. Indeed, Nathaniel Hayward's grant of slaves and a rice plantation (Silk Hope) in 1827 to his recently wed daughter Elizabeth was a principal source of Charles Manigault's prosperity. Although Manigault did not actually gain legal title to the property until Heyward's death in 1851, he and his wife, Elizabeth, always enjoyed the income from Silk Hope; and Charles governed Silk Hope, giving orders to its overseer, and deporting sixty-eight of the Silk Hope slaves to work his Gowrie plantation.

Even before marrying Heyward's daughter—and during the one year's engagement which Elizabeth's parents imposed as the price for their consent to Elizabeth's marriage—Charles Manigault was already contemplating how an investment in river embankments could enrich an entrepreneur with an eye to the future. Nathaniel Heyward had spent eighteen months in Europe as a young man, and in 1824 he urged his nephew to do likewise. "Deeply interested in all pertaining to the banking of riceland," Heyward suggested to Manigault that "whilst in England he should visit the lowlands along the borders of the river Humber, observe the size and shape of the banks, the heighth [sic] of the tides, etc." The wish of the father-in-law-to-be was the young man's command. Manigault recorded in his travel journal how each retiring tide in the muddy Humber left "a sediment ¾ of an inch thick, which is rich and adds greatly to the fertility of the soil. Near the river Trent," Manigault continued, thinking expectantly of the South Carolina parallel,

> a body of land which until a few years [ago] has been considered a useless morass . . . has lately been banked and ditched and the river water let into it, which after depositing its alluvial soil for a time . . . , at the expense of £20 an acre, has now made this land of several hundred acres worth £100 per acre.[5]

Like uncle, like nephew: here in 1824 was a quintessentially capitalist mind, speculating how a judicious investment in embankments and ditches might quickly magnify itself fivefold.

During Charles Manigault's career as a rice planter, the example of his uncle—nearly thirty years his senior—loomed large in his imagination. In their maturity the two men both sought to secure their children's futures, yet they balanced capitalist and gentry ideals differently. Heyward was an entrepreneur who aimed to buy his children's way into the highest echelons of Carolina society; Manigault, on the other hand, was already socially secure, and he invested in Gowrie to improve the economic prospects of his children. As Charles Manigault's life became intertwined with Heyward's for more than a quarter of a century—and as Heyward was the largest rice planter the United States has ever seen—the older man's career deserves a moment's consideration.

Relatively uncultivated Nathaniel Heyward may have been, but his was scarcely a "rags to riches" story: for when he was a boy in the 1770s his father, Daniel Heyward, owned 999 slaves. Many of these descended to Nathaniel's much older half brother Judge Thomas Heyward, who as a signer of the Declaration of Independence has remained far better known to posterity than the entrepreneurial Nathaniel. An elder brother James also inherited a goodly fortune. Yet it was only by the inflated standards of the rice kingdom that Nathaniel could pretend not to have been born with a silver spoon in his mouth, for he inherited about 200 slaves from his father,[6] plus two rice plantations. And at the age of thirty, in 1796, he inherited another 256 slaves from his brother James, who had died without a male heir. Nathaniel's marriage in 1788 to Henrietta Manigault (a well-endowed sister of Charles Manigault's father) brought him a fifty-thousand-dollar dowry which—had he used it solely for purchasing slaves—might have given him another 200 of them.[7] As Heyward's grandson acknowledged, Nathaniel Heyward was born well off and "his associations had always been with the well-to-do and wealthy."[8] A total of some 656 slaves—either inherited or secured by marrying an heiress— was not to be sniffed at even in South Carolina.

What did cause well-bred Charlestonian sniffs was Nathaniel Hayward's lack of genteel culture. A man of simple tastes, he had been raised in an inland area—on the Combahee River—where women talked crudely and openly of sex. Nathaniel's father "lived altogether in the country"; the father's "home was plain and unpretentious," Nathaniel's grandson wrote years later,

> and many subjects were there discussed and remarks made, by the female members of the family which in course of time [after Nathaniel had made an acquaintance with polite society at his brother William's house in Charleston], he discovered very improper for those believing themselves to be ladies.[9]

Heyward's driving purposes, then, became to build his own fortune through forward-looking entrepreneurship, and subsequently to use this money to gain entrée for his children into posh Carolina society. Capitalist investment (in land and slaves) and meticulous, businesslike attention to detail ran hand in hand with a passion for gentility.

Heyward's career contrasted sharply with that of his brother-in-law Joseph Manigault. Both inherited inland rice plantations (Joseph's being the larger), both inherited many slaves from their fathers (Joseph rather more), and both came into their inheritances in the late 1780s. Joseph, an amiable, well-bred man with a taste for comfortable urban living, stuck mainly by his inland plantation and saw his fortune melt away: for inland rice production was rapidly being superseded by the new tidal ventures—rather as a twentieth-century heir to an old urban dockyard might have watched his capitalist enterprise succumb to the burgeoning new cargo-container business. Inland plantations depended upon damming streams and collecting the rainwater into reservoirs for use in irrigation. But these reservoirs drowned half of the swampland; and, even so, the amount of water they made available for flooding the rice fields—for example, just after the seed had been planted—was smaller than the supply furnished to the new tidal plantations by the great adjacent rivers. Furthermore, the inland planter had no way to drain an inland field quickly if too much rain had caused a flood. The young Nathaniel Heyward had indeed lost his first crop, on his inland plantation, to the super-abundant rain that drowned his rice: he could not get rid of the excess water because his land was not close enough to the ocean to benefit measurably from low tides. Heyward had instantly resolved to turn his back on inland culture. By 1788 he had transferred his slaves to his second plantation, where tidal methods could be practiced, and he energetically threw himself into experiments with the new techniques.[10]

Here he profited again from being the son of a wealthy man. Although Nathaniel's principal inherited plantation, far from the sea, had proved almost valueless; and although his second plantation, where he *could* practice tidal culture, was relatively small—yet his family connection enabled him to administer (for his two elder brothers, who did not share his dedication to rice planting) the large and brilliantly profitable tidal plantations they had inherited from their father. The new tidal industry was in the throes of development, and Heyward placed himself in the vanguard of the innovative entrepreneurs.

Three problems had to be solved. The planters must learn how to build embankments strong enough to avoid the disastrous breaks which at first bedeviled their enterprises—and here the experience of Dutch dike builders was of critical importance. Then a system of wooden sluices (trunks) and floodgates must be devised—"a matter that was experimental at first, and which became better understood only after repeated failures." Finally, a new system of "flowing" the fields must be discovered, wherewith water might drown the weeds when the rice was first sprouting. On inland plantations slaves were forced to pull out these little weeds, a task which even a defender of slavery acknowledged "required much labor . . . of a most fatiguing kind to stoop over and pick out the grasses by hand." Once a "point flow" had been devised for the new tidal estates (lasting ten to fourteen days just after the rice had been planted), the tidal planters found they needed only half as many slaves per acre—yet on the rich soil enclosed by the new embankments they could grow twice as much rice per acre—as on inland plantations.[11] Nathaniel Heyward vigorously helped to perfect the new techniques—he was especially influential in developing the point flow—and by 1800 he was splendidly situated to profit from the high cereal prices which accompanied the Napoleonic Wars and their aftermath. The price of rice reached nineteenth-century peaks between 1801 and 1805, and again in 1817–18, and by then Heyward was well on his way to becoming a millionaire.[12]

Fortunately for him (if not for thousands of Africans), Pierce Butler and the other Carolina and Georgia delegates to the U.S. Constitutional Convention of 1787 had demanded that no national ban be fixed upon the African slave trade until 1808. Although South Carolina imposed a local ban until 1804, doubtless some Africans imported into Georgia before 1804 were sent across the border into Carolina; others were illegally smuggled directly into the latter state; and forty thousand more Africans were rushed into Carolina from 1804 to 1807, when the local ban was lifted. During these years Heyward bought scores, perhaps hundreds, of Africans at lower prices than would have prevailed had his supply been confined to slaves imported from Virginia. Heyward often bestowed a satirical sobriquet upon a newly arrived African: "Greek and Roman history as well as Shakespeare and the Bible were ransacked for names," which were then written on a card worn for a time around the slave's neck. Often in those days, Heyward's grandson related, one would see a planter, who could not yet remember the name of a newly imported African, "go up to a field hand, whether man or woman, and insert his forefinger under the collar of the shirt to draw out the card containing the name." Heyward was clear about his motives for investing capital in a fresh supply of bondsmen and women. The richest of his rice plantations were, he said, "gold mines."[13] The mines would have been valueless had there been no slaves laboriously to construct the huge new embankments, and to try to cope with the malaria bred in the flooded rice swamps.

The fortune built upon enslaved black backs by this energetic entrepreneur was immense. By the time Heyward died in 1851 (at the age of eighty-five), he had acquired some 2,340 bondsmen and women, financially worth over one million dollars at the prices then prevailing. He had accumulated seventeen rice plantations (ranging in quality from the "gold mines" to a couple of residential farms whose rice production was minimal), where about 1,900 of his slaves labored. Two hundred more of his bondsmen and women worked on other rice plantations owned by two of his children. Heyward's other slaves were scattered over one or two sea-island cotton plantations and another provision farm or two, while seventeen were house servants at the Charleston town house which he occupied when not at his beloved "Bluff" plantation on the Combahee River. His fortune in 1851—unencumbered by debts—also included $70,000 in cash, some landed property in Charleston, and "an enormous amount in stocks." Even when based on the executors' undervaluation of his slaves, Heyward's fortune was worth $2,018,000.[14]

After Heyward's wife died in 1827, he seems to have turned his affections particularly toward his youngest and probably favorite daughter, Elizabeth—who that year was eighteen and had been married for two years to Charles Manigault. Elizabeth constantly visited her father at his country estate, and he constantly showered gifts upon her and her children. In addition to his gift in 1827 of the old Silk Hope plantation and its 126 slaves, he presented her in 1837 with the beautiful Parker-Drayton House, which can still be glimpsed on

Charleston's Gibbes Street. The peninsula had not yet been filled in at that point of the city, and the house then commanded a splendid view over the Ashley River.[15] In the 1830s Heyward offered his daughter Marshlands Farm with its fine, spacious dwelling only seven miles from Charleston; but as Marshlands was a small, rather unproductive rice and cotton plantation, and as Charles Manigault had his hands full attending to Gowrie, he and his wife declined the offer at this time: they did not come into its possession until Heyward's death in 1851. Meanwhile, the old man lavished cash gifts on Elizabeth and her children: for example, two thousand dollars to help her pay the cost of bringing her family back home from France to America in 1848; and the four thousand dollars to Louis Manigault which enabled him in 1850 and 1851 to retrace his father's footsteps through China and South America. When Nathaniel died in 1851 he left Elizabeth another thirty-five thousand dollars![16]

Heyward spoiled his sons too, and only one of those who survived him (Charles Heyward) displayed any of his father's business enterprise.[17] The old man—ill educated and not much polished by his eighteen months in Europe—was, like many another successful rice planter, a man enthralled by embankments, trunks, point flows, and the governing of slaves but increasingly taciturn after the premature deaths of his two eldest sons. His dream was to establish his children so securely in their inherited wealth that they—distancing themselves from his own hard-driving entrepreneurial career—could become full-fledged members of the gentry; and he looked to Britain for the model of social excellence. Besides plantations and slaves, his children and grandchildren must have big houses in Charleston, and Heyward bought up about ten (like the Parker-Drayton House) to bestow individually upon them. Although Nathaniel could not trace a high pedigree to his British ancestors, these big houses made the Heywards "one of the conspicuous families in the city." A grandson tried to fathom Heyward's motives. "As the landowners in England . . . had been the dominant class socially there," Dr. Gabriel Manigault mused in 1884,

> so were they also in South Carolina. . . . With this prestige of the planting or slaveholding class was associated a large amount of family pride, and there were a few old families in the State, especially among the rice planters, who from having been able to retain their wealth for several generations, and in consequence of being able to trace their descent to people of position in England, were generally looked up to, as the titled and land owning classes are looked up to there. . . .
>
> Mr. Heyward, having been under the English rule, and associating throughout his entire life with persons who had been similarly circumstanced, leaned naturally toward English methods of thought, and English views, as to what the objects of life were. He had in these the great example of the English selfmade men, who as eminent lawyers, had obtained positions as equals among the peers of the realm. The great purpose of all of these, after finding themselves in the proud atmosphere of inherited wealth, was to found, and endow families of their own. . . .[18]

In pursuit of this goal, Nathaniel Heyward doubtless relished marrying two of his daughters to their Manigault first cousins,[19] for these alliances might fix the Heywards more surely in the social firmament than had his own marriage to Henrietta Manigault. Charles Manigault—who Heyward probably hoped would quietly adorn the Heyward wealth—proved, however, to hanker after making a little fortune of his own with which to endow his own children. Although Charles Manigault, unlike his father-in-law, was a cultivated gentleman, he ran Gowrie on the same capitalist principles which had proved so lucrative to Heyward: but he had to do so over Heyward's deep-seated opposition.

Against the brilliant example of Nathaniel Heyward, Charles Manigault might set the dim careers of various other members of his family: rice grandees whose fortunes had withered. The estate of Manigault's grandfather, Senator Ralph Izard—a gentleman who was "Stern, Positive & too Dictatorial & ready for a fight," according to Charles Manigault—had become much diminished by the time of Izard's death in 1804. And Ralph Izard's eldest son, Henry (rebelling against a dictatorial father?), ruined himself and his own family by gambling: he committed suicide in 1826.[20] Charles's uncle Joseph Manigault— "highly educated [an] accomplished schollar [*sic*]," but in Charles's view "little calculated to struggle with the clashing interests and rude realities of practical life"—had inherited almost half of Gabriel Manigault I's fortune, including 245 slaves: yet he died in 1843 nearly ruined, his estate encumbered with debts.[21] Charles's own father—a gifted amateur architect who had inherited nearly another half of that fortune but who too was not a dedicated rice planter—and Charles's mother had witnessed the diminution of Gabriel II's fortune of $272,000 in 1788 to about $175,000 by the time they were both dead in 1824. By contrast to these improvident relatives, Charles Manigault prided himself on his own "systematic habits" and his capacity to "*calculate results.*" He set great store on his Huguenot ancestry, whence he believed he had inherited perseverance, self-control, and a capacity for hard work. He was confident that a genteel Carolinian with capital to invest in a rice plantation could easily prosper, "with prudence and industry, *provided* one has only a moderate sum to lay down upon the stump on entering the swamp, after which a few years only must be devoted to self-denial and economy." He himself might have lived off his inherited fortune and his wife's dowry, but instead he had chosen to invest in Gowrie in order to give his children a comfortable start in life. He hoped in future years they would say of him: Our father has "sacrificed *his* time and comfort for *our* benefit."[22]

The "moderate sum" required to launch a rice-planting enterprise might most readily be found from two sources: either from a family inheritance or from marriage to an heiress. Charles Manigault utilized both sources. His family was rich, and as a child he had been accustomed to living in style. The summer residence which his father established in 1807 was a 360-acre estate along the Delaware River, seventeen miles north of Philadelphia, graced by "a Magnificent Dwelling" with rooms "of palatial proportions."[23] The family continued to own a big rice plantation on a tributary of South Carolina's Edisto River; it also received annual installments from Nathaniel Heyward in payment for Silk

Hope; and Charles's father invested heavily in Pennsylvania lands. In 1804 Charles's mother inherited her father's (Senator Ralph Izards's) big Charleston house. Charles's mother had built up a library of some twenty-five hundred volumes—nearly two-fifths the size of the more famous collection of Thomas Jefferson[24]—all of which came into Charles Manigault's possession soon after her death in 1824. The family's luxurious taste for oil portraiture was best exemplified in the large picture (measuring seven and one half feet by five feet) of Charles's grandparents—Ralph Izard and his DeLancey wife—which they had had Copley paint in Rome in 1775.

In such circumstances, anxious concern for family wills, inheritances, and dowries—and flaming rows among jealous legatees—were as common as in a Victorian novel; and Charles Manigault depended more on the traditional avenues to comfort—inheritance or marriage—than he cared to acknowledge. His father's will in 1809 apportioned 9/27 of the estate to Charles's mother, 6/27 to Charles's elder brother, Harry, 4/27 to Charles himself, and 2/27 to each of Charles's four sisters. This seemed to promise Charles about forty thousand dollars; but the value of Pennsylvania lands fell drastically during the depression of 1819, and when the estate was finally settled in 1826, Charles's portion turned out to be only about twenty-eight thousand dollars. Of this Charles had already lost fifteen thousand dollars in his disastrous Far Eastern mercantile speculations.[25] He therefore depended substantially on his mother to promote his fortunes.

To manage her husband's estate, she had at first turned to her elder son, Harry; and she lent Harry money to buy, for himself, the family's rice plantation near the Edisto River. But Harry turned out to be a wastrel, who gambled away his prospective fortune at cards.[26] By 1816 Harry's misadventures led to the appointment of a South Carolina administrator. The subsequent decade of careful management ensured that by 1826—to the family's relief, and despite the fall in Pennsylvania land values—the estate's settlement realized $190,000; of this, Charles Manigault's share was the aforementioned $28,000.[27]

Charles's patrimony was smaller than Harry's, and the disparity had grown when their mother had imprudently lent Harry money which might never be repaid. She tried to even things out by favoring Charles in her own will, bequeathing half her fortune to Charles and only one-quarter to Harry.[28] Thus when she died in 1824, twenty-five thousand dollars would theoretically be Charles's to add to the remainder of his father's legacy; but whether Charles would actually receive all of this money depended on whether Harry would pay the debt he owed to their mother's estate. An unseemly row transpired, with Charles suing Harry. In 1826 the Pennsylvania court gave Charles his main object: he secured an order obliging Harry to pay Charles the thirteen thousand dollars Harry owed.[29]

At Christmas 1823 this unedifying family quarrel had already been brewing backstage when Charles—recently returned to his mother's embraces after six years abroad—set off from Philadelphia for South Carolina to bolster his slightly precarious financial position. For decades the prospect of nourishing themselves from Nathaniel Heyward's cornucopia caused hungry suitors to flock toward unmarried Heyward women like autumnal bobolinks to the heavily laden rice fields of Nathaniel's seventeen rice plantations. As early as 1817, Charles's brother, Harry, had wed Nathaniel's sixteen-year-old daughter Ann. (This union proved a trial to Heyward; for Harry—everyone believed—used his connection to the rich old man to save himself from financial ruin. After Harry died in 1834, the slaves Heyward had given him and Ann had to be auctioned to pay Harry's debts. At the sale Nathaniel Heyward bought them all and gave them a second time to his daughter Ann, but that was the last big gift he made her.)[30] And, as late as 1846, Charles Manigault's cousin Anthony Barclay was writing to Charles with an eye on Heyward's fortune. Barclay, discussing the marriage prospects of his son, Henry Barclay, openly avowed his own motives. The young man, Anthony Barclay observed,

> has shown some disposition to be *spoony* with the fair sex. I should have no objection certainly, if he can find one who is well provided for. I have heard of a Miss Heyward, who . . . is said to have a good Plantation or two, with the proper appendages [i.e., slaves to work the land]. If the story be correct, and you can get him introduced to her. . . .[31]

Charles Manigault's own parent had not hesitated in 1824 to direct Charles's eyes toward the attractive Heyward rice fields, their "appendages," and the largesse of their proprietor. Nathaniel Heyward, Charles's mother wrote to Charles on April 2, "enjoys the happiness of benefitting all who belong to him [i.e., his children and their spouses] and that is a noble pleasure."[32] Charles required no prompting, and this letter probably had not yet reached him in South Carolina when on April 7 he proposed to Nathaniel's fifteen-and-a-half-year-old daughter Elizabeth. During the three brief months of their acquaintance Manigault, nearly twenty-nine, had doubtless regaled the young girl with tales of adventure in Canton and the Dutch East Indies, and of his horseback journey across the Andes. No doubt he spoke

> of the Cannibals, that each other eat; The Anthropophagi, and men whose heads Do grow beneath their shoulders; this to hear Would [Elizabeth] seriously incline; . . . And often did [I] beguile her of her tears, When I did speak of some distressed stroke That my youth suffered.

On Manigault's twenty-ninth birthday, in the garden of Elizabeth's "Aunt Tom" Heyward's plantation, he then popped the question. Elizabeth said, " 'Oh cousin I am too young' [Charles reported to his mother], and I then 'argefied' the topic with her by telling of several ladies of my acquaintance who had married before they had attained their 15th year, for instance Mrs. William Elliott, Mrs. John Parker, etc., etc." Manigault bolstered this argument to Elizabeth by claiming that, despite their brief courtship, he and his first cousin were perfectly acquainted with each other's character and disposition, through family report.[33]

Although Charles succeeded quickly in overcoming Elizabeth's scruples, her parents did not believe she was old enough to know her own mind.

Sixteen was a splendid age for an heiress to marry, but fifteen? The young couple must wait a year. Nathaniel Heyward, having already suggested to Charles that the young man complete his education by making a European tour, now put his hand into his pocket: out came $1,700 to finance just such a trip—the first of Nathaniel's many splendid supports to Charles Manigault.[34] And when Charles, returning from Europe to find Elizabeth true to him, married her on his thirtieth birthday, his fortune was made. By 1861 Manigault reckoned he was worth nearly half a million dollars, and while his investment at Gowrie (including his deportation of sixty-eight of Nathaniel Heyward's slaves from Silk Hope to Gowrie) contributed some $266,000 of that sum, he owed most of the rest to Nathaniel Heyward's munificence.

The heiress who brought him this decisive part of his fortune had, as a child, attended Madame Talande's elegant girls' school in Charleston; yet she was ill educated, mousy, and dependent, and her son Dr. Gabriel Manigault could not in later years avoid patronizing her. Her four European tours, after she married Charles Manigault, were "much to her improvement," Gabriel wrote sniffily.[35]

Her pleasures were homely ones. She always loved to get away from Charleston to pay country visits at her sisters' plantations, or to her beloved father, Nathaniel, who was a widower for the last twenty-four years of his life. "Tall and angular. Not, pretty," Elizabeth (according to a Heyward grand-nephew) "was very domestic and never went out much." Charles Manigault, this same grand-nephew declared, was "a very repressive sort of man" to whom Elizabeth "made a good wife . . . because she was willing to let him have his own way."[36]

The tone with which Elizabeth addressed her husband in 1845—after twenty years of marriage—was cool even by the standards of Victorian propriety. Writing from her father's Bluff plantation on New Years Day, she began:

> I received your letter written on Christmas day, and I wish you in return a happy New year. I did not think you had such a good memory about the time I had promised to write to you, and shall behave better another time. . . .
>
> believe me
Yours very sincerely.[37]

Although a good measure of her affection was poured into cherishing her father—and perhaps into her "kind of companion[ship]" with Victoire Gautier, a French peasant woman who served as Elizabeth's maid from 1836 to 1866—Elizabeth was not quite the cipher her grand-nephew suggested. By gentle means she could sometimes cause her husband to change course. When they first arrived in Paris, she (noticing that Charles Manigault's French accent was not readily intelligible to the French shopkeepers) took secret lessons in pronunciation from their chambermaid, "which she incidentally would rehearse for her husband."[38] Later Elizabeth's hostility to mulattoes impelled Charles Manigault, against his will, to find a new Parisian school for their two boys, where they would not have brown Caribbean schoolmates. Creditably, however, Elizabeth dissuaded her husband in the 1850s from shipping two or three Marshlands slaves to Gowrie. Charles did in fact deport sixty-eight Silk Hope bondsmen and women to his Savannah River plantation, mainly in the 1830s and 1840s; but after Nathaniel Heyward's death in 1851, Manigault felt financially so secure that he was willing to be swayed by his wife's wishes.[39]

Elizabeth presented her husband with seven children, one of whom died in childhood. (The contrast with the child mortality rate at Gowrie was striking, as will become evident.) Those of her children who survived were four boys—Charles Jr.,[40] Louis, (Dr.) Gabriel, and Alfred—and two girls, Harriet and Emma. No doubt Charles Manigault's repressive character affected these children as much as it did his wife and his slaves. He was determined to instill into his sons his own prudent, calculating, entrepreneurial spirit, and he destined his two elder boys—after they finished their academic education—to the same type of commercial apprenticeship he himself had enjoyed. This, he felt, would be their best training for a businesslike approach to life and would be a boon to them should they later become rice planters. But he did not want them to be provincial, and he lavished foreign travel on all of his children. In 1847–48, for example, when Charles Jr. had just graduated from Yale and Louis had completed two years there, he took these two young men, as well as his wife and two of their other children, on a year's tour unusual in scope: from Paris through Greece to Egypt, then back to Paris via Naples, Spain, and southern France. His investment at Gowrie was intended to enable him to bequeath his children substantial property when he died. A parent, he declared, "should make every honest exertion to set each son up in the world upon the same footing as his father did for him. I have four sons to provide for." In return Manigault insisted that his sons be workers, and he brooked no challenge to this fundament of his belief. No doubt his long, embittered struggle with his spendthrift brother had determined him that no son of his own should emulate Harry Manigault: "Any property I may have Created, or Inherited," he avowed grimly, "I would rather, see *it sink in the ocean* than go to an idle, loafer of a Son."[41]

When he penned this threat, probably in 1847, Charles Manigault may already have had a presentiment of the thunderous storm which later drove his eldest son, Charles Jr., from the family's shelter. The young man, having been kept on a short tether at home, appears to have bolted for a kind of freedom soon after being pastured in Connecticut as a Yale undergraduate. His bad example at that distant college later impelled Charles Manigault to place his third son, Gabriel, under his own surveillance at the College of Charleston. As Gabriel recounted, his father had been very disappointed in Yale and "wanted me to remain under his eye and control": the consequence was that the third son, in contrast to his elder brother, "never gave way to any of the temptations to which a youth is exposed when he first leaves the parental roof."[42]

To what temptations Charles Jr. succumbed is not clear. After graduating from Yale, and after returning from the family's long trip to Egypt, he entered a mercantile house as his father wished—first in Charleston and later in New

York City—but his several years in countinghouses did not suit his temperament. He was much happier pursuing buffaloes on horseback in the Wild
West, as he did in 1853.[43] His family believed his character gravely flawed; but
whether gambling, drunkenness, wild adventures, or some combination of
these was at the center of the trouble remains uncertain. In the winter of
1855–56 the young man became crippled during some escapade—possibly
when drunk on horseback. Among other things, he smashed a big toe. He
lived for a time at Marshlands, jovially chatting with relatives in the family
mansion;[44] but eventually Charles Manigault threw him out of the house.
Charles Jr.'s twenty-three-year-old younger brother, Dr. Gabriel Manigault—
then making a grand tour through Constantinople and Russia—addressed the
following admirably clear-sighted, tactful remonstrance to their imperious
father:

> I cannot exactly agree with you in your determination to exclude Charles
> from living with the family in town. That he will be a helpless cripple for the
> rest of his life is quite plain, from the nature of the accident, but that it will
> have some salutary effect in the reformation of his character, I sincerely
> doubt. It certainly is very melancholy that [after all the pains you have taken
> to give us] correct ideas of our duty to ourselves and to society, one of us
> should act as Charles has done. . . . I think your feelings quite natural. But
> [may you not go too far in your determination] to turn from home a son who
> requires, though it be from his own self-abandonment, the constant assis-
> tance of an attendant.[45]

These unillusioned, yet compassionate, words fell on deaf ears. That summer Charles Jr. went to a Virginia Springs resort, where his brother Louis
kept him company; but there was no welcome from Gibbes Street. Instead the
young Charles later went to a boarding house in New York City, where in
December he died alone[46]—a suicide? The Manigault records, so full in other
regards, are silent respecting this terrible family tragedy, which no doubt
seared the memory of the elder Charles Manigault until his dying day nearly
eighteen years later.

But the father reared, in his second son, Louis, a child after his own heart.
When Louis was eleven, Charles Manigault took him in a gig on the three-day
overland journey to Gowrie, the first time Louis had ever seen the plantation
and the first time he had ever been under Charles's exclusive care; and the boy
remembered this trip ever afterward. A gang of sixteen slaves bought in
Savannah had recently arrived at Gowrie, including the thirteen-year-old
Cato (who later became the plantation's trusted miller) and an eighteen-year-
old apprentice carpenter named Jack Savage, whom Louis later came to fear.
In December 1839, however, the slaves had the obligatory smiles on their
faces; and many years later, in the disillusioning wartime year of 1863 (and
only a few weeks after the Manigaults had finally sold Jack Savage in consequence of his having successfully fled Gowrie for an eighteen-month sojourn
in the swamp: his version of foreign travel), Louis fondly recalled "that journey [with my Dear Father], and the care my Father took of me (it being the

first time I had been solely under his care, and separated from my Mother)—
and then again my boyish pleasures at the plantation, where all seemed happiness and contentment." Louis believed he resembled his father "in character
as well as looks much more than any of my brothers [did]." Louis was once
described as "reserved . . . quiet and unassuming," and the first two of these
adjectives might equally well have been applied to Charles Manigault. A
deeply affectionate tone subsisted in the correspondence of father and son.
"Now my old Cricket," Charles addressed Louis from New York in August
1853. "It's bloody hot here." Louis declared that, even as a man of thirty-six,
he was "more thankful for a compliment from My Father, than to be praised
by any one else."[47]

Charles Manigault lavished upon this son the same openhanded generosity
which Nathaniel Heyward had demonstrated toward Heyward's daughter
Elizabeth: thus in May 1858 Charles gave Louis the magnificent sum of ten
thousand dollars with which to take Louis's new bride on a European wedding
trip.[48] Even more important to the young man was his father's personal kindness. Thus when Louis had to leave Charleston very early one December
morning in 1863 to visit Gowrie, he found that at 4 A.M. his father was already
up and dressed to take an affectionate leave of him. He had been raised under
his father's "especial care," Louis wrote that same year;

> perhaps no Son could have been more with a parent than were we two together,
> throughout my Youth and until my Marriage. . . . My constant travels to
> Europe under his guardianship and the numerous advantages I have enjoyed,
> should alone cause me to cling with fondness to his memory. But far more than
> this. . . . The similarity of our educations [during our mercantile trips to
> China] has the more firmly riveted my attachment for him.[49]

Louis paid a price for the perhaps obsequious manner in which he (unlike his
elder brother) cultivated good relations with their father. He dedicated what to
a subsequent age might appear extravagent attention to the details of family
genealogy; and never during his career as rice planter, wartime secretary to the
Confederate Surgeon Major Joseph Jones, and postwar functionary in a
Charleston mercantile firm did Louis show the acuity and relative independence of spirit which characterized his younger brother, Dr. Gabriel Manigault.

Gabriel devoted much of his later life to public service for his native city.
The tone of his quiet protest against his father's slamming the door in the face of
the crippled Charles Jr.—good-hearted yet wholly realistic—is extraordinarily
attractive. No doubt Gabriel's professional training as a medical doctor had
fostered in him a capacity for rational analysis, but the letter bespoke also an
inner security which medical school alone could never have instilled. Gabriel
was as ardent a defender of slavery as every other member of his family, and he
paid a price for his convictions. As a Confederate cavalryman, he was wounded
at Louisa Court House, Virginia, in June 1864, and incarcerated at Fort Delaware for several months. (His treatment there, however, contrasted with that of
the Union prisoners whose plight Louis Manigault stonily surveyed at Ander-
sonville prison.) After the war Gabriel was as keen as everyone else in his

family to restore blacks to subordination. Yet his good works in postwar Charleston—as curator of the Charleston Museum, as a principal patron of the Gibbes Art Museum, and as a professor at the College of Charleston—and the lucidity of his unpublished family memoirs mark him as a man of public worth and some private distinction.

Charles Manigault's three other children led more obscure lives. In 1864 his son Alfred, another Confederate cavalryman, contracted malaria during summer duty in the swamplands, and the desperate Confederate military authorities did not grant him sufficient leave to recuperate properly. Their error of judgment led to his futile death in 1865, after a chilling horseback ride through a stream: a chill that would not have killed a soldier in good health. When Charles Manigault received word several weeks later that his twenty-four-year-old son had perished, he repressed every written expression of emotion: "I do not touch upon the afflicting subject of your Letter," was his only reply to his son Gabriel's notification of Alfred's death. Yet when Alfred's remains were later interred at Charleston's St. Philips Church, Louis said he "had never before seen My Father so deeply afflicted."[50] A stiff upper lip had been as thoroughly bred into this—in some ways personally vulnerable—Charleston aristocrat as into the most Victorian of English gentlemen.

Whether family reserve and aloofness (or even paternal intervention) contributed to Harriet's and Emma's long spinsterhoods is uncertain. Charles Manigault's plans for his daughters' lives blended a portion of enlightenment with a considerable measure of traditional patriarchal authority. On the one hand, he wished to endow his two girls so generously—with "perhaps a larger share of my property than my sons"—that they would not need to marry for money. On the other hand, his list of the essential requisites for an acceptable suitor afforded ample scope for a parental veto: the young man, Manigault declared, might be "as poor as may be, but with some profession or solid pursuit, and with that Huguenot kind of industry, perseverance, training, propriety of deportment, and virtuous Control over all his actions."[51] The two girls, like all of Manigault's children, were put into Parisian schools, and they continued to talk French as their first language within the family until their dying days in the 1880s. Harriet became such a good pianist that she could play through whole operas in piano transcription. She was courted by one of the young Charleston Vander Horsts, but in 1861 at the age of thirty she remained unmarried, and so did her twenty-two-year-old sister Emma; nor did either woman marry during the turbulent wartime and postwar years. When Louis Manigault's wife died in 1868, Emma found a vocation in raising his three surviving young children.[52] The continued presence of Harriet and of Emma at 6 Gibbes Street brightened Charles Manigault's declining years; and in 1870 he still had enough money to hire four black servants—a cook, a chambermaid, a washerwoman, and a yard man—so that his daughters could lead lives of gentility. Manigault had aimed to provide his girls with the economic independence that they might "have it in their power . . . to chuse their own husbands . . . as poor as may be";[53] and they had exercised this power in a way he had not designed.

Thus, if Charles Manigault had been able to forget the traumas associated with his eldest son's demise, he might have felt that he had splendidly fulfilled a parent's duties; and that the rewards to him of fatherhood, though mixed, were substantial. In many other respects, too, his was a happy life. His most distinctive pleasure—one he indulged to the full—was foreign travel. Even by the standards of a later century, his journeys were remarkable. At twenty-two he sailed around the Cape of Good Hope to Canton; and during the next four and a half years mercantile ventures took him to Calcutta, Manila, Batavia, and New South Wales. At Ile de France he invested his own ten thousand dollars, and borrowed five thousand dollars more, in purchasing a load of cloves, and a ship to carry them to China and Manila—where prices proved disastrously lower than anticipated. Manigault spent the rest of his years in the Orient trying to recover from this financial catastrophe. His mother implored him to return to Philadelphia, and he finally abandoned his hope of recouping his lost fortune in the Far East. He then searched nine months to locate a ship bound from the Orient for Peru, which would carry a small cargo of his own; his profit from this venture furnished him the means for a year's travel in South America. He rode horseback from Valparaiso across the Andes to Buenos Aires, sojourned there, then journeyed home via Brazil. By the time he reached Philadelphia in 1823 he was astonishingly well traveled and financially more prudent: wiser but much less rich than when he had set off in 1817. And incidentally, in addition to his other accomplishments, he had become by now a guitarist, a notable dancer, an excellent whist player, and a worthy chess player. (At the age of twenty-eight he had already spent 916 days aboard ship, where he could improve the latter two skills.) His had thus far been a life that might turn many a young person—and not only in 1823—green with envy.[54]

Thereafter Manigault directed his wanderlust eastward. Nathaniel Heyward first sent him across the Atlantic in 1824, but Manigault surely developed his passion for European travel principally from the example of his own parents, especially his mother. From the age of three until fifteen she had lived in Europe; she was remarkably cosmopolitan in her intellectual tastes; and to her Charles Manigault "always looked . . . as being the true standard of a perfect woman, both in intelligence and knowledge of the world."[55]

Manigault took his own family to stay in Europe for seven years, spread over four separate journeys: 1828–30 (two and a half years), 1835–36 (one and a half years), 1846–48 (two and a half years), and 1855 (half a year). This he did partly for his wife's education, then for his children's—and always for his own mental stimulation. A person will "*stagnate, in mind* (if not in body)," he wrote from Europe in 1847, "by remaining *too sedentary* for ten years at home winter and summer pretty much in the same place, and a trip *like this* always has the effect *with me* of sweeping out *much* useless lumber from the mind, replacing it with a fresh stock of ideas to go upon for perhaps ten years to come."[56]

His stock of ideas was a curious mélange of Federalist social prejudice with robust pride in the laissez-faire achievements of American society. Manigault's father was a Federalist member of the South Carolina convention that in 1788 narrowly ratified the new American Constitution; and his maternal grandfather, Ralph Izard, had subsequently, in the U.S. Senate, been a stalwart, anti-democratic, Federalist supporter of President George Washington. In 1847 Charles Manigault expressed their Federalist snobbery in his unbounded contempt for jumped-up Southern colonels—a stance congruent with his boasting, like a courtier, of proximity to regal favor. He had recently attended "a magnificent Ball and supper given by the Royal Family [Louis Philippe's]," he complacently wrote to his Savannah factor from Paris in 1847,

> at the Palace of the Tuileries . . . , to which Mrs. M and myself were invited. . . . Gentlemen all go in [military] uniform, or in an established Court dress. And as I never gouged a man, nor killed a rattle snake, nor drove regularly a four horse stage, nor kept a tavern, I therefore have no *legitimate* right to be dubbed "Colonel"; therefore being thus excluded from this notable Class in my own Country I got an embroidered Court Dress made.[57]

The means to buy a Court outfit, probably worn by Manigault only once in his life, were readily available to him from Silk Hope's profits.

Laissez-faire ideology was as well adapted to protect these profits from government intervention as it later proved in defending those of industrial capitalists; yet Manigault's attachment to laissez-faire grew into a passion deeper than sheer rationalization of his own economic interest. His admiration for the American minister to England—the patriotic historian George Bancroft of Massachusetts—was heartfelt; and European travel reaffirmed the Carolinian's pride in the strength of many American social institutions. Manigault, having achieved an invitation to the Tuileries, could now deny that he was impressed by "the splendour, and tinsel, the pomp and parade of high life *here,* where embroidery and decorations (many no doubt obtained thro[ugh] favor, and intrigue) *may have* dazzled *those* who have a taste and devotion for *such things.*" By contrast with this European tinsel, Manigault was delighted by George Bancroft, then visiting Paris—"this unaffected well-informed representative of our country." Perhaps under the influence of Bancroft's after-dinner oratory, Manigault temporarily forgot about the jumped-up Colonels; instead, he radiated pride in

> our Country, its institutions and . . . our state of social advancement in every thing—such for instance as our encouragement to science, our enormous sums devoted to education, the maintenance of religion, [our country's] churches, and schools, and charitable institutions, *all* sustained by the mass of society, and all in the most flourishing Condition, *unaided by Government.*[58]

Manigault's trip to Egypt the next year gave him a more personal reason for satisfaction at how Americans did things. His tactic was always to do favors for well-placed people, then to seek reciprocal favors for himself. Thus he occasionally sent Mr. Greene, an American banker in Paris, "some of Uncle [Nathaniel] Heyward's oldest and best" Madeira, which Greene then used for sumptuous entertainments: for example, to entertain George Bancroft in 1847.[59] No doubt this was why Manigault was invited to meet Bancroft. (Thus the sweat of black people in Heyward's rice swamps lubricated the wheels of American self-congratulation about the strength of America's social institutions.) Perhaps by similar assiduous attention to another person of influence—this time, the American consul in Cairo—Manigault secured an interview with Mahomet Ali, the modernizing ruler of Egypt, in 1848. The pasha then granted him permission to inspect rice-milling machinery recently installed by British engineers at Alexandria. Manigault's delight in the superiority of the machine he himself had just introduced at Gowrie was boundless, and his Savannah "factor" soon received from him a self-satisfied letter, which also canvassed the prospect of unwelcome Egyptian competition in world rice markets.

Had the author been a Northern manufacturer of fine cotton goods, writing to Boston from Lancashire and assessing the worth of modern British technology—and had American cotton technology been much better than in fact it was—the Northern capitalist might have reported scornfully, "I have had some conversation with Robert Owen respecting his cotton mills. I visited his mill at New Lanark, which . . . was coarsely made with none of our modern American improvements." The actual words of the letter, however, were those of a keen Southern capitalist whose mill was operated by slave labor. "[I] had some conversation with the Pasha," Charles Manigault informed Robert Habersham in Savannah

respecting his Steam Rice Mills. . . . I visited his mill at Alexandria . . . which tho[ugh] Constructed by first rate English Engineers and . . . working with great ease and rapidity, still it was coarsely made with none of our modern improvements in Brushes, &c., &c. And the Rice was every Grain Deep Red, shewing from long neglect & ignorance in not changing the seed, Volunteer Rice [i.e., inferior rice sprouted from a previous year's planting] has now become the Rice of this Country. . . . But they never can interfere with us in this article [in world markets], for they want all they produce.[60]

The comforts which the Manigaults enjoyed during their European journeys may be estimated by their traveling style in the United States. In September 1853 the family found itself luxuriously ensconced at New York's elite St. Nicholas Hotel, thanks to Charles Manigault's careful preparations (and to his bulging pocketbook). "All the [New York] Hotels overflowing. But I know how *to fix them*," he reported cheerily to Louis,

and have always got *first rate rooms*. I write a stylish Note, on my Stampt [i.e., engraved] Paper, put it in the Stampt envelope, address it to The "Proprietor" of said Hotel, tell him that since leaving Charleston with my family of 6 we have made it a point to select *the most celebrated* Hotels and *theirs* having been particularly named to me by one of *their friends*, I beg him to select two *such Bed*-rooms as will suit my wife and daughters, and lock them up at my expense the moment they may be vacant—so that they think me a "Hell of a fellow" and we find it *all right* on my arrival. We have beautiful rooms. . . .[61]

Wealth enabled Manigault to indulge not only in costly hotel life but in many of the other pleasures of conspicuous consumption. When, in 1841, he had commissioned his cousin Anthony Barclay to buy a pair of carriage horses in New York City and to ship them to Charleston, his instructions were: " 'Damn the Expense.' " The resultant bill for the two horses—$540[62]—was about the same as it had recently cost Manigault to build five two-room frame houses to accommodate forty of his slaves at Gowrie. (A two-room house for eight slaves cost about $108; the Marshlands house where the Manigaults spent their winters during the 1850s—with its mahogany staircase and its "lavish and excellently executed gouge work . . . to supplement its more formal Adam embellishments"—had cost the wealthy rice planter John Ball nearly $10,000 to build in 1810.)[63] And in 1859 Manigault paid $160 for a gold hunting lever watch and chain—rather more than the $139 he spent that same year on furnishing the then ninety-six Gowrie slaves with the tobacco and molasses which were their equivalent luxuries.[64]

A capitalist entrepreneur with a taste for expensive living, clinging to a slave system which he knew was condemned by much of the world, might be expected to justify himself by claims of altruism and the fulfillment of onerous duty toward the subject caste. This, indeed, is how Charles Manigault appeared in a memoir he wrote in 1870, seeking to explain himself to his descendants. His two hundred slaves (including those at Silk Hope and Marshlands) were, he said, mainly "*Descendants* from *those Negroes* owned formerly by my ancestors . . . and to the present day, they have ever been treated (sick, or well) most kindly & liberally, well clothed & fed, & particularly at *Silk Hope* permitted to plant a little for *themselves* & to raise poultry, & a hog or two for some of them." Marshlands Farm, he declared,

> was never of any profit to me. It hardly paid its expenses & I wanted to move 2 or 3 of its Negroes to Savannah River *where their Work* would be productive, & valuable to me. But, My Wife said, "Though they are doing so little *here* on the Farm, yet, as they were a Gift to us from My Father, dont let us separate any of them from Each other." And *there* they Every one Remained.

This scenario of Carolinian masters' long attachment to their "numerous faithful ancestral family Negroes" differed sharply, in Manigault's eyes, from the callousness of absentee British planters toward their West Indian slaves. Manigault's portrayal of American slavery was a stereotypical tableau of cheerful bondsmen and women freely maintained by careworn paternalist masters. "Even while *we were* Slave Colonies of Great Britain," he declaimed,

> *We, here at the South,* in most instances, resided with our families *half the year on Our Plantations,* Surrounded by Our Negroes, attending personally to their comforts. *We saw that* they ever received good, wholesome food, & the

Sick & aged attended to. And as *Our own Children* (to a certain extent) were playmates with *theirs,* on the Plantation, *All this, naturally resulted,* in mutual family interests, and kind personal feelings So generally prevailing (*until recently*) between *Masters & their Slaves* amongst *us. But, Emancipation* has Distroyed [*sic*] *All this.* . . . Their Heads & Hearts are turned against *us* their former protectors & friends. . . . *While we owned them, their prosperity,* as well *as Ours* were *mutual & reciprocal.* Their Lives, & well-being, were cherished (as their *wonderful Increase* [in population] shews. . . .[65]

This retrospective view of slavery contrasts starkly with the picture that emerges from Charles Manigault's own carefully compiled contemporary records of life at Gowrie.

3

The Charnel House

Callousness, not paternalist benevolence, was the hallmark of many American masters' relation to their slaves. Edwin Epps, a small Louisiana cotton farmer in 1850, brutally flogged a helpless slave woman Patsey of whom he was sexually jealous, and stabbed the unoffending elderly slave Abram during one of Epps's regular drunken fits. The rich and genteel Louisiana planter Bennet Barrow and his neighbor Ruffin exhibited their own heartlessness in pursuing Ruffin's fugitive slave with dogs, twice ordering the beasts to chew the black man when they caught him. When the dogs had tracked the fugitive, they soon "had him up & a going, And never in my life did I ever see as excited beings as R[uffin] and myself, ran 1/2 miles & caught him. Dogs soon tore him naked, took him Home Before the other negro[es] at dark & made the dogs give him another over hauling."[1] The savagery of an Epps or a Barrow was not uncommon in the burgeoning Southwest, where the mid-nineteenth-century cotton boom impelled masters to push their slaves ruthlessly. But well-bred planters on the long-settled Atlantic coast could have been expected to display a more benevolent spirit than those of the Southwest. The Atlantic coast was the stronghold of paternalist ideology,[2] and one might have supposed that the masters' conduct there would reflect their paternalist rhetoric.

Yet although Charles and Louis Manigault were neither Edwin Eppses nor Bennet Barrows, their stance toward their bondsmen and women was akin to that of Barrow: fundamentally, slaves were instruments to be employed for the master's enrichment; they must be firmly disciplined, and if a number of slaves died untimely deaths while laboring to increase the master's profits, that was the slaves' own bad luck. The clearest evidence of the Manigaults' callousness lies in the astonishing record of slave mortality at Gowrie. In 1849 the eminent British geologist Charles Lyell made himself a mouthpiece for proslavery propaganda: the Georgia "rice grounds," Lyell asseverated,

> are salubrious to the negroes as compared to the whites. In this lower region the increase of the slaves is rapid, for they are well fed, fitted for a southern climate, and free from care. . . . Such advantages, however, would be of no avail, in rendering them prolific, if they were overworked and harshly treated.[3]

The annual lists of Gowrie's slaves inscribed by the Manigaults from 1833 to 1861 show that the premise of Lyell's argument—prolific "increase"—was far from evident at that plantation.[4]

In 1833 Charles Manigault launched his enterprise on the Savannah River with a capital investment of some thirty-two thousand dollars, plus a further twenty thousand dollars of borrowed money. Just over half of the total was investment in slaves: seventy-two of them. He bought fifty for fifteen thousand dollars (with the plantation) and culled the other twenty-two from his father-in-law's Silk Hope estate—nearly all young "prime hands," worth perhaps twelve thousand dollars. His stock declined during the first year, for nine slaves died and only five were born. To instill proper discipline among his new bondsmen and women, he sold one of them (the twenty-six-year-old Friday) because he was a "runaway." He therefore had only sixty-seven slaves left at the end of his first year, and he soon sold another slave, the twenty-six-year-old Minda, no doubt also for disciplinary reasons.[5]

In 1834 disaster struck. The Asiatic cholera, crossing the ocean from Europe, hit Gowrie in September. Fifteen slaves died during a dreadful fortnight in mid-September—most of them "prime hands" no more than thirty-two years old—and three more perished later in the epidemic. Because nine other slaves also died that year from other illnesses, while just two were born, only forty-one slaves were still alive on New Year's Day 1835—only a little more than half of the original number.

Manigault was nevertheless making good enough rice crops at his wife's Silk Hope plantation that he felt able to take his family for a one-and-one-half-year sojourn in France from May 1835 to December 1836. Returning to America, he instituted the policy of filling the ranks at Gowrie with new recruits. By purchasing twenty-seven bondsmen and women and deporting eighteen others from Silk Hope, he had by 1842 restored his slaveholdings at Gowrie to the original seventy-two, even though many more slaves continued to die than were born.

During the next three years he felt he had turned an important corner, for during that period the sixteen deaths of slaves were offset by seventeen births. In 1845, indeed, the excess of births over deaths was three. This sounded better expressed as a percentage. "Of late years," he exulted to a Carolinian acquaintance, births had exceeded deaths, and owing to his "own peculiar care & management [the increase] was last year 4 per cent."[6]

These words—penned in Europe, where Silk Hope's rice profits permitted Manigault to take his family for a two-and-a-half-year trip from May 1846 through November 1848—were belied by, among other things, a measles and dysentery epidemic in 1848. These and other diseases from 1846 until early 1849 killed one-third of the slaves.

Nothing daunted, Manigault nearly doubled the scale of his capital investment in 1848. He bought the plantation adjacent to Gowrie, purchased 52 new slaves for it, and dispatched six more from Silk Hope. He felt that 119 bondsmen and women would be enough to farm the new estate successfully, but the appalling health conditions at Gowrie prevented him from ever keeping as many living slaves there as he wished. In 1850 disease struck down 21 bondsmen and women, while only 7 were born. In 1852, 21 more slaves died—8 in an epidemic supposed to have been "cholera"; in 1853 the toll was 19; and 1854 was nearly Gowrie's worst year, with about 25 percent of the slaves dying (13 from another "cholera" epidemic).

In the face of this horrific death rate, the only way to keep up the slave force was to resort to massive importation of new slaves. Manigault sent 45 such recruits to Gowrie from 1851 to 1854, and as soon as his finances could accomplish it he sent 21 more early in 1857. Even during the last six years before the Civil War 52 slaves died while only 39 were born. The pattern continued into the war itself.[7]

The melancholy record from 1833 to 1861 appears in table 5. This shows that, during a period of nearly thirty years, nearly twice as many bondsmen and women died at Gowrie as were born: about 294 perished there, while some 148 babies came into the world. The original stock of the plantation— 72 slaves in 1833 and 58 more added in 1848 when the size of the plantation was doubled—could not quite be maintained even by the massive net importation of 110 new slaves to take the places of most of those who died so fast.

How conditions at Gowrie affected the slaves' health is evident in this consideration: had Manigault managed to bring down the number of deaths so that it equaled the number of births, 240 slaves would have been alive in 1861. But, in fact, all except 94 had perished.

The vicissitudes of the slaves' lives, from year to year, may be seen in table 6.[8] The death tolls of 1834, 1846–48, 1850, and 1852–54 stand out, but deaths almost always exceeded births—the striking exception being in 1845, when, for a solitary year, the increase of the slave population had indeed amounted to 4 percent. Manigault's management had not proved salutary to his slaves in other years, and one must attempt to determine why this was so.

A principal source of misery to Gowrie's slave parents was that they found it nearly impossible to keep their children alive. For example, among the original group of slaves at Gowrie in 1833 were 6 "infants" (under three years old); not one of them survived until 1835. Only one of these six died of Asiatic cholera. And malaria and enteric diseases—probably responsible for most of the other five deaths—continued to kill off Gowrie's youngsters at an almost

TABLE 5.   Gowrie's Slave Population, 1833–61 (Summary)

Original stock (incl. 72 slaves to stock "original Gowrie" in 1833, and 58 slaves to stock East Hermitage in 1848)		130
Slaves *imported,* 1836–61	+129	
Slaves *exported,* 1833–61	−19	
Net imports		+110
Total stock		240
Births (estimated), 1833–61	+148	
Deaths (estimated), 1833–61	−294	
Net natural decrease of slave population		−146
Total slaves still alive at Gowrie, April 1861		94

Note: See appendixes B and C for the sources of these estimates.

unbelievable rate so long as slave masters confined the children to the dank rice swamps.

Thirteen infants (under age three), born elsewhere, were imported into Gowrie with their parents between 1833 and 1855, and with one exception every one of them died before reaching the age of sixteen. The sole survivor, Sam, lived until the age of twenty-two, when he contracted pneumonia during the winter—no doubt from doing wet ditching work in the cold, windswept rice fields—and he died in March 1858. None of these 13 infants therefore survived to see freedom.

About 109 other infants were born at Gowrie from 1833 to 1855, and 97 of them succumbed before reaching the age of sixteen. Of the dozen survivors, two more died before reaching the age of twenty-six—one of them a suicide. A third survivor, Sam's brother Fortune, was sold as a habitual runaway. Two others were sent back to South Carolina as young children to escape Gowrie's deathly "miasma." Thus only 7 of the original 109 babies were still alive in Georgia when General Sherman's army arrived there to liberate them in December 1864.

Most of this record is summarized in table 7, showing a horrific child mortality rate (to age sixteen): 90 percent.[9] Lest this dismal statistic be regarded as incredible, the names of all 69 dead children who can be identified are printed in appendix C, where specialists can check them; appendix B explains the reasons for estimating that 46 other infants died before the lists were compiled.

Though a child mortality rate of 90 percent was ghastly enough, this number does not fully measure the sorrows of the slave women, for it takes no account of stillbirths (like Joaney's in the summer of 1845). The number of stillbirths was almost certainly at least 5 percent as large as the total number of live births.[10] Nor does the child mortality rate of 90 percent take into account miscarriages (like Linda's in June 1852). Miscarriages were seldom mentioned in the Manigault records, but their frequency—among pregnant women who worked in the fields until shortly before the anticipated birth—is suggested by Frances Kemble, who spent several months at another low-country Georgia

TABLE 6.   Gowrie's Annual Slave Population, 1833–61

Year*	(a) No. of slaves at start of year	(b) Births (est.)	(c) Deaths (est.)	(d) Imports	(e) Exports
1833	72	5	9	0	1
1834	67	2	27	0	1
1835–36	41	5	5	8	1
1837	48	2	3	10	0
1838	57	9	9	0	0
1839	57	3	8	17	0
1840	69	6	8	0	0
1841	67	4	7	1	0
1842	65	4	6	9	0
1843	72	4	3	0	0
1844	73	6	9	5	1
1845	74	7	4	5	0
1846–48	82	11	31	0	1
1849	119**	8	10	1	0
1850	118	7	21	4	2
1851	106	7	11	7	2
1852	107	9	21	19	0
1853	114	6	19	19	4
1854	116	4	31	0	1
1855	88	4	12	0	3
1856	77	9	10	21	0
1857	97	7	6	0	0
1858	98	7	10	1	0
1859	96	6	5	1	0
1860	98	6	9	1	2
1861 (April)	94	—	—	—	—
TOTAL		148	294	129	19

Note: See appendix B for sources.

* Beginning in 1849, the "Year" normally begins in April and ends in April of the next calendar year. Before 1849 the "Year" normally runs from December to December. (Thus "1841" = Dec. 1840 to Dec. 1841.)

**Includes 61 still alive at end of 1848, plus 58 slaves brought in to stock the new East Hermitage section of the plantation.

plantation. Kemble reported (in a striking passage of her *Journal of a Residence on a Georgian Plantation*) the experiences of nine slave women who talked to her one evening in 1839. Gowrie's record suggests that these nine women did not exaggerate to Kemble their stories of misfortune. Altogether the nine women had had 55 children, of whom five were stillborn and 24 more had already died by the time Kemble spoke to them. These women also reported twelve miscarriages—one and one-third per woman—and again, more will have taken place before the women left childbearing age.[11] When the baby of another slave woman (the mother of thirteen children, many

TABLE 7.   Gowrie's Estimated Child Mortality (to age 16), 1833–64
(of children born before April 1855)

	Number of Infants			(d) Child mortality rate to age 16 (b/a)
	(a) Total (est.)	(b) Died before age 16 (est.)	(c) Alive at age 16	
Infants (under 3 years) at Gowrie, Jan. 1, 1833	6	6	0	100%
Infants (under 3 years) imported into Gowrie, 1833–April 1855	13	12	1	92
Infants born at Gowrie, 1833– April 1855	109	97	12	89
TOTAL	128	115	13	90

Note: Gowrie's lists of living slaves—annual except for one twenty-seven-month gap (1835–37) and one forty-month gap (1845–49)—show that 63 children were born there from 1833 to April 1855 and survived long enough to be recorded in the subsequent annual list; of these, only 12 survived until age sixteen.

I estimate that 46 other babies were born at Gowrie during this same period but died before their names could be recorded in the subsequent lists. Thus a total of 109 babies were born (63 listed and 46 unlisted), of whom 12 survived to age sixteen. This information is printed on the next–to–last line of table 7.

Because of the high infant mortality on rice plantations (e.g., at Pierce Butler's "Butler Island" plantation 32.6 percent of the infants perished during their first six months), a large number of babies certainly died before their names could be placed on Gowrie's annual lists. (Every new baby whom the Manigaults recorded on an annual list was, on average, six months old; the proportion of live births whose names were omitted from the annual list therefore would have been about 32.6 percent, if Gowrie's infant mortality rate were no worse than at Butler Island.) An even larger proportion of Gowrie's births will have been unrecorded in the 1837 and 1849 lists because, during the twenty-seven- and forty-month intervals when Manigault was in Europe, even more babies are sure to have died than during the usual twelve-month interval.

My estimate that 46 Gowrie babies (born 1833–April 1855) died before their names could be recorded in the subsequent lists is fully explained in appendix B; the estimated number of such unrecorded births, for each year from 1833 through April 1855, is printed in appendix table 1, column d (see appendix B).

already dead) expired, she "merely repeated [to Kemble] over and over again: 'I've lost a many; they all goes so.' "[12] The sentiment is sure to have been common at Gowrie.

Few of the approximately 115 Gowrie children who died during this period saw a doctor during their final illness. Their medical care was entrusted to the overseer, who sometimes had more pressing duties; to Binah, an elderly slave woman, whose services cost nothing, and in the efficacy of whose remedies as plantation nurse Charles Manigault had considerable (if unfounded) faith; and to the children's parents during whatever waking hours they may have been away from the fields. The causes of the children's massive death toll are not at first evident. Tetanus—caused by unhygienic cutting of the umbilical cord—probably killed about 3 percent of Gowrie's infants during the first eighteen days of their lives, as it appears to have done on other rice planta- tions;[13] but this disease cannot explain the subsequent toll. The feebleness of the infants at birth—resulting from their mothers' chronic malaria, or their

exhaustion from arduous field labor during the last months of pregnancy—
was doubtless a major cause of infant mortality.[14] Overseers' reports at
Gowrie occasionally suggested teething, or worms, as reasons for children's
deaths; and several years after nurse Binah's death in 1853 of "old Age" (at
sixty-three), Manigault recommended the reinstatement of her annual dosage
of the children with "vermifuge" to expel worms. Yet almost surely two other
maladies were (directly or indirectly) the principal killers: malaria, and bowel
complaints.

That Charles Manigault suspected malaria is evident in his reference to
"the bad summer climate of our rice fields *for children.*"[15] Summer was the
time when every white person who could afford to do so left the region to
avoid the "country fever" (malaria); and the remedy Manigault adopted for
a time in the 1840s to protect the slave children was identical to the defense
adopted by white people against malaria: summer residence on high ground
(where the breezes blew away the anopheles mosquitoes). The time for
taking the slave children to the high land was mid-May[16]—the moment
chosen by whites to flee the malarial swamps; and the time for bringing them
home was the moment chosen by whites for their own return, when frosts in
October or November routed the mosquitoes. The planters supposed they
were escaping swamp "miasma": no one then knew that mosquitoes carried
malaria, but these precautions make plain that malaria was the summer
disease feared among slave children. Some blacks inherited a genetic partial
defense—the sickle-cell trait—against malaria; and some acquired from
their mothers' blood, through the umbilical cord, antibodies conferring a
certain nongenetic resistance against the disease (if the mother herself had
survived attacks of malaria);[17] but most adult blacks in the malarial regions
are likely to have had childhood bouts with the disease before building up
enough immunity to gain for themselves a certain protection against fatal
encounters in later life.

Doubtless these childhood bouts were numerous among the summer maladies fatal to many Gowrie children. "Fevers plagues the children very much,"
wrote the overseer in the summer of 1852.[18] Such fevers plagued adult slaves
too, and sometimes were certainly malarial. Clear instances of malarial intermittent fever—in an adult and a child slave later deported to Gowrie—were
mentioned by the Silk Hope overseer in autumn 1835: "Betsey is better—but
has frequent attacks of Fever and ague. Her smallest child [Hagar] is also
frequently down with it."[19] Roswell King Jr., the intelligent agent who ran
Pierce Butler's huge Georgia rice plantation during the 1830s, believed black
children were susceptible to country fever: he therefore "advocated the [sum-
mertime] removal of children from Butler's Island to high ground." Frederick
Olmsted, too—probably deriving his views from his Georgia host, the rice
planter Richard J. Arnold—believed malaria killed many black infants: "The
greater difficulty with which [the Negroes'] lives are preserved [on rice plantations than elsewhere], *through infancy especially,* shows that the subtle poison
of the miasma is not innocuous to them." And the postbellum Carolina rice
planter Duncan Heyward acknowledged from his own experience that even

after 1888 black "children suffered from [malaria] to some extent, and with infants it was often fatal."[20] So pestilential was malaria on the Savannah River that the Savannah City Council, in the 1820s, had passed " 'dry culture' ordinances prohibiting the flooding of rice fields within one mile of the city"— rules which no doubt saved white people's lives in Savannah but did nothing for Gowrie's children eight miles upstream.[21] Malaria may have been even more common at Gowrie than on rice plantations elsewhere in the low country, because Manigault housed his slaves on the swampy island instead of sheltering them in pine woods on mainland riverbanks, or on rises a little above the swamp.

Infants imported into Gowrie died even faster than those born there after 1833 (see table 7), and perhaps part of the explanation lies in fatal enteric diseases. These may have been even more common on the Savannah River than elsewhere, and possibly some of the native born built up a certain resistance against them. Thus when Charles Manigault finally bought a pineland camp in 1856 and sent children there during subsequent summers, this probably protected them not only from malaria but from enteric diseases spread by polluted water in the river swamps.[22] For several years child mortality declined substantially.

Then in 1860 a new killer struck: seven children died that year (all born since 1855 and none therefore included in table 7); most of them died suddenly at the pineland. No doubt influenced by the overseer's report, Louis Manigault at first confidently attributed these deaths to poisoning by the slave Old Betsey, the cook at the summer camp (the "Betsey" whose malarial attack in 1835 has just been mentioned). Yet there is no record of Manigault's seeking a criminal prosecution of Betsey, nor of punishing her himself; and several years later Louis modified the accusation: Betsey, he wrote, was "*said* to have poisoned several Children."[23] In the unlikely event that Betsey ever thought of striking at Charles Manigault by killing some of his "property," her main reason for anger had been removed before the children's deaths: for Manigault had already relented from his earlier intention of selling Betsey's son, driver George.[24]

If the children's sudden deaths were caused by poisoning, a malevolent white pineland neighbor was far more likely to have been the poisoner. As early as 1843 Manigault had encountered opposition to his sending Gowrie slaves into the pineland, from the proprietor of a plantation adjacent to land which Manigault then rented as a summer refuge for Gowrie's children. The neighbor—one of the Heywards—insisted that Manigault move a newly constructed house four to five hundred yards away, so that the Gowrie slave children would not mix with Heyward's own bondsmen and women.[25] And in 1852 highland farmers proved most reluctant to rent Manigault land as a "cholera" refuge for his slaves.[26] Had "cholera" struck in 1860, Manigault would surely have evacuated his Gowrie slaves to his new pineland "camp"; the wish to discourage him from doing so may have impelled a white neighbor to poison the Gowrie children. Gowrie's overseer, however, had every reason to accuse Betsey, the mother of his enemy George,[27] of a crime which a white man probably committed. Whatever caused the children to perish, the only certain thing is that this form of death would have been avoided had the children not been forcibly separated from the care of their own mothers. Here was an example of why freedwomen after 1865 sought more time to nurture their own young children.[28]

Charles Manigault lived to the ripe old age of eighty-five, but the term "old" meant something different when applied to his slaves. "old Abram" was fifty-one, Harriet at fifty was an "old Woman"; and the Hannah who had lived at Gowrie since before 1833 was "old" at fifty.[29] A stronger term had to be used for a slave who survived much longer: thus Ned, who died in 1849 at the unusually advanced age of sixty-seven, was "very old." The origin of this usage becomes evident from Louis Manigault's tabulation of the ages of Gowrie's slaves in 1855. Eighty-seven slaves then lived at Gowrie, but not one of them was as old as fifty-eight.[30]

Part of the explanation was that in Charles Manigault's first decade of proprietorship—when he supplemented Gowrie's original set of slaves with others imported from Silk Hope or purchased at auctions—the newcomers were nearly all young "prime hands" who would not have been much over fifty by 1855. But those already at Gowrie included many who by 1855 would have been over fifty-seven had they survived; and Manigault acquired several relatively old slaves after 1839. Altogether twenty-three of the slaves owned by Manigault at Gowrie would have been over fifty-seven in 1855 if they had lived that long; but all had died.[31] Gowrie was inhospitable to the elderly as well as to the very young.[32]

Neither was it salubrious for "prime hands." The Savannah River was thought to be for slaves unusually unhealthy even by the standards of the rice kingdom. In 1832 Charles Manigault's nephew, a low-country South Carolina planter, declined to purchase a plantation on the Savannah River because the slaves' death rate there was so high. This did not deter Manigault from buying Gowrie, nor were other planters put off; and by 1859 more acres were planted in rice on the Savannah than on any other river in America. But in 1845 a nearby planter thought it worth mentioning—and Manigault thought it worth recording in his journal—that the former's slave force had actually grown slightly in numbers over a seven-year period. The opposite experience was the norm. One neighbor's stock of slaves had declined from 95 to only 65 by 1844, within six years. Manigault heard of another nearby planter who had lost forty "prime hands" within eight years, out of a total force which probably had numbered in 1836 about 115.[33] Manigault was therefore exultant in 1847 when he persuaded himself that Gowrie's slave force was finally beginning to grow naturally.

As we have seen, his hope was quickly shattered. Twenty-eight slaves—more than one-third of the whole plantation—caught measles in an 1848 epidemic; driver Renty died of it, "being struck suddenly in one of the lungs & bowels which no remedy could remove." Before the slaves recovered from measles, many got dysentery, and at least six died within a fortnight. There seems to have been no supply of unpolluted water; overseer Cooper probably failed to give the slaves enough "flax, sage & other teas" to slake their burning thirst with boiled water; some slaves in despair probably drank ditch water; and Cooper then blamed them for self-destruction. It was not the picture of a cheerful slave community:

> Sickness to an alarming extent prevails at Gowrie—disease *Measles super-ceded [sic] by dysentery.* The latter has proven fatal . . . upon two Women & a Girl. [June 20, 1848]

> Our sick house being full these taken [sick] afterwards were compelled to remain in their own houses. . . . Our old & only nurse [Binah], from constant worrying was attacked with appoplexy, a disease she has long been subject to. . . . [I set two field slaves, inexperienced at nursing, to take her place,] one to attend to the sick house, the other, to the numerous cases scattered throughout the settlement. [The slaves] would come out of their houses at night, regardless of the weather (for it was constantly raining) & go even to the ditches & drink their fill. . . . I look upon their deaths as suicidal acts. [June 30, 1848]

At first Cooper delayed calling a doctor, but by June 20 he had summoned the experienced Dr. Pritchard, who now resided eighteen miles from Gowrie. Charles Manigault, who had not yet learned the scale of the epidemic, urged the overseer to avoid spending more money on a doctor than necessary. "You have indeed had much sickness to contend with," Manigault replied to Cooper's letter of June 18 (a missive which probably had understated the seriousness of the epidemic), "& I am glad to think your experience enables you to contend with it, without calling in the Doctor for every Case which does not actually require his presence."[34]

Although Dr. Pritchard's services enabled Gowrie's slaves to escape the Asiatic cholera epidemic of 1849, Manigault appears to have dropped him in the spring of 1850 in order to cut his medical bill. Fevers (malarial?) plagued Gowrie all that summer. Blaming the slaves' troubles on a so-called "broken bone fever [then prevalent in Charleston] in consequence of low and damp situations," the overseer tried to maintain an upbeat tone. But Cooper had been quite ill himself, he was anxious about the harvest (which proved alarmingly small), and he seemed almost unhinged by the horrors of the slaves' lives:

> The health of the Island has somewhat improved [he reported in mid-June]. We have only thirteen [hands] at this time down. We have had over 20 at a time. [Gowrie's workforce was then equivalent to 73 "prime hands."] I have had no physician as yet and have thus far been blest with success, although I must say that I find the duties in that department more worrying mentally and physically, than my planting duties. [June 17, 1850]

> With us in many cases it was [three to six weeks] before people recovered [he wrote early in September]. [Though we do not have an epidemic,] frequent cases of fevers occur. . . . It has been with sorrowing heart that I have walked through the fields and looked upon this one, that one, and another, and so

on, and see their attenuated frames, hardly able to drag along through the small portion [of work] they seem able to do, brought down by disease, and although at that time convalescent, had to come out to make room for others worse off than themselves [i.e., were coerced by Cooper to stagger into the fields in order to cut the ripe rice]. This state of things as well as the backward state [of the harvest], and the amount of work before us, has operated upon my mental feelings. [Sept. 4, 1850][35]

Nineteen bondsmen and women, including the usual toll of infants, died that year—15 percent of the plantation. Vibrant community indeed, when even the overseer who forced the slaves from their sickbeds to their harvesttime toil was shaken by their misery!

Twenty-eight more slaves died in 1851 and 1852 (eight of them in the "cholera" epidemic of 1852). To fill the depleted ranks Manigault—in miniature like the relentless General Douglas Haig—sent more recruits (see table 8). Over the years, importation had proved essential to keep Gowrie functioning.

The importations after 1849 worsened Gowrie's already dismal health record: for all of these imported slaves came from the South Carolina low country, and slaves from Carolina died even faster at Gowrie than did the native born. Nine infants, under age three, were brought with their mothers between 1849 and 1855; every one of these children was dead by 1855. Early in 1854 Manigault bought the trusted driver of a Carolina plantation and five members of his family. Within a year all had died: five from consumption and the sixth, Rebecca, during the chaos of the 1854 "cholera" epidemic. She contracted that disease at Gowrie and was transferred to the pinelands. (To remove them from the epidemic, the overseer had desperately shifted all of the slaves on December 18 and 21 to pinelands with "good water," but there were no dwellings until the slaves hastily erected some: "When Rebecca reached the Pine Land, the Camps had not been put up, & she suffered much from exposure &c. &c.," and she died by Christmas.)[36]

In 1854 Manigault had also bought, at unusually high prices, the thirteen members of a promising extended family: a "truly fine family & well worth" their price.[37] These slaves had been owned by a Northern-born lawyer, Benjamin Faneuil Hunt, who bore in the name his proud family connection to Boston's Faneuil Hall. He had become one of the great rice planters on South Carolina's Pee Dee River, possessing 234 slaves in 1850. Retiring from planting four years later, Hunt wished to realize the cash value of his assets by selling his land to a prosperous neighbor, and his slaves where they would fetch a good price. If this meant that the 13 members of the "Hunt family" must be torn away from their community on the Pee Dee and deported nearly two hundred miles to pestilential Gowrie, so be it.[38] Within about a year 8 of these 13 Hunt slaves were dead, 4 from "cholera." Indeed, newcomers to Gowrie were especially susceptible to the "cholera" of 1854: of the thirteen deaths in that epidemic, twelve were among slaves imported to Gowrie in 1849 or thereafter. For this reason, when the time approached for sending survivors back from the pineland "cholera" camp to Gowrie, to test whether the epidemic

TABLE 8. Slaves Imported into Gowrie, 1836–60*

	Number imported	From Silk Hope	Bought in Savannah	Bought in Charleston
1836–42	45	18	19	8
1843–50	15	15	—	—
1851–54	45	7	—	38
1855–60	24	1	—	23
Total imports	129	41**	19	69
Less exports, 1833–60	19***			
Net imports	110			

* Does not include the 72 slaves with which Manigault launched his enterprise in 1833 (22 from Silk Hope and 50 purchased with Gowrie); nor the 58 slaves with which he stocked his new East Hermitage tract in 1848–49 (6 from Silk Hope and 52 bought in Charleston).

** Because one slave (imported in 1842, exported in 1846–48, and imported again in 1849) has had to be double counted here, the actual number of individuals imported from Silk Hope was 40. Thus the total number moved from Silk Hope comprised these 40, plus the 22 in 1833, and the 6 in 1849: a grand total of 68.

*** Ten of these were sold for insubordination, and 9 were sent back to Manigault's properties in South Carolina.

was over, the doctor cautiously advised Louis Manigault "to send a detachment of the real Georgia Negroes first."[39]

The most spectacular death tolls at Gowrie resulted from what was believed to be Asiatic cholera. The first epidemic of that disease reached American seaports from Europe in 1833. Because it spread principally through infected water, its ravages were concentrated near rivers; and the Savannah River was hard hit in 1834. Gowrie then lost eighteen slaves. The second epidemic arrived at American ports in 1848, and when it came to the Savannah River in 1849 the two Pringle Smith plantations on the river's Carolina shore lost a total of fifty slaves.[40] That year Gowrie's slaves were quickly evacuated to a nearby cholera camp with clean water supplies, run by Dr. Pritchard (who in 1834 had borne much responsibility for combating the epidemic in Charleston), and none of Manigault's slaves died. Three years later cholera may have returned to the river, but the overseer did not recognize the danger. Manigault misunderstood "cholera," supposing that it, like malaria, was innocuous after the autumnal frosts.[41] Presumably his overseers shared this notion and were unprepared for epidemics in November 1852 or December 1854. More important, Manigault had discouraged his overseers from spending much money on doctors; he himself preferred not to spend the money to buy a permanent pineland camp as a refuge for the slave children or their parents; he no longer even rented such a camp. It was not surprising, therefore, that the overseer in November 1852 dallied before calling in a competent doctor and that he waited even longer before he was able to rent a camp to which the slaves could be evacuated.[42] Eight slaves died, most of them surely unnecessarily. And history repeated itself under a different overseer in 1854. This man neglected to call in a doctor soon enough and failed to evacuate the plantation until it was too late. The first victim—driver Robert's wife—died on December 5, 1854, yet a fortnight later the masters were still negotiating for a pineland refuge. "There has been seven cases since yesterday morning," the overseer's wife wrote from Gowrie on December 18. "Cuffe died . . . yesterday morning. Eve is the worse now." (Eve soon died.) Mrs. Clark promised to send a letter to the father of the previous overseer, no doubt searching for a camp to which the slaves could be evacuated. By the time this could be accomplished and a competent doctor was engaged, thirteen slaves had died.[43] Louis Manigault reached Savannah from Charleston on Christmas Eve. "The Dr. [Bullock] has been telling me just what I know already," Louis reported to his father, "that we must have [i.e., buy] a tract of land. . . . When (says Dr. B.) You loose one prime hand & another is about to be taken down with Cholera, go at once to the Pine Land." Louis concluded soberly. "Had We moved out sooner, I think we would hardly have lost any."[44]

The year 1854 was the nadir of the most ghastly extended period in Gowrie's history: during the seven years after Charles Manigault bought East Hermitage 115 slaves died, while only 35 were born. "Cholera" in 1852 and 1854 claimed altogether 21 of these lives but obviously was not the only killer.

Indeed, whether the epidemics in 1852 and 1854 were Asiatic cholera is uncertain. Joseph Waring's "Asiatic Cholera in South Carolina" suggests that the spasmodic cholera of 1852 on South Carolina's Pee Dee River may not have been the Asiatic variant; possibly that on the Savannah River was not either. There is even more reason to doubt that Gowrie slaves died of Asiatic cholera in 1854. Savannah's Dr. William Bullock then reported that— according to two overseers—"all the other plantations are quite healthy";[45] and Waring's article mentions no Asiatic cholera in South Carolina in 1854. Dr. Bullock suspected that unsanitary conditions were at the heart of the matter, for, indeed, fatal enteric diseases were common at Gowrie. One wonders whether the 1854 outbreak, and perhaps also that of 1852, were simply epidemic manifestations of a chronic problem, not always thought to be worth a doctor's attention:

[1846] The negroes have been very much effected with Diarroahs & Dysentery [the overseer reported]. The children (those at home) are at present considerably effected with it & I fear Nancy's child will die. Mom Banah [the plantation nurse] has really managed the desease remarkably well.

[1847] We have had dysentery very severe on the plantation for the last month or six weeks and it presents itself in the most obstinate form I ever seen it. Some of the negroes have had it 2 & 3 weeks at a time, and . . . it has taken off Jackson he died on the 14th Inst. It is very prevalent among the children but have lost none of them as yet. Dr. Pritchard is in attendance.

[1853] There is considerable sickness among the Negroes at this time [overseer Stephen Clark reported]. I have lost 3 children within the week passed. Bowel Complaint the principle cause.[46]

Apparently slaves and overseers alike depended on the river—supplemented perhaps by whatever rainwater could be collected in barrels—for their water supplies until after the 1849 cholera scare. Upon their return from the cholera camp that year the overseer had a spring dug at both slave settlements. "The water in them," he assured Manigault, "filters through coarse gravel & sand. It is almost as clear as rain water, quite cool, & far preferable to the warm & muddy river water."⁴⁷ Yet living conditions at the plantation remained often noxious.

One problem was that the mud dikes were inefficient in keeping out the river water. "I have as usual too much Sickness,—[malarial?] fever & diarrhea," overseer Skinner reported in midsummer 1851. Four slaves doing carpentry on the new brick thresher had all been ill. Ever since the fields nearest the East Hermitage slave houses had been most recently "flowed" (in one of their several annual regularly planned periods of being covered by irrigation water), the settlement

has been very disagreeable [Skinner acknowledged], oweing to the water oozeing through the bank and keeping the ground under the Negro Houses soft and wet, which emits an effluvia which is certainly poisonous. I have kept the weeds cut down and have had small gutters cut to get all the water into the large ditch, but I cant begin to get the ground dry under the houses.⁴⁸

As though this were not enough, Gowrie was subject to periodic unplanned floodings, when everything was inundated (including the slave quarters themselves) except the threshing mound and the pounding mill. The masters' and slaves' houses were built on stilts to protect them from these freshets, but the protection was incomplete. A flood might last a week or ten days, and there were serious ones at least in 1833 (and probably in late June 1835), 1840, September 1841, April 1844, March 1850, September 1852, March 1854, September 1854, and February 1861. "Every thing is nasty & dirty about the [slaves'] settlement . . . ," Louis reported after the flood subsided in March 1854. It was the planting season, however, and "We have no more time now for this year to whitewash & all will now remain dirty & dingy until next Fall." Two days later he exclaimed, "Every thing is Covered with the Freshet sediment & the fields 'Stink!' "⁴⁹ Relief did not in fact come that autumn, for in September 1854 a hurricane deluged the island again, sweeping two-thirds of the harvest into the river and covering everything again in muck. The new spring near the pounding mill was probably, like everything else, covered by the filthy waters. Can the inundations of 1852 and 1854 have been wholly unrelated to the spread of devastating enteric epidemics in November 1852 and December 1854?

Other possible carriers of disease were rats. They were not in short supply. "The audacious rats have cut a good deal of [rice] off near water mark," the overseer reported, as the 1851 harvesttime approached, "& [they] continue to cut away. It is the only way they can subsist at this season." Manigault's neighbor once devised an incentive scheme to spur the zeal of his own ratcatcher. "The old [slave] man at Mr. McAlpin's killed between Harvest & then planting again fully 4000 Rats (four thousand)," Manigault had written with ill-concealed dissatisfaction in 1844, "while at my place old Abram only killed about 1000. Mr. McAlpin instructed [his overseer] to pay one lb. of tobacco for every 100 rats." The idea of keeping up with the McAlpins led the next winter to a flurry of activity at Gowrie, and for a time rats were dispatched more efficiently than settlement ditches were cleaned: "The number of dead Rats brought in by old Abram & his pack of 5 Curs . . . from the 1st Jany. to this date. . . ," Manigault chortled the next April Fools' Day, "is 2700 (two thousand & seven hundred rats!!)." But Manigault was soon in Europe, while "old" Abram shortly went blind, and no record remains of further rodent eradication. No doubt the slaves were obliged to regard rats as an inevitable component of life down by the riverside.[50]

Filthy water seemed to Louis Manigault the likely carrier of "cholera," and poor sanitation was for him the heart of the matter. Although he blamed this on the overseers, he (like many contemporary whites) could not refrain from blaming the slaves too for their own deaths. Gowrie presumably had no outdoor privies, settlement ditches being used for the purpose. The overseer reported cleaning these ditches in February 1852, but the job may have been done inefficiently—and at one of the two settlements probably not at all. Robert (the Gowrie driver) told Louis during the 1854 epidemic that

> the Gowrie Settlement ditches have not been Cleaned out since Mr. Bagshaw's time [i.e., since 1844], nor has Hermitage Settlement [the second settlement on the plantation] been Cleaned either for several years. Mr. Bagshaw made it a rule to Clean out those ditches every Spring but that rule has never been followed out.
>
> The rule is to have the ditches always perfectly Clean & allow fresh water from the river to flow in & out at times through little plug trunks. This has not been attended to at Gowrie. Ducks even are no longer raised at Gowrie owing (says Robert) to the ditches being so dirty. . . . Now Can that be a Cause?
>
> . . . The Negroes, You know, put all sorts of nasty things in the ditches & then dip up (I am Confident) the same water to drink.

In 1845 Charles Manigault had applauded the energy of Bagshaw's successor in digging out the canals and in "half quarter draining" the fields, for efficient irrigation had high priority; but clean settlement ditches did not then loom large on the master's horizon.[51]

Louis Manigault implied that driver Robert's wife, and the "truly fine family" bought in 1854, were especially imprudent about drinking water; for she was the first victim in 1854, and four of the nine adults in that family also perished during the epidemic. Instead of blaming the victims for their own deaths, Louis might have indicted himself as manager, or his father as Gowrie's proprietor. Had the slaves not been compelled to live there, many would have drifted away to more healthful regions—as happened after 1865, leading soon after 1900 toward the virtual extinction of low-country rice culture.[52] Any free laborer on Gowrie could have fled at the first suspicion of an epidemic instead of remaining until the overseer and the owner—whose interest in the matter was less exigent—decided what to do. If the Manigaults had permitted the blacks to live scattered around the countryside—as happened all over the South as soon as slavery was abolished—epidemics would have spread less speedily. Thus in January 1854 Manigault bought the adjacent Legaré plantation with 148 acres of rice fields and its own settlement of slave houses; but instead of letting some of his own bondsmen and women live there—where they might have escaped the "cholera" that December—he tore down all the newly acquired houses and used the material to build extra dwellings beside those at East Hermitage. He was determined to concentrate the slaves into just two settlements (Gowrie and East Hermitage), where their doings could be closely supervised—even though this meant that any epidemic would be sure to spread quickly.

If Manigault had supplied as many mules as his overseer had requested in 1852,[53] slaves released from "mashing" the soil with their hoes would have had time to clean out the settlement ditches each winter, and the two later "cholera" epidemics might never have occurred. And had Charles Manigault had been willing to spend the money to buy a pineland refuge for his slaves (to replace the one he ceased renting from Dr. Pritchard about 1850), he could have evacuated the slaves immediately in 1852 and 1854, as he had done in 1849. In the absence of such a refuge the overseers dithered: days were wasted and many lives lost while the overseers tried to find a piney woods proprietor willing to rent even empty pineland for occupation by a plantation of slaves stricken with the dread "cholera." "The delay of two days . . . , in search of some high-growing retreat, greatly increased our Mortality [from the 1852 "cholera"]," Louis Manigault later admitted. He attributed the delay to "the natural unwillingness of the Georgia high-land farmers to allow an infected Gang of Negroes to camp on their lands." Even when the land was finally found, more time had to be wasted in hastily throwing up the seven triangular log "Tents" meant to shelter from the winter the one hundred miserable refugees.[54]

Because Louis felt anxious about his own drinking water, his younger brother Gabriel—a medical doctor traveling in Europe—dispatched in October 1854 from Paris, for Louis's own use, a porous stone water filter. This did the slaves no good that December, for it did not arrive soon enough to be installed, and in any case was meant for the master, not the slaves. After thirteen slaves died in that year's epidemic, Louis bought a second filter "for my plantation," which may perhaps thereafter have produced a small supply of clean water. But the problem had certainly not been solved by 1859, for in that year Charles Manigault was still urging Louis to get some kind of water filter for a prospective overseer who had discovered from previous experience on the Savannah River "the muddy nature at times of our river water."[55]

Another cause for unnecessary deaths was the tardiness with which competent medical assistance was secured. The first "cholera" victim (driver Robert's wife) died on December 5, 1854, but no doctor was summoned until December 10, by which time the epidemic was well launched. At first the overseer then called in a Dr. Gregoire—probably a local resident and relatively cheap—for daily visits to the plantation, and it was only after the overseer had moved half of the slaves to the pineland camp that he secured the services of the esteemed, and doubtless expensive, Dr. William Bullock of Savannah. Bullock went down well with the slaves: "All the People seem to like Dr. Bullock very much," Louis reported on Christmas Day. "He knows a great deal about the Cholera, moreover he is so successful."[56]

In every age physicians are criticized, sometimes rightly. The appalling bloodletting therapies, the immense lacunae in doctors' knowledge, and the prostitution of some medical "science" to proslavery purposes—these all make it easy for a later age to scorn physicians of the mid–nineteenth century. We may do them an injustice, for their perceptions were often clearer than those of the planters. That the diet of field hands lacked adequate nutritive value was clear, for example, to Dr. Gabriel Manigault, Louis's brother. In 1860 he was thinking of making a house servant out of a fifteen- or sixteen-year-old youth, "but, I am sorry to say, [he] is not well grown for his age. He ought soon to take a start though, as Robert [a young Silk Hope house servant] has done since he has been with me, and the good food that he is likely to have as a house servant ought to accelerate his growth."[57] Medical doctors like Gabriel Manigault, through a combination of education, experience, and common sense, some- times penetrated walls of planter self-interest in order to enunciate simple truths easily overlooked. This was a principal service they could render the slaves: they could present a point of view independent from the wishes of planters to maximize profits, and of overseers to "make a crop." Dr. Bullock made clear to Louis Manigault that prompt removal from Gowrie would have saved the lives of most of the thirteen bondsmen and women who died in the 1854 epidemic; his insistence that the Manigaults purchase a pineland tract of their own led (two years later) to their doing so.

How a doctor's advice might save a slave's life—because he was indepen- dent from a planter's self-interest—appeared in an anecdote of the traveler Frederick Olmsted. A yellow fever epidemic about 1853 killed several slaves confined in jail at Natchez, Mississippi. A physician therefore advised the captor of a fugitive slave not to lodge him in the jail, for fear he too would die. The captor heeded this advice; the fugitive thereupon escaped again, and the fugitive's owner (subsequently learning what had happened) was enraged that the doctor's advice had been followed. "Whenever you catch a nigger again," the owner angrily lectured the captor, "you send him to jail, no matter what's to be feared. If he dies in the jail, you are not responsible. You've done your duty. . . ." Duty, to the planter, consisted in maintaining plantation discipline, and a slave dead in jail was worth more to him than one alive in the swamp. Duty to the doctor, by contrast, lay in keeping a human being alive, even if this might conflict with the dictates of plantation discipline.[58]

At first glance it might appear that Charles Manigault was scrupulous in securing independent advice for his slaves, for he did indeed lavish medical care upon certain of his bondsmen and women. His doctor's bill (excluding medicines) for his eight Charleston house slaves in 1858 reached perhaps nineteen dollars per slave.[59] He spent forty-one dollars to have Dr. Bullock attend to the eye of Hector, Louis's favored boatman and companion; and he sent Betty—driver George's wife, and one of the Manigaults' two most esteemed slave women at Gowrie—to Charleston for expert medical attention to an injured shoulder.[60]

Yet he was not eager to secure for his slaves frequent recourse to the services and independent opinions of medical doctors, and he mingled one portion of openhandedness with a dozen of parsimony. In 1845 Dr. Pritchard lived just across the river on the Carolina shore, but Manigault declined his offer of medical attendance on Gowrie slaves at $1.25 per head per year. The annual expense in 1845 would have been less than $100—a small sum for a plantation whose net profits reached a peak of $13,500 that year—but Manigault preferred to pay for each visit, and to try to keep the number of visits small.[61] This attempt at economy failed, for during the next four years Pritchard had to visit Gowrie so often that his annual bills averaged just over $2.00 per slave.[62] In the late 1850s (when Manigault no longer employed Pritchard), he held the Gowrie doctors' bill per slave down to about $1.50— and in some years less than $1.00.[63] The overseers understood that Manigault valued their being medically self-reliant: "We have been able to controle [an outburst of dysentery] so far without the aid of Dr. Pritchard," James Haynes pridefully reported in mid-1846. The next overseer, Jesse Cooper, was anxious to assure Manigault in August 1849 that "up to the time of our removal out here [to Dr. Pritchard's camp to escape cholera] I had never called in a Physician . . . this year, neither have I done so as yet to any of your people in Camp. . . . I have attended to & prescribed for all myself." These boasts were often, of course, accompanied by vows that a doctor would be summoned if really necessary.[64]

Although evacuating the slaves to Dr. Pritchard's camp saved them from the Asiatic cholera in 1849, Manigault was soon embroiled in a dispute with their medical benefactor. Dr. Pritchard, overseer Cooper informed Manigault in March 1850,

> disapproved entirely of the course I [acting on Manigault's instructions] had pursued the past year of managing all the sickness myself [except when the slaves were at Pritchard's cholera camp]. I told him we differed upon that point, that . . . when I found the disease would yield to the influence of medicines under my own direction and treatment, I deemed it altogether unnecessary to trouble him with such cases.—It is true the responsibility is a great one.

Apparently this dispute led to a rupture between Manigault and Pritchard, and to termination of the summertime practice of sending the slave children to a camp away from Gowrie's malarial swamp.[65]

How the system of relying on an overseer's medical judgment could work in practice was illustrated in the case of Pride, a carpenter, who "was layed up of Fever severe, and slight pain in his right side," on Tuesday, September 2,

1851. This was harvesttime, and any manager of slaves—even the estimable overseer K. W. Skinner—would think twice before taking boat hands away from the pressing harvest labor to fetch a doctor. For five days Skinner failed to get one. "I attended him until this morning," Skinner wrote on Sunday, September 7, "when I found his case desperate. I immediately dispatched your boat & 5 hands to Town for Doct. Wrag. . . . He arrived half past 12 P.M." It was too late, and Pride died at eight o'clock the next morning of peripneumonia, evidently a victim of the overseer's negligence, the pressures of the annual harvest, and above all of Charles Manigault's insistence that overseers take the place of medical doctors whenever they—ill judging as they often proved to be—imagined they could do so without a valuable slave's dying.[66]

The next spring Skinner ventured to send Ralph—a good worker who was later made driver at the Hermitage tract—to Savannah for at least a week for medical treatment of a "most awfully swollen" penis. Skinner's liberality with his employer's money apparently elicited from Charles Manigault a reprimand and an order to avoid Savannah doctors whenever feasible; after receiving Manigault's missive, the overseer hastened to make the fateful promise that "I will avoid sending any one down to the Doct. as much as possible. I know how extortionate they are in their charges."[67]

Five months later, having harvested the 1852 crop and stacked the cut rice at the threshing mill, Skinner was frantically preoccupied with finding an engineer to repair the steam thresher: its breakdown paralyzed the whole threshing operation. A crisis like this one in getting the valuable crop to market—not the health of one or two slaves—was the recurrent nightmare of an overseer's life. "Your work must go forward . . . ," Skinner wrote anxiously on October 31, 1852. "Nothing can be done in the threshing line until a competent Engineer comes on." To add to Skinner's worries, the grinding stones in the pounding mill were out of line and "must be put in first-rate order by a first-rate mill-wright, before I can have any rice ground." Four days later Skinner journeyed to Savannah and pinned down the errant white engineer; the thresher was repaired within a few hours. Beset by annual crises of this sort, the overseer was relieved finally to have things running smoothly again and he mentioned in passing the least of his concerns, the life of an infant slave. He also explained why he summoned a local—probably young, inexperienced, and relatively cheap—doctor for Cicero instead of getting a good doctor from Savannah. "Now I am threshing," he reported to Manigault with satisfaction on November 4, "& hope to go on well, &cs. I have been very busy with the hands at important work, &cs. Die's child died to day. Cicero is very ill, —something like an Epidemic & I have sent for Doct. Magilo just above here, who is a good Physician. I cant spare 4 hands to go to Town for Doct. Wragg."[68]

The diagnosis of diarrheic complaints was complicated by the existence of a relatively mild disease called "cholera" (not the Asiatic variant), which seems to have been endemic at Gowrie: thus in May Skinner had reported without alarm three cases of "cholera morbus." Skinner and Dr. Magilo—

whose name never appeared before or afterward in the Manigault records—
seem not to have recognized in Cicero the symptoms of a virulent disease.
Eleven days later the plantation had been evacuated in desperation, yet not
until November 18 did Skinner have the skilled Dr. Bullock of Savannah
attend the stricken pineland "cholera" camp.[69] No doubt Manigault's reprimand about extortionate Savannah doctors had been fresh in Skinner's mind
early in November, and the 1852 "cholera" epidemic was permitted to gain a
running start before effective action was taken. Eight Gowrie slaves perished.

Besides these eight, eleven other slaves died in the year beginning April
1852. Only seven were born. Yet the excess of twelve deaths over births, while
uncomfortable to the Manigaults, was not a financial catastrophe. Although
some of the 1852 crop was damaged by the September freshet and had to be
sold cheap (and although the slaves' thirty-five-day absence at the pineland
"cholera" camp obliged Manigault to have most of the crop milled expen-
sively at Savannah and Charleston, rather than free in Gowrie's own pounding
mill), nevertheless the year's profits—even after deducting six thousand dollars for the net loss of the dead slaves—were eighty-seven hundred dollars.[70]
This sum enabled Manigault to purchase nineteen new slaves in 1853. The
master was considerably better off after the epidemic and the other deaths
than before.

Although Skinner left the Manigaults' employ in December 1852, this was
partly because his own health had been undermined by malaria, contracted
during his summertime plantation work. Charles Manigault probably distrusted Skinner, believing he had deceived him about how much rice had been
soaked in the September freshet,[71] but he does not appear to have sacked
Skinner because of his handling of the "cholera" epidemic. Certainly, when
hiring Skinner's successor, Manigault was not chastened by recent experiences: the contract of Stephen Clark, the new overseer, made plain how
future illnesses of the slaves were to be handled. "There being no physician
engaged on the place," Clark had to agree in his contract. "I will provide
myself with a good book of Medical instruction and be careful to have at hand
the few requisite Plantation Medicines and I will attend myself to mixing and
instructing the nurses how to administer them."[72] Broken bones were a different matter: in such cases Clark was enjoined to hurry the patient to Dr.
Bullock in Savannah.

Besides the supposed economy of depending on the overseer's medical
skill (except for broken bones and emergency cases), another reason to mini-
mize dealings with Savannah doctors was that slaves might get the wrong idea;
they might conclude that a mysterious malady, accompanied by a jolly excursion down the river to town, would furnish an attractive alternative to life at
Gowrie. "I have had Amos quite sick here with a stricture," Louis Manigault
notified his father in March 1853,

> & I fear it will lead to retention of urine. I thought it prudent to send him to
> Dr. Bullock. I have done so (although I hate to do a thing like that very
> much) three times. . . . I shall not send Amos to town again unless I find him

in great danger. I think it will be best to send Amos to Charleston for it will never do for me to send him to Savannah so often.[73]

In view of the strict terms of his contract, and of the Manigaults' clear desire to avoid superfluous dealings with Savannah doctors, it was understandable that overseer Clark let Robert's wife die on December 5, 1854, without calling in a doctor, and that none was secured until five days later, when the next "cholera" epidemic was well under way. The Manigaults' distaste for securing regular medical attendance for their slaves was a principal cause for the death toll in December 1854. They did not blame Clark for the slaves' deaths: instead, they hired him again for 1855, even though some fifty slaves had died since Clark had begun overseeing Gowrie two years earlier; when Clark himself died of consumption at Gowrie in December 1855, Louis Manigault penned in his plantation book the unique compliment: "A good Overseer."

One slave who survived a bout of "cholera" in 1854, but whose life nevertheless was marked by the effects of his masters' neglect, was Abel Hunt. Abel was one of the thirteen members of the high-priced extended family proudly purchased earlier that year by the Manigaults and shipped off from South Carolina to replace slaves who had died at Gowrie in 1852 and 1853. The father, George Hunt, at fifty was an experienced "trunk minder" (controller of the irrigation sluices) who immediately assumed one of these posts at Gowrie. His wife, Flora, took over the job of plantation nurse from old Binah, who died just after the Hunts arrived. The Hunts' eight children included two sets of twins—Adam and Eve, and Cain and Abel; and there were also a son-in-law and two infant grandchildren.

The two grandchildren, like all other very young children imported into Gowrie during this period, died not long after their arrival. So did one of the Hunts' elder daughters. Her husband, Anthony, father of one of the infants who died, perversely seems not to have cared for Gowrie; he attempted to flee and, as Louis noted laconically, "died from it, died in Charleston."[74] When "cholera" struck Gowrie at the end of 1854, nineteen-year-old Abel Hunt was very sick but lived. Early in December his mother died in the epidemic. So did his twin brother, Cain, and, within a few days, his father, George. His sister, twenty years old and a "remarkable woman" in Louis's words, died a day or two later. Thus eight of the thirteen Hunts died within a year, and Abel's seventeen-year-old sister Nancy and his eight-year-old sister Fanny were also stricken with "cholera" but survived. On December 25 Louis Manigault arrived at the impromptu pineland camp from Charleston to spread Christmas cheer among those still alive, but Abel Hunt did not respond with the "broad grin" which was de rigueur for slaves, and with which his sister Nancy managed to greet her master that day.[75] Abel, having by December 26 nearly recovered from his own serious illness, "now begins to feel the loss of his Parents. Poor Fellow, he was rolling on the ground almost like a Crazy person & Calling his Father and Mother." Two days later Louis Manigault seemed surprised that Abel still had something on his mind, and he sought to get him to keep his troubles to himself. Acknowledging nevertheless that slaves could have the same feelings as other people, Louis turned to the writings of South Carolina's best-known author, William Gilmore Simms, for a parallel. "I have never seen a person in Able's situation," Louis reflected,

> but Simms gives a Character in one of his Novels that is similar. "Able" appears to be quite well, but he seems to be deranged at times. Something is troubling his mind & he imagines he sees his Father & Mother & that they are talking to him, & then he will strike up the funeral hymn. I find I can only make him hush up for a while.[76]

No doubt the reason the Manigaults did not sack Clark was that he raised good crops (except when freshets and hurricanes intervened). Clark nevertheless may have been uneasy about the large number of slaves who had died, and when he wrote to his employers in the summer of 1855 it behooved him to assure them of his concern for the slaves' health. His real anxieties, however, focused on the possibility of another flood, and on the perpetual conflict between getting the harvest in and keeping the slaves alive. "I expect a fine crop," Clark predicted nervously in July 1855,

> if we have no Freshet which I sincerly [sic] hope we will not have though in dayly dread of it. . . . It is very provoking to live in such constant dread. The Negros have generall keept well which has been every thing for me (thus far) though August & September is trying month, a time of such intense interest to me.

His ambiguous location of "thus far" suggested Clark's sense that in August and September the harvest must be secured, and health might then have to take a second place. A pregnant "prime hand" had been so ill that Clark had even called the doctor for a visit. The Manigaults had owned this slave woman for only six years, and Clark thought he'd better remind Louis who she was. "There has been a few cases of Fever among them," he continued, "& that woman Phillis who cooked for me has been very sick. I had to call Dr. Gregorie to her. She is still sick though not under the Dr." Clark's subsequent medical care was not more salutary to her than the doctor's would have been, and within four weeks the overseer had the same number of deaths to report:

> The woman Ph[i]llis who cooked for me is dead. I carried her out to the pine Land as soon after her confinement as I though[t] proper but she took the Bowel Complaint which carried her off in short time. Mingos Phillis [aged twenty] is dead too. I have lost Charle's Child Ralph and one of Die's Twins. . . .[77]

After Clark's own death in December 1855, Charles Manigault placed his dependence upon the medical skills of the next overseer, Leonard Venters, whose bulletins unfortunately tended toward the cryptic. "I must say to you," Venters informed his employer during the 1857 harvest, that

> I have lost to[o] since my last to you old Hannah [she was fifty] & little Jackson [thirteen years old] who has Decease and Departed this life. I am

sorry But I can not helpe it as you may Know or will Know when you come to
learn. I have had some very sick since my last to you. But some has Recovered & some has Dide.[78]

Exasperated, the Manigaults decided five weeks later to get rid of Venters,
but the offense for which he was fired was the unforgivable one of undermining plantation discipline, not the relatively unimportant one of medical
ineffectuality.

A further factor contributing to Gowrie's death toll among adult slaves—
beyond the prevalence of enteric diseases and the Manigaults' heavy medical
reliance on their overseers instead of doctors—arose from the conditions of
labor in the waterlogged fields. The problem was most acute in winter and the
early spring. Respiratory illness was so common among low-country slaves as to
cause frequent comment by overseers and masters. Thus "Mr. McA[lpin] has
lost this winter 7 prime hands" (out of forty-six) by pleurisy, Manigault noted in
1844. Two years later Manigault's overseer—overoptimistically—speculated
that, in doing away with the hand flail, Gowrie's new threshing machine might
"do away with that horrible disease Pneumonia." The overseer reported in
March 1847 that six prime hands owned by another of Manigault's neighbors,
Dr. King, had recently died of pneumonia; this was more than one-sixth of
King's effective labor force. Dr. King, no doubt correctly, blamed his overseer
and sacked him, but of course this remedial action did not bring the slaves back
to life—and no one would have thought of charging with manslaughter a negli-
gent overseer, or the employer responsible for hiring him. If low-country slaves
died in the winter, respiratory illness was presupposed a likely cause: for example, Charles Manigault reported early in March 1859—of a Savannah River
neighbor recently returned to Charleston—"Since A[llan] Izard left his Plantation he has lost 3 more negroes, by Pneumonia I presume."[79]

The nine exhausting weeks of the harvest were succeeded late in October
each year—even after 1846, when at Gowrie threshing machinery replaced
hand flailing—by the frantic work of threshing: "The hurry of threshing equals
the hurry of harvesting," Charles Manigault once acknowledged. Yet the winter
labors after the threshing were probably the most hated by the slaves. On
cotton plantations winter work might be less unpleasant than in the summer
and autumn, but on rice plantations things were different. The river embankments must be mended, the irrigation ditches cleaned, the canals deepened, the
floodgates and culverts repaired, and all of this done in the wet mud, often
barefoot at the coldest time of the year. Even the overseers admitted the work
was disagreeable. "The women are rakeing out the vines, &cs. which grew in
the large ditches,—the rakeing of which is quite a job," Skinner acknowledged
early one February. Overseers minimized the risk to the slaves' lives:

> Our Hands have been steadily employed on Canal work since my last [Jesse
> Cooper reported in midwinter 1850]. We have had considerable sickness
> amongst the people of both places, but all are doing well again. [Feb. 14,
> 1850]

The heavy mud of the canal has made [a] good many of both places sick though nothing very serious. [Mar. 1, 1850][80]

If a virgin field was being cleared, ditches must be made; and an individual slave's daily task was the digging and removal of six hundred cubic feet of earth. No wheelbarrows were used to move the mud, and the heavy "spades" supplied—more difficult for a recalcitrant slave to sabotage than a light "shovel"—were exhausting to use. When, after the war, in 1876, Louis Manigault resorted for one year to the disastrously expensive expedient of hiring Irish immigrants for ditching, he was astonished by their laborsaving equipment. The "manner of work . . . is all quite new to me," he marveled. "The Irishman works with a shovel (and long bent handle) and wheelbarrow"! No such miraculous technology had been furnished Gowrie's slaves when they ditched the four new fields in 1839–41. The smallest ditches ("quarter drains") were 3 feet in depth and an average of 18 inches wide. Each slave had to dig out a 133-foot length of this ditch to complete the daily task. Tangled cypress roots exacerbated the slaves' difficulties. "Where there are stumps or trees," Charles Manigault admitted, "the full task cannot be done." The main ditches were much larger than quarter drains—often 5 feet deep and an average of 5 feet wide, and a ditcher was compelled to finish a 24-foot length of such a ditch in a day's muddy labor.[81]

Canal building seems to have been even more onerous, for only the strongest males were set to this work: each was expected to dig, in one day, a 10-foot length of a canal wide and deep enough to accommodate the great flatboat which carried cut rice to the barnyard. When overseer Washington Skinner started a new canal on November 11, 1851, he set his fourteen best men to digging, while women worked at the sides, building banks with the earth dug out by the men. The steam thresher had freed the strongest field hands to undertake this backbreaking work by November; "I have all of the inferior hands about the Thresher," Skinner reported with satisfaction.[82] If the best hands had had to waste their labor at the ancient hand flailing of the grain, the essential winter's work of cleaning the ditches and canals could never—at Gowrie, which perpetually suffered a labor shortage—have been completed before the fields must be prepared for the next spring's sowing.

Hot as the plantation was in summer, it could be icy in the winter. Ben, a thirty-year-old slave, was rated as only a half hand because his hands and feet were frostbitten. There was snow on January 13, 1852, and on January 20 the land was so frozen that the plows couldn't work. "The weather has been quite severe . . . ," the overseer reported. "The cold affects the negroes very much, and causes the sick house to be well occupied. Jack [Savage]'s child Affy died on the 10th." On the flat island in the middle of the river the slaves were "exposed to the cold pierceing wind. They are coughing, blowing, sneezeing, and shivering. . . . There is any quantity of Ice in the canals & ditches."[83] When the weather was at its very worst slaves might be set indoor tasks—Skinner had them finish the threshing in January 1852—but outdoor work was the rule during most of the winter. Anticipating this annual problem, overseer

Cooper tried late one November to turn to advantage the disaster of a month's breakdown in the threshing process[84] by putting slaves to ditching earlier than usual: "In the absence of threshing," he assured Manigault, "it is desirable that we should do as much of that cold & muddy work [ditching] as possible before the chilling frosts of winter sets in with much severity." Work began not at sunrise but earlier, at "day light";[85] repairing the embankments was probably done in gangs until nightfall (as the individualistic task system was ill suited to collective labor); and the weather—as all the evidence attests—could be frightful. A principal benefit of slavery to rice planters was that they could coerce the laborers into doing this miserable, wet, wintry work; and the rapid decline of low-country rice plantations after 1865 resulted in substantial measure because free black laborers were very reluctant to do it, as the tidal irrigation system required. The exultation of the slaves at their emancipation by Sherman's army was matched by cries of frustration from every low-country rice planter. "Probably few of your readers, who have not themselves beheld the wonders and intricacies of the [tidal] cultivation of the rice plant, have any idea of the immense labor requisite. . . ," one planter lamented in the summer of 1865:

> Miles on miles of powerful dykes [e.g., more than three miles of dikes around Gowrie, according to Louis Manigault's calculation, which he pasted beside this newspaper clipping in his journal], with multitudinous sluices and flood-gates in every direction, tell a wondrous tale of diligence, skill and untiring perseverance. . . . Amid the malarial exhalations of the artificial rice swamps, it was only by black labor [he alleged] that these vast fields for the amphibious plant could have been reclaimed and constructed. . . .
>
> Nay, the rice planters all say, with one accord, that not only must they have black labor to succeed, but compulsory black labor, and nothing else. . . . Compulsory labor being . . . "played out," it is clear that the rice planters are in a very bad way, and that unless something should turn up to prevent, the culture of rice in South Carolina [the writer prophetically observed] will, ere long, be a thing of the past.[86]

One benefit of slavery to the Manigaults was that, after employing certain slave children in their Charleston mansion until they grew to full size, they could then deport these town-bred house servants to the mud of Gowrie—a destination no Charleston youth would voluntarily have chosen. The masters could gamble with the lives of their workers in ways the workers themselves would have been loath to do. Every enslaved field worker had to become inured to working in the rain and cold, and if a Charleston house servant were moved to Gowrie, she must be broken in to the conditions which field hands regularly experienced. Sending Nanny—a strong, healthy, sixteen-year-old house girl—to Gowrie in December 1858, Charles Manigault at first exempted her from field labor until the weather became warmer in April, because she was "as yet unaccustomed to exposure." But the demand for outdoor workers was exigent, and Manigault quickly changed his mind. "The best thing," he then advised, "is to inniciate her into plantation work as soon as possible, but not to expose her during *this* winter to any rainy weather, or Cold as She is not accustomed to out door work."[87] Similarly, the life of a convalescent slave would be in danger should she be put back too soon into the ditch. Thus the Silk Hope overseer had warned Manigault in 1845 that Hester (who was being sent after a seven-month separation to join her husband Robert at Gowrie) has "been quite sick and I would advise you not to work her in the mud for one or two weeks." Heaven forbid, however, that concern for a slave's life should foster malingering: "Keep her on dry land as much as possible [the overseer continued], tho she should not know of your reasons for doing so or she will make a handle of it and shuffle."[88]

There was constant tension between the masters' desire to get plantation work done and their wish to keep most of the slaves alive. The overseer "told me he intended to fix a weak place in the . . . Canal Bank," Charles wrote in January 1859, "—& to fix the Stopping of the Mill Race way—& to dig out a shoal place in the Canal. . . . I cautioned him against putting the hands to work in water during winter." Manigault could not know whether the overseer had taken any notice of his advice. He was sure, however, that the slaves often got completely soaked in a rainstorm: "Always after a complete wetting particularly in cold rainy weather, in winter or spring," he acknowledged, "one or more of [the slaves] are made sick . . . and at times serious illness ensues." He therefore wrote into the overseer's contract that "whenever a hard storm of rain sets in and does not clear off towards the afternoon," the slaves should be sent home for the rest of the afternoon. The force of this instruction was vitiated, however, by Manigault's clear exception of those times when slaves were "at some very pressing and important work." Knowing the overseer was likely to disobey even this watered-down injunction, Charles set his son Louis to oversee the overseer. In February 1853 one of the more valued slaves, Short Jack, had pneumonia. February and March "are very trying, & dangerous. . . ," Charles admonished his son; "if you find [the slaves] working in a cold rainy windy spell call them in early."[89]

The decision whether or not to work in the cold rain was not the slave's but the overseer's; and when Short Jack seemed to have recovered from pneumonia, the decision when to go back to work was not his but the white people's: a power of life or death. "It is a dangerous Disease Pneumonia," Charles exhorted his son, "& you must be careful not to turn [Short Jack] out to work too soon." Charles's protestations that his slaves must not be pushed too hard in winter arose from repeated melancholy experience. In January 1857—soon after she arrived at Gowrie from the Charleston slave market (and during a particularly cold, snowy, wet spell)—a newly purchased, twenty-one-year-old slave woman caught a severe case of pneumonia, "that dreadful disease [Charles lamented to Louis], from which we all suffer so much on Savh River. . . . [As I believe the slaves] are liable to a relapse, I advise you not putting her to work again for some time, or such delicate work as will not expose her to wetting her feet &c." Year after year the master repeated his refrain: "It is so dangerous putting Negroes in Cold & wet ditches during Cold weather," he wrote in January 1859, "that raking out with the hoe [instead of digging them out more thoroughly] will have to answer with most of the Ditches now." And year after year slaves died of pneumonia despite Manigault's fair words: William, a thirty-two-year-old field hand, contracted pneumonia soon after this letter was written and died in March 1859; and Rhina, a thirty-nine-year-old female field hand, perished from pneumonia a month after William's decease.[90]

Many other illnesses attacked Gowrie's slaves. Of these malaria was surely the most serious, but information about it is hard to evaluate. Historians now know that some American blacks had genetic or acquired defenses against malaria,[91] but this should not lead one to underestimate the incidence of that disease among those slaves partially or wholly susceptible to one of its several variants. Overseers' letters infrequently provide firm evidence, for they seldom distinguish malarial from other fevers. Yet when a candid overseer like K. W. Skinner acknowledged the prevalence of summer fevers, he must often have been referring to malaria. "The health of the people is not good," he reported soon after the beginning of the malarial season in 1851. "I have had a good many cases of fever . . . as well as some of other complaints." Two months later the slaves' ill health fed Skinner's concern about what was really important to him—securing the crop: "I have a great deal of fever among the negroes,—some very obstinate cases, which puts the [harvest] work behind hand." Conditions the next summer were similar. By late July (well into the malarial season) many children had fevers, and two weeks later the overseer acknowledged that adults were ill too: "There is a good deal of fever among the negroes, and some diarreah." Sickness did not always ensure that a slave would be sent home to recover. Although two carpenters had been ill and off work, a third slave "keeps up, but looks badly, and is quite weak."[92]

Three weeks later, Skinner's report showed clearly that these fevers were sometimes malarial. "I have had a deal of sickness among these people— fever mostly," he declared early in September. "Ben [thirty-three years old] has been sick for weeks. [Three other named slaves—all in their forties— have been ill, and the engineer, thirty-three-year-old] Jimmy has been sick [for ten days] of fever-remittent." Frederick Olmsted, observing that "the negroes do not enjoy as good health on rice plantations as elsewhere," attributed this ill health to "the malaria" (which he, like everyone else, thought an emanation from the swamps).[93] Although malaria may not have killed vast numbers of grown slaves, a nonlethal variant of chronic malaria probably undermined the health of many adults, gravely weakening their resistance to the respiratory illnesses which then often proved fatal. Thus Frances Kemble, at her husband's Georgia rice plantation, was amazed at the quick death of a young adult: "A very valuable slave called Shadrach was seized with a disease which is frequent, and very apt to be fatal here—peripneumonia," she wrote in January 1839, "and, in spite of all that could be done to save him, sank rapidly, and died after an acute illness of only three days. . . . It is astonishing how much less power of resistance to disease they seem to possess than we do." Olmsted perceived that among low-country white overseers, malaria "shatters the constitution, and renders them peculiarly liable to pneumonia, or other complaints which are fatal."[94] Olmsted might almost have been quoting a letter penned a dozen years earlier at the Butler Island rice plantation, whose overseer Thomas Oden had in January 1841 just died of one of "those pleurasy's so fatal amongst the negroes." The overseer's attack of pleurisy "was not," according to his employer, "a violent one. [Yet] his constitution being much broken by previous attacks of fever, he finally succumbed."[95] The same shattering of the slaves' constitutions by malaria surely had for them the same effect. Chronic malaria was almost certainly a principal source for the slaves' "dreadful mortality" on rice plantations.[96]

Four further health problems at Gowrie may be sketched. A Louisiana plantation manager told Frederick Olmsted in 1853 that black women had relatively little trouble with childbirth, because field labor made them physically strong.[97] One might therefore be tempted to suppose that many slave women were exempt from the terrors of childbed, but the Manigault records challenge any such inference. Eight slave women died at Gowrie very soon after the birth of a baby, out of a total of 33 women of childbearing age who died between 1835 and 1862.[98] Thus—even more than the "cholera" epidemics of 1852 and 1854, which killed six of these women of childbearing age—childbirth and subsequent complications were probably the greatest threats to the women's health. They caused or contributed to the deaths of some 30 percent of these women who did not succumb to "cholera."[99]

Gynecologic complaints, often caused or aggravated by childbirth, seem to have afflicted innumerable slave women. Their coerced return (within a few weeks of confinement) to labor in the muddy, often flooded rice fields subjected them to greater danger of infection than on a cotton plantation. In 1844 Gowrie's overseer correctly predicted that a thirty-seven-year-old grandmother was likely to die soon: "I am afraid I will loose [*sic*] . . . Katy," A. R. Bagshaw reported matter-of-factly, "with the Same [gynecologic] disease she has been labouring under for the last two years. I have not imployed any Doctor for I dont think any one Can doe her any good. . . ." Masters and overseers took for granted that in such cases overseers would inspect the slave women's private parts. Bagshaw's successor reluctantly reported to Manigault in 1846 a "rather serious" case of "chronic affection of the womb, & that is the woman Nelly [the mother of Jack Savage]. She has had for some time a discharge from the utera similar to that of [Katy, who had finally died in 1845] but not of that mucus appearance as hers was but blood." Nelly died the next year, in all likelihood another victim of the hard field work demanded of childbearing women.[100]

The Savannah River presented another health hazard to Gowrie's island-bound slaves. The recently purchased twenty-three-year-old Anthony drowned in 1850 after about a year at Gowrie; in 1852 the very young child Cosum drowned in a settlement ditch; Cato the miller perished the same year while poling a flatboat up the treacherous river at midnight on plantation business; Bob, after an illicit trading trip to Savannah in 1853, was also drowned at night; the twenty-two-year-old London committed suicide by drowning himself in the river in 1860; the twenty-five-year-old Parker (who fled the plantation for three months in 1863) drowned in 1864—possibly in a renewed attempt to escape; and Big Sampson had been the river's victim in the early hours of September 30, 1847. Sampson, formerly the highly responsible driver at Silk Hope, had been deported to Gowrie in 1839 and reduced to field labor, no doubt as punishment for some supposed offense. By 1846, having won the favor of Gowrie's overseer, he was a bird minder entrusted with a gun: he burned his "hands and face badly . . . with [gun]powder," the overseer reported that year. In 1847 he was a plantation watchman, and on September 29 he made an unauthorized visit to his forty-seven-year-old wife, who had been sent away from him across Savannah Back River during the long summer to tend Gowrie's children at a rented summer camp. The boat he used to cross the river apparently was missing when he returned very early the next morning; fearing a flogging if his absence were discovered at the morning roll call, Sampson—probably in his early fifties—desperately tried to swim across the swift current. His wish to be with his wife ended in sudden death: his corpse was found three days later floating on the river with arms "extended wide as in the attitude of swiming [sic] and his features bearing every mark of fright."[101]

Sunstroke was another menace to the health of slaves forced to labor at hours when they would not voluntarily have done so. On one hot July day two women, "Cotta and Sarey, received a stroke of the sun. Sarey recovered early. Cotta is yet on hand," the overseer wrote five days later, "and recovering slowly,—many of the other negroes staggered about considerably."[102] In such weather the overseer might—rarely—give the slaves a two-hour break at midday, but here again the life-or-death decision was in the hands of the white person. Primus, a forty-four-year-old field hand and trunk minder, died of sunstroke in the summer of 1861.

The appalling record of deaths at Gowrie—a child mortality rate (to age sixteen) of 90 percent, many deaths of slaves during their most productive years, the infrequency of a slave's surviving to age sixty, and the huge excess of deaths over births—impels the question, Why? Why didn't Charles and Louis Manigault do something about it?

Neither malice, sadism, nor any other psychic perversity can be the answer. Charles Manigault was a cool, intelligent, rational entrepreneur. He thought carefully about his capital investments at Gowrie in slaves, land, and equipment, applying there the lessons in business management he had learned in his earlier career as a merchant. He had the self-confidence of a successful innovator, brooking for years family opposition against his initial purchase of Gowrie and challenging Savannah River custom in his introduction of advanced threshing machinery. He prided himself on feeding his slaves their preferred rice instead of less expensive corn, and on giving them better clothing material than some of his neighbors did. He trusted a slave like the carpenter, John Izard, to travel unaccompanied back and forth between Charleston and Savannah; he was prepared to spend a substantial sum for the medical treatment of a favored slave like the boatman Hector; and he would sometimes listen to a slave's story and act upon what he heard—as when in the summer of 1860 he let the demoted driver George persuade him not to sell him, as overseer Capers was urging Manigault to do. Louis Manigault cultivated a jocular relation with his favorite, the boatman Hector, and he liked to surround himself in the evening with singing slave children. He cautiously brought unpalatable truths to his father's attention, as when he passed on driver Robert's plaint about the many years when the settlement ditches had never been cleaned out, and when Dr. Bullock urgently recommended that Charles Manigault spend some money buying a camp to which the slaves could immediately be evacuated in the event of another "cholera" epidemic.

In the absence of psychological perversity, entrepreneurs are supposed to act in accord with their own economic interest; and at first it would seem self-evident that a dead slave had less economic value to its master than one who was alive and strong. But the question of economic interest is much less straightforward than these propositions might imply. For one thing, the owner's economic interest in keeping his slave alive was far weaker than the slave's own interest in survival. This became especially plain during the "cholera" epidemics: doubtless free laborers would have fled the plantation at the first sign of epidemic, but the white people took their own time (and the slaves' lives) before concluding that evacuation was necessary.

Furthermore, the owner's economic interest in maintaining plantation discipline took priority over his interest in keeping an individual slave alive. Thus when Will fled the plantation in the summer of 1854, it was in Charles Manigault's economic interest to recapture him in order to deter other slaves from attempting to escape. If Will died a few months later (as he did in the "cholera" of that year), his recapture had nevertheless helped to maintain plantation discipline: Will was of more economic value to Manigault dead at Gowrie than he would have been free and alive somewhere in the swamp. Plantation slaves were forced to live in "settlements" where they could be kept under surveillance, rather than scattered in isolated cabins (where they would have been less vulnerable to the risks of contagion and of bad sanitation). Dysentery and repeated "cholera" epidemics never for a moment suggested to Charles Manigault the notion of relaxing discipline by spreading out the slaves' cabins.

If the master's economic interest impelled him to maintain "good order" at whatever cost to the slaves' health, even more did his interest require securing a big crop each year. Rice planting was a hazardous enterprise beset by horrendous risks; and when a planter attacked his manifold problems, he was likely to focus on those which had a more obvious solution than did his slaves' ill health. If there was danger of a freshet, the manifest requirement was to strengthen the embankments. If the tidal irrigation system was inefficient, the canals must be deepened. If drainage didn't function properly, more ditches had to be dug. If a trunk seemed likely to give way, it must be renewed and its emplacement strengthened. Any one of these problems might lead to a crisis costing the plantation thousands of dollars; by contrast, the economic loss when a slave died was relatively small. All of this seemed obvious, and gave owners and overseers plenty to do without their attacking the much more problematic causes of their slaves' ill health.

Another explanation for the slaves' continued plight was that Charles Manigault, like many a businessman, cut corners in his pursuit of profit. If meat was costly, why bother to supply it regularly? After all, fish were abundant in the river. If rice land was immensely profitable, why reduce revenues by turning over good rice land to the slaves for vegetable plots? If doctors were avaricious, and if the medical services of the overseer and of Binah the plantation nurse were free, why employ doctors except for emergencies? Charles Manigault may have pinched pennies even harder than some of his neighbors, but the fault lay in the system, not in the individual slave master. In an era of unconstrained individualism, the planter was the most unconstrained of all. His laborers had no wages which they might decide to spend on meat or on a doctor, no chance to rent a vegetable plot, no opportunity to leave Gowrie to see whether they could find a healthier place to live and work. And, of course, no government regulation impinged upon Manigault's mastery over the lives and health of his slaves.

Moreover, Charles Manigault seldom resided at Gowrie and he was therefore ill situated to keep an eye on the slaves' health. In 1844 the overseer A. R. Bagshaw might institute a rule that settlement ditches were to be cleaned out every year, but Manigault's two-and-a-half-year European trip in 1846–48 ushered in a long period when the rule was not implemented. Manigault could declare that the overseers were not to keep the slaves in the fields on cold, wet, wintry afternoons, but he was not present to prevent them from doing so. The problem of absenteeism was endemic in the rice kingdom, where it was an axiom that rich planters would leave the immediate vicinity of the malarial swamps from May until November each year. The only way an owner could supervise his plantation during this period was to purchase a summer residence close enough for a daily trip of inspection—yet high enough, or sufficiently near the ocean, for breezes that would scatter the mosquitoes. In the Georgetown district of South Carolina some planters bought summer houses facing the ocean: then they could travel each day to the plantation, returning before the mosquitoes swarmed at sundown. But Charles Manigault was a civilized gentleman who did not dream of leaving Charleston to live in the wilds of Georgia during the dangerous summer months. Thus, in this respect, the master's lifestyle did impinge upon his economic interest. But lifestyle was not alone at issue—the planter's life itself was at stake. Charles Manigault lived to the advanced age of eighty-five, while planters who risked living near their plantations during the summer did not always evade malaria, and they tended to die younger than he did. Manigault, not surprisingly, preferred to risk his "negroes' " lives rather than his own, and the system gave him the power to do so.

Other factors militating against the slaves' health were the masters' rural inertia, and their racial attitudes. The sheer force of custom made it improbable that Manigault would institute vigorous reforms of diet, housing, and sanitation. Some Southern agricultural reformers were captivated by experiments with fertilizer and crop rotation; a few—like South Carolina's Governor James

Hammond, a cotton planter farther up the Savannah River—did try to combat the terrific slave mortality; but Manigault's reforming imagination was captured instead by threshing machinery and "open planting" as means of reducing Gowrie's labor requirements. Behind his inertia toward the conditions affecting his workers' health lay Manigault's attitude toward the slaves themselves: they were "negroes," and they were factors of production. He was not ill disposed toward obedient slaves, certainly not malicious—though, as will appear, he took pleasure in showing a recalcitrant black how easily a bit of "discipline" could reduce the slave to docility; but the slaves' lives did not deeply interest him. What fired his imagination was the prospect of quickly turning an initial capital investment of his own twenty thousand dollars into an annual return of fifteen thousand dollars. He felt no such interest in whether an individual slave stayed alive or not. He was no Simon Legree; but his economic interest, and above all his situation of uncontrolled power over other people's lives, made him essentially indifferent to those lives. The stark contrast between the colorful picture of antebellum plantation life painted in 1870 by Charles Manigault—"faithful ancestral family Negroes"; "*we . . .* attending personally to their comforts"; "their Lives . . . cherished (as their *wonderful Increase* shews)"—and Gowrie's gray reality illustrates the human capacity for selective perception. Although Harriet Beecher Stowe's lurid fiction stirred hearts in the North, the sober record of life and death at Gowrie is ultimately more chilling, because the slaves' ill health arose not from malignity but from power and economic interest.

Slaves' death rates in the rice kingdom helped to shape the history of the new republic from the moment the Constitution was written in 1787. Rice plantations then had a poor reputation. Oliver Ellsworth of Connecticut advocated—during the secret debates at the Constitutional Convention—a further period during which bondsmen and women might be freely imported from Africa. Slaves, he believed, died so fast "in the sickly rice swamp [that] foreign supplies are necessary." Not everyone agreed with Ellsworth's political judgment, but no delegate to the convention appears to have doubted that the rice swamps were deadly for the slaves. "South Carolina & Georgia cannot do without [importing] slaves," Carolina's General C. C. Pinckney averred, and his position was supported by nearly every delegate from those states. The demand of rice planters for more Africans, and their threat not to ratify the Constitution unless they had their way, defeated all proposals at the convention to ban the African slave trade before 1808.[103]

Yet nearly two centuries later the reputation of the rice plantations appeared to enjoy a surprising reversal. Eugene Genovese stressed the length to which some paternalist planters, including rice planters, went in order to make life tolerable for their wards. Philip Morgan showed how the task system, ubiquitous in the rice kingdom, gave some slaves enough time to work for themselves and to acquire property of their own. Julia Smith concluded that slaves on Georgia rice plantations were better fed, clothed, and housed than those in the cotton belt. Charles Joyner found little evidence[104] of active discontent among slaves on South Carolina's Waccamaw River, and a reader of his illuminating study of slave culture might infer that the morale of slaves on rice plantations was better than that of free black sharecroppers in the twentieth century.

The death rate among Gowrie's slaves may suggest caution about accepting such a view of life in the rice swamps. The Manigaults' careful records show beyond doubt that child mortality on the plantation was fearsome—almost incredibly high to an American eye of a later century—and that enteric and respiratory diseases, aggravated by medical neglect and probably also by chronic malaria, had devastating effects upon the lives of adult slaves. Death rates of this order must have profoundly shaken the slaves' morale and influenced every aspect of their lives. The effect upon family life was certainly marked, as will become evident in the next chapter.

No doubt health was even worse at Gowrie than on most of its contemporary rice plantations. Yet recent demographic studies remind one of what everyone knew in the eighteenth century, that slaves died much faster in the rice region than elsewhere in the American South. A conservative modern estimate suggests that at least 55 percent of the children born on nineteenth-century rice plantations died by age fifteen. (By contrast, the same study implies that about 38 percent of children born on large cotton and sugar plantations died by age fifteen.)[105] The true figure for the rice plantations is surely higher even than a 55 percent child mortality rate, for even the best plantation records probably omitted many deaths which occurred during the first four weeks of infancy; and the Balls, who kept the best records, are likely to have been less uncaring about their slaves' health than were most other South Carolina rice planters. Probably about two-thirds—perhaps more—of the slave children born on rice plantations during the nineteenth century were dead by age fifteen.[106]

Before the 1970s, knowledge of American slavery was based almost exclusively on nineteenth-century records. Yet slavery in the eighteenth century was an even grimmer institution than in the mid–nineteenth century. In recent years historians have ingeniously tried to show the institution as it was in its earlier years, before the reform movement after 1820 modified some of its features; but eighteenth-century records are sparse. Only one full plantation record of slaves' birth and death dates survives from before 1803, and that one—for a sea-island cotton plantation, where mortality rates were less frightful than on rice plantations—goes back only to 1786.[107] A principal value of the Manigault records, therefore, is that they suggest health conditions that probably were widespread in the rice kingdom during its early years: if 90 percent of Gowrie's slaves died before they were sixteen years old, comparable death rates are likely to have been common in the low country during the eighteenth century.

Even in the nineteenth century the reputation of Georgia's rice plantations was not enviable. "The cultivation of rice was described to me as by far the most unhealthy work in which the slaves were employed," the archconservative Scottish naval captain Basil Hall reported in 1829, and, in spite of every care, that they sank under it in great numbers. The causes of this dreadful mortality, are the constant moisture and heat of the atmosphere, together with the alternate floodings and dryings of the fields, on which the negroes are perpetually at work, often ankle deep in mud. . . .

Great numbers [of slaves imported from the border states] are . . . absorbed by South Carolina and Georgia, where the cultivation of rice thins the black population so fast, as to render a constant fresh supply of negroes indispensable. . . .

[The slaves on these rice plantations] are sometimes overworked, in order to "meet the season," as it is called, and upon these occasions they sink rapidly under their complicated hardships. [A Savannah medical doctor] told me of a friend of his who had lost 40 out of 300 slaves last year.[108]

An incident from 1846 illustrates Georgia's reputation then. Sidney Fisher, the Philadelphia diarist, owned a free-labor farm in Maryland, and two of the black men hired on this farm were married to slave women from a nearby plantation. One of these women lived with her husband at Fisher's farm. When Fisher's neighbor (a Mr. Forman) died, he left his plantation to a Georgia rice planter, Thomas Bryan, the son of one of Forman's natural children. Bryan, delighted to acquire at no cost a new supply of laborers for his rice plantation, ordered the two slave women back to the home plantation in Maryland, then swiftly shipped them (with others) to Georgia, thus separating forever the two women from their husbands. Sidney Fisher, deeply racist though he was, and a believer in slavery, nevertheless disapproved of this transaction. The Negroes in Maryland "dread nothing on earth so much" as being sent to the Deep South: "the poor fellows," Fisher exclaimed,

who heard it only this even'g are in terrible distress & have gone over to take leave [of their wives. All the women's] friends & relations are here [in Maryland]. They regard the [Deep] South with perfect horror, and to be sent there is considered as the worst punishment inflicted on them, & is reserved for one offence alone by the custom of the neighborhood, an attempt to run away.

Part of these slaves' horror of the deep South arose from loyalty to relatives and friends in Maryland, but Gowrie's records make plain that slaves had other reasons as well to dread a Georgia rice plantation.[109]

Beauty lies in the eye of the beholder, it is said, but not even the fond eye of Louis Manigault perceived Gowrie as a lovely plantation. He tried to beautify the area around his own house and the slave settlements, planting one hundred trees (especially water oaks), cultivating a rose garden, and training ivy to grow up the brick foundations of his house. Nevertheless, "there is very little of interest at this season of the year," he acknowledged sadly in December 1863,

to behold on a Rice plantation such as Gowrie, the entire tract being low Rice fields every foot of which is cultivated in rice. You ride from bank to bank, and square to square, each field presenting a great similarity to the other, with its "Face-ditches" and "Quarter-drains" in regular order, passing now

and then near a "Trunk," "Flood-Gate," or over some rude bridge, which
traverses a Canal, distinguished perhaps for its great want of architectural
beauty. . . .[110]

The impression of dullness is today even more powerful, for the flat, monoto-
nous, former rice land has returned to swamp. Reeds of uniform height grow
everywhere now, only an isolated small tree or two varying the scene, and not
even a brick can be perceived where the brick thresher once stood. Argyle
Island is now a National Wildlife Refuge, and one is strenuously enjoined not
even to set foot on the old plantation for fear of the deadly reptiles which have
recovered tenure from its transitory human proprietors. At best one can stand
at the border of U.S. 17 where it crosses the island half a mile south of
Gowrie—a relatively untraveled and neglected road, because almost everyone now uses the big interstate highways miles away. Occasionally a long
truck thunders southwestward on Route 17, transporting South Carolina's
rich natural produce—great timbers now from its forests, no longer heavy
barrels of rice from the swamps—to distant markets. No freshly painted "big
house" remains at Gowrie (indeed, there never was one, only a modest dwelling for Charles or Louis Manigault's occasional residence, and long since
disappeared) to mislead a later century about the slaves' lives: only the dank
swamp itself.

One can infer, beholding the treeless, flattened wasteland, why slaves'
lives were even shorter at Gowrie than at some other rice plantations. For the
Savannah is the greatest of the sixteen rivers where rice was grown, and its
islands were wider and more solid than those, say, between the Pee Dee and
Waccamaw Rivers (where only Sandy Island offered the prospect of yearlong
residence). Near Georgetown, South Carolina, no one could keep slaves permanently on the islands south of Sandy Island: instead, slaves like those of
Robert Allston lived on the mainland, and went by flatboat across the Pee
Dee each day to do their involuntary labor on the rice islands. At Argyle
Island, by contrast, a proprietor might keep his slaves yearlong on the island,
as Charles Manigault did. This meant, however, that the slaves slept at night
far from the pineland woods which, thinning the mosquitoes, offered a partial
protection against malaria to those slaves—like Allston's—whose settlements
were built among pine trees. And mainland residence probably gave slaves
access to a less polluted water supply than that available on a river island such
as Argyle, thus lessening the incidence of those bowel diseases—dysentery,
diarrhea, "cholera"—which mowed down the Gowrie slaves. Had Charles
Manigault spent the money to house his bondsmen and women on the mainland, he surely would have lengthened their lives.

This was what his neighbor James Potter did, domiciling his slaves (except
during harvesttime nights) on the Georgia mainland and boating them each
morning to his Argyle Island rice fields, just across the southernmost Gowrie
canal which divided it from the Potter estate. Finding a mainland tract, however, might have been difficult for Manigault; it certainly would have been
costly; it would have aggravated his overseers' problems in disciplining their

(more scattered) slaves; and it would have "wasted" the slaves' time in lengthy boat trips. For more than twenty years Manigault failed even to purchase a pineland summer retreat for the slave children—though he rented one for a few years—and eventually he did so only under the urging of Dr. Bullock, who finally persuaded him that a pineland base for temporary retreat would be a way of nipping a future "cholera" epidemic in the bud. Manigault's slaves paid a fearful price for his obstinacy. His doggedness in pursuing his Savannah River enterprise, in the face of Nathaniel Heyward's disapproval, may be admired if one's criterion is—as Manigault's was—the financially successful carrying through of a bold capitalist venture. But if one's criterion were genuine respect for the lives of the human beings he controlled—or even a mere paternalist regard for the welfare of his dependents—one is likely to be struck by the heartlessness of this polished gentleman in sending, year after year, fresh "supplies"[111] of human beings to their deaths.

4

Unhappy Families

Slavery, scholars once supposed, largely destroyed nuclear family structures among its victims. Opinion later swung to an opposite extreme. The bondsmen and women, heroically resisting the destructive tendencies of slavery, were now seen as active shapers of their own destinies, forging resilient family institutions which continued effectively to serve black people well into the twentieth century. But a more realistic reassessment of the slaves' family lives may be under way. Certainly the Manigault records lend little support to an optimistic view of the bondsmen and women's family circumstances. So much is known about those sixty-one slaves living at Gowrie late in 1848 that one can reconstruct their family histories perhaps more completely than at any other plantation in America.[1] The annual slave lists, and the overseers' letters to their employers, present an appalling picture of family hardship. And the masters' policy—far from strengthening the slaves' family institutions through paternalistic benevolence—surely weakened them.

Nearly all of these sixty-one slaves were members of six extended families. Three were already at Gowrie when Manigault bought it in 1833; a fourth comprised the "Savage gang" (Georgia slaves whom Manigault purchased from the William Savage estate in 1839); and two came from Silk Hope, Manigault's principal South Carolina plantation, whence he had deported them to supply Gowrie's voracious appetite for new slaves.

Child mortality devastated these families, so that the most common nuclear grouping was a husband and a wife with *no* surviving children. So many adults died young, and so many couples split up voluntarily, that over half the women who reached the age of twenty-eight married at least twice, and not uncommonly three, four, or even five times.[2]

The extent of tragedy within these families was certainly very much greater even than the following pages will suggest, because on average each woman mentioned here bore some 66 percent more babies than appear in the slave lists—and all of these unmentioned infants died before the subsequent list was compiled.[3] Thus Jack Savage's wife, Amey (who is reported as having borne four children), probably in fact bore at least six, more likely seven, perhaps even eight babies. Every one of her children died before reaching the age of fifteen, and her grief at their deaths almost surely was repeated much more often than the annual lists indicate.

At the Manigaults' home plantations in South Carolina a demarcation may well have tended to separate the families of privileged slaves—especially house servants—from those of ordinary field hands; but at Gowrie no such line could be drawn. The following sketches of three extended families show (and the same was true of the other three main families) that all contained members with relatively privileged occupations—for example, drivers, cooks, artisans, or nurses; and every family also contained substantial numbers of field hands.

Within these extended families one can make an acquaintance—however brief—with nearly every slave who lived at Gowrie in November 1848. And from these acquaintances, one can begin to apprehend the tenor of life at this plantation in a way possibly unique in the annals of slavery.

Old Ned's Family

Born about 1782, and trunk minder at Gowrie late in the 1830s, Ned was the eldest member of an extended family which included several key slaves in the plantation hierarchy (see genealogical table 9). An unusual proportion of this family's members had stable, long-enduring marriages. Ned's younger brother, Harry, was Gowrie's head driver for over thirteen years, before 1846; and Harry's sister-in-law Binah remained the plantation nurse until her death in 1853.[4] But because all of Harry's children had died by 1850[5]—as had his sole grandchild—Ned's three surviving children were the only ones left to carry on the family. These were Stephen the miller; captain Hector (the chief boathand), who was Louis Manigault's favorite; and Nancy, married to a slave named Jacob whom Charles Manigault praised as "smart & intelligent."[6]

These three children of Ned's all had long marriages. The miller Stephen was married to Binah Currie (not to be confused with Binah the nurse) for at least twenty-seven years. Hector the boatman—after a brief marriage to a woman who died, perhaps in childbirth, in 1841—was married to Joaney for twenty-one years before her death in 1862. And Nancy had been married to Jacob for fifteen years before he was sent away from Gowrie (because he was "disorderly");[7] she seems to have been loyal to him for the six remaining years of her life.

TABLE 9.   Old Ned's Family

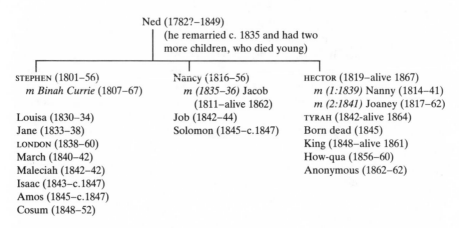

Ned (1782?–1849)
(he remarried c. 1835 and had two
more children, who died young)

STEPHEN (1801–56)	Nancy (1816–56)	HECTOR (1819–alive 1867)
m Binah Currie (1807–67)	m (1835–36) Jacob	m (1:1839) Nanny (1814–41)
	(1811–alive 1862)	m (2:1841) Joaney (1817–62)
Louisa (1830–34)	Job (1842–44)	TYRAH (1842-alive 1864)
Jane (1833–38)	Solomon (1845–c.1847)	Born dead (1845)
LONDON (1838–60)		King (1848–alive 1861)
March (1840–42)		How-qua (1856–60)
Maleciah (1842–42)		Anonymous (1862–62)
Isaac (1843–c.1847)		
Amos (1845–c.1847)		
Cosum (1848–52)		

Yet these families were not happy ones. Binah Currie bore at least eight children to Stephen the miller, but every one of them died before reaching the age of twenty-three. By about 1847 six had perished, none surviving more than five years. Then in 1852 three-year-old Cosum drowned in the settlement ditch. The miller's wife was not exempt from field labor, and no doubt the child had been left to the halfhearted care of some old woman no longer fit to work in the field—or to chase a lively child. (One begins to infer why a prime demand of freedwomen after 1865 was to have more time for their own infants instead of letting their children be shunted off to someone else's inattention.)[8] Thus Binah was left with only one child; at the age of twenty-two this son, London, committed suicide in defying what he thought an unjust whipping. His mother was left without a single descendant to cherish in her old age. Neither of Nancy and Jacob's two children lived more than a couple of years.

Hector was therefore the only one of Ned's offspring to produce surviving children; and not even he and his wife Joaney—a "little Runt," according to Charles Manigault—led extraordinarily sunny lives. Their child Tyrah did reach adulthood, but Joaney's next child was born dead. The white sub-overseer, whose wife had just died of malaria, then forced Joaney to suckle his own three-month-old child—a form of coerced labor about whose "propriety or impropriety" the head overseer professed to be uncertain.[9] Joaney and Hector both survived bouts of "cholera" in 1852. When their child King was five in 1854, he too was stricken with this disease. King did not die, but he was still a dwarf six years later, apparently unfit even to be trained for house service. Manigault had sent King to his South Carolina plantation at the age of five, to recover from the "cholera," and his mother, Joaney, never saw him again during the remaining seven years of her life.

Meanwhile, Joaney and Hector had their fourth child, whom they named

"How-qua." In so doing, they cunningly served two masters: for "How-qua" was the name of Louis Manigault's six-oared racing boat (captained by Hector), and Louis was delighted they had chosen this name for the child. Yet the Gullah pronunciation of How-qua (Huh-ka) was so close to the pronunciation of Hector (Huh-kta) that the parents doubtless reveled in naming the child after his own father. This trick did not protect How-qua from Gowrie's plagues, and he died when he was four. Late in 1861 Louis Manigault deported Hector—formerly his most highly favored slave—to South Carolina to prevent his escaping to the nearby Yankee military forces, and Hector never saw his wife again. Within a few months their fifth child was born, but it soon died. So did Joaney—perhaps from complications following the birth.

Thus although Ned's children had included privileged slaves—the boatman and the miller—their privileges could not secure the health of their offspring. At least twelve of Ned's grandchildren died young (not counting Joaney's stillbirth), one was a dwarf, and only one lived to become a healthy adult.[10]

The Savage Family

In 1839 Charles Manigault bought sixteen members of an extended family from the estate of William Savage, an Ogeechee River (Georgia) rice planter. This "Savage gang" seemed to Manigault an unusually good buy, partly since it included a skilled forty-one-year-old carpenter named Brave Boy, but mainly because it contained eleven cousins aged between eight and twenty-one—old enough that they had a good chance of surviving Gowrie's childhood plagues, yet sufficiently young that they promised to supply many future years of labor (see genealogical table 10). Although four of the cousins nevertheless perished during the Savages' first decade at Gowrie, the other seven lived so long, and their experiences ranged so widely, that their lives are worth outlining. Their reactions to slavery covered the spectrum from sullen resistance to an apparently tractable accommodation.

Among many remarkable characters at Gowrie, *Jack Savage,* a youth of eighteen, developed into perhaps the most striking of all. Jack's father, who had previously been separated from the family (probably by a sale), lived in Savannah, where Jack cannot have seen much of him. Jack was trained by his uncle Brave Boy to be a carpenter and cooper, and he appears to have lived in Brave Boy's family. Jack became Gowrie's most skilled artisan.

His talent became evident in his construction of wooden floodgates and smaller trunks, which were indispensable to tidal irrigation. (These latter were wooden culverts eight feet wide and two feet deep—emplaced in a mud embankment—with clever doors at front and back, which could be regulated to let river water into the fields at high tide and to drain the water out when the tide was low.) "The Trunks built by Jack Savage after the 'McAlpin pattern,' with Arms to slip in and out," Louis Manigault later exclaimed, "were perfect, and his large Flood-Gates were all that one could desire and specimens of

TABLE 10. The Savage Family

Nelly ([c. 1805?]*–47)	Nelly's sister (d before 1839)	Brave Boy (Nelly's brother) (1798–1841)
Her children:	Her children (adopted by Nelly):	m Phillis (1803–alive 1864)
JACK SAVAGE (1820–alive 1867)	BETTY (1827–alive 1867)	Their children and stepchildren:
m(1844) Amey (1823–alive 1862)	m(1845) (Cooper) George (1822–alive 1867)	Primus (1817–61) (Brave Boy's son by another
Harry (1844–58)	Louisa (Simmons) (1829–alive 1875)	woman)
Affy (1850–52)	m(c.1847) Short Jack (1817–63)	m(1841) Big Lucy (1812–c.1863)
Brister (1854–55)	Elizabeth (1849–52)	Lappo (1819–39)
Mary (1857–59)	Minna (1851–53)	Pompey (1820–48) (Phillis's son by another
ISHMAEL (1822–alive 1867)	Mendoza (1854–alive 1861)	man)
m(1845) Crecie (1828–54)	Elizabeth (1857–58)	m(1844) Rhina (1819–59)
Nelly (1848–49)	Rebecca (1857–60)	Jack Jon (1822–c.1847)
Betsey (1851–alive 1861)		CATO (1826–52) (Brave Boy's son by another
Cato (1854–alive 1861)		woman)
Affey (1828–40)		m(c.1847) Catherine (1828–alive 1875)
Sary (1831–86)		Chloe (1837[?]–39)
m(1849) William (1826–59)		Anonymous (1840–40)
m(1851) Pompey (1831–alive 1864)		
Edward (1853–56)		
Anonymous (1856–57)		
Jane (1857–c.1862)		
Pussy (1859–alive 1864)		

* I infer that Nelly's vendor in 1839 understated her age—a more common practice then among slave vendors than among the used-car salesmen of a later epoch. (He claimed she was thirty.)

good work." When Charles Manigault brought Jack temporarily to South Carolina to build a trunk for his Marshlands farm, a white neighbor was impressed. "Jack made a beautiful Trunk" on the Savannah River model, Manigault declared with pride (though his pride was as much in the design of the trunk by the former owner of Gowrie, Henry McAlpin, as in Jack's execution of that design): the neighbor "was so much struck with its strength, efficiency, & simplicity, that he measured it throughout, & made a Drawing of it while in my yard. Our Trunks on Savh. River I consider Perfect in all respects."[11]

A splendid carpenter, Jack Savage was also the most ungovernable slave on the estate. "He was the only Negro ever in our possession who I considered capable of Murdering me," Louis Manigault later reflected, "or burning my dwelling at night, or capable of committing any act." He was also excessively lazy (in his masters' eyes), excusing himself—when he was working together with the other good carpenter, John Izard—by falsely claiming of himself (using Gullah grammar), " 'him one had all the work to do.' " The way to attack this problem, overseer Skinner believed, was to divide and conquer. Jack's younger brother, Ishmael, was then the second driver, in charge of the East Hermitage tract: "I had Ishmeal [*sic*] to whip Jack well . . . ," Skinner reported laconically in 1852; "Jack has did well since."[12] The soil of fraternal rancor was thus cultivated for a renewed flowering of the hardy Cain and Abel perennial nine years later.

Jack's wife, Amey, appears to have been an Amazon: she was "5 ft. $7\frac{7}{8}$ In. in height," Louis noted; and as this was the only slave's height he ever recorded, she must have been remarkably tall for a female slave, probably the tallest woman at Gowrie.[13] Three years Jack's junior, she was twenty when she married him. They lived together for eighteen years until his hatred for the slave regime led him in 1862 to flee Gowrie for an eighteen-month sojourn in the swamp. During their marriage Jack and Amey had at least four children, but unsurprisingly all four died: three in infancy and one at the age of fourteen. The most common family pattern at Gowrie being that of a man and his wife with no surviving children, Jack and Amey had attained this status by the time Jack was thirty-nine.

Ishmael, Jack's brother, was more fortunate with his children, though less lucky in his marriage. Like Jack, Ishmael proved difficult for his masters to fathom. That he was "very intelligent" (in Louis Manigault's words) there can be no doubt, but opinions differed as to his other capabilities. After Ishmael had been trained for some time under cooper George's tutelage, the overseer complained that the twenty-two-year-old trainee "never will make a good Cooper"; yet eight years later Louis was certain he was "first rate" in that occupation. Meanwhile, however, Ishmael's leadership ability had caused him to be selected (at the age of twenty-six) to be the driver of the new gang of slaves Manigault had bought to work his newly purchased East Hermitage land. The post of driver at Gowrie was nearly as unstable as that of overseer, and within four years Ishmael had been demoted—he was "a pretty good for nothing Driver," Louis Manigault came to believe. Nevertheless in 1867, as a freedman, Ishmael was made one of the five "foremen" under whose direction the free-labor system then functioned.[14]

In March 1845 the twenty-two-year-old Ishmael had first set eyes on a seventeen-year-old girl, Crecie, who had just been imported from Silk Hope. In keeping with the pattern of early marriage of women at Gowrie, the two were living together within a few months. During the nine years of their marriage they had at least three children, all of whom were given names of Crecie's relatives. Nelly, named after Crecie's younger sister who had recently died at Gowrie at the age of sixteen, died herself at the age of one. Betsey, named after Crecie's mother, was removed from Gowrie to Silk Hope at the age of three,[15] probably to recover from "cholera," and she was still alive there six years later. Cato, born in 1854, was named after the recently drowned slave who had been the husband of Crecie's first cousin, Catherine. The child Cato was still alive in 1861, but complications from his birth may have been the cause of Crecie's death in 1854, at the age of twenty-six.

Ishmael, who with Crecie had returned to the original Gowrie settlement after he was sacked as the Hermitage driver, had lived there in the house of Crecie's mother, Betsey. But soon after Crecie's death he left the infant Cato in Old Betsey's care and moved back to the Hermitage tract, half a mile away, where he lived for six years in the house of the old settlement nurse. Probably he entered an abroad marriage with a woman on a plantation adjoining East Hermitage. The strength of this new attachment may have led him to betray his brother, Jack, in 1861, in order to ingratiate himself with the overseer and to avoid being deported from Georgia. Historians like to discover solidarity among the slaves, but slaves were human like everyone else; and the masters' determined efforts to divide one slave from another were a principal means of their maintaining their hegemony. Ishmael's betrayal[16] of his brother, Jack Savage, was but Gowrie's most dramatic illustration of how successful the masters could sometimes be.

Sary, a younger sister of Jack Savage's, lived to the ripe old age of fifty-five. When she was seventeen, William, a twenty-two-year-old slave who had just been deported from Silk Hope, split up with his pregnant wife to move in with Sary. William, however, left Sary after a year or two to marry a different woman. A year later Sary married a man of her own age, Pompey, who gained the Manigaults' confidence to such an extent that they made him "postboy" in 1861, when they reluctantly concluded that captain Hector could no longer be trusted. While the other slaves were laboring in the fields, Pompey had the enviable job of walking every day the nine or ten miles overland to Savannah to fetch letters and papers, with a pass enabling him to enter the nervous wartime city. Pompey and Sary had four children in the 1850s. The first three died quickly, as usual, but the last one had reached the advanced age of five, still alive in 1864 when the record ceases.

Louisa was an orphaned cousin of Jack Savage's whom Jack's mother adopted and raised. Louisa worked for many years as a field hand, but in 1861 was finally elevated to the post of Louis Manigault's washerwoman in Charleston. She had a relatively long marriage—sixteen years. When about eighteen, she wed a thirty-year-old widower named Short Jack and became stepmother to his child, Little Mary. (Little Mary's life, like that of Louisa herself, illustrated the important role of foster mothers and stepmothers at Gowrie: for when Short Jack's first wife had died soon after Little Mary's birth, the baby had at first been cared for by a young foster mother whose own infant had just died. And when this young woman also died within a few years, Little Mary—after a spell with an aunt—was raised by Louisa.) Louisa and Short Jack then added five children of their own.

Their married life at Gowrie was not trouble-free. Jack survived a bout of "cholera" in 1852, a bad case of pneumonia in 1853, and a somewhat less severe case of pneumonia in 1854. Originally from Silk Hope, Short Jack did not feel that life at Gowrie suited him: one and a half years after his second case of pneumonia, he ran away for a few days, then returned voluntarily—"rested"[17]—to face his whipping. Meanwhile, Louisa's and his children nearly all died, as did Little Mary. Their only child to live for anything near seven years was Mendoza, who had reached that age when he went with his washerwoman mother to Charleston in 1861, leaving his father at Gowrie.

Short Jack, mistrusted by Louis Manigault as a "bad Negro," was one of the first slaves sent away from the plantation in November 1861 to prevent his trying to reach Yankee war vessels. A few weeks later, when the military alarm had abated, Louis wanted Jack back to labor at Gowrie. To get Jack into a properly docile frame of mind, Louis recommended his father to put "Short Jack in the dark-hole [in the Charleston workhouse] for a month" before returning him to Gowrie.[18] After Jack came back to the plantation, a new military alarm supervened and he was sent with Louisa to the relatively secure Silk Hope plantation, where Jack died in 1863 at the age of forty-seven. Louisa's sixteen years of marriage thus produced a single surviving child who probably, like Louisa herself, lived long enough to witness emancipation.

Betty, Louisa's sister, was probably spared a mother's griefs, for she appears never to have had a child. At the age of eighteen she married cooper George; and the reason why her marriage—which lasted for at least twenty-two years—was unfruitful may have been that, when George was a young man, a hoop pole had seriously injured his testicle. Betty survived a bout of "cholera" in 1852. She was regarded by Charles Manigault as one of his two best slave women at Gowrie—the sort of slave on whose health the Manigaults spent time and trouble; and in 1858, eighteen months after she had suffered a painful shoulder injury (caused by her getting caught in the thresher's conveyor belt), her master finally decided to have her sent from Gowrie to their trusted doctor in Charleston to ensure that no bone had been broken.

Yet Manigault was sufficiently indifferent to the slaves' marriage ties that he threatened even his most esteemed slaves with separating them from their spouses. When Manigault had troubled to transport Betty to Charleston for medical attention, Betty's husband, George, had recently been made Gowrie's head driver, and their master doubtless aimed to sweeten George and Betty in this way. (The principle was the name as when Manigault had supplied Mr. Greene, the Parisian banker, with some of Nathaniel Heyward's choice

Madeira, and had secured for himself in return an invitation to the Bancroft dinner.) Yet Manigault menaced even Betty with separation from her husband, and Betty knew the threat was a credible one. "The Dr. says Betty is well," Charles notified Louis Manigault from Charleston: "I gave her a threat to send her to Silk Hope [separating her from George at Gowrie], that I thought she was shamming, or making too much fuss. She begged off hard from that, and promised to do all her tasks well and fully, except any straining work, which she says will swell her arms again."[19]

Betty's alleged "shamming" did not affect the Manigaults' feelings about her; and Louis's regard for her appeared years later, in 1867, when he first revisited Gowrie after the war. As he approached the devastated buildings, Louis and his own eight-year-old son got their feet soaked walking through flooded fields, and Louis left his boy at Betty's cabin and in her care for several hours, while he tramped around the old estate with his white agent. Louis encountered averted gazes from some of his former slaves, who were little pleased to see their old master back again; but Betty, "a woman I had known for many years and who always bore a good character . . . , [Louis reported with relief] made a fire for [Louis's child] in her house, dried his shoes & stockings and as I learnt afterwards boiled several eggs for him to his great delight."[20] Having had no children of her own, Betty may have enjoyed being kindly to the child of her former master. Her forgiving conduct resembled, perhaps, that of Cordelia toward the errant King Lear.

The family circumstances of *Primus,* another cousin of Jack Savage's, are confusing. If the information recorded by Charles Manigault at the time he bought the Savage slaves was correct, Primus's carpenter father, Brave Boy, had children by another woman than his wife, Phillis, both before and after he had a child by her; and Primus's stepmother, Phillis, had a child by another man between those she bore to Brave Boy. (Old Phillis lived to be at least sixty-one and had seven children and stepchildren; yet if she had any grandchildren, not a single one survived to carry on her branch of the family.)

Primus, Phillis's stepson, was the most long-lived of her children and stepchildren, not dying until he was forty-four. At twenty-four he had married a twenty-nine-year-old widow, Big Lucy.[21] Both Lucy and Primus worked nearly always as field hands, though the latter sometimes helped get the mill ready to grind and was once listed as the second trunk minder; and Lucy at forty-eight served a year as the overseer's cook. This marriage was a long one, enduring from 1841 until Primus died from sunstroke in 1861. If Primus ever had children, none lived past infancy: Primus and Big Lucy provided, therefore, another example of the dominant Gowrie pattern of a couple without surviving children.

Cato, another stepson of Old Phillis's, was like his cousin Betty one of the Manigaults' most esteemed slaves. His life, brief though it was, may have given Old Phillis great pleasure; for a large part of the satisfaction of some bondswomen was in raising children in whom they could take pride, and Phillis was likely to have been happy about Cato. At the age of only twenty-four he was appointed the plantation miller, replacing Stephen, who was old (forty-nine) and asthmatic, and whom the Manigaults may have suspected of stealing rice to sell in Savannah.[22] Cato appears to have been honest and fully reliable, and when he drowned two years later in a flatboat accident, the lament of the overseer was heartfelt. "Your best most honest & confidential servant Cato is no more," the overseer—anxious to deny responsibility for the drowning—notified Charles Manigault. And Cato's wife, Catherine, was almost as highly regarded by the masters as Cato himself—for Catherine and Cato's cousin Betty were, according to Charles Manigault, "the two primest, & best Negresses on the place."[23]

In the ethical morass produced by slavery, it would be too easy to dismiss Betty's kindness to the little Manigault boy, and Cato and Catherine's honesty and reliability, as the conduct of Aunt Chloes and Uncle Toms. There was, of course, an honorable place for stealing and other types of dissidence among the slaves. But there may also have been a place for the generous spirit of Betty toward the white child, and the honesty of her cousin Cato in his milling operations; and Betty's and Cato's parents, foster parents, and stepparents are likely to have been proud of inculcating these qualities into their children.

The members of the Savage family and their spouses thus included several slaves in positions of responsibility: the carpenters Brave Boy and Jack Savage; the drivers Ishmael and cooper George; Cato the miller; Louisa, who eventually escaped plantation labor as a washerwoman; and Sary, whose husband had at the age of thirty won the Manigaults' trust as postboy. Yet the family did not comprise a self-contained slave "elite." All of the women did hard field labor during most of their adult lives as slaves (Old Phillis herself was still a full hand at forty-six and a half hand at fifty-one), and so did Short Jack and Pompey, before his elevation to post boy. Even Cato's position as miller, and Betty's husband George's job as cooper, did not exempt these men from a great deal of heavy, dangerous work, as the injury to George's testicle and Cato's drowning bore witness.

Even for slaves in relatively privileged positions, family life was no bed of roses. If Cato had any children, none survived; the same was true of Betty and of Primus. Jack Savage's four children all died young. Of Ishmael's, Sary's, and Louisa's twelve children, eight are known to have died young (the others having reached the ages of five, seven, seven, and ten when the record ends). The privilege which really mattered was that of being sent away from Gowrie: for of the four surviving children, three had been sent to Manigault's properties in South Carolina.

The response of the Savage slaves toward slavery ran the gamut from Jack Savage's inveterate dissidence to the accommodating stance of Cato. Although Cato, his wife, Catherine, and his cousin Betty were highly esteemed by the Manigaults, and both Louisa and Pompey (Sary's husband) were entrusted by the masters with jobs taking them away from routine field labor, this was by no means the whole story. Catherine and Betty pretty surely helped once to sabotage the threshing machine, when they were assigned to feed sheaves of rice into it, and Short Jack also contributed to a slowdown at that machine. Short Jack ran away once and earned the Manigaults' mistrust

in other ways. Ishmael's conduct was ambiguous, for although he once betrayed his brother, Jack Savage, a forbidden supply of gunpowder had previously been discovered in his cabin.[24] And although Betty's husband, cooper
George, was elevated to the post of head driver for three years, he was later
demoted; and—as will appear in the next chapter—George then tenaciously
sustained a feud with the overseer, ran away, and was jailed in Charleston and
nearly sold. The conduct of the Savage slaves and their spouses fitted into no
neat twentieth-century categories.

Betsey's Family

Betsey (Crecie's mother) was the matriarch of a family—high in the plantation's occupational hierarchy—that had been shipped bit by bit from Silk Hope
between 1835 and 1849 to help fill gaping holes in the ranks (see genealogical
table 11). So vivid to the slaves was the danger of family breakup (and such a
horror did they doubtless feel for the unhealthy Savannah River plantation)
that in 1835 Betsey's thirty-seven-year-old husband, a cooper at Silk Hope, had
been reduced to tears at the prospect of being sent on his own, even temporarily, to Gowrie. In the previous winter Manigault had indeed sent George for a
spell to make barrels at Gowrie, and the overseer was impressed by his skill. In
September 1835 Manigault, then in Europe, sent word that George was again
to be sent to the Savannah River. "I was affraid he would Run away and not go
to Savannah at all," the Silk Hope overseer reported, "as he started off Crying,
and said if you had not left positive directions when he was to be sent back, that
he was sure your overseer [at Gowrie] would keep him, having proved him to be
a Smart Cooper last Winter."[25]

Upon Manigault's return to Charleston he dealt in a different way with the
awkward problem of George's attachment to his family: Manigault deported
the cooper permanently to Gowrie with his wife, Betsey, and their two teenage children—seventeen-year-old Matty and fifteen-year-old George (named
after his father, and soon trained to his father's trade); but he split up the
family by keeping back in South Carolina Betsey's daughter Jane (for domestic service), and Betsey's three youngest children, who were then nine, five,
and three years old. He separated the three young children from their mother
for eight years; they never saw their father again, for he died (at the age of
thirty-nine) a year after arriving at Gowrie. Manigault doubtless calculated
that the three youngest children, still useless to him in the rice fields, were less
likely to die at Silk Hope than at Gowrie: for his policy was always to select
"prime hands" at Silk Hope for deportation, and if parents must be separated
from young children, so be it. By 1845, however, Betsey's youngest children
were old enough—seventeen, thirteen, and eleven by then—that he shipped
them too to Gowrie. He had had good reason to fear for the young slaves'
lives: for the thirteen-year-old and the eleven-year-old girls both died within
four years of their arrival.

Soon after Betsey's husband died in 1838, she bore his posthumous child,

TABLE 11. Betsey's Family

```
                          BETSEY (1802-alive 1867)                    Betsey's sibling
                                    |
              |---------------------|
[George's sibling]            —— m George (1799-1838)          CATHERINE (Pendergrath)
                                                               (1828-alive 1875)
ROBERT (1814-57)              Matty (1820-44)                  m(1: c.1847) Cato (1826-52)
m(1:) Hester (1819-54)       m(by 1842) JOHN IZARD             m(2: 1853) Joe (1831-53)
   Nelly (1843[?]-45)           (1815-alive 1877)              m(3: 1855) Robert (1814-57)
   Matty (1852-52)              Patty (1844-44)                m(4: 1856) Tommy (Pendergrath)
m(2:1855) Catherine          JANE (1821-sold 1854)               (1821-alive 1867)
   (1828-alive 1875)         (COOPER) GEORGE                      Lucy (1858-59)
m(3:1856) Clary                 (1822-alive 1867)                 Paul (1863-alive 1864)
   (1801-alive 1864)         m(1845) BETTY
                                (1827-alive 1867)
                             Crecie (1828-54)
                             m(1845) Ishmael
                                (1822-alive 1867)
                                Nelly (1848-49)
                                Betsey (1851-alive 1861)
                                Cato (1854-alive 1864)
                             Ellen (1832-c.1848)
                             Hagar (1834-c.1848)
                             Paul (1839-9)
```

who survived only a few months. The family's size was augmented in 1841 by
the importation of Betsey's thirteen-year-old niece Catherine from Silk Hope.
But Betsey's family quickly left her hearth: her daughter Matty married John
Izard—the most versatile artisan at Gowrie—by 1842; her son cooper George
married the eighteen-year-old Betty (Jack Savage's cousin) in 1845; Betsey's
seventeen-year-old daughter Crecie married Ishmael within months of arriving at Gowrie in 1845; and her niece Catherine was married to Cato the miller
at about nineteen. Betsey was made Gowrie's plantation cook and housekeeper, so that all surviving members of her family held (or—in the case of
Catherine—were married to a person soon to hold) privileged positions
within the occupational hierarchy. The features of the five more remarkable
members of this family can still be discerned after nearly a century and a half.

   John Izard, Matty's husband, held perhaps the most privileged position
among all the Gowrie slaves. Not quite so skilled a carpenter as Jack Savage,
John was a much steadier worker; and whenever a white artisan was hired for
a spell at Gowrie the Manigaults took the opportunity to train John to a new
trade, whether it be bricklaying, painting, or repairing the threshing machine.
He became Gowrie's "chief engineer." His artisan skills were often needed at
Silk Hope, and Charles Manigault took for granted that John would be trusted
to travel long distances on his own (but, of course, with a pass). In the 1830s,
when it had taken the Manigault slaves six and a half days to walk—in a
guarded group—from Silk Hope to Gowrie, John Izard cut a couple of days
off the trip by taking a boat from Silk Hope to Charleston, whence he was
allowed to walk alone for four days to Gowrie; and in later years he was sent
alone by steamboat between Savannah and Charleston.

   These privileges could not protect John from the family disasters experienced by almost every other slave at Gowrie. John was married at least three
times but his partners all died, none living to be more than thirty-two. Matty,
Betsey's daughter, was the first of John's wives. They had been married for
several years[26] before Matty finally became pregnant, and the overseer did not
miss the opportunity to express contempt for even the most reliable of
Gowrie's slave artisans. "Carpenter John has got his wife up at last," overseer
Bagshaw wrote in July 1844. "I expect he thinks he is a man now."[27]
Bagshaw's jest turned sour soon after Matty's child was born, for the exhausted mother contracted pleurisy and was dead four days later. The baby
quickly followed her, and John Izard was for the first time a childless widower.

   Matty's sister Jane, who had been kept in Charleston as a house servant,
incurred Charles Manigault's displeasure and—after a spell in the fields at
Silk Hope—in 1849 was deported to Gowrie. From house service she was
reduced to working in the "mud & water of the swamp,"[28] a demotion against
which she waged a long, ingenious, and for a time successful struggle. John
Izard, her brother-in-law, was soon living with her, but he seems to have told
his masters that she was his "sister," not his wife; and they then spoke of her
satirically as "Sister Jane."[29] As though to show they were wrong in their
assumptions, John Izard soon married another woman, Margaret, who came
to live in the house with him and Jane.

Relatively independent himself, John Izard seems to have had a taste for independent souls, and both Margaret and John's third wife were—like "Sister Jane"—among those Gowrie women whom the Manigaults found difficult to govern. Early in 1852 Margaret and another slave woman were sent to the Savannah jail to be whipped and "cooled," possibly as punishment for assisting two of Gowrie's slaves who were then hiding in the swamps. That September Margaret's child by John Izard was born. Margaret died three months later, at the age of twenty-two, of "cholera." Their infant was dead within a year ("I think it was its teeth," the overseer surmised), and John was for the second time a childless widower.[30]

John's next wife was Judy, whom Manigault had bought in 1853 with her husband, Amos, and their three children. Judy's two youngest children had died within a year of arriving at Gowrie, and her husband followed in the "cholera" epidemic of 1854. Judy had no reason to cherish Gowrie, and a few months later she ran away with forty-year-old Julia. But trying to stay alive in the snake-infested swamp—and sharing one's abode with the numerous rats—was also an uncongenial existence, and she returned after a month. Judy soon married John Izard and presented him with a daughter. But Judy died of dysentery in 1858, at the age of thirty-two, and the child perished before she was five. John himself survived pneumonia in the winter of 1853–54 and once again (or another serious illness) in 1859. After his last child's death John was for the third time a childless widower, though he continued to care for his stepdaughter.[31] This tie was not strong enough to attach him to the Manigaults, and he ran away in 1863. Captured after two weeks, John Izard was incarcerated for a time in a South Carolina jail, but unlike Jack Savage he was not then sold. His Izard blood protected him from the wrath of Charles Izard Manigault.[32]

Jane, Betsey's eldest surviving child after Matty's death, did not wait so long as John Izard to flee the Manigaults' service. More than any other of the Gowrie slaves, Jane appears to have felt herself above the lot of an ordinary field hand. She was also the only young woman at Gowrie who held herself aloof from marrying any of the slave men. Her campaign for special treatment was successful in 1849, and she was removed from field labor to be a house servant, cook, and nurse. But her complaints and alleged malingering led to her being demoted again to field labor in 1854, whereupon she promptly ran away, was captured, was subjected to six months of discipline in the Savannah jail, and then was sold to New Orleans.[33] Special privilege did not reconcile either Jane or John Izard to the slave regime.

Betsey's nephew *Robert* was another Silk Hope slave fallen from Manigault's favor, who had been deported to do field labor at Gowrie. His response, however, was different from Jane's. A "very determined" man,[34] Robert proved nevertheless to be more accommodating than Jane. He was thirty, and had been Charles Manigault's house servant in South Carolina during the previous seven years, when he suddenly was sent to Gowrie in 1844. Part of the punishment was to separate Robert from his wife, Hester, and his child Nelly, who were kept at Silk Hope. Manigault watched to see whether removing

Robert's feet from the polished floors of the master's South Carolina residences to the flooded fields of Gowrie would cool his temper.

Overseer Bagshaw reported cautiously at first that "Robert gets along tolerable well but I See he is getting a little tame, not quite so firerey [*sic*] as when he first Come." Bagshaw thought the demoted house servant was fussy about the boring food rations doled out to Gowrie's slaves: "A negroe never Knows when he is well off," the overseer ruminated. But Robert quickly decided to make the best of a bad job, and Bagshaw was amazed at what a house servant could do in the field:

> Robert does his work as well as any of them. . . . [Aug. 24, 1844]

> Robert bids fair to make a very Prime hand. He has got on astonishing in the harvest. [Sept. 14, 1844]

> Robert is very near as good a hand to work as I have got. [Oct. 20, 1844]

The overseer started thinking how Robert's capability could be better employed—perhaps he should be placed under cooper George for training in George's trade? This idea fell on deaf ears; but by 1848 Robert had so thoroughly regained Manigault's confidence that, when driver Renty suddenly died that year, Robert was made head driver—a post he held until his own death nine years later. He won the younger Manigault's confidence too, and when in 1852 Louis Manigault was trying to persuade his father to sack Ishmael as "second driver" (in charge of the East Hermitage tract), he assured Charles Manigault that "Robert Could easily look after both Gangs—at least for a while."[35]

To reward Robert's newfound tractability, the elder Manigault had sent on his wife, Hester, and child Nelly from Silk Hope after seven months of separation. As with every other very young child imported into Gowrie during this period, death quickly seized Nelly from her mother's arms. Robert and Hester later had at least one other child; but she and any other babies of theirs died during infancy. Robert and Hester—like John Izard and his wives, Jack Savage and his wife, and the majority of Gowrie couples—had no surviving children. Hester had "cholera" in 1852 but did not succumb to it. Robert had a very bad case of pneumonia in February 1854; as he was the driver, the Manigaults were genuinely anxious about his illness. He recovered, but during the same year his wife, Hester, was again stricken with "cholera" and this time she died, at the age of thirty-five. This left Robert a childless widower.

Within twenty weeks Betsey's niece Catherine appears to have married Robert, but she stayed with him less than a year, and Robert perhaps turned morose. The next year the plantation cook Clary, a fifty-five-year-old widow who was thirteen years older than Robert, was moved into his house, but this may not have been a real marriage.

Robert died suddenly in 1857 at the age of forty-three. Quite possibly he killed himself; certainly something out of the ordinary had occurred. The Methodist Bishop Andrew visited Gowrie a few days later but was tight-lipped about the atmosphere there into which he had stumbled. Charles Manigault was almost equally cryptic: "Have the House [Robert's] cleaned out & put [the new driver] in it at once," Manigault ordered his son Louis. "After any thing of the kind occurring in a house if it remains shut up any time the Negroes will get up a story of its being haunted, & none will wish to go there."[36]

The new driver was *cooper George*—Betsey's thirty-five-year-old son—a first cousin of Robert's and, like him, a "very determined" man. Although George was Louis Manigault's own choice as driver, within a few years the master had lost faith in him. By 1860 George had been dismissed from his post and was nearly sold. He resented his demotion, challenged the overseer's authority, tried to run away, and in 1861 was put for "3 months in Dark Solitary Confinement" in the Charleston workhouse. Louis decided that George's mother, Betsey, was "a very wicked Woman" whom he (almost certainly falsely) suspected of poisoning several slave children in the summer of 1860.[37]

This tangle of passions can scarcely be unraveled. Soon after George became driver in 1857, he seems to have had disciplinary problems with the other slaves. Surprisingly enough, overseer Leonard Venters apparently sided with the slaves against the driver (or, at least, some of the slaves later reported him as having done so). While Louis Manigault was taking a long trip in Europe during the summer of 1857, Venters—a twenty-five-year-old man with little previous overseeing experience, and the least literate of the Manigaults' overseers—allegedly was overcome with religious feeling, and he began joining the slaves in their prayer meetings. He also started sleeping with a twenty-two-year-old field hand, Harriet; their child, James, was born in 1858. Meanwhile, Louis returned from Europe and promptly sacked Venters for undermining plantation discipline.[38] One supposes that driver George helped persuade Louis that Venters was not the man for Gowrie.

George also outlasted the next overseer, William Bryan, whom the Manigaults fired in disgust after only one year's service. They concluded that Bryan neglected his plantation duties, spending far more time than was allowed with his family at Bryan's pineland summer residence, leaving the plantation too long under the charge of George and the other black driver.

George probably never got on with the next overseer, William Capers, a genteel Carolinian who preened himself on his knowledge of the slaves' character, but whose six-year stint at Gowrie was marked by more turbulence among the slaves than any other period of the Manigaults' proprietorship. George's halfheartedness in enforcing Capers's edicts may have compounded the trouble—certainly Capers was quick to blame George for the defiant suicide of twenty-two-year-old London in 1860—but the slaves' unruliness continued long after George had been demoted from being driver; indeed, George was later a leading spirit in the slaves' unrest. His mother, Betsey (who would scarcely have forgiven the Manigaults for the sale of her daughter Jane to New Orleans), surely sided with George in his feud with overseer Capers, and this was probably why Capers blamed her for the sudden deaths of several slave children under her care during the summer of 1860. Yet when Louis Manigault returned to Gowrie for his first postwar visit in 1867, George—who was then one of the five "foremen" each managing one-fifth of the free-labor plantation—agreed to carry Louis's son on his back, and then

Louis himself, across the most flooded of the fields, to save them from getting even more thoroughly soaked than they already were. No doubt George remembered vividly the three months he had spent in the "dark hole" of the Charleston workhouse at the Manigaults' behest, and his long feud with Louis Manigault's esteemed overseer, Capers; yet this did not deter him from acting in a generous way to his former master.

When, in 1867, cooper George was walking more than knee-deep through the flooded field carrying Louis Manigault on his back, Louis may have fancied for a moment that he was again in the saddle, and that nothing had changed. An hour later, as he tramped around the old plantation with the white man who was managing Gowrie, and with the black men who as foremen subcontracted under the white manager, Louis was overcome by happy nostalgia. Even the weather suited the symbolism of the occasion; the Savannah church seemed to have lent divine sanction to the old social system; and only the absence of his horse, so that he could have been fully in the saddle, marred Louis's pleasure. "Proceeding in front of [the white manager]," Louis recalled,

> and followed by some of his "Foremen" (none other than our former Negroes "Driver John," "George" Cooper, "Big Hector," and "Charles" the Trunk Minder) I imagined myself for the moment a Planter once more as if followed by Overseer and Driver. The weather was most beautiful, not a cloud on the Horizon, and so clear and pure the atmosphere that the Presbyterian Church Steeple in Savannah loomed up as if one half its distance. I wished my horse with me to ride over the entire Tract as of yore. But these were only passing momentary thoughts, & soon dispelled by the sad reality of affairs.[39]

The "sad" fact was that cooper George was now relatively free. He carried Louis physically on his back not because he was slavishly following orders but because from his relative abundance he could freely spare something: he could be charitable toward the man who had jailed him in Charleston, and could savor the satisfaction of being the giver, not the powerless receiver, of small favors.

Betsey's niece *Catherine,* it will be recalled, was in Charles Manigaults' eyes one of the two best slave women at Gowrie. This did not ensure that the Manigaults would treat her with respect. Catherine had been deported to Gowrie from Silk Hope at the age of thirteen to live with Betsey; if any members of Catherine's own family at Silk Hope were still alive—as was probable—she was then separated from them. At about nineteen she married Cato the miller, and they lived with Cato's stepmother, Phillis. When Cato drowned in 1852, Catherine continued living with Phillis. Six months later, Charles Manigault purchased thirty-two slaves in Charleston and shipped them to Gowrie; one of them, Joe, at twenty-three, was exactly Catherine's age. Within six weeks Louis notified his father that, after having put Joe briefly at the Hermitage tract with the other new slaves, he was about to "place [Joe] here at Gowrie with Cathrina, & old Maum Phillis." The plan of coupling Joe with Catherine was unsuccessful. Joe does not appear to have relished life at Gowrie, and three months later he perished in an unsuccessful attempt to escape.[40]

Catherine's next partner was driver Robert, whom she seems to have married soon after his wife, Hester, had died of "cholera." But apparently they did not get on, and within a year Catherine had left the driver and was married instead to a field hand named Tommy.[41] This marriage lasted at least eleven years and produced two recorded infants, one of whom was still alive in 1864.[42] Catherine was not therefore sterile, and the fact that no other child appears in the record of her four marriages suggests that she had miscarriages, or other babies who died very young, as did so many other women at Gowrie. Before settling down with Tommy at the age of twenty-eight, Catherine had had three previous marriages broken, respectively, by death, the flight and death of a fugitive slave, and voluntary separation.

Thus, the only surviving children in old Betsey's extended family, two generations after Betsey, were her daughter Crecie's two children and Catherine's infant; for neither Betsey's other six children, nor her nephew Robert, nor her son-in-law John Izard had any surviving children. And although Betsey's family contained many privileged slaves—cooper George, driver Robert, house servant Jane, and the wives of carpenter John Izard, of Cato the miller, and of driver Ishmael—it was not a docile group. When Louis Manigault concluded in 1867 that Betsey was "very wicked,"[43] he may have blamed her for fostering their independence.

Old Mary's Family

This family included her three daughters and a son, Charles. While the daughters were field hands, Charles had already by the age of twenty-one been appointed Gowrie's "second driver" (under driver Harry). Thirteen years later, he briefly succeeded Harry as head driver, though the masters soon demoted him from that post. He and his wife, Juna, had at least eight children, but not one survived to age five. (Altogether Old Mary's children and their spouses produced sixteen known offspring, but as none of the grandchildren survived to age twenty, the family became extinct.)[44]

Old Scotland's Family

This family comprised his three daughters, whose lives suggested how fragile marriage could be at Gowrie. *Hannah* apparently had an "abroad" marriage— her spouse living on another plantation, owned by a different master. This union seems to have been broken up by the removal of Hannah's husband from East Hermitage in 1848 when she was pregnant with their fifth child.[45] *Minty* had five children by three different fathers, and was recently married to a fourth man when she died in 1851, at the age of forty-three. *Rhina* had seen three husbands to the grave—two of them drowned—by the time she was thirty-four.

Her fourth marriage ended in voluntary separation. Her fifth union lasted less than two years because she, at age thirty-nine, contracted pneumonia and died in the spring of 1859, soon after Charles Manigault had made yet another of his futile exhortations to the overseers to keep the slaves out of wet winter weather and cold March winds. Rhina may have had a series of miscarriages; if she ever had a live birth, no infant of hers survived long enough to find its way into Manigault's annual lists. Hers would not have been the kind of life to make a Maryland slave woman enthusiastic about being deported to a Georgia rice plantation.

Old Fortune's Family

Fortune and her three teenage daughters—euphoniously named Joaney, Juna, and Julia—were deported from Silk Hope to Gowrie in 1833. Two of the daughters have already been mentioned: for Joaney married captain Hector, while Juna became driver Charles's wife. Julia, the third daughter, was as unsuccessful as Juna in saving any of her children from Gowrie's plagues; and she suffered the added sorrow that by the time she was forty-four her three husbands, too, had all died, one after another.

Smaller Families

In addition to the six principal families, there were three smaller groups at Gowrie in November 1848, each stricken by family tragedy.

Bob, sent to Gowrie in 1833, appears to have been separated at age thirty from a pregnant wife and two very young children when Charles Manigault culled the Silk Hope slaves, selecting able-bodied workers like Bob for Gowrie and leaving almost every young child behind. About three years later, with no prospect of ever seeing his wife again, Bob married a Gowrie woman named Binkey. She soon became a cripple, and she died at forty-two. Bob later espoused Rhina. He was apprehended selling stolen rice in Savannah, and subsequently he drowned when returning from another illicit boat trip.[46]

The mother of a boy named *Fortune* apparently died of complications following his birth in 1840. Fortune's father, Renty, became Gowrie's head driver in 1848 and died in a dysentery epidemic the same year. Fortune, orphaned at eight, was then cared for by a succession of four women who all expired or became incapacitated, one after another, during the next seven years. His siblings were all dead by 1858, the elder brother succumbing that year (at age twenty-two) to pneumonia—doubtless contracted while he was doing wet ditching in February blasts. Fortune embarked upon a career as the most persistent absentee among Manigault's slaves. In every year from 1857 to 1859 he ran away; and when he did so again in April 1860, Louis Manigault resorted to the standard remedy—taken for granted by even the most paternalist of slaveholders. He sold Fortune in Savannah for twelve hundred dollars "as he was always running off."[47]

Posh, a bird minder entrusted to go "Round the fields with a gun at the black birds," also held privileged jobs as cooper, trunk minder, and watchman. Apparently he abandoned his first wife, Pender, to father a child by Peggy, the seventeen-year-old daughter of old driver Harry. Peggy died at twenty-two, and their child perished in the same year. Posh entered a long feud with a new overseer (who accused him of malingering), ran away at least twice, and was then sold—the masters' standard way for converting an otherwise valueless property into cash.[48]

Unlike the rest of the Americas, the United States witnessed in the nineteenth century a rapid natural growth of its slave population (though not as rapid as that of its free inhabitants). One therefore might think of the slaves as prolific, and envisage slave parents surrounded by large numbers of children—something like the rural families one can still find in the Austrian Alps, where a father and a vigorous, radiant mother are surrounded by fifteen hearty children, only one of their original sixteen children having died. The reality at Gowrie was different. Only one woman of childbearing age there in 1848 had as many as three children who reached the age of twenty-one, or who at least survived until 1864.[49] Only three other mothers had as many as two survivors. Of the other fifteen women of childbearing age in 1848, three had one surviving child; the great majority—twelve women—had none at all.[50]

All twelve of these women were married[51] and at least eight of them had children, but the children did not live long. Juna had at least nine children (not including her foster child), Binah Currie at least eight, Amey (Jack Savage's wife) at least four: but every one of these twenty-one children died. The same was true of the children of Hester (driver Robert's wife), Nancy, Julia, Peggy, and Big Lucy. If the other four wives ever bore children, they did not live even long enough to be recorded in the annual lists.[52] Here again it must be remembered that the actual number of children borne by these women was on average some 66 percent more than indicated by the annual lists. Thus Juna may actually have borne not nine but say fifteen children, all of whom died young. And women like Rhina and Pender, who appear to have been infertile, may in fact have had a series of miscarriages, stillbirths, and babies who died too young to be listed.

The number of babies listed for these nineteen married women was small (an average of three per woman), the majority of these women seeming to have had no more than two live births (see table 12). The surprisingly small number of children *recorded* in the annual lists is therefore strong evidence—in a noncontraceptive society—that these women suffered from a frightful number of miscarriages, stillbirths, and deaths of children from feebleness at birth, or from malaria, winter fevers, tetanus, and other killers of infants in the first months of their lives: mishaps not recorded in the annual lists.[53]

The small size of these women's families did not arise from late marriage. On the contrary, at Gowrie virtually every woman was married by the age of

TABLE 12.   Apparent Fertility of
Gowrie Women

	Number
with 0–2 recorded live births	10
" 3–5 " " "	7
" 6 or more " " "	2
TOTAL	19

twenty. Almost a third were married, or had conceived a child, by seventeen, and almost half by eighteen.

Reasonably accurate dates are known for twenty-five women.[54] Not one of these women remained unmarried; twenty-three of them were married by about age twenty, or had conceived a child by then.[55] Phillis may have been only fifteen; Jenny and Fortune were probably not more than sixteen; and Juna, Crecie, Peggy, and probably two others were no more than seventeen when they married or conceived their first children. At the other extreme, Rhina and Joaney were both about twenty-four when their first known marriages occurred, but special factors probably were at work. Rhina (who subsequently had five marriages) may have had an earlier "abroad" marriage, of the sort which both of her sisters apparently established. And Joaney was a "Little Runt" who may not have attracted a marriage partner until she was about twenty-four. None of the other women was over about twenty, and the median age of marriage or first conception was barely nineteen, as becomes evident in table 13.[56] These figures support the conclusion of other historians[57] that most slave women had sex young and married young. They had few incentives to do otherwise.

Customarily women married men who were much older than themselves. The age gap was usually at least five years and often nine or more. Ned was at least thirty-three years older than Julia, Bob seventeen years older than Rhina, and driver Robert fourteen years older than Catherine; while driver Harry's wife, Betsey, seems to have been married successively to two men, each twenty or more years older than she. In 20 percent of the marriages for which data are available, the husbands were at least nine years older than the wives, and for another 30 percent the age gap was five to eight years.[58] Julia, Rhina, and Catherine had all been separated at an early age from their fathers—probably, in each case, by deportation or death—and in marrying relatively old men they may in part have sought substitutes for their own lost fathers.

Three other instances of wide age gaps stand forth in the later Manigault records (not included in the group already discussed). In 1860 Manigault, dismissing cooper George as the head driver, bought a forty-four-year-old South Carolina slave named John to take George's place. (If driver John had a family in South Carolina, he was separated from them.) Within a few months

John married the twenty-three-year-old Nancy Hunt, a survivor from the ill-fated family which had been decimated in 1854.

When in 1849 Manigault bought the family of Die, a twenty-seven-year-old South Carolina slave, she had already been married for at least eight years to the sixty-year-old Joe, and they had three children.

In 1857 Manigault purchased a group of slaves including the elderly Daniel, so old that he was added—free—to the parcel of others. Daniel pretty surely was therefore at least fifty-five, probably older. He was married to the twenty-one-year-old Miley; they had been married since she was fifteen, and their previous owner said that "they are both much attached to each other."

Thus the age gaps in these three marriages were twenty-one years, thirty-three years, and probably more than thirty-four years. If older men tend to dominate younger wives, the seeds of male chauvinism had been planted deep at Gowrie.

On the other hand, a surprising number of the wives—nearly a quarter of them—were older than their husbands, and typically the gap was five years or more (see table 14).[59] After old Ned's death, Julia married a man nine years younger than she; Rhina, after the deaths of three previous husbands, also married someone nine years her junior. Minty was forty-one when she married the twenty-eight-year-old Tommy, she having had three previous marriages.

Abroad marriages were common in most of the Old South; and the

TABLE 13.   Gowrie Women's
Age at First-Known Marriage
or Conception of
First-Known Child*

Age	No. of Women
24	2**
20	5***
19	6
18	4
17	5
16	2
15	1
TOTAL	25

*If both a woman's age at first marriage and her age at conception of first child are known, the earlier is used.

**Rhina was 24 or 25; Joaney was 23 or 24.

***Amey was 20 or 21, Julia was 19 to 21, and Matty was 19 or 20; while Pender and Minty were no more than 20, but quite possibly younger.

TABLE 14.   Age Differences of Gowrie Marriage Partners

	No. of Marriages
MAN OLDER THAN WIFE	
14–33 years older	5
9–13 " "	4
5–8 " "	15
1–4 " "	9
SAME AGE	3
WOMAN OLDER THAN HUSBAND	
1–4 years older	3
5–8 " "	3
9–13 " "	5
TOTAL MARRIAGES	47

inevitable strains on marriage when husband and wife did not live together (except on weekends and perhaps on one midweek night) were central to the lives of many slaves. Several of these marriages existed at Gowrie in 1833 when Manigault bought the estate: thus, in seeking to track down two fugitives that year, Manigault learned that Elick's wife lived across the river on Isla Island, and that Minda "has a husband . . . in the Georgia Pine barren and has a sweet heart . . . at Judge Berryan's place."[60] But Manigault sold Minda in 1834, Elick died of Asiatic cholera that year, and their master instituted and enforced a rule that no Gowrie woman was to marry a slave unknown to the overseer.[61] Abroad marriages became rare: Hannah and Minty probably had them, Romeo and Cicero established brief ones before their early deaths, and Rhina, Ishmael (after Crecie's death), and Little Lucy may also have done so; but these were perhaps the only ones in the 1840s and 1850s. Instead of the strains of abroad marriages, Manigault substituted at Gowrie the strains from marriage within a very limited marriage market. The master's concern was plantation discipline, not the strength of the slaves' family life. The number of available marriage partners of one's own age being tiny, many slaves tried to solve the problem by marrying someone much older than themselves.

Another reason for wide age gaps was that first marriages often ended abruptly, and the relatively old survivor then commonly married a young new partner. Thus when at the age of thirty Bob was shipped from Silk Hope to Gowrie—pretty surely being separated from a pregnant wife, Betty, and her two very young children there[62]—he found as his new wife Binkey, six years younger than he was. By the time she died, Bob was old enough to marry Rhina, seventeen years his junior. Driver Harry's wife, Patty, died in 1834, and he later married a widow, Betsey, who was about twenty years younger than he. And after driver Robert's wife, Hester, died in the "cholera" of 1854, he married Catherine, who at twenty-seven was fourteen years his junior; but this marriage of unequal partners quickly broke down.[63]

Though Charles Manigault often preserved family groupings among his slaves, he destroyed family ties when it suited him to do so. He often split up families in selling a slave for insubordination; and he did so sometimes too simply to serve his own pecuniary interest. Thus when he deported thirty-year-old Moses from Silk Hope to Gowrie in 1833, he separated Moses from a wife and child in Carolina. Moses had an abroad marriage to a slave woman owned by the Silk Hope overseer, who three years later offered to buy Moses from Manigault in order to reunite him with his wife. She "seems to have a great attachment to him," the overseer pointed out. But Manigault kept Moses—whom he regarded as "slow & complaining"—at Gowrie: why should a "negro" complain about being separated from his spouse? A year or two later Moses, with no chance of rejoining his wife, entered an unsuccessful marriage with a Gowrie woman, but it broke down in 1840; he died in 1844 without ever seeing his first wife or child again.[64]

As Manigault had done to Moses, so he probably also did to Bob, another thirty-year-old man sent from Silk Hope to Gowrie in 1833. This separation arose from the master's policy of culling Silk Hope slaves, selecting youthful, able-bodied workers for Gowrie, and leaving nearly all young children behind in South Carolina. (Of the twenty-two slaves deported from Silk Hope in 1833, nineteen were aged between fourteen and thirty, two were [still-productive] mothers sent to accompany their families of "prime hands," and only one[65] was under fourteen years old.) Manigault's policy of leaving infants and young children at Silk Hope was sure to break up families.

The Silk Hope woman from whom Bob seems to have been separated was named Betty (a different Betty from cooper George's wife). Betty at Silk Hope was the mother of a young boy and of the one-year-old Margaret; and when Bob was sent to Gowrie in 1833 Betty was pregnant with another child, soon to be named Ralph.[66] Sixteen years later, when Margaret had reached an age to be worth her master's deporting her to the Savannah River plantation, she came to live with Bob and his new wife, and Ralph followed two years later. Their both being housed with Bob can scarcely be explained except by their being close relations of his. That Bob was their father, not an uncle, may be inferred from the facts that a thirty-year-old Silk Hope male was unlikely to be a bachelor, and that Manigault clearly did not scruple sometimes to separate a husband from his wife—as he had done to Moses—when he thought this necessary to secure enough "prime hands" at Gowrie. From the master's point of view, to send the pregnant Betty and her two young children to Gowrie with Bob would have defeated the purpose of culling.[67] When Manigault was in Europe in 1835, Betsey's husband, George, had known Bob's and Moses's family circumstances; and George's weeping then, when the overseer had sent him alone to Gowrie, makes plain that George feared he—like they—would be permanently separated from his wife.

Other cases of family breakups occurred later. When Manigault sent

George and Betsey to Gowrie in 1837, he separated Betsey from her three youngest children for eight years. In 1844 the master deported Robert (later the head driver) to Gowrie, separating him from his wife, Hester, and their child; Hester was permitted to rejoin her husband only after Robert had knuckled under to plantation discipline in the Georgia rice swamp. In 1858 Manigault threatened to separate driver George from his wife because he believed the latter was malingering. And this enumeration takes no account of instances when Manigault purchased a parcel of slaves that included a mother and child but not the child's father.

The master's policy contributed to the fragility of marriage at Gowrie. Nineteen women of childbearing age lived there on November 30, 1848, and probably 21 percent of them experienced the breakup of a marriage (or of a relationship which had produced a child) by the master's deporting—or acquiescing in the deportation of—one of the partners (see table 15). When in 1833 Manigault sent eighteen-year-old Juna from Silk Hope to Gowrie with her infant daughter, he separated Juna from the child's father; and Juna—with no prospect of ever seeing him again—two years later married someone else. Nancy's husband, the "smart & intelligent" Jacob, was deported from Gowrie back to Silk Hope for disorderliness, after Nancy had been married to him for about fifteen years: they never saw each other again. Amey had been married to Jack Savage for eighteen years when he fled for eighteen months to the swamp; and when, gaunt and haggard, he finally returned, the Manigaults broke up the marriage by selling Jack. Hannah, who never was listed as living with a Gowrie man, probably had an abroad marriage, which seems to have been broken up by the removal and sale of her husband by his owner when she was pregnant with their fifth child. Hannah's husband probably lived at East Hermitage and was among the slaves owned by Henry McAlpin, offered for sale to Manigault when the latter bought that tract in 1848;[68] but Manigault thought he could purchase new slaves cheaper elsewhere, and therefore Hannah probably never saw her husband again.[69]

Manigault's policy, however, was not the only reason that Gowrie's marriages were precarious. At least 26 percent of the Gowrie group[70] experienced the voluntary breakup of a marriage, or of a relationship which had produced a child. In 1849 Jack Savage's sister Sary split up with her first husband, William (who had already had a previous unsuccessful marriage). Pender apparently was deserted by the bird minder Posh when he fathered a child by Peggy. Minty, after producing four children by two different fathers, married a third man in 1840. Rhina's fourth marriage ended voluntarily after only about a year. And Catherine's third marriage—to driver Robert—also survived only about a year.

Probably 37 percent of the women experienced the breakup of a marriage—when they were still in their twenties—because one of the partners died. Pender was twenty-eight and in her second marriage when she died of "cholera" in 1852. Crecie was twenty-six at her own death, and Peggy succumbed at only twenty-two. The first of Rhina's five marriages ended with her husband's death when she was twenty-nine. Big Lucy's first

TABLE 15.   Nineteen Women's Experience of Marriage (or of a Relationship Which Produced a Child)

	Number	Percentage*
A marriage broken by deportation of one partner	4**	21
A marriage broken voluntarily	5	26
A marriage broken by death of one partner when wife was in her twenties	7***	37
A marriage broken by death of one partner when wife was in her thirties	4	21
A "long" first marriage—i.e., 16 or more years	6****	32
A "long" second marriage	2	11

*These percentages add up to more than 100 percent because several women fall into more than one category.

**As previously explained, I infer that Hannah had an abroad marriage broken by the deportation of her husband in 1848.

***I infer that Binkey had a marriage prior to the one she entered at age twenty-seven with Bob, and I guess that this first marriage was broken by death rather than voluntarily or by deportation.

****Of these long marriages, two (Nancy's and Amey's) were subsequently broken by the deportation of the husbands.

husband perished when she was twenty-eight. Catherine was just twenty-four when her husband Cato drowned—and twenty-five when her second husband (Joe) died in consequence of his unsuccessful attempt at flight. Binkey was probably married to someone prior to her marriage (at twenty-seven) to Bob; this earlier marriage may well have been ended by the husband's death rather than by voluntary separation or by his deportation.

Probably another 21 percent of the women experienced their griefs a little later in life: they or their husbands perished during their thirties. Julia saw three husbands die, one after another within a decade, the first when she was thirty-four. Driver Robert's wife, Hester, succumbed to her second bout of "cholera" when she was thirty-five, while Rhina died at thirty-nine. And Sary's second husband, the "postboy" Pompey, probably died when she was thirty-three or thirty-four.

Because of these various disruptions, no more than 32 percent[71] of these women enjoyed a relatively "long" first marriage—that is, one which endured sixteen years or more. Binah Currie had been married to Stephen the miller for at least twenty-six years when he died in 1856. Betty's childless marriage to cooper George survived at least twenty-two years; Joaney had been married to captain Hector for twenty-one years before her death in 1862; Amey's marriage to Jack Savage had lasted nineteen years when Manigault sold him in 1863; and Louisa had been wed to Short Jack for about sixteen years when he died in 1863. And although Hester is only known with certainty to have been married to driver Robert for eleven years before she died in 1854, the marriage probably had in fact survived about sixteen years.

Another 11 percent of the women established a "long" second marriage after an earlier one had been ended by deportation or death. Thus Juna, after being separated from the father of her first child at Silk Hope, settled down to at least twenty-eight years of marriage to the sometime driver Charles. And Big Lucy, after the death of her first husband, remarried and lived with the field hand Primus for twenty years until his death in 1861. Even the term "long marriage," however, is relative, for only three of these nineteen women were married for as long as twenty-two years.

The experiences of other Gowrie slaves, not included in the group of nineteen women already discussed, indicate that family life was even more fragile than the previous statistics may suggest. Driver Charles's sister Maria had at least three marriages: she had a child by one man; a brief marriage to a second person, dissolved voluntarily; and a third marriage ended by her husband's drowning after he had paid her an unauthorized visit (when she had been sent to mind slave children at a pineland camp miles away from Gowrie). Maria's sister Susey also had at least three marriages: she bore two children by one man; another baby by a second person; then a child by a third man (probably Short Jack, whom she married later that year); and finally, another child by Short Jack after they were married. Similarly, John Izard had three marriages, as did driver Robert; and driver Harry's wife, Betsey, had at least three marriages, if one includes her period of living with Prince.

The slaves who have been mentioned differed in one significant way from most other Gowrie bondsmen and women: nearly all had lived at Gowrie for their whole lives (having been owned there by McAlpin before he sold them with the plantation to Manigault in 1833), *or* they had lived their whole lives under Heyward/Manigault proprietorship (first at Silk Hope, then at Gowrie). By contrast, the 113 slaves whom Charles Manigault bought between 1849 and 1860 changed both owner and residence when they were sold; their removal to Gowrie, therefore, was especially likely to exacerbate family instability.

The contrast is not, however, an absolute one, because even the deportation of slaves from Silk Hope to Gowrie broke up a number of marriages— surely Moses's, almost certainly Bob's, probably others. It also separated mothers from young children: certainly Betsey for eight years from her three young daughters; certainly Maretta permanently from her two daughters (then fifteen and nine years old);[72] and probably others.

Yet family separations—of husbands from wives, and of parents from children—were even more common among the slaves whom Manigault bought after 1849. And this was true even though many of the newly purchased slaves appeared to be sold in family groups. For example, Bess—a twenty-two-year-old woman whom Manigault acquired in 1853—was the sister of Jimmy (the fireman at the steam thresher's boiler), who had been bought in 1849; and Bess's purchase might therefore seem to have restored a shattered family bond. The parcel for which Manigault had paid, however, included only Bess and her infant, Charles, but not the baby's father. After living for a few weeks with her brother Jimmy, Bess then found a new husband. This man soon incurred the Manigaults' displeasure and was sold before he and Bess had been together a full year. Presently Bess married a man six years her junior; but after only a couple of years he died of pneumonia at the age of twenty-two, leaving a posthumous child. Bess later had two other children by a fourth man—either in an abroad marriage or by a man with whom she was not living regularly.

A comparable case was that of Phillis, a thirty-one-year-old woman whom Manigault bought in 1849. This time the parcel comprised Phillis and her two young children, but again not their father. Phillis was pregnant when she was separated from her husband, and on February 15, 1849—the very day she was auctioned in Charleston—she gave birth there to the baby Moses. Soon after arriving at Gowrie she married a man nine years younger than she, but he died in 1850, leaving a posthumous child. Within a few months Phillis then married the newly widowed Stafford (whose previous wife and their infant had both also died in 1850, along with fifteen more slaves in that dreadful year). Stafford survived two years but died of "cholera" in 1852. Phillis's fourth marriage, which she entered not long after Stafford's death, was also brief: she died in 1855 of a bowel complaint which dispatched her soon after the birth of another infant.

The tragedies and instabilities of Bess's and Phillis's family lives obviously were aggravated by their being sold separately from their first husbands. A different kind of family disruption occurred in 1857 when Manigault acquired twenty-one new slaves to fill the ranks depleted during the ghastly year of 1854 (when thirty-two Gowrie slaves had died). One parcel on offer at the Charleston auction included Will, a prime twenty-eight-year-old field hand, and his sickly forty-four-year-old mother, Susanna. Charles Manigault insisted— contrary to the vendor's intention—that the family be split so that he would not be lumbered with an unhealthy "old" woman. He purchased Will but refused to buy Susanna, and presumably she never saw her son again. Will soon earned the Manigaults' distrust: he ran away for several weeks in the winter of 1860–61; the next year he was one of the five slaves about whose inclination to flee to the Yankees the masters were so anxious that they kept him inland at Silk Hope during the whole winter of 1861–62.[73]

The parcels which Manigault bought after 1849 did fairly often, however, include both husband and wife—for the practice of selling couples together was more common in the Charleston market for rice slaves than in the much larger western slave markets for cotton slaves. Perhaps this was because rice slaves had so many other reasons for profound discontent that masters hesitated to push them too far by destroying the family ties of too large a proportion of them.[74] The experiences of Bess, Phillis, and Will were more disrupting than usual among Gowrie's newly purchased slaves. Yet taken as a whole, the 113 bondsmen and women Manigault acquired after 1849 surely suffered family instability even worse than was common among the slaves previously settled there.

Miscegenation was important in the lives of some slaves. The power of white men to force sex upon slave women was the heart of the matter, and Charles Manigault certainly mistrusted the overseer class in this regard. He hired a succession of young men as suboverseers, but by 1848 had "never yet found one who gave entire satisfaction." They were especially tiresome, he thought, if they resided anywhere near Gowrie, "for in this case while on the place their friends & acquaintances are constantly coming to see them—or they take my Negroes & slip off in a boat to visit their friends. I could say much more on this subject. . . ." Obviously Manigault believed the local poor whites were using his slave women to make their own lives jollier.[75]

He required his overseers to sign a contract limiting their access to female field hands. Thus in 1853 the new overseer had to agree that the "woman exclusively devoted to washing and cooking for me [is] never to be a field hand"; and the overseer was banned from employing any other slave besides his cook for any of his household affairs.[76] Such rules were wholly ineffective in stopping overseer Venters from sleeping with the field hand Harriet in 1857, and producing a child by her.

Venters's was the second case where the Manigault records give clear proof of an overseer's fathering a child by a slave woman. The first known instance was in 1837, when the Silk Hope overseer Thomas R. Heargroves made pregnant a girl of seventeen or eighteen named Elsey. She was a younger sister of the Jacob whom Manigault had characterized as "smart & intelligent." Elsey, having reached the age at which "prime hands" were useful at Gowrie, was sent there from Silk Hope in December 1837, perhaps before her pregnancy became known. Heargroves's child Nat was born at Gowrie, and Elsey's misery was made complete when she died, either in childbirth or soon thereafter. Nat was then given a foster mother, Juna, whose newborn baby, Nelly, had to share Juna's milk with Nat. Nelly died the next year and so did Nat—the third and fourth of Juna's ten children and foster children to perish in the rice swamps.[77] The only survivor of this sorry episode, therefore, was Heargroves, the overseer who could—if he chose—oblige slave women to have sex with him. Heargroves's conduct did not lead to his dismissal; on the contrary, Manigault kept him on as the Silk Hope overseer, and, indeed, in 1840 he promoted him by making him overseer at the more productive Gowrie plantation. Clearly, on Manigault's plantations, as on every other plantation where white men had power over slave women, these women's sexual decisions could not be very largely their own.

A slave woman might be tempted to, or think it in her interest to, cultivate familiar relations with a white man. Betsey's daughter Jane—formerly a house servant in Charleston but briefly demoted to field labor at Gowrie, and then restored to lighter duties—was the only slave woman who seems to have adopted a more confidential tone toward the Manigaults than other slave women would have assumed. She sought special treatment from the moment she arrived at Gowrie in 1849, and the overseer felt he "must . . . in candour say" that for a house servant like Jane, representing herself to be in feeble health and classed at the age of twenty-eight as only a half hand, "this kind of work will never answer for her, her constitution will never bear the mud & water of the swamp." Although Jane was soon made a house servant and nurse at Gowrie, this did not terminate her requests for favor. In 1853 Louis Manigault's younger brother Gabriel—who at the age of twenty was already a medical doctor—was planning to come from South Carolina to pay Louis a visit at Gowrie. Can medical attention have been the only thing in Jane's mind when she asked Louis to send a message to Gabriel? " 'Sister Jane' Came to me this morning," Louis reported, "& told me in a very melancholy way that she had a violent head ache & she asked me when Mas. Gabriel was Coming. She said that Mas. Gabriel had told her that Frog liver was good for head ache & that she wanted Mas. Gabriel to kill a frog for her."[78]

Another slave woman whose relation with the young Manigault men may have become familiar was Dolly, Jane's successor as the bachelor Louis Manigault's cook. Dolly, too, was a Silk Hope house servant, deported at the age of nineteen to Gowrie with her husband in 1852. Suffering from unaccountable fevers within a few weeks, she was sent back to Silk Hope for her health. While she was there her marriage dissolved, her husband at Gowrie moving in with the widow of an 1852 "cholera" victim. Dolly, meanwhile, was establishing the principle—perhaps made credible to the Manigaults because she was a mulatto—that her health made her "not . . . able to remain on Plantation during the Summer." When Dolly returned to Gowrie late in 1853, she became Louis's cook and washerwoman, and began moving back and forth with him from Gowrie in wintertime to South Carolina during the summer. For the summer of 1854 Louis tried to arrange for her to live at his guitar teacher's house in Charleston (where he would be sure to run into her three times a week when he came for guitar lessons); when this plan fell through, a place was found for her instead in Friend Street, Charleston. The next summer Dolly was sent to Silk Hope. This pattern—of Dolly's cooking and washing for Louis at Gowrie during each winter, and returning to South Carolina during the malarial season—continued until the summer of 1857, when Louis became engaged to a white Georgia woman. Before bringing his new bride to Gowrie in December 1857, Louis evinced a strong desire to get Dolly out of his plantation kitchen; on about October 1 he ordered the overseer to "move Dolly & [the twelve-year-old house girl] over to East Hermitage" where she would become the overseer's cook; the overseer's male cook, Simon, could then take over in Louis's own kitchen. Dolly may have had her own thoughts about why Louis was suddenly keen to install a male cook at Gowrie to greet the new Mrs. Manigault. Dolly became ill. This gave the overseer Leonard Venters a good excuse to send her off to the pineland "camp"; and this suited his own purposes, for he had no wish to have Dolly in his own house while he was sleeping with the field hand Harriet. As soon as Dolly recovered at the end of October, Venters put her back into the Gowrie kitchen pending the arrival of Charles Manigault.[79] If this irritated Louis Manigault, he made the best of it. He sacked Venters (for other reasons) but decided to keep Dolly on as his washerwoman, with Simon doing the cooking; and in the summers, apparently, he continued taking Dolly to Charleston, leaving the rest of his house servants at Gowrie.

There was only enough space in Charles Manigault's Charleston house for Louis to bring one house servant with him from Gowrie, and that one— Charles presumed—"no doubt will be 'Dolly' as She can wash, & do other things for you." In fact, Louis assigned her to care for his infant. How Dolly felt about minding Mrs. Louis Manigault's firstborn child is unknown, but Dolly's health declined and in the midsummer of 1860 she was sent back from Charleston, looking "quite badly," to stay at the pineland "camp," and help cooper George's mother, Betsey, take care of the slave children there. Although Dolly is supposed to have become an invalid before 1863, this did not deter her that year, at the age of thirty, from running away from Louis: the only one of the Manigault slaves who appears to have made good a permanent escape from their masters.[80] Louis's relation to Dolly, and the Manigault young men's earlier relation to Jane, may have been no more complicated than the usual relation between a master and a slave; but the exposed position of slave women, and especially of unmarried house servants like Jane and Dolly (after her husband's remarriage), put them in a position loaded with apparent opportunities and evident dangers.

Famous passages in the diary of the South Carolina aristocrat Mary Chesnut have made well known the tensions within the white elite centering on the planters' use of slave women for sex. "Ours is a *monstrous* system & wrong & iniquity," Chesnut exclaimed angrily in March 1861.

> Like the patriarchs of old our men live all in one house with their wives & their concubines, & the Mulattoes one sees in every family exactly resemble the white children—& every lady tells you who is the father of all the Mulatto children in every body's household, but those in her own, she seems to think drop from the clouds or pretends so to think.[81]

Though cross with the white men who produced these mulattoes, Chesnut reserved her deepest loathing for "those beastly negress beauties" who, she felt, ensnared the white men. For mulattoes Chesnut had little sympathy: she referred scornfully, for example, to a "stately yellow gentleman"—a slave whose inflated self-esteem, Chesnut believed, had caused him foolishly to flee relatively comfortable circumstances because his master never gave him cash.[82] The Manigault records illustrate how very differently a planter and his wife might feel about the mulatto offspring of a planter and a slave woman.

Charles Manigault, unlike his wife, believed mulattoes should be treated as a third caste, neither white nor black. He believed that their white ancestry made mulattoes racially superior to blacks, and therefore deserving special treatment so long as they held themselves apart from the blacks. "Their intelligence and respectful Deportment," he wrote of the mulattoes (many of whom were free), "are appreciated by the [white] community. Tho Distinct from Us, They will not associate with the Negro, either in Church or else where." Charles Manigault's sense of mulattoes as a third caste had deep roots in his family. In the 1760s his rich great-grandfather had given a mulatto slave named James to Charles's father, Gabriel, when "they both were little children, & of course were often playmates together & apparently Much attached to Each Other." Many years later, when Charles himself was a boy, he had witnessed James—now Gabriel's body servant—rearranging the master's queue and powdering his hair before dinner. Although James's attachment to Gabriel was insufficiently strong to prevent his bolting for freedom when the Manigaults moved to Pennsylvania in 1807, Charles's anger at James's alleged perfidy did not alter his deep sense that mulattoes of good blood were rather special.[83]

When a family imbroglio developed in 1846, Manigault even invoked the Declaration of Independence to support the rights of brown people. The Manigaults were spending the year in Paris, and it turned out that two Cuban mulatto boys were enrolled at the school where the Carolinians had placed their son Gabriel. Mrs. Manigault kicked up a fuss; but Charles Manigault urged the young Gabriel to accept the situation at the school,

> taking my text from our Declaration of Independence that "all men are born equal," and that He should always try to make the best of such things, & telling him that whatever *we* might feel or resolve respecting Slavery, that nevertheless nearly the whole of the Christian world (in ignorance and prejudice) are against us and that in Europe Negroes are generally regarded as our equals.

These arguments cut no ice with Mrs. Manigault, and the usually imperious Charles Manigault backed down, moving Gabriel to another school. His discomfiture at having to concede a point to his wife expressed itself in irritation at the Cuban boys: "Your Mama," he explained to an older son, "never could reconcile herself to these two Niggers."[84]

A similar family dispute had a rather different outcome early in 1864. John Izard, the trusted mulatto carpenter who had served as chief engineer at Gowrie, ran away from Silk Hope before Christmas 1863 but was caught and jailed after a fortnight of freedom. His fate must be decided. Three months earlier Charles Manigault had impatiently sold Jack Savage, just as he had sold any number of other fugitives in earlier years. But John Izard was different, and a principal difference was that he was pretty surely a first or second cousin (perhaps once removed) of his master. This earned him special consideration in the eyes of both Charles Manigault and his son Louis, but not in those of Mrs. Manigault. Charles felt there was some justification for John's flight, because the wartime overseer at Silk Hope was a "miserable fellow." He therefore suggested to his wife that John Izard be moved to Marshlands, where special privileges would keep him from running away again; but Mrs. Manigault would not accept the idea. "[John] is a well meaning poor fellow," Charles wrote to Louis. "I proposed to your mama to have him in our yard as a general factotum, and somewhat of a Carpenter. But She objected; in fact She does not appreciate or fully understand the merits of the true Izard blood."[85] Charles Izard Manigault's family pride embraced the mulatto offspring of the distinguished Izard family; the clear presumption was that a planter need feel no shame in having sex with a slave woman. Mrs. Manigault understandably did not buy this sexual ethic. Fortunately for John Izard, however, Louis Manigault shared his father's view. John—far from being sold like Jack Savage—was rewarded for his flight by being taken to Augusta, Georgia, to work around Louis's wartime domicile there. "*That* was a good plan," Charles chortled; and a consequence was that John Izard chose to continue working for the Manigaults at Silk Hope from time to time in the 1870s—a dozen years after emancipation—when his wage as a carpenter was double that paid to unskilled laborers.[86]

The strength of the slaves' family institutions depended partly on their sexual customs, but the Manigault records are cryptic about this matter. It is evident, however, that Louis Manigault was willing to encourage adultery among his own slaves. Early in 1853 he received from Charleston a shipment of nineteen newly purchased blacks, and there seemed not quite enough room for all of them at the East Hermitage tract. Nancy, a thirty-four-year-old woman long married to Ben (they had been deported together from Silk Hope to Gowrie in 1848), happened to be living on her own: her only Gowrie child had died in 1850, and her husband, Ben, had been so seriously ill in 1852 that he had been sent back to South Carolina—where it was hoped that proper food and medical attention might save his life. Thus there was space at Nancy's into which the newly purchased twenty-five-year-old Frederick might be moved: mayhap he could afford Nancy consolation in her husband's absence, and perhaps Nancy's comforts might reconcile Frederick to being torn away from brother, sister, and friends in South Carolina? Louis "placed [Frederick] for present with Nancy (Ben's)," he inscribed, but nothing came of this arrangement. Nancy remained loyal to Ben and seems to have malingered in the (unavailing) hope of being sent back to South Carolina to rejoin her husband;[87] while Frederick quickly found another woman with whom to live.[88]

Louis Manigault believed the slaves were promiscuous, and not just before marriage. Thus when in the summer of 1853 overseer Clark went away from the plantation each evening to escape malaria, Louis was "Certain there are many things going on that neither You [Charles Manigault] nor I, nor Clark know of. I know that when I am not here there is more visiting going on than we would allow." Just south of Gowrie was one of the several rice plantations owned by the wealthy planter James Potter, perhaps 66 of whose 440 slaves—resident on the Georgia side of the river—came each day to work on Argyle Island. Louis was convinced that during the harvest, when he was away and the overseer left driver Robert in charge at night, Robert's rule was lax: "I dare say that when Potter's People Cut rice on Argyle one half sleep at Gowrie."[89]

Louis Manigault's implication about the slaves' sexual conduct might easily be dismissed as the ignorant prejudice of a white man who wished to believe ill of the slaves. Recent historians have worked effectively to combat slander of the slaves. But here, as in many facets of the slaves' lives, there may be a danger of romanticizing the realities. Nearly all Gowrie slave women—except for an occasional house servant like Jane—were married or had children by twenty, and usually much sooner. Why should they not start sexual relations as soon as they wished? They had few of the economic incentives which impelled many early-modern French peasant women to defer marriage until well into their twenties.[90] Some young slave women (like Juna) had a child by one man before settling down with another. Gowrie's slaves often lived together soon after making each other's acquaintance: thus in 1853 Catherine was living with Joe two months after his arrival at Gowrie, and the same was true of Julia and her third husband, Mathias. The interval between a spouse's death and remarriage to a new partner was often brief. Joe was living with Catherine within eight months of Cato's drowning, and Mathias was living with Julia five months after her husband, Jingo, had succumbed to "cholera." A considerable number of marriages dissolved when one spouse— like Dolly's husband, or Pender's, or Sary's—found a different partner.

All of these facts suggest that most Gowrie slaves had an easy attitude toward sexuality. No doubt many marriages on the plantation were long-enduring. But Gowrie's records tell little about the extramarital sexual conduct which may have been thought consonant with continuation of a relatively stable marriage. Driver Robert will not have felt it his duty to inquire where each of James Potter's slaves was sleeping when they stayed at Gowrie. Louis Manigault may have indulged a fantasy about the nightlife on his plantation; but a late-twentieth-century reader, conscious of the easy sexuality which flourishes in many communities and in many different social classes when modern circumstances permit, will be wary of imputing a Victorian morality to most slaves who had few Victorian incentives to chastity. (The example of Nate Shaw's father, born a slave in 1850, does not suggest that this individual brought with him from slavery a strong Victorian code.)[91] Perhaps the reality at Gowrie was that some long-married slave couples cherished each other with Victorian fidelity, and that a substantial number of others maintained a long, and even a good, marriage without feeling that uninterrupted chastity was essential.

Eight days after the capture of Fort Sumter by Confederate forces, Louis Manigault recorded with unusual emotion the performance of a semiannual ritual at Gowrie: "Gave out Summer Clothes this Sunday 21st April 1861, being the first year of the sovereignty and Independence of the Confederate States of America, Praise God for same!"[92] One slave to whom he gave the usual allowance of cloth was an eighteen-year-old woman Tyrah, the daughter of Louis's favorite slave, captain Hector, and of Hector's wife, Joaney, the plantation cook. Tyrah was still unmarried, and it is challenging to try to see her marriage and mothering prospects as she, talking with her own mother, may have viewed them in 1861—on the assumption that slavery would continue into the indefinite future.

Tyrah had grown up in a stable family. Joaney and Hector had been married for twenty years (Hector's first wife having died after only two years of marriage), and had been unusually fortunate in rearing two children who were still alive: the dwarf King (Tyrah's twelve-year-old brother), who had been at Silk Hope for the last six years, and Tyrah herself. More than one-third of the families at Gowrie[93] were something like Tyrah's—with stable, long-enduring marriages between partners who had not been married before (or where one partner, like Hector, had previously been widowed). Such marriages were especially common in families—such as captain Hector's—where the man held a privileged job.[94]

A long-enduring, stable marriage between partners previously unmarried (or widowed) was not, however, the typical pattern at Gowrie. Nearly two-thirds of the women had had experiences which, at one extreme, were not vastly different from those of Tyrah's mother, Joaney, but at the other extreme were unstable indeed. The pattern (among these two-thirds of the women) closest to Joaney's was that of her sister Juna and of Jack Savage's sister Sary. These two women had each had a brief connection with a previous man— Juna had a child at seventeen, before she was deported from Silk Hope, and Sary was married for a year or two to William before he left her to marry Cotta; but after these early relationships the women had each settled down in a long-enduring marriage with a second man. This pattern has been identified by Herbert Gutman as common on other plantations.[95]

More usual at Gowrie, however, was a marriage terminated prematurely by the forced removal of the husband or by one partner's death. Tyrah's aunt Nancy had been married to Jacob for fifteen years when Manigault deported him back to Silk Hope as a troublemaker, and she never saw him again. Another of Tyrah's aunts, Julia, had three husbands, all of whom died; and the marriages of Binkey, Crecie, and Peggy were all ended by these women's early demise (at ages forty-two, twenty-six, and twenty-two).

Almost equally common at Gowrie were marriages of considerable insta-bility. Pender had been married to Posh the trunk minder for only two or three years before he left her and married Peggy, driver Harry's daughter. Presently Pender married the half-incapacitated twenty-eight-year-old Mingo, but she died three years later when she herself was only twenty-eight. Catherine had four marriages, and so probably did Minty. Minty's sister Rhina, who died at thirty-nine, had during this time at least five marriages, none of which had lasted longer than four years.

The final family pattern was for a woman never to have a man perma-nently in the house. This was the situation of Minty's sister Hannah, who bore at least five children. She probably had an abroad marriage, ended by her husband's removal and sale in 1848. If her husband had previously been with her each week only on Saturday night, Sunday, and perhaps one midweek night—a common pattern in abroad marriages—the potential strains on the two partners were obvious, as was the probable attenuation of the bond between father and children.

As the eighteen-year-old Tyrah surveyed her prospects, therefore, her mood may have been sober. On the one hand, there was the strong tradition, strengthened by her parents' example and that of more than one-third of the Gowrie slaves, of building a stable, long-enduring family. There was, further-more, the escape route taken by her aunt Juna; a young woman who had a child but no husband was not thereby disgraced, and she could well build a second, stable and long-lasting relationship, as Juna had done. But at Gowrie the chances were against such an outcome. A wife was likely to die young, or to find her husband permanently deported—as happened to Tyrah's aunt

Nancy—or to lose a succession of husbands by death, as had happened to another of Tyrah's aunts, Julia. A woman was equally likely to experience a long series of relatively short relationships, broken up by death or voluntary separation, or to raise children without a man permanently in the house. And these statements ignore the sorrows a Gowrie woman was sure to experience with family illness and death.

The loss of young children by their mothers was universal. Fifteen of the nineteen married women are known to have borne children, and of these fifteen every one lost at least one child. As previously mentioned, Tyrah's aunt Juna lost all ten of her children (including her foster child) by the time she was forty-one years old, Binah Currie lost all of her eight, and Amey all four. Altogether the nineteen women had only twelve surviving children by 1864, out of perhaps ninety-five whom they had borne.[96] Nineteen married women should be producing at least thirty-eight surviving children if the population is to reproduce itself: obviously no such thing was happening at Gowrie.

The most important function of the family is to nurture children, and one may inquire how well this function could be performed at Gowrie. Tyrah might have felt, from her own experience, that a stable family could function effectively, even though she herself had had some acquaintance with the tribulations of family life. During Tyrah's childhood her mother had experienced a stillbirth and a case of the fearsome "cholera." When Tyrah was eight her father had nearly died: "I have never had such a desperate case of Diarrhea," the overseer had exclaimed of Hector's illness;[97] and eighteen months later Hector was stricken with "cholera." One of Tyrah's brothers had been sent permanently to South Carolina for his health, and another (How-qua) perished in 1860—probably one of those young children who died suddenly at the summer "camp." In 1862 Tyrah's mother, Joaney, had another child who died quickly, as did Joaney herself, perhaps from complications following the child's birth. Yet Tyrah's experience of family tragedy was mild compared with what happened in most Gowrie families, and her experience of being raised in a stable family environment was untypical.

Of the twelve children (of these nineteen women) who survived until 1864, only three others were reared in a stable family. The eldest of them, Mendoza, was the sole survivor of the five children in Louisa and Short Jack's stable, long-enduring marriage. The family was disrupted in the spring of 1861, when the seven-year-old Mendoza was taken with his mother to Charleston (where she was installed as Louis Manigault's washerwoman). Short Jack was sent inland to Silk Hope for much of the Civil War, and he may have managed to see Louisa and Mendoza occasionally before his own death at Silk Hope in 1863. Although Mendoza's family life may not appear a model of stability, it was so by Gowrie's standards.

Another child reared in a stable family was Pussy, born in 1859 to the long-married Sary and Pompey. After Sary's brief marriage to William had dissolved, she had been living with Pompey for thirteen years by 1864. By then all three of their other children had died; Pompey, too, seems to have died soon, though perhaps not until after the war's end. Sary and Pompey were thus able to provide a stable family for Pussy until she was at least five. Another child in a situation comparable to Pussy's was Catherine's son Paul, born in about 1863. Catherine's family life had been unstable before her fourth marriage, but by 1863 she had been settled for seven years with her husband Tommy, and was situated to furnish Paul a stable family environment. Whether Pussy or Paul would have survived to adulthood as slaves at Gowrie was another question: they were so young in 1864 that an actuary would not have laid long odds on their doing so.

Three other children were raised in an unstable two-parent family. These were Minty's offspring—Billy the carpenter and Scotland the cook—and her stepchild Fortune, the perennial fugitive. By the time Billy was twenty-one his own father had long been missing—he may have had an abroad marriage with Minty that quickly dissolved—and Billy's stepfather had died. Billy's much younger half brother Scotland probably was more fortunate, because during most of his childhood Minty had a husband in the house with her. Scotland's stepbrother Fortune, however, moved from pillar to post during his teens; his frequent attempts at flight, and his final sale at Savannah in 1860, may have had some of their origins in the instability of his family life after his father's death in 1848.

Two other children were reared by their mother with no man permanently in the house; these were Hannah's. Probably neither of the children (the elder of whom was then eleven) ever saw their father after 1848, when McAlpin sold his East Hermitage slaves.

The remaining three children were not raised by either of their parents after the age of six. When Crecie died in 1854, her baby, Cato, was removed from his father, Ishmael's, care and was raised instead for four years by his grandmother Betsey. Cato was then sent—from age four until probably age ten—to the pineland camp Manigault had bought, where he seems to have been reared by his great-aunt Phillis. Meanwhile, Crecie's three-year-old daughter, Little Betsey, instead of being raised by the grandmother after whom she was named, was sent to Silk Hope for her health, where perhaps she too was reared by a great-aunt. And Tyrah's own brother King was also sent to Silk Hope for his health after the 1854 epidemic, when he was six. He never saw his mother again (she died in 1862), and can seldom have seen his father either; if he was raised by relatives at Silk Hope, they would have been distant ones who had not seen his mother, Joaney, since her deportation from Silk Hope twenty-two years earlier.

Evidently the Manigaults did not feel it was very important for parents to raise their own children. When mother and father were both in the fields, their young children were always shunted off during each working day to be watched by some old woman who was worthless for field labor. "The other old Woman is not much," Louis declared scornfully when he surveyed the most valueless of a batch of nineteen slaves his father had just dispatched from South Carolina: "She can mind all these Children."[98] Such a woman's heart was not likely to be in the task of unremunerated supervision of other people's infants—witness the drowning of Binah Currie's three-year-old child in a settlement ditch, and the sudden, unexplained deaths of several young children at the pineland camp in 1860. From the masters' point of view, the object of raising slave children was not to stimulate their imaginations nor to develop their personalities, but simply to try to feed them and keep them out of mischief—with the least possible waste of the time of good plantation laborers, who were in short supply. The Manigaults did ship a few sickly children of favored parents to Silk Hope, in order to try to keep them from dying as fast as was customary at Gowrie, but this bespoke no concern to strengthen the fragile bonds between parents and their children.

Thus only one-third of these children—four out of the twelve—could have been raised in a relatively stable two-parent family. Three were reared in an unstable two-parent family, two in a family with the father not permanently at home (and probably *never* at home after the elder child was eleven), and three not raised by their parents at all. It could scarcely be said that these twelve children carried from slavery into freedom a thriving tradition of stable two-parent family life.

Historians have done splendid work in recent years showing how bravely the slaves battled against adverse circumstances to make their families a refuge against the blows inflicted by masters and overseers. These authors' treatment of slaves as active shapers of their own destinies—not as mere passive victims of circumstance—has surely been welcome. Yet there may be a danger of exaggerating how much the slaves were able to achieve against the odds. Gowrie's records suggest that neither in creating favorable circumstances for marriage partners to cherish each other nor in making a stable environment for rearing children could the slaves' family institutions operate as effectively as some recent books have implied.[99]

Gowrie was not, of course, a typical plantation. But historians constantly lament the absence of reliable information about slaves' lives, and Gowrie's records may be the best for any plantation in the United States; and it would be perverse to dismiss Gowrie's experience as simply unrepresentative. These records have a tremendous advantage over travelers' reports or slave narratives in that they are in some respects demonstrably objective, and they are sufficiently complete that one can quantify with more than usual confidence. The records, moreover, are direct: one does not need to depend on roundabout mathematical calculations, which have sometimes been used to excellent effect, but where the chain of logic is necessarily inferential.[100]

No doubt Gowrie's high death rate lends it a certain macabre distinction. But most rice plantations probably had horrific death rates in the eighteenth century, and many in the nineteenth century as well. Nor can Gowrie's record be explained away by the incidence of exceptional "cholera" epidemics, because most of the adults did not die of "cholera," nor did scarcely any of the children. If, in addition to enteric diseases, malaria was a principal cause for the children's deaths, the consequences for understanding the slaves' health problems are far-reaching: for malaria was by no means confined to the Savannah River. High death rates were one reason that the slaves' family institutions were less resilient than the slaves would have wished.

5

Dissidence

In order to refute the old canard that American slaves were content with their lot, historians have carefully attended all evidence of an insurrectionary spirit among the bondsmen and women. The one time in American history when slaves killed a substantial number of whites—the Nat Turner insurrection of 1831, when about fifty-five whites perished—has been studied in loving detail, and has even produced a well-known historical novel. A few facts have been recovered about the only other sizeable nineteenth-century insurrection (near New Orleans in 1811). The stories of two abortive nineteenth-century conspiracies (at Richmond, Virginia, in 1800 and Charleston, South Carolina, in 1822) have been endlessly rehearsed, and the only important eighteenth-century rebellions (at New York City in 1712 and Stono, South Carolina, in 1739) are also well known. Insurrection panics swept nineteenth-century Southern white communities from time to time, and Southern demagogues surely extracted every possible drop of electoral advantage from stirring the deep pool of latent white anxiety.

Yet the late–twentieth century's preoccupation with slave rebellions may reflect more accurately twentieth-century concerns—pride in the slaves' insubordination, preoccupation with modern urban riots—than nineteenth-century realities. Unlike Santo Domingo—where just a few thousand whites were scattered among a vastly larger number of slaves, and where from 1791 to 1804 those slaves heroically carried through a successful insurrection—the American South contained by 1860 eight million whites whose numbers and military organization rendered successful rebellion inconceivable. Not a single substantial slave insurrection occurred in the United States between 1831 and

1865. Everything depended on the military balance of power between masters and slaves, and before November 1861 (when the invasion of Port Royal Island off the South Carolina coast abruptly altered that balance in the rice kingdom) the overseers at Gowrie appear to have enjoyed a sense of total security, even when surrounded by a huge majority of slaves. There is no evidence that any male Gowrie slave even struck any white man in anger (though—after November 1861—one female did so, and one male slave struck a black driver).

This does not mean that Gowrie's bondsmen and women were content. On the contrary, there is overwhelming evidence of their profound alienation from the slave regime: but their dissidence took nonviolent forms. Slaves regularly obstructed plantation operations, and a remarkable number fled temporarily to the swamps. Suicide was not unknown, and there was even a significant tradition of collective nonviolent protest.

The twentieth-century term "resistance" obscures the character of this dissidence. When a master spoke in the mid–nineteenth century of a slave's "resisting," he was thinking of overt physical resistance; and on a plantation like Gowrie—so long as whites could maintain the peacetime military balance of power—such resistance was virtually nonexistent. Slaves evidently drew a sharp line between overt physical "resistance"—which they knew would be crushed with draconian severity—and nonviolent dissidence, which was ubiquitous. To a later generation it may seem astonishing that a single white overseer could stride forth among a hundred slaves, imposing his will upon them with scarcely a moment's anxiety that they might "resist" him. Only by examining the instruments of Charles Manigault's regime—his power to inflict excruciating physical pain upon another human being, his threat to tear an individual forever from her or his most precious ties (by deportation to New Orleans), and his ultimate menace that a recalcitrant slave might die (as Joe did in 1853 and Anthony in 1854)—can one understand why slaves sharply distinguished nonviolent dissidence from those forms of resistance which seemed practically beyond the pale.

Proud to think his slaves unusually well disciplined, Charles Manigault fondly quoted the alluring maxim "A good slave makes a good master." A "good" slave was imbued with the sense of duty to his owner, and performed his obligations cheerfully.

To instill a slave new to Gowrie with a proper sense of subordination, Manigault recommended his agent to conduct a "plantation talk." Here the fresh "Negro" learned that his fate was in his own hands: all he had to do was be dutiful and cheerful, and good treatment would follow. But the slave should understand that failure to fulfill his duties would forfeit the privileges otherwise within his grasp. Nothing was easier, the slave must understand, than to reduce a nonconformist to submission.

If subordination did not appear spontaneously, the simplest way to elicit it was, as on virtually every other Southern plantation, to inflict pain with a whip. When a new overseer was installed in 1859, Charles advised Louis to have him order the driver to flog a couple of slaves in Louis's presence: then all the slaves would know that—when Louis later left the plantation for one of his usual lengthy absences—the overseer was having them whipped with Louis's full assent. As further sanctions Charles Manigault depended on two other disciplinary measures: imposing a term in the Savannah jail (or the Charleston "workhouse"), and selling recalcitrant slaves. He supplemented these punishments with a range of other measures, seeking always to divide and conquer.

Manigault's overseers, quickly learning the principles on which their employer ran his plantation, hastened to adopt his own language. Thus Jesse Cooper boasted during his second year of overseeing Gowrie that his considerate treatment of the slaves had instilled into them the proper attitudes. "I believe each one feels it a duty incumbent upon them," he claimed—employing twice the key word in Manigault's lexicon—"to discharge their duties faithfully & with cheerfulness on their part." But overseers knew there was a sharp line between proper consideration of the slaves and spoiling them, the latter being wholly unacceptable. Charles Manigault contrasted his own practice with that of his uncle Alfred Huger, whose slaves had much less rice land to cultivate, per slave, than did the slaves at Gowrie. "I consider his Negroes petted," Charles wrote disapprovingly, "& spoilt, and not accustomed to work." He was equally critical of how Louis Manigault's in-laws, the Habershams, managed their house servants in Savannah. Two of the Habershams were merchants and the third a medical doctor: "They spoil their servants so," Charles Manigault groused, "& have not time to supervise their movements."[1]

Manigault's regimen included the award of privileges to selected slaves, but he was determined they should never suppose they had a right to special treatment. Privilege was a gift of the master;[2] it could always be withdrawn at the master's fiat; and the slave must first earn the privilege by proper subordination in the humblest of positions. Thus when in 1854 Manigault bought two groups of slaves—including George Hunt and the fifty-year-old Jupiter, who both had previous service as drivers—he immediately reduced these two men to the status of field hands: they must not imagine they had any claim to privilege beyond what they might earn by future good conduct. He intended eventually to make either George Hunt or Jupiter the driver at Marshlands, but first they must show that they were not proud. Manigault had already had trouble with Jupiter's family, whose self-esteem had evolved from Jupiter's status as driver at his previous plantation: he was, according to the Silk Hope overseer, "a highly confidential Driver, who is sober, honest, & trust worthy who was intrusted with the Keys." Jupiter's family had also developed pride from their ability to accumulate household property, even though they were only slaves. One way for Manigault to put them down was to ridicule their names: although Jupiter's wife was called Binkey, the master thought it amusing to pretend she was "Juno." Manigault and a trusted slave received Jupiter's family from the Cooper River steamer at the Charleston pier and conveyed them to the Savannah steamer for Gowrie. "We received Jupiter Juno & the 2 young goddesses," he announced, "with a quantity of Baggage, filling two drays, & [the trusted slave] going before, & I bringing up the rear, & the drays stopping 6 times to adjust the bedstead & other traps, tumbling out in the streets." The master brought up the rear to be sure Jupiter's family did not try to escape again, as they had done a few days earlier.

When they had learned they were being sent away from South Carolina to Georgia, Jupiter's wife and their four children had all fled from Silk Hope to find the wife of their previous master, appealing to her against deportation: "they were afraid of going to Savannah River." Jupiter himself had not participated in this—unavailing—act of insubordination, but "even Jupiter," Manigault complained, "said something to me about his not being a field Hand (he has been a Driver, & [the Silk Hope overseer] says a very good one). But so was Ishm[a]el a Driver, & many others. Now he [Jupiter] must go in the field, & his wife also." Manigault was not, he thought, vindictive: he would expect these two "old" slaves to accomplish only one full "task" between the two of them. But they must learn their place. Charles's advice to his son encapsulated several of his central tenets: subordination must be inculcated from the outset; although it was "best to favour all New Commers a little," nevertheless a slave's duty to his master was paramount, and only in consequence of duty faithfully performed might a slave hope for the grant of real privilege; and if the slave were slow to get the message, a whipping and incarceration in the Savannah jail would speedily set things to right. "The old woman . . . ," Manigault exclaimed of Jupiter's forty-eight-year-old wife,

> must be brought to her bearings, & Jupiter too, & you just give them both a plantation talk, & tell them that a good Negro makes a good Master & the straight path is always easy, but the crooked path is full of trouble, & if either of them hang back you will put them in a boat & send them down to the Savannah Jail for a month or two, until they come to their senses. . . . It's best always in these cases to begin at once to put things straight with them.[3]

The success of this particular application of Manigault's precepts cannot be evaluated, for George Hunt died of "cholera" in December; and Jupiter, his wife, Binkey, and three of their four children all died of consumption within a few months of George Hunt. Jupiter's fourth child, Rebecca—a "prime hand"—died of "cholera" (and exposure to December blasts before shelters could be erected at the pineland camp) a few days after George Hunt. They had had reason to be afraid of going to Gowrie.

Manigault spelled out the role of the Savannah jail in a letter written from Paris in 1847 for the instruction of a young overseer. This epistle enumerated a series of measures by which an overseer might handle a disorderly slave. Manigault's policy of dividing to conquer impelled him to prefer dirty work at Gowrie—like whippings—to be done wherever possible by one slave upon another. And an advantage of the Savannah jail was that a severe whipping could there be imposed by a stranger: the slave's violent resentment would not be concentrated upon the overseer. But if an unpleasant spell at the Savannah jail, culminating in a final flogging, chanced not to have the desired effect, the New Orleans slave market was the ultimate sanction. In disciplining a nonconforming slave like Jacob (the husband of Jacob's Nancy),

Manigault thought instinctively of the discipline of schoolchildren; and such a slave must be dealt with by cunning. "Keep in mind the important old plantation maxim," he admonished the overseer,

> viz., "Never to threaten a Negro" or he will do as you & I would under such circumstances when at school[:] he will run. But with such a one whenever things get too bad, you should take a certain opportunity, when for instance he is with the Driver in the provision room, and you at the door, with a string [rope] in your own pocket—then pull it out & order him tied—for if in such a case a Negro succeeds in dodging & running from you, the anoyance [sic] is great. But having got him, if you wish to make an example of him take him with you down to the Savannah Jail, & give him prison discipline [obviously including flogging] & by all means solitary Confinement for 3 weeks, when he will be glad to get home again—but previous to his coming out let them jog his memory again. [Then] tell him that you & he are quits . . . & all depends on himself, for he now sees how easy it is to fix "a bad disposed nigger." Then give my Compliments to him & tell him . . . I say if he don't change for the better, I'll sell him to a slave trader who will send him to New Orleans, where I have already sent several of the gang for their misconduct, or their running away for no cause.[4]

Explicit though Manigault was about the Savannah jail, he was a little less clear about administering whippings at Gowrie: overseers could be expected to know the ropes without further instruction. The overseers themselves tended to be reticent about this side of their management. Ten letters from the overseer Stephen Clark—extending from June through October 1853—reported his plantation activities to Louis Manigault during the latter's long summer absence. Clark said not one word about whipping or any other form of disciplinary action, and he mentioned only one case of a slave's insubordination—the flight of the recently purchased Joe. Yet Clark was struck by "the brisk way" a neighbor's slaves worked, and it is highly probable that he himself was whipping Gowrie slaves a good deal in order to impel them to equally brisk labor. Certainly discontent built up at Gowrie that summer, unreported by the overseer. Prince, Louis Manigault later learned, "has been of late leaving Plantation without any cause"; Frederick shortly thereafter was punished at the Savannah jail "for 'kicking up the devil' here"; and Quash's William was simultaneously despatched to Charleston, where all three were sold.[5] Three months later, Betsey's daughter Jane ran away, and she too was sold after her capture. The disciplinary sale within a year of four adults and (at about the same time) the flights and subsequent deaths of two more adults (Joe and Anthony) from a group which then, including children and "old" slaves, numbered 116 indicate widespread discontent, surely related to unreported floggings.

Whipping was like defecating: it happened regularly but one did not usually talk about it. Louis Manigault, for example, was reluctant to name a spade a spade. When in 1862 the stock tender allowed eight pigs to disappear—probably having killed them himself to supply fugitives then successfully hiding in a nearby swamp—Louis avoided the word "whipping": instead he noted in his plantation journal that the stock tender had "received his due punishment."

An overseer feared getting into trouble with his employer if he flogged slaves too often; yet everyone knew that whipping was indispensable. The overseer's trick was to persuade the employer that he was restrained in his administration of this terrible punishment. Both a boast and a menace had lain behind A. R. Bagshaw's claim in 1842 that "I seldom have a Negro corrected [i.e., whipped] for not getting through with his task for several reasons." The overseer claimed, that is, that slaves under his management nearly always completed their quotas; and no doubt the severity of Bagshaw's whippings impelled most slaves to toe the line. Early in 1859 the Manigaults, after having sacked in rapid succession both Leonard Venters and William Bryan, were on the lookout for a new overseer. Louis Manigault managed Gowrie for three months on his own, while his father scrabbled around trying to find a new overseer; and Louis reported that some of the slaves were unruly. When William Capers was finally hired for the job, the new overseer presented himself to Charles Manigault as the employer would wish to see him. Capers "said he would soon put [the unruliness] to rights, but that he dont resort to the lash, except where occasion really requires it."[6]

Restraint by the overseer might be appropriate, but of course Charles Manigault knew whipping of field hands would occur whenever his agent judged it necessary. He instructed his son to legitimate the new overseer's authority in the eyes of the slaves. "You aluded [*sic*] to one or two fractious negroes," he wrote two days later. "The way to fix them is . . . ," when they all assembled to get their weekly food allowance, to have the hands of the fractious slaves

> tied before them in the provision room, waiting there before all the others. Lastly preach them a short sermon on the propriety of Conduct, & make the Driver proceed with them. This done thoroughly, in presence of the new Overseer will have the best effect, or they will say hereafter that he does what Massa never would have done.[7]

There seems to have been an understanding between overseer and master that field hands could be whipped at the overseer's discretion, but that slaves in privileged positions were to be whipped just occasionally. An overseer usually bothered to mention a whipping only in the case of privileged slaves, when the action might seem to require justification. "One day last week I found it absolutely necessary to take hold of Carpenter Jack [Savage]," the overseer Skinner reported in 1852,

> and learn him how to progress more rapidly with his work, as he did but little. . . . John [Izard] being away [at Silk Hope], I found that John did the most of the work when he was here. I had Ishmeal [*sic;* Jack Savage's brother] to whip Jack well, and then Amos [a less skilled carpenter] slightly. Jack has did well since. Amos has been laying up of his old complaint since Sunday night last (Asthma).[8]

William Capers was less circumspect than most overseers about his practices. He did not cavil at whipping a slave belonging to Manigault's neighbor,

James Potter. Apparently a row with Potter had ensued, and Capers hastened to explain himself to Louis Manigault. "I chastised a negro of Mr. Potter's," Capers declared, "for insolence to my Son and myself, also disobeyed my order. The negro bei[ng] old saved him from as *much* as a *negro* should [get?] at *one time* whence he received [only?] 20 Stripes with a Whip taken from him and [kept?] at the Camp for the inspection of your Father." The other whippings which Capers troubled himself to mention always involved privileged slaves. Boatman Hector allegedly having been drunk when collecting the post in Savannah and having broken two five-gallon jugs of rum, Capers had confined him in the threshing mill: "I gave him [a good?] strapping. . . . I do not think he cares for the Strap."⁹ Capers had to explain the next year how the twenty-two-year-old house servant London (formerly Louis Manigault's cook) had defied a whipping which the drivers—no doubt enforcing Capers's edicts—had threatened. Seventeen months later the demoted head driver, cooper George (whom Capers had been trying to persuade Manigault to sell) ran away from the overseer in the presence of the other slaves and was rewarded—according to Capers—with sixty lashes. And in 1863 the overseer found the opportunity to test his precepts on Rose, who had been the nursemaid for Louis Manigault's young child at Augusta, Georgia. Louis's cook Dolly seemed to have made good her escape from Augusta, and Capers feared Rose would follow her example. "Without you manage Rose," Capers thundered to Louis, "you need not expect any Servant will stay with you, give her the devil. But few Negroes are ever satisfied, the Kindest treatment makes them worse." Capers advocated intimidating Rose (and Louis's other domestic servants) to get her to rat on Dolly. Louis, apparently mistrusting Rose, sent her back to the pineland summer camp, where Capers kept "her closely watched." Soon Capers incarcerated her: "I have Rose in confinement at this place. I had an occasion to whip her and she refused to be tied and fought me until she had not a rag of clothes on." To have all of her clothes torn off was not enough indignity: Capers evidently intended to repeat the whipping, and to imprint on Rose's consciousness the racial degradation of being a slave: "Before she is turned loose," he concluded, "she will know she is a negroe."¹⁰

Indispensable though whipping might have been, it did not always secure the desired subordination. The next step in the escalation of punishments was the Savannah jail, or—an even more powerful deterrent—the Charleston workhouse. "Workhouse" was a euphemism to cloak the building's real purpose—the administration of "discipline" out of earshot of one's urban neighbors, or more horrific than might readily be achieved at a plantation. Thus Charles Manigault acknowledged privately that he had on occasion "had Joe, & Dublin, Stepney, &c. [his Charleston house servants] flogged at the workhouse." The workhouse was a fearsome place meant to instill even more terror than a master's or overseer's whippings could achieve. Jackmore, a Cooper River slave, had been three weeks in the Charleston workhouse in 1835: "If this does not satisfy Jackmore," the Silk Hope overseer wrote, "I don't know what will." Cooper George's offense, in 1861, of publicly defying the overseer and seeking to flee was judged so serious that after his sixty lashes at Gowrie he was sent (at Charles Manigault's direction) to the Charleston workhouse for "3 months in Dark Solitary Confinement . . . , which is known to be very severe."[11] Jack Savage, who tried to escape on the same day as cooper George and who resisted the driver's capturing him, was also given three months of solitary confinement at the Charleston workhouse. Afterward Charles Manigault believed this treatment had been efficacious: the two slaves "profess great Penitence." These deceptive utterances reassured Manigault, for he concluded that—even in the restless wartime atmosphere of early 1862—the two slaves "now see clearly how easy it is to fix a bad Negro. Just put handcuffs on them," he advised Louis, "& deliver them to the Express . . . for delivery in Chtn. Work House. Or in Solitary in Savh. Jail, might answer just as well."[12]

Charles's words fell upon receptive ears, for Louis's mood was bellicose. "The unrighteous and diabolical War now waging between our Confederate States and the United States is causing great distress amongst the Sea Coast Plantations," he lamented near this time. The insubordination of certain Gowrie slaves had led the overseer to complain about the laxity of even the awesome Charleston workhouse: "The three Negroes now Confined [George Hunt's son Little George being jailed there, as well as Jack Savage and cooper George] should by no means be allowed at any moment to Converse or see each other," Louis warned his father: overseer Capers "says they sometimes allow it." Concluding that plantation discipline had been altogether too lax during peacetime, Louis now felt that three slaves in the workhouse was not enough. "In January you Can put Big Hector & Short Jack in the dark-hole for a month"; this would put them in a proper state of mind to resume their plantation duties in February.[13]

Disciplinary resort to urban jails was not confined to wartime, as Short Jack knew only too well. The accompanying photograph of a Savannah jail receipt shows that Short Jack—a "bad Negro" (according to Louis Manigault), who had previously been known to flee to the swamp for several days—had been in serious trouble in 1860. The jailer's bill included a fee for whipping the forty-three-year-old "Boy" (who by then had been married to Louisa for some thirteen years and had fathered a boy, and four girls, of his own).[14]

To avoid incurring hefty bills like this one, an overseer could of course lock up a recalcitrant slave at the plantation. Capers's plan—after the aforementioned whipping of boatman Hector and his demotion to field labor—was to keep Hector on a short tether: "I . . . intend working him daily and confine him [at night]." Equipment was available to deter angry slaves from escaping. Early in 1861, soon after the nineteen-year-old Little George Hunt (a survivor from the ill-fated Hunt family purchased in 1854) had returned from a three-month sojourn in the swamp, Louis Manigault feared he would try to escape again, and began to confine him in irons at nighttime. George, who was being trained as a "carpenter boy," had fallen under the influence of the spirited carpenter Jack Savage. "You do the only thing with the Carpenter Boy . . . ," Charles Manigault congratulated Louis, "and I think that Sulky fellow 'Will' (I think is his name) should be treated with Irons also if there is any probability of his running again." (Having owned Will only four years, Manigault was

Mr Manigo

To Chatham County Jail Dr

for Imprisonment of his Boy Jack 11 Days at

30 cents per Day   330

      Key   120

      Blanket   150

      Whipping   100

      officers fees   125

Sat January

31st 1860   Received payment $ 825

                  Peter Lucddy Deputy Jailer

Chatham County Jail receipt

not quite sure of his name, and may have forgotten his own refusal to buy Will's mother at the Charleston auction in 1857, permanently separating the two. He remembered, however, that Will had recently fled Gowrie to spend a month in the swamp, returning with the "Carpenter Boy.")[15]

The beauty of the Savannah jail, from the masters' point of view, was that a series of floggings could be inflicted, yet there need be no anxiety that the angry victim could escape at night—for even a slave confined in irons might find a confederate to help her at the plantation. One of Gowrie's recurrent periods of slave unrest had been in the winter of 1851–52, when both Cicero and Posh ran away, and two slave women—probably angrily disobedient—were then consigned by overseer Skinner to the Savannah jail. The punishment included repeated whippings. "I went down . . . ," Skinner later reported with satisfaction,

> where I found Betty [Brister] & Margaret appearantly [sic] in a state of true repentance. The jailor had allowed them to go to the fire, as it was very cold [plowing at Gowrie having stopped the previous day because the land was frozen] and he thought they had received enough of the Strap, and was quite willing to let them off. . . . They appeared to be well "cooled" and no mistake.[16]

Late in 1855 Gowrie was unusually short of labor, for thirty-one slaves had died in 1854 (hardly balanced by four births) and no new slaves had yet been sent to take their places. The labor shortage probably impelled Louis

Manigault to send two captured fugitives to the Savannah jail for a severe bout of flogging, instead of dispatching them for sale to New Orleans. This policy won his father's approval. No paternalist tone (toward the slaves) entered Charles's voice as he contemplated the whipping of Judy and of Tyrah's aunt Julia, who had escaped from Gowrie for a month. "The two runaways you fixed admirably," Charles crowed. "A full allowance of all Jail discipline will bring them to holesome [*sic*] conclusions."[17]

Yet whipping—at Gowrie or at the Savannah jail—did not bring every slave into a wholesome state of mind, and Charles Manigault regularly sold nonconforming slaves to New Orleans, ridding himself of them and (he hoped) intimidating the others. "Negroes" had a duty to be docile; if they failed in their duty, it was to Manigault axiomatic that they and their families had no claim to remain together. Jack Savage had been married to Amey for nineteen years when the Manigaults sold him to a trader on the understanding that "the negro [is] to be sent away, far from us." Everywhere in the low country it was taken for granted, by the most respectable of planters, that of course a slave would be sold—rupturing every family tie—if he or she fled repeatedly to the swamps. In September 1837, for example—when Jack Savage was sixteen and still lived on the Ogeechee River, owned by Mr. William Savage—one of Jack's fellow slaves named Simon was caught just a few miles from home. Simon "has run away three times," a neighbor wrote, without a shadow of embarrassment, to the most paternalist of rice planters, Richard J. Arnold, "& I presume will now be shipped." Charles Manigault boasted in 1847 of his own practice: "I always made it a rule to sell every runaway—and they are fully aware of this." Believing Gowrie's slaves remarkably orderly, he attributed his success to his firm policy of sale.[18]

Although dearth of labor after 1854 diminished Manigault's single-mindedness in enforcing this policy, he and Louis sent altogether about a dozen Gowrie slaves to the auction block, of whom one-third were women.[19] Louis expected the auctioneer to lie in order to secure the highest price for the spurned slaves. If an adult male were sold on his own, a potential buyer in Charleston might be suspicious of being landed with an insubordinate slave; in 1854, therefore, the Manigaults waited until they had assembled a little group of three nonconformists—Prince, William, and Frederick (Bess's husband)— to auction in a single parcel. Buyers would not divine that three lemons had rotted simultaneously. "I am persuaded that the three, if sold together will bring a pretty good price," Louis assured his father, "for in truth they are prime hands, at least the Auctioneer will swear that they are." Like superficial defects on a used car in a later century, obvious physical faults must be put right before the sale. "They all three have sore feet. I must cure them first," Charles notified his impatient son. And like a defective used car, the slave must be given a new external appearance. "If you have 3 [new] Suits of Jackets & Trousers, & Shirt left," Charles requested Louis, "I should like to have them here [in Charleston], to shew them off to the best advantage, & Caps too."[20]

A network of white people's community institutions and customs strengthened the Manigaults' control over their slaves. Every white person could challenge every black person to show a pass authorizing absence from the plantation. Thus a Mr. Zipro captured Posh, a fugitive from Gowrie, and carried him to the Savannah jail in January 1852. And about two years later another white man apprehended Prince and—to save the Manigaults a jail fee—sent the fugitive directly back to Gowrie the next morning. If, when the Manigaults were absent in Charleston, they wanted an insubordinate slave sent to them from Savannah, the Adams Express Company would guarantee safe delivery for a price. The respectable urban "factors" who handled the plantation's commercial business were perfectly willing to act as agents in expediting a slave sale. "The man Prince [who had been shipped from Gowrie to Charleston] was immediately sent to the work house," the Charleston firm of Middleton and Company notified Louis Manigault a few days after Prince's capture. And after Jane, the demoted house servant, had languished six months in the Savannah jail—waiting for the winter slave-trading season to begin—the esteemed factors R. Habersham and Son assured Manigault, "We shall avail of the first opportunity of sending y[ou]r woman to New Orleans." When the Manigaults dispatched a free Charleston black to hang paper at Gowrie, they had a white person obtain clearance for him to return on the steamer from Savannah: thus the chance of a slave's escaping by steamship was minimized.[21] The local patrol, on which Gowrie's overseer was expected to serve, hindered slaves from making unauthorized trips to Savannah or to other plantations.

Although gentlemen evaded service on routine patrols,[22] they might occasionally join an informal posse to search for fugitive slaves. "It is hard to catch [fugitives] again if they are out from spring to winter," Charles once grumbled, for not enough white people remained at the plantations to form these posses. Thus in late September 1837 a leading Georgia rice planter had notified an absent neighbor that it was still too early in the year to track down several fugitives: "It is intended," he assured Richard Arnold, "as soon as the accumulation of frost will render it safe [from malaria], to hunt for them by detachments until they are all caught or driven away."[23] Louis Manigault's brother Gabriel, who was managing Silk Hope in January 1861, explained then to Louis the principles upon which these posses operated. Four of Gowrie's slaves were at that moment in the swamps, two of them having been there since October. As the sale of Fortune—a frequent fugitive—in May 1860 had not deterred these other slaves from fleeing, Gabriel was convinced that Louis must now hunt them with dogs. In November 1860 Gabriel had himself gone hunting near Silk Hope "with a parcel of overseers and three professional negro hunters with nine dogs"; and he had learned from these men—what gentlemen did not always know—the common lore of the slave-hunting "profession."[24] Dr. Gabriel Manigault became one of the principal figures in the cultural life of postbellum Charleston—a professor at Charleston College, curator of the Charleston Museum, and a leading member of the Gibbes Art Museum, where a plaque by the entrance door still commemorates his good work for that institution. He was also a man of compassion, as he had proved by his admirably self-respecting, tactful plea to his father not to slam the door permanently in the face of Gabriel's eldest brother during a flaming family row. The tone of Gabriel's advice to Louis about slave hunting is therefore the more striking, coming from a man in other ways so estimable.

"It is absolutely necessary to go armed with a double barrelled gun," Gabriel advised,

> loaded with duck shot at least, with the intention of shooting in the leg, or in a vital part if necessary, any negro who attempts to resist or to escape after being caught. . . .
>
> The dogs are usually harmless hounds who are simply trained to follow the negro scent, and usually if there is water in the neighborhood the negroes will take to it and hide so effectually among the reeds that you might be in the immediate neighborhood of one and not discover him. The dogs do not follow them in the water, and when once there, it is no easy matter to lay your hands upon one.
>
> . . . I think that there should be at least six in the party [all armed], in order that, in searching a piece of ground, all of the avenues of [e]gress may be guarded.[25]

The four Gowrie slaves did not believe the hounds would be harmless—dogs are well known to have chewed up fugitive slaves elsewhere in the South[26]— and fear of dogs impelled them to return to Gowrie on January 25 to face their whippings.[27]

The practice of poor men's serving on patrols, and the legal right of any white person to challenge any black person to produce a pass, encouraged nonslaveholding whites to intimidate slaves. Thus when the Gowrie slaves were evacuated to an impromptu pineland camp during the "cholera" epidemic of 1852, the owner of some nearby pigs ("a real Cracker," in Louis Manigault's opinion) threatened to take the law into his own hands if any slave touched his pigs. He told them (in his own words), " 'If dey Catch my pigs I'll Cut their throats, & they never trouble me.' "[28]

Besides depending on local whites to apprehend fugitives, the Manigaults could sometimes turn to black drivers of nearby plantations to do the same job. Thus in 1849 they paid Frank (the driver of the Williamson rice plantation, on the Carolina bank of the Savannah River) $1.50 for "taking" a Gowrie woman—probably one of those recently purchased in Charleston to stock the new East Hermitage tract. Frank's was a bargain rate, for the fee to a Savannah constable for "taking up" a Gowrie slave in 1846 was $3.00. When, therefore, the Manigaults paid the same driver Frank $10.00 in 1851 for an unspecified service, this is probably a sign that he then helped them to recapture a good-sized group of fugitives, of whom no other record has survived.[29]

The ultimate way of teaching subordination, behind this tissue of surveillance and menace, was the threat of military force. Although Louis Manigault feared Jack Savage, and Gowrie's overseers experienced many forms of slave dissidence, these overseers almost never gave a thought to the possibility of slave insurrection. The dangers of freshets, the uncertainties of tidal irrigation, the anxieties of harvest time, the overseers' concern to keep their own health and that of their families, the problems posed by the slaves' daily negligence of their plantation "duties"—these real problems kept the overseers on the jump without their exercising themselves over the chimera of rebellion. Even in the eighteenth-century South Carolina low country, scattered white men could speedily organize and concentrate themselves on horseback (as happened in 1739 during the abortive Stono rebellion); and once steamships and railways brought swift transportation into play, the chances of plantation slaves' standing against the quickly massed formations of South Carolina's or Georgia's military forces were minuscule.

Every opportunity was seized to overawe slaves by displays of military force. Thus when two men were hanged at Walterborough, South Carolina, in March 1854, Charles Manigault's cousin Arthur (later a brigadier general in the Confederate army) was sent two days beforehand from Charleston "in command of a body of troops in a Steamboat which also conveyed the two men to be hung." No doubt slaves at Charleston, at Walterborough, and at every steamboat stop between the two towns were suitably impressed. On December 26 of that year there was a military display in Savannah, allegedly for the "fun" of slaves making merry at Christmas, but obviously intended to remind all blacks of the white people's military might. As soon as Yankee forces made their appearance along the coast in November 1861, a Confederate military detachment visited Gowrie to overawe the restless slaves. One night "Eight Men all in uniforms, and armed with Sabre, Revolver, &c., made their appearance at Gowrie, & East Hermitage, searched all the Houses on these two places, & at Mr. Barclay's [the next plantation to the north] & were here all night."[30] Military force was, of course, even more evident during the war than in peacetime; but its existence, and its capacity for rapid deployment, was the decisive deterrent to insurrection. The absence of uprisings during the antebellum period, and during the Civil War itself, need have surprised no one.

If insurrection was out of the question, less dramatic forms of dissidence were nevertheless endemic. Day-to-day obstructiveness—ranging from deliberately sloppy work to large-scale theft—was chronic at Gowrie and affected every aspect of production. Discussion of this dissidence cannot be separated from a long-standing controversy among historians over the "efficiency" of slave labor.

Classical advocates of the free marketplace, going back most famously to Adam Smith in 1776, argued that slave labor must inevitably be inefficient because slaves had no strong incentives—such as wages—to impel them to efficiency. The most powerful statement of this view appeared in the writings of the American traveler Frederick Olmsted, whose influential *Cotton Kingdom* (1861)—and the three travelogues of the 1850s from which it was distilled—reported case after case of the slaves' (often deliberate) inefficiency. The most vigorous assault upon this view of slave labor appeared in the much-discussed *Time on the Cross* (1974). The authors there argued that Olmsted, in electing not to travel in the Deep South during the (malarial) harvest season, unwittingly cut himself off from the opportunity to see slaves at their most productive.[31]

A claim that slaves were inefficient has sometimes been associated with racial prejudice; and although Olmsted was less racially prejudiced[32] than most nineteenth-century travelers in the Deep South, it is nevertheless obvious that prejudice substantially affected his writings. His picture of slave women doing road labor inland in South Carolina shows how easily his distaste for many African-Americans might be interwoven with his view of the inefficiency of the slaves' labor: "Clumsy, awkward, gross, elephantine in all their movements; pouting, grinning, and leering at us; sly, sensual, and shameless, in all their expressions and demeanor; I never before had witnessed, I thought, anything more revolting than the whole scene."[33]

The modern assault upon racial prejudice has led, entirely reasonably, to a questioning of whether Olmsted denigrated the achievements of the slaves. Perhaps they were, after all, remarkably productive? Perhaps the average slave produced as much as, or more than, the average white farmer on a midwestern farm? Perhaps Olmsted mistakenly attributed to slavery and to racial characteristics that periodic idleness which arose rather from the age-old work rhythms of every preindustrial people? Before the introduction of time clocks and factory discipline, workers always alternated between spells of quiet and periods of frenzied activity; did not Olmsted himself acknowledge that those slaves quickly loading logs onto a Mississippi River steamboat (to fuel its furnaces) worked for a time with a vigor that would have shamed a free-labor work gang?[34] Rice plantations could certainly be very profitable:[35] must not the labor of rice slaves, therefore, have been "efficient"?

Yet when Olmsted, in 1853, visited the rice plantation of Richard J. Arnold on Georgia's Ogeechee River—only a few miles from Gowrie—he found that Arnold's slaves left gates open (with the result that animals might trample seedlings in newly planted fields); fence rails were stolen for firewood; and new fence rails were deposited in the wrong place, so that completion of repair work would take much longer than necessary. Furthermore, draft animals were lamed and tools broken by "careless" usage; a large, ill-secured boat was left to drift out into the river (doubtless to the slaves' vast amusement); and a vital repair to an embankment was deliberately botched, with the consequence that an inundation of that field might later destroy its crop.[36] Olmsted, despite his racial bias, was a remarkably candid and clear-eyed observer, and his detailed account of the slaves' doings at Arnold's plantation cannot be doubted. Furthermore, Olmsted's report is wholly consistent with a mass of evidence from plantations everywhere else in the South.[37] Can Olmsted's report of the slaves' "inefficiency" be reconciled with the planters' nevertheless reaping big profits from slave labor?

Economic historians' long-established distinction between "efficiency" and profitability goes far toward clarifying this matter, for slave labor could theoretically be profoundly inefficient, yet highly profitable. The cost of using slave labor was low because no wages had to be paid; even a relatively small gross revenue might therefore lead to a high profit: Gross revenue (per slave) − Cost (per slave) = Profit (per slave). Profitability would be enhanced if—as in the case of American cotton during most antebellum years—world demand was high and Lancashire (and Massachusetts) manufacturers could find few alternative sources of supply. The voracious demand for cotton would then keep its price high, and cotton planters could reap high profits even with inefficient slave labor.[38] Rice plantations became unprofitable soon after slavery was abolished, and part of the explanation was that free laborers cost a planter much more than had slaves. Work on rice plantations was unhealthy; free workers would naturally drift away from the region, or turn to healthier work on any patch of nearby land to which they could stake a claim;[39] and the wages of a worker remaining on a rice plantation would far exceed the costs to a slaveholder of maintaining a prewar "prime hand."

The profitability of slave labor on rice plantations does not therefore prove that slave labor was efficient. Yet the controversial question of efficiency may never be resolved until a further distinction is established between "efficiency" and "productivity." Slaves may truly have been highly "productive"—as modern critics of Olmsted have claimed—but they may simultaneously have been very "inefficient," as Olmsted constantly reiterated. Slave labor was not only much more profitable at Gowrie than free labor proved to be, but it probably was also much more "productive." Productivity arose directly from coercion. The clearest example arose from the hateful winter work of ditching, and of strengthening the mud embankments. Slaves could be forced to do this labor, and if some of them died from pneumonia, this was to the owner a small price to pay for work which was essential to the long-term productivity of the plantation. Freedmen and women proved deeply reluctant to perform this indispensable element in the annual cycle of tidal rice production. After the war, when Louis Manigault once impatiently hired white laborers to do the job, the high wage bill contributed to his staggering deficit, and he quickly abandoned the experiment. Throughout the rice region the difficulty of getting freedmen and women to clean the ditches and repair the embankments was the greatest single factor causing low production of rice per acre in the postwar period. Coerced slave labor at Gowrie, and throughout the rice kingdom, was therefore more "productive" than free labor proved to be. But it may simultaneously have been less "efficient" (if one measures "efficiency" by comparing achievements of slaves with those of Northern laborers at agricultural tasks common to North and South: there were no rice swamps to be ditched in the North, and no mud embankments to be reinforced in February).

Charles Manigault certainly believed his slaves—however productive—to be grossly inefficient. They would always, he thought, create a foul-up if offered any excuse for doing so. He therefore advised a new suboverseer to give the slaves their head at first: the suboverseer ought not, at the outset, to interfere much with work the slaves were doing, "as all negroes will be quite satisfied to go wrong if they can put it on any one else."[40]

One might be tempted to dismiss such an utterance as a mere outburst of racial prejudice, were not the evidence overwhelming that Gowrie's slaves did indeed create foul-ups at every stage of the productive process. When the veteran overseer William Capers first arrived at Gowrie in April 1859, he "pointed out to [the less experienced Louis Manigault] that the ploughs had been skipping ground, & doing very bad work." Eugene Genovese has demonstrated that during the 1850s Deep South cotton planters turned increasingly to mules instead of horses as work animals, because "as most contemporaries admitted [mules] withstood more readily the punishment inflicted by the slaves." The slaves seemed (in Genovese's words) "to have taken the greatest delight in abusing the horses, oxen, and mules." Charles Manigault's views were identical. The mules, he thought, must be inspected every day to see whether sores had developed, for the slaves were likely to wound the animals with the chains, or by beating them. A mule was likely to plunge into a ditch because the board used as a bridge was too narrow, and the plowmen ("boys," he called these adult men) loved to get a mule deliberately bogged in a ditch. When the mules came home they were likely to be obliged to slake their thirst with dirty, hot water. When Charles Manigault advised Louis how to keep the white overseer on his toes so as to avoid the consequences of the slaves' deliberate inefficiency, Olmsted himself might have been speaking: Manigault wanted the overseer

[1] to try to see the mules each day, if galled or not—

[2] & make the Boys have always a [wide] board Bridge . . . to cross the Ditches . . . ,

[3] & have always a Tub of water at the Stable for them to drink as they arrive home, to be put in fresh every day, & not drinking the same hot & dirty water remaining in part from day to day,

[4] never to Jump the mules over a ditch, or let them go in one to drink, these two last things the boys think high fun, to bog a mule. . . .

[5] Watch that they dont strike the mules in the same spot to make it raw . . .

[6] & see that the chains trace dont wound the Side or the Legs of the mule.[41]

Obstacles to plantation efficiency appeared equally clearly during the harvest and threshing seasons, when the slaves' conduct sometimes verged on sabotage. One January Louis Manigault found that a good deal of the harvested rice had become "mow-burnt." The overseer, Louis was convinced, had failed to watch constantly when the cut rice was being stacked, and the slaves had seized their opportunity: "That rice must have been put in the stacks wet," Louis sadly concluded. "A sheaf of wet rice will destroy several bushels in a stack."[42] At other times the slaves merely sought to reduce their labors. Before threshing machinery was introduced, one way of measuring a "task" was to require a "prime hand" to thresh six hundred sheaves of rice per day. The size of this task depended on the size of a sheaf, and "Negroes are cunning enough," Charles Manigault sighed, "to remember that what they are harvesting they will have to thresh, & will tie as small sheaves as they can."

The overseer threatened to impose a 10 percent increase in the size of the task "if they went on tieing such small sheaves."

To avoid this problem, one might define the "task" in an entirely different way; but then the slaves' wish to avoid work could lead to sabotage. Thus a "task" might be defined as the volume of threshed rice—before winnowing—which the overseer estimated would produce twelve bushels after winnowing. Slaves unfortunately exhibited an irritating disregard for natural justice: if this method of measuring the "task" were used, "the negro will then knock away so as to break up & intermix the greatest possible quantity of cut straw &c. with his days task & thus defeat justice by rendering things uncertain & unequal."[43]

Two years after penning this lament, Charles Manigault—as keen as any Northern capitalist to reap the benefits of new technology if only his slaves would permit him to do so—introduced a newly invented threshing machine. He was cunning enough to foresee that the slaves, in turn, would introduce new methods to reduce plantation efficiency. The machine "must be fed by the two feeding-hands with a Constant supply of sheaves—," he instructed the overseer, "the head of the one touching the but[t] of the foremost sheave just as it is about to disappear in the thresher. . . . I am sure one of the most difficult things will be to make the Negroes feed properly."[44] This tidal-powered threshing machine had the disadvantage of slowing down the older tidal-powered pounding mill, to which it had been attached; and not long after Manigault's 1849 purchase of a steam-powered thresher (at the East Hermitage tract), he transferred all threshing operations to the new site.

The slaves' inefficiency, and their propensity to sabotage plantation operations, proved at least as great as their master had anticipated. Straw was used to feed the furnace, and the fireman did not perform his duties properly. Even the two most trustworthy slave women would sabotage the machine if they were given the chance. Manigault used the term "accidental," but he knew better; for if these women failed to keep the beater fully occupied, the machine would gradually wreck itself. Short Jack was supposed to keep the women working constantly, but someone had to be present every minute to ensure that Short Jack was holding the women up to the mark. It seemed to the master like trying to whip a bunch of schoolchildren into order. Manigault tried to persuade himself that the problem was the slaves' ignorance, but he knew in his heart that they loved to undermine plantation efficiency. "I hope the Thresher will go on well," he wrote doubtfully to Louis,

> after all the trouble it has given us. But it has to contend against all kinds of contrariété—Ignorance amongst the whole of them. And even if it goes on well they wont in the first place feed up with straw properly, nor will even the two primest, & best Negresses on the place (Betty & Cathrina) continue to place the shieves regularly on the India Rubber conveyer. But if they think they are not watched they will let the Beater wear itself out in turning uselessly, while the conveying cloth goes up nearly empty. And "Short Jack" whose station is at the feeding Rollers will never call out to them to feed up

unless he thinks that he is watched by any one and so it goes! Any accidental stopping pleases them all I fear, just as it used to be with us all at school I suppose. When any thing happened to the master, or any thing else in the concern, so as to cause a stoppage we subordinates all looked at each other & grinned with delight.

Such was the inefficiency of slave labor, Manigault tended to believe, that in many cases "where Negroes are concerned . . . , manual labour is better than any out of the way attempt at machinery."[45]

Slave artisans could be as inefficient as the machine operators and field hands. "I got perfectly disgusted with Amos & Billy," Louis once wrote of two carpenters who had been building a garden fence for his Gowrie residence: "I have not time to be watching them all the while and Amos (the Old Fool) put almost every post down Crooked." The excellent craftsmanship of carpenter Jack Savage presented a welcome contrast to the sloppiness of Amos and Billy and to the low standard of most plantation labor. Thus when a gang of Charles Manigault's slaves embedded into the bank of his South Carolina plantation a culvert built by Jack, he reported that "Jack made a beautiful Trunk, which . . . after some bungling, & much caving in, & delay the Gang got it in its place."[46] Yet Jack Savage, skilled artisan though he was, often worked at a maddeningly slow pace; and Louis Manigault was intimidated by him. John Izard was almost the only artisan whom the Manigaults fully trusted, and the overseers sometimes lodged complaints at even his slowness.[47]

Malingering was a perennial form of day-to-day dissidence at Gowrie. Overseers and masters repeatedly racked their brains trying to determine whether a slave's complaint was fake or not. Jane "still represents herself as being in a feeble state of health . . . ," the overseer ruminated in 1849: "From her own statements, she does not know what a well day is. . . . I must say that her looks denies the assertion. . . . She may possibly be diseased, or have some object in view."[48] A different overseer in 1852 accused Posh of lying about the cause of his involuntary urination, and the dispute led to Posh's flight and subsequent sale. The next year Louis Manigault speculated about the source of Nancy's peculiar complaint. She and her husband, Ben, had been deported from Silk Hope to Gowrie in 1848, but Ben was sent back to Silk Hope in 1852 to try to recover from an illness; Nancy seems to have hoped to follow him. She was in the sick house and Dr. Bullock had given her medicine, but Louis Manigault suspected "there is some humbug about Nancy, altho' true! her Complaint is a very difficult thing to get at. . . . It lasts for months & even years at times," Louis continued, "but I think that Nancy thinks You may take her to Silk Hope to recruit &c., & do nothing." Charles Manigault was impatient with his son's uncertainties: "Shove her out with the trash gang from moping all the time in the house," he urged. Louis heeded his father's injunction, put her to work at Gowrie instead of returning her to Silk Hope,[49] and was thus responsible for her death in Gowrie's "cholera" epidemic of 1854.

Unlike some other forms of dissidence, malingering was an act which hurt the interests of other slaves. Thus when Jane said she was feeling bad during the 1852 "cholera" epidemic, the overseer was certain to regard her complaint with skepticism, and this doubtless contributed to his tardiness in treating the epidemic seriously. In 1856 Charles Manigault, suffering from a chronic labor shortage at Gowrie, sent ten "prime hands" from Silk Hope to help out for six weeks during the harvest. Nine of the ten went to the sick house during their brief sojourn in Georgia, and the overseer quickly came to disbelieve their complaints. "At first some of those new comers Tryed to lie up," Leonard Venters blustered. "But they are getting on Tolerable well at this [time] being they find it no use in Triffling." Determination to prevent "Triffling" surely contributed to the overseers' shocking record of misdiagnosing genuine illness. For example, when Charles Manigault bought eight slaves in March 1842, one of them—Lucy, a twenty-five-year-old "prime hand"—alleged she was sick. Three months later Manigault suggested that overseer Bagshaw make her a "¾ hand," thus reducing by 25 percent the task she was expected to accomplish each day. Bagshaw objected that leniency would produce a crop of malingerers: "I think it would have a tendency to injure and we would soon have more of them kind. I can point out several that does [i.e., finishes] there [sic] task that I doe not think abler than Lucy." Manigault then decided that Lucy was "pretending." She died the next year at twenty-six, her death no doubt speeded by her masters' anxiety that a slave might cheat them of a day's work.[50]

Besides working inefficiently, Gowrie's slaves obstructed plantation discipline in countless other ways. They often left Gowrie on unauthorized trips to other plantations (or even to Savannah), and they obtained cash by trading with slaves on these plantations. They sometimes "borrowed" Manigault's plantation flatboats to make an unsanctioned journey, and—against the rules—they also constructed canoes to facilitate illicit travel. They stole corn from the mules, and rice from the plantation seed supply, to fill their stomachs. And they appear to have organized a ring to steal larger quantities of rice from the mill for illegal sale in Savannah. The overseers tried to control the extent of these activities, but an air of weary resignation prevailed: such things were inevitable concomitants of the slave regime. If a bondswoman from a neighboring plantation was drowned in a gale while making an illicit trip to Savannah, the response of Gowrie's overseer was a nonchalant, slightly triumphant "So much for their excessive canoeing to Town." Venters, an overseer whose orthography was undistinguished, seemed to congratulate himself that one group of absentees from Gowrie had all returned voluntarily, and that he had not even had to pay a white person—as had happened another time—to return the plantation flatboat. "I have all heare know [now] safe," he assured Charles, "& non are not missing heare at this presant time. [Yesterday] she [the boat] where [were] presant & nothing to pay for her."[51]

The furnishings of an overseer's house were, to a slave's eye, palatial; and when overseer Stephen Clark died in December 1855, a dispute quickly flared between Clark's widow and Charles Manigault about whether his slaves had stolen a long list of the Clarks' possessions. She claimed that on February 8,

1856, when the slaves loaded her goods onto a sailing vessel which carried rough rice to Charleston, the following items had vanished:

1 Carpet
1 Broom 2 Milk pans 10 jugs
6 Bottles Med[icine] 2 Jars
3 Bottles Whiskey, 1 Bottle ——?——
[6 bottles Wine?] Vinegar ——?——
10 lbs Coffee 30 lbs flour 25 lbs Crush Sugar
1 Wire Safe
2 Flat Irons 2 Coffee Mills
1 Wire ——?——.

Mrs. Clark's suspicion that slaves had stolen these goods was plausible, for Louis Manigault had been attending the balls in Charleston that day and—in the absence of a new overseer—Gowrie's slaves had been under the temporary supervision of a neighbor's overseer, who no doubt had other duties to claim his attention.[52]

The complex operations of a rice plantation presented innumerable opportunities for theft and petty vandalism. When a double quantity of barrel staves was mistakenly delivered at Gowrie in 1842, the overseer was perplexed whether or not to return the extra ones, for they would be useful for making barrels the following year: "It would not be a bad plan to keep them all [he mused] if we *could* keep them but that is almost impossible. The more there is the more will be waisted, burnt, etc."[53] When slate roofs were being put on the slaves' houses early in 1861, Charles Manigault admonished his son to "keep an eye to the waste, and theft by negroes of those copper nails [which] cost more than their weight in Copper Money." And when John Izard was painting the pounding mill early in the summer of 1842, part of the job had to be left incomplete until a resident suboverseer could be hired for the harvesttime: "I cant open [those rooms] untill I get some one on the spot," Bagshaw, the nonresident head overseer, explained. Otherwise, "no doubt there would be Robbing committed with the provision." That thievery of rice was endemic was shown in Charles Manigault's advice to his son: one advantage of claying the seed rice (for use in the so-called open planting technique) was that the slaves "cant steal it so easily, without detection of it in their possession, or in their preparation in cooking it."[54]

Of more concern to Manigault, however, was large-scale theft from the mill, and transportation of the booty for sale in Savannah. "I allow . . . none of [my Negroes] to keep a boat . . . ," he informed a new overseer in 1848:

Cut up, or lock up in the mill any Negro Canoe found anywhere on my place, & particularly near the Mill—whether it be on my land or on "Mr. Potter's" [whose land adjoined Gowrie just south of the canal where Manigault's mill was situated], as that gentleman requested me, to do so, if I found any near my Mill on his land.

Apparently Manigault was concerned about the recent report of the outgoing overseer: about 10 percent of the milled rice seemed to be disappearing. "Somehow or other Stephen [the slave miller] cannot make [the threshed rice] hold out to measurement . . . ," the overseer had complained in puzzlement. It took Stephen twenty-two or twenty-three bushels of threshed rice to produce one barrel of milled rice, "which in my judgment is too much. Clay ground rice ought not to take over 20 bushels pr. barrel and frequently even less. I can never think that Stephen and the other mill hands acts perfectly honest with the rice in the mill." If a group of slaves was stealing anything near 10 percent of Manigault's rice and selling it in Savannah, even the drastically reduced price they could obtain from illicit sale to a white trader would have netted them magnificent sums.[55] By 1851 Manigault had demoted Stephen from the post of miller, replacing him with the trusted Cato.

This shift in personnel seems to have led the rice thieves to change their operations from polished rice (at the Gowrie mill) to "rough rice"—threshed but not yet milled—which they could purloin from the brick threshing building at East Hermitage. In May 1851 the overseer reported that although certain bags "were counted sometime ago, and locked up in the Corn Room, one of each parcel was missing." One of these sacks was probably used by Bob when, early one Sunday morning in 1852, he was "apprehended in Town with a boat and 8 or 9 bushels of Rough Rice and lodged in jail by one of the constables." The overseer whipped Bob and hoped for his reformation, but he disbelieved Bob's story that he himself had stolen the rice from the brick threshing building. Bob probably was covering up for an accomplice; and an accessory to the fact may have been the Manigaults' esteemed John Izard (who had been entrusted with the keys to this building). That Bob's capture in 1852 did not end theft from the threshing building is suggested by his unauthorized boat trip to Savannah on the night of Sunday, April 24, 1853.[56]

Olmsted's view of the "inefficiency" of slave labor thus finds copious substantiation in the Manigault records. Bondsmen and women could be forced into the wet ditches in January, and were therefore more productive on rice plantations than free workers proved to be, yet they were thoroughly inefficient.

The slaves' custom of making unsanctioned journeys away from the plantation—like the previously mentioned trip of Sampson to visit his wife, Maria, at the summer "camp," which had led to his drowning in 1847—merged into the surprisingly common practice of fleeing into the swamp for extended periods. Historians believe that, between 1830 and 1860, one or two thousand fugitive slaves per year made their way successfully to freedom north of the Mason-Dixon line (or in Mexico), but this was a mere trickle from among the millions of slaves—and nearly all of these successful fugitives fled from border states like Maryland, Virginia, and Kentucky.[57] With practically no slaves from the Deep South able to reach the North or Canada, one might wonder why politicians in the Deep South felt so strongly about the fugitive slave issue, and why they insisted that Congress enact the noxious Fugitive Slave Act of 1850. No doubt much of their feeling arose because this issue symbolized for them—as the territorial slavery issue did for many Northern politicians—the whole slavery question. Furthermore, the "personal liberty laws," designed in some Northern states to obstruct enforcement of fugitive slave laws, offered secessionists a perfect rationale for their policy. If the North violated its contractual obligation to return fugitive slaves, then (secessionists averred) the constitutional contract could no longer bind the South: Southern independence seemed constitutionally justified. Yet the sensitivity of Deep South planters to the fugitive slave issue had other origins than these political ones. Slave owners were aroused because thousands and thousands of slaves did in fact run away from plantations in the Deep South. The idea of permanent escape—least of all to the far-distant North—impelled only a few of these flights (until the Civil War brought Northern war vessels and soldiers into the South). The fugitives sought instead simple short-term relief from the plantation: almost all knew that sooner or later they would once again be subject to the authority of a slave master.

The hazards of swimming a broad and turbulent river, or concealing oneself for weeks at a time in the dank swampland, might readily be underestimated by those unfamiliar with the alligators, water moccasins, and ubiquitous rattlesnakes of the antebellum low country. The intrepid Frances Kemble testified to a slave companion's fear of straying from open roads on Georgia's St. Simons Island, where snakes were to be encountered. "The wood paths are as tempting as paths into Paradise," she wrote enthusiastically in March 1839, "but Jack is in such deadly terror about the snakes . . . that he will not follow me off the open road, and twice today scared me back from charming wood paths I ventured to explore with his exclamations of terrified warning."[58] That flight from Gowrie was perilous is clear from the fates of the dissidents Joe and Anthony. The former fled his new Georgia domicile five months after being shipped there from the Charleston auction block in 1853: "The new comer Joe walked off some time agoe," overseer Clark reported that summer. "He took the small flat[boat] across the river [to South Carolina]. I got it back. I have not heard of him since." But no peacetime fugitive from Gowrie ever escaped permanently. Joe perished in consequence of his flight—probably in the swamp, or possibly from a severe whipping after being captured: "He is a scoundrel!" Louis Manigault insouciantly wrote in his notebook. "He has died."[59]

A year later history repeated itself with another unhappy deportee to Gowrie, and this time Louis made no pretense of high spirits. Tersely he inscribed upon the 1854 slave list:

> Anthony   P[rime]   35 Yrs.
> Runaway Died from it
> died in Charleston.

Once again the master's note leaves uncertain whether death eventuated from the hazards of flight or the severity of punishment after the fugitive was captured.[60]

Dolly, Louis's thirty-year-old "invalid" washerwoman—who fled from him when he was living at Augusta, Georgia, in 1863—probably escaped unharmed. If so, she appears to have been the only Manigault slave ever to have made good a permanent escape, without suffering permanent injury. Her nearest counterpart was July, a twenty-seven-year-old field hand who fled by boat late in 1864 and was shot in the leg by a Confederate soldier; the leg had to be amputated in the "Yankee hospital" set up in Savannah by General Sherman. Fortune, who ran away every year from 1857 to 1860, was falsely reported to have drowned in 1860;[61] evading this very real danger, he was captured and later sold to New Orleans, where perhaps he soon pitted himself against the hazards of a Louisiana bayou instead of those of a Georgia swamp.

Against the perils of flight the slaves could set the dangers of the plantation. Cicero, who ran away in 1852, might have stayed alive had he escaped permanently; but, returned to Gowrie, he succumbed there a few months later to "cholera." His sister Phoebe, who ran away with him in 1852, was captured; she died at Gowrie of "cholera" in February 1855. By contrast, the four fugitives whom the Manigaults sold in 1854 avoided exposure to the deadly "cholera" epidemic later that year which claimed Phoebe's life.

Despite the hazards of flight, probably at least two dozen Gowrie slaves spent periods in the swamp between 1851 and October 1861, and there may well have been others.[62] Seven more tried to escape between November 1861 and late 1864.[63] Furthermore, a group of ten slaves (seven of them among the fugitives already mentioned) were credibly suspected in November 1861 of planning to escape: they were then deported inland to South Carolina to prevent their doing so.[64] And just before Christmas in 1864—Sherman's army having arrived in the vicinity—Gowrie's bondsmen and women (except those who had been impressed into Confederate service to build fortifications) dug a great hole in the embankment and floated a flatboat through it. Then all dusted their feet of the plantation: every one of them boarded the boat and set off for Savannah or the seacoast. This was no small record of discontent in a slave force which seldom during the 1850s numbered more than seventy-five able-bodied adult slaves.[65] At least twenty-three of the fugitives (between 1851 and 1864, before Sherman arrived) were male:[66] thus the record of discontent among Gowrie's able-bodied adult men—usually numbering about thirty-five at any one moment—was striking indeed.

The most circumstantial account of fugitives' doings was given to Charles Manigault in 1833—the very year he acquired Gowrie—by the twenty-six-year-old Friday. Manigault was preparing to sell Friday as a habitual runaway. Two other Gowrie slaves had disappeared, and Friday probably sought to avoid sale by telling Manigault where they might be found. He also talked about two other slaves who had fled temporarily during the previous year. Although he may have fabricated certain details in order to mislead his master, Friday's acquaintance in the neighborhood was evidently extensive, and the gist of his account is plausible.

Two of the other four fugitives had abroad marriages. Three of them were women. They had allies: for at one plantation the slaves were sure to help, while Gowrie's driver Harry lent tacit assistance, and a white shopkeeper probably traded with the runaways. Clearly there was a large enough supply of illicit homemade canoes that the slaves could often cross the river. To escape the perils of the swamps, fugitives often sought out high ground, woods, or the buildings of a neighboring plantation. Charles Manigault, still new at Gowrie, recorded the slave's words with fascination: "Friday," he wrote, as a notary might record the testimony of a witness in a court case,

> says that the place that he generally went to when he ran away was at a swamp which has some dry noles [knolls] in it which lies between Mr. J[ames] Potter's place [on the Georgia side of the river] and the place just below it. . . . That there is a man by the name of Jefferson who keeps a store near where Gordon's road joins the broad road who is the best acquainted with the swamp and the best person to tell [i.e., to notify] if any of our Negroes are out. Friday says that my [small, uninhabited, wooded] Island opposite Mr. Marchant's is a great [Manigault, who could not be expected to share Friday's enthusiasm for a great hiding place, struck out "great" and substituted here "good"] place [to hide] and that as Alick [one of Manigault's fugitives, a thirty-year-old cooper] has a wife at Mr. Marchant's named Katy that he is probably there and sleeps on Mr. Marchant's every night. That Mr. Marchant's negroes will always help the runaways. That when Maria and Betsey [two other youngish slaves whom Manigault had purchased with Gowrie] ran away last year they were out two or three months and [visited?] Mr. Marchant's *settlement* and often hid in the kitchen as it was known that search would only be made for them in the negro houses. That Minda [another of Manigault's newly acquired slaves, twenty-six years old] has a husband at Mr. Ulmer's place in the Georgia Pine barren named Abraham, and has a sweetheart named Daniel at Judge Berryan's[67] place. Friday also says that [driver] Harry never stops a negro or tries to talk him out of it when he knows that he is going to run away.[68]

Intriguing though this glimpse of the fugitives' world might be, Charles Manigault did not allow it to deflect him from his purpose: he sold Friday in July 1833. He also sold the last-named fugitive—Minda—six months later (separating her from husband and sweetheart); and three years after that he sold Friday's sister Charlotte. Gowrie's slaves must be made to understand discipline.

Although gaps in the records make it impossible to determine how many slaves fled Gowrie during the seventeen years after 1833, fragmentary evidence suggests that flight was not uncommon. Simon, a twenty-one-year-old Silk Hope slave deported to Gowrie in 1833, was incarcerated in the Savannah jail three times during the summer of 1834, quite possibly as punishment for repeatedly running away. If Manigault intended to sell him that winter, the plan was interrupted by the Asiatic cholera epidemic. Simon perished on September 15, 1834. In the spring of 1844 Manigault punished two Silk Hope fugitives, Posh and Quash, by deporting them to Gowrie. "Pos[h] has runaway for ten days past," the Silk Hope overseer had complained to his employer: "I wish you would take him to Savannah [River, i.e., to Gowrie] for he has so many a[c]quaintances there."[69] Manigault followed this advice, and privileges at Gowrie temporarily pacified Posh. Quash's stay at Gowrie was briefer. He, like Posh, at first made a good impression on Gowrie's overseer—"Your man Quash dose very well, has not Run, and behaves him Self," Bagshaw reported in July 1844; but probably he ran soon thereafter and was sold.[70] Other Gowrie fugitives were certainly captured in 1846 and 1849; possibly also in 1834 and 1835; and probably a group of fugitives was betrayed by a neighbor's driver in 1851.[71]

When Louis Manigault took over Gowrie's management, he, unlike his father, kept rather complete records of flight; these show that during no year from 1851 was Gowrie without at least one fugitive. Most of the flights occurred under the management of overseers Stephen Clark in 1853–55, and of William Capers in 1859–64.

Before Capers's arrival the fugitives were usually relative newcomers to Gowrie. Two of them, Posh the trunk minder and Jane (John Izard's sister-in-law), had been deported from Silk Hope in the 1840s. Posh lasted at Gowrie for more than seven years but ran away in 1851 and again early in 1852 because the overseer thought he was malingering. Posh claimed to suffer from involuntary urination "brought on by straining when he was Trunk Minder." Overseer Skinner disbelieved this story and ordered Posh back to work at what Skinner considered a suitably light job. Posh, cross, fled that night. A white man demanded his pass, then jailed him, and Manigault sold him in South Carolina. Jane, deported to Gowrie in 1849, was a persistent nonconformist, also accused of malingering, who finally fled in 1854; Louis Manigault jailed her, then sold her to New Orleans.[72]

Four Cooper River slaves bought in 1849 fled Gowrie within a few years of their purchase. Twenty-five-year-old Cicero ran in December 1851 and managed to survive in the swamp for nearly three months before voluntarily returning. His sister, eighteen, and a fifteen-year-old girl apparently joined him in his hideout for a short time before they were taken. (All three of these thwarted young dissidents perished at Gowrie before 1856.) Meanwhile, the fifteen-year-old's uncle, Prince, had fallen into the habit of "leaving Plantation without any cause," and for this offense he was sold.[73]

To repair the ravages of Gowrie's plagues, Charles Manigault purchased in 1853 what proved an unusually recalcitrant group of nineteen slaves. Their intractability was almost surely occasioned by the stringency of the overseer, Stephen Clark, who held sway at Gowrie from the beginning of 1853 until his death in December 1855. The discontent of three of the unmarried men was aggravated by their having been torn away from their natal families in South Carolina.[74] Although Joe soon espoused the miller Cato's widow, Catherine, and Frederick quickly married a woman who had just been sold away from the father of her infant, these new connections did not attach Joe and Frederick to Gowrie. As has been stated, Joe managed in July 1853 to escape across the river but died in consequence of his flight.

Later that year Frederick joined William, Prince, and some other Gowrie slaves in nocturnal disorders maddening to the local overseers. Possibly Frederick and William were not fugitives in the conventional sense; for although they left the plantation frequently at night, probably they often returned to work the next day. This cut no ice with the overseer at "Ricedale," the northernmost plantation on Argyle Island. Your slaves "are a great trouble to others," he wrote angrily to Stephen Clark,

> breaking open my yard gate, tearing and littering my Land, running and whis[p]ering around my House and preventing rest, breaking into the cow lot and turning out the cattle. Two nights they have slept in my Land and one in the cow lot, within a few days. I cannot tell how many times they have slept in my Land in the past few weeks.

Stephen Clark and Louis Manigault may also have been made the butt of these nighttime sorties, and Louis felt strong measures were required. On December 7 he shipped Prince to Charleston for sale, but this did not pacify the others; on the contrary, the rowdiness of Gowrie's slaves reached a climax during the next few days. Louis now dispatched Frederick to the Savannah jail for a stiff dose of discipline, and then sent him to Charleston for sale (thus permanently separating him from his wife, who was pregnant); and Manigault shipped William to Charleston on January 6 to complete the parcel of three "prime hands" being readied for the auction block.[75]

Dissidence was not a male preserve; and although young unattached women were the most likely females to run, they were not the only ones of their gender to flee the plantation's rigors. In 1853 Joe's sister Judy arrived at Gowrie, at the age of twenty-six, with a husband and three children. The two younger children died within a year, and her husband perished in the 1854 "cholera." During the next frantic harvest season Judy fled, leaving behind a fourteen-year-old daughter. Overseer Clark supposed she had gone to get a rest from the harvest labor. A few weeks later she was joined in the swamp by the forty-year-old Julia, who had lived at Gowrie for twenty-two years, who had already seen two husbands and at least two children to the grave, and who left behind the husband—a man much younger than herself—whom she had recently married. Judy probably stayed in the swamp for more than two months. When she and Julia returned, Louis Manigault "fixed" them with "a full allowance of all Jail discipline."[76]

Of Gowrie's thirty-five fugitives whose gender is known, ten were women: 29 percent of the total.[77] Judy was the only woman with a living child—and Judy's was nearly old enough to fend for herself. Julia was one of the only two of these ten women who was married to a Gowrie slave at the moment she fled to the swamps.[78] Obviously the reluctance of mothers to leave behind young children largely explains why the proportion of females among the fugitives was not even higher than 29 percent. And perhaps marriage attached women to the plantation more than was true for men. The striking fact, however, is that many slave women were not genteel, timid females terrified of the lonely, dangerous life of an outlaw. On the contrary, the harsh conditions of slavery bred into them a willingness to pit their resources against those of the swamp and of their masters.

Anthony, the husband of one of the Hunt daughters, was—like Joe in

1853—a dissident who succumbed to the perils of flight. Within months of his family's arrival at Gowrie his wife had perished in the "cholera" of 1854, while his infant child died during the same year; it was probably after these deaths that Anthony fled the doom-laden plantation. He was the fugitive who "died from it . . . in Charleston." The deaths of two fugitives—Joe in 1853 and Anthony a year later—show how dangerous flight might be: discontent at Gowrie was surely profound, when slaves continued to flee year after year despite such perils.[79]

Even under the relatively lax rule of overseers Venters and Bryan, at least two slaves fled. These were Celim, another dissentient member of the 1853 gang, who went to the swamp for a time in 1856, and the youth Fortune, who ran away in both 1857 and 1858.

More insubordination occurred under William Capers's overseership (which began in April 1859) than even under Stephen Clark's, and the practice of fleeing extended from newcomers to a substantial number of slaves long resident at Gowrie. An early dissident was young Fortune, who fled again twice during Capers's first year and was sold to New Orleans in May 1860.[80] The next month a serious incident transpired—probably related to Fortune's sale, and involving several members of Fortune's wider family.

One of the protagonists was London, a young man of Fortune's age who for eight years had enjoyed positions of privilege at Gowrie. Son of Stephen the miller (and named after Stephen's brother, who had preceded Stephen as miller), London had been selected at the age of fourteen—in 1852—to be Louis Manigault's houseboy. The young planter took pride in fitting up London to play the part: "I have My Boy London dressed in Blue with a white shirt. I make him wait on table, sweep out the rooms &c. He also sleeps in the House. I think in the Course of time I shall hardly need Jane in the House, only to make up beds &c." Louis sometimes took London to Charleston to serve him as houseboy during his long "summer" residence there, and the young slave remained continuously as the houseboy at Gowrie until 1860.[81]

London's job threw him into the company of Fortune and of Fortune's stepcousins. Before Capers's arrival in 1859, Fortune did the same houseboy's job for the overseer at East Hermitage which London did for Louis at Gowrie; and most of the other Gowrie house servants were related to Fortune.[82] These close associations make it probable that London felt strongly when Fortune was sold at Savannah in the spring of 1860. London also had a grievance of his own, for he was banned from Charleston during the summer of 1860 (Charles Manigault having permitted Louis to bring only Dolly). Capers had no doubt demoted the privileged houseboy to field labor during Louis Manigault's long absence from the plantation.

A second protagonist was cooper George, who had become Gowrie's head driver after driver Robert's sudden death in 1857. Both George and his "second driver" Ralph (supervisor of the Hermitage tract) had been raised at Silk Hope—George not having been sent to Gowrie until he was fifteen, and Ralph not until eighteen—and there may have been tension between them and slaves like Fortune and London, whose families had been at Gowrie since before 1833.[83]

The third protagonist was the new overseer William Capers. There had probably been friction between the drivers and one of Capers's predecessors, and such rivalry was certainly exacerbated with Capers's arrival. Thus Leonard Venters had allegedly sided with the ordinary slaves against the drivers, and this had led to Venters's being sacked as overseer in December 1857. (Drivers George and Ralph also held their posts longer than did Venters's successor, William Bryan, whom the Manigaults impatiently dismissed in 1858 for absenting himself too long from the plantation, leaving the two drivers in charge.)[84] But when Charles Manigault finally hired his own second cousin, the genteel William Capers, to take over as Gowrie's overseer in April 1859, the drivers were unlikely to continue to have things their own way. Capers, aged forty-four, had long experience as an overseer, having most recently managed for two years the large rice plantation of South Carolina's former governor, William Aiken. The new overseer was embroiled in a lawsuit when Manigault hired him: he "has numerous enemies but even by these he is recognized as a Competent Manager of a Rice Crop, & a Capable & intelligent Man."[85] Capers soon added driver George to the list of his enemies.

Charles Manigault paid Capers more than three times as large a wage as the inexperienced Venters (the twenty-four-year-old Venters having received three hundred dollars a year, and Capers one thousand dollars: "the highest Salary we have yet paid"); but Capers raised rather less rice in 1859 and 1860 than Venters had achieved in 1856 and 1857.[86] "Bad management & most miserable overseer in every respect," Louis Manigault had fumed of Venters, but Louis accepted with little hesitation the excuses which Capers—who "belonged to the best blood of Carolina"—was quick to offer for his own failures.[87] Capers claimed that the poor condition in which he found Gowrie in 1859—some fields were overrun with "volunteer" rice—accounted for the poor crop that year; and he attributed the disappointments of 1860 to a bad localized hailstorm in July (whose depredations neither of the Manigaults was present to witness for himself, and which did not hurt the adjacent rice plantations). In truth Capers's troubles about managing the slaves surely contributed substantially to his relatively poor production record; yet Louis Manigault never lost faith in Capers's self-fulfilling maxims about the character defects of "the Negro." (Charles Manigault, however, came to believe Capers a chronic purveyor of falsehoods.)[88]

Capers spent the night of Sunday, June 10, 1860, at the pineland camp and did not reach Gowrie until late the next morning. Upon his arrival he found that the twenty-two-year-old London was dead, his body floating in the river. Capers ordered that "no one is to touch the corpse and [it] will remain if not taken off by the next tide. This I have done to let the negroes see when a negro takes his own life they will be treated in this manner." Capers immediately seized the opportunity to recommend that driver George be dismissed and sold: he "is a bad negro, he would command a good price in Savannah where he can be sold in a quiet manner."

A "bad Negro" could be a synonym for a "determined Negro": "Jack Savage is a bad Negro," Louis Manigault wrote to his father seventeen months later, "and would do almost any thing. Big George [the driver in 1860] is also a very determined Negro, much of the Character of Robert [the driver until his death in 1857]."[89] The problem was that in the low country—where rice planters fled the malarial swamps for months at a time[90] and overseers were thinly scattered among the slaves—heavy responsibilities had to be delegated to the drivers. A driver must be a sturdy leader, and such a man was likely to be high-spirited. A spineless slave would not make a good driver; the planters therefore were pushed toward experimenting with men of independent spirit—"determined" men like Robert, whom Manigault had dismissed from a house servant's job in South Carolina and exiled as a field hand in Gowrie's swamps for four years before establishing him as the driver.

A determined man such as driver George, with a mind of his own, might be halfhearted in enforcing the edicts of a martinet like Capers. George evidently disagreed with the second driver, Ralph, about how far they should cooperate with the overseer. And yet London, at the moment he killed himself, was probably enraged with both Ralph and George for playing ball with Capers as far as they did. "Divide and conquer" being Manigault's practice, floggings were normally administered by the drivers. Hatred was to be directed by the tortured black victim of the whip against his black tormenter, wherever possible, rather than against the white overseer.

Capers was himself a determined man—he was set to get George's scalp—and no doubt he adjusted his picture of London's death to place George in the most compromising position. Capers's first word after mentioning London's death—the cause of that event, he implied—was "George":

> George brought London & Nat [a young field hand, and probably a good friend of London's] to Ralph, saying they deserved punishment, they were taken to the Barn, when Ralph went for the key to put them in George allowed London to leave him, and when spoken to by Ralph about not making an exertion to stop London his answer was he would not dust his feet to stop him. London . . . took the River at the mouth of the canal, in the presents of some of Mr. Barclay's negroes [slaves on the plantation on the northern side of the canal, adjacent to Gowrie] and Ralph, who told him to return, George should not whip him until my return, his ans[wer] was he would drown himself before he would and he sank soon after. . . . My advice to you about George is to ship him, he is of no use to you as a driver and is a bad negro.[91]

George was thus, in Capers's book, quadruply responsible: his threat of a whipping goaded London into a temper, yet his slackness about controlling London, his unslavish sense of superiority ("he would not dust his feet"), and his lack of solidarity with Ralph permitted London to perform a public act of defiance. Manigault was robbed of a valuable asset, and an intolerable example of insubordination had been witnessed by the local "negroes."

George's motives are hard to deduce. Probably he was fed up with Capers's new regime and lacked conviction in enforcing the new plantation discipline. No doubt London and Nat—for the reasons previously suggested—had committed some infraction of Capers's rules which George reluctantly felt could not be overlooked. George and Ralph seem to have tried to pass the buck about who would do the dirty work of inflicting the whipping. George, as head driver (with the same authority over Ralph which Robert, as "first" driver, had earlier exercised over Ralph as "second" driver), may have told Ralph to whip London and Nat; Ralph, one conjectures, may have told George to do it himself, if he thought it worth making a fuss over a minor infraction; George may have thought that, if Ralph would not do as George ordered, why should George cooperate with Ralph? No doubt both drivers regretted the good old days under Venters and Bryan, when the drivers could get on with plantation affairs at their own pace, without constant efforts by the tiresome Capers to tighten up discipline and tell the drivers how to run the show.

Years earlier, when new and relatively inexperienced overseers had come to Gowrie, Charles Manigault had warned them not to interfere much with the way the leading slaves conducted matters. Even in 1856, after Louis had been managing Gowrie for four years, Charles Manigault had still urged him to depend heavily on the advice of driver Robert: "You cant go wrong with Roberts experience, if you only keep him up to all he knows by talking to him." Two months later, when the Hermitage boiler and its brick surrounds were about to be rebuilt, Charles thought that driver Robert and carpenter Jack Savage would be at least as much use as overseer Venters in ensuring that the itinerant boilermakers and bricklayer would do the job properly. And as recently as March 1859 (before they had any idea they would be able to hire William Capers), Charles and Louis Manigault were both of the opinion that their new overseer—who was likely to be some young man—"must submit to the advice of those on the Place who know all about it" (e.g., driver George, carpenter Jack Savage, and trunk minder Charles).[92] But there was no chance that the forty-four-year-old, experienced, and opinionated William Capers would submit to George's advice. George might well be exasperated with Capers, and halfhearted in enforcing his edicts.

The results were tragedy for London and for his mother, Binah Currie, who thus experienced the death of the last one of her eight children. And Capers now had a splendid opportunity to rid himself of his awkward subaltern. After London's suicide Charles Manigault quickly traveled by steamboat to Savannah, whither he summoned Capers for consultation. (Manigault would not venture to Gowrie itself during the malarial season.) The proprietor then returned to Charleston, Capers went back to Gowrie, and George was dispatched for a spell in the Savannah jail. Capers advised that a high enough price for George was not, after all, available in Savannah—the slave trader Joseph Bryan perhaps having learned that a recalcitrant slave was on offer—and George was sent to the Charleston workhouse until he could be sold.

Things were going nicely for Capers: he wrote sanguinely to Manigault in July that "George should command $1,500 at any market. Would advise you not to take less." But when George finally had the opportunity in Charleston to tell the master his side of the story, he persuaded Manigault not to sell him. Probably George blamed Ralph, for a little later Ralph was sacked as the Hermitage driver. George nevertheless bore, in his master's eyes, a share of the responsibility. He must be humbled. George's quick talk had forestalled his sale, but he could no longer be driver; instead of returning him to his cooper's trade, Manigault reduced him to field labor.

George did not easily bend. "He was not respectfull," Capers complained a few days later, "when I met him at Savannah River." Furthermore, George seized at once the driver's prerogative in a symbolic act of defiance. "The morning after his arrival," the thwarted overseer grieved, George "Rang the Bell in answer to Ralphs Hour, when during his absence I made Charles (Trunk M[in]d[er]) Ring in answer to the Hour." George "must know his place [in the field]," Capers insisted. "George is a negro you will yet have trouble with."[93]

This prophecy was quickly fulfilled, but first a new driver must be found. Capers recommended the forty-four-year-old South Carolina slave John, who had seventeen years of experience as a driver, and who several years previously had filled that post under Capers on a Santee River plantation. Unlike George, John had the virtues—in Capers's view—of "strictly obeying orders and [being] attentive to his business." John had a deceptively slow appearance: "In speaking with John he does not answer like a smart negro but he is quite so." Since Capers had left the Santee River, John had acquired the reputation of a drunkard; and he appears to have tried to put off Manigault by claiming that he was ruptured. Capers was sure he could wean John from the bottle. Manigault bought John alone, separating him from any family or relations he may have had in South Carolina, and dispatched him to Gowrie minus his watch and some of his clothes (which the master held for a time in Charleston as hostages to John's good behavior). John proved the very man Capers was seeking, and after one and a half years Manigault sent along his watch and clothes; probably he also then rewarded John with boots, a coat, and a hat, as Louis recommended.[94] Most slaves at Gowrie, however, do not appear to have greeted John's arrival with equal enthusiasm.

That summer Capers "had much trouble with the Negroes . . . and several Runaways." The first of these fugitives was Daniel, who was so old that Manigault had paid nothing for him when he came as part of a parcel of twenty-one slaves purchased in 1857. Daniel had been assigned to live the whole year away from Gowrie, as guardian of Manigault's newly acquired pineland camp. He raised vegetables, flowers, and ducks; and his wife Miley, a field hand more than thirty years younger than he, was authorized to visit him on Sundays—a different version of the "abroad" marriage. Within a year of Capers's arrival the overseer was already at loggerheads with Daniel, who did not supply ducks for Capers to send to the Manigaults in Charleston as Capers requested. In August Daniel deliberately broke up Capers's buggy by "quietly turn[ing] the Mule loose," and he then fled for several weeks to postpone the consequences.

The rot spread to slaves who, unlike Daniel, had lived at Gowrie for many years. Louis Manigault's favorite slave, captain Hector (the chief boathand), got into trouble with Capers—so the overseer informed Louis—for "injureing one of your Plants in the Flour Garden, Drunkeness, & disobeying orders." The morning after Daniel had fled, Hector also departed. "Have no doubt he has gone to Savannah where he will soon be caught," Capers opined. In fact Hector returned the next night after only a thirty-six-hour absence; but disaffection in a slave so much "indulged" (Louis Manigault's word) by the master was a harbinger of further trouble. At least one other slave ran away that summer. And a symptom of discontent was that Capers—who in 1859 evidently had bought chickens on credit from the Gowrie slaves for his own family's consumption—was unable to obtain any the next year. Manigault always withheld his overseer's salary until the end of the year to ensure satisfactory performance of duty until the end of the annual term, and Capers was short of cash. Gowrie's slaves (surprisingly) ran short of fowl, and the slaves on neighboring plantations were uncooperative. "Your Negroes have no Chickens," the overseer grumbled, "& those around us will only sell for cash & I am entirely out of money."[95]

Three weeks later, Little George Hunt and "Big Hector" (not to be confused with captain Hector) fled to the swamp; they disappeared for three months. Capers knew flight was often provoked by a whipping or the threat of one, but these two slaves, he protested, had left "without one word being said to them." Eighteen-year-old Little George was the youngest son of the trunk minder George Hunt, whose "truly fine family" Manigault had bought in 1854. Little George had been singled out at the age of thirteen for training as a carpenter; but from the Manigaults' point of view this proved questionable policy, for it brought Little George under the subversive influence of the skilled carpenter Jack Savage. Little George had seen eight of the other twelve members of his family die within about a year of their arrival at Gowrie; two more had been sent back to South Carolina after the 1854 "cholera." The only members of his family still at Gowrie, therefore, were his "fine looking" elder sister Nancy (who had barely survived her case of "cholera" in 1854) and his elder brother Abel (who had temporarily gone out of his mind during that epidemic).[96] In October 1860 Little George may have been cross with his sister Nancy, for at about this time she married the unpopular new driver John.[97]

Little George's companion in flight was the thirty-two-year-old Big Hector, a Silk Hope slave deported to Gowrie in 1852 with his wife, Dolly. Hector had managed to survive a bad case of "cholera" that year, but his marriage did not long continue. Earlier in 1852 Dolly, as previously mentioned, had been sent back to Silk Hope with strange fevers; when she finally returned, Louis Manigault made her his cook and washerwoman, and took her away to Charleston for the whole long summer. By 1854 Hector had left Dolly and was married to the widow of a "cholera" victim, but she soon died. He then married the widow of yet another of the 1852 "cholera" victims, and this marriage endured at least eleven years.

Big Hector appears to have been another "determined" slave—like driver Robert and driver George—with a hot-tempered independence of spirit. Louis Manigault's opinion of him fluctuated according to whether or not Hector was accommodating to the plantation regime. Louis had already known Big Hector when they were at Silk Hope, the two men having been born in the same year. In November 1852, when Louis arrived from South Carolina at the stricken "cholera" camp, he mentioned foremost Hector among those whom he had attended. Bringing Hector news of his wife, Dolly—who was still recuperating at Silk Hope—Louis relished the role of benefactor to the husband of a young woman whom he would soon make his own house servant. Hector "is still very sick . . . ," Louis wrote to his father. "I sat by him a good while today [in his hut] & told him how finely his wife was getting on &c. &c. & all about Silk Hope &c. He seemed to Cheer up a little." Fifteen years later, in 1867, when slavery was dead, Hector's leadership was acknowledged, and he—along with three former drivers (John, cooper George, and Charles the trunk minder)—was made one of the five foremen of the free-labor plantation. He was, Louis wrote in 1867, "a fine Man." Yet in 1861 Louis had regarded him as a "bad Negro" and had advised his father to "put Big Hector . . . in the dark-hole [of the Charleston workhouse] for a month." He thought Hector had a "bad influence" on other slaves.[98]

Big Hector was no doubt the leading spirit when he and the much younger Little George set off for the swamp on October 26, 1860. They hid not far from Gowrie. A week after their departure Capers reported that "Hector has been on the Plantation since he left and says he will not be taken." Capers claimed to believe a story which slaves sympathetic to Hector may have fed the overseer in order to intimidate him—Capers professing himself fearless: Hector "had a p[ai]r of Pistols & Sword. His being armed I care not for if I can only put my Eyes on him." But as Charles Manigault later came to believe Capers a habitual liar, there is no real evidence that Capers actually believed Hector to be armed, and even less evidence that Hector really did possess a weapon. Capers wanted to give the contest between himself and Big Hector more the character of a public joust than it already had, and to put pressure on Gowrie's slaves to side with him. "Would it not be a good plan," he suggested, "[to] send no small Rice to the Plantation until he is taken?" A week later Capers fulminated (of Hector and Little George), "All that I wish is to get my hands on them."[99]

Big Hector and Little George eluded Capers's grasp for weeks. Meanwhile, three other slaves ran away, joining one by one those already in the swamp. The thirty-one-year-old field hand Will, a relative newcomer to Gowrie, left in December; this was his second flight within the year. Charles Manigault had separated Will from his mother when buying him in Charleston in 1857. Within a few weeks of coming to Gowrie Will had married Rhina, but after her death from pneumonia in 1859 Will had no remaining family tie there. The next slave to flee—on January 2, 1861—was Simon, Louis's twenty-four-year-old cook. He was quick-minded and more knowledgeable than most of the bondsmen and women. Louis regarded him as somewhat untrustworthy without being "bad"—a "Great Rascal," Louis later wrote, with amusement rather than hostility. Simon, married to Fortune's stepcousin, "lived [according to Louis] rather freely." He was "smart," and reliable enough that Louis thought he could be trusted to work at Gowrie early in 1862, even though Northern military forces lurked not far away; yet he was not sufficiently reliable to travel alone from South Carolina to Gowrie: "A fellow, of his Cunning & knowledge, going alone," Charles Manigault then apprehended, "might dodge off & no one know his whereabouts."[100]

Simon's whereabouts in the swamp in January 1861 had remained unknown to the Manigaults for more than three weeks, yet some of their slaves knew it; and another of them—Jimmy, the fireman at the steam thresher—joined the four other fugitives on January 11. Jimmy, purchased at twenty-three in 1849 along with his wife, Dinah, had at first been entrusted with running the steam thresher, but by 1852 Louis deemed him undependable: "He has a way every now and then of going to sleep, even while the engine is going."[101] He was therefore demoted to the position of fireman, John Izard supplanting him as engineer. Dinah had died from pneumonia in January 1857, and about three months later Jimmy had married Tilla (fifteen years his junior). Unlike the other fugitives in 1861, Jimmy remained only a week in the swamp, returning voluntarily to Gowrie on January 18. No doubt he vividly remembered Dinah's vainly struggling to catch her breath four Januarys earlier, and he may have decided not to take further risk of contracting pneumonia himself by remaining in the swamp during that wintry month. Louis rewarded his quick return by not having him whipped, but Louis never fully trusted Jimmy again.

By this time Big Hector and Little George had been gone nearly three months, and the Manigaults began to lose their cool. Slaves from other Savannah River plantations appear to have run away too, while "many Negroes" were out on South Carolina's Cooper River; there were also, Charles Manigault believed, unusual numbers of fugitives elsewhere in the South. This wave of insubordination he attributed to Abraham Lincoln's election: the slaves, he claimed, "have very generally got the idea of being emancipated when 'Lincoln' comes in."[102] He endorsed rigorous suppression: "To hunt with Dogs seems to be the plan in all directions now & with Loaded guns also." He warned Louis of the fugitives' network of support, extending to the house slaves. "No overseer, or Planter should speak on such subjects even before a small house boy, or girl, as they communicate all that they hear to others, who convey it to the spies of the runaways, who are still at home." A slave-chasing expedition must be sprung upon the runaways without warning: "If any preparation for hunting them be made the day before, they will be informed that night." Charles's son Dr. Gabriel Manigault had recently been out hunting fugitives on the Cooper River, and he counseled Louis (as previously quoted) to use shotguns and dogs. This advice was effective, for the idea of being chewed and mangled by dogs—added to the normal dangers of the swamp, and the hazards of frost and disease in January—impelled Gowrie's four remaining fugitives to return to the plantation on January 25. Louis did not "let [them] off," as he had done to Jimmy.[103]

The last slave to flee from the Manigaults before November 1861—when Northern military forces altered the balance of power between master and subordinate—was the twenty-two-year-old Martha, "a fine Mulatto Woman" whom Charles gave Louis in 1859 to care for Louis's first baby. Louis had been delighted with her and wanted to keep her as a nurse for his future children. In addition to her child-care abilities, Martha "washes and sews beautifully," and was a good pastry cook. More important, she was properly deferential, which Louis associated with her being a relatively dark-skinned mulatto: "She is darker than Dolly and a perfect Negro [i.e., a perfect slave] in manners," he enthused. What was more, she interested Louis because she was a woman of some mental ability: she had "more ideas" than the usual submissive house servant.[104]

A problem arose over where Martha was to stay during the long summer of 1860, when Louis planned to bring his family to live with his father at 6 Gibbes Street, Charleston. Set against Martha's excellent qualities was, to Charles Manigault's ear, one drawback: she was an incessant talker. Her "eternal & untireing tongue" had recently led the Charleston lady, from whom Charles had bought Martha, to have her "well flogged" at the work-house. Charles kept this whipping secret for a time from Louis, and he told Martha he would do so. Charles later denied that Martha's having required a flogging diminished her real value: "Her good qualities render that a trifle."[105] But he knew Louis might look a gift horse in the mouth, and undervalue a slave nurse who had recently needed "discipline." Charles also felt that, by promising Martha to keep the matter a secret, he could make her feel she had a good reputation to live up to.

Evidently both genteel masters and privileged Charleston house slaves felt that if such a slave had a decent master, the slave might hope by exemplary conduct to escape flogging; and if the slave forfeited by misconduct her exemption from whipping, she diminished her own market value and claim to special favor. Charles, believing genteel Charlestonian masters too squeamish about administering an occasional whipping to their house slaves, drew once again a misleading parallel to the disciplining of schoolchildren (he denied that the different severity of a house slave's whipping from that of a schoolchild rendered the two transactions different in kind). When Charles finally disclosed Martha's flogging to Louis, he testily defended his earlier secrecy. He accounted for his not having told Louis sooner by declaring that, years earlier, he had not felt obliged "to disclose . . . to anyone when you used to get so flogged by Mr. Cotes [the master of Charleston's poshest boys' school] as to leave the black & white marks on your arms & back for some time afterwards. Nor did I disclose that I had [my Charleston house slaves] flogged at the workhouse."[106]

Splendid, therefore, though Martha might be in every other respect, Charles Manigault could not tolerate having her tongue in his own house when Louis came for his annual six-month sojourn in 1860. Her loquacity was sure to upset the smooth functioning of Charles's household, where his own "very quiet & orderly crowd of servants" were, he thought, admirably disciplined. But it would not do, either, to lend Martha for the summer to the Habershams—Mrs. Louis Manigault's mercantile and medical family in Savannah—for "they spoil their servants so, & have not time to supervise their movements." Louis rejected his father's suggestion that Martha be left at Gowrie to serve the overseer's wife: Louis insisted upon keeping her in contact with people of their own class, so that her manners would not deteriorate. But neither would he ever "for a moment allow her to remain at all in Savannah" during the summer, for she wouldn't be properly watched there: city life would undermine the strict discipline to which he subjected her.[107] He discovered instead the happy—for himself, if not for Martha—solution of placing her that summer ten miles from Savannah with his wife's uncle, a naval captain, who was no doubt a proper disciplinarian.

Martha did indeed have more ideas than a stereotypical submissive house servant. These thoughts disturbed her sleep, and when she first rejoined Louis's wife for a brief stay at Savannah in November 1860, she—although very useful to her mistress—upset her. "Both nights," Fanny Manigault wrote anxiously, "Martha has had night-mear [nightmares], I do not know how to spell it; but it is very disagreeable indeed and she frightens me very much. It is so strange."[108] Six months later, when it was time for Louis and Fanny to leave Gowrie for the summer, they expectantly set off for Charleston, taking Martha with them this time: for they finally felt financially able to live in a summer house of their own in Charleston—just across the street from Charles Manigault—and Martha therefore came with them.

Martha, exiled from Charleston for eighteen months, was at least as eager to return to the city as Louis was to set himself up in his new "charming residence," but she was less happy with the thought of returning to Gowrie the next winter. Louis's family and house slaves had scarcely arrived at Charleston when Martha fled. She evaded capture for four months; she was then caught and sold.[109]

This record of at least twenty-four[110] fugitives within a decade demonstrates very substantial discontent at Gowrie; yet there is no indication in the Manigault records that they ever advertised in the newspapers for any of these absentees.[111] Knowing that a fugitive from Gowrie had almost no chance of escaping to permanent freedom—the free states were too far away—the masters normally relied on two powerful instruments for securing the escapees' return: the intense danger in the swamp (snakes, frost, famine, disease) and the surveillance exercised by every white person in the South over every black stranger (e.g., Mr. Zipro's accosting Posh in 1852 and jailing him until claimed). Apparently only once, in January 1861, did the perennial fugitive problem impel the Manigaults to hire dogs; and fear of those dogs quickly brought in the five absentees. If (as seems probable) the Manigaults seldom or never advertised in a newspaper for their fugitives, advertisements are a poor measure of discontent. The swamp would eventually drive most fugitives home again, or local whites would apprehend them: why should a genteel master waste money, and incur embarrassment, by newspaper advertisement?

Inefficient work and flight into the swamps were much the most common ways of expressing discontent at Gowrie, but there was also a significant tradition of collective nonviolent dissidence. Slave women were heavily involved in this form of insubordination—just as Binkey and her children (but not her husband, Jupiter) protested collectively against their deportation to Gowrie in 1854.

In the mid-1830s Charles Manigault was even less successful than in the 1850s in securing a regular overseer. Each year from 1833 to 1835 he had to hire a new one, and in 1836 there were two. The first of these 1836 overseers was a Mr. Gibbons. Although Manigault then did most of his buying and selling through a merchant in Charleston, he relied on a businessman in Savannah (almost within hail of Gowrie) to perform one crucial service. When Manigault was absent each summer, he needed a reliable local agent to whom he could depute ultimate authority over the overseer; the factors Habersham and Son performed this function in Savannah. In the summer of 1836 the overseer gave the Gowrie slaves "a Real Cause of complaint" (Manigault's words), and in consequence "almost every grown Negro (male & female, principally the latter) pushed off in a body & went to Savannah with serious Charges against . . . Gibbons, who was then overseer at Gowrie while I was in Europe." The slaves probably seized a plantation flatboat at night, evaded challenge from land-bound white planters and itinerants by floating and poling the eight miles downstream to Savannah, and put in their appearance at Habersham's office the next morning before the overseer could stop them. They persuaded Habersham of the justice of their charges: perhaps Gibbons had inflicted unfair, indiscriminate, unusually severe whippings, and probably he had indulged in more-than-ordinary sexual abuse of the women. Habersham sacked the overseer and engaged instead for Gowrie the part-time services of A. R. Bagshaw, who was also overseer for a neighbor of Manigault's. (Bagshaw continued to be Manigault's part-time overseer for seven of the next eight years).[112]

Far from objecting to this nonviolent protest, Manigault—at least in retrospect—seems wholly to have approved it. Like the British Foreign Minister Lord Castlereagh, trying after Napoleon's downfall to arrange a "balance of power" across the English Channel to serve British interests, so Manigault at a distance from Gowrie sought to balance the power of overseers with that of his Savannah agent and with those of the drivers and of the rest of the slaves themselves, in order to secure his own ends. Like Castlereagh, Manigault fully trusted none of the powers whom he tried to set off against one another. Habitually, and with reason, he distrusted his overseers; and eleven years after this nonviolent resistance had led to Gibbons's dismissal, Manigault deliberately invoked the chance of his slaves' again protesting to

Habersham as a means of controlling another overseer. But Manigault certainly did not trust his slaves either, and in 1847 he coupled his veiled threat to the overseer with ruthless instructions about how that same overseer should deal with any truly "bad disposed nigger."[113]

By now Bagshaw had quit Manigault's service and James Haynes had succeeded to his position.[114] Manigault's policy at this time (before he bought the East Hermitage tract from Henry McAlpin) was to depend during most of the year on a part-time overseer—first Bagshaw, later Haynes, finally Jesse Cooper— who did not reside at Gowrie. The overseer normally (Manigault explained) "walk[ed] through [Gowrie] once a day" but otherwise left Gowrie's slaves under the direction of their black driver. Then at harvesttime the proprietor would hire for a few months, on the cheap, a young suboverseer who would reside at Gowrie and work under the direction of the more experienced chief overseer. In December 1846 Manigault's overseer, James Haynes, lived at the adjacent plantation of Manigault's cousin, Anthony Barclay, overseeing Barclay's slaves and visiting Gowrie daily.

During the Christmas holidays (the slaves' only real break all year: just three working days at Gowrie and on many other rice plantations), exuberant celebration was the norm. The escaped Maryland slave Frederick Douglass believed masters encouraged the bondsmen and women to have a drunken Christmas binge, in hopes that the slaves' hangovers, and their disgust with the consequences of their saturnalia, would reconcile them to another year of bondage. During the Christmas holiday of 1846, trouble brewed at Barclay's plantation, caused (Haynes claimed) by the slaves being "as usual ever ripe for a 'blow out.' " They tended in any case to leave Barclay's plantation for unauthorized trips, and this tendency no doubt found exaggerated expression during the Yuletide. Haynes and the black driver disagreed about how to keep things from getting out of hand; the driver, Haynes claimed, used "insolent language" to him; and Haynes (he himself admitted) struck the driver.[115]

Barclay was nowhere near, but Mrs. Barclay resided at "Rockingham," on the nearby Ogeechee River. In the early hours of New Year's Day a group of thirteen Barclay slaves (doubtless recalling the successful nonviolent dissidence at Gowrie a decade earlier) slipped off from Barclay's plantation and made their way to Mrs. Barclay. "To those who ran off," Haynes alleged, "there was not a word spoken"—they were simply demonstrating solidarity with their driver. They persuaded Mrs. Barclay that Haynes had excessively and unfairly abused the driver. Just as a nonviolent protest had convinced Habersham in 1836, so this nonviolent protest in 1847 convinced Mrs. Barclay: she dismissed Haynes out of hand. Haynes, of course, was outraged—it would not have happened, he blustered, if Mr. Barclay had been there to control his wife. Haynes's words may carry little conviction; but his diction, his syntax, and even his alliteration show that not all overseers were destitute of education: Haynes obviously had missed a career as a political journalist. "The charge made against me," he expostulated to Manigault, "is utterly without foundation, a fabrication of falsehoods hatched by the negroes and told to Mrs. Barclay who believed every word as truth, & without a propper investigation, or any question whatever being asked me, unhesitatingly discharged me." Though Haynes might fulminate, the slaves' successful protest meant that he must hurriedly pack his bags to leave Barclay's place; and for lack of anywhere better to go, he and his family moved with their effects into the empty overseer's house at Gowrie. Haynes anxiously hoped Manigault (then in Paris) would not object.[116]

When Habersham sent his version of events to Paris, Manigault gave warning to both Haynes and Barclay. He did not wish to see at Gowrie a recurrence of the events at Barclay's plantation. Habersham, Manigault threatened Haynes, "has full powers over all my Concerns on Savannah River, even to changing an Overseer." Although Haynes had written in December that Gowrie's slaves "have behaved very well up to this time," Manigault distrusted them. "I am glad to think that my people Continue orderly & industrious," he wrote skeptically, "but they are up to the same thing which has occurred recently with you at Mr. Barclay's." Manigault then told Haynes how Gowrie's slaves had in 1836 gone to Habersham with "serious Charges" against the then overseer, whom Habersham as a result had sacked. No matter how much Manigault couched his threat in terms disrespectful toward the slaves—and interspersed them with stern words about curbing some slaves' disorderliness—he certainly was using the menace of the slaves' collective nonviolent protest as a means of curbing the overseer.[117]

To his cousin Barclay, Manigault addressed a different admonition. More sternness toward slaves, he thought, was required on Barclay's part. No doubt Haynes's conduct toward Barclay's slaves was "quite sufficient for a discharge," Manigault mollified Barclay; but Barclay himself was partly to blame for allowing the situation to arise where his slaves had provoked the overseer: "I believe your gang has some in it fond of absenting themselves, & [Haynes] accuses them also of insolence to himself." If Barclay had followed Manigault's rigorous practice, the slaves' fondness for wandering would have been controlled, and trouble avoided. "I always made it a rule to sell every runaway—," Manigault boasted with some exaggeration, "and they are fully aware of this."[118] The good order at Gowrie on which Manigault prided himself in 1847 was the product, he believed, of his firmness toward both slaves and overseers, balancing each against the other.

Although these utterances reek of self-congratulation and not a little self-delusion, Manigault had certain grounds for satisfaction. "Resistance" in the nineteenth-century South signified something very different from what a later century means by that word.[119] "Resistance" then denoted overt physical resistance; thus when, in January 1861, Dr. Gabriel Manigault instructed his brother Louis about hunting fugitives with a loaded double-barreled shotgun, he declared it was essential to go "with the intention of shooting . . . any negro who attempts to resist. . . ."[120] In this sense of "resist," Charles Manigault was almost wholly successful in eliminating resistance from Gowrie. The slaves expressed massive discontent—through inefficiency, sabotage of the work routine, theft, and malingering; through fleeing to the swamp; and occasionally through collective nonviolent protest—but overt physical resistance was beyond the pale. It rarely occurred, and everyone knew it would be savagely suppressed.

Occasionally overt "resistance" did, of course, take place on other rice plantations (as it did everywhere else in the South). Thus, in 1853 a drunken rice planter's unprovoked attack upon several of his slaves, only a few miles from Gowrie, led one of them to resist. Olmsted reported that at the time of his visit to Richard Arnold, a neighbor of Arnold's,

> while in a drunken frolic, not only flogged a number of his negroes, without cause, but attempted to shoot and stab them; and if he did not succeed in killing any of them outright, was only prevented from doing so by what the law would have considered—and often has considered—an act of insubordination to be justifiably punished with death.

And another Georgia rice planter acknowledged to Sidney Fisher in 1852 that "he had himself known instances of slaves being whipped to death, and of their being tied before a fire for the purposes of torture. But he added that persons guilty of such barbarities were . . . generally murdered by the slaves. . . ." Of slaves who resisted in this way he declared: "Of course, . . . we are obliged to put them to death." Draconian suppression of resistance meant that both slaves and masters knew its futility. The former bondsman Henry Bibb, for example, employed the words "resist" and "resistance" in their nineteenth-century sense: "The only weapon of self defense that I [as a slave] could use successfully," Bibb declared, "was that of deception. It is useless for a poor helpless slave, to resist a white man in a slaveholding State. Public opinion and the law is against him; and resistance in many cases is death to the slave, while the law declares, that he shall submit or die." With such an apparatus of control, there should be no surprise that masters normally enjoyed a sense of total security.[121]

Gowrie's slaves were not "cowed": most of this chapter has explored the range of their vigorously subversive activities. But there were clearly understood limits beyond which subversion was not tolerated. The overseer therefore confidently placed a shotgun in the hands of the principal bird minder every spring and autumn, to limit the depredations of the ravenous rice birds (who would devour the crop if given half a chance). What caused anxiety to the overseer—the only white man within half a mile, and surrounded by about a hundred slaves—was the rice birds, not the armed bird minder. The overseer annually dreaded a sudden freshet that might sweep away thousands of dollars' worth of rice, but seldom apprehended a sudden overflow of rebellion from the slaves. This explains the Manigaults' toleration of day-to-day dissidence, short-run absenteeism, and even collective nonviolent protest. The regime was—within well-defined limits—lax: bondsmen often roamed the country roads around Savannah at night; and the Savannah River was covered, so to speak, with slaves making boat trips, authorized and unauthorized, in every direction. In December 1861 (when wartime regulations had put an end to such traffic), Louis Manigault exulted that "none of the numerous boats are now to be seen on the River."[122] By contrast, before the war even so firm a disciplinarian as Charles Manigault had learned to live with a certain amount of short-term absenteeism, and with an occasional fugitive in the swamp. The planters' capacity to concentrate military force gave them confidence that "resistance" (in the nineteenth-century sense) was almost unthinkable; and nonviolent dissidence could, they thought, be tolerated with impunity, so clear was the line between overt "resistance" and the usual forms of dissent.

The first Northern military incursion into the low country in November 1861 seemed briefly to change all this. For, just as Manigault's control of the plantation had depended on a balance of forces between the overseer and the slaves, so the slaves' response had depended on a balance of military force between the local slaveholders and any possible outside allies of the slaves. The Spanish garrison in eighteenth-century Florida, British military power during the American Revolution and again during the War of 1812, the chance of French naval intervention in 1802:[123] these were the military forces which might alter the local balance of power; and when Northern naval vessels and soldiers appeared along the rice coast in November 1861, alarm suddenly struck the breasts of planters and overseers who had slept easily—surrounded by dissident but not overtly "resisting" slaves—for years before the war. This wartime experience hardened Charles Manigault's heart: after the South won the war, he vowed in January 1862, it must replace with "a new Code of management, of the strictest nature" the regime—"too slack entirely"—which in retrospect he felt had existed before the war.[124] The clear line between nonviolent insubordination and overt resistance threatened in the winter of 1861–62 to dissolve all too quickly: the slaves' easygoing prewar noncooperation had disclosed an alarming tendency to slide, almost overnight, into forms of dissent beyond the pale.

In August 1861 Capers paid twenty-four dollars for two bags of gun shot and twenty-five pounds of gunpowder: doubtless he was stockpiling commodities, soon likely to be in short supply, which were essential for scaring off rice birds. Some of the shot and powder soon found its way into the cabin of Ishmael, a former driver. Ishmael—"very intelligent," according to Louis Manigault (who bestowed no such encomium on any other slave)[125]—was the younger brother of the skilled carpenter, Jack Savage. Ishmael had been the Manigaults' driver on the East Hermitage tract from 1849 to 1853, and later (in 1867) he was made one of the five "foremen" of their free-labor force. Capers did not discover the shot and powder in Ishmael's cabin until November 1861.

Early that month a Northern seaborne military force occupied Port Royal, a South Carolina sea island not far north of Savannah, and the shock reverberated through the low country. Fearing a wave of disaffection among Gowrie's slaves, Capers searched the cabins, found Ishmael's secret hoard, and no doubt whipped him severely. Ishmael admitted he had been planning to escape, and Capers quickly concluded that Louis Manigault's trusted boatman captain Hector (who had run away for a night in the summer of 1860) and a number of other slaves also meditated flight. (A low-country fugitive, seeking at about this time the location of Yankee pickets, improvised a splendid simulation of terror when he learned from a gullible planter that they were nearby: far be it from him to flee *toward* the enemy!)[126] Louis Manigault appeared at Savannah—the nearest a planter would dare to approach the swamps until the season's third frost ended the malarial season—to consult with Capers, and they decided to remove from temptation nearly a dozen of the most untrustworthy slaves, deporting them to Silk Hope, forty miles inland from Charleston. By about November 12 this group of slaves—including Jack Savage, Big George (the recently sacked driver), and Little George Hunt—had been readied for the journey.

To carry messages to Louis Manigault in Savannah, Capers could no longer depend on captain Hector, for he—thought to be the very first of the slaves to project flight—was among the group selected for deportation. Capers therefore picked as messenger the nineteen-year-old Joe, son of a former trunk minder and of the former plantation cook at East Hermitage. At about this time Capers had an urgent message for Manigault: Jack Savage,[127] the most skilled artisan on the plantation, and his assistant carpenter, Little George Hunt, had fled to escape deportation; and then, in the presence of the other slaves and of Capers himself, Big George had also run. Whether or not this was Joe's message to Louis Manigault on November 12, Joe that day played the role of Sambo to perfection. "I . . . am very vexed today," Louis sputtered that evening to his wife, turning to *Hamlet* to elucidate his experiences: "Capers has sent that stupid dirty Negro Joe to me with no letter & absolutely nothing & Joe you Know is Brother to Rose[n]crantz and I ask him a question & he opens his big Cat-fish mouth and says "I do no Sa! I aint see am." So I have just written Capers to Come down here tomorrow . . . & see me." Joe may thus have shown solidarity with the fugitives, trying to delay the moment when Louis could send assistance to Capers. But Ishmael did not ally himself with the escapees. Capers intended to deport him too, and Ishmael was desperate not to be exiled from Gowrie: he "begged to remain." Possibly he had an abroad wife from whom he did not wish to be separated. Probably there was bad blood between him and his brother: as early as 1852, when Ishmael was driver, he had been made by the overseer to "whip Jack [Savage] well," and rancor probably had festered between the two. Possibly Jack Savage had stolen the shot and powder and had hidden it in Ishmael's cabin to divert suspicion from himself. Whatever the reasons, Ishmael betrayed the whereabouts of his brother, Jack, and of Little George Hunt, winning thereby his master's goodwill and reprieve from exile: Ishmael "is a completely changed individual," Louis later effused. By November 14 driver John had captured all three fugitives: Jack Savage and Little George down by the riverside, and John's predecessor as driver—Big George—immediately after George's bolt for freedom, between the conveyor house and the door of the threshing building. Once again the policy of divide and conquer had succeeded, as the Manigaults relied on the new black driver, informed by the self-interested and perhaps embittered brother of an escapee, to capture runaway slaves. Jack Savage was the only fugitive to offer overt physical resistance to his capture: he resisted (unavailingly) not the white overseer but the black driver who had ferreted out his whereabouts.[128]

As previously recounted, Capers himself gave Big George at least sixty lashes in front of the entire Gowrie gang, and doubtless Jack Savage and Little George received the same—or in Jack's case worse—when they were caught. Handcuffed, the three captured men accompanied seven other deportees by an inland route to Silk Hope, whence the three fugitives were sent on to the Charleston "workhouse" for weeks of solitary confinement, together no doubt with further "discipline." The twenty-one-year-old Little George— whom the Manigaults probably thought young enough to have been influenced by carpenter Jack Savage—was sent back to Silk Hope before the other two, but Jack and Big George each languished in his "dark hole" until late January. Charles Manigault would have sold them (as, in the case of Big George, Capers had long advised); but prices plummeted when Port Royal was captured and Manigault balked at "sacrific[ing them] for a trifling sum."[129]

The flood of anxiety on the Savannah River subsided by January 1862, and Charles Manigault sent Jack Savage, Big George, and several other slaves back to Gowrie. But only a few weeks later a new Yankee incursion caused fresh consternation: nineteen of the mistrusted "prime hands" (including Jack Savage and his wife, Amey) were hastily sent on February 20 to the pineland camp for deportation by rail to South Carolina the next day. On February 21 all of them made the journey to Carolina except Jack Savage, for he had stealthily escaped the previous night. He was gone from Gowrie eighteen months, living most of that time at a remote spot on another Savannah River plantation, "in the dense Carolina Swamp."[130]

Slaves at Gowrie sent food to Jack, across the Savannah Back River, with the connivance of the stock minder Charles Lucas. Louis Manigault's confidence in his own slaves had dissipated, and he and Capers molded all of the lead weights on the slaves' fishnets into bullets for their own pistols. That spring Louis sold the six Gowrie cows "through fear of their being all stolen some night by our Negroes." Then in September 1862 Charles Lucas permitted eight hogs to "depart from the plantation in some unaccountable manner": Louis suspected Charles of killing them himself. Charles was whipped. He fled without delay and remained in the swamp with Jack Savage for nearly a year. Parker—who like Charles Lucas was a relative newcomer to Gowrie— ran away in May 1863 and apparently joined Charles and Jack in their maroon, where some escapees from other plantations also hid. Three months later Charles Lucas was captured; Parker eventually returned; and eleven days after Lucas's capture Jack Savage himself (probably discouraged by his friend's capture, and no longer able to use the long-established lair at McPherson's plantation) finally went back to Gowrie.[131]

He had not, however, been inactive during the days which immediately preceded his return. In the summer of 1863, exhausted and fed up with the miserable life of a fugitive, Jack Savage had sought to extend his network of allies to include some white people. A Mr. Winkler, who owned a small plantation—very near Gowrie but on the Georgia side of the river—kept a shop there where he traded with slaves. A slave carpenter of Winkler's was among the group of fugitives known to Jack Savage. Jack talked with Winkler—indeed, stayed with him for several days—and tried to get Winkler to buy him from Charles Manigault, promising that if Winkler did so, Jack would persuade Winkler's carpenter to return to Winkler. Winkler wrote to Charles Manigault, offering to buy Jack Savage, but Manigault repulsed the offer, replying "that I never sold a corrupt Negro to reside . . . even on the same river with my Plantation, to avoid the corruption that such a Negro would effect on his former companions on my Plantation."[132]

Matters stood thus when Jack Savage—miserable, bedraggled, "looking half starved and wretched in the extreme"—finally gave himself up to Capers. He seemed at first penitent, but food and proper sleep did wonders to restore his spirits. Within a month Capers was complaining that the returned slave had been "impertinent" to a white workman repairing the engine, and that Jack had told "old Charles," the fifty-two-year-old trunk minder and an untrustworthy confidant of Jack's, that "he had not come home to be killed up with work." A fortnight later the Manigaults sold Jack at a bargain price,[133] his spirit unbroken to the last. He tried to frustrate the sale when the buyer first set eyes on him. "It would have provoked you," Capers fumed, "to have heard Jack's lies of his inability &c."

But wheels were here working within wheels. Capers, whom Charles Manigault came to believe an inveterate liar, may have been conspiring with Winkler to frustrate Manigault's purpose. Capers's instructions from his employer were that the slave trader who bought Jack Savage was to remove him immediately from the vicinity of Gowrie. It was Capers who found the trader and negotiated with him a price probably a good deal lower than the going market price. Smelling a rat, Manigault told Capers after the sale to be sure that Winkler had not bought Jack Savage and kept him on his own place. Three months later Manigault vowed to Louis that—if the trader had sold Jack to Winkler—an experienced constable would come to Winkler's and "seize the nigger and pop him in Jail, to await the trial." Manigault believed Jack Savage probably *had* been bought by Winkler and was on his plantation, just across the river from Gowrie, but he could not get a straight word from Capers on the subject.[134] Although there is no way to determine what really happened, one is tempted to believe that Jack Savage, playing on the cupidity of Winkler and of Capers—who may have found it financially advantageous to sell Jack cheap to Winkler via an intermediary—had the last laugh on his master.

Dolly, Louis Manigault's cook and washerwoman, appears to have had an even heartier laugh a little earlier in the same year. She is the only Gowrie slave for whom a photograph is extant—for Louis affixed it to the notice he posted in the Augusta police station after she escaped on April 7, 1863. Only six weeks earlier Louis had imported another slave washerwoman from

Gowrie to Augusta (where Louis's wife and children had sought wartime refuge, and where Dolly was a house servant). Dolly probably feared that, if she did not flee, she would be displaced from her position in the city and sent back to Gowrie, as had happened to her in the summer of 1860. Louis was absent from Augusta on April 7, and Dolly's departure was sufficiently leisurely that she had time to take "with her an ample wardrobe of her own Clothes." On the fugitive slave notice Louis expressed the view that this mulatto woman of "light complexion" was "rather good looking, with a fine set of teeth"; unsurprisingly, Louis thought she would be attractive to a white man, by whom she might have been "enticed off."[135]

Rose, an eighteen-year-old slave woman who had been working around Louis's house in Augusta, was back at Gowrie when Dolly escaped; and overseer Capers bullied her into telling him about Dolly's life in Augusta. Rose thought that Ralph (the former driver of the East Hermitage tract, who was now in charge of Louis Manigault's yard slaves in Augusta) or Captain (another house servant at Augusta) might know the name of a man who had been courting Dolly there. White people—overseers and gentlemen alike—took for granted that it was justifiable to whip a story out of a slave: "I should certainly endeavor to *extract* at least a portion of what they [Captain and the cook Scotland] know," Louis's brother-in-law John Habersham advised him. Capers was more blunt: "Make these negroes point out this man."[136]

The man in question, according to Ralph, proved to be not a white man as Louis had speculated but "Mr. Lewis . . . , an omnibus driver of L. L. Hotel—black Man. —Dolly remarked, 'There is Mr. Lewis—he is Courting me.' " "Mr." Lewis was a slave. Seventy years later it was still not "etiquette" for Southern whites to award the title "Mr." to a black man, yet here were house slaves addressing another slave as "Mr.": a clear assertion of the same burning pride which in Mississippi (in a well-known anecdote of Susan Smedes) led the self-respecting Mammy Maria to insist on calling her brother Henry "Mr. Ferguson" on his wedding day. According to Rose, Dolly had been "Washing and Sewing" for the man who for some time had been visiting her. Three months later, nothing more having been heard of Dolly, Capers advised Louis that "if you think Rose [who by now had returned to Augusta] knows anything of Dolly, she should be made to confess."[137]

Apparently Dolly escaped permanently, the only Manigault slave ever to have done so. Capers feared that others—for example, Rose—would follow suit. "Without you manage Rose you need not expect any Servant will stay with you, give her the devil," was his refrain. That autumn Louis Manigault planned to bring carpenter Billy's wife, Jenny, and her new infant to Augusta to help with the domestic burdens entailed by the prospective arrival of Louis's mother and sister from Charleston. Louis intended Jenny's four-year-old daughter to remain at Gowrie; but Dolly's example encouraged Jenny to threaten that she too would run away if separated from the four-year-old. Capers's mood was less steamy than usual: "I think you will have trouble with her if the [four-year-old] child is taken from her. . . . In these times [we mus]t be carefull with Negroes. There is so many chan[ces for] them to make their way to the Yankees."[138] Jenny's threat—and Capers's advice—caused Louis to back down and to let Jenny bring the four-year-old child as well as the suckling.

As Capers became more pragmatic in his handling of slaves, he became more fiery in his denunciation of the Yankees—and especially of the black soldiers whose presence at the recent battle of Fort Wagner had contributed to the decision of Louis's mother and sister (and of Capers's daughter) to leave Charleston. "I cannot see how our Men can take prisoners," Capers ejaculated, "Negro prisoners particularly. It strikes me if I had a Son in service and he took prisoner a Negro I could never know him again." That Capers was not alone in these sentiments was shown by the repeated massacres of black Union prisoners during the war.[139]

After the capture of Charles Lucas and the return of Jack Savage and of Parker, the next fugitive was the most trusted of all Gowrie slaves—John Izard. As recently as December 1860 Manigault had allowed John to set off alone from Charleston on the railway as far as the Savannah River bridge (some miles north of Gowrie), whence he was to board any chance vessel which might take him downstream to the plantation. Perhaps it was on a similar journey from Silk Hope, supposedly to Gowrie, that John disappeared in December 1863; but his flight was foiled by Confederate soldiers, who lodged him in jail at the county seat of Beaufort District. Charles Manigault had always tempered his threat to sell a fugitive with his own escape clause: he would sell a slave for "running away *for no cause.*"[140] In the case of John Izard, Manigault felt—as previously mentioned—that there was cause for flight: the employer thoroughly distrusted his wartime overseer at Silk Hope; and in any case John's "good" Izard blood strongly predisposed Charles Izard Manigault to leniency. Instead of being sold like Jack Savage, John Izard ended up working in Louis Manigault's yard in Augusta.

The last of Gowrie's fugitives was July, who in December 1864 suffered an amputated leg as the price of his bid for freedom; yet Jack Savage's long vigil in the swamp—coming as it did long before General Sherman reached Georgia—remained perhaps the most remarkable defiance of Gowrie's discipline. The Confederates had fortified Savannah early in 1862 against the Union navy, and after May of that year the Savannah River plantations were more secure than most of those elsewhere in the low country. Gowrie produced substantial rice crops in both 1862 and 1863. Although the masters had panicked for a few months in the winter of 1861–62, the renewal of military order allowed the restoration of discipline; and as late as the spring of 1864, "such a degree of security was felt by the Rice Planters for this section [along the Savannah River] that nearly all of the Plantations were working their entire Gangs."[141] The sharp line between nonviolent dissent and overt resistance had for a moment seemed ready to dissolve, but it was quickly redrawn. Except for Jack Savage, who resisted capture by driver John in 1861, and

Rose, who resisted being whipped by Capers, no Gowrie slave appears to have lifted a hand against the masters or their agents during the war—and Jack had resisted the black driver, not a white man.

When Capers entered a protracted and fatal illness in the summer of 1864, however, the slaves' customary inefficiency reached new heights. Under lax overseers from 1856 through 1858—when driver Robert and then driver George had been in office—the slaves had produced only moderate crops. Capers's relatively strict discipline, under driver John, boomeranged in 1864: during Capers's sickness, driver John was unable to get Gowrie's slaves to work even in the way they had done from 1856 to 1858. Capers died on October 30, 1864, and when Louis Manigault came to Gowrie a week or two later he "saw plainly that during Mr. Capers' long illness of the past summer little or no work had been done."[142] Even less was done after Capers's death, until a new agent was installed; and the arrival of Sherman's army only a few weeks later changed everything again, irreversibly. Yet the slaves' slowdown during the summer of 1864 was of a piece with their long prewar tradition of "day-to-day dissidence": they were reacting in the summer and harvesttime of 1864 not so much to General Sherman's movements as to the incapacitation of a martinet against whom they had struggled nonviolently since 1859.

The many flights from Gowrie between 1851 and 1864 are clear evidence of the slaves' discontent. So great were the hazards of fleeing, so painful the punishments when the fugitives were finally obliged to surrender, that only deep loathing for the regime could explain the frequency of flight. Hatred of slavery drove both men and women, both privileged slaves and ordinary field hands, to take desperate measures for relief.

Jack Savage remained, in Louis Manigault's mind, Gowrie's most alarming dissenter. Language failed to express Louis's sentiments: Jack was "the greatest Villain on the Plantation, the most notoriously bad character & worst Negro of the place." After the war Jack returned to Gowrie (from Winkler's?), and when the Manigaults tried to raise their first postwar crop in 1867, Jack immediately recorded his protest by causing a greatly disruptive flooding of the land which the Manigaults were now reclaiming (after abandoning it to the black squatters in 1865 and 1866). When Jack had been a slave, Louis had tried to buy him off with tiny privileges, whose extent suggests the scantiness of the regular supplies at Gowrie: "I always gave him many presents," Louis sadly reminisced, "such as bacon, & tobacco & rice." These privileges had not ended Jack's "laziness" nor his intimidating deportment. Freedom, in Louis Manigault's judgment, had completed Jack's ruin: "Tall, black, lousy, in rags, & [with] uncombed, kinky, knotty-hair," there appeared before Manigault's blinking eyes in 1867 the same man whom he had consigned to Charleston's "dark hole" in 1861, whom he had not seen since 1862, and who had defied him for eighteen months in the swamp during the war. To Manigault's astonishment, Jack was one of the dozen blacks who advanced to meet him at East Hermitage, shook hands, and—unlike some of the sullen young women who refused to lift their heads as their former master passed—seemed glad to exchange friendly remarks.[143]

What had been the effect of slavery upon Jack Savage's character? Historians have suggested at least three answers to such a question. Some authors discern a continuum extending from the submissive "Sambo" to the rebellious "Nat Turner": no slave was likely to be wholly a Nat Turner nor—least of all— wholly a Sambo; instead an individual might oscillate, perhaps unpredictably, between these two extremes. American slavery's most influential student, while not denying that the Sambo–Nat Turner polarity may sometimes be illuminating, has called attention to a rather different "type": the heroic accommodator—the slave, usually a member of the slave elite, who played ball with the masters to a considerable extent but who tenaciously exercised her or his plantation privileges to benefit the accommodator's enslaved comrades. The aforementioned Mammy Maria—a sort of "prime minister" on Thomas Dabney's cotton plantation in Mississippi, who insisted on calling her brother "Mr. Ferguson"—was but the most vivid example of such an accommodator; and many a heroic driver or slave preacher, in Eugene Genovese's view, adopted a similar stance toward the slave regime.[144] A third group of historians—most prominently, Orlando Patterson—are deeply suspicious of any attempt to fathom a slave's character. They believe the evidence is too sparse; and that talk about "the slave character" may degenerate all too quickly into an exercise by white, or black, historians in projecting their own predilections upon the helpless (because long-since dead) slaves. An individual slave's mentality will always remain impenetrable, Patterson argues; the most that historians might responsibly essay is to study the political psychology of slaves, considering them as a group but not as individuals.[145]

While each of these approaches has something to be said in its favor, none appears to shed much light upon the characters of Gowrie's slaves. No Nat Turner lived at Gowrie, and although Jack Savage was the nearest to a Nat, he was not very close. Jack's brother, Ishmael, might be thought of as a Sambo: but a Sambo who acknowledged late in 1861 that he had been planning permanent flight? The image of a slave suddenly oscillating between a Nat Turner and a Sambo might fit Ishmael a little better, but does it really lead far toward understanding? Nor was there a Mammy Maria at Gowrie: the white folks did not stay there long enough each year to create a stable "big house" from which a Mammy might have exercised her dominion. The role of the esteemed plantation nurse Binah was far more constricted than that of Dabney's Mammy Maria. A trusted driver may sometimes indeed—accommodating to the system—have exerted power on behalf of his people. But driver George, a resolute opponent of overseer Capers, bore also a certain (perhaps substantial) responsibility for London's suicide; and the position of driver was so unstable that many drivers were never able to build for themselves the authority of the stereotypical heroic driver/accommodator. One might be tempted, then, to heed the warnings of Orlando Patterson, and eschew individual psychology altogether.

Yet slavery certainly helped to shape the characters of many members of the master class, as Thomas Jefferson had been quick to appreciate. The child of a slave master saw his parent exercising (in Jefferson's words) "the most boisterous passions, the most unremitting despotism" toward the slaves; and the white child "thus nursed, educated, and daily exercised in tyranny, cannot but be stamped by it with odious peculiarities. The man must be a prodigy who can retain his manners and morals undepraved by such circumstances."[146] If the system thus affected the masters, may it not have affected slaves too? The most rewarding approach may be to attempt to define not a single polarity of character types but, as Jefferson seemed to imply in the case of the masters, a range of different types corresponding to the manifold variability of human nature.

One significant type at Gowrie—a variant of the heroic accommodator— was the hot-temperred, "determined" slave, of considerable leadership ability, whom the Manigaults sometimes tried to co-opt into helping them run the plantation. The ratio of slaves to whites on a rice plantation was so high, and the complexity of the annual production cycle so great, that no master could envisage managing the show without deputing considerable responsibilities to certain slaves. The masters oscillated between imposing painful punishment upon such "determined" slaves and awarding them what they imagined were substantial privileges. Robert, the fiery South Carolina house servant, was remanded for a time to the hell of Gowrie's rice fields before Charles Manigault elevated him to the purgatorial post of driver. Manigault served his own interests—but simultaneously rewarded Robert in the currency of genuine esteem—when he advised his son and his overseer to depend heavily on Robert's experienced judgment in making plantation decisions. Louis must talk constantly to Robert in order to keep the driver "up to all he knows."[147]

Is Robert to have been judged heroic? What alternatives were there, one might ask, for a fiery-tempered man? Once he came to Gowrie, the banished house servant worked with a will, and after four years was given great authority over the other slaves. Ought he instead to have taken the stance of Jack Savage, working often skillfully at his trade, yet continually shirking responsibility and seeking to intimidate the masters by his unsmiling visage? Would Robert have died a happier man had he fled to the Carolina swamp and moldered there, dodging snakes and rats, as Jack Savage later did? Robert decided instead to accept responsibilities within the regime. The Manigaults suspected that their driver drove with a light rein when the overseer was absent. Yet a relatively lax regime might sometimes hurt the slaves. Thus Robert complained after the 1854 "cholera" that for years the overseer had not ordered the settlement ditch cleaned out; but an energetic driver, responsible for his people's interests, might have persuaded the overseer to undertake this elementary measure of sanitation. Field hands sometimes showed solidarity with a driver, as Barclay's slaves did when they mounted their nonviolent protest in 1847; but Robert may have become somewhat isolated from his "Gang," and he probably died a saddened man, quite possibly a suicide.[148] Although there is not enough evidence to plumb

Robert's mind, his career suggests some of the dilemmas with which slavery confronted a "determined" man.

Robert's first cousin, Big George, was another high-spirited man, long co-opted into the system, who also had a falling-out with his master. Robert had a good house job in South Carolina, ran into a squall, then was reinstated as driver at Gowrie; George was driver, ran into a typhoon with overseer Capers, but lived to be co-opted again into the plantation hierarchy as one of the free-labor "foremen" in 1867. The cooper's high temper evidently complemented a somewhat incautious disposition: at twenty-three George badly injured his testicle with a hoop pole, and a year later he "carelessly cut his foot with a drawing Knife by steping [*sic*] on it in the dark." Religion probably meant less to him than to many other slaves: he seems to have been the only one of the five flatboat hands not singing a hymn at the moment miller Cato slipped overboard and drowned in 1852. One might have supposed that George's nearly three months of confinement in Charleston's dark hole would have ended forever both his and his master's willingness to cooperate in running the plantation. Yet in 1867 cooper George, a "foreman" at Gowrie, was carrying Louis Manigault on his back across a flooded field. This was by no stretch of the imagination the conduct of a Sambo, nor was George's spirited dissidence in 1860 and 1861 that of a Nat Turner. George was a high-tempered, "determined" man, with some independence of character, but he made compromises imposed on him by the system. After cooper George and Jack Savage had had nearly three months of "very severe," "Dark Solitary Confinement," Charles Manigault came to the Charleston workhouse to discuss with them their future. Though prices were too low for Manigault to wish to sell them, George and Jack would not have known this, and Manigault doubtless threatened them with sale unless they promised to turn over a new leaf. Even a high-spirited man would eat mud if he was made to do so. They "profess great Contrition for their misconduct," Charles Manigault reported with relish, "which they both acknowledge to have been bad, & . . . promise now never to give offense or trouble again, & . . . now see how easy a thing it is to fix a bad Negro."[149]

Jack Savage—cooper George's companion in this ritual of subordination and dishonor—was at this time associated in Louis Manigault's mind with the two other "determined" men who have been discussed. But Jack Savage's character was shaped by slavery rather differently from those of either Robert or George. Not only did Jack never assume leadership responsibilities, as did Robert and George, but his demeanor and conduct were different. If Robert and George were "determined" men, Jack might be denominated the "truculent" slave. Jack "was always giving trouble," Louis Manigault recalled, "& ever appeared dissatisfied."[150] Cooper George, after his three months in the Charleston workhouse, appears to have undergone a change of heart, like the one Robert experienced after he was sent from the Carolina "big house" to plod in the mud of Gowrie. But Jack Savage, within four weeks of his professing "great Contrition," had escaped to begin his eighteen-month ordeal in the swamp. Doubtless his life in hiding was sometimes even more unpleasant than the Charleston workhouse. Jack had seen all four of his children to the grave, and he left his wife, Amey—to whom he had been married eighteen years—mayhap never to see her again. He probably calculated that if he did not escape in February 1862, when Yankee soldiers were nearby, he might never again in his life have a chance to gain permanent freedom. His intrepidity—and the self-assertiveness which caused Louis Manigault to fear his own murder or the rape of Mrs. Louis Manigault—excite more interest, possibly more admiration, than one may feel for any other Gowrie slave.

But in personal terms Jack Savage paid a heavy price for his course of action, and he probably did not win the admiration of certain other slaves. He tried to blame John Izard for being a slow worker, when he was himself the slower one; he fell out with his own brother, Ishmael, to such an extent that Ishmael betrayed him in November 1861; Jack sought to barter the freedom of Winkler's fugitive carpenter in order to improve his own future; trunk minder Charles abetted Jack's sale in 1863 by telling the overseer about his continued grumbling; and Jack's disheveled appearance in 1867 may have betokened a certain lack of self-respect, coexisting with his truculence. Louis Manigault had no understanding of the moral ambiguities forced upon the blacks by slavery, and he dismissed Jack Savage as "a bad Negro [who] would do almost any thing."[151] A different century might be tempted to substitute "good" every time Manigault wrote "bad"—and "bad" every time Manigault wrote "good." But such a substitution might betray almost as little understanding of the slaves' dilemmas as Manigault himself possessed. Lying, truculence, unwillingness to assume responsibility: these character traits cannot always be virtues, though they might often be so for a slave. The high human cost paid for his independence by Jack Savage—the most skilled workman at Gowrie and potentially one of its most admirable characters—condemns slavery as much as the institution's more obvious iniquities.

A third type at Gowrie—beyond the "determined" and the "truculent"—was the "cunning" slave. Captain Hector was the most notable example, and trunk minder Charles a shadowy illustration, of this type. Nearly always more supple in character—less willing to cause offense—than the determined Robert and George, captain Hector and Charles appear to have pursued self-interest steadily by keeping in with the master. Yet neither deserves to be dismissed as a mere Sambo. Hector, the younger brother of Stephen the miller, was thirteen when Manigault bought Gowrie in 1833, and he was then serving as the overseer's waiting boy. He soon became the chief boat hand; and Louis Manigault's first trip to Gowrie in 1839, as a boy of eleven, indelibly impressed upon the child the happy memory of being rowed upriver from Savannah by the nineteen-year-old youth who soon became his favorite slave.

"Always spoiled by my Father and Myself, greatly indulged," Hector received many of those gifts with which masters signified their favor. One present was an old coat of Charles Manigault's, and as Hector wore it, he puffed himself up so that the Manigaults could indulge themselves in the beguiling pleasure of laughing at him. Slaves, they thought, had no honor;[152] if slaves nevertheless pretended to be honorable, it was good fun to ridicule their pretensions; and Hector was up to playing the required role in order to make his masters feel good. Upon Louis's return to the plantation in 1852, after two years in China and Latin America, he described his reception at Savannah by Hector and the other five boat hands who were to row him upstream to Gowrie. "I knew Hector a great distance off," Louis happily observed to his father, "from your old brown coat with brass buttons, buttoned up to the throat, and a large straw hat painted black & burned up at the sides; truly he thinks himself a great fellow in that dress." The slaves were keen Louis should think that seeing him gave them the greatest pleasure in the world, and a continuous burst of song was their instrument to achieve this purpose. "Well!" Louis exclaimed, "the boys seemed delighted to see me again, and they began to sing as soon as we left the wharf and hardly stopt at all all the way."[153] These men were to Louis "boys," and a few years later captain Hector, at the age of thirty-six, was the "postboy" entrusted with frequent trips on his own, from Gowrie to Savannah, to fetch letters and do errands.

Before Louis Manigault married in 1857, he made Hector "my constant companion when . . . I would be quite alone upon the plantation" (the overseer residing half a mile away at East Hermitage). When Louis returned to Georgia after one of his long summer absences, he expected Hector to tell him how things had been going in his absence, and especially to give a spy's report on the overseer. Thus, when Louis stopped in Savannah in mid-October 1856 (on his way from Augusta to Charleston—the season was, of course, still too malarial for him to go to Gowrie), Charles Manigault presumed Louis and Hector would have private conversation in the new overseer's absence: "I am sure you took good Care to intercept 'Hector' on his trip from the plantation to Savannah today, so as to have a Plantation talk with him." Flexile, ingratiating, Hector nevertheless immediately got into trouble with Capers, who accused him of drunkenness and demoted him at least temporarily to field work. Hector ran away from Gowrie one night in 1860, and in the autumn of 1861 was the first Gowrie slave who, Louis believed, aimed to flee to the Yankees. "A great Rascal," Louis called Hector in 1867: this was a term by which the master designated a slave who was slippery but not threatening (as a "determined" slave like Robert or George might be). Hector, Louis wrote with disillusion in 1867—but not with antagonism—had proved "as cunning as Negroes can be."[154]

Quite different in character was the "upright conformist" to plantation discipline, such as Cato. In the summer of 1852 Cato, then twenty-eight, had recently been elevated to the post of miller, replacing Stephen, who at fifty-one was getting old and asthmatic, and whom the overseer suspected of stealing rice for sale in town. Cato, by contrast, appears to have been reliable and honest. On Thursday, August 19, Cato, with cooper George, Short Jack, and two other boat hands, took the old flatboat on plantation business to Savannah. They placed on board two hundred bushels of corn, as well as two barrels of molasses and a supply of tobacco; then they spent the afternoon until sunset loading the flatboat with lumber (perhaps four thousand feet of one-inch boards). They could not load it quite full, as the old boat "leaks very much" (it had to be sent for repairs three weeks later). Waiting until the tide turned, they set off for Gowrie at 8 P.M. At midnight, as they neared home (poling), Cato and three others (but not cooper George) were singing a hymn in which Jesus—like the boatmen—labored with a little group of coworkers:

> When Christ the Lord was here below
> About the work He came to do
> Before He left this little band
> He gave to them his great command.

Cato heaved the heavy pole to fix it in the mud at the river's edge, slipped on the leaky, wet flatboat, and despite his friends' efforts, drowned in the swift current. His body was recovered two days later: Manigault's "best most honest & confidential servant" had perished, the overseer reported anxiously. Even the overseer avoided the word "slave," and he sought, too, to avoid his employer's wrath, protesting his own innocence. If slaves had to work at midnight on treacherous rivers in old, leaky flatboats to make a few white people wealthy, the "accident" which ensued was simply a stroke of fortune: "I regret it very much. What an unfortunate event! His place can't be well filled. You will most undoubtedly be very much chagrined about the fatal occurence [sic] but it could not be avoided. . . ." If Cato set about the work he came to do honestly—and if to some degree he cherished the ethical ideals practiced so ill by those whom his labor enriched—was his life less admirable than that of a Nat Turner?[155]

Slavery did not always ennoble its subjects, and a fifth type was the "demoralized opportunist." Yet at the age of thirty Bob, a field hand, had appeared to his master "slow, honest, good."[156] In 1833 Charles Manigault uprooted Bob from his home (probably separating him from a pregnant wife and two young children at Silk Hope) and placed him, with his mother and four of her other children between the ages of fourteen and twenty-two, in the mud of Gowrie. Bob's brother Latrance died in the first year, and his forty-six-year-old mother perished a few months later. His three remaining siblings escaped the Asiatic cholera of 1834 (which mowed down nearly one-third of the other slaves newly deported from Silk Hope); but within a few years two of these siblings had died, and even the third did not survive past the age of thirty. Binkey, the first woman Bob married at Gowrie, was by the age of thirty-seven a cripple useless to the Manigaults, and she died at forty-two.

These experiences did not benefit Bob's character, and when he was fifty-four this man—"honest" and "good" in his earlier years—was to Louis Manigault "a great Rascal." Though Manigault applied to Bob the same term he later used for "cunning" slaves (like captain Hector, Charles the trunk minder, and Simon the cook), Bob's character evidently differed from theirs. In May 1852 he was apprehended in Savannah with eight or nine bushels of rice (worth altogether about six and a half dollars to a Savannah trader) stolen from Manigault's supplies. A couple of days in jail, a whipping from the overseer, and promises of good behavior do not appear to have altered his conduct. His life might encourage him to spend the proceeds of illicit trade on whiskey. Sneaking home on a Sunday night the next spring (and not inconceivably drunk), after another unauthorized trip "to trade &c., &c." in Savannah, Bob—like Cato eight months earlier but this time not in a leaky plantation flatboat (probably instead in one of those "Negro canoes" of the slaves' own construction which Manigault unsuccessfully tried to outlaw)—fell into the swift-flowing river and drowned. He combated slavery by unauthorized trips, theft, and illegal trading; his life was a horror, and one may feel compassion for what his experiences did to him; but was Cato less exemplary than the dissident Bob? Crecie, a first cousin of the miller's widow, did not think so: upon her infant, born March 4, 1854, was bestowed the honored name "Cato."[157]

A sixth character type was the "proud" slave, holding herself or himself somewhat aloof from the other bondsmen and women. Louis Manigault's cook Jane provided Gowrie's most eminent illustration of this response to slavery. Jane—daughter to a cooper, sister to cooper George, cousin of driver Robert, and sister-in-law to the versatile artisan John Izard—was originally a Charleston house servant who almost surely thought herself a cut above ordinary slaves. She was virtually the only woman not to have married by the age of twenty, and her mien toward the young Manigault men was exceptional.[158] In 1846, when Jane was twenty-five, Charles Manigault had taken his family for a long trip to Europe, and he had sent her (with several other slaves) from domestic service in Charleston to field labor at Silk Hope. She complained to the Silk Hope overseer, but Manigault's tone, when he replied, was steely: "Jane and Malsey had better accustom themselves to field work, for they will never see town again."[159]

In Jane's battle for special treatment, her principal weapon appears to have been the claim of ill health. By 1849 Charles Manigault had come to think her a chronic malingerer, and this surmise was probably the cause of his deporting her that year from Silk Hope to Gowrie—as punishment to her, and as a warning to other house servants (or to former house servants like Malsey) of the fate which lay in store if they did not toe the line. Manigault was not perfectly sure, however, that Jane was malingering; he therefore instructed the Gowrie overseer to require of the twenty-eight-year-old woman only half the labors of a "prime hand." This order did not sit well with overseer Jesse Cooper, who misdoubted securing proper work from other slaves if Jane could get away with half tasks. Cooper's principal interest was to impel the gang to work, not to guard Jane's health, and his advice to Manigault was therefore suffused with contradiction. She must be treated with "severity"; her constitution would not stand "the mud & water of the swamp"; she probably was not diseased; "would it not be well to dispose of her to some kind person who may require her as a House Servant or Nurse"?[160] Like the impatient junior minister of an imperial power wavering in its handling of a minor colonial rebellion, Cooper felt anything would be better than his boss's halfway policy of "leniency."

Matters were complicated by the intervention of Dr. Pritchard, a veteran battler against South Carolina's cholera epidemics, at whose cholera camp on the river's Carolina side Gowrie's slaves were domiciled during the 1849 epidemic. Dr. Pritchard examined Jane and thought her complaint was probably genuine. Jane, disliking field work, may have put into Pritchard's mind the idea of his buying her at half price from Manigault on a speculation that her health would improve. The overseer, probably knowing that Manigault on principle did not sell slaves except for misconduct (but underestimating the force of that conviction), cautiously communicated Pritchard's offer to Manigault, and thereby provoked a storm. Manigault was profoundly unwilling to let his other slaves get the idea that, if they did not fancy the discipline at Gowrie, they need only seek out a purchaser in order to secure relief: selling Jane to Pritchard was therefore wholly out of the question.[161] Perpetually mistrusting his overseers, Manigault probably also suspected Cooper of conspiring with Pritchard to get Pritchard a good slave at a bargain price. Jane—Manigault was pretty sure— was malingering; and neither she nor Pritchard was to profit by her pretense of illness. Manigault promptly slammed the door against Pritchard's offer; his wrath with the doctor may well have led to Manigault's disastrous failures in 1852 and 1854 to organize in time a "cholera" camp of the sort which Pritchard had so successfully (for a price) rented to him in 1849.

Her hopes of acquiring a new master frustrated, Jane nevertheless managed in due course to get out of the swamp and under a roof. When Louis Manigault established himself at Gowrie in 1852, she became his cook and house servant. But this was an unstable relation; Louis soon aimed to make Jane only his bedmaker, bringing in the fourteen-year-old London as his houseboy, and appointing Dolly (Big Hector's former wife) as his cook. Meanwhile, Jane's complaints continued apace: when "cholera" struck Gowrie in 1852, Jane said she felt bad too, though nothing was diagnosed; and in 1853 she told Louis "in a very melancholy way" of a (migraine?) headache, which she thought Dr. Gabriel Manigault's remedy might cure. When "old" Binah died, Jane became the plantation nurse, but (jealous of Dolly?) she continued to complain. "I had a little trouble here about a week ago with Sister Jane," Louis finally reported in 1854; "she did not attend to the sick at all." Louis congratulated himself on the decision with which he had handled Jane's renewed skirmishing for special treatment: "Caramba! I put her on the field, & I tell You what, it is one of the best Changes ever made."

A few hours after Louis wrote these self-satisfied words, Jane—who continued to think herself above field work—ran away. As indicated earlier, she was caught, given six months of "discipline" at the Savannah jail, and sold to New Orleans.[162] Doubtless Louis Manigault kept her in jail for half a year because prices (compared with those earlier in the season) were higher in December, when buyers flocked to the Charleston and Savannah slave markets. But in keeping Jane incarcerated so long, Louis probably could not avoid the pleasure of humbling her pride—of proving to Jane that he, not she, had had the last word: of showing, in Charles Manigault's words, "how easy it is to fix 'a bad-disposed nigger.' " Jane's tenacious battle, using whatever nonviolent methods she found at her disposal, may arouse simultaneously one's esteem for her pertinacity, doubts about her claim to special treatment, and sorrow for the waste of her unrealized human potential.

These six different responses to slavery—hot-tempered determination, trucu-lence, cunning, upright conformity, demoralized opportunism, or pride—were surely only a handful among the numerous character types developed at Gowrie.[163] Even this incomplete outline, however, should make clear how unsatisfactory the Sambo–Nat Turner polarity might be as a framework for discussing the slaves' characters.[164] Nor can a category like "heroic accom-modator" adequately describe the complexity of character developed by those determined, yet accommodating, and sometimes admirable men, driver Rob-ert and cooper George. Above all, the range of the slaves' responses to their condition was wider than might be suggested by any singular denomination of *the* slave character. Slaves, like other human beings, responded to their circum-stances in a profusion of ways, and the six types here suggested merely scratch the surface of human variety.

Yet these six types have a common feature: in every instance the growth of the slave's character was in some degree stunted. No doubt the same has been true of most human beings throughout history, but the thwarting of these slaves' development was marked. Jack Savage, evidently a man of unusual ability, was driven to shirking and negativity. Cooper George was not loved by the suicide, London, and he was obliged to squander much of his talent and energy in a long-standing feud with overseer Capers. A cunning slave like captain Hector probably told tales on other slaves (as well as on the overseer) to secure his own privileged place in Gowrie's hierarchy of privilege.[165] Cato the miller was honor-able by his own lights and by the ethical standards of most of the world; but slavery produced its own ethics, where stealing was to the slaves their "right" (most of them feeling that they had been "taught" to steal by their masters' example). Cato's honesty may therefore have been resented by some slaves like the former miller Stephen and the peripatetic Bob; and a high-spirited man like cooper George may have thought Cato paid a high personal price for the conformity which won his masters' regard. Bob's personal development was probably more constricted than Cato's, for Bob was impelled to find in theft, unauthorized excursions, and perhaps whiskey the opportunities for expression so limited elsewhere in his life. Nor is one likely to feel that Jane's long struggle for special treatment greatly improved her character. Slaves combated the restrictions upon their lives with many instruments,[166] but their struggle was an unequal one. The masters, seeking to reduce their slaves to subordination, aimed to close from their bondsmen and women most avenues for personal growth. The Manigault records suggest that the stunting of human potential, no less than the profligate waste of human life itself, exacted a dismal toll in Gowrie's swamps. The abolition of slavery in 1865—after a dreadful, fratricidal war inspired by those who sought to perpetuate the system—was not just a minor shift in the form of labor exploitation.

6

Privilege

The Manigaults, of course, did not govern their slaves solely with the whip, the Charleston "dark hole," and the threat of sale. Less important in securing subordination—but often effective in winning the grin which was supposed to accompany subordination—was their granting of privileges. For most bondsmen and women these might do little more than slightly ease their straitened circumstances, but for a few slaves privileges opened substantial opportunities to escape the full rigor of bondage. The concept of "privilege" has led to two much-discussed theories about slavery.

The principal source of human rights, Edmund Burke had argued in the eighteenth century, was the gradual transformation of a privilege, by long usage, into a claim so firmly established in custom that the grantor of the privilege could no longer easily withdraw it: a "privilege" had become transmuted into a "right." Burke's idea has been fruitfully applied to the history of slavery. Slaves surely acquired certain de facto prerogatives, limiting their masters' power. In the colonial period, for example, some masters might grant their slaves the privilege of not working on Sundays, and in due course the custom of a Sabbath holiday (or a holiday on another day, if the harvest demanded labor on a particular Sunday) became deeply embedded in local custom. Few masters would then deny their slaves what the latter had come to regard as their right.

A second and related theory has also shaped the understanding of slavery, resembling labor historians' long-established distinction between an "aristocracy" of skilled artisans and the mass of unskilled workers. Privileged slaves, it has often been said—house servants, drivers, artisans, preachers, conjurors—

formed a special group, a "slave elite," set off from the mass of field hands. Controversy has simmered over the relation between the slave elite and the field hands: did the former selfishly betray the latter (in order to feather their own nests), or did members of the elite often prove loyal comrades to their brothers and sisters in bondage? In whatever way this question is answered, few writers have disputed the existence of a "slave elite."

Gowrie's records suggest caution in the use of both of these theories. Although Charles Manigault depended heavily upon the grant of privilege as an instrument in governing his slaves, he was determined that each privilege should remain just that. A "privilege" was the free gift of the powerful master, and could at any moment be withdrawn. Manigault granted privileges in order to make his slaves more dependent upon himself, not to convert his slaves into the independent possessors of customary rights.

Nor does the concept of a "slave elite" prove as applicable to Gowrie's social structure as might be expected. The term implies not only a distinguishing of the elite from the mass but a certain solidity of structure. As has already been shown, however, most families at Gowrie included both field hands and people who held privileged positions; and the privilege of holding a relatively good job could easily be lost. Although the situation of a driver was not so uncertain as that of an overseer, it was far from assured. Harry—Gowrie's driver when Manigault bought it in 1833—did, to be sure, hold office continuously until ill health prevented his doing so in 1846; and during that period he had outlasted seven overseers and witnessed the installation of an eighth. Thereafter, however, considerable instability ensued, eight drivers serving during the next eighteen years. Whereas a displaced overseer always left the plantation, the social structure of Gowrie was confused by the plenitude of displaced drivers remaining there, often working as field hands. When John was imposed as driver in 1860, he held sway over no less than five men who had held his office since 1846 (and this number did not include Renty and Robert, the two drivers whom death had removed from office since 1846). Charles, who succeeded the ailing Harry as driver in 1846, was dismissed in 1848; in 1860 he was the principal trunk minder. Ishmael, appointed driver of East Hermitage in 1849, was reduced to the ranks in 1853. His successor, Stephney, held office only until 1855, when he was demoted to plowman. And Ralph, who replaced Stephney, was reduced to field labor in 1860, soon after Big George had suffered the same punishment.[1] Privilege granted was readily withdrawn. Instead of using a term like "slave elite"—whose implications appear to be misleading—one might better speak of the "privileged slaves" at Gowrie, keeping thus constantly in mind that what the master gave to a slave he might take away.

Privileges were of two sorts: those extended to the whole gang, and those granted only to selected individuals. Those awarded to the gang focused on food and clothing rations, while the most important privileges given to the chosen few concerned their jobs on the plantation.

Wherever feasible, Manigault treated the provision of food and clothing as though the rations were privileges rather than rights. The edifice of privilege thus constructed at Gowrie arose upon diverse foundations: some furnished by nature, some regulated by local custom, and others deliberately designed by Manigault to serve his own interest. Nature decreed that Gowrie was on an island in the middle of a river full of fish. Nature also determined that tidal rice culture—with its massive investment in mud embankments and laboriously devised ditches—would be confined to a narrow coastal strip which (because of the swamps, and the covering of fields with nearly stagnant water) was murderously malarial. And nature declared that a single slave could cultivate a much larger acreage of rice than of sugar: close supervision of labor was therefore much more difficult to achieve in the rice kingdom than on Caribbean sugar plantations.[2] Large numbers of slaves, who could not be closely supervised by the (relatively tiny) class of white overseers who had built up a certain resistance to malaria: this was a formula for the growth of a "task system"; and during major parts of each year slaves worked under black drivers with comparatively little white overseership. Those slaves who finished their allotted day's "task" before dusk were permitted to leave the fields upon its completion. Local practice crystallized into binding local custom, and Manigault never thought of trying to abandon the principle of a task system.

Charles Manigault was free, however, to decide where to buy land and what use to make of it. He chose to buy only richly productive rice land on Argyle Island. He did not buy—in addition to Gowrie—a "farm" on the South Carolina or Georgia side of the Savannah River, where he might have raised corn and pigs to feed his slaves. (To cultivate a "farm" in Georgia was the pattern of Manigault's neighbor James Potter—whose slaves lived on the Georgia side of the river and traveled each day to work on Potter's Argyle Island rice plantation. And many other rice planters, like South Carolina's Robert Allston,[3] bought land near their rice plantations which was unfit for rice production, and there raised provisions for the slaves who were growing rice.) Furthermore, Manigault did not allocate appreciable patches of land to individual slaves as garden plots. No doubt he calculated that every spot of soil fit for raising rice was a tiny gold mine: and who would imagine letting a slave raise sweet potatoes in a gold mine?

Consequently, Gowrie's slaves—if they were to eat the corn and pork standard to the South—must usually be fed corn bought in the Charleston market and shipped by sea to Gowrie. Similarly, hogsheads of pork normally had to be bought in Savannah or Charleston, and this was expensive.[4] Manigault's unwillingness to buy a farm gave him a powerful incentive to cut costs by limiting the meat ration: indeed, there was no regular ration. God had provided fish in the river, and the task system gave men time, during long stretches of the year, to fish. Pork therefore was not a right but a privilege, to be doled out at the overseer's discretion. In 1844 the overseer gave adult slaves three pounds of pork as a Christmas treat; three pounds each fortnight during the harvest (when everyone was much too busy to fish); and an unspecified amount "once or twice during the summer when the work is hard in hoeing &c." A bit of unexpected meat (or molasses) might then be proferred the slaves to forestall discontent. The summer heat, for example, did not improve the quality of Gowrie's corn: "I have got some more bacon and molasses for [the slaves]," the overseer explained in late June 1842, "as the corn is so bad. What there is of it now is almost spoiled after being spread and stirred up every week." Everything was arranged to stress the master's authority, not the slaves' right, over the quantity of meat distributed. And skimpy meat rations were, in fact, common throughout the low country: as the task system gave masters less direct control over their slaves' time than in most of the South, the slaves were obliged to use their own time to supplement the basic corn ration. Thus a former slave testified, "No meat whatsoever was issued," by the wealthy Colonel Henry DuBignon, a neighbor of Pierce Butler's on Georgia's St. Simons Island. "It was up to the slaves to catch fish, oysters and other sea food for their meat supply."[5]

Charles Manigault was impatient with slaves who tried to improve their ration: the whole business of distributing food must be got through expeditiously. When Louis Manigault began to manage Gowrie he suggested giving out both pork and mackerel during the planting season, a half ration of each, but Charles vetoed the notion that both should be distributed on the same day. "Allowance is at best a troublesome job," he admonished the young man, "& should be got over as quick as possible. The Negroes should have no picking & chusing." Nor was any meat to be wasted on the children: "It is only the grown ones that draw meat you know." This last rule might be modified if a child were looking unwell, but here again the meat ration was a privilege, not a right. "I give all the Children molasses," the overseer wrote later that year, "and if any seem drooping, meat."[6]

Molasses and tobacco, like meat, were distributed irregularly: at Christmas and, at the overseer's discretion, two or three times during the rest of the year. In addition, molasses was distributed fortnightly during the exhausting harvest season to restore the slaves' dwindling energy. Another special feature of harvesttime was that "Dirty Rice"—of relatively low commercial value, left over from the previous year's milling—was given them instead of corn. When the slaves were working at the task system, they must fill any spare time with fishing, sewing clothes, and grinding corn; but at harvesttime the task system apparently was abandoned, everyone laboring from dawn until dusk. "The Dirty Rice," Manigault explained, "amounting usually to 10 or 12 Barrels [about 2 percent of the annual production], is always kept for them at harvest when hard work don't give them time to grind Corn."[7]

Cutting costs on meat, on feeding children, and by limiting the distribution of molasses and tobacco to special occasions and monopolizing all the land for rice production, instead of giving the slaves garden plots—Manigault then felt free to grant his slaves certain substantial privileges which might win their cheerful submission to the regime. But if the gang became querulous, the privileges could be withdrawn. In parts of many years before 1855, Manigault prided himself on feeding his slaves "small rice" (which had fallen through the mill's strainer) instead of corn, even though small rice was usually more expensive.[8] The slaves liked the rice better, and might have been expected by Manigault to be grateful. But in December 1845, instead of displaying gratitude, they complained (perhaps about the paucity of their meat supply). Manigault thereupon withdrew the privilege of small rice, reducing the slaves to a corn diet for a year. The privilege was then restored with a flourish, as a sign to the slaves of Manigault's fondness for them. The whole idea of renewing the privilege was to secure uncomplaining subordination. When the privilege was restored, the overseer was to tell the slaves this was done because of their good conduct, which had led the master to decide to grant them the small rice again—"on trial; & it depends entirely on them whether they shall have it in future or not."[9]

His slaves' privilege of raising poultry was one which Manigault valued as a means of granting them a tiny "stake in society." The overseer at Gowrie must forgo an overseer's usual right to raise chickens, for otherwise there would be endless disputes with the slaves over the ownership of fowl. Manigault granted the privilege exclusively to his slaves because he refused to give them garden plots. Poultry, he acknowledged, "is the only thing my people can raise for themselves (they having no spot to plant) except the trifle near their houses & near my dwelling. [Raising chickens] enable[s] them to procure some little extra Comforts for themselves, & . . . tends to attach them to their homes."[10] Although a few slaves on certain other low-country plantations managed to accumulate perceptible amounts of property (especially livestock), such was not the case at Gowrie. No Gowrie slave owned a horse, a cow, or even a pig—the slaves' stake in society being confined there to the possession of a few chickens.[11]

The master himself might occasionally supply other food and drink—always as a special privilege. At the end of the 1835 harvest there was fresh beef, and again for the Christmas of 1836; but these appear to have been the only times that fresh meat was offered during the six years from 1833 through 1838. In 1851 (and again in 1852) Manigault permitted overseer Skinner to spend eleven dollars on a thirty-nine-gallon barrel of whiskey to spread autumnal cheer among the slaves, but there is no record that this treat was granted in other years. The slaves' consumption of some mackerel in 1853 was also an unusual privilege, for Louis Manigault did not even know that year how much each slave should be given. In 1856 Charles Manigault lavished ten dollars on turkeys so that his slaves could celebrate the end of the harvest (the master's net revenues that year being ninety-four hundred dollars).[12]

When the slaves were sent to Dr. Pritchard's cholera camp in 1849, they received fresh beef. This special provision had been intended, however, to save Manigault money by sparing him the purchase of the pork which Dr. Pritchard evidently had recommended: "Our arrangement about fresh beef," the overseer assured his employer, "will curtail the heavy expense proposed from bacon." When the slaves were in the "cholera" camp again after the epidemic of 1852, they were given the outlandish treat of coffee twice a day, a luxury unheard of except to boost spirits at a time of catastrophe. Shocked by his experiences at the "cholera" camp, Louis Manigault also gave every slave a new blanket that December (instead of operating the usual system by which one-third received a blanket each year). He even went so far as to kill a cow for a Christmas treat in 1852: probably one of the first times since 1836 that Gowrie's slaves had enjoyed fresh beef at Christmas.[13]

In the absence of individual garden plots, Charles Manigault sometimes supplied a few vegetables from a small garden near his house, but he set a low priority on doing so. He suggested to the overseer in 1848 that some vegetables might improve the slaves' health, and they should be raised "if you have anyone who has nothing else to do (such as 'Old Ned')." Ned, "very old" at sixty-six, had been useless to Manigault for years; but as he died not long afterward, the vegetable garden may have remained untended. In 1857 and 1859 the slaves enjoyed the rare privilege of eating cowpeas—and, in 1860, sweet potatoes too. These crops had been planted in a few fields not to improve the slaves' diet but to rid these fields of "volunteer" rice, which lowered the price Charleston rice merchants would pay for Gowrie's produce. Everyone understood that, in spite of a few special privileges, food supplies at Gowrie were not splendid for the slaves' health. When Scipio was unable to work for two or three months in 1852 because of a slightly swollen stomach, "The Dr. advised that he should be removed to some other place [e.g., the Manigaults' Marshlands farm near Charleston] where he Could have a Change of food &c."[14]

Besides small rice and a rare culinary treat like cowpeas, another privilege granted Manigault's slaves was relatively good cloth. The women were obliged to use their spare time to sew all of their own clothes, all of their childrens', and all of their husbands' summer clothes: only the men's winter clothing was purchased ready-made. The master thus again lessened the disadvantage to him of the task system.[15] His manner of supplying the summer cloth showed once more that the grant of a privilege was intended to govern the slaves' conduct; and if the desired conduct was not forthcoming, the privilege could be withdrawn. Some of the slave women did not care to devote their spare time, after completing the daily task, to the sewing which Manigault demanded of them. Charles therefore advised Louis to withhold some of the cloth until the women had finished sewing the first allotment: "When they each bring them to you all made up then give them their . . . Summer Cloth besides. . . . The parents of the children will have to be watched, or their little things wont be made up for them."[16]

The master's distribution of cloth in the spring, and of cloth and men's clothing in December, was an important ritual symbolizing his largesse. It was always performed on a Sunday (not a Saturday), in order to discourage the slaves from leaving Gowrie for the weekend and improvidently trading off some of the good cloth or clothing. If the weather turned cold in December before one of the Manigaults arrived from Charleston to perform the semiannual ceremony, the slaves must freeze for a few days: it would not do for the overseer to give out cloth too soon, lessening the slaves' sense of being granted a privilege by Master himself.[17] Knowing how cold Argyle Island— low-lying and windswept—could be in the winter, and having sometimes suffered himself from the cold there, Manigault apparently calculated that a dollar spent on good cloth would be better for the slaves than a dollar spent on meat. The slaves themselves had no choice in the matter (unless they traded their cloth ration for other goods), and Gowrie's health record does not suggest that Manigault's policy was a blazing success; but the master convinced himself that the privileges he allowed his slaves were in their interest.

In 1848, however, he was willing to make a slight concession about the meat. Apparently the slaves complained again, making invidious comparisons with the ration supplied on a neighboring plantation by Manigault's cousin, Anthony Barclay; and the overseer probably suggested less infrequent distribution of meat at Gowrie. " 'Mr. Barclay' gives more meat than I do," Manigault acknowledged,

> but my people besides being the best clothed in the [Savannah River] Country have other advantages—for instance, I keep all the small Rice for them, unless on one or two occasions when they have done anything wrong, when I have sold the whole of it. . . . But you will give them meat, now & then, when you think proper.

Never routinized, the slaves' occasional privilege of eating meat remained at the overseer's discretion, intended to prod them into a display of gratitude; and as late as 1856, when a ration of pork was about to be distributed—as was usual during the harvest season—the overseer notified Manigault that the slaves "seams che[e]r[e]d up of the Idea of giting meat."[18]

Louis Manigault was gratified that, during the Civil War, his slaves experienced a substantial diminution in the quality of their food. Although cowpeas were raised, any meat for the slaves was now out of the question,[19] and so of course were molasses and tobacco. The slaves could no longer fish, for hooks were unobtainable; and the master and overseer shaped the weights essential for the slaves' fish pots into bullets for their own armament. Blaming the slaves for the war, Louis Manigault derived satisfaction at the termination of their culinary privileges. He regretted only that the slaves did not, in his opinion, suffer as much as did the white people: "Thus does the Negro, to some extent, experience his share of privation, during the continuance of this [unrighteous and diabolical] War."[20]

Before the war, slaves groused about poor shoes as well as about the shortage of meat. They were, of course, expected to go barefoot in the summer, but a pair of shoes had to be supplied each winter if their feet were not to be damaged by the cold. Sometimes the shoes did not fit properly. Slaves could not test shoes for size themselves at a shop; instead they must depend on white people—whose interests might be contrary to their own—to supply them. The overseer cut flexible material (perhaps remnants of cloth) the length of each adult slave's foot and sent these to the master; the master then took them to a shoe merchant. If the vendor did not have enough shoes of correct size at hand, he might scrunch up the flexible measure so that a shoe would fit it; in such cases the slave ended up scrunching her or his feet into shoes that were too small. The unusual overseer Washington Skinner tried, by selecting strong material for the measures he sent to Manigault, to prevent a merchant from cheating. "The measure should be put into the Shoe," he instructed his employer in 1851, "just tight enough to keep it fast. [The measures] are strong, and cant be bent so as to be forced into a Small Shoe, as I have seen [done]."[21]

Although the shoes may have been correctly fitted that winter, they did not last long. The quality of shoes was variable, and it now occurred to Skinner that the slaves' customary right of receiving an ordinary low-grade pair of winter shoes might be converted into the privilege of receiving a relatively durable pair. The idea of buying better shoes did not occur to Charles Manigault unprompted: it was one of the virtues of K. W. Skinner as overseer that he dared communicate the slaves' complaints to his employer. "The shoes for last season (I believe) were not of the best quality," Skinner ventured to report in 1852, "as they wore out in a very short time. I had frequently heard the negroes makeing remarks about their shoes breaking so early in the winter." Several years later Manigault finally discovered that he had been buying "an ordinary kind of Shoe, the Leather rather thin." He then decided to pay about a 15 percent higher price for less skimpy footwear, and his slaves thus gained the privilege of wearing shoes which had a chance of lasting as long as did the cold weather.[22]

Usually the huts of slaves in the rice kingdom were less wretched than those elsewhere in the South, because the low country was so unhealthy that masters sought to give their bondsmen and women at least some compensatory protection against the cold and the mud. And rice planters were usually rich enough to afford better housing than that offered by many a scrabbling short-staple cotton farmer.[23] From 1837 to 1861 slaves at the original Gowrie tract lived in eighteen-by-eighteen-foot dwellings intended for four inhabitants—somewhat larger than the fifteen-by-fifteen-foot hut typical of the cotton kingdom. Probably each such "house" comprised a single room, above which there may have been a loft.[24] Two such dwellings were built side by side, in a wooden frame structure with a shingle roof and a brick chimney in the middle, which opened into both of the adjacent houses. Commonly four people—not necessarily all in the same family—lived in each half of a double house, and if a family was large it occupied both halves of the house.[25]

Henry McAlpin, the proprietor of the East Hermitage tract until 1848, owned a brickyard near Savannah, and in 1843 he built brick huts for his slaves at East Hermitage. When Manigault bought the tract in 1848, he therefore came into possession of seven brick double houses, built on brick stilts six and a half feet above the ground. Presumably here, too, each dwelling comprised a single room. As more than fifty-six slaves were destined for East Hermitage, there were sometimes at first more than four slaves to a room; but in 1850 15 percent of the plantation's slaves died, and thereafter there were seldom more than four slaves per dwelling.[26] Early in 1861 the Manigaults built four brick double houses at the original Gowrie tract to replace some of their wooden buildings. Unlike the pillars under the previous frame huts, the brick foundations for these new houses were high enough to elevate them above freshets; and the masters took the unusual step of supplying the buildings with slate roofs. So long as slavery continued, Charles Manigault referred to the slaves' dwellings as "houses"; but his wrath at the revolution of 1865 once impelled him to candor. In February 1865, when the Confederate army evacuated the Charleston area, the Silk Hope slaves broke open all the boxes where their master's possessions were stored. Charles Manigault wrote in disbelief: "My own Negro, who had been previously *the Driver* at Silk Hope . . . Seized My Portrait [painted by Thomas Sully in 1817] as His Share of the Spoils, & . . . [kept] it a little while to ornament *His Hut*."[27]

Assiduous in devising food, clothing, and perhaps "hut" privileges, Charles Manigault was less willing to extend the principle by granting much time off work. Slaves, by custom, had to be given a Christmas holiday—often a week elsewhere in the South (it being their only substantial vacation throughout the year) but frequently only three days in the rice kingdom. Here again rice planters compensated themselves for the disadvantages of a task system by limiting the slaves' other prerogatives. Accordingly, Gowrie's Yuletide recess was confined to three working days (including December 25), and the Manigaults always feared disorder during even this short period. In 1852 they managed virtually to eliminate frivolity. The slaves "have been employed for the past three days in Cleaning their houses, &c., &c.," Louis wrote with satisfaction on December 28: thus the slaves' long absence from Gowrie (at the "cholera" camp before December 20) was compensated by work at Christmas. "Christmas is always a very bad time for Negroes," Louis Manigault sighed in December 1861, "and it is always a God-Send (any Year, but far more so this) when that Holyday is over, and we all resume our quiet plantation work."[28] Sunday and nighttime work might, of course, be demanded of slaves during an emergency on any plantation; and Gowrie, like other rice plantations, was peculiarly susceptible to emergencies.[29] Furthermore, not even at high summer noonday did Gowrie's overseers normally decree a siesta. It was a matter of unusual and extended comment by Louis Manigault that in July 1860 the heat was "so intense that the Negroes were not allowed to work from 12 until 2 for several days." To justify the grant of this extraordinary privilege, Louis explained that "Mr. Edward Barnwell (a very experienced Planter on the Pon Pon River) tells us that he did the same thing, and I dare say other Planters also."[30]

The man who best understood how privileges might oil the plantation machinery was K. W. Skinner, Manigault's overseer in 1851 and 1852. Skinner's deportment was distinguished by the absence of obsequiousness toward his employer. To be sure, he was as willing as any other overseer to impose whippings (e.g., when Ishmael was made to flog his brother, Jack Savage), and he bore—along with Charles Manigault—substantial responsibility for the "cholera" disaster of 1852; but his candor in addressing Manigault, his evident skill in directing the complex operations of tidal rice culture, and his astute granting of privilege may stimulate a measure of esteem rarely felt for any other Gowrie overseer. Skinner was the manager who tried to induce Manigault to improve the quality of the slaves' footwear; he seems to have instituted for two years a whiskey ration during the harvest (like the well-known, but exceptional, one at fodder-pulling time on Thomas Dabney's Mississippi plantation); and he acknowledged how hard female slaves had to work in very cold weather.[31]

Skinner also extended further than previously to Gowrie's slaves the privilege—early in the season—of substituting quadruped for human labor. In so doing, Skinner had to combat Charles Manigault's parsimony, for Manigault (like numerous rice planters) was reluctant to supply many mules and plows. For a time after a rice field had been flooded, it was too soggy for a draft animal to pull a plow, and this led some planters to claim that plows were not suited to rice culture. The claim was false at the beginning of the season, when the fields were relatively dry; but rice planters were loath to use plows and mules to break up the earth because there would be little use for these implements and animals later in the year. Why not let slaves—who, unlike mules, could work throughout the year—do the backbreaking labor of break-ing up the soil with a heavy hoe? The South's richest rice planter, Nathaniel Heyward, had never at the time of his death in 1851 employed a plow, and as late as 1861 some other rice planters still had never done so. By contrast, Skinner, within a few weeks of taking over Gowrie in January 1851, addressed to Charles Manigault a peremptory request: "I must now ask you to put two more mules on your plantation as early as they can be purchased." Within a year Skinner had secured Manigault's agreement to place a total of three mules at Gowrie, but the overseer believed this was only half as many as needed. "With the present two and the 3rd one when it arrives," he wrote impatiently, "you will scarcely get the land ploughed, and none harrowed." Skinner's motive was not to spare the slaves but to increase the crop. Slaves taken from "mashing" the earth with a heavy hoe could be set instead at wintry ditching work, which at the shorthanded Gowrie would otherwise be neglected. "The more you harrow [with mules]," he exhorted his employer,

> the more work can be done with the hands, such as makeing banks, raising banks, cleaning ditches, etc., etc. Mules can draw harrows, but they can't clean ditches, raise and make banks. If you dont have mules to do the harrow-ing, the hands will have to mash the ground (half an acre to each hand), which is slow business where hands are scarce, and *work* far behind-hand.

Manigault promptly sent a fourth mule!

Skinner made plain that—contrary to slavery's apologists—the "task" of a slave on a rice plantation might well be too large for some slaves to complete. "I could not get half acre [of hoeing] to every hand in the unploughed ground," Skinner reported in mid-May 1852 (hoping thus to confirm Manigault in the new practice of committing four mules to plowing), "but after they got into the ploughed ground, they gave the half acre easily." This blunt appeal to Manigault's self-interest did indeed prevent retrogression; but not until prepar-ing for the 1860 crop did the master finally equip Gowrie with the six mules Skinner had requested in 1852. By 1876 there were ten mules to work the 350 acres then planted at Gowrie by free labor: yet in 1858 Manigault had supplied only four mules to till the 624 acres then cultivated by slaves. Only by the low standards of a slave system could the master's provision of these few mules have been considered noteworthy.[32]

Besides diminishing the slaves' labor by increased use of mules, Skinner was adept at granting the privilege of a holiday, within the framework of the plantation's stringent annual routine. Gowrie's slaves, both male and female, had to do six full tasks per week, with no diminution on Saturday. This was more demanding than on some plantations, where the women might be given a half day's respite on Saturday for their sewing, washing, and household chores. The custom at Gowrie was that all slaves might be granted one day's holiday in the spring and another one at the end of the harvest, at the overseer's discretion. In Skinner's first year at Gowrie, however, he contrived to give the slaves an extra springtime holiday, and the grant of this privilege doubtless helped him to secure a less grudging subordination from them than usual. He had intended to let the slaves have a holiday on Thursday, May 30, 1851, when any who wished could go to Savannah; but a smallpox epidemic in that town gave him a plausible excuse for granting bondsmen and women the privilege of an unexpected second day's vacation. "The Hands did so well in [hoeing] those very foul [fields]," he wrote on May 30, "that I am induced to give them to day for holiday, but none to go to Town (at their own request) [because of the epidemic]. I will give them a day to go to Town when I get well ahead [with the hoeing] & the Small Pox disappears."[33]

Reluctant—except under the prodding of an overseer like Skinner—to grant many holidays to his slaves, Manigault was also averse to exempting children from plantation work. A contrast is sometimes drawn between the exploitation of children in Britain's early Industrial Revolution and a putative freedom of American slave children from labor, but Gowrie's records lend little support to such a distinction. Manigault was as prepared as any industrialist to employ a child at the first moment the young slave was old enough to be useful. In his rice mill there was a screen through which the dark and inferior grains of "small rice" were supposed to fall. If the screen became clogged, this inferior rice would pollute the better-quality grains, reducing the price a merchant would pay. Manigault might have instructed his miller to stop the mill periodically to scrape the screen; or else he might have tried installing a mechanical device to clean the screen regularly during the milling; but he preferred to use "2 small Boys" so that one of them could be present "all the time . . . to clean it." The tidal mill had to be run when the tide was low (when the water in the canal was thus several feet below the level of water in the mill ponds); and if it was to be run twice a day, this often meant working through the night. One of the demerits of Stephen the miller, the Manigaults felt, was that he lacked their enthusiasm for child labor in the middle of the night: sometimes he seems to have let the child go to sleep.[34] That the Manigaults' rice might consequently lose some of its commercial value was not much skin off Stephen's nose.

If a child was big enough, the Manigaults believed the age of nine was not too soon for her or him to be put to work. But in 1860 Betsey, the nine-year-old daughter of the former driver Ishmael, did not seem to Dr. Gabriel

Manigault—who as a medical man might be more fastidious about these matters than most rice planters—quite developed enough for house service. She "has grown a little," he notified his brother Louis, "but looks quite delicate. She might learn how to sew in the house, but is still too small to be of much use."[35] The principle of child labor was taken for granted by Charles Manigault. In claying the rice seed for use in the open-planting technique, he advised Louis that "little hands can help much." And during the annual harvesttime crises, any child who could help was made to do so. The ripe rice "comes on our hands faster than we can cut, tie, & stack in the [fields]," Skinner reported desperately in 1851. "I will make every thing [i.e., everyone] that can tie a sheaf of rice do it."[36]

A different function performed by certain young slave children—surprising to those unfamiliar with antebellum customs—was to help white women entertain their own children. Probably in 1862, when Louis Manigault's first son was almost four, Louis commandeered a slave child named Cuffy—a year older than Louis's boy—to fulfill this role. Cuffy had been named in memory of his father's brother, who had died in the "cholera" of 1854; but as Louis did not like the name, he changed it to Casar (thus flouting the intention of Cuffy's father, William, who, having died of pneumonia in 1859, was unable to protest). Cuffy's new name created a problem, however; for he had a younger, crippled brother who was already named Casar. No matter: the original Casar could be given a new name too; and Louis Manigault—no doubt thinking derisively of the crippled fort in Charleston harbor—renamed the crippled infant Sumter. He then took the newly named Casar away from his mother, Cotta, transported him to Augusta, and kept him there for about three years as companion to his own son, until the abolition of slavery in 1865 terminated a master's right to dispose of a black child in this way.[37]

Thus the Manigaults—regarding even a mother's claim to raise her own young child not as a right but as a favor that might be withdrawn to suit the master's interest—were parsimonious in the extension of privileges to their slaves. Children worked as soon as they could; a full day's work on Saturday by both men and women was taken for granted; the Christmas holiday was short; and there were few other holidays except at the behest of a relatively enlightened overseer like Skinner. Meat was in short supply, there were no vegetable patches, and if cloth was better than average, it was distributed on the strict understanding that a woman must finish her daily task quickly enough to leave time for sewing up all her own and her children's clothes, and some of her husband's. The elements within this stringent regimen were constantly manipulated by Charles Manigault to make the slaves feel he granted them privileges which he might at any moment withdraw. They must not complain gratuitously, or they might lose the privilege of eating small rice. The women must do their tasks quickly and sew up their cloth, or they would find themselves short in the summer distribution. The slaves must all submit cheerfully to their lot, or they might find themselves deprived of one of the discretionary holidays, or stinted in the discretionary supply of meat. Privilege, like the whip, was indispensable to plantation management; and at

Gowrie it probably often (except under a particularly aggressive overseer like Capers) helped elicit the required facade of cheerful subordination.

Even more important in plantation management than the grant of privileges to the whole gang was the extension of special favors to selected individuals. Such privileges included better-than-average clothing, cash, and special medical care. In contrast to the short jackets given to other adult males for the winter, long coats were procured for the drivers—symbolizing their favored position and protecting their health less inefficiently than the field hands' from the cold rains and winds. In November 1861—when panic suddenly struck the low country and gunpowder was found in Ishmael's cabin, while unrest clutched a dozen slaves, including even captain Hector—Louis Manigault and William Capers appealed crassly to the self-interest of the new driver John, in order to keep the others under control. Charles Manigault still possessed John's watch and some clothing, which he had held in Charleston since 1860 as guarantee of John's good behavior at Gowrie. Louis wrote anxiously to his father that, according to Capers, driver John "is still the Same," unmoved by the North's invasion of the sea islands:

> John is a Man of great importance to us [Louis continued nervously], and he stands much in need of a pair of boots, & a Coat & Common hat. His measure is 11 Inches, and I would Certainly recommend your sending the above to me, . . . & you Can also send what Clothes you have. He asked me particularly after his watch & is now using Mr. Capers' Son's watch.[38]

Although the Manigaults never otherwise expressed so starkly—as in this panicky letter of Louis's—the idea of "divide and conquer," the principle was long established. Thus at the November 1833 distribution of cloth at Silk Hope, four leading slaves (the driver, the chief carpenter, the bricklayer, and the housekeeper) were each given the bonus of one yard of *white* cloth, over and above the five or six yards of blue cloth allotted to every adult slave. In the 1830s Charles Manigault occasionally spent $.25 on a gift of tobacco for Gowrie's driver Harry; he also appropriated a total of $.35—$.11⅔ each—to buying driver Harry and two other privileged slaves slightly better-quality shoes than those furnished Gowrie's other adults. A larger bonus went to the Silk Hope cooper, whom Manigault dispatched to Gowrie to make barrels during the winter of 1835–36, and whom he offered $.25 (the standard commercial price) for every barrel more than his "task." As the cooper made thirty-five extra barrels, he received $8.75—a substantial privilege indeed by the slave's standards. This principle of rewarding artisans was sustained in later years: Charles Manigault once paid Jack Savage $3.00 for hoop poles made during his own time, and on another occasion he gave Jack the not inconsiderable sum of $5.00 for his part in building a boat (as well as $2.00 to John Izard).[39]

Special medical care was the most costly privilege which might be granted a slave. In 1857 the Manigaults spent $10.00 to have the high-priced Dr. Bullock attend Louis's cook Dolly at Gowrie. Later that year they paid him

$41.00 for extensive treatment in Savannah of an eye injury to Louis's favorite slave, captain Hector. And the next year they paid their own Dr. Ogier in Charleston to diagnose the extent of the shoulder injury suffered by driver George's wife from the thresher's conveyor belt.[40]

It might be tempting to conclude that these grants of special treatment were ineffectual: for ex-driver George tried to flee in 1861, Jack Savage ran away for eighteen months in 1862, Dolly escaped in 1863, John Izard tried unsuccessfully to abscond in the same year, and Louis Manigault was convinced that captain Hector would have fled had he not been prevented from doing so. No doubt the privileges had failed of their long-term purpose, once the Civil War changed the military balance of power. But during peacetime the grant of special favors enabled low-country planters successfully to co-opt many able slaves into the system.

For some slaves the most important privilege conferred by the Manigaults was a measure of esteem. How the masters' regard for a slave was intermixed with other gifts may be seen in the careers of the mulatto John Izard and of Charles the trunk minder. John, the versatile carpenter, engineer, and jack-of-all-trades, was one of the most favored slaves at Gowrie, and his first privilege was a recognized surname. This was a symbol of respect withheld from nearly all other slaves because slavery involved dishonor. Slaves must usually be denied the distinction of a surname, the masters felt, or they would get too big for their boots; but a handful might be accorded the special privilege to set them off from the others. John Izard was permitted to travel alone by steamship, back and forth from Savannah to Charleston (with a letter of permission from his master or overseer), in order to work at whichever of the Manigault plantations currently required his skilled labor. He was given cash gifts for his work (e.g., the two dollars paid him for his part in building a boat). He was made chief engineer of the steam thresher (supplanting the allegedly somnolent Jimmy), and he was entrusted with the keys to the building. After recovering from a serious illness in 1859—probably another case of pneumonia, like the one he had had in 1853—John was instructed by Charles Manigault (via Louis) "to tell the head Stewart [on the Savannah to Charleston steamboat] that he belongs to me, & they will blow out John Izard first rate with supper" at Manigault's expense. John was given opportunities to extend the range of his skills—for example, to bricklaying—and the Manigaults then used him to save themselves the expense of hiring a specialist. When the thresher needed painting, overseer Skinner cut the cost by buying oil and paint separately, "as John says he can mix it." John evidently took pride in his versatility, and probably to him his most valuable privilege was the esteem of his masters and of some of the overseers, which no doubt also increased his standing with some of the other slaves. Louis Manigault depended as much on John Izard's judgment as on that of overseer Stephen Clark in deciding whether a cogwheel in the thresher needed replacement: "Neither Clark, John Izard or Myself," Louis told his father, "think there is any use to have another made." Slavery was designed to undermine the self-esteem of most slaves; and the privilege of winning the master's genuine respect was sweeter to certain estimable slaves than the small tip, or rare "blowout," by which favor normally was marked.[41]

Another privileged slave was Charles the trunk minder—a "cunning" man like captain Hector—who was willing to tell tales on other slaves to secure his own advantage.[42] When Manigault bought Gowrie in 1833, Charles was already serving as second driver (under Harry), and when dysentery disabled Harry in 1846, the overseer promoted Charles to head driver. Charles Manigault, then in Europe, did not think his namesake the right man for the job, and two years later he fully approved when another overseer "broke" Charles and replaced him by the "remarkable" Renty, reducing Charles to the rank of field hand. Not until six years later was Charles restored to privilege— being then made trunk minder.

Meanwhile, he had gradually gained the Manigaults' confidence by assuming limited responsibilities. In 1852, for example, he was entrusted to bring back from Savannah the third mule, which Skinner had persuaded Charles Manigault to ship from South Carolina. And it was the slave Charles who came at midnight on Sunday, March 5, 1854, to warn Louis Manigault that an embankment was broken: the slaves must immediately flee to the pounding mill, as the freshet would quickly inundate all the rest of the plantation. Charles's initiative probably persuaded the Manigaults to restore him to privilege, and seven weeks later he held the post of trunk minder.[43] A trunk minder needed to know when to flood and drain the fields, and how fast, but did not have to be good at wielding authority over other slaves; and Charles won the Manigaults' esteem in this more limited role. They came to rely heavily on his judgment, more so than they would have done for an ordinary trunk minder, because Charles had had years of experience as the second driver, and even two years as head driver.

How much Charles Manigault depended on him became evident in 1859. By January of that year Louis Manigault had been managing Gowrie for seven years, but he still had much to learn from the privileged slaves. That month Gowrie was without an overseer (William Bryan having been peremptorily sacked, and no replacement having yet been found), and Louis would soon have to assume an overseer's responsibility for the three plantings of the new crop. Charles Manigault took for granted that in these delicate operations (which must each be synchronized with the high tides) Louis would rely heavily on the two slaves most knowledgeable about tidal rice culture. "You have Considerable experience now," Manigault encouraged his son, "& with the experience of 'Charles' & 'George' [the head driver since Robert's death in 1857] you can plant perfectly the first & 2d &c." Twelve weeks later Charles Manigault had still not succeeded in hiring a new overseer, and as the time rapidly approached when Louis would have to flee the malarial swamp, the elder Manigault contemplated—reluctantly, but without alarm—the prospect that Gowrie might have to be left under the sole control of two slaves for all the rest of the year. The law required a white man to be present on every plantation, but Manigault planned to fulfill this requirement only nominally, paying lip service to a law he did not believe in. "It is a common thing with persons in our predicament," he explained to Louis,

> with a well trained, & disposed gang, to get what is called a "Key Keeper," just to scrdne the law of having a white man on ones plantation, who under written instructions will be guided by the experience of the Driver (& in our case Charles with him) as to the management of the Crop. Joe Huger did this last year. And Walter Blake [another big South Carolina rice planter] has done so, & McM[illan] King told me that he has had to do the same.

Reluctant Manigault might be, but he would depend solely on driver George and trunk minder Charles, with no overseer, if he must.[44]

To have deputed great responsibility in 1859 to one or two slaves would have been consonant with Manigault's earlier practice. For nine of the dozen years before 1849—when Bagshaw, then Haynes, and then Jesse Cooper were overseers—no white man had resided at Gowrie during eight or nine months of each year. Only at the harvest and milling seasons was a suboverseer hired for a few months to live on the plantation. Bagshaw, Haynes, and Cooper resided on nearby estates and combined the part-time overseership of Gowrie with overseeing other plantations. For most of the year the Gowrie drivers supervised the field hands each day, largely on their own. "I always preferred being without a resident overseer," Manigault had informed his cousin in 1847,

> & having a neighbour's Overseer to manage for me, who at harvest & while the mill is at work always hires an assistant to live on the plantation, & attend to these things for 3 or 4 months. And this has been my plan for many years. [Manigault explained that he, in contrast to many rice planters, had only a] little place, . . . small & compact . . . , requiring in general merely a walk through it once a day by the manager, who sees that all is right, & gives orders for the morrow—the driver going to him in the evening to make his report. . . . Mr. Bagshaw who previously managed in this way 6 years for me . . . had four places to attend to.[45]

The scarcity of good overseers—combined with Manigault's congenital distrust of those whom he did finally manage to hire—had prompted this course of action. The wife of a resident overseer was sure to wish to raise chickens, and this would inevitably lead to disputes with the slaves. A resident overseer, furthermore, was likely to rob Manigault of his slaves' time, commandeering some of them to make boat trips to Savannah to carry provisions for the overseer's family. And an overseer might ruffle the feathers of the slaves, interfering with routines the slaves understood as well as, or better than, the white man. A new suboverseer must not "meddle too much with any work the Negroes may be doing until he gets more experience in Rice Plantation work," Manigault instructed in 1845; and in 1853 he was singing the same tune. The new overseer that year had to agree to "be careful not to interfere too much with the beating and management of the Rice Mill in cases where I am unacquainted with such machinery and the working of it, as the Negroes in charge have much experience therein."[46]

Even when, in 1849, Manigault shifted to requiring his overseer (or at least a suboverseer) to reside at Gowrie throughout the year,[47] substantial responsibilities continued to devolve upon the driver. The overseer always departed the island at nighttime during the long malarial season, taking refuge at a pineland camp on the mainland, and leaving the driver in charge until after work had started the next morning. And in making plantation decisions the Manigaults always relied a good deal on the driver's judgment, especially—as has been shown—from 1848 to 1857, when Robert was the head driver. If Louis Manigault wished to persuade his father that he was acting prudently, he was likely to invoke Robert's authority in addition to that of the overseer. Thus when Louis projected a staged return from the "cholera" camp to Gowrie after the 1854 epidemic, he assured Charles Manigault that "both Clark [the overseer] & Robert . . . think my plan good."

When the new overseer in 1856 (Venters) seemed to be making a muck of things, the problem—Charles Manigault thought—might have been that Venters was not paying enough attention to the advice of Robert, and of Charles the trunk minder. Robert's opinion must cautiously be sounded. The 1856 crop had proved smaller than expected, and although Charles Manigault tried to appear evenhanded between the overseer and the driver, he obviously was predisposed to trust driver Robert more than Venters. Louis should "ferret out this mystery," Charles Manigault urged him,

> by enquiring of the driver [Robert], trunkminder [Charles], &c. [probably referring to captain Hector, the chief boat hand], without shewing that you believe in the Overseers incapasity. Then make up your mind whether he is an imbécille, or whether he be not in fault & all other qualities are tolerable. . . .

> You will find out, slowly, Cautiously, & clearly, whether Venters & Robert pulled together, or not, so as to have rendered available or not for general interests & results, the information & local experience of all Roberts requisite knowledge, &c. tending towards the prosperity of the Crop, &c. & whether any insolence was shewn on Robert's side, or any assumption or pretence of knowing every thing led Venters to rush on to the Consummation of a failure by holding in Contempt Roberts, & Charles', practical experience.

This delicate inquiry convinced Louis that Venters had "made two great and fatal mistakes." Early in the season he had drained the fields too fast, "prostrating his rice to the ground"; and then he had left the fields dry too long. He had failed to heed the sensible counsel of the leading slaves.[48]

The grant of special privileges to drivers, trunk minders, house servants, and artisans was thus a vital element in the Manigaults' management of Gowrie. Without the assistance of the leading slaves, plantation operations could not have proceeded. How, then, should one regard these privileged bondsmen and women? Are they to be seen as quislings—traitorous collaborators with an enemy regime?

The analogy to the Nazi occupation of Europe is unconvincing. The conquered people of Holland in 1940 were born free, and they might reasonably hope to regain freedom within a few years. By contrast, the residents of Gowrie—born enslaved, and of enslaved ancestors—were likely, so far as they could see, to remain slaves for the rest of their lives. Insurrection was not an option at Gowrie; overt physical resistance seemed beyond the pale; and flight could lead only to temporary relief. No BBC broadcasts honestly reported the progress of a war of liberation to clandestine listeners in the huts of Argyle Island, and indeed (until 1861) there was no war to bring hope to the subjugated. Under such desperate circumstances, ought every slave to have refused a position of responsibility within the plantation regime, and to have plodded hopelessly, monotonously, stultifyingly in the mud swamps for day after day, until death offered surcease? Are only those slaves to be admired who sought solace in the illusory hope of life after death?

One of the strengths of Eugene Genovese's *Roll, Jordan, Roll* is its author's understanding of the dilemmas faced by privileged slaves. Perceiving that a degree of accommodation to the slave regime was inevitable, Genovese has celebrated the "resistance within accommodation" of many bondsmen and women like Thomas Dabney's Mammy Maria, who used her privileged position to benefit the wider slave community.[49]

Surely, however, most slaves who accepted a position of responsibility aimed to develop and exercise their own human talents; to escape exhausting, boring, unskilled labor; and to improve the material condition of themselves and of their families. These were secular, not religious, purposes; and they were probably on the whole self-interested (and family-oriented) rather than inspired by devotion to the welfare of the whole slave community. Were such aims less admirable for being this-worldly and individualistic?

Within an enslaved working class at Gowrie arose figures like driver Robert, trunk minder Charles, engineer John Izard, the nurse Old Binah, the house servant Jane, her brother cooper George, washerwoman Dolly, carpenter Jack Savage, the miller Cato, and the boatman captain Hector, all of whom accepted positions of responsibility and privilege. When one contemplates the only alternative available to them—endless dreary labor in the wet, stinking, malarial miasma—one can scarcely begrudge these human beings their aspirations to a less degraded existence. And this remains true even though surely not every one of them used her or his privileges to promote the general interest of the slave community. All aspired to human dignity by exercising skills beyond those of menial labor. Although some of them doubtless pursued self-interest at the expense of their fellows, taken as a group these were perhaps among the most admirable of slaves, combating through their own personal development their masters' impulse to render slaves wholly powerless and dishonored.

A defense of slaves who accepted positions of responsibility does not, however, mean that every such slave was a splendid worker, nor does it imply the existence at Gowrie of a socially distinct "slave elite." The skill and efficiency of the privileged bondsmen and women should not be exaggerated. When a master relied on his own artisans, he often did so with no great esteem for their workmanship, and only because of the scarcity of competent free tradesmen. Thus in 1835, when Silk Hope's leading artisan died, the overseer's comment was ambivalent: the deceased chief carpenter "was but an inferior Carpenter but will be greatly miss[ed] here, as [the bricklayer] is [as a carpenter] only a Jobber." At Gowrie Jack Savage often did excellent (albeit slow) carpentry, and John Izard was also a good workman, but the craftsmanship of Manigault's other carpenters like Amos, Pride, and Willey was only fair. Masters and overseers made plain that Jack Savage, unlike several of the others, was no mere "plantation carpenter," for this was a term implying mediocrity. When two leaky old plantation flatboats were repaired and recaulked in 1851, overseer Skinner wanted the job done "in a very superior mode" compared to what plantation carpenters would do, and he persuaded Manigault to send the flats to a Savannah shipyard instead of relying on the Gowrie workmen. He was greatly disappointed, to be sure, for not only were the shipyard's charges—in his view—extortionate but the "work was done below plantation workmanship, being slight & rough."[50]

Although masters gladly used slave artisans when a job (like building a wharf) was "so plain and simple [that] we need no workmen but our own," they usually sought to hire free artisans—often whites—for highly skilled work. For example, keeping the pounding mill in good order was a perennial problem, Stephen the miller being better at operating the machinery than at repairing it. In 1843 Manigault apparently was unsuccessful in his efforts to hire a white man to overhaul the machinery. The next year, however, he succeeded in bypassing Stephen, employing a white artisan for a fourteen-week repair job. In 1849 a white workman spent two weeks at Gowrie, readying the mill for that year's operations. And three years later John Izard and the then engineer, Jimmy, tried for a long time—but failed—to repair the pumps in the steam thresher. Although overseer Skinner praised John for his good work—John "stopped [the old joints] with hot lead, then put all together nicely & faithfully. . . . John exerted himself"—the overseer had to report that John could not get the pumps to work. A more skilled engineer must be hired to do the job: "A proper person" must be dispatched from Charleston to Gowrie "to put everything in perfect order . . . ," Skinner implored. "It will require a most competent person for this case."[51]

Similar problems beset the tidal pounding mill. The quality and quantity of grain milled by Stephen the miller had more than once been criticized in the 1840s, and in 1852 he was unable to get the top millstone properly aligned with the bottom stone.[52] "They must be put in first-rate order," Skinner advised, "by a first-rate mill-wright, before I can have any rice ground. Stephen Tommy & Primus have been endeavouring to fix them and can't do so. Stephen says that it will take a mill-wright to fix them properly."[53]

For skilled brickworkers to rebuild East Hermitage's brick thresher in 1856,[54] Manigault felt obliged to turn to black artisans in Charleston— probably free men, though one may have been a slave authorized to hire out his own time. The choice seemed to be between an independent-minded man ("Ellick the Mulatto") whom a Charleston machinist firm declared "was the only man whom they employed to do their Brickwork," and another black man named Tom: "Ellick knows more of Steam thresher brick works than Tom [Manigault reflected], for he put up the brick work of 2 or 3 Steam Threshers [which the machinist firm] built. But he is a slippery dodging fellow, & I . . . prefer Tom." If he could pin down one or both of these black men, Charles Manigault would rather have hired them than a Savannah bricklayer named Henry Sharp (probably white), because they were cheaper: and no Gowrie slave, not even John Izard, had the requisite skills.[55]

Gowrie's drivers, too, had their limitations, of which the most poignant illustration was the partial responsibility of drivers George and Ralph for London's suicide in 1860. Of course, drivers often failed to perform their duties as the master would wish, and Manigault—contrary to his later claim to his cousin—had in 1845 embarked with enthusiasm upon the experiment of hiring a year-round resident suboverseer to accomplish jobs the drivers had neglected.[56] The new suboverseer, Manigault exclaimed cheerfully in 1845, had had canals dug out which hadn't been done since before 1833, and he had also begun to "half quarter drain" the fields. Driver Harry, in other words, had sensibly failed to require of the slaves as much cold, unhealthy winter work as was essential to the plantation's long-term profitability.[57] Less understandably, drivers Harry, Charles, Robert, Ishmael, and Stephney were inefficient in getting even the settlement ditches cleaned out to protect the slaves' health. The drivers, like the artisans, held privileged and responsible positions, but like everyone else they were fallible: their efficiency ought not to be overstated.

The evidence may appear contradictory about whether privilege sharply divided some slaves from others. No doubt being selected as a house servant to accompany Louis Manigault, for half the year, to Charleston was a privilege indeed: one which might even save a slave's life. This was evident in 1860 when Charles Manigault recommended the fifteen-year-old son of the Silk Hope driver (to replace the suicide London, who had *not* been taken to Charleston that summer) as Louis Manigault's valet: the fifteen-year-old "is rather delicate looking," Charles observed, "& cannot remain on Savannah River in Summer." No doubt, too, a massive favor was conferred upon a slave by his or her selection for certain of Gowrie's other jobs. Thus when Capers demoted captain Hector to field work in 1859, the former boatman "begged" to be restored to his privileged position. The regard which some privileged slaves might feel for another privileged bondsman is suggested by the naming of two babies "Harry" in 1845—presumably for Gowrie's aging driver—even though none of the four parents seems to have been a relative of Harry's. The second driver Charles and his wife, Juna, named their infant Harry, and so did carpenter Jack Savage and his wife, Amey. And the masters' attempt to separate domestic servants from field hands was evident in their building a "servant house" at Gowrie, set a little apart from the houses where the other slaves lived.[58]

Yet it would be rash to infer from this evidence that the holders of privileged positions formed a special stratum in Gowrie's social structure. A bird minder with a gun in his hand, like Posh, might be pleased by the privilege in the spring and in the autumn when the bobolinks were migrating, but he was still a field hand most of the year (until he was promoted to being a trunk minder). No doubt a plowman exercised skill and judgment in this job, but during most months Gowrie's plows remained in the shed; thus when Stephney lost his privileged position as the East Hermitage driver in 1855 and was demoted to plowman, this meant that most of the year he worked with the field hands. The coopers were skilled artisans, yet both at planting time and during the harvest they worked as field hands, building barrels only during certain slack times before the harvest and after the milling. Even the most skilled artisan at Gowrie, Jack Savage, was taken away from carpentry to do ordinary field labor at harvesttime, and the less skilled carpenters spent even more time in the field than did Jack.[59]

The blurred line between field hands and the privileged was even more indistinct for female slaves. The title "plantation cook," "overseer's cook." or "plantation nurse" might sound impressive; but it soon becomes evident that—just as there was a high turnover among drivers—so there was an even higher turnover among the holders of these apparently favored women's jobs. In fact, nearly every "plantation cook" or "overseer's cook" at Gowrie had been a field worker but was now too old or too unhealthy to serve any longer as a "prime hand." The same was true of most of those women who successively were denominated "plantation nurse." This was almost surely true even of the Manigaults' esteemed "Old Binah," who seems still to have been a "prime" field hand at the age of 42.[60] The one year of "Sister Jane's" work as plantation nurse was a partial exception to the rule that this job was reserved for the elderly and the disabled;[61] but Jane herself was obliged to do field labor both before and after her serving as Louis Manigault's house cook and as nurse.

Even in one of the rare instances when Charles Manigault betrayed real human feeling for one of his slaves, he was careful to specify that this woman (formerly a house servant in Charleston) was not to be exempted from field labor. His concern for the sixteen-year-old Nanny—he was quick to assure Louis—arose only from his worry about the health of a girl unaccustomed to the mud and wintry winds of Argyle Island. "She from a Child has only been in our house," he wrote in December 1858, "& you will see what you Can do with her & if best she can go in the field in April, but not before. She is as yet unaccustomed to exposure, but strong, healthy, & quite a young woman." A week later Charles urged Louis "only [to] give her half task, should She not be employed at indoor plantation work (at the Thresher, &c.)." But he hastened to add a postscript, protesting that he did not intend her to be kept indoors now that she was old enough to make a field laborer. "You must not think I want 'Nanny' to be a house servant. . . . I merely wish great care taken of her at first going off She thus far being a stranger to field work, to the climate, the water, & to exposure." It was all right for a female to be a house servant when she was a girl, and again when she was superannuated; but "prime" females must work in the field, and it was time for a sixteen-year-old woman to be broken in to the rigors of the life which faced her.[62]

The principal institution dissolving a line between privileged slaves and field hands was marriage. In April 1852 the wife of each especially privileged male was a field hand: this was true of Hester (driver Robert's wife), Crecie (driver Ishmael's wife), Amey (Jack Savage's wife), Margaret (John Izard's wife), Catherine (miller Cato's wife), Joaney (boat captain Hector's wife), Betty (cooper George's wife), Die (trunk minder Joe's wife), and Dinah (engineer Jimmy's wife).[63]

A high turnover in office was another force impeding the formation of sharp class distinctions within the slave community. In April 1852—the month just discussed—Charles (who had been broken as driver in 1848) was a field hand, but he was restored to a privileged position (as trunk minder) in 1854. By that time Ishmael had been reduced to the rank of field hand, and Cato the miller was dead. A year later trunk minder Joe had died; by 1856 Jimmy had been degraded from engineer to fireman; and by 1857 Robert was dead. Captain Hector was demoted to field work in 1859, and cooper George—after a spell as driver—was reduced to field work in 1860. Flux, not stasis, was the rule at Gowrie.

So impermanent was the line between privileged slaves and field hands that—as has previously been indicated—every one of the six principal families resident at Gowrie on November 30, 1848, contained both types of slaves. Minty, for example, was a field hand all her life; there is no sign that her parental family enjoyed privilege; and three of her four husbands were probably field hands. Yet she was also, for eight years, the wife of Renty (driver briefly in 1848, until his death from measles); and several of her children and stepchildren were granted privileges. Her son Billy was trained as a carpenter; her son Scotland became Louis Manigault's esteemed house cook; and her stepson Fortune served several years as the overseer's houseboy, before his repeated flights led to his sale in 1860. People in this family—like those in most other Gowrie families—were members neither of an "elite" nor of an undifferentiated mass of field hands. Rather, privilege was a gift of the master which might be extended to, and then withdrawn from, more than one member of most families. The selective granting of privilege was a means of dividing to conquer; it did not, at Gowrie, provide the foundation for fixed divisions between different social classes among the enslaved.[64]

Gowrie's bondsmen and women were all in the same boat. It was not a coal-burning ocean liner, with engine room below deck, seamen above them, and cabin crew on top. It was not even a modified Venetian trireme, with enslaved oarsmen below and a differentiated "slave elite" above. The metaphor of layered social "stratification" is misleading for Gowrie, whose society resembled a single-tiered Viking war vessel with two smallish compartments amidships, setting off two social groups which essentially were on the same level as the mass of the slave population. In one of these compartments were a handful of the artisans and house servants, distinguished from other slaves by their training, culture, or ancestry (e.g., the mulatto John Izard—at once carpenter, engineer, bricklayer, paint mixer—and his sister-in-law Jane, an unmarried house servant whose stance toward the Manigaults was more familiar than that of most slaves). In a second compartment were males like driver Robert, driver George, and Charles the trunk minder, whose distinction lay not in an artisan's training (though George had been a cooper) nor in assimilation to their masters' culture, but in personal qualities of leadership, and in the acquisition of agricultural lore through long years of responsibility within the plantation regime. There was no sharp separation between the slaves in these two compartments and those in other parts of the single-tiered vessel. Robert, George, Charles, and John Izard were all married to field hands, and anyone in the two compartments might at any moment be plucked by the Manigaults out of his or her compartment and placed in the main part of the boat with all the other slaves. This was what happened to Jane in 1846 (when she was exiled from house service in Charleston to field labor at Silk Hope, and later at Gowrie) and again (after a spell in a special compartment) in 1854; and it happened to driver George in 1860. To be in one of the two special compartments was a privilege decreed by the master that might readily be withdrawn; it was not a solid, fixed position in a layered geologic stratification system.

The Viking ship did not sail sedately across a calm North Sea from Scandinavia to England. The journey, on the contrary, was stormy; the ship was disease-stricken; and sailors constantly dropped into the sea and were lost from sight. The number of dead children tossed overboard was legion, and adults were also likely to perish in untimely fashion. Death—unlike the Manigaults—played no favorites with those in the two special compartments: Charles the trunk minder lost overboard all nine of his children;[65] Robert lost all his children and his first two wives; and John Izard lost all three of his own children and all three of his wives—one to pleurisy, a second to "cholera," and the third to dysentery.

The vessel had therefore to return periodically to some Norwegian fjord to pick up new crew members—those purchased irregularly by Charles Manigault in Charleston, or culled from his gang at Silk Hope—to replace those left dead in the North Sea. There was a sort of grim game of musical chairs on board the ship, with one piano played by Death and a second one played by Charles Manigault, determining who would drop overboard, and who would sit in one of the two compartments: would the driver at East Hermitage be Ishmael (1849), or Stephney (1853), or Ralph (1855), or (in 1860) the new driver John? Life was not the static, unchanging routine of some fabled "organic" society. On the contrary, instability was the norm, an instability in some ways matching and in some ways exceeding that of proletarian wage laborers in an industrializing "community." New overseers arrived every few years, each one introducing modifications into the system of subordination and privilege. The coming of a new overseer might presage a period of relaxed discipline, as apparently occurred under Venters and William Bryan; but it might usher in a long struggle between overseer, drivers, and field hands, as happened in 1859 with the arrival of William Capers. Drivers were changed frequently, and each new driver brought with him further disciplinary changes. Slaves died like flies; scores of new slaves were imported into Gowrie; some slaves moved back and forth between South Carolina and Georgia, like the ten Silk Hope hands Manigault sent to help with Gowrie's harvest in 1856;[66] a significant number of slaves were sold to New Orleans; and an even larger number fled for weeks into the swamps. Husbands, wives, and children were separated, often by death, sometimes by sale, not infrequently by the voluntary action of the slaves themselves. Life was confined within the sides of a narrow vessel, but it was by no means unchanging.

Thus Gowrie was not the stable, patriarchal society dear to the florid imagination of the antebellum Virginia theorist George Fitzhugh. The slaves, on the contrary, were locked into a class conflict of epic proportions, pitting a largely homogeneous class of slaves against profit-seeking masters whose interests seldom coincided with those of their bondsmen and women. This conflict expressed itself over a range of issues, from the frequency of a meat ration to the severity of punishing fugitives; but its clearest sign was the enthusiasm and bellicosity with which in 1861 rice planters armed the low country for a war to keep the slaves enslaved.

In this struggle the weapons of Gowrie's slaves were not insurrection or— except most unusually—overt resistance. Many slaves fled to the swamp for temporary relief, and there was a significant tradition of collective, nonviolent resistance. But the contest was an unequal one, and the slaves' principal weapon was to work inefficiently. Gowrie's slaves did not free themselves, nor had they any chance of doing so. They were freed by General Sherman's army: they were freed, that is, mainly by white soldiers, deeply imbued with their own racial prejudices, acting upon the orders of political leaders who blended idealism with a powerful appeal to the self-interest of Northern whites. Northern soldiers finally defeated—but only barely so—those masters whose class interest was to preserve slavery, and those other Southern whites who felt they shared that interest.

Because a great historian of American slavery has incautiously introduced— into his brilliant cultural analysis of the world the slaves made—a dubious portrayal of the slaveholders' regime, it may be necessary to consider briefly the term "paternalism." This word has sometimes been employed to denominate three concepts which need clear demarcation from each other: (1) the slaveholders' ideology, (2) their motives, and (3) the system of punishments, allowances, and privileges which the planters imposed on their bondsmen and women.

"Paternalism" is not used in the third sense here, because doing so might confuse analysis. In popular usage "paternalism" is heavily freighted with value judgments: "paternalism" was benevolent conduct, and a "paternalist" was a person with (admirably) benevolent motives, whose behavior could be likened to that of a kindly father acting for the welfare of dependent children.

No matter how much a historian may seek to use the word in a value-free sense, popular understanding of the term makes it almost impossible to do so. Eugene Genovese has compounded this difficulty by arguing that the conduct of many slaveholders was surprisingly benevolent; he thus slips uncomfortably back and forth between a value-free analysis of the system of allowances and privileges, and a value-laden discussion of planters' motives.[67]

A way to avoid confusion may be to employ three different terms for the three concepts. (1) "Paternalist ideology" is an appropriate phrase for analyzing the beliefs of many proslavery publicists, and of some planters. (2) "Paternalism" is similarly useful for analyzing the motives of planters. Benevolent motives *were* indeed salient in shaping the conduct of some slaveholders; they also existed—though not prominently so—among the motives of many other masters; and these impulses may properly be called "paternalist." But the term should be rigorously limited to a discussion of motives. (3) If muddy water is to be avoided, therefore, the system itself should be called something else; and whenever the short word "slavery" is insufficient, a value-free term like "system of punishments, allowances, and privileges" is essential.[68]

In the first sense, then, did the Manigaults subscribe to a paternalist ideology? As we have seen, such a theory did indeed—in 1870—furnish Charles Manigault a ready-made garb within whose folds he might dress himself before his descendants' gaze.[69] This was not, however, the clothing he had worn before the Civil War, when he was an active entrepreneur. Paternalist theory would posit a morally binding obligation on both master and slave toward each other—but this was not how Charles Manigault saw things. In his eyes the slave's duty to the master preceded that of the master to the slave, and if the former was not fulfilled, the latter was nugatory. Manigault expressed this view in his favorite maxim: "A good Negro [i.e., slave] makes a good master";[70] and he genuinely felt that slaves had a moral duty to work well and be obedient. The source of the slave's prior duty was that he or she was a "negro."

The Manigaults and their overseers almost never used the word "slave." Occasionally they said "servant" (as in the overseer's letter announcing the drowning of Cato the miller);[71] sometimes they referred to their slaves as "the people"; but by far the preferred term was "negro." Thus when Louis's brother Dr. Gabriel Manigault went hunting for fugitive slaves along the Cooper River in November 1860, he went "with a parcel of overseers and three professional negro hunters with nine dogs." By South Carolina law the word "negro" meant "slave,"[72] and a deep-rooted popular usage underlay the legal terminology. Determined as they were to preserve slavery, and hostile as many of them were to democratic principles, the low-country planters nevertheless sensed that slavery, pure and simple, was not consonant with the values of their century. Few of them felt real guilt about slavery, but they— like the authors of the American Constitution in 1787—were squeamish about the word "slave": better, the low-country planters thought, to say "negro" and remind oneself that the source of the slave's duty lay in her or his race.

One consequence of this usage was that the lessons the Manigaults and their overseers thought they learned from their dealings with slaves were nearly always racial ones. This was most evident in Louis Manigault's relation to the overseer William Capers—in Louis's words "a perfect Gentleman," who as Charles Manigault's second cousin "belonged to the best blood of Carolina." Although Capers never secured unusually large crops, and his reign from 1859 was attended by a sustained bout of dissidence from the slaves, these facts did not diminish Louis's confidence in Capers's understanding of how to manage bondsmen and women. If Capers had written to Louis that "all slaves must be watched," the sentiment would have been unexceptionable; but when in 1860 he wrote (of the boatman) that "Hector is doing as well as he can but like all negroes must be watched," the lesson was racial. Capers's favorite saying—which Louis applauded—would again have shown his insight had the word been "slave"; but the implications were very different in Capers's formulation: "If a Man put his confidence in a Negro He was simply a Damned Fool."[73] Louis had once placed confidence in Hector and a few other slaves, but their evident disloyalty to him—when Yankee military force made its presence felt in the low country in November 1861—caused Louis in June 1862 to ground himself upon the ideological bedrock of South Carolina's nineteenth-century plantation slavery: not genuinely paternalist, but racial, ideology.[74] He was distressed to find that house servants "are often the first to have their minds polluted with evil thoughts. For my own part," he concluded emphatically, "I am more than ever convinced that the only suitable occupation for the Negro is to be a Laborer of the Earth, and to work as a field hand upon a well disciplined plantation." In 1862 Louis Manigault needed the nervous relief of expressing emotion; for, were Negroes not what he said they were, what was he?[75]

If the Manigaults were not essentially paternalist in their ideology, were they so in their motives? "Paternalism" might seem to suggest a "traditional," noncapitalist set of motives: but evidently the Manigaults' purposes were something very different. As has been shown, Charles Manigault was among the leaders—though in a smaller way than Nathaniel Heyward on the Combahee River, Governor Robert Allston on the Pee Dee, or J. J. Ward on the Waccamaw—of the vigorous agricultural capitalism which dominated the antebellum low country. The slave-based variant of capitalism did not contain within itself that capacity wholly to transform the modern world which Marx and other writers rightly attributed to free-labor capitalism. Yet this incapacity need not distract one's attention from the fact that Charles Manigault (like other successful rice planters) was a shrewd businessman with a sharp eye for (more or less) maximizing his returns upon his large capital investment. Capitalist motives, not paternalist ones, were at the heart of his enterprise. And although Karl Marx defined "the capitalist mode of production" as a free-labor system, this matter is too important to be settled by the definition of a nineteenth-century economist, without historical investigation of the actual purposes guiding slaveholders.

The rice planters' motives were easily misunderstood, because they operated within a society suffused with gentry ideals. Everywhere Charles Manigault looked about him—whether in his own family or elsewhere in the low country—he could find lazy, improvident sons who squandered their patrimony, probably doing so even more regularly than the same thing was done by the improvident sons of wealthy Northern capitalists. The ethos of South Carolina obviously was not that of Massachusetts. A slave-based agricultural capitalism of great landed estates naturally had a spirit different from the free-labor capitalism of Massachusetts, where Puritan principles and propitious circumstances had in the seventeenth century shaped a rare society, the great majority of whose adult males had been landowning farmers working for themselves, and employing few laborers outside the family. The prominence of gentry ideals in the low country need not blind one to the profit-seeking motives of the great rice planters.

To be sure, a capitalist profit seeker might also be a "paternalist," in the strict sense of acting benevolently toward his workforce. One may doubt, however, whether paternalist motives prominently marked the regime at Gowrie. For one thing, during the nineteen years before Louis Manigault began in 1852 to manage the Savannah River plantation, the masters were to a substantial degree absentee owners. Mrs. Charles Manigault probably never in her life visited Gowrie, except possibly once in 1857.[76] Nor did Charles's children go there when they were little—Louis's first visit was when he was eleven—and generally they showed little interest in returning. Even Charles Manigault himself did not spend a great deal of time there. In 1833 he visited his new plantation only four times, for about a fortnight each. When he had had a suitable—though relatively simple—house built for himself at the plantation, his stays did become longer. Yet Charles's family knew so little about Gowrie that they "used to joke me," he reminisced, "by saying 'they did not believe *I had* any plantation on Savannah [River].' "[77]

Charles Manigault established at Gowrie a carefully calibrated system of privilege which—in conjunction with the even more important grid work of fearsome punishments—was remarkably successful during peacetime in confining dissidence within well-understood boundaries. But this whole chapter suggests that the motives of Gowrie's masters, in granting these privileges, were only to a most limited degree benevolent. Calculation was evident everywhere, whether in the slaughtering of a cow for Christmas after the "cholera" disaster of 1852, in the sudden production of special clothes for driver John during the panic of November 1861, or in the cultivation of captain Hector as a spy on the overseer. This was a moneymaking enterprise where the grant of certain privileges to the Gowrie gang—such as ready-made winter clothing for the adult males—and even the conferring of some genuine esteem upon a man like driver Robert were consonant with rational, profit-seeking entrepreneurship.

The few privileges Manigault granted his slaves were so clearly motivated by self-interest that they were scarcely paternalistic. Thus in December 1845 he stopped giving his bondsmen and women their preferred small rice; he sold it and bought corn for them instead. This saved him about $350, a welcome though small contribution toward the plantation's profitability. At the beginning of 1847 he resumed the small rice ration, but only on condition of good behavior; and he explained to overseer James Haynes why he had stopped the ration a year earlier. When Charles Manigault had visited Gowrie in December 1845, at the end of Haynes's first year of service, many slaves had complained to him of their new overseer's conduct. These complaints probably were well justified,[78] but in 1845 Manigault supposed them to be groundless. He attributed his slaves' criticisms of Haynes to the instigation of A. R. Bagshaw, the previous overseer, who still worked in the neighborhood and was a rival of Haynes's. Slaves who bellyached deserved punishment, in Manigault's view, and he had stopped everyone's small rice to discourage anyone from expressing discontent. When a year later he renewed the privilege, he sought to buy the slaves' goodwill toward Haynes and himself: in stopping the ration, he had "wished the Negroes to see . . . how they are favored by me in food & clothing . . . ," he wrote to Haynes from Paris; "but now I wish you to tell them that tho I can sell [the small rice] & with half the money buy Corn instead, & put thereby half the money in my pocket, that you wrote to me stating their good Conduct, & that I have decided to let them now have all the small Rice again—on trial." Thus the grant of a privilege was prompted not so much by benevolence as by a wish to secure "good Conduct" among the slaves.[79]

Toward a handful of privileged slaves the Manigaults showed genuine human feeling. Even overseers might share this sentiment for a few bondsmen and women, but overseers and masters were conscious as well of these slaves' economic value. A clear illustration was the overseer's genuine regret for the accidental drowning of the young slave miller, Cato, in 1852.[80] Similarly, when the trusted driver Robert was gravely ill from pneumonia, the overseer wrote with real concern, which the Manigaults doubtless shared. Human feelings as well as economic considerations moved Louis Manigault as he inscribed the letter "c" beside various names on the 1854 slave list: "c. stands for Cholera by which we have lost Twelve. . . . This list fills me with melancholy as I recall some sad scenes." But Louis could not long repress economic calculations. Disaster in Europe happily compensated disaster at home: "Considering the immense losses we have experienced during the past three years," he consoled himself in spring 1856, "the Cholera having swept off in 1852 and in 1854 many of our very best hands, [and considering the freshet of 1852 and the hurricane of 1854], I do not complain of our present crop. Rice this year, caused as is supposed by the now pending Crimean War has been very high, & our entire crop has sold well." Louis once more assessed death among the slaves in economic terms: "Since the last Cholera (Dec'r, 1854)," he continued cheerfully, "we have lost no one of any Consequence." Stephen, who had served another term as miller after Cato's death, had himself died three months before Louis wrote this passage in 1856; but as Stephen was old by Gowrie's standards (fifty-five years of age) and asthmatic, and had been by now pensioned off to the insignificant role of ratcatcher, his death was of no consequence.[81]

The best general study of the conditions imposed upon American slaves quotes the callous economic reasoning of one slave owner, published in a

Southern agricultural journal in 1849: "The time has been that the farmer could kill up and wear out one Negro to buy another; but it is not so now. Negroes are too high in proportion to the price of cotton, and it behooves those who own them to make them last as long as possible." The genteel Charles Manigault would not have publicly uttered such words; yet this was his reasoning, too, as he privately warned Louis of the economic consequences of pneumonia: "Negroes are too valuable *now*," he wrote in 1856, "to run any risk to their health, & pneumonia is auful [*sic*]" (Yet Charles's exhortation did not prevent the deaths from pneumonia—usually induced by wintry forced labor on the ditches and embankments, or by wet field work in the March winds—of five adult Gowrie hands, whose average age was only thirty-two, during the next three years.)[82]

The gentleman capitalists of the rice kingdom exercised immense power over their slaves. In recent years historians have done splendid work in uncovering the rich culture which black people developed within the system of slavery. This scholarship, however, has sometimes been associated with a surprisingly uncritical analysis of the system which masters tried to impose upon their bondsmen and women. The Gowrie records suggest that—no matter how affectionate Charles Manigault was toward his son Louis, no matter how honorable the Manigaults may have been in relation to those they regarded as their peers, no matter how clever they were in devising privileges which helped them to govern their slaves—the system itself was harsh to a degree that no language of "paternalism" should be allowed to obscure.

The Manigaults' slaves supplied abundant evidence, during the turbulent months from December 1864 through April 1865, of how they assessed their masters' motives. Early in December 1864 Louis Manigault briefly left Augusta and Charleston to visit Gowrie, where "all was excitement on account of the approaching Enemy": General Sherman's army. On December 6, five weeks after Capers's death, Louis installed J. W. Bandy as the new overseer, and young Manigault "encouraged the Negroes to remain on the place." Although sounds of artillery and musketry were soon to be heard, he then believed the slaves were "still pleased to see me"; but later Louis acknowledged that "we Southerners knew nothing of the Negro character," because under slavery "fear in a great measure guided the action of the Negro & we Planters could never get at the truth." After the Confederate army abandoned Savannah on December 20, much of the slaves' fear fell away, and their real feelings became evident. Gowrie's bondsmen and women felt at liberty, finally, at some point during the next three days, to act out old dreams. They dug a great hole in an embankment, floated a flatboat through it, and set off for Savannah or Hilton Head, and freedom.[83]

To Louis Manigault, the saddest event in the history of Gowrie was the destruction of the fine wooden pounding mill which for some fifty-five years had dominated the scene, representing the old regime. The event was richly symbolic, partly because the mill was totally anachronistic (having not been operated since 1855, as Gowrie's rice was milled thereafter at Charleston or

Savannah). And just as slavery was ultimately destroyed by those rice planters and others who spurred the attack on Fort Sumter, so the pounding mill—Louis strongly suspected, though he hated to admit it to himself—was in all likelihood fired by the Confederates themselves, acting under written instructions from General W. J. Hardee that plantation property was to be destroyed to prevent its falling into the hands of the hated Yankees. As a detachment of Sherman's army occupied Gowrie on December 24, Confederate forces retreated to the Carolina side of the Savannah River, from where one of their artillery shells probably started the spectacular conflagration that consumed not only the mill but Louis's house, the separate kitchen building, and the servant house as well. Sherman's forces deliberately continued the work of destruction, setting fire to the three-story brick thresher at East Hermitage. Eleven of the slaves' brick "double houses"—seven at East Hermitage and four at Gowrie—were all that remained.[84]

The revolution reached Charleston eight weeks later, when on February 17, 1865, Confederate forces evacuated the area. Charles Manigault—who had been residing at his Marshlands plantation seven miles north of Charleston—immediately abandoned his isolated rural retreat and took his wife, two grown daughters, and their French servant back to town to occupy the posh house on Gibbes Street. They were dismayed to find that "every one of our house & yard Negroes immediately left us." Years later Manigault still could not forgive them. Bitterly and with little paternalist spirit, he wrote that "all our Domestic Servants (5 grown & 2 children) March[ed] out of Our yard. . . . How they get on since? I know nor care not." To Louis the most painful defection was that of Joe Rile, for thirty years the butler in Charleston. "Although he used to take me to School," the younger Manigault exclaimed in disbelief, "he was one of the first to go to the Yankees upon the [Confederate] evacuation of the city!!" One of the several reasons that Joe Rile's attachment to his masters proved tenuous may be found in an earlier wartime duty of his. Two Union shells, each seven inches in diameter and fifteen inches long, had passed through the Manigault house during the bombardment of Charleston in 1863 and had buried themselves unexploded in the garden. Charles Manigault had had Joe Rile dig them up: "quite a dangerous operation . . . ," Louis conceded, "as the least stroke of the spade upon the concealed cap-point would have caused them to explode."

So angry were the Manigaults at being deserted by slaves like Joe Rile—privileged, to be sure!—that "we are all resolved," Charles expostulated in April 1865, "never to have a Negro in our house again." Although the difficulty of finding cheap, governable white house servants quickly demolished this resolution, it nevertheless reflected accurately the masters' indignation at bondsmen and women whom they supposed they had treated well.[85] Their slaves' sentiments soon became as clear at Marshlands and Silk Hope as had already emerged at Gowrie and in Charleston.

Charles Manigault's most valuable possessions—at a time when Confederate currency was becoming worthless, while Gowrie's 1864 crop was in Sherman's hands, and no cash crop at all would be grown in 1865—had seemed to be his two thousand bottles of Madeira, "some very old." Eight hundred of them were secreted in a pre-Revolutionary powder cellar at the old Izard house in Charleston, and twelve hundred had been transported to Marshlands. Those in Charleston, however, were all lost to thieves at about the time the Manigaults returned to Gibbes Street; and the ones at Marshlands were also in jeopardy. In the first days after the Union army occupied Charleston, Manigault secured a special and rare permission to drive his carriage several times through the Union fortifications so as to haul small possessions from Marshlands to Gibbes Street; in this way he rescued four hundred bottles of Madeira—though eight hundred more were lost to thieves at Marshlands. What Manigault saved he did by his own exertion, and with the help of certain Northern army officers, but not through the vigilance of blacks loyal to their old master. A principal assistant to him was a Northern officer, Captain Niles Parker (who later as state treasurer of South Carolina during Reconstruction was at the center of disgraceful financial scandals, but who in 1865 apparently was not yet corrupt). Donning civilian clothes, Parker accompanied Manigault to Marshlands to help him recover his property. Manigault tried to pay him back with a dozen bottles of Madeira, but Parker refused—accepting only two or three to show his friends the quality of a rice planter's wine cellar.

These journeys to Marshlands could not long continue, for, as Manigault explained two months later,

> Our own and neighbouring Negroes soon began pilfering, and soldiers from the lines carried off at least 800 Bottles [of old Wine], and many other things, when lastly came a large boat from Town which carried off the heavy furniture—tables, bedsteads, chairs, etc., and now the Farm [i.e., the Marshlands blacks] and other strange Negroes have complete possession of the Place, and I never go there.

During the course of these depredations—Manigault groaned with quadruple emphasis—there did not occur "a Solitary instance on Either Plantation [Marshlands and Silk Hope] of any one of Our Negroes preserving for us a single thing." The former driver of Marshlands, Frederick, proved—to Manigault's astonishment—to be "ringleader . . . of all the iniquity committed there. —He encouraged all the Negroes to believe that the Farm, and every thing on it, now since Emancipation, belonged Solely to them." But the freedmen and women did not destroy the beautiful "big house" at Marshlands. (And indeed visitors can still see it at Fort Johnson—across the Ashley River from Charleston—where conservationists in 1961 carefully removed it from the grounds of the modern Charleston Navy Yard.) Neither were other buildings razed, nor were any white people hurt. Fourteen alien freedmen and women, however, lived for a couple of months in the "big house," invited there by ex-driver Frederick to labor on shares at Marshlands under his direction; movable property was carried away; and the blacks used force to intimidate their former master. Two or three freedmen had loaded guns, and " 'Moses' (one of the principal hands) stated loudly on all occasions that 'if ever I threatened to Move *Him* off the Place, he would Shuit me on the spot.' " In the good old days of bondage, Charles Manigault lamented, the little slave children "used to watch for my coming [from Charleston], to open the Gates, & climb on the Sulky to take a little ride." Now, alas, they were "taught [by their elders] to shun Me, & never to call me 'Master' again. 'Heddy [Howdy] Mossa' was Dead and gone."

Not only were the gratifying visages of grinning slaves no longer visible, but "a Negro Woman (Peggy) seized as her part of the Spoils My Wife's Large and handsome Mahogany Bedstead and Mattrass and arranged *it* in her own Negro House on which She Slept for some time." Manigault, recalling later this dreadful demonstration of Peggy's true lack of attachment to her mistress, could scarcely conceal his satisfaction that—only two months after committing this lèse-majesté—Peggy had died.[86]

From his point of view, matters stood even worse at Silk Hope. Believing that its location forty miles up the Cooper River would guard it during the war from Northern naval incursions, Manigault had shipped to Silk Hope boxloads of family portraits and other valuables, which no doubt he instructed his leading slaves to protect. Yet as the liberating army approached, the blacks forced their overseer to flee; and in February 1865, even

> before any of the enemy [Union soldiers] got there, [our Negroes,] instead of securing or secreting any thing of ours, they immediately broke into Our Dwelling, forced open these Boxes, & seized every Picture. Some of them, they hung up in their Negro Houses, while Some of the Family Portraits (as if to turn them into redicule [*sic*]) they left out, Night and Day, exposed to the open air.

Manigault believed Northern soldiers stole two valuable horses, and he implied that his own trusted slaves had pointed out to the thieves a boxful of valuable souvenirs from their master's foreign travels. His indignation focused upon the conduct of the Silk Hope blacks—a driver once again in the forefront. Manigault now felt as little respect for driver Peter as Peter had proved to feel for his master. The driver—having taken Thomas Sully's 1817 portrait of Charles Manigault to adorn his own house—had told a female friend that "*she* must take this Portrait home with her, TO REMEMBER HIM!! She Did So. . . . My Portrait, to remember this Nigger!" Lèse-majesté indeed![87]

Although the revolution of 1865—a genuine social revolution, and the only one the United States has ever witnessed—was imposed by military force from above, the contribution of slaves like those of Charles Manigault was an indispensable element in the transformation. Black civilians generally confined themselves to nonviolent (and often symbolic) acts of self-assertion, because the powerful Union army governed the South: it quickly exercised its authority to restore property to the planters. To be sure, Charles Manigault said that two Union soldiers stole valuables from Silk Hope, that others drunkenly participated in the looting of his wine cellar at Marshlands, and that a provost marshal once told the Marshlands blacks that Manigault had no right to dispossess them. Yet Charles Manigault also acknowledged that he and his relations had enjoyed substantial protection from the Union army.

Under the federal occupation Manigault's family remained "quite undisturbed in our [Gibbes Street] dwelling," and General Hatch had returned to Charles Manigault a valuable gold watch which a Northern soldier had stolen from Charles's cousin Heyward Manigault. General Rufus Saxton had ordered some Northern officers out of the house of the wife of Manigault's cousin, Tom Middleton. A Northern quartermaster eventually helped Charles to repossess Marshlands from the blacks, supplying two army wagons for the purpose; and the quartermaster had done this out of admiration for the gallantry in battle of another cousin, the Confederate Major Edward Manigault. The social revolution proceeded only within those sharply defined limits quickly fixed by the conquerors.[88]

During the chaotic first weeks of the Northern occupation, however, Manigault's slaves had enjoyed a certain latitude in expressing hitherto concealed emotions. The stock of family portraits had offered Manigault's bondsmen and women a safe way to let off steam. Like a throng of visitors to an exhibition of Madame Tussaud's waxworks, simulating unwonted intimacy with figures of the great—but with a depth of feeling that no crowd of mere sightseers could rival—the Silk Hope slaves roughly nailed oil portraits of the Manigaults onto the walls of their cramped dwellings, sold some of the portraits cheap (no doubt thinking ironically of the old slave auctions), gave them away as curiosities, or let them lie for days in the rain. They "scattered Them in Every direction," Charles Manigault mourned, "to Shew their hatred of their former master & of all his family."[89]

II

BUTLER ISLAND

7

Frances Kemble

Sixty miles south of Gowrie, and athwart Georgia's Altamaha River, lay a rice plantation which gained notoriety in 1859 through the well-publicized, two-day auction of hundreds of its slaves, reported at length in the *New York Tribune*. Permanent fame came to Butler Island four years later when a re-markable Englishwoman, Frances Kemble, published her *Journal of a Residence on a Georgian Plantation in 1838–1839*. The estate described by Kemble was indirectly connected to Charles Manigault's family: for a favorite niece of Charles's, Gabriella Manigault Morris (Butler), was married to its coproprietor, John Butler of Philadelphia.[1] In 1834 the actress Frances Kemble—a younger member of Britain's foremost acting family—had ruined her life by marrying the other proprietor, Pierce Butler, thus setting the stage for her traumatic confrontation with life on a Georgia rice plantation (see genealogical table 16).

John and Pierce Butler—absentee owners—lived with their wives in Phila-delphia, where they were well known to the diarist Sidney Fisher. Fisher did not greatly esteem either man, but he admired Mrs. John Butler (Gabriella) and, for different reasons, Mrs. Pierce Butler (Frances Kemble). Well situ-ated to observe the doings of Philadelphia's proslavery aristocracy,[2] the diarist recorded the uses to which the riches generated by the rice plantation were turned. "Jno. Butler's [costume] was the most splendid I ever saw," Fisher exclaimed after attending a fancy-dress ball at Newport, Rhode Island, in 1844. A rice planter might spend twelve dollars to keep each of his slaves fed and clothed for a full year, but Butler appropriated perhaps forty times that sum to this single appearance at Newport. The costume, Fisher explained,

TABLE 16.   The Butler Family

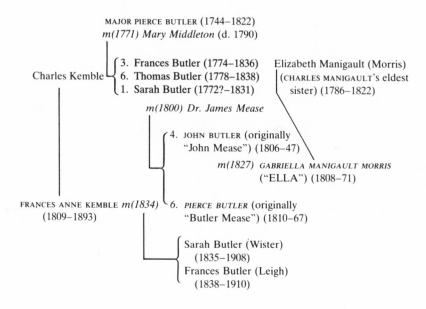

MAJOR PIERCE BUTLER (1744–1822)
m(1771) Mary Middleton (d. 1790)

Charles Kemble ⎨ 3. Frances Butler (1774–1836)   Elizabeth Manigault (Morris)
6. Thomas Butler (1778–1838)   (CHARLES MANIGAULT'S eldest
1. Sarah Butler (1772?–1831)   sister) (1786–1822)

m(1800) Dr. James Mease

4. JOHN BUTLER (originally
"John Mease") (1806–47)

m(1827) GABRIELLA MANIGAULT MORRIS
("ELLA") (1808–71)

FRANCES ANNE KEMBLE m(1834) 6. PIERCE BUTLER (originally
(1809–1893)   "Butler Mease") (1810–67)

Sarah Butler (Wister)
(1835–1908)
Frances Butler (Leigh)
(1838–1910)

was that of a knight of the 15th century, a helmet, cuirass, I believe it was called, covering the back & chest to the waist, and armor for the thighs, all of polished steel, over a dress of buckskin embroidered with gold lace, a glittering sword, buckskin boots & gold spurs and towering plume formed of red & white ostrich feathers. He has a fine figure & graceful manner & I never saw a more splendid looking fellow than he was that night. The dress was made in London & cost him 4 or $500.

John Butler's half share in the biggest estate on the Altamaha River—stocked in 1839 with some 715 slaves who worked a sea-island cotton plantation on St. Simons Island as well as the rice plantation on Butler Island—made him "enormously rich." One emblem of his wealth was his wife's "magnificent dress of crimson velvet" worn at a Philadelphia soirée by the "queenly and superb" Mrs. John Butler—"blazed with jewels"—before the stunned gaze of Sidney Fisher. "She is certainly one of the most beautiful women in the *world*." Nine days later, when Fisher renewed acquaintance with her, she was still "looking magnificent." The diarist gasped: "The most splendid figure I ever saw. . . . Tho she has no mind, she has the ease & high breeding of the southern aristocracy, a manner produced by birth, early habit, & wealth."[3]

A much larger sum than that expended upon Gabriella's jewel-bedizened dresses or her husband's medieval costume was swallowed by the ill-conceived stock market speculations (and gambling at cards) of Pierce Butler, John's younger brother. Pierce could not plead the panic of 1857 as excuse for his financial follies, because he had already squandered some three hundred thousand dollars—a great fortune—by 1856, when his affairs had to be put into the hands of three trustees to ensure he did not further jeopardize his family's welfare. The sale of 436 of his slaves in Savannah in 1859—America's greatest recorded slave auction—was his way of saving his own skin. At the end of the proceedings he put four shiny new silver quarter dollars of conscience money into the palm of each adult slave sold away from the community he had shattered.[4]

Gabriella's wealth—though derived in part from Manigault rice lands in South Carolina[5]—depended principally at midcentury upon one thousand acres of Butler Island rice land in Georgia.[6] This plantation had been developed in the 1790s by Major Pierce Butler, the Butler brothers' grandfather. Major Butler, as a South Carolina delegate to the Philadelphia Convention of 1787, had already made his mark by writing the United States Constitution's famous fugitive slave clause, and he was a U.S. senator from South Carolina from 1789 to 1796—a contemporary of Charles Manigault's grandfather, Senator Ralph Izard. A political career had come naturally to Major Pierce Butler, for he was the third son of an Irish Protestant member of Parliament, Sir Richard Butler. Major Butler had cherished a lifelong antipathy to primogeniture, and had had to make his fortune by another means than an inheritance of his own: he had sought instead the money of a rice heiress.

First coming to the American colonies with his British regiment during the French and Indian War, Butler once tried unsuccessfully to elope with a rich fifteen-year-old South Carolina girl, Elizabeth Izard. Some time after this enterprise had foundered, he managed to espouse Mary Middleton, the inheriting daughter of one of South Carolina's biggest African slave traders. By selling his British commission two years later, in 1773, Major Butler got the money to buy a seventeen-hundred-acre sea-island cotton plantation on St. Simons Island, Georgia; and in 1791 he bought, not far from St. Simons, what became the jewel of his estate—Butler Island. He seems to have achieved the purchase and development of this rice plantation by appropriating to his own use South Carolina land and slaves left in trust by his dead wife for their children.

Never considering permanent residence on malarial Butler Island, the major—who relished the sound of his own name—built instead a big house at "Butler Point" on St. Simons Island, where Atlantic breezes scattered the mosquitoes. Here he provided his old friend Vice-President Aaron Burr a haven in 1804, when Burr's killing of Alexander Hamilton in a duel made him persona non grata in the North. But the major, "very polite and well bred, his manners exceedingly polished indeed" (according to a Philadelphia neighbor), preferred cosmopolitan life to that on St. Simons Island; and about 1804 he purchased a mansion on Philadelphia's Chestnut Street—as well as a country house a few miles away named, unsurprisingly, "Butler Place"—whence he directed plantation affairs through an agent. Increasingly a mere absentee, Butler visited his rice and cotton plantations only once between 1810 and his death in 1822. He was in 1812 master of 638 slaves, and consequently was one of the richest men in the United States.[7]

His principal agents in improving his fortunes were an entrepreneur from

New England, Roswell King, and Roswell King Jr., who managed the Butler plantations for nearly fifty years. The first King, son of a Connecticut sea captain, emigrated as an impecunious young man in 1789 to the tiny seaport of Darien, Georgia, where he established himself as a commission merchant and building contractor. Becoming Butler's manager in 1802, King received a much higher salary than a mere overseer, and he enriched himself in Butler's service. By 1819, when he turned over the plantations' management to his own son, King was wealthy enough to found the town of Roswell, Georgia, twenty miles north of Atlanta, where he built flour and cotton mills and erected for himself a "splendid mansion."[8] Roswell King Jr., who was only twenty-three when he assumed management of the Butler estate, eventually became rich enough to establish his own low-country plantation, twenty-five miles from Butler Island. At his death in 1854 the younger King and his wife owned 179 slaves; and, as one of Georgia's great planters, he lived on terms of social equality with his neighbor, the Reverend C. C. Jones—a Presbyterian divine and the South's most famous advocate of *The Religious Instruction of the Negroes*.[9] The best proof of the younger King's acceptance within the low-country gentry was the Reverend Jones's willingness to hire jointly with King the tutor who privately educated both their broods of children.

Quarrels disrupted Major Butler's family as in a Victorian novel, and—as in a novel—the disputes often centered upon inheritance. Butler's son, Thomas, claimed that the old man always demanded "blind obedience," and that to refuse this "was sufficient to Excite his lasting Displeasure." Privately educated in London for eleven years, Thomas Butler had returned to America at seventeen, in 1795, and quickly became alienated from his imperious father. Thomas eventually secured his finances by marrying a woman with a French title and a slave plantation in Martinique. Refusing to be reconciled with Major Butler, Thomas received only a relatively small inheritance when his father died in 1822. The major gave his fortune instead to two grandsons, but only on condition that they abandon their own surnames and assume the mellifluous "Butler": the gift was not to take effect until the death of Major Butler's favorite unmarried daughter, which finally occurred in 1836.[10]

When Frances Kemble married the major's grandson Pierce (Mease) Butler in 1834, the bridegroom was therefore not yet—as he became two years later—the joint owner of nearly seven hundred slaves. Kemble knew the young Philadelphian was rich, but he seems not to have told her the source of his income. He was a reserved man, and he believed literally in a bride's vow of obedience to her husband. He could not believe that even a "woman of genius"—his ambivalent characterization of his wife—would feel so strongly about slavery as to challenge his authority, and to detonate thereby one explosion after another during their embattled fifteen years of marriage.[11]

The younger Pierce Butler combined diverse, not always estimable, traits. He was handsome, wealthy, "clever, most gentlemanlike in his manners," but by Sidney Fisher's standards "entirely without education." He was sometimes extremely generous, as in 1831 when he had allowed his older brother, John Mease, a half share of the fortune—which would otherwise have been

Pierce's alone—by permitting him to adopt the Butler surname several years later than the major's will had stipulated. Pierce Butler appears to have been repeatedly unfaithful to his wife—as early, according to Kemble, as 1835 when she had their first baby—and he was supposed in 1842 to be keeping a mistress. In 1844 a James Schott of Philadelphia claimed he had found his own wife in a compromising situation with Pierce Butler at a New York hotel: Butler, who (though born and bred in Philadelphia) thought himself a Southern gentleman, challenged Schott to a duel. This took place at a famous dueling spot in Maryland, but without harm to either party.[12] Pierce Butler was "often in dire financial straits [according to the family's biographer, Malcolm Bell] from consistent losses at cards." Why it was deemed essential by 1856 to put his financial affairs into the hands of three trustees may be inferred from the tale—evidently printed in the *New York Herald*—of his "once losing $24,000 at one hand of poker." The celebrated English diarist Charles Greville, who knew the Butlers in London in 1841, regarded Pierce as "a weak, dawdling, ignorant, violent tempered man."[13]

Well known within the pro-Southern wing of Philadelphia's Democratic Party, Pierce Butler was nominated and elected in 1856 as one of Pennsylvania's presidential electors. In December 1860 he returned to Philadelphia from the Deep South—six days after South Carolina's secession—a keen supporter of disrupting the Union. Then fifty years old, he told Sidney Fisher that he came back "only to *buy arms* and intends to return [to Georgia] immediately and join the army. He will take his [twenty-two-year-old] daughter Fanny with him and has bought a rifle for *her,* too." Although Butler did go South, he returned again to Philadelphia soon after the first Battle of Bull Run and openly "expressed . . . the strongest opinions in favor of the southern cause and wishes for its success in earnest language." This led federal authorities to incarcerate him for about five weeks, until Philadelphia's biggest private banker (a heavy contributor to the Republican Party, but also one of Butler's three financial trustees) secured his release. For the rest of the war Butler kept his opinions to himself, but he was almost the only Philadelphian to refuse to put a black bow at his window as a sign of respect when Lincoln was assassinated. Only intervention by an antislavery former Congressman prevented an enraged crowd from storming Butler's house.[14]

How, one might ask, could a person so intelligent and talented as Frances Kemble have got herself tied up with a man so much her inferior as Pierce Butler? No doubt a large part of the answer was money. Although Frances Kemble was a famous actress both in Britain and during her two-year American tour with her father, Charles Kemble (whose precarious finances as manager of London's Covent Garden Theatre she was trying to rescue for him), she had an aversion to the stage. She had had a genteel education in Paris (her elder brother, educated at Trinity College, Cambridge, was a friend there of Tennyson's), and she yearned to be a member of the gentry. She was an ambitious writer and, if freed from the need to support herself by acting, she might more readily fulfill her literary ambitions. (Eventually she published a dozen volumes of plays, poems, fiction, travel journals, and autobiographical writings. She later became a good friend of Henry James, who wrote an acute forty-two-page obituary-article and literary appreciation, upon her death in 1893.)[15] Besides wealth, Pierce Butler had attractive personal characteristics: from time to time—and certainly in his determined pursuit of Kemble—he showed "a great deal of energy & character"; he played the flute well enough to get a chair with the orchestra when Kemble was performing in the New York and Boston theaters; he had qualities which subsequently won the devotion of at least one of their two daughters; he was capable of considerate behavior (for example, he later showed more regard for some of his slaves than did many a master); and he and Frances were no doubt deeply in love at the beginning of their life together. Perhaps because of her long and close professional association with her father, Frances Kemble was emotionally starved in 1832, as she approached her twenty-third birthday; and she conceived for Pierce Butler a "violent passion which," she declared as late as 1840, "has scarce grown into anything deserving a calmer name."[16] Whatever wretchedness Kemble suffered from her marriage, no one today seeking to understand human bondage can regret her youthful folly; for the product of her union with Pierce Butler was the most vivid report ever written about slavery on an American plantation.

Its author must be known if Frances Kemble's Georgian *Journal* is to be fathomed. Except by those who have read this *Journal,* Kemble is remembered simply as an actress, and as a "reader" of Shakespearean drama. Her acting career was compressed into the five years before 1834, when marriage allowed her to retire at the age of twenty-four; and into a single year, 1847–48, when the collapse of that marriage led her once again to seek an independent income. This income she secured for many years after 1848 by her one-person public readings of Shakespearean plays, which in their day were nearly as famous as her acting had been. Although her grandfather, her aunt Sarah (Kemble) Siddons, her uncle John Kemble, and both her father, Charles Kemble, and her French mother were theater people—the most famous family of actors in Britain—Frances was intended for gentility; she went onto the stage at nineteen only because her father's threatened bankruptcy (as a proprietor of Covent Garden) impelled him to test her as a way of drawing larger crowds to the theater. She had little training as an actress, nor did she ever develop much interest in theatrical technique. Her power arose instead from her personality: from the mobility of her facial expressions, her vitality, the vehemence and force of her voice.

Time and again acquaintances remarked upon her "masculine" characteristics. The British actor Henry Irving remembered her—from one of her Shakespearean readings—as "a lady with an extraordinarily flashing eye, a masculine and muscular outside." Years earlier, in 1840—when she was in the sixth year of her marriage and had two small children—Sidney Fisher commented that she was "very independent & rides about [the Philadelphia countryside] constantly unattended. . . . Her costume was becoming & peculiar. A green cloth riding habit, with rolling collar & open in front, under it a *man's* waistcoat." She had "a powerful physique," Fisher observed a few years later, "is accustomed to a great deal of exercise and her whole appearance and bearing are the reverse of feminine." Kemble acknowledged a love of riding—"I am never in health, looks, or spirits without daily hard exercise on horseback," she wrote in 1841 to Harriet St. Leger, an intimate Irish friend who herself had "affected a mannish, austere style of dress" and whose boots were "made by a man's boot maker." Kemble's zest in controlling a horse was transparent, and she was glad to ride a stallion if no suitable mare were available. "The death I should prefer," she once wrote, "would be to break my neck off the back of my horse at a full gallop on a fine day." Controlling a horse gratified the depths of her being: when the stallion tried to buck her, she reported that his "opposition very presently aroused the Amazon which is both natural and acquired in me."[17]

Kemble's mental strength was as marked as her physical vigor. She was steeped in Shakespeare and in French classical drama (she spoke French as readily as English), and to discourse with her about the true nature of art was, to the thirsty Sidney Fisher, like finding an oasis in the mindless desert of Philadelphia's upper-crust society. She held vehement antislavery opinions and argued them ably. The English actor William Macready, however, thought her tactless in expressing these ideas—to her husband's discomfiture—when in 1843 the Butlers attended a New York dinner party with Longfellow and William Cullen Bryant. "Mrs. Butler spoke admirably well," Macready confided to his diary, "but quite like a man. She is a woman of most extraordinary mind. What she said on most subjects was true, the stern truth, but what in the spirit of charity should not have been said in the presence of one who was obliged to listen to it."[18]

Males might believe Kemble should defer to her husband at dinner, but the force of her personality was what captivated them when she was safely upon a stage. She had taken London by storm when she first appeared at Covent Garden at nineteen, and she filled the theater many a night for the best part of three years. When her father then brought her across the Atlantic for their American tour, her fame had preceded her. Philip Hone, the New York diarist, recorded the response on first night. "Her display of the strong feelings which belong to the part"—Bianca in H. H. Milman's *Fazio*—"was great beyond description, and the expression of her wonderful face would have been a rich treat if her tongue had uttered no sound. The fifth act was such an expression of female powers as we have never before witnessed, and the curtain fell among deafening shouts and plaudits of an astonished audience." Kemble's declamatory power was not to everyone's taste. The young Henry Irving—not yet launched upon his own, greater, acting career—found her tastelessly grandiloquent when, many years later, he heard her read *Hamlet*. But for many people, listening to Kemble was an unforgettable experience. A journalist, for example, recalled to Henry James having seen Kemble act Lady Macbeth in 1848. The manner of her reading the letter at Lady Macbeth's entrance, James quoted the journalist, "the tones that reached his ears, held him motionless and spell-bound till she had finished. To nothing more beautiful had he ever listened, nothing more beautiful was he ever to hear again."[19]

Pierce Butler, too, had been spellbound by the actress's force of personality. Philadelphia aristocrats did not marry actresses, but Kemble was no ordinary actress: she was a woman of breeding who might lend to Butler's drawing room even greater luster than his sister-in-law—the magnificent Gabriella—transmitted to John Butler's. Rarely has a marriage been built upon more infirm foundations. If Kemble supposed Pierce Butler a stallion to be subdued by "a due administration of both spur and whip, attended with a judicious combination of coaxing pats on his great crested neck, and endearing commendations of his beauty," she had mistaken this reserved, obstinate, resentful man. And if Butler supposed that retirement from the stage would long curb his bride's independence of spirit, he soon discovered otherwise.[20]

Their marriage might have turned out differently had Butler possessed a great landed estate in England, with hundreds of dependent agricultural laborers on whom Kemble could lavish paternalist benevolence, as enjoined by her evangelical conscience—and had the intellectual radiance of London been near to her eye. But the rural American working people near Butler Place—the newlyweds' country house a few miles north of downtown Philadelphia—repelled Kemble's offers to teach their children reading: they had imbibed a democratic ethos, could send their children to the local school, and did not want to be patronized by an English Lady Bountiful. Except for a handful of intrepid spirits like the Quaker abolitionist Lucretia Mott, or a few cultivated gentlemen like Sidney Fisher, Philadelphia offered Kemble nothing that matched the stimulus of London. Pierce Butler, his wife had discovered by 1837, was "a person of no brilliancy of intellect"; and—ill educated, conventional, and domineering as he was—he repressed the flow of her spirits. He insisted upon suppressing an antislavery treatise which she had planned to publish during the second year of their married life, at the same moment when she issued her "American *Journal*." (This "American *Journal*"—a youthful travelogue—is not to be confused with her later and much more famous Georgian *Journal*.) Butler claimed that an antiabolitionist mob would tear down their house and burn its furniture, were the antislavery tract published. Kemble was impatient to write her third play—*An English Tragedy*—but could find inspiration neither at Butler Place nor in Philadelphia. Yet as soon as she returned to London in 1836–37, she made rapid progress on the play. (The Butler brothers, inspecting their newly inherited plantations in Georgia, had refused to take Kemble with them; she therefore revisited the British metropolis during their absence.) Once she had returned from London to life with Butler in Philadelphia, "all things [she complained obliquely] tend to check any utterance of my thoughts, spoken or written." It took her nearly a year to put the finishing touches to the play.[21]

When Kemble had learned in 1836 that Pierce had inherited his half share of the huge Georgia estate, her heart quickened: here was a new and grander field for philanthropy than could be found in rural Philadelphia County. Loathing the idea of slavery, she raced ahead in her thoughts to the good influence she might exercise upon the lives of hundreds of Pierce Butler's dependents. Gradual emancipation (something like that then transpiring in the West Indies by act of the British Parliament) might be effected by her own act: or, at least, by her husband's—this qualification did not yet cause her imagination to stumble. The Butler slaves might be taken to the southwestern United States, where Frances could gradually free "those into whom I had been able to instill industrious and economical habits." Though she communicated these ideas to Harriet St. Leger, Frances failed to mention them to Pierce and John Butler. As she claimed forty-five years later, she did not yet have "the remotest suspicion of,—the amazement and dismay, the terror and disgust, with which such theories . . . must have filled every member of the [Butler] family."[22]

Pierce Butler cherished a corresponding illusion. Although he knew that Frances disliked slavery—indeed, they had a big row about it in October 1838—he supposed that her contact with the slaves would quickly alter her convictions. When she persuaded him, that year, to take her and their two young children for a sixteen-week sojourn upon their Georgia estate, he thought she would soon discover that blacks needed to be disciplined and controlled by the white race: that slavery served the best interests of the slaves as much as it benefited the financial interests of the Butlers themselves. "I am told," Frances wrote skeptically to a friend after a month in Georgia, "that a total change in my opinions upon slavery was anticipated from my residence on a plantation."[23]

After arriving at Butler Island on December 30, 1838, Frances threw herself into good works. Appalled at the filth and discomfort of the slaves' "sick house," she instituted a cleanup campaign, spending hours supervising the sweeping, scrubbing, and tidying of the Augean stables. She persuaded her husband to try the radical experiment of substituting mules for human labor in plowing some of the rice fields. The slaves—and especially the women—began to confide in their unconventional mistress. For one exhausted mother Frances later succeeded in getting the usual respite from field labor extended for an additional week after childbirth. Another slave woman, however, was whipped after complaining to Frances of her hard lot; and the indignant Englishwoman had to swallow her husband's explanation that the flogging was for the woman's failure to do her full quota of work, not for the complaint itself.[24]

Seven weeks of confinement upon the flat, aesthetically boring, nearly treeless rice island were succeeded by a nine-week residence at the Butlers' sea-island cotton plantation on St. Simons Island (fifteen miles by boat down winding river channels), where Frances was able to renew her beloved horseback riding. The two enduring passions of her life were Shakespeare and the beauties of nature; and although St. Simons Island was not the Alps (where later in life she passed three months every year in rambling) nor even the hills of western Massachusetts (which Frances loved with passionate intensity), it did offer exotic beauties of its own. Frances's Georgian *Journal* testifies to the many hours she spent, day after day, exploring with fascination the wild landscape. Seldom, however, could she shake out of her head her responsibility to the slaves. Horrified by the gynecologic disorders of the slave women, she tried to secure to all mothers, after childbirth, an extra week's surcease from field labor. When Pierce was absent at the rice island, she started reading prayers on Sunday mornings to twenty or thirty slaves (whom the Butler plantation rules banned from attending the island's only church services, at Christ Church). She even (behind her husband's back) started to teach her seventeen-year-old waiter—at his request—to read. This was Aleck Alexander, who as late as 1896 was still writing long deferential letters from Georgia to Frances's daughter Sarah in Philadelphia.

Frances's philanthropy led to flaming rows between her and Pierce. Trouble smoldered at Butler Island, and quickly reached tinder point when she and Pierce moved to St. Simons. The slave women flocked after work to beg their surprising mistress for flannel (probably for menstrual bleeding or to make underclothing), bits of sugar, and meat (which—as on the Manigault plantation—was rarely distributed to Butler slaves). Frances asked them how many children they had had, how many miscarriages, how many children dead; and she carried some of their petitions to her husband. Although Butler tried hard to propitiate his wife and made some concessions, he and the two overseers thought Frances was undermining plantation discipline; and on February 26, 1839, he finally refused to listen to any more pleas from her on the slaves' behalf. "Why do you believe such trash?" he angrily demanded. "Don't you know the niggers are all d[amne]d liars?" Frances was not one to control her own emotions. It was true, she later acknowledged, that the slaves' sufferings and especially the injustice done to them

> have filled my heart with bitterness and indignation that have overflowed my lips, till, I suppose, [Mr. Butler] is weary of hearing what he has never heard before, the voice of passionate expostulation and importunate pleading against wrongs that he will not even acknowledge, and for creatures [in] whose common humanity with his own I half think he does not believe.[25]

Shaking with fury at Pierce's peremptory edict, she bolted like a stallion. Frances entrusted her two children temporarily to the care of their Irish nurse and had the slave boatmen row her fifteen miles to Darien, where she would take a steamboat for the North. No such vessel, however, was expected for three or four days: this gave her time to cool off and for the tug of her children to reassert itself. After a night at Butler Island—only a mile from Darien— she returned to St. Simons. In Pierce's absence she had the slaves move her bed and furniture upstairs (presumably to keep at a distance from him on those nights when he returned from the rice plantation to sleep at St. Simons), and it was during these last weeks at St. Simons that she inquired most closely after the slave women's health, started reading religious services on Sunday morning, and dared to teach Aleck his alphabet.

Like the Grimké sisters of South Carolina—but unlike nearly all wives of slave masters—Frances soon began to realize that paternalism was no satisfactory channel for antislavery conviction. She then resuscitated an idea already canvassed with her Massachusetts friend Elizabeth Sedgwick before Frances had departed for Georgia.[26] Inveterate writer as she was—with a two-volume *American Journal* of travels recently published and her third play just completed—Frances had, of course, been keeping a daily journal of her observations in Georgia. Could she not fill in these notes, write them up properly when she returned to the North, and publish to the world an account of what a rice plantation was really like? Here might be a way of fulfilling, to the satisfaction of her Christian conscience, that duty to her slaves which residence in Georgia showed could be fulfilled in no other wise.

For months after returning North from the Butler estate Frances worked hard at filling in, rearranging, and rewriting her plantation journal. She tried to persuade Pierce to let her accompany him for a second visit in 1839–40— when she would be able to add to her store of observation and to improve her new *Journal*—but John Butler absolutely forbade her such a trip. (Or more likely, Pierce—fearing that another appearance by Frances in Georgia would further undermine plantation discipline and alienate the overseers—got John to bear the responsibility for frustrating Frances's wishes.) By this time it had already "been suggested to me," Frances wrote, "that such an account of a Southern plantation might be worth publishing. . . . So I am . . . making a fair copy of my Georgia Journal." But she felt that "such a publication would be a breach of confidence."[27] She was still uncertain what to do with her manuscript when she and Pierce sailed for England late in 1840.

Kemble had probably completed the manuscript early in 1840 (when Pierce Butler was still away in Georgia) or soon thereafter. Receiving in London a request from Lydia Maria Child, editor of the *National Anti-Slavery Standard,* to print parts of the new journal, Kemble wrote a letter in November 1841 offering for publication her general reflections on slavery, and a description only of her overland journey from Philadelphia until the moment of her arrival at Butler Island.[28] She did not feel free to publish the rest of the manuscript (although it was surely ready for publication).[29] Pierce Butler secretly intercepted this letter. Kemble found the letter in his desk, posted it anyway, and told him that she had done so. Butler declared that "my sending that letter to Mrs. Child put an end to our living together."[30]

London society watched the marital struggle escalate as Frances moved away from Pierce, then back together with him, bolted by train to catch the steamer for America from Liverpool, but was dramatically overtaken by her husband at Birmingham. Pierce fell back increasingly upon the principle that a wife was contracted to obey her husband. Frances did not deny the general principle but introduced a Protestant escape clause: the wife was not bound to do any act which violated her conscience. When the Butlers returned together to America in 1843, their renewed marital negotiations resembled the diplomatic treaties of two foreign nations. Pierce demanded, and Frances agreed that year, that

    a. she would not go back onto the stage;

    b. she would not publish abolitionist views; and

    c. she would publish nothing without her husband's consent.[31]

This treaty, which set out starkly the obstacles in 1843 to a wife's pursuing an independent career—either as an actress or as a writer—kept the peace for only a few months. Pierce, who had been trained as a lawyer, knew Pennsylvania law much better than did Frances. He managed—by his control over money, and his legal right to control their children's contact with Frances—to outmaneuver her, so that when the divorce finally came in 1849 he was able to sue her for desertion; she gave up her defense of the case in order to secure access to the children from time to time.

Butler's charge of desertion astonished Sidney Fisher: "It is quite notorious," the diarist wrote, "that she was driven from [Pierce Butler's] house by his own barbarous treatment." This view of the matter finds confirmation in an 1845 report by Kemble's friend Rebecca Gratz. Pierce Butler, according to Gratz, had sent his and Frances Kemble's children "for two months away in the country where she is not permitted to visit them so that the whole object of her residence in his house is defeated. . . . It would be in vain [for her] to stay [in America any longer] pining after duties [to her children] she is not permitted to perform."[32]

To Sidney Fisher the fault seemed, however, to be not solely Pierce's: Fisher had always thought Frances too *prononcée;* she lacked tact, and was herself "somewhat dictatorial"; she was divorced "by reason of her own fiery & impetuous temper" as well as by "her husband's dogged & iron will." Yet Fisher could not withhold sympathy from this remarkable woman. She has "too much will & vitality & force of character . . . ," he wrote in 1860, "to be very happy in domestic life, more especially with such a man as Butler, her inferior far in all intellectual endowments, but her equal in firmness & strength of character. She is not a person to be governed by force."[33] Pierce Butler died of malaria on Butler Island in August 1867. Frances soon thereafter made another journey to Philadelphia to see her daughters, and Fisher was anxious how she would fit in. She quickly regained his admiration: "A person of overwhelming vitality . . . ," he concluded:

> She is a grand creature, full of intellect & passion, cultivated and accomplished, with all her faculties strengthened & trained by exercise. [Since her separation from Butler she has won not just a living but] wealth by her readings of Shakspeare [sic], unequalled in force & beauty by any artist before or since. What a giant is such a woman compared to ladies of ordinary experience, however clever & cultivated & elegant in person & manners.[34]

Because Pierce Butler controlled the movements of their younger daughter until she reached twenty-one in 1859, Frances could not risk publishing her Georgia *Journal* before then; and she did nothing for three years thereafter. But during the American Civil War the sympathy exhibited by most genteel Britons for the South posed, by 1862, a real threat that the British navy might be employed to break the blockade that cut off Southern cotton from the Lancashire mills. Britain's "sentimental apologists" for slavery (Kemble's words) put an end to her indecision. "The ignorant and mischievous nonsense I was continually compelled to hear upon the subject of slavery in the seceding

States," she later explained, "determined me to publish my own observation of it." The *Journal* appeared in London in May 1863 and in New York at the beginning of July. Six weeks later Sidney Fisher had "a great deal of talk" with John Butler's widow, Gabriella: he wanted to see what she made of her sister-in-law's book. Gabriella said, according to Fisher's record, that "Mrs. Kemble's description of the treatment of the Negroes & their condition on the Butler estate is true, & she [Gabriella] ought to know as she owns half the property, or did before the war, & has frequently resided on the estate."[35]

That the *Journal* is a fundamentally correct statement of Kemble's experiences upon the Butler estate is not to be doubted (albeit significant qualifications must be made). Pierce Butler was still alive in 1863 (a hearty fifty-three); and had he thought worth doing so, he might have challenged his former wife's veracity—as in 1850 he had challenged her account of their married life with his 183-page printed *Statement*. But in Kemble's *Journal* she acknowledged that the Butler slaves were better treated than she believed was common elsewhere; and her book shows the feeling and regard for her husband (interspersed, of course, with impatient outbursts) which she still felt for him in 1839 and 1840. She knew Butler was the kind of master who might stay up all night caring for an ill slave, or who might even bring a sickly slave to Philadelphia in the hopes of improving his health, and she said so in her *Journal*.[36] Gabriella Butler's testimony is sufficient proof that Kemble told the essential truth about the estate, and the Butler family records in Philadelphia lend powerful corroboration.[37]

These records give glimpses of the later (and earlier) lives of slaves named in Kemble's *Journal*. Ten years after Kemble left Georgia, headman Frank—who impressed her more than any other slave—was still head driver at the rice plantation; and even though he was by now fifty-one, his official monetary value was the highest on the estate.[38] His wife, Betty, and five of her children were still living in 1849. Betty—whose cleanliness and tidiness had won Kemble's esteem in 1839—was the central figure in one of the apparently less credible assertions of Kemble's *Journal*. Kemble reported that when [in 1817] Roswell King Jr. sired a mulatto child by Betty, Betty was already married to Frank. Kemble's source for this claim was an elderly slave woman, Old House Molly; and one might be tempted to speculate that Molly—twenty-two years after the event—had sought to magnify King's culpability by accusing him not only of forcing a slave woman to have sex with him, but of forcing a married woman to do so, thus displaying his contempt for her relation to her husband. Yet the Butler records confirm that Betty was indeed married to Frank in 1817, and had had a child by him a year before her mulatto child was conceived.[39]

A slave retained by Gabriella Butler in 1859—when she and Pierce Butler divided the then 919 slaves into two portions prior to auctioning Pierce's half—was Aleck, to whom Kemble had taught the alphabet twenty years earlier. In 1859 Aleck was a thirty-seven-year-old house servant. He and his wife Daphne (a mulatto child of Roswell King Jr.'s) and their daughters kept in touch with Kemble's daughter Sarah after the Civil War; and this contact enabled the Alexanders—in 1899 when a black man in Darien was with flagrant injustice accused of rape—to secure money from a knot of Northern abolitionists to hire the lawyer who won the man's acquittal. Excellent photographs of Aleck Alexander, his wife, Daphne (whom Kemble had also known), and two of their children are extant.[40]

One of Kemble's best-known stories finds corroboration in a contemporary letter of Pierce Butler's. Kemble narrates a complex tale of a slave woman named Psyche, who was nearly separated permanently from her husband, Joe, by the actions of their white masters. This tragedy was avoided by Joe's resolute protest, by Kemble's impassioned intervention, and by Pierce Butler's purchasing Psyche and her children from the overseer, who had recently bought them from the younger King. So complicated is the story that one might speculate that these details had been elaborated by Kemble; yet Pierce Butler's letter of February 17, 1839, to King confirms that Butler had indeed just bought Psyche and her children from the overseer, who in turn had bought them from King.[41]

The Butler slaves had soon discovered that Kemble was no ordinary plantation mistress, and some of them—especially women—came to believe they could tell her uncomfortable truths without getting whipped for daring to do so. Thus on March 2, 1839, she asked nine slave women how many children they had had, and how many were still alive; and lists of the slaves (and of births and deaths) in the Butler Papers enable one to identify every one of the nine women, and often to furnish their children's names and their birth and death dates.[42] In case after case like these, slaves described by Kemble can be identified in the Butler Papers, which contain further details about their lives and make it resoundingly clear that Kemble had recorded with considerable accuracy her experiences at the estate.

For example, corroboration of one of her important stories appears in a letter Roswell King Jr. wrote to Pierce Butler in 1839. The slave woman Judy had told Kemble that her mulatto child had been the product of her being raped by the estate's manager. Later the slave Sophy declared that Judy's and two other mulatto children had all been born on the plantation within a month of each other—one of these others also sired (by the same manager) to a slave named Sinder, and the other (Sophy's own child) fathered by a white man named Walker, who had been employed at the mill. Sophy said that she, Judy, and Sinder had all been severely whipped at the order of Mrs. King and exiled, as punishment, to a remote and isolated part of the estate called Five Pound (at the western end of the otherwise virtually uninhabited Little St. Simons Island). While Pierce Butler and his wife were still at the estate in 1839, Pierce wrote to Roswell King Jr.—whom he greatly esteemed—to elicit his response to the story about Judy's child. King replied that three slave women had given birth to mulatto children, more or less simultaneously, in about August 1814. He also confirmed that they had all been exiled to Five Pound (for five years). "This punishment," he said, "was at the express desire of your Grandfather." Stating that he—then eighteen—had been absent at the time the women became pregnant, King claimed that he "therefore [could] not say anything farther on the subject." As to the paternity of the children, perhaps the slave women Judy and Sophy, speaking to Kemble, were more credible witnesses than King, and they said King's father (Roswell King Sr.) was the father of Judy's and Sinder's mulatto children. Kemble named the three women, but she had the third name wrong: it was Sinder, not "Scylla" as she reported. More significant, when in 1853 Kemble wrote an appendix to her *Journal,* she forgot that Roswell King Sr. (sire of Judy's and Sinder's mulatto infants) was not the father of Sophy's child too.[43]

No doubt the *Journal* abounds in small errors of this sort. Among some 715 slaves in 1839, many with biblical names, and almost none with a surname known to Kemble, it would have been surprising had she not occasionally confused one Abraham or Jacob with another. She reported correctly that Major Butler gave Morris a silver cup—cherished years later by Morris's descendants—for saving over 100 slaves for his owner but was mistaken as to the circumstances. (Morris saved these slaves' lives during a hurricane in 1804; it was one of the Abrahams, not Morris, who saved many slaves for Major Butler by persuading them not to join the 138 other Butler slaves who did escape with the British army in 1815.) Abraham was later freed by Butler for loyal conduct—but probably not for actual payment of cash he had earned, as Kemble believed. In order to protect Roswell King Jr.'s anonymity, Kemble deliberately mislocated his own plantation. (She said "Mr. K____'s" new estate was in Alabama, when she knew King's plantation was in Georgia, twenty-five miles north of the Butler estate.)[44]

Harder to comprehend were deliberate distortions of fact which Kemble introduced for artistic effect. She was not a scientific scholar, aiming to state every fact precisely, but a literary artist seeking to convey the essential truth about her husband's plantation in readable, memorable vignettes. Her *Journal* took the form of letters to her Massachusetts friend Elizabeth Sedgwick; but the "letters" had never been posted, and this was just a literary device— like the epistolary form of Goethe's novel *The Sorrows of Young Werther*—for giving the *Journal's* reader a sense of immediacy. Her artistic practice in 1839 and 1840, when she expanded and rearranged her plantation notes, becomes evident when the published *Journal* is compared with contemporary records. Kemble sometimes conflated the events of several days into one, to make them more vivid; or she spread the events of a single day over several, to increase their dramatic impact. When she attended the funeral services for Shadrach—a young, capable worker who, like so many of the Manigault rice slaves, died suddenly in winter of peripneumonia—two or three black men, including cooper London, officiated. In her published account, however, Kemble chose to conflate these into the single figure of the cooper.[45]

More striking was Kemble's altering the dates when one St. Simons planter killed another one, and when the jury acquitted the killer, so as to weave into the fabric of her narrative these two events, one of which, in fact, occurred just before she arrived in Georgia and the other just after she left. The extenuation offered by an able editor of her *Journal*—that she sought thus to disguise her own strong emotions about the duel Pierce Butler fought in 1844—will not convince every reader: for Kemble wrote the *Journal* in 1839 and 1840, and evidently it was ready for publication in 1841. There is no clear evidence that she made any substantial alterations after 1841, except for adding a few footnotes, two concluding paragraphs and two appendixes, and deleting certain passages deemed too personal for publication. The more probable explanation for her changing the date of the killing was artistic. She sought to tell an important truth about the Southern ethos, which justified one gentleman's killing another upon a point of honor (the dead man had struck the other with a cane and spat in his face): but she chose to do so in a dramatic narrative rather than in a cold retrospective analysis.[46] Kemble seems also to have altered an important fact in her story of the rescue of a party from the sinking steamer *Pulaski*. In so doing she magnified the heroism of her esteemed Georgia neighbor, the renowned rice planter James Hamilton Couper.[47]

Kemble's *Journal* therefore is no passionless report from a painstaking modern scholar. Instead it is slippery and hard to grasp—like every other piece of evidence on slavery, whether from nineteenth-century proslavery Southern whites or from aged former slaves interviewed with questionable methods in 1937. This problem is exacerbated by Kemble's tendency to overstate a contrast, and by her hyperbole. She herself was subject to "inconceivable rapidity of emotion," oscillating from despair at the plight of slave women to enchantment with the beauty of the low country during the springtime; and when she pointed an absolute contrast between the self-respect of headman Frank and the degradation of most slaves, she ran the danger of projecting upon the slaves' world the marked contrasts of her own temperament. The strength of her feelings occasionally led her to generalize recklessly, and her inconsistencies were readily discernible. When it seemed to her that "There is not a girl of sixteen on the plantations but has children, nor a woman of thirty but has grandchildren," she obviously had not done her sums; she was engaging in the same hyperbole which led Shakespeare to declare the heroine of *Romeo and Juliet* to be just thirteen. Kemble's unconvincing allegation, that for the slaves parenthood became "mere breeding, bearing, suckling, and there an end," was patently inconsistent with the words concluding her *Journal*—that the passionate attachment of a slave woman to her children was the master's best guarantee the mother would not flee.[48]

These scholarly problems in interpreting Kemble's *Journal* are compounded by an artistic one, arising from its author's egocentricity and her sententiousness. Constantly she protests she will let the facts speak for themselves; yet she cannot refrain from recording her emotional reaction to those facts. Sometimes this is moving, for she felt strongly and deeply, and her strangely modern frame of mind—her groping toward a genuine egalitarianism, her strong social conscience, her anguish at her incapacity to help the slaves—can give a reader a sense of what it might feel like to be transported backward a century and a half to the rice kingdom. Too often, however, one longs for the lachrymose Kemble to weep privately and not call attention to her tears. The depth of her Christian conviction was one source for those tears; but the 1830s and 1840s were a didactic era, and Kemble had acquired in her correspondence with people like even the estimable Mrs. Jameson a tone of moral uplift which offends the modern temper: if only she would drop the preaching!

This profound artistic weakness has presented some twentieth-century historians a reason to undervalue the sharp observations of the remarkable Englishwoman. The supercilious and sexist tone with which Ulrich Phillips in 1929 dismissed the testimony of "this visiting lady" comes as no surprise, for Kemble said what Phillips did not wish to hear.[49] But even a great modern historian risks patronizing Kemble when her testimony contradicts his own considered conclusions. Would any historian familiarly denominate Kemble's male contemporary, Frederick Law Olmsted—author of *The Cotton Kingdom* (1861)—"Freddie Olmsted"? Yet Eugene Genovese, minimizing or overlooking some of the evidence Kemble presented that slave drivers on the Butler estate abused their power, and that they inspired other slaves with fear,[50] alleges that "Fanny Kemble allowed herself to be deceived" by the tone slave drivers used toward other slaves. No doubt the Victorian public referred to its stage heroine as "Fanny Kemble"; but she was not only a public idol, she was a sharp-witted author, and she printed her name on the title page of her book: Frances Anne Kemble.[51]

Although Kemble's attitudes toward blacks are rightly unacceptable to a modern reader, she was in her own day a pioneer in racial egalitarianism. In this respect she stands out from other nineteenth-century observers of slavery. Famous British travelers of genteel background, like Captain Basil Hall and Sir Charles Lyell, squandered page after page upon proving to their own satisfaction that blacks were, after all, human beings—not a separate creation—and that the slave masters (although situated on the uncivilized side of the Atlantic Ocean) acted in a surprisingly gentlemanly fashion toward their dependents. Even Frederick Olmsted, despite his environmentalism, betrayed deep racial bias. By contrast, Kemble spent far more time than any of these gentlemen in talking with the blacks themselves—especially the women—and she actively tried to combat the self-denigration which to her was the most pernicious effect of slavery upon those subject to it.[52]

Yet at first blush Kemble appears to be nothing but a conventional racist. Her journey from Philadelphia toward Butler Island in 1838 took her South on a new railway; and at a small Virginia town "the Negroes gathered in admiring crowds round the railroad carriages," she remarked. "They seem full of idle merriment and unmeaning glee. . . . As my child leaned from the carriage window, her brilliant complexion drew forth sundry exclamations of delight from the sooty circle below, and one woman, grinning from ear to ear, and displaying a most dazzling set of grinders [etc., etc.]." Kemble deplored the resemblance between the slaves' lives and those of animals, a parallel which offended her Victorian sense of decency: "You see them," she wrote, boys and girls from the youngest age to seventeen and eighteen, rolling, tumbling, kicking, and wallowing in the dust, regardless alike of decency, and incapable of any more rational amusement; or lolling, with half-closed eyes, like so many cats and dogs, against a wall, or upon a bank in the sun, dozing away their short leisure hour, until called to resume their labors in the field or the mill.

Nor did Kemble hesitate to make the comparison—beloved by the most bigoted racist—of blacks to monkeys and apes. She once met at Butler's pineland tract

a creature which *was* a woman, but looked like a crooked, ill-built figure set up in a field to scare crows, with a face infinitely more like a mere animal's than any human countenance I ever beheld, and with that peculiar, wild, restless look of indefinite and, at the same time, intense sadness that is so remarkable in the countenance of some monkeys.[53]

Kemble came to Butler Island, one might believe, carrying with her every racial stereotype in the book. One's first, modern impulse might therefore be to dump her *Journal* into the river and be done with it. How—any racial egalitarian might inquire—can value be attributed to a report whose author betrayed such blatant racial biases?

Before dumping the *Journal,* however, one might observe that this is almost exactly what certain defenders of the South's old racial order sought to do in 1959 and 1960, when Alfred Knopf essayed to publish a modern edition of the controversial work. So hostile to Kemble's portrayal of slavery and of slaveholders was the local St. Simons Island historian, Margaret Davis Cate, that she seemed in 1959 to threaten to institute legal proceedings against republication of the book. Cate had discovered Kemble's misdatings of the killing of John Wylly and the acquittal of his killer, and to her these discredited Kemble's whole *Journal.* The eminent Southern white historian E. Merton Coulter—author of numberless books on Southern history and editor, in 1959, of the *Georgia Historical Quarterly*—was delighted at Cate's discovery. Coulter made his *Quarterly* the vehicle for Cate, promising to feature her attack upon the *Journal* as the first article in a forthcoming issue of the *Quarterly* (March 1960). Coulter mistakenly believed that major portions of the *Journal* had not been composed until 1862; and that Kemble had written them then (when she could no longer recall accurately events from twenty-three years earlier) as anti-Southern propaganda, designed to prevent Britain from intervening on the Southern side in the American Civil War. Coulter did not know that (except for a few footnotes and a couple of concluding paragraphs added by Kemble in 1862) the *Journal* was essentially complete by 1841. Nor was he aware how far the Butler Papers would corroborate Kemble's report. And (because Sidney Fisher's diary had not yet been published) he had not seen Gabriella Butler's testimony confirming the accuracy of the *Journal.* When Cate's article appeared in the *Georgia Historical Quarterly,* Cate sent copies to newspaper editors all over the South and elicited from a number of them enthusiastic replies, together with favorable notices of her article printed in their newspapers. As the civil rights movement gained momentum in 1959 and 1960, Coulter and Cate evidently felt that a well-publicized assault upon Kemble's *Journal* would deliver a sharp blow against the rising forces of racial egalitarianism.[54]

The explanation for their hostility toward Kemble's *Journal* is that the Englishwoman brought with her to Georgia not only those noxious racial stereotypes already illustrated but other baggage as well. Kemble was a subversive, whose luggage in 1838 contained an environmentalist theory; a capacity to see with her naked eye (as even the details of her observation of the scarecrow woman might suggest); a respect for human worth wherever found; and the rudiments of an egalitarian hypothesis. She perceived that the slaves' outrageous flattery of their masters was the product not of nature but of their dependent status. She challenged the belief of her Georgia neighbor, James Hamilton Couper, in the blacks' native "incapacity for progress": the same thing, she averred, had been said of the Irish, yet within two generations in the different environment of the northern United States the Irish immigrants had progressed rapidly. A comparable change, she implied, would occur among the blacks if they were not subject to an oppressive environment. She became "sick and weary of [the] cruel and ignorant folly" of Southern whites who blamed upon allegedly "natural defects of the Negro race" incapacities which were evidently the product of slavery. Admiring the intelligence, trustworthiness, and sobriety of headman Frank—the chief driver, who at Butler Island, as at other rice estates, bore full responsibility for running the plantation in the overseer's absence—Kemble satirized those who supposed blacks congenitally inferior. Slavery, she believed, destroyed virtues among many slaves, but because headman Frank had been entrusted with heavy responsibilities, his character had not atrophied. "Thus you see," she addressed Elizabeth Sedgwick—alluding sarcastically to the views of racist theorists—"among these *inferior* creatures, their own masters yet look to find, surviving all their best efforts to destroy them, good sense, honesty, self-denial, and all the qualities, mental and moral, that make one man worthy to be trusted by another."[55]

Although Kemble thought black people not beautiful, she tried to open her eyes, and to distinguish what was natural from what was acquired. She disliked the blacks' hair and the shapes of their mouths and noses; but after she had instituted a campaign to get the children to wash their faces and hands—by paying them a penny when they passed inspection—she came to believe the skins of most blacks "infinitely finer and softer than the skins of white people." And she continued: "I have seen many babies on this plantation who were quite as pretty as white children, and this very day stooped to kiss a little sleeping creature that lay on its mother's knees in the infirmary—as beautiful a specimen of a sleeping infant as I ever saw." Some of the blacks had a "finely-shaped oval face" and she also found "very considerable beauty in the make of the [women's] hands." Though she thought their feet often ill shaped, she attributed this to their seldom wearing shoes. The women carried themselves erect and very well, and this too she believed an acquired characteristic: it resulted from "the habit they have of balancing great weights on their heads." Kemble watched carefully the reactions of her young daughters to the blacks. "I cannot perceive, in observing my children," she reported, "that they exhibit the slightest repugnance or dislike to these swarthy dependents of theirs, which they surely would do if, as is so often pretended, there is an inherent, irreconcilable repulsion on the part of the white toward the Negro race." This was the language of a person, writing still with fastidious condescension, but trying to perceive reality beneath stereotype.[56]

Kemble's intercourse with the slaves resembled nothing they had previously experienced from a white person. First to become well acquainted with her was Jack, the son of the previous head driver, whom Pierce Butler assigned to attend his wife on her walks and rowing expeditions. As quick-minded as his father had been, Jack plied Kemble with questions about the wider world, and she came to relish his company. Finding him more sympathetic than the proslavery women in Darien to whom she occasionally paid a social call, she was wont to refresh herself "with a row on the broad Altamaha and the conversation of my slave Jack." Jack taught her to paddle a canoe, whereupon she ironically acknowledged a kind of equality between him and Pierce Butler, her lord and master. With her usual intrepidity she had gone paddling alone with her three-year-old daughter, and because of her inexperience had nearly got them both drowned: since then, she told Elizabeth, "I have taken no more paddling lessons without my slave and master, Jack." Their nautical camaraderie came to resemble that of Huck Finn with the slave Jim. Jack was a lad "of great natural shrewdness and no little humour," she wrote six weeks later to an English friend. He "was out fishing with me the other day, and after about two hours' silent and unsuccessful watching of our floats, he gravely remarked, 'Fishing bery good fun, when de fish him bite,'— an observation so ludicrous under the circumstances, that we both burst out laughing as soon as he uttered it."[57]

By this time Kemble had won the admiration of a number of other blacks on the estate. "My lady neighbors in these parts . . . have expressed unbounded astonishment," she reported, at the "perfect confidence" with which she went among the male slaves. Nine of them had rowed her the fifteen miles to Darien when she sought to flee North; the next day, when they rowed her back to St. Simons, they were caught up in a dangerous storm, and afterward it was not just the slaves' customary flattery of their masters which impelled them to declare "they were pleased because there was not another planter's lady in all Georgia who would have gone through the storm all alone with them in a boat; i.e., without the protecting presence of a white man." Most evenings slave women came to Kemble with petitions, and there was also another kind of visitation to her study at St. Simons when her husband was staying at Butler Island. "Often in the evening," she reported,

> when my bairns are asleep, and M[argery O'Brien, her children's Irish-Protestant nurse] upstairs keeping watch over them, and I sit writing this [journal] . . . , the door of the great barnlike room is opened stealthily, and one after another, men and women come trooping silently in, their naked feet

falling all but inaudibly on the bare boards as they betake themselves to the hearth, where they squat down on their hams in a circle. . . . I have had as many as fourteen at a time squatting silently there for nearly half an hour, watching me writing at the other end of the room. . . . I very often take no notice of them at all, and they seem perfectly absorbed in contemplating me. . . . Sometimes at the end of my day's journal I look up and say suddenly: "Well, what do you want?" when each black figure springs up at once . . . ; they all answer: "Me come say ha do (how d'ye do), missis"; and then they troop out as noiselessly as they entered.

Perhaps the social distance between Kemble and the blacks brought out the best side of her nature. She was capable of brusquerie toward her social equals, of turning her satire savagely against those who rubbed her the wrong way. But with the slaves she sought to reach across the chasm separating them, hoping they would learn "that there are beings in the world, even with skins of a different color from their own, who have sympathy for their misfortunes, love for their virtues, and respect for their common nature." This regard for the slaves' virtues—this nascent egalitarianism—alarmed Pierce Butler. "I remember hearing at the time," Sidney Fisher recalled years later, "that her conduct at the plantation had enraged Butler & the overseers & caused much dissatisfaction among neighboring gentlemen as she put dangerous notions into the minds of the slaves."[58]

The notions she inculcated were environmentalist. When Abraham, her cook, told her that "we colored people" gladly ate certain fish which white people disliked, she challenged him. Her experience as an actress helped her to adopt Abraham's idiom. "Why do you say we colored people?" she inquired.

"Because, missis, white people won't touch what we too glad of."

"That," Kemble asserted, "is because you are poor, and do not often have meat to eat, not because you are colored, Abraham; rich white folks will not touch what poor white folks are too glad of; it has nothing in the world to do with color."[59]

Repeatedly the blacks told her they were naturally inferior to whites. No doubt this was done partly to flatter and partly to ward off extra demands upon their time. When Kemble urged three teenage girls—"rudely playing and romping with each other" during their lunch break—to clean and tidy their filthy house, the girls countered ingeniously:

They said they had seen buckree (white) women's houses just as dirty, and they could not be expected to be cleaner than white women. I then told them that the only difference between themselves and buckree women was, that the latter were generally better informed, and, for that reason alone, it was more disgraceful to them to be disorderly and dirty. They seemed to listen to me attentively, and one of them exclaimed, with great satisfaction, that they saw I made no difference between them and white girls, and that they never had been so treated before.

Kemble believed that the blacks, considering themselves different from whites, set themselves low standards. "Self-love," she thought, "is not so vile a sin as self-neglecting." Therefore, whenever the slaves spoke disparagingly of themselves as congenitally squalid or knavish, she replied to them that "white people are as dirty and as dishonest as colored folks, when they have suffered the same lack of decent training." But the slaves did not quickly expunge their years of indoctrination: Kemble despaired that she could not find even one slave woman who believed "that she was neither more nor less than my equal." Thomas Oden, the Butler Island overseer, knew the slaves must be rigidly indoctrinated if order were to be upheld. He was sure to disapprove Kemble's "way of speaking to the people, of treating them, or living with them, the appeals [she made] to their sense of truth, of duty, of self-respect." Oden—unlike Roswell King Jr.—was of a wholly different social class from the Butlers and he was expected to behave deferentially to his employer and his wife; once, however, he dared to hint the truth to Kemble: her "existence among slaves was an element of danger to the 'institution.' "[60]

Kemble's existence among the Butler slaves was, however, a boon to those seeking to understand slavery: for although she was partially imprisoned by Victorian ideology, her egalitarian strivings and her protofeminist deportment marked hers as, in some respects, a remarkably modern sensibility. Her apprehension of the blacks' lives was surely more acute than that of most whites who interviewed former slaves for the Works Progress Administration (WPA) a century later; and one might lose much, were one to disregard her testimony.

8

Mothers and Children

Kemble was appalled by her experiences on the Butler estate. Child mortality
was frightful. The health of female slaves was shattered by the field labor
required of them until soon before, and again soon after, their frequent pregnancies. Not even the most estimable slave woman could defend herself
against the sexual demands of white overseers. Slaves were subject to revolting physical punishment and to degrading callousness. Both children and the
aged were shockingly neglected. Worst of all, slaves were systematically
taught to devalue themselves, and their demoralization often expressed itself
in filth, nervelessness, and a brutalized style of life. If certain admirable slaves
managed to preserve self-respect against every force tending to undermine it,
their condition was the more deplorable: conscious of degradation, they
showed in their countenances sadness, fear, and pathos.

This picture of slavery has been not wholly to the taste of any twentieth-
century reader—surely not to slavery's apologist Ulrich Phillips, but neither
to modern students of black culture. Kemble's *Journal* challenges criticism
whenever it conflicts with a reader's deepest convictions about slavery.

The frequency with which children died, dismaying though it was to Kemble,
should surprise no one acquainted with the rice kingdom.[1] One evening a
series of nine slave women came to Kemble after their work was done, peti-
tioning her for bits of cloth and morsels of food, or simply paying her a visit.
She asked each one her childbearing experiences. All nine women can be
identified, a century and a half later, in the Butler records in Philadelphia; and
with the possible exception of one (Sukey), the stories they told Kemble

about the number of children they had borne appear to be consistent with the
records of births and deaths kept by Roswell King Jr. from 1819 to 1834. The
thirty-three-year-old Molly, for example, was the most fortunate of these
women, because only three of her nine children had died. (Her nine children,
the Butler records show, were born in 1824, 1826, 1828, 1830, 1831, 1833,
1834, 1836, and 1837: of these, the ones who had died by the time of Kemble's
trip were those born in 1830, 1833, and 1834. A fourth child—the one born in
1831—died subsequent to Kemble's visit but before reaching adulthood.)
Sophy was not quite so lucky, for five of her ten children were already dead.
Thirty-two-year-old Sukey said she had needed fifteen pregnancies to produce
six living children: she had had four miscarriages, and five live children had
later expired.[2]

These were the only ones of the nine women who still had large families
when Kemble spoke to them. Leah, twenty-six years old, had lost three of her
six children, while Nanny at twenty-eight had seen two of her three die.
(Nanny, Kemble noted, "came to implore that the rule of sending them into
the field three weeks after their confinement might be altered.") Forty-eight-
year-old Charlotte had had only two pregnancies, both ending in miscarriages.
Sally at forty-four had also had two miscarriages, and one of her three live
children had died. Fanny, thirty-eight years old, told Kemble that five of her
six children had died. Her sole living child, the Butler records show, was her
two-year-old Wallace.[3]

The thirty-nine-year-old Sarah had had perhaps the hardest life of all those
to whom Kemble spoke that evening. Her first husband, carpenter Ben, had
died in 1825. Their only child had perished in infancy, and Sarah probably had
also had several miscarriages before her husband's death. By a second husband Sarah bore children in 1827, 1828, 1830, 1832, 1833, and probably about
1836, of whom only two were still alive in 1839. Thus by the time she spoke to
Kemble she had been pregnant eleven times, had had four miscarriages, and
had seen five of her seven children die. Pregnant once again, Sarah

> complained of dreadful pains in the back, and an internal tumor which swells
> with the exertion of working in the fields; probably, I think, she is ruptured.
> She told me she had once been mad and had run into the woods, where she
> contrived to elude discovery for some time, but was at last tracked and
> brought back, when she was tied up by the arms, and heavy logs fastened to
> her feet, and was severely flogged. After this she contrived to escape again,
> and lived for some time skulking in the woods, and she supposes mad, for
> when she was taken again she was entirely naked. . . . I suppose her constant
> childbearing and hard labor in the fields at the same time may have produced
> the temporary insanity.[4]

This record of human misery undermines the claim of the eminent British
geologist Sir Charles Lyell that the rapid growth of the slave population
proved the happy condition of low-country slaves.[5] The lives of these nine
women—who among them had experienced twelve miscarriages and five stillbirths, and seen twenty-four more children die—were scarcely models of

felicity; yet the nine women had produced twenty-six living children, far more than required to sustain the estate's labor force. As at Gowrie, the majority of these families became small through dreadful child mortality; and the high incidence of miscarriage—suffered by four of these nine women—suggests an added dimension to the maternal woes of women at Gowrie, where miscarriages seldom found their way into the plantation records. Yet on the Butler estate, unlike Gowrie, enough slave women were able to keep four, five, or even six children alive to replenish, and more than replenish, the slave population. The Butlers' white managers sometimes worried about the high death rate, and in certain years—as in 1821, 1822, and 1825—deaths on the estate exceeded births; but normally the managers expected a steady, if not spectacular, increase in the number of slaves. From 1824 to 1859 the Butler slave population increased at a rate of 14.5 percent per decade, probably wholly through natural increase.[6] This was much less than the growth of the American slave population, which during this period was at a rate of 26.6 percent per decade.[7] If the number of Butler slaves on the St. Simons cotton plantations grew at nearly the national average, then those at the Butler Island rice plantation increased at a rate of some 10.5 percent per decade. (Two-thirds of the infants were born at Butler Island, and rice plantations, as everyone knew, were the most unhealthy for slaves). "The proportion of sick is always greater here," Kemble reported from Butler Island, "than on the cotton plantation, and the invalids of this place are not unfrequently sent down to St. Simons to recover their strength."[8] Kemble's *Journal* suggests the human realities disguised by the statistics of an expanding slave population.

The Butler records from 1819 to 1834 help to explain the slave women's travail. At the St. Simons cotton plantations—where five of Kemble's nine interlocutors had worked—one-third of the children died before reaching the age of six. Yet the situation was even worse at the Butler Island rice plantation,[9] as is evident in table 17. During the infants' first two weeks, over 16 percent of those born alive at Butler Island perished; and at every subsequent stage a young child on the rice plantation was much more likely to die than at St. Simons. The difference was most marked during the first six months; and over half of the children at Butler Island had succumbed before age six (see table 18).

Yet the figures on "children born alive" always understate the hardships experienced by the slave women, for they include neither stillbirths nor miscarriages. Stillbirths on the Butler estate—with no significant difference *here* between the rice and the cotton plantations—numbered 5.3 percent of live births.[10] And although the managers did not record miscarriages, Kemble's *Journal* suggests that the total number of miscarriages was substantially larger than the total number of mothers. Thus, perhaps 22 percent of the Butler Island slave women's pregnancies terminated in either stillbirth or miscarriage—and the same was probably true throughout the rice kingdom.[11]

It has never been sufficiently realized how devastating infant mortality was on nineteenth-century rice plantations. Even Richard Steckel—whose valuable studies have done most to call attention to the phenomenon—originally

TABLE 17.   Child Mortality Rates (to age 6)
(1819–34, Butler Estate)

	Sea-island cotton (St. Simons Island) (%)	Rice (Butler Island) (%)
Mortality rates, first 6 months (Dead/all children born alive)		
Weeks 1–2	11.4	16.3
Remainder of first 6 months	6.3	16.3
Mortality rate, months 7–12	4.7	8.1
(Dead/those alive after 6 months)		
Mortality rate, years 2–3	10.4	12.7
(Dead/those alive at first birthday)		
Mortality rate, years 4–6	5.9	8.0
(Dead/those alive at third birthday)		

Note: Mortality rate for the first six months of an infant's life are based upon 158 live births at St. Simons and 331 live births at Butler Island. Details are in appendix D (appendix table 3).

suggested an infant mortality rate on rice plantations (to age one) of 31 percent; yet this figure, high though it seems, was surely an underestimate. The records Steckel analyzed—as he himself pointed out—probably underreported early deaths; and the very complete Butler lists show that 38 percent of infants at that large rice plantation died during their first year.[12] There is no reason to suppose that Butler Island was especially unhealthy, compared with other rice plantations; indeed, infants elsewhere in the rice kingdom probably perished even faster than at Butler Island. The Butlers' agents confidently pointed to the increase in their slave population to prove that they were more successful than most managers of rice plantations. "Doctor Grant, who is rather indulgent, has told me that his gang diminished," Roswell King Jr. assured the Butlers in 1834. "At Hopeton [a model rice plantation managed by the renowned James Hamilton Couper] where greater expense, than with us, has been gone to, they decrease. A planter three years from Georgetown, S.C[arolin]a told me that his gang had diminished 10 p[er] C[ent] anually [*sic*], particularly among children."[13] The Manigaults' Gowrie plantation was certainly even more unhealthy for children than Butler Island (61 percent of Butler Island children died by age sixteen, while about 90 percent of Gowrie children perished before that age). Just as infant mortality on most American nonrice plantations was surely even higher than on the Butlers' sea-island cotton plantation, so infant mortality on the typical rice plantation was probably even worse than at Butler Island.[14]

No doubt an even larger proportion of infants would have died at the Butler estate had the managers not granted pregnant mothers a certain respite from field labor. So clear was it that arduous labor in muddy or flooded rice fields would impair the health of pregnant women and their babies that—

according to the younger Roswell King—"the labour of pregnant women is reduced one half, and they are put to work in dry situations." This sounded sensible, so far as it went; but how was King to determine whether a woman was pregnant? Evidently he had at first relied upon the women to notify him when a baby was on its way, and apparently as many as one-third of them had then pretended to be pregnant before they actually were. Dido's infant, King reported with exasperation in 1822, had been "15 mo[nths] breeding," Tina's 11 months, Elce's 17 months, and Mary's 16 months. Malingering seems to have been practiced even by the wives of the most trusted artisans. The admirable Betty (wife of that carpenter Frank whom King later promoted to be the head driver at Butler Island) was 12 months in breeding her infant; while the wife of carpenter Ned—later appointed chief engineer of the rice mill—took 15 months between the time she said her pregnancy had begun and the moment the child appeared. However much one may smile appreciatively at these women's successful deception of their master, this form of day-to-day resistance could be counterproductive; for it might impel the suspicious white man never to reduce a woman's task until he could see with his own eyes that she was indeed pregnant.[15]

The terrific infant mortality at the Butler estate—which occurred despite the reduction in the pregnant women's task—demands explanation. King sought to exculpate himself by blaming the slaves themselves for infants' deaths, and in 1833 he pointed his finger particularly at the mothers. "The mortality is very great . . . ," he acknowledged. "It appears difficult to save the lives of the young negroes. . . . Not until the parents become more careful can it be effected. Towards themselves, they are thoughtless in the extreme." A year

TABLE 18. Cumulative Child Mortality Rates (to age 21)*
(of children born 1819–34, Butler Estate)
(dead/all children born alive)

	Sea-island cotton (St. Simons Island) (%)	Rice (Butler Island) (%)
Died during first 6 months	17.7	32.6
Died before first birthday	21.6	38.1
Died before third birthday	29.7	45.9
Died before sixth birthday	33.9	50.3
Died before sixteenth birthday (est.)	—	61.0**
Died before 21st birthday (est.)	—	63.8**

*Except for the last two lines of this table, the cumulative rates are derived from the mortality rates in table 17. But the cumulative rate is *not* the sum of the rates printed in table 17 because, in order to calculate it, each of those rates must be multiplied by the proportion of children still alive at the relevant age. The methods of calculation are shown in appendix D (appendix table 4).

**The sources for these estimates—based upon 105 children born (from 1819 to 1834) to a sample of 24 Butler Island women—are explained in appendix D.

later he accused those slaves especially charged with medical duties. "The great mortality among the infants . . . ," he alleged,

> originates from inattention on the part of the midwife and nurse. . . . The first 9 days is the most critical time, a neglect of the umbilical chord (*sic*] I think is the cause of the loss of so many Infants. Threatening the missis has very little effect. Negroes are as great Predistinarians [*sic*], as the Turks, all must die when their time arrives, none before.[16]

King's careful death records (where he specified the supposed cause of each infant's demise) offer important clues to the causes of infant mortality, and they enable one to challenge his own theories. To be sure—as medical historians would expect—lockjaw (i.e., tetanus caused by unsterile cutting of the umbilical cord) was a substantial killer at Butler Island, mowing down 3 percent of the infants within eighteen days of birth. Yet lockjaw cannot have caused the distinctively high death rate on rice plantations, for it killed almost the same proportion of infants at the sea-island cotton plantations (as may be seen in table 19).

Bowel diseases, perhaps resulting from polluted river water, were indeed more common at the rice plantation than at St. Simons, killing nearly 2 percent of the Butler Island babies. Two other factors, however, seem to have been the principal sources of rice's macabre record. One was malaria; the other was the infants' feebleness at birth, probably caused partly by the mothers' debility from chronic malaria, and partly by their general exhaustion during pregnancy.

Summer fevers dispatched over 4 percent of Butler Island infants during their first year yet killed scarcely a single child at St. Simons. This striking difference is testimony to the lethal effects of mosquitoes (bred in the stagnant rice swamps) upon the black children. And those infants who survived the malarial fevers transmitted by those mosquitoes had lower resistance to other diseases, which may explain the higher death rate on the rice island from winter fevers, whooping cough, and convulsions.

The second principal factor was the infants' feebleness. Puniness, or illness at birth, caused the deaths of over 5 percent of the babies within two weeks of birth, and of another 4 percent during the remainder of their first year. In itself, however, this does not really distinguish rice from cotton, for nearly as high a proportion of very young infants died from these causes at St. Simons. The big difference lay in unexplained deaths, which within the first two weeks killed 5 percent of all infants at Butler Island, but which almost never occurred at St. Simons (nor at Butler Island after the first fortnight). These deaths were unlikely to have resulted either from lockjaw or from a high fever—whose striking symptoms were clearly identifiable. Instead, these were probably the deaths of infants who seemed so unpromising at birth that no special explanation was required to account for their rapid demise. Richard Steckel proves—from twentieth-century studies of malaria—that mothers suffering chronic malaria are likely to produce stunted children who die unusually quickly. And Frances Kemble showed that the relative ill health of mothers on the rice plantation was well understood at the Butler estate. Butler Island women, she reported, were

TABLE 19.   Causes of Infant Mortality (to age 1)
(Butler Estate, 1819–34)

Proportion of Live Births Who Died from Specified Causes

Cause	Sea-island cotton (St. Simons Island)		Rice (Butler Island)	
	Died before first birthday	Among whom, died in weeks 1–2	Died before first birthday	Among whom, died in weeks 1–2
Lockjaw	2.5%	(2.5%)	3.0%	(2.7%)
Bowel diseases, dysentery	—	(—)	1.8%	(—)
Summer* fevers	0.6%	(—)	4.3%	(0.3%)
Winter fevers, coughs, colds	3.8%	(2.5%)	4.9%	(1.2%)
Whooping cough	1.3%	(—)	2.4%	(0.3%)
Influenza	0.6%	(—)	0.9%	(—)
Convulsions, fits	—	(—)	1.5%	(0.6%)
Puny, feeble, deformed	5.7%	(3.2%)	5.5%	(3.3%)
Ill at birth	1.9%	(1.9%)	3.7%	(2.1%)
Unspecified	0.6%	(0.6%)	5.8%	(5.2%)
Injury	1.3%	(—)	1.2%	(—)
Miscellaneous**	3.3%	(0.7%)	3.1%	(0.6%)
TOTAL	21.6%	(11.4%)	38.1%	(16.3%)

Sources: Lists of births and deaths, 1819–34, Butler MS (HSP).

Note: Figures for deaths (to Dec. 31, 1834) during the first 6 months are based on 158 live births (1819–June 30, 1834) to St. Simons mothers and 331 live births to Butler Island mothers. For deaths (to Dec. 31, 1834) during months 7–12, figures are based on 128 infants born 1819–33, who were still alive at end of 6 months, to St. Simons mothers, and 210 such infants to Butler Island mothers. For each disease, the percentages derived from these two sets of figures are combined by the procedure specified in appendix D, appendix table 4, lines d, e, and f.

*Malarial season: Deaths occurred June 18–Nov. 20.

**Thrush, teething, sudden death, ulcerated, refusal to nurse, sore mouth, abscess on thigh.

always given maternity leave for one week longer than those at St. Simons: no doubt in an effort to compensate them for the special rigors of working in the rice swamps. The relatively unhealthy mothers at Butlers Island were even more likely than at St. Simons to produce feeble infants, who died without explanation soon after birth.[17]

If these deaths from unspecified causes were indeed the result of the infants' feebleness at birth, one can begin to comprehend the horrific infant mortality rate on rice plantations. Probably nearly 15 percent of the babies died during their first year because they were puny or ill at birth; perhaps 4 percent more from malaria; 8 percent more from winter fevers, whooping cough, and influenza (where presumably the infants' resistance had often been undermined by malaria); 3 percent from lockjaw; and about 2 percent from bowel diseases. These were the main reasons that nearly two-fifths of all the babies died before their first birthday. The great majority of these dead infants had not survived for even six months.[18]

Kemble's evening conversations with the nine slave women suggest the impact of their children's deaths upon these mothers. But the only systematic way to assess the family lives of the Butler Island women is to examine a representative sample of those women. Such a scrutiny—based on the childbearing histories of twenty-four typical young Butler Island women, taken from the 1821 slave list—shows that their experiences were even harsher than Kemble had inferred.[19]

One reason was that a number of these young women had died before 1839, and were therefore no longer available for conversation when Kemble visited Georgia that year. From the sample of twenty-four women, four had died while still in their twenties. Sue died at twenty-three, of "continued fever and subject to vomiting blood." Hagar perished suddenly at twenty-eight, of "violent pain in the head and stomach." The twenty-seven-year-old Esther died, five days after giving birth to her fourth child, from "influenza and childbed." And the same influenza epidemic (which generally was fatal only to slaves already weak from other causes) killed one other young mother, the twenty-five-year-old Dido.[20]

These four women died too soon to have very big families—they produced altogether eleven children, of whom only two survived to adulthood; and a fifth woman appears to have been sterile. The other nineteen women in the sample, by contrast, gave birth to large numbers of children. Four of them each bore a dozen or more live infants; and the norm—for these nineteen women—was to mother nine children.

To keep their children alive was another matter. Sinder, for example, bore about sixteen infants, but her experiences were dismal. Apart from any possible miscarriages (which would not appear in the records), she bore four children from 1820 to 1827, all of whom died young: the first child, Nancy, encountered one of the rice plantation's peculiar dangers, and "drowned in [a] ditch" at eighteen months; Rina was ulcerated at birth and survived only seven months; Priamus died of summer fever—probably malaria—at fifteen months; and an anonymous child succumbed to whooping cough when only one week old. Meanwhile, Sinder's husband, cooper Lewis, had died of apoplexy at age twenty-seven. She remarried, and from 1829 through 1834 bore a child every year. Without fail, each one quickly died, usually because puny at birth. One might have supposed that with this record of ten dead children in a row, Sinder would never have produced a surviving child; but, in fact, her next half dozen or so pregnancies resulted in two children who actually survived (at least to the ages of eleven and five)—a substantial compensation to a woman whose existence had been grim almost beyond reckoning.

Another woman whose life was not a carefree idyll was Tina, who bore her first eight children within ten years. The firstborn (when Tina was eighteen) was premature and died after just one day. The next was stillborn (and therefore is not included in my figures on "live births"). Three other infants died young—of whooping cough, fits, and a cough and cold—while two more survived well into childhood but then perished. Tina's eighth child, therefore, was the first to reach the age of fifteen. Yet Tina persisted, and about five more pregnancies produced three other children who survived infancy. Thus by the time Tina was forty-five years old, her thirteen known pregnancies had left her with four living children, aged fifteen, ten, three, and one.[21]

Tina's, and even Sinder's, lives suggest a substantial difference between Butler Island and the Manigaults' Gowrie plantation: at Butler Island a woman's experiences might be harrowing, yet—by contrast to the situation at Gowrie—she stood a good chance of having a few children left alive at the end of her life. On average (and the figures refer now to all twenty-four women in the sample, including the four who died in their twenties) these Butler Island women had 7.2 babies born alive. Of these, 4.6 children, on average, died before reaching the age of twenty-one. But this meant that each woman bore, on average, 2.6 children who survived to age twenty-one. Harsh though life might be, and painful as were the frequent deaths of children, enough children nevertheless survived that, as table 20 indicates, most women might look forward to bearing at least two who would reach adulthood.

Thus, although nearly 40 percent of these mothers did not raise even as many as two surviving children, just over 40 percent bore two to four survivors; and about 20 percent raised five or six children to maturity.

A woman of childbearing age needed to mother only two surviving children in order to replenish the slave population. The Butler Island women, producing an average of 2.6 surviving children, therefore ensured that the slave population would increase steadily—even on a rice plantation—at a decennial rate of some 10.5 percent.[22] An agent like Roswell King Jr., or a gullible foreign traveler like Sir Charles Lyell, could—by ignoring the women's hardships—reassure himself that the growth of the slave population was proof of the slaves' felicitous condition.

Kemble's conversations with other slave women illustrated the rigors which might accompany a woman's raising a handful of children to maturity. One mother—who had had two miscarriages, and all but one of whose children had died—suggested the causal connection between the women's hours of field labor and the dreadful mortality rate among their infants. "Missis," she addressed Kemble, "we hab um pickaninny—tree weeks in de ospital, and den right out upon the hoe again—*can we strong* dat way, missis? No!" The experiences of a woman named Die resembled those of Sinder (mentioned previously), whose first ten children had all perished one after another

TABLE 20.   Size of Families (children who survived to age 21)
(Estimated number of children born 1819/49 to a sample
of 24 Butler Island women born between 1799 and 1806)*

Size of Family (i.e., no. of children who survived to age 21)	No. of women whose family was this size	Proportion of the women whose families were this size	Total no. of children in these women's families		
			Who survived to age 21	Who died before age 21	Total no. of live births
Average number of children per woman			2.6	4.6	7.2
0	3	12.5%	0	3	3
1	6	25.0	6	29	35
2	3	12.5	6	18	24
3	4	16.7	12	26	38
4	3	12.5	12	9	21
5	3	12.5	15	16	31
6	2	8.3	12	10	22
TOTAL	24	100.0	63	111	174

*The estimates are derived as follows:

(a) The sample of twenty-four women includes every Butler Island female worker aged twenty-one or under on the 1821 list.

(b) The names and birthdays of their 105 live births, 1819–34, are taken from the birth lists for those years; and the 47 of these children who died before January 1835 are identified from the death lists for the same years.

(c) An additional 19 of these original 105 live births who had died by 1849 are identified by names missing from the 1849 slave list.

(d) Thus 39 of the original 105 children survived to 1849. Their ages are specified in the 1849 list. Fourteen of them were then under twenty-one years old, and I estimate (from age-specific mortality rates of other slaves) that one of them died before age twenty-one, raising the total number of dead children to 67 and reducing the number of survivors to 38.

(e) Twenty of the twenty-four women were alive in Jan. 1835, and from the 1849 slave list one can determine that between 1835 and 1849 these women bore 31 more children who were still alive in 1849.

(f) The ages of these 31 children—ranging from one to fourteen years—are specified in the 1849 slave list. By applying to each of them Butler Island's age-specific mortality rates (derived from tables 17 and 18), one can estimate that six of these children died before reaching age twenty-one. The families to which these 6 dead children are most likely to have belonged can be identified from the ages of each child, and from the number of such children in each family.

(g) From the preceding paragraph, one estimates that 25 of the children born after 1835 survived to age twenty-one. By applying Butler Island's cumulative mortality rate to age twenty-one (63.8 percent, as stated in table 18), one can estimate that the twenty women still alive in 1835 must have borne a total of about 69 children between 1835 and 1849, in order to produce the 25 survivors.

(h) In order to estimate roughly how many of these 69 children were born after 1835 to each of the twenty mothers, I have taken into account: (1) the number of a woman's children born during that period who were still alive in 1849; (2) the woman's fertility from 1819 to 1834; and (3) her age in 1835.

(j) The total number of the twenty-four women's live births from 1819 to 1849 must have been about 174 (i.e., the 105 before 1835 plus the estimated 69 thereafter). Of these, the number who reached age twenty-one must have been about 63 (i.e., 38 of those born before 1835 plus 25 born after 1835). (I have ignored the—probably negligible—number of live births which these twenty-four women may have had before 1819 or after 1849.)

(k) I have estimated each woman's total number of live births, and the total number of her children who survived to age twenty-one, by combining the figures derived by the procedures described in each of the preceding paragraphs. By adding up the number of these women who fell into each category, one reaches the figures printed in table 20.

but whose later pregnancies had finally produced two survivors. Die's twenty pregnancies had left her, too, she told Kemble, with but two living children: fourteen were dead, and she had had four miscarriages. One of these

> had been caused with falling down with a very heavy burden on her head, and one from having her arms strained up to be lashed. I asked her what she meant by having her arms tied up. She said their hands were first tied together, sometimes by the wrists, and sometimes, which was worse, by the thumbs, and they were then drawn up to a tree or post, so as almost to swing them off the ground, and then their clothes rolled round their waist, and a man with a cowhide stands and stripes them. . . . She did not speak of this as of anything strange, unusual, or especially horrid and abominable; and when I said: "Did they do that to you when you were with child?" she simply replied: "Yes, missis."[23]

Slavery induced a kind of dumb patience in many of its victims, but Kemble knew this did not imply lack of strong family feeling. One January afternoon she visited a settlement on Butler Island where many children were ill, and where an unusually large number had succumbed during the winter. "In one miserable hut I heard that the baby was just dead," she wrote gloomily:

> it was one of thirteen, many of whom had [died] like itself. . . . The father and mother, and old Rose, the nurse, who was their little baby's grandmother, all seemed apathetic, and apparently indifferent to the event. The mother merely repeated over and over again: "I've lost a many; they all goes so"; and the father, without word or comment, went out to his enforced labor.

Numbed by "frequent repetition of similar losses," and sensing that life would have offered little to the enslaved infant, the parents were battered into silence.[24]

To deflect their minds from present conditions, the slaves cherished the vision of a sort of golden age before old Major Butler had died in 1822. The major had allowed the Hampton slave women four weeks after confinement before they had to return to field labor, and even then their hours were lightened: they did not need to be in the field before sunrise (i.e., they did not have to start work at dawn like the other slaves) nor to work after sunset. And on the unhealthy rice island the maternity leave had been stretched to five full weeks. After the major's death, however, Roswell King Jr. had lopped a week off from their leave, both at Hampton and at Butler Island. Now the slaves' energies—as so often elsewhere in slavery—were channeled into seeking the grant of a privilege, rather than in openly combating the system itself. The pregnant women who spoke to Kemble on March 1 begged her

> to have the sentence (what else can I call it?) modified which condemns them to resume their labor of hoeing in the fields three weeks after their confinement. . . . Their sole entreaty was that I would use my influence with Mr. [Butler] to obtain for them a month's respite from labor in the field after childbearing. Their principal spokeswoman, a woman with a bright sweet

face, called Mary, and a very sweet voice, which is by no means an uncommon excellence among them, appealed to my own experience. . . . I held the table before me so hard in order not to cry that I think my fingers ought to have left a mark on it.[25]

The brevity of maternity leave was obviously related to the prevalence of gynecologic complaints among the slave women. Victorian prudery sheltered white male observers from learning the facts of the slave women's lives, and thus blunted the edge of antislavery criticism. Even Kemble was constrained to write obliquely, but it is evident that excessive menstrual bleeding afflicted innumerable slave women, that chronic menstrual backache made many mothers' lives miserable, and that fallen wombs were common. All this was on top of rheumatism, which cursed young and old rice workers alike, and was probably more usual among women than men. One slave woman after another petitioned Kemble for menstrual flannel. Her principal help to Charlotte and Judy was to give them "the bandages they especially begged for": they had come to Kemble, she reported indirectly, with "a complaint, which it really seems to me every other woman on the estate is cursed with, and which is a direct result of . . . sending women to labor in the fields [three weeks] after their confinement."[26] Although Auber looked so elderly that Kemble supposed she had stopped menstruating, the woman "complained of flooding, of intolerable backache." Kemble was "surprised to hear of [these] complaints, for she seemed to me like quite an old woman; but [their life] ages these poor creatures prematurely." A few days later one of the new admissions into the Hampton sick house was the slave Priscilla, who "had come out of the fields today scarcely able to crawl; she has been losing blood for a whole fortnight without intermission, and, until today, was laboring in the fields." Sally was another slave woman who "came complaining of incessant pain and weakness in her back."[27]

Many slave women, Kemble learned, were "victims to falling of the womb and weakness in the spine." No slave woman would have demonstrated her gynecologic problems to a male visitor like Sir Charles Lyell or Frederick Olmsted, but this was what Teresa, an "emaciated-looking" woman, did to Kemble. The slaves—delighted that Pierce Butler had married and produced two children and that they might therefore be safe from an auctioneer's hammer for another generation—had overwhelmed Kemble by their servile effusions of joy when she had first landed at Butler Island; and the most demonstrative of all had been Teresa, tall and gaunt, who "flew to us, parting the throng on either side, and embraced us in her arms. I believe I was almost frightened." A few days later Teresa visited Kemble on the porch of the overseer's house, where the Butlers lived:

She appeared very ill today, and [unfolded] a most distressing history of bodily afflictions. She was the mother of a very large family, and complained to me that, what with childbearing and hard field labor, her back was almost broken in two. With an almost savage vehemence of gesticulation, she suddenly tore up her scanty clothing, and exhibited a spectacle with which I was inconceivably shocked and sickened. . . . These are natural results, inevitable and irremediable ones, of improper treatment of the female frame.[28]

Sackey, for many years one of the chief nurses, explained to Kemble that Roswell King Jr. had reduced the women's maternity leave. Their quick return to field work after confinement, she convincingly declared,

> "is why, missis, so many of the women have falling of the womb and weakness in the back". . . . Sometimes, after sending them back into the field at the expiration of their three weeks, they would work for a day or two, she said, and then fall down in the field with exhaustion, and be brought to the hospital almost at the point of death.

Within a month of young Pierce Butler's arrival at the rice island a gang of pregnant women had come to him in the evening to complain of overwork, but he had not budged; he had intoned instead their "duty" to fulfill the tasks set them. This, as has been seen, did not stop the women from seeking to influence Butler through his wife, but he banned her on February 26, 1839, from presenting any more of their petitions.[29]

After her abortive attempt to flee to the North, Kemble listened more seriously than ever to the women's stories of hardship, often uttered with patient resignation. Thus Peggy—an "exceedingly decent woman" married to the literate carpenter John, who was one of Butler's most valuable slaves—suffered ill health in 1839 and said "she had been broken down ever since the birth of her last child." Asked how long after the confinement she returned to field work, "she answered very quietly, but with a deep sigh: 'Three weeks, missis; de usual time.' " Shocked by the sufferings of Mile and especially of Die (the woman whose miscarriage had been induced by a whipping), and shaken still by the explosion when Butler had refused her permission to intercede for the slaves, Kemble tried to "walk off some of the weight of horror and depression [she felt] surrounded by all this misery and degradation that I can neither help nor hinder." In the woods, the frightfulness of how people treat their own kind mingled with the horror nature sometimes displays. "Treacherous white moss"—like white slaveholders living off their slaves—parasitically depended from the "noble live oaks" of St. Simons Island and finally conquered them, "stripping [their] huge limbs bare." The seventh circle of Dante's hell came to Kemble's mind, where suicides, converted into trees, cried for compassion: *"Non hai tu spirto di pietate alcuno?"*—Have you no pity?[30]

9

Degradation

The masters' indifference toward the health of black women and their children was one strand in a more general pattern of dishonoring slaves. At first sight the motives for this degradation might appear straightforward. If an overseer forced sex upon a slave woman, his purpose was apparent. Similarly, whipping a slave was obviously aimed at impelling harder work. And money saved on furnishing the slaves' infirmary might pay for the master's expensive medieval ball costume. Yet the degradation of slaves served other functions beyond these uncomplicated ones. When a master had the power to act contemptuously toward a slave, might there not sometimes be satisfaction in doing so? And if black people could be made to feel their degradation, might they not become easier to govern? Kemble's long stay at the Butler estate offered her more opportunities to observe this dishonoring of slaves than were afforded to transient visitors like Sir Charles Lyell or even Frederick Olmsted. She learned something of miscegenation, much about discipline, and even more about the whole system of degrading the slaves.

Although the Kings were of a higher social class than the usual overseer, Kemble discovered that their class position did not constrain them from taking advantage of bondswomen under their power. Roswell King Sr. was the father of three mulatto slaves by three different slave women: Venus, Judy, and Sinder. Venus's mulatto child, born in 1812, was Bram, who later became a driver; King's other two mulatto children were born in 1814. Judy said that King "forced her [and] flogged her severely for having resisted him." The product of this rape, Jim Valiant, was Judy's first child.

Mrs. Roswell King Sr. appears to have borne her last child to her husband in 1810, when she was thirty-four, and she may have decided not to sleep with him regularly thereafter. Whether or not this prompted King to turn to slave women for sex, it did not lessen his wife's jealousy. Soon after Jim Valiant and the other mulatto baby were born in 1814—and "in her husband's temporary absence from the estate"—Mrs. King went to the infirmary, personally supervised a severe flogging of both Judy and Sinder (and of Sophy as well, who had just borne a mulatto baby sired by a white worker at the rice mill), and had the three women exiled as punishment to the remote "Five Pound" plantation, with orders for a week of further floggings there.[1]

Roswell King Jr. was also the father of three mulatto slaves, by two different slave women—Betty and Minda. Betty's child Renty was probably born in 1818, and the twins, Daphne and Ben, were born to Minda on July 12, 1824. These children were all produced before King's own marriage in 1825. Although Betty was only fifteen or sixteen when the twenty-one-year-old King sired Renty, she was already married to the twenty-year-old slave Frank (and was already the mother by Frank of a healthy infant), when in 1817 the manager's son took her for his own pleasure. Frank later became the head driver at Butler Island. Kemble esteemed him and his wife, Betty, above all other slaves on the estate. Roswell King Jr. esteemed them too: King "was emphatic in his praise of both Frank and his wife . . . ," Kemble reported drily, Betty "having, as he declared, by way of climax to his eulogies, quite the principles of a white woman. Perhaps she imbibed them from his excellent influence over her."[2]

The Butler slaves regarded themselves as better treated than many other bondsmen and women, and Kemble shared this judgment. One sign that they were relatively well off was Renty's request that he be allowed to have the gun which Roswell King Jr. left at the estate when he retired from managing it in 1838. Knowing that the blacks were banned from possessing firearms, Renty argued to Pierce Butler that his white blood should entitle him to special privilege. This did not wash with Pierce Butler, and Renty "departed with some severe reflections on Mr. K[ing], his father, for not having left him his gun as a keepsake, in token of paternal affection, when he left the plantation." The Manigaults, to be sure, let their chief bird minder keep a gun, and the Georgia rice planter Richard Arnold allowed several slaves the privilege; but not many planters did so, and Renty's openly expressed hope for a gun implied that the Butler estate was in certain respects less restrictive than most. The understanding between Renty and Pierce Butler that King was Renty's father also suggested that even hypocrisy had its limits. Major Butler, finding in 1819 that the infant Renty was a mulatto, had obliged King to acknowledge paternity.

But King never admitted his siring of Daphne and Ben, for by then the major had died. The absentee owners in Philadelphia made no inquiries; and by then King's own marriage was impending—to the sixteen-year-old daughter of a well-to-do Georgia slaveholder, Colonel Audley Maxwell. Best to keep quiet about recent doings on Butler Island.[3] If the King men left a trail of sorrow behind them in the slave quarters—if Betty and headman Frank never could regard King without thinking of the wrong he had done them, and if Daphne Alexander could never think of her father without bitterness—the slave women knew that compassion for their sorrows was in short supply.

The most important way of dishonoring the slaves was to subject them to harsh physical punishments, and the discipline imposed upon the Butler slaves resembled that common elsewhere in the rice kingdom. Planters and managers liked, however, to draw fine distinctions between one plantation's regime and another, and in 1828 Roswell King Jr. publicly lauded the superiority of his father's and his own management of the Butler estate over what had subsisted there before 1802. In the first volume of a new journal, the *Southern Agriculturist,* the younger King contrasted his father's regime with the "brutality and licentiousness [theretofore] practiced by the principal men on [the Butler estate before 1802]; (say the drivers and tradesmen)."[4] Licentiousness evidently came in various degrees. The Butler estate may well have been even worse before the Kings took over than it was afterward. King's accusation of the previous regime was ambiguous—it was safer to blame black drivers and artisans than to point the finger at white men like William Page (Major Butler's manager from 1796 to 1802), who had given a reference for King when the latter assumed the estate's management in 1819, and whose daughter—still living on St. Simons in 1828—might take offense.

The virtues which King claimed for his management of slaves focused upon his limiting the use of the whip. He thoroughly mistrusted the ordinary drivers, believing them likely to demand extra work from some slaves in order to favor others, and to lash any slave who complained about this unfair division of labor. Drivers therefore, King alleged, were not permitted to whip a slave at the Butler estate "until after a regular trial." King himself, of course, used the lash, but he publicly preferred to dwell upon those other penalties which ate into a slave's spare time. The offender might be forced to clear trash around the settlement or to dig tree stumps, on a Sunday or after finishing the regular task. The estate was known locally for the isolation the Butlers sought to impose upon their bondsmen and women who, the son of a neighboring slaveholder later wrote, "were governed by laws more arbitrary than elsewhere enforced. By their owners' orders no intercourse with the neighboring plantations was permitted." A few Butler slaves were, however, allowed to go to Darien on Sunday morning to sell eggs, chickens, or works of carpentry, "but must be home by 12 o'clock [noon], unless by special permit"; and Sunday trips were allowed once a month back and forth between Butler Island and the Butler cotton plantations downstream at St. Simons Island. A ban upon even this limited Sunday travel was, King declared, a severe penalty for a recalcitrant slave, who might be confined at home "six months to twelve months, or longer." A slave returning intoxicated from Darien "goes into stocks, and [is] not allowed to leave home for twelve months."[5]

In composing—for the edification of other planters and of his employer,

Frances Butler (the dead major's daughter)—his paean to his father's and his own exemplary conduct, and to the Butler slaves' submissiveness, King omitted one or two facts that might have confused the issue. In late January 1815 a British military detachment, whose commanding admiral arrived on the Georgia coast fresh from burning the White House in Washington, had occupied St. Simons Island and offered freedom to any slave who cared to come aboard the British vessels. Almost all of the able-bodied field workers at Hampton (Major Butler's main cotton plantation on St. Simons) and a substantial number of the privileged artisans accepted this offer: 139 men, women, and children. Roswell King Sr. remonstrated with the male slaves who—like Adam blaming Eve, but with bondsmen's skilled pretense of attachment to their masters: "sorry, solemn, and often crying"—guilefully explained to King that they had to leave Hampton not because they wanted to (heavens, no!) but because they must: "Some said they must follow their daughters, others, their wives." It was even more dangerous for a male slave than for a female to defy authority; to the women, therefore, must be attributed the responsibility.[6]

Unrest had spread instantly to the rice workers fifteen miles away at Butler Island. Abraham, a carpenter, tried to dissuade his fellow slaves there from following the Hampton slaves (and seven years later was rewarded for his loyalty by a grant of manumission, in Major Butler's will; but as that document freed neither Abraham's wife nor his children, the old man ended his days with them on the Hampton plantation, legally free). King knew that despite Abraham's suasion most Butler Island slaves "would have gone off [to the British] if they only had a chance." He reported angrily in early March 1815 that they "have been very Rebelious, did but little for some weeks, some totally refused to work." Maddened by the island's "ungrateful rascals," King responded to the British invasion as Louis Manigault later did to the proximity of Northern troops in 1862: "Those animals," King vowed, "must be ruled with a rod of iron." As for the Hampton slaves who had fled, he fulminated, "How it will please me to have the pleasure to git your Negroes back and pick out one husband, one wife, one fellow, one Wench and sell them—leaving there children or parents behind as it may happen, to reflect on there wanton, Impudent folly."[7]

The British allowed two St. Simons planters to board ship and try to persuade the hundreds of fugitives to return to their masters. Only one of Hampton's 139 refugees agreed to do so—a bricklayer whose conduct was part of a general pattern: Major Butler's privileged slaves were not quite so willing to gamble on freedom as those who had even less to lose. Later in the year King—hoping that the inhospitality of Nova Scotia would cause a change of heart among the fugitives whom the British had dumped at that frigid outpost—wrote to agents there, but learned "that they can find none that wish to return except some old ones that are not worth sending." King knew that cash value, not a paternalist ethos, motivated Major Butler; and none of the handful who wished to return was sent for. The major instead lodged an inflated claim against the British of some fifty-six thousand dollars: for their taking his slaves, and for robbing him of the cotton those slaves might have produced in 1815, had they not fled. Eleven years later Britain, under the treaty ending the War of 1812, paid to his estate one-eighth of this sum.[8]

Another clear instance of slaves' discontent appeared in November 1816 when, according to the death list, two slaves each "Drowned self." Whether they succumbed to despair or through an unsuccessful attempt to escape remains uncertain. The elder King tried to pass the buck for their deaths to Butler Island's head driver Harry, "in one of his tiranacal fits." The two slaves were sheep minders; and Harry, finding they had failed to send every sheep to St. Simons as instructed, had ordered them to make a special trip there to take the last sheep. After completing this task the men—a thirty-nine-year-old and his sixteen-year-old assistant—disappeared. "As the weather was so moderate," King explained, accidental death had seemed improbable, and some thought the two men had fled. King, however, was convinced the two men had drowned, and he ordered the search which led to their bodies being found. So stern was King in punishing fugitives that "no Negro," he boasted, "dare run way from me." He communicated these words to Major Butler, because he knew that draconian punishments for flight would win the old man's approval.[9]

It was in 1828, then, that Roswell King Jr. published his boast that the Butler estate was scarcely troubled by a fugitive problem. Other deterrents to flight—in addition to the terror which the older King had sought to instill, and to the slaves' "stake in society" (their poultry and their vegetable gardens, to which the younger King publicly attributed their alleged docility)—were the rattlesnakes in the woods, and the alligators and water moccasins in the rivers. "Lor, missis, taint no use—," old House Molly protested to Kemble in 1839, "what use nigger run away? —de swamp all round; dey get in dar, an' dey starve to def, or de snakes eat 'em up." Everyone on St. Simons warned Kemble of the rattlesnakes, who were already active in February and became even more vicious in the heat of July and August; and her slave companion Jack was terrified lest he be held responsible for her incurring snakebite by wandering off the roads during their daily excursions.[10] Yet within a month of King's public boast of good order, a group of seven slaves had fled the estate: in midwinter, to be sure.

Their leader was a man named Sampson, and among those accompanying him was Sampson's twelve-year-old son, Emanuel, who doubtless was bursting with pride at the opportunity to go with his father on a thrilling adult adventure. King was cross that these "few malignant, ungrateful Scoundrels" might destroy the subordination he had worked so hard to establish. "I am obliged to be very strict," he had written to the proprietress in 1824. "Allow no intercourse with other Negroes. None allowed to go off [the estate] without asking permission, and stating his business abroad, and every Negro to be home before night." When the seven fugitives were captured, therefore, King punished them severely. No doubt he flogged them thoroughly, though he claimed that "I never use the whip without giving me pains. I put it off to the very last." He also punished some of them by a method of his own contrivance: "The cold bath is solely my punishment, never used by anyone else."

In consequence of the bath administered from a bucket of cold water in January 1829, doubtless after a whipping, the twelve-year-old fugitive (the boy Emanuel) died—presumably of shock. King alleged, in the death list, that Emanuel had died of "Worms, ill 24 hours"! Subsequently he had to explain this incident more candidly to the proprietors in Philadelphia, but it did not lead to his indictment and conviction for manslaughter, as in justice it should have done. It did not even lead to his dismissal—no more so than had the Maryland overseer Orson Gore's killing in 1823 a (nonviolently) defiant slave, later reported in Frederick Douglass's autobiography.[11] On the contrary, the proprietors thought King an admirable manager, and Pierce Butler was so sorry when this paragon left the Butlers' employ in 1838 that he gave a present of a valuable young slave, Joe, to the departing King as a sign of his esteem. That King's accepting this gift would tear Joe away from his wife and their two children did not trouble King's conscience; and only Joe's anguished remonstrance and Kemble's intervention caused King and Pierce Butler to abandon this plan.[12]

Kemble's husband was capable of impulsive generosity to the slaves as well as to King, and he was almost certainly regarded by them as a better master than most. During his first trip to the plantation in 1836–37, he diverged from low-country custom and from previous practice on the Butler estate by decreeing that the "task" of an able-bodied female slave be smaller than that of an able-bodied male. Because Pierce Butler was an absentee who until the age of twenty-six had never visited the plantation, he appeared as a deus ex machina, possessing power to relax regulations long enforced by Roswell King Jr. And insofar as Butler in 1839 responded to Frances Kemble's interventions, this would have raised his stock further with his bondsmen and women. The grandson of a neighboring planter later declared—with less exaggeration than might at first appear—that Butler's being a rich absentee had nourished in his slaves "loyalty, affection and pride in their owner's name and wealth."[13] Though one might dismiss many other encomia written by members of the planter class about other members of their own class, this one cannot be so quickly spurned: for (as will appear) its author, Charles Spalding Wylly, sharply criticized the fundamental principles of the Butler regime; and insofar as Wylly lauded Butler, his praise received a certain corroboration through an abolitionist source.

Soon before Robert Gould Shaw led the fatal attack of his black regiment upon Fort Wagner near Charleston in 1863, the Massachusetts colonel talked at St. Simons Island to some former slaves of Pierce Butler. They no longer needed to, yet they did nevertheless assure Shaw, he wrote home, "that 'Massa Butler was a good Massa' and they would give anything to see him again." Bram, the driver at Hampton, was another black man "loyal" to Butler: for the testimony by Butler's daughter Frances of Bram's and other blacks' feelings toward Butler after the war—myopic though Frances Butler Leigh was—cannot be wholly dismissed. And the steadiness with which Aleck Alexander (whom Kemble had taught his alphabet) and his wife, Daphne (Roswell King Jr.'s daughter), and their children maintained contact with the

Butlers' daughter Sarah, right into the twentieth century, is further evidence
of some blacks' positive feelings toward the Butler family.[14]

Kemble regarded the estate as being "under the best and most humane
administration," and she believed there was an "absence of all voluntary or
even conscious cruelty on the part of the master." She said "the owners are
supposed to be humane, the overseer efficient and kind, and the Negroes
remarkably well cared for and comfortable." Though she changed her mind
about King's kindness, and though she knew the "comfort" of Butler's slaves
was only relative, her observation of other Altamaha River estates confirmed
her original impression that her husband's bondsmen and women were comparatively well treated. One illustration was the plantation rule, instituted by
Major Butler, that the head driver could inflict no more than thirty-six lashes
at his own discretion, and the subdrivers twelve.[15] Another sign of Pierce
Butler's unusual handling of his slaves was that, when he decided in 1853 to
sell Glasgow as an incorrigible runaway, he permitted Glasgow's wife and/or
his fourteen-year-old son to be sold with him if they wished.[16] When the
Manigaults sold Jack Savage in 1863, there was no thought of letting Jack's
wife, Amey, accompany him; nor did the Manigaults—or almost any other
slaveholders—ever flinch from separating husband and wife when a runaway
was to be sold.

But the death of the twelve-year-old fugitive Emanuel (after whipping and
a cold bath) and the sale of Glasgow illustrate the limits of the Butlers'
"indulgence" of their slaves. Overseers and drivers flogged slaves on the
Butler estate, sometimes terribly, as a matter of course: for the whole system
depended upon inflicting shocking physical pain as a way of governing an
unwilling labor force. And recalcitrant slaves were sold from the Butler estate
as from almost every other one in the South, for this was the most profitable
means of securing subordination. In place of futile contrasts between the
comparative lenity of one master and the severity of another (though these
were vitally important to the slaves involved), the disciplinary methods shared
by the Butlers with most other rice planters—and the consequences for the
slaves—need further exploration.

Old Major Butler had early stated his ideal of absolute subordination: "The
master will give what is needed—what is not given is not to be desired."[17] The
major was adept at devising nonviolent punishments, such as cutting off the
clothing ration, as a way of disciplining his slaves; but as late as the last few
months of his life he remained clear that whipping was the ultimate means for
securing his ends. In 1821 cotton production on Little St. Simons Island was
not what Butler thought it should be, and Roswell King Jr. blamed the male
cotton pickers. "If [deprivation] will have no effect," the major instructed his
twenty-five-year-old manager, "the unpleasant alternative of punishment
must be resorted to. They must be brought under." This echoed the language
the elder King had used fifteen years earlier about a young slave whose work
did not give satisfaction. "A little whipping" had not done the trick, King then
remarked. And although an older slave might become unconquerable and

have to be sold, a severe whipping would be just the medicine for this youth: "He is a very likely lad of about 18 . . . , young enough to be conquered." In 1808 another young man stole half a barrel of rice and absconded for two days: "I gave him a severe whipping," King reported, confident the major would approve.[18]

Skillful manipulation of the system of deputing authority to black drivers was another indispensable disciplinary tool. Masters everywhere in the South liked to focus their slaves' resentments upon the overseer, against whose authority the owner—as benevolent court of last resort—might occasionally intervene on the slaves' behalf. The elder King operated a similar system with his black drivers. Once, when a driver was left in charge of Butler Island, a slave fled for a week to the woodland. Not many days after King's return to the island, the slave surrendered voluntarily, claiming he had merely got affronted with the driver; and instead of inflicting the customary severe whipping, King let Jimoney pay off the lost time in Sunday labor. At other times, however, King conspired with the drivers against the field workers. When the slaves came to him to complain, he boasted to Major Butler, "I talk smoothly to them, and behind their backs, tell their drivers to push them up."[19]

King did not always talk smoothly. His feelings toward insubordination resembled those of the Manigaults' gentlemanly overseer, William Capers, when Louis Manigault's house servant London committed suicide. Before King took over in 1802, Butler Island slaves seem to have been permitted to travel to St. Simons (in a relatively safe plantation boat) during the Christmas holiday; but King apparently removed this privilege as part of his policy of keeping the Butler slaves on a short tether. Defying a ban against travel to St. Simons on any small boat, five slaves (four of them teenagers) set off for the fifteen-mile journey on Sunday, December 24, 1808, in a tippy dugout. The weather was bad, the dugout overturned, and all five were drowned. King's reaction to this challenge to his authority was not sorrow but rage: he told the slaves "that there [*sic*] friends might find the bodies and bury them like *dogs,* for not one of them should have a Coffin . . . , and that the next got Drowned in violation of [Orders], I would sell the Bodies to be Cut to pieces by the Doctors."[20] This was a threat after Major Butler's own heart, for the major did not approve of doctors and would not let them be employed for his slaves—except for broken bones and venereal complaints. (This did not, however, save his slaves from bleedings: Butler insisted the bleedings must be administered by his untrained managers rather than by professional doctors.)[21]

The tradition of stringent control of the slaves, instituted by the elder King with Major Butler's full support, was continued and intensified by King's son. One of his first problems was to cope with the Butlers' version of Jack Savage, an indomitable slave who escaped "several times, and skulked starving in the woods and morasses, but had always been tracked and brought back, and flogged almost to death, and finally sold as an incorrigible runaway." King gained permission to sell him away from his wife, Molly, who never saw him again. Yet whipping was not the invariable punishment for flight, if mitigating circumstances could be adduced. Judy—whose rape by the elder King had led to the birth of the mulatto Jim Valiant—was later married to a slave, but she went mad. He left her. "While out of her mind," Kemble went on, Judy "escaped into the jungle, and contrived to secrete herself there for some time, but was finally tracked and caught." In this instance, instead of a whipping, the younger King made her "sit, day after day, for hours in the stocks."[22]

Whipping and the threat of sale remained, however, the pillars of the system, while flight and poor work remained the slaves' principal forms of dissidence. "It is to be regretted that two such healthy tough men [as London and Scipio] cannot be tamed," Roswell King Jr. lamented to his employer in 1835. What alarmed him about their repeated absenteeism was not that they would make a permanent escape but that they might die by snakebite, drowning, starvation, or disease; and the owner's investment in them (each had cost $450) would then be sunk. "The risk of loss in these erratick excurtions," he mused, "is very great." The usual whippings were insufficient to pacify these two men, and if he gave them a truly horrific whipping, their resentment (or merely their sullenness) would infect the other slaves and be counterproductive. "I can keep them at home and get their work," he congratulated himself, "but"—obliquely—"it is attended with much trouble." Might it not be best to sell them as he had done with Molly's husband? There was, moreover, a worse problem to hand. "Our chief blacksmith Jack," King continued, "has not for 20 years give the satisfaction he ought to have done. Talking to him does no good. Last summer I had to give him a sound flogging, but that has not mended him." Major Butler had threatened Jack with sale fifteen years earlier—was it not time now to carry out this threat?[23]

The Butlers' slaves had been better off—according to their estimable neighbor, John Couper—while Major Butler had actively supervised the estate, than later when it fell under the virtually unconstrained dominion of the two Kings. Couper had tried to persuade Major Butler to raise turnips and peaches at Hampton for the benefit of the slaves, but these plans "had been obstructed and finally put entirely aside by old Mr. K[ing] and his son." The Kings grew rich while managing the Butlers' property, but they took little interest in the slaves' welfare. Roswell King Jr. was not necessarily responsible for the one substantial improvement since Major Butler's death—the employment on an annual salary of a competent medical doctor—for this may have been done at the instigation of Major Butler's daughter, or his son, in Philadelphia. The younger King, who chopped a week off the women's maternity leave, evinced no concern about cleaning or repairing the filthy infirmaries to which ill slaves were consigned.[24]

That the slaves' welfare had deteriorated since Major Butler's death was reported by the slaves too. "Major [Butler] was considerate and humane to his people," Kemble was told by Venus and Tressa (who knew no slave had ever been whipped for praising a master); and

> the women were especially carefully treated. But they said Mr. K[ing Jr.] had ruined all the young women with working them too soon after their confinements; and as for the older ones, he would kick them, curse them, turn their

clothes over their heads, flog them unmercifully himself, and abuse them shamefully, no matter what condition they were in. They both ended with fervent thanks to God that he had left the estate.[25]

A slave might escape punishment for condemning a former manager, but to criticize the present overseer was riskier business. If the overseer flogged a slave who had just complained to Kemble, a legalistic dispute might ensue over the grounds for the whipping. Thus, soon after Teresa said she was ill and overworked, and showed Kemble her bodily afflictions as evidence, the overseer Thomas Oden (who knew of Teresa's complaining) had her whipped. The instrument used "was a short stick of moderate size, with a thick square [i.e., rectangular] leather thong attached to it." Teresa went to Kemble "in a dreadful state of excitement . . . because she said Mr. O[den] had ordered her to be flogged for having complained to me." Pierce Butler, however, argued to his enraged wife that Teresa had failed to perform her allotted task and was whipped for this reason alone, not because she had complained; and Kemble, silenced on this particular issue, "resorted, in my distress and indignation, to the abstract question; . . . the brutal inhumanity of allowing a man to strip and lash a woman, the mother of ten children; to exact from her, toil, which was to maintain in luxury two idle young men, the owners of the plantation."[26]

Another case—that of Harriet—was harder for Butler to explain away. Kemble, finding this woman in the infirmary ill, with her infant also ill, had criticized her for "the horribly dirty condition of her baby." Harriet had excused herself by saying the slave women did field work from daybreak till evening: they could not clean their children because "then they were too tired and worn out to do anything but throw themselves down and sleep." Overseer Oden, irritated by this excuse, vehemently denied to Kemble that the slave women had to work as long as Harriet said. The next morning he whipped Harriet in the infirmary, and according to the slave women this was punishment for her complaining to her mistress. Their story provoked Kemble's first threat to leave the plantation—"if the people were to be chastised for anything they said to me."

The situation looked different to Thomas Oden: Harriet was, in his view, whipped for an impudent answer to his orders, not for having complained to her mistress. The overseer was plagued by a constant struggle with the slaves over their chronic malingering (and by the women's repeatedly pretending they were pregnant to get increased rations and decreased labor); and on the morning after Harriet's complaint to Kemble he had decided the slave woman was once again fit for field labor. He commanded Harriet to set off from the infirmary for work, but instead of silently and cheerfully obeying orders as all slaves were supposed to do, she had the impertinence to answer him back. She

said she was ill and could not work; . . . he retorted he knew better, and bade her get up and go to work; she replied: "Very well, I'll go, but I shall just come back again!" meaning that when in the field she would be unable to work, and obliged to return to the hospital.

"For this reply," Mr. O[den] said, "I gave her a good lashing; it was her

business to have gone into the field without answering me, and then we
should have soon seen whether she could work or not; I gave it to Chloe too
for some such impudence."

Teresa, in anger, had misled Kemble about the cause of her own flogging; but
did Harriet, weeping bitterly in the infirmary just after Oden had horse-
whipped her, misunderstand the fundamental reason for *that* event?[27]

Although neither the overseers nor the slaves informed Kemble of routine
floggings during her sojourn, four other whippings did nevertheless come to
her attention. Cook John, one victim, was a member of a highly privileged
slave family. His grandfather Abraham was the slave freed for dissuading
Butler Island slaves from fleeing in 1815; John's father was the respected "old
Jacob"; and his brothers were Psyche's Joe (one of the most manful slaves at
Butler Island), carpenter Abraham, and the wagon driver Israel. To his master's astonishment, John stole a ham from the Butlers:

> Mr. [Butler] was in a state of towering anger and indignation, and, besides a
> flogging, sentenced the unhappy cook to degradation from his high and digni-
> fied position (and, alas! all its sweets of comparatively easy labor and good
> living from the remains of our table) to the hard toil, coarse scanty fare, and
> despised position of a common field hand.[28]

Another whipped slave was Louisa, "a remarkably intelligent, nice-
looking young girl," who was the grandchild of the esteemed house servant
old House Molly. As at Gowrie, no sharp line could be drawn between the
families of house servants and field hands, and old Molly's granddaughter was
an ordinary worker in the Hampton cotton fields. One day Louisa felt ill and
unable to complete her task, and driver Bram severely whipped her for her
failure to do so. The slaves "were fastened up by their wrists to a beam or a
branch of a tree," Louisa explained to Kemble,

> their feet barely touching the ground, so as to allow them no purchase for
> resistance or evasion of the lash, their clothes turned over their heads, and
> their backs scored with a leather thong, either by the driver himself, or, if he
> pleases [by] any of the men he may choose to summon to the office; it might
> be father, brother, husband, or lover, if the overseer so ordered it.

The next day this "slender young slip of a lassie, with her poor piteous face and
murmuring, pleading voice" felt again unable to complete her task, and Bram's
threat of another flogging caused her to flee to the swamp despite the rattlesnakes: "Oh, missis, me no tink of dem; me forget all 'bout dem for de fretting."
After a few days, famished, Louisa staggered back to the hospital: "Me starve
with hunger, me most dead with hunger before me come back." One of the
privileges overseers might extend to slaves—oil to keep the machinery
running—was remission of the whipping which everyone took for granted as
the penalty for flight. Louisa (not a threatening, defiant male but a submissive-
looking lassie) was "sick so long" in the infirmary after starving in the swamp
that the overseer called it quits; no further whipping was imposed.[29]

The third of these punishments reported to Kemble was a man's "very severe" whipping at Butler Island, caused by his getting his wife baptized without securing the overseer's permission. Hampton slaves were allowed once a month to attend the blacks' Baptist church at Darien, where they were preached to by a white man, but they were barred from going to the only church on St. Simons Island (at Frederica, several miles from Hampton). Allegedly this ban was just part of the general policy of hindering contact between Butler slaves and those from other plantations; but more was at stake, for the younger King rejected an offer by the Frederica minister to conduct special services at Hampton. Although no missionary was permitted to set foot on Butler Island, and although Pierce Butler rejected his slaves' petition that he build a church on the island, the slaves there were less illiberally treated than at Hampton: for in addition to a monthly trip to Darien they were allowed to hold their own Methodist Sunday service at cooper London's house, and also a nighttime prayer and hymn meeting during the week.

Both Kings had disapproved of religion for slaves. Thus the elder King had requested Major Butler in 1804 to let him buy a dozen cheap fiddles: he was determined to "try to break up so much preaching as there is on your Estate. Some of your Negroes die for the Love of God and others through feir [*sic*] of Him. Something must be done. I think Dancing will give the Negroes a better appetite for sleep than preaching." The younger King was indifferent to religious or moral training for the slaves—"his only notion upon the subject of religion," John Couper's daughter declared, "was that it was something *not bad* for white women and children." The feelings of Thomas Oden, the overseer in 1839, were if anything stronger than those of the Kings—he was wholly hostile to any religious instruction of slaves.

Local planters were divided upon the subject: two black preachers (evidently missionaries) had recently been expelled from Darien; two white clergymen there solicited Pierce Butler's support for their preaching to slaves, and received contributions from him; but Butler defended his reluctance to build a church on Butler Island by saying his neighbors would disapprove. At Butler Island the master's permission was required for a slave to be baptized. The whipping reported to Kemble was therefore another of those floggings interpreted differently by slaves than by the overseer. The slaves saw it as a punishment for baptism, while Oden doubtless felt he was simply repressing disobedience: the requirement of prior permission was not to be flouted.[30]

The last whipping Kemble reported, for which she did not learn the offense, was inflicted upon a man named Glasgow, the slave who was finally sold as unconquerable in 1853. It is difficult for a later century—when physical punishment even of children is often frowned upon—to understand how on the rice plantations a handful of whites could have imposed their wills over hundreds of apparently intimidated slaves. The answer lies largely in the power of physical pain. At the turn of the twentieth century lynching was a central element in subordinating blacks, and two lynchings a week (over the period 1880–1910, each one well publicized) sent tremors throughout the

Southern black community. Under slavery whippings performed a similar function, and even more effectively. Floggings were vastly more numerous than postbellum lynchings; yet the number of particularly savage floggings need not have been enormous in order to impress upon slaves the peril of challenging authority. Our century needs only observe the desperation with which we sometimes seek sexual pleasure, in order to imagine more readily the desperation with which other human beings may sometimes have sought to avoid excruciating physical pain. Although the Butlers' slave Glasgow may himself have been an indomitable character, the price he paid for his independence—quickly known throughout the Butler estate—was certain to breed caution in others. "Jack gave me a terrible account of a flogging that . . . Glasgow had received yesterday," Kemble recounted. Jack "seemed awfully impressed with it, so I suppose it must have been an unusually severe punishment."[31]

To impress the blacks with their powerlessness by imposing upon them fearsome physical pain was the most important element in a more general system of degradation. At the Butler estate, its young neighbor Charles Spalding Wylly later testified, "Discipline was supreme. . . . Every step [by a slave] toward individuality, self-reliance or independence was repressed and checked." Wylly contrasted the situation of slaves on rice plantations (subject to the overseers' unconstrained dominion) with that on some nearby sea-island cotton plantations (such as his grandfather Thomas Spalding's), where the constant presence of the master might mitigate the harshness of the system. The condition of the Butler slaves probably typified those at other rice plantations, though Wylly felt that—partly because of the isolation imposed by the Butlers on their bondsmen and women—they were in certain respects even worse off than elsewhere in the rice kingdom. The language of the Butler slaves

> was absolutely unintelligible to one not long conversant with them. In their training no attention at all had been paid to morals, religion or to the improvement of their minds; industry and thrift had been inculcated, but every sign of independence or personality in character was checked and discouraged, and, in many ways, this large estate represented some of the worst features of the "System."[32]

On the Butler estate, Kemble showed, the slaves were to be treated with contempt, and their spirits crushed. Her illustrations were taken from the St. Simons cotton plantation as well as from the Butler Island rice plantation, and she often described practices common throughout the South, not just on an absentee plantation. White people, for example, had surnames, but the Butler slaves scarcely ever. White people were "Mr." and "Mrs.," but blacks never. At the Hampton burial ground Kemble was amazed to find that, although Roswell King had put a little fence around the graves of two white workmen to keep the cows off, the cattle trampled at will upon the blacks' graves. The two white men "were strangers," Kemble angrily reflected, and of course utterly indifferent to the people here; but by virtue of their white skins, their resting place was protected from the hoofs of the cattle, while the [relatives of the slaves] might see the graves of those they loved trampled upon and browsed over, desecrated and defiled, from morning till night.[33]

If the dead were disdained, the lives of the very old were treated with almost equal contempt. Even the most privileged of the elderly slaves, old House Molly, was ill used. She had been a functionary in the "big house" on Butler Point, in the good old days when Major Butler had sometimes resided there and entertained in style; and he had promised that she would be well cared for in her old age. But of course slaves had no legal right to enforce such a promise: special privilege inculcated special dependence, and the goodwill of white people was the only—fragile—guarantee of a promise. Major Butler's vow was poorly kept: no one from Philadelphia visited the estate for nearly seventeen years, and though the younger King professed esteem for Molly, he was essentially indifferent except to her financial value. He reported in 1835 that she (though more than seventy) greatly helped in raising her grandchildren and great-grandchildren, thus "much more than paying her expenses." Compensated for her life of service with "a most wretched hovel . . . , [lacking] every decency and every comfort," Molly was left in 1839, Kemble found, "most miserably off in her infirm years."[34]

Slaves knew even more pathos at the ends of their lives than is the usual lot of humankind, for they had never worked for themselves, only for others—or sometimes to fulfill an ideal of what they themselves considered "good work." Kemble visited an old woman, Nancy, in her hut at Hampton; the latter was experiencing the wretchedness of any shattered human being: "exceedingly infirm and miserable, suffering from sore limbs and an ulcerated leg so cruelly that she can hardly find rest in any position from the constant pain." But Nancy's burden was heavier because of what her life had been: "As I bent over her today," Kemble wrote,

> trying to prop her into some posture where she might find some ease, she took hold of my hand, and with the tears streaming over her face, said: "I have worked every day through dew and damp, and sand and heat, and done good work; but oh, missis, me old and broken now; no tongue can tell how much I suffer."[35]

Though a white person might occasionally make a gesture of reconciliation, like Kemble's, across the chasm dividing slave from free, the message most old slaves received was that they were worthless. On Thursday, March 28, 1839, Kemble entered a room of the slaves' infirmary at Hampton,

> the walls of which were simply mud and laths; the floor, the soil itself, damp with perpetual drippings from the holes in the roof; and the open space which served for a window was protected only by a broken shutter, which, in order to exclude the cold, was drawn so near as almost to exclude the light at the same time. Upon this earthen floor, with nothing but its hard, damp surface

beneath him, no covering but a tattered shirt and trousers, and a few sticks
under his head for a pillow, lay an old man [named Friday] of upward of
seventy, dying. When I first looked at him I thought, by the glazed stare of his
eyes, and the flies that had gathered round his half-open mouth, that he was
dead.

It being a workday, no relative or friend of the old man's was allowed to leave
the fields to comfort him. Apologists for slavery liked to compare (favorably)
the lives of American slaves with those of European peasants; but Kemble
thought the true comparison was with animals. As she bent over Friday, the
last faint struggle of life ceased.

Not a creature [except the flies around his mouth] was near him. There he
lay—the worn-out slave, whose life had been spent in unrequited labor for
me and mine, without one physical alleviation, one Christian solace, one
human sympathy, to cheer him in his extremity—panting out the last breath
of his wretched existence like some forsaken, overworked, wearied-out beast
of burden, rotting where it falls![36]

Children, too, were treated like animals. Their mothers torn away from
them for most of the day, and any kind of schooling denied them, the children
under twelve were left to roll, "like dogs or cats, in the sand and the sun." At
Butler Island the only employment of the children aged eight to twelve was
"what they call 'tend baby,' ":

The poor little Negro sucklings were cared for (I leave to your own judgment
how efficiently or how tenderly) by these half-savage slips of slavery—carried
by them to the fields where their mothers were working under the lash, to
receive their needful nourishment, and then carried back again to the "settlement," . . . where they wallowed unheeded in utter filth and neglect until the
time again returned for their being carried to their mother's breast.

Some of the old women having been removed to Hampton, the babies and
baby minders at Butler Island were left totally unsupervised except by Rose,
the old midwife in charge of the sick house.[37]

The neglect of their infirmaries gave further notice to the slaves of the
dishonor of their condition. Unlike the infirmary on St. Simons, the principal
one at Butler Island did at least have a wooden floor, for even the masters
could see that the rice island was too damp to make an earthen floor feasible.
The two-story building was whitewashed. On each story were two rooms,
twenty feet square, women on the ground floor and men above. The infirmary
was heavily used, and even Pierce Butler grudgingly acknowledged the slaves'
ill health that winter. Bondsmen and women at Butler Island then numbered
430: "For several weeks," their master wrote from the island on February 17,
"our hospital list numbered fifty and upwards daily, and very little shamming." The Butler Island sick house was probably better than slaves commonly enjoyed in the South, for half of the downstairs windows were glazed—
a rare privilege for the women, which was not extended to the men on the
second floor. In other respects, however, the Butlers had not been prodigal of

expense. There were no bedsteads, mattresses, or pillows, and the blankets were filthy and tattered. There were no chairs with backs—which might have supported a person weak with age and illness—only benches without backs, and not enough of these. Because of the building's slipshod construction slaves with fevers were exposed to chilling drafts. On a winter day the men upstairs lay in darkness, the shutters being closed to stop the wind from roaring through the unglazed windows. The fire was inadequately made up. So callous were the masters, so demoralized the slaves, that filth and vermin abounded. On the morning early in January when Kemble first visited the infirmary, those downstairs windows which did have glazing

> were obscured with dirt, almost as much as the other window-less ones were darkened by the dingy shutters, which the shivering inmates had fastened to in order to protect themselves from the cold. In the enormous chimney glimmered the powerless embers of a few sticks of wood, round which, how-ever, as many of the sick women as could approach were cowering, some on wooden settles [backless benches], most of them on the ground, excluding those who were too ill to rise; and these last poor wretches lay prostrate on the floor. . . . Here lay some burning with fever, others chilled with cold and aching with rheumatism, upon the hard cold ground, the draughts and damp-ness of the atmosphere increasing their sufferings, and dirt, noise, and stench, and every aggravation of which sickness is capable, combined in their condition—here they lay like brute beasts. . . .[38]

If there were a crisis—such as the time when Shadrach, a valuable young slave, was suddenly felled by the rice islands' winter scourge of peripneumonia—the doctor might be summoned from Darien three days in a row, and Pierce Butler probably stayed up all night as Shadrach was dying. But no slave could fail to apprehend—from the condition of the infirmary—the indifference with which their rich masters normally regarded them. The prevailing custom was to treat most slaves as though they were filthy, subhuman creatures. A master was rare who stood out against custom.

Since the Hampton cotton plantation was less profitable than the rice island, conditions there were worse. Everything was run down. The floor of the Hampton infirmary

> (which was not boarded, but merely the damp hard earth itself) was strewn with wretched women, who, but for their moans of pain, and uneasy, restless motions, might very well each have been taken for a mere heap of filthy rags; the chimney refusing passage to the smoke from the pine-wood fire, it puffed out in clouds through the room, where it circled and hung, only gradually oozing away through the windows [in which] there was not a single whole pane of glass.

That these infirmaries were not what they might have been was perceived by the Butler Island overseer Thomas Oden. For fourteen years he had worked for the unusual John Couper (adjacent to Hampton), and he knew from Couper's practice that God had not universally ordained filth and neglect for black people. Oden told Kemble, when she stormed to his house after her first visit to the Butler Island infirmary,

> that the condition of the hospital had appeared to him, from his first entering upon his situation (only within the last year), to require a reform, and that he had proposed it to the former manager, Mr. K[ing], and Mr. [Pierce Butler]'s brother . . . , but, receiving no encouragement from them, had supposed that it was a matter of indifference to the owners, and had left it in the condition in which he had found it.[39]

Under Kemble's prodding Oden acted to remedy the worst negligence. Apparently he provided the sick houses with mattress covers and pillowcases, which the slaves could stuff with moss to make mattresses and pillows. But Oden was a drunkard,[40] unlikely to put his heart into improving conditions for the slaves once the surprising Englishwoman had departed for Philadelphia. Nor did he survive long enough to pursue any reforms, for rice plantations were unhealthy to overseers as well as slaves: Oden—like H. W. Crum, T. R. Heargroves, Stephen Clark, and William Capers at Gowrie—lost his health relatively early in life and was in his grave by 1841. When Oden died, coproprietor John Butler confirmed that conditions on the whole estate had indeed demanded reform. He doubted, however, that Oden had achieved much at the rice plantation: "The improvement at Hampton is more perceptible [than at Butler Island] from its former disorder and want of attention."[41]

Despite John Butler's fair words, negligence persisted. The estate's inventory in 1849 showed that Kemble's innovations had not been renewed during the decade since her departure: the hospitals' "38 Mattras covers, 58 pillow cases (of oznaburghs), in use 10 years," were valued at only twenty-four dollars. The worth of the thirty-one blankets, "all more or less worn," was estimated at a dollar each, while all of the tubs, pails, lamps, pots and kettles, and spoons were valued at fifteen dollars: a total of seventy dollars for the furnishings of all of the sick houses at both Butler Island and Hampton. By comparison, a single flatboat for the harvest was worth one hundred dollars and a good mule fifty dollars. The investment in hospital furnishings, as of 1849, was scarcely extravagant.[42] Evidently most Butler slaves had been relegated to a subhuman status: they were essentially instruments of production—useful to their masters for a period, but discardable when worn out.

10

Morale

The physical and mental tyranny—the brutality, "contempt and neglect" to which the blacks were habitually exposed—were consciously and unconsciously employed by the masters to shape the slaves' character for life. That slavery left a permanent mark was understood, in both the nineteenth and the twentieth centuries, by many blacks who knew whereof they spoke. The sharecropper Nate Shaw realized that his father, born in 1850, suffered a "back yonder 'ism' " bred into him by slavery, that impelled him to flinch before white neighbors like Jim Flint and to lead an improvident life. The Northern-born black clergyman Henry Turner (later bishop of the African Methodist Episcopal Church) lamented in 1865—from his observation as an army chaplain in the South—that the "old servile fear still twirls itself around the heart strings [of many freedmen and women], and fills with terror the entire soul at a white man's frown. Just let him say stop, and every fibre is palsied, and this will be the case till they all die."[1]

Kemble, too, believed the imprint of slavery was deep, upon both master and slave. This is the point on which her testimony may be the most important, and is certainly the most contentious; for a modern impulse has been to deny that Nate Shaw and Bishop Turner understood their own people. In 1959 Stanley Elkins raised the question of slavery's psychological effects, but he vitiated (by great overstatement, and by inadequate research) his claim that many slaves became servile. Since 1959, generations of undergraduates, graduates, and historians have flayed Elkins's dead horse, and the principal influence of his book has been in the number of excellent rebuttals it has inspired.[2] The late twentieth century has rightly wished to stress the slaves' often heroic dissidence against slavery, and this has led to vastly improved understanding of "the world the slaves made." But perversely, and unnecessarily, the new scholarship—swinging from one extreme to another—has sometimes seemed to assert that the effects of living under the slave regime penetrated only skin deep. Kemble, by contrast, apprehended the profound and tragic impact of slavery—"the miserable results of the system on everything connected with it—the souls, minds, bodies, and estates of both races of men."[3]

She was struck by the extravagance with which the powerless flattered their masters. For almost seventeen years—from early 1820 until late 1836—no Butler had visited the estate, and even when the new heirs had appeared in the latter year, neither Pierce nor John Butler had brought his wife. The arrival at the island, therefore (on the last day of 1838), from the distant North, of not only Pierce Butler but also his wife and their two young children resembled the descent of gods from the heavens before the dazzled eyes of the beholders. Like powerful, fickle, untrustworthy deities, they must be propitiated. As the white family first approached Butler Island on the plantation boat from Darien, the wharf

> began to be crowded with Negroes, jumping, dancing, shouting, laughing, and clapping their hands . . . , and using the most extravagant . . . gesticulations to express their ecstasy at our arrival.
>
> On our landing from the boat, the crowd thronged about us like a swarm of bees; we were seized, pulled, pushed, carried, dragged, and all but lifted in the air by the clamorous multitude. . . . They seized our clothes, kissed them—then our hands, and almost wrung them off.

Reporting this reception, Kemble mixed an outrageous Victorian snobbery toward the Irish with a modern environmentalism that attributed the slaves' sycophancy to their circumstances, not their genes. Frances Kemble's skin was so dark that she claimed she could be mistaken for a mulatto; but in the slaves' obeisance to their masters, white was right: and when Pierce Butler introduced his young wife to the fat, good-humored old midwife Rose, she shrieked out,

> "Oh massa!" . . . in a paroxysm of admiration, "where you get this lilly alabaster baby!"
>
> . . . This superlative apostrophe was elicited by the fairness of *my skin* [Kemble observed]. The mere quality of mistress must have had a most miraculous effect upon my skin in the eyes of poor Rose. But this species of outrageous flattery is as usual with these people as with the low Irish, and arises from the ignorant desire, common to both the races, of propitiating at all costs the fellow creature who is to them as a Providence.

This scene was reenacted one January Sunday when a boatload of Hampton slaves, making their monthly pilgrimage to the Darien church, came to Butler Island to pay their respects to massa and missis. "The expressions of devotion and delight of these poor people," Kemble exclaimed, "are the most fervent you can imagine. One of them, speaking to me of Mr. [Butler], and saying that they had heard that he had not been well, added: 'Oh! we hear so, missis, and we not know what to do. Oh! missis, massa sick, all him people *broken!* " Old House Molly, Major Butler's old servant—who Kemble came to believe one of the least servile slaves on the estate—"absolutely embraced [Pierce Butler], and seemed unable sufficiently to express her ecstasy at seeing him again."[4]

Kemble was scathing toward white people who mistook such conduct as genuine affection for the absentee masters. Self-interest was evidently at stake: "The owner who at . . . distant intervals of months or years revisits his estate," she later reflected,

> is looked upon as a returning providence by the poor Negroes. They have no experience of his character to destroy their hopes in his goodness, and all possible and impossible ameliorations of their condition are anticipated from his advent. . . .
>
> I once heard a slave on the plantation of an absentee express the most lively distress at hearing that his master was ill. Before, however, I had recovered from my surprise at this warm "attachment" to a distant and all but unknown proprietor, the man added: "Massa die, what become of all him people?"

Gratitude, Kemble understood, could be "a lively sense of benefits to come." The abject fawning of some of the slaves—their transparent linking of obeisance to material self-interest—reached its nadir when the Butlers visited some decrepit old slave women at the remote plantation of Woodville. "One of these old crones," Kemble wrote with revulsion,

> a hideous, withered, wrinkled piece of womanhood, [said]: "Missus, tho' we no able to work, we make little niggers for massa." Her joy at seeing her present owner was unbounded, and she kept clapping her horny hands together and exclaiming: "While there is life there is hope; we seen massa before we die." These demonstrations of regard were followed up by piteous complaints of hunger and rheumatism, and their usual requests for pittances of food and clothing. . . .[5]

Flattery was linked to "the utter subserviency of [the] slaves"; here again Kemble was amazed at what she found. Israel, the son of a literate slave, and—as a wagon driver—himself one of the most privileged men on the estate, enunciated to Kemble (with Gullah grammar) the basic principle: "What de white man dat goberns de estate him seem to like and favor, dat de people find out bery soon and do it." The carpenter Abraham, for example—who doubled as butcher but was unable to cut up a sheep to Kemble's satisfaction—kept trying "to find out 'zackly wot de missis do want," and finally "declared his misery at being unable to cut it as I wished, and his readiness to conform for the future to whatever *patterns* of mutton 'de missis would only please to give him.' " Kemble's daughter Sarah, just under four, risked being quickly corrupted by the slaves' obeisance. "I . . . saw, with dismay," Kemble recounted one Sunday, "the universal eagerness with which they sprang to obey her little gestures of command. She said something about a swing, and in less than five minutes headman Frank had erected it for her, and a dozen young slaves were ready to swing little 'missis.' "⁶

The slaves seemed to take almost masochistic satisfaction in abasing themselves, insisting that they, not the mistress, were to fulfill the servile role. At the infirmary in January—full of sick women and those recovering from childbirth—Kemble wanted to make up a proper fire from the embers in the fireplace. "Upon my lifting a log . . . ," she said, "there was one universal outcry of horror, and old Rose [the midwife], attempting to snatch it from me, exclaimed: 'Let alone, missis—let be; what for you lift wood? you have nigger enough, missis, to do it!' " A comparable scene was enacted some weeks later at Hampton. Kemble, riding alone on her horse about a mile south of Butler Point, came to a place that was too boggy for her to traverse. A nearby field worker, Charlotte, suggested that Kemble, rather than turn around, should commandeer enough slaves to build a plank road over which she could proceed. No doubt Charlotte sought for the slaves the variety, interest, and probably relaxed discipline of getting off from their routine tasks to undertake an unusual job; but she seemed also to take pleasure in abasing herself before the mistress, probably hoping that this would earn her goodwill: "You no turn back, missis,' Charlotte shouted at the top of her voice; 'if you want to go through, send, missis, send; you hab slave enough, nigger enough, let 'em come, let 'em fetch planks, and make de bridge; what you say dey must do— send, missis, send, missis!' "

Servility reached its apogee when Kemble—ever adventurous and unconventional—conceived the scheme of crossing, with her young daughter Sarah, the expanse of eastern Little St. Simons Island (wild, desolate, and uninhabited except by one slave family) in order to view the Atlantic Ocean from its beach. A group of slave men under Israel's direction put her wagon on a boat to carry her across the river from Great St. Simons Island; deposited the wagon with Kemble and Sarah on Little St. Simons Island; and with enormous effort carved a path for the wagon through the woods to reach the appointed destination about a mile away. To her mortification, Kemble then learned that, "by taking the tide in proper season, and going by boat," she could have reached the island's Atlantic coast easily, in half the time, and without imposing herculean labor upon the slaves; "but because, being of course absolutely ignorant of this, I had expressed a desire to go through the wood, not a syllable of remonstrance was uttered by anyone; and the men . . . underwent the labor of cutting a path for the wagon and dragging it through and over all the impediments we encountered." At a ditch in a tract of salt marsh several of them even entreated her "to let them lie down and make a bridge with their bodies for me to walk over." Kemble supposed that at least a privileged slave like Israel would have shown some independence; but "When I expressed my astonishment at their not having remonstrated against my order, and explained how I could best achieve the purpose I had in view, the sole answer I got even from Israel was: 'Missis say so, so me do; missis say me go through the wood, me no tell missis go another way.' "⁷

Powerless, undervalued, despised, many slaves came to esteem themselves for some of the same qualities the whites valued in them. The women at Woodville were not the only ones to recognize their worth as broodmares. "They have all of them a most distinct and perfect knowledge of their value to their owners as property," Kemble observed,

and a woman thinks, and not much amiss, that the more frequently she adds to the number of her master's livestock by bringing new slaves into the world, the more claims she will have upon his consideration and good will. This was perfectly evident to me from the meritorious air with which the women always made haste to inform me of the number of children they had borne, and the frequent occasions on which the older slaves would direct my attention to their children, exclaiming: "Look, missis! little niggers for you and massa; plenty little niggers for you and little missis!"

Every clear-eyed visitor to the South reported the same phenomenon. A sixty-year-old slave blacksmith took pride, talking to Frederick Olmsted, in the high price he had fetched on the auction block in Virginia, and the even higher price for which he had been sold in Louisiana. The resentment lurking behind the blacksmith's jovial facade could not disguise his pride in his own monetary value: "Ho, ho! He [the slave trader] did well that time." Another Louisiana slave, knowing that masters valued slaves for their productivity and therefore regarded old slaves as worthless, thought in the same terms. Lauding the economic value of his master's sugar plantation and its workforce, Olmsted's interlocutor acknowledged that "some few of [the slaves], whom his master had brought from his former plantation, were old; but altogether, they were 'as right good a lot of niggers' as could be found anywhere."[8]

Besides taking pride in their economic value, slaves could augment their diminished self-esteem by identifying with the master's greatness. When old House Molly showed Kemble through the tottering ruins of the old mansion at Butler Point, where Major Butler had once lived, the overwhelming message she conveyed was "her impression of the immeasurable grandeur and nobility of the house she served." The old people's "tales of the former grandeur of the estate and family," Kemble observed, "are like things one reads of in novels." One old slave woman had worked for Major Butler at his Philadelphia establishment, and she "told with infinite pride of having waited [there] upon his daughters and granddaughters." This was not just a put-on to court Kemble's favor, nor was the mentality confined to house servants. Frederick Douglass, the escaped Maryland slave, testified that even among themselves the blacks associated their own worth with their masters'. When Colonel Lloyd's slaves met those from an adjacent plantation (Fayette Gibson's), they boasted that they were better than Gibson's slaves because their master was richer than Gibson. To this the neighbor's slaves retorted that their master was smarter and stronger than Lloyd: they "would boast [Gibson's] ability to whip Colonel Lloyd. . . . They seemed to think that the greatness of their masters was transferable to themselves."[9]

Lacking a sense of full worth except insofar as valuable to their masters,

some slaves avowed their inferiority to white people. Even old House Molly—
who retained from her previous service to Major Butler "a certain dignified
courtesy," and who had little about her of "cringing servility"—apologized

> with great gravity for her mispronunciation, modestly suggesting that *white
> words* were impossible to the organs of speech of black folks. It is curious
> [Kemble remarked] how universally any theory, no matter how absurd, is
> accepted by these people . . . in which the contemptuous supremacy of the
> dominant race is admitted. . . . Their acquiescence in the theory of their own
> incorrigible baseness is . . . complete.[10]

To have white blood gave one claim to special regard. The mulatto daughter
of a white workman petitioned to be taken from the fields and given house
work " '*on account of her color*'. . . . These people . . . have accepted the
contempt of their masters to that degree," Kemble complained, "that they
profess, and really seem to feel it for themselves, [that] the faintest admixture
of white blood in their black veins appears at once, by common consent of
their own race, to raise them in the scale of humanity." Although Renty, the
mulatto son of Roswell King Jr., had other grounds for carrying himself with
an easy condescension almost unique among the slaves, Kemble believed his
"very decidedly mulatto tinge" substantially contributed to "the peculiar
disinvoltura of his carriage and manner; he was evidently, in his own opinion,
a very superior creature." The idea that a white admixture enhanced the
worth of black blood was not confined to possessors of this blend. A song of
the black boatmen proclaimed that "twenty-six black girls not make mulatto
yellow girl": the despondent Kemble could understand these words only as
the product of the boatmen's "desperate tendency to despise and undervalue
their own race and color."[11]

If blacks were—in the eyes of many slaves—worth less than whites, they
need not be treated by slaves with the same show of respect accorded to
whites. Kemble was impressed by the tact and courtesy slaves had developed
in addressing whites, but to each other their manner was different—and
especially if entrusted with authority over other slaves. With whip in hand, a
subdriver might address his underlings tyrannically: "The command of one
slave to another is altogether [a] most uncompromising utterance of insolent
truculent despotism. . . . 'You nigger—I say, you black nigger—you no hear
me call you—what for you no run quick?' " A later century would like to
believe this a put-on, for drivers sometimes deceived their masters into thinking them harsher than they really were. (The best-known example was the
Louisiana driver Solomon Northup's "throwing the lash within a hair's
breadth of the back, the ear, the nose, without, however, touching either of
them": the faked screams of the slave whose punishment was being simulated
made the distant master believe Northup was enforcing strict discipline.) But
Sophy's report of being raped by another driver, and Louisa's flight from
driver Bram, and Jack's fear of one of the drivers—his reluctance to meddle
with an animal trap owned by that functionary—all suggest that the driver's

despotic tone (though perhaps exaggerated for Kemble's benefit) was no charade.[12]

Slaves without authority over others were almost as unfeeling in their address to each other as the drivers. Kemble hired five Hampton youths to work for wages for her, after they had finished their daily tasks in the cotton fields; she was "struck with the insolent tyranny of their demeanor toward each other. This is almost a universal characteristic of the manner of the Negroes among themselves. They are diabolically cruel to animals too." One slave calling to another at a distance would shout, "You niggar, you hear? hi! you niggar!" in a tone of "despotic insolence."[13]

The all-embracing atmosphere of callous physical punishment, scorn, and contempt was certain to eat like acid into the souls of many blacks. Even a privileged slave such as Israel, who was deputed to accompany Kemble on many of her horseback rides at Hampton, was not unaffected by the enveloping miasma. His father, old Jacob, knew how to read, but Israel had never had the assurance to get his father to teach him. No doubt fear that Roswell King Jr. would whip them was a major deterrent, but even more important was Israel's diminished self-confidence. As Kemble rode horseback beside him, coming home from the church at Frederica, she asked Israel why he had never learned to read, and the slave enunciated in 1839 the argument which finally moved the United State Supreme Court more than a century later, in its 1954 school desegregation decision. "Suddenly stopping, and pulling up his horse," Israel said: " 'Missis, what for me learn to read? me have no prospect.' "[14]

If Israel's morale was undermined, this was even more true of most Butler slaves. To Kemble the most striking symptom was the squalor in which many of them lived. The housing accommodation was, of course, crowded—two families normally shared the three small rooms plus children's loft which were standard at the principal settlement on Butler Island. The largest room, shared by the two families, was about twelve feet by fifteen feet, while the two bedrooms—one for each family—were "closets smaller and closer than the staterooms of a ship. . . . They have almost all of them a rude bedstead, with the gray moss of the forests for mattress, and filthy, pestilential-looking blankets for covering." What struck Kemble was not so much the overcrowding as the dirt and disorder which most slaves tolerated—signs, to her, of their demoralization:

> Such of these dwellings as I visited today were filthy and wretched in the extreme. . . . Instead of the order, neatness, and ingenuity which might convert even these miserable hovels into tolerable residences, there was the careless, reckless, filthy indolence which even the brutes do not exhibit in their lairs and nests. . . . Firewood and shavings lay littered about the floors, while the half-naked children were cowering round two or three smouldering cinders. The moss with which the chinks and crannies of their ill-protecting dwellings might have been stuffed was trailing in dirt and dust about the ground, while the back door of the huts, opening upon a most unsightly ditch, was left wide open for the fowls and ducks, which they are allowed to raise, to

travel in and out, increasing the filth of the cabin by what they brought and left in every direction.[15]

That slaves might live differently from this—as Kemble urged upon them—was to many of them a startling thought. The older children in these houses were dumbfounded at Kemble's pressing them to "Kindle up the fire, sweep the floor, and expel the poultry. For a long time my very words seemed unintelligible to them, till, when I began to sweep and make up the fire, etc., they first fell to laughing, and then imitating me."

The principal obstacle to tidiness might have seemed to be the slaves' want of instruction, but Kemble knew the real problems were morale and the adults' long hours of field labor. The same factors explained many slaves' lack of personal hygiene. It was not the custom for slaves to wash themselves very much. When Kemble insisted that the midwife give a warm-water tub bath to two slave infants, their "mothers looked on in unutterable dismay." Kemble examined a slave woman experiencing terrible earache and found her swollen face and neck "begrimed with filth. . . . The first process, of course, was washing [warm-water sponging], which, however, appeared to her so very unusual an operation, that I had to perform it for her myself." A clothing allowance was distributed twice a year and Kemble came to believe that, except for Sundays, the slaves wore the same undergarments—virtually without washing—from one distribution until the next. The women seemed surprised at her suggesting "the possibility of a change of the nethermost as well as the uppermost garment." One consequence of these customs was that ordinary slaves like Dorcas were filthy. Kemble offered this old woman (who had walked a mile to Butler Point to beg some sugar) a ride home with her in her cart, and had to "endure her abominable dirt and foulness in the closest proximity."[16]

Even the two house servant grandchildren of old House Molly—a cleanly woman because, as she said, Major Butler had insisted on his house servants being clean—suffered from Dorcas's affliction. Seventeen-year-old Aleck (whom Kemble esteemed in every other way, and to whom she later taught the alphabet) and his sister Mary (the housemaid) and the other youthful footman at Butler Island were all dirty. Kemble's language was strong: "The two young lads . . . who wait upon us . . . are perfectly filthy in their persons and clothes—their faces, hands, and naked feet being literally incrusted with dirt. . . . Mary, too, is so intolerably offensive in her person that it is impossible to endure her proximity."

The slaves' degradation was thus expressed in the physical condition of their persons and their houses as much as in their subservience, servility, and lack of faith in their own race. A later century does not wish to hear this about the slaves, and one might be tempted to dismiss Kemble's report as factually incorrect. Her statements did not arise principally, however, from racism, for she was careful in these passages to deny that she was talking of racial characteristics: "The stench in an Irish, Scotch, Italian, or French hovel is quite as intolerable as any I ever found in our Negro houses." Nor were bodily smells racially determined, as slavery's apologists claimed, for the Englishwoman found that "thorough ablutions and change of linen, when tried, [have] been perfectly successful in removing all such objections." Kemble was in many ways sympathetic to the slaves and—as will soon be shown again—she was quick to praise what she found laudable in their lives. May not her account of the squalor in which many of them lived have been close to the mark?[17]

Kemble's explanations for the conditions she reported are, however, highly controversial. She was never consistent in her theories. At one moment she said ignorance was the only cause for poor hygiene. On another page she declared it "hopeless to attempt to reform [the mothers'] habits or improve their condition while the women are condemned to field labor." And in another mood she blamed everything on the demoralization bred by slavery:

> A total absence of self-respect begets these hateful physical results. . . . Well-being, freedom, and industry induce self-respect, self-respect induces cleanliness and personal attention, so that slavery is answerable for all the evils that exhibit themselves where it exists—from lying, thieving, and adultery, to dirty houses, ragged clothes, and foul smells.[18]

One might well deride Kemble's logical inconsistencies and accuse her of simply importing into a cultural context—where it was alien—the Victorian precept that cleanliness was next to godliness.

But may she not have been right? Perhaps the problem was not just ignorance, or the mothers' exhaustion at the end of the day—though both were powerful factors. Perhaps there really was a question of morale. Perhaps slavery did indeed sap the self-esteem of many slaves, and so discourage them that they did not feel it worth the effort to tidy things up. When the overseer lost his temper at Harriet for claiming the slave women never had enough energy to clean their babies, perhaps he was not entirely ignorant of the factors accounting for dirty infants. At certain times of the year the task system permitted some field workers to get home in the midafternoon (after starting at dawn), if they worked hard. Kemble repeatedly observed this at Hampton; and when she offered cash payments to youths there, for work voluntarily undertaken for her after they completed their normal tasks, she found a good number of takers for the offer. Had the laborers worked with a will, there would at these seasons have been the time to make things less uncomfortable at home, and there might have been the energy if it had seemed worthwhile. But why bother?

The spirits of many slaves—men and women—were probably undermined. Negligence became for these people a way of life, reflecting the demoralization that issued naturally from the terror, contempt, and dishonor imposed upon slaves. Every scholar of the Southern sharecropping system acknowledges that that regime broke the spirits of many a cropper. Would it be surprising if slavery—an even more intensive system of labor coercion—sapped the morale of an even larger proportion of those subjected to it? This is what Nate Shaw testified when he condemned the slavery-bred "back yonder 'ism' " of his father's generation.

The many admirable characters Kemble met among the slaves stand out the more sharply—often heroically—against the dark background she painted of widespread demoralization. Foremost among those Kemble esteemed was forty-one-year-old headman Frank, who next to the white overseer bore principal responsibility for the day-to-day functioning of the rice plantation. Frank was in complete charge of Butler Island from dusk until morning every day from late spring until the November frosts, during which period Thomas Oden—like nearly every other overseer in the rice kingdom—made his nightly retreat to the pinelands to avoid malaria. Frank, who kept the keys to the food stores, was responsible both for distributing the weekly food ration to the slaves and for providing the food for the overseer's house, where Pierce Butler and his family lived during their stay at the island. With some 430 slaves spread over the four settlements on Butler Island—the furthermost village located one and two-thirds miles from the main settlement, and the farthest northwestern field nearly four miles by foot from the tidal rice mill at the other end of the boomerang-shaped island[19]—the one white overseer could not possibly supervise the whole complex operation of rice growing; heavy duties inevitably fell upon Frank and the four drivers under him. Even in the steam pounding mill, which the skilled slave engineer Ned kept in good running order, headman Frank was in charge of supervising the mill workers. The head driver and his assistants were the most important slaves to their masters; and ten years later (when Frank was fifty-one), he was still officially valued—along with two younger drivers and a much younger blacksmith—as the most valuable bondsman on the estate: worth a thousand dollars, when even good young carpenters and coopers were rated at only seven to eight hundred dollars, when the best young male field hands were valued at six hundred dollars, and the best young females at only five hundred dollars.[20]

The Butlers had always depended heavily on their drivers. When in 1791 Major Butler was first shifting his plantation operations from South Carolina toward his new estate in Georgia, he turned to his established driver Sambo for advice: "Let Sambo point out a Driver for Hampton," he instructed his agent. "He knows better than I do who will answer best." Dependence did not, of course, preclude dissatisfaction. Although Sambo was soon put in charge—virtually without white supervision—of a gang of ditchers reclaiming the swampland of Butler Island for cultivation, he achieved fewer results than Butler expected. The major believed Sambo drank too much. And in 1806 Roswell King Sr. suspected that Sambo had "whipped several of your prime men *when drunk.*"[21]

Here was another of the rice kingdom's chronic feuds between overseer and driver. King, unable to prove that Sambo had been drunk, complained to Major Butler that "A *Driver* is more *Absolute* than the *Deay of Algiers.* It is very difficult to find a Negroe that dare tell upon them." This was the background to the younger King's claim that his father, upon taking over the estate's management in 1802, had had to suppress the brutality and licentiousness of some of the drivers and slave artisans there. But another driver, Morris, won Major Butler's lasting gratitude by his coolheadedness in the hurricane of 1804. Morris exercised his despotic powers to quell a panic of the one hundred slaves under his command at Little St. Simons Island, forcing them to remain unwillingly on the island in a relatively protected place where nearly all survived, while scores of slaves on Great St. Simons perished. Butler presented the literate Morris with an inscribed silver cup, which was cherished by Morris's descendants many years later. And a different Sambo, the head driver in 1821, gained the masters' esteem to such a degree that they later placed a *stone* marker at his burial place.[22]

The tyrannical powers conferred upon them undoubtedly corrupted many a driver, rather as overseers were often corrupted by their even more absolute authority. The responsibility for such undermining of a driver's character obviously rested upon the masters, whose profits demanded despotism. One of the great privileges a rice planter could grant his slaves was a decent driver, and in this respect the Butlers' record was patchy. Morris's son (also named Morris), the driver at Five Pound, raped the slave woman Sophy in about 1817. When Kemble asked Sophy if she didn't know it was wrong to have sex with a man not her husband, Sophy seized Kemble "vehemently by the wrist" and spoke with a "voice and look of abject misery": " 'Oh yes, missis, we know . . . ; but we do anything to get our poor flesh some rest from de whip; when he made me follow him into de bush, what use me tell him no? he have strength to make me.' " Neither did Bram, the twenty-seven-year-old head driver at Hampton, impress Kemble as a savory character.[23]

But in making Frank the head driver of the rice plantation, the Butlers appear to have alighted upon a man of real merit. Years of responsibility for plantation operations, and of daily contact with the younger Roswell King, made Frank extraordinarily capable and quick-minded, and King could not sing his praises too highly. Although Kemble remarked the irony of the former manager's encomium—that Frank "had quite the principles of a white man"—she shared King's regard for the head driver. Frank was

> clear-headed, well judging, active, intelligent, extremely well-mannered, and, being respected, he respects himself. He is as ignorant as the rest of the slaves; but he is always clean and tidy in his person, with a courteousness of demeanor far removed from servility. . . . I was in his house today, and the same superiority in cleanliness, comfort, and propriety exhibited itself in his dwelling as in his own personal appearance and that of his wife—a most active, trustworthy, excellent woman.[24]

Frank and his wife, Betty, had by this time had at least eight children of their own, in addition to Betty's child by Roswell King Jr.; and of these nine the remarkable number of five survived to adulthood. One of Betty's children was stillborn, two others died while still less than five days old, and one other apparently perished as a teenager; yet by the time Betty reached the age of forty-seven in 1849, her five living children and her nine young grandchildren made her family a flourishing concern. Her eldest child (born when Betty was almost fifteen) became a skilled carpenter like his father, while her mulatto son, Renty, was also a (less skilled) carpenter, and Betty's elder daughter,

Phoebe was married to another carpenter. (Phoebe's marriage—like those of several women at Gowrie—was with a man much her elder: when Phoebe was twenty-three, her husband was forty-seven.) Betty's fourteen-year-old son still lived at home. Betty's eighteen-year-old daughter, Philada (named for the distant city where the masters lived?), who married a field hand, was therefore the exception in an extended family which otherwise seemed to present a rare illustration of the concept "an enslaved aristocracy of labor." In one generation was headman Frank and his wife, Betty (probably the daughter of a St. Simons driver, and thus the granddaughter of the driver Morris to whom Major Butler had presented a silver cup), while in the next generation three of the four adult sons, or sons-in-law, were skilled carpenters.[25]

Headman Frank often kept himself apart from the other slaves, and his visage contrasted with the grinning Sambo image which slaves were normally expected to cultivate. Seeing him once, in his leisure, "looking, with a countenance of deep thought, . . . over the broad river, which is to him as a prison wall, to the fields and forest beyond," Kemble was struck by Frank's "grave, sad," sober appearance. She came to believe this sadness characteristic of the most self-respecting slaves on the Butler estate. (A factor doubtless magnifying Frank's sorrow was the limitation upon his authority to ameliorate the condition of the slaves under his jurisdiction. The overseer was more powerful than he; and Butler Island's overseer, Thomas Oden—like so many others of his profession—was often inebriated. Oden was "very intemperate" during the summer of 1840, according to the local doctor, "and on one occasion in Darien, I had to take him from [the tavern] to my house, until he was in a condition to go home." The doctor partially attributed Oden's death [during his convalescence from a respiratory disease] to his body's incapacity to respond to brandy, because he had habitually drunk spirits so heavily.)[26]

Engineer Ned was another slave whose intelligence and trustworthiness won Kemble's esteem. At forty-eight, he looked ten years younger and attributed this to "his never having done . . . field work, or been exposed, as the common gang Negroes are, to the hardships of their all but brutish existence. He said his former master had brought him up very kindly." He was a carpenter selected by the younger King to learn to tend the engines from the white men who installed the steam mill in 1833–34. Impressed though Kemble was by Ned's "sagacious clever" mien, she did not present him as a paragon of personal hygiene. While conversing at the mill she acquired from Ned fleas, and perhaps also another type of insect (lice?) so abhorrent to her that she would not name them. Had Ned been an artisan in a free society, he could have used his earning power to benefit his spouse; but Ned's forty-year-old wife, Eve—like the wives of all the privileged males at the Manigaults' Gowrie—was an ordinary field hand. Powerless over her condition, Ned could only solicit Pierce Butler's goodwill. His wife, he told Kemble,

> was "most broke in two" with labor, and exposure, and hard work while with child, and hard work just directly after childbearing; he said she could hardly crawl, and he urged me very much to speak a kind word for her to massa. [Of

the eight children Eve had borne between 1820 and 1832, three survived to adulthood, while five had died in infancy.] She was almost all the time in the hospital, and he thought she could not live long.[27]

An artisan even more impressive to Kemble was the fifty-one-year-old cooper London, a lay Methodist preacher. To London's "exemplary conduct and character," Kemble reported, "there is but one concurrent testimony all over the plantation." London was a splendid example of the slave middlemen who—as Eugene Genovese has shown—often used their position of trust within the plantation hierarchy to benefit their fellow slaves. London knew how to read, and he was determined to teach other slaves this skill. The Bible being the slaves' primer (as exemplified at Frederick Douglass's secret Sabbath school, where he helped his fellow slaves "to learn how to read the will of God"), London wanted more of them. When Kemble departed from Butler Island, London's last request to her was that she send him "a lot of Bibles and Prayer Books" from Philadelphia.

Even to a well-disposed white person like Kemble, however, London would give no inkling of how he had learned to read. The person who taught him must be protected, and "Heaven" might be invoked here, as in almost every other instance when the slaves wished to call upon an external power to attenuate the starkness of the master-slave polarity. "Well, missis, me learn," London unexceptionably replied to Kemble's inquiries about the source of his book learning: " 'Well, missis, me try'; and finally, 'Well, missis, me 'spose Heaven help me'; to which I could only reply that I knew Heaven was helpful, but very hardly to the tune of teaching folks their letters. I got no satisfaction."[28]

London won Kemble's regard not only for his discretion but, even more, for his religious leadership of his people. When the young, "valuable" slave Shadrach succumbed to peripneumonia in January 1839, his body had to be buried quickly to prevent putrefaction. After the slaves had finished their field labor that evening there were twin ceremonies, first in front of cooper London's house, and then at the graveyard. The scene was awesome; and Kemble, only recently arrived at Butler Island, was impressionable. The first service began just as evening turned into total darkness, and numerous slave men carried pinewood torches. The scores of slaves in the assemblage had been to many a funeral, but never one attended by their master and mistress, and their eyes were fixed upon the two white people. The Englishwoman listened as "the whole congregation uplifted their voices in a hymn, the first high wailing notes of which—sung all in unison, in the midst of these unwonted surroundings—sent a thrill through all my nerves." During the prayers every slave knelt in the sand and so did Kemble, Pierce Butler alone remaining erect. Butler's Unitarian upbringing discouraged people's abasing themselves before the Deity, but everyone present knew the real meaning of the contrast between upright master and obeisant slave. "I cannot tell you how profoundly the whole ceremony . . . affected me," Kemble wrote,

and there was nothing in the simple and pathetic supplication of the poor black artisan to check or interfere with the solemn influences of the whole

scene. It was a sort of conventional Methodist prayer, and probably quite as
conventional as all the rest was the closing invocation of God's blessing upon
their master, their mistress, and our children; but this fairly overcame my
composure, and I began to cry very bitterly.

London's prayer resembled Cordelia's asking a benediction from King Lear,
when Lear was the one who needed to ask forgiveness.

London's message of Christian charity was resumed when the congregation walked to the graveyard for the burial service. Kemble was moved by

an indescribable sensation of wonder at finding myself on this slave soil,
surrounded by *my* slaves, among whom again I knelt while the words pro-
claiming to the living and the dead the everlasting covenant of freedom, "I
am the resurrection and the life," sounded over the prostrate throng, and
mingled with the heavy flowing of the vast river sweeping, not far from where
we stood, through the darkness by which we were now encompassed (beyond
the immediate circle of our torchbearers).

White preachers in the South told the slaves that God wanted them to work
hard and not to lie and steal from the masters, and the slaves universally saw
through the hypocrisy usually involved. Every black preacher was expected to
preach the same gospel, and a white person was supposed always to be present
to ensure that the black man's message was a safe one. Kemble therefore had
grounds to suppose London's blessing purely conventional: but was it? The
burial service

ended with a short address from London upon the subject of Lazarus, and the
confirmation which the story of his resurrection afforded our hopes. The
words were simple and rustic . . . ; but there was nothing in the slightest
degree incongruous or grotesque in the matter or manner, and the exhortations not to steal, or lie, or neglect to work well for massa, with which the
glorious hope of immortality was blended in the poor slave preacher's closing
address, was a moral adaptation, as wholesome as it was touching, of the
great Christian theory to the capacities and consciences of his hearers.

No doubt the presence of white people demanded of London his blessing of
massa and missis, and his exhortations to work well; but the slave preacher
may nevertheless have been sincere. His greatest service to his people was to
combat the pressures toward demoralization attacking them from every side
of their squalid, demeaned existence. Circumstances change ethics, and the
slaves, of course, had a moral right to steal, lie, and shirk, when their masters
stole their freedom, lied in justification, and squandered fortunes on medieval
ball costumes, jewel-bedizened dresses, and gambling on the stock market.
But London was urging upon his people a higher ethic: he worked at rebuilding their morale, by impelling them to grasp ideals of honesty, industry, and
compassion in the teeth of every force assaulting those virtues.[29]

Although the self-respecting attitudes of headman Frank and his wife,
Betty, engineer Ned, and cooper London could scarcely flourish widely upon
the Butler estate, Kemble was surprised by the number of other slaves who

managed to keep their heads above the level to which circumstances seemed to doom them. Notable among these were the children and grandchildren of old House Molly and of her brother, old Jacob. Molly's daughter was Hannah, the widow of Sauney, who had been the best violinist on the estate. Hannah was the washerwoman/house servant whose care and kindliness to the younger Roswell King when he was ill had won King's gratitude—"Kindness to a sick person is as good as medicine," he had written in 1824—and she was equally kind to Pierce Butler when he was sick at the rice plantation in 1839. Her children included Aleck (later Aleck Alexander), whom Kemble tutored in 1839.[30]

Molly's brother old Jacob, who was literate, continued to perform store-keeping duties at Hampton well into his seventies. His children—besides cook John (demoted for stealing a ham at Butler Island), carpenter Abraham (confidently believed by Kemble to have stolen mutton at Hampton), and wagon driver Israel (the slave who explained to Kemble why he had never learned to read from his father)—included another Hannah and a young man named Joe. Joe was married to Kemble's undernursemaid Psyche.

Psyche, just over twenty, helped Kemble's Irish nurse, Margery O'Brien, to care for Kemble's daughters. Psyche's own two children appeared to Kemble to be "really as neat and tidy as children of the bettermost class of artisans among ourselves [in Britain]." When Kemble moved from Butler Island to Hampton, Psyche came with her and lived at the house of her sister-in-law Hannah, whose gentility impressed Kemble as much as did Psyche's. Hannah's cabin was "as tidy and comfortable as it could be made, and their [Hannah's and Psyche's] children, as usual, neat and clean; they are capital women, both of them, with an innate love of cleanliness and order most uncommon among these people." Psyche, like headman Frank, often looked somber:

> She is always serious, not to say sad and silent, and has always an air of melancholy and timidity, that has frequently struck me very much. . . . Just in proportion as I have found the slaves on this plantation intelligent and advanced beyond the general brutish level of the majority, I have observed this pathetic expression of countenance in them, a mixture of sadness and fear, the involuntary exhibition of the two feelings, which I suppose must be the predominant experience of their whole lives, regret and apprehension, not the less heavy, either of them, for being, in some degree, vague and indefinite—a sense of incalculable past loss and injury, and a dread of incalculable future loss and injury.[31]

Psyche's situation in 1839 gave her immediate cause for apprehension. She was a slave of the younger Roswell King, and ever since his departure from the Butler's employ in 1838 she had wondered whether she and her two children were to be taken to King's own plantation, twenty-five miles away, where she would be permanently separated from her husband, Joe. When Pierce Butler came to the estate, he invited King to pay him a visit, and as a token of his gratitude for King's nineteen years of service he planned to give

Joe to King as a present. This would have put Psyche and Joe under the same owner. But unbeknownst to anyone else—least of all to Psyche—King had already sold her to the new overseer, Thomas Oden. Butler's gift of Joe to King, therefore, far from solving Psyche's problem, aggravated it, for King fully expected to take Joe with him to his own plantation, leaving Psyche and her children behind at Butler Island with Thomas Oden.

When Joe learned from King what was afoot, and discovered that Psyche's new owner was Thomas Oden, he burst into the room where Pierce Butler received his slaves' petitions. Joe was a son of the highly esteemed old Jacob, and consequently he possessed more assurance than most slaves. Kemble, startled by hearing loud voices in the next room, heard the din increase

> until there was an absolute cry of despair uttered by some man. I . . . opened the door of communication and saw Joe, the young man, poor Psyche's husband, raving almost in a state of frenzy, and in a voice broken with sobs and almost inarticulate with passion, reiterating his determination never to leave this plantation, never to go to [King's plantation], never to leave his old father and mother, his poor wife and children, and dashing his hat, which he was wringing like a cloth in his hands, upon the ground, he declared he would kill himself if he was compelled to follow Mr. K[ing]. [Mr. Butler] was standing, leaning against a table with his arms folded, occasionally uttering a few words of counsel to his slave to be quiet and not fret, and not make a fuss about what there was no help for.

Although Pierce Butler probably had heard from King of Psyche's sale to Oden, he kept his cards close to his chest. King certainly had known Joe and Psyche were to be separated and had batted no eyelash, for the "property" rights of white people authorized breaking the marriage of slaves. (Indeed, when King had established his own plantation, he had sent there from the Butler estate one of his own slaves, married to a Butler slave woman named Oney, thus permanently breaking up their marriage; and he was perfectly prepared to do the same thing with Joe and Psyche.)

But Kemble intervened after Joe left the room. She appealed successfully to her husband's better nature, persuading him to buy Psyche and her children from Oden; and King then relented. In Thomas Oden's words, King " 'heard that [Joe] had kicked up a fuss about it . . . and said that if the fellow wasn't willing to go with him, he did not wish to be bothered with any niggers down there who were to be troublesome, so he might stay behind.' "[32]

Joe's manful protest succeeded partly because Pierce Butler was a more than usually receptive master, and Kemble was an extraordinary advocate; and King was less hard-hearted than he might have been. Yet there was another reason for the protest's success. Joe and Psyche were part of the relatively small group of slaves whose normally accommodating conduct earned for them the opportunity occasionally to press for a favor—Joe's stormy interview without peremptory dismissal, London's request for a load of Bibles, engineer Ned's petition that his wife's labor be lightened.

The unpalatable fact was that, however little "prospect" any slave had, there was almost no prospect at all unless one usually cooperated with the system. Headman Frank, cooper London, old House Molly, Joe's Psyche, engineer Ned—all had been confronted with choices most human beings are not called upon to make. All had chosen a path of accommodation. This did not make them fawning Uncle Toms and Aunt Jemimahs. On the contrary, all of these—and a good many others, like old Jacob, Jacob's daughter Hannah, and old Molly's daughter Hannah—had developed skills, undertaken responsibilities, and found roles within the regime which offered at least minimal satisfactions. As a group they were extraordinarily self-respecting. Nor were they feathering their nests at the expense of their people. Cooper London was not doing so when he taught others to read, nor when he tried to inculcate into his people values which would resist slavery's corrosive effects upon their morale. Headman Frank probably used his authority to make the system less oppressive than it would have been in the hands of another head driver. Ned's training as engineer helped the slaves to run a steam mill, which diminished the labor of pounding rice in the tidal mill (or of doing so by hand!); and it helped to create within the slave community a group of artisans whose expertise demonstrated to the slaves their own human potential. The skill and kindliness with which old House Molly and her daughter Hannah performed their duties as house servants helped to create tenuous bonds of sympathy between masters and slaves. Psyche, her sister-in-law Hannah (old Jacob's daughter), headman Frank's wife, Betty, and certain other slave women created oases of order and dignity in a world that scarcely nourished such qualities.

Were these not some of the most admirable dissidents against slavery—people who dissented not by futile insurrection, not by physical "resistance" in its narrow nineteenth-century sense; and not by lying, theft, and slipshod work; but by combating slavery's assault upon the slaves' morale? They developed within an enslaved working class the allegedly bourgeois values of intelligent industry, sobriety, order, responsibility, self-respect. Here is one of the deepest traditions of America's black people. Although these slaves' route to self-respect was not the only such path, it was one of the most important. It may merit the honor of African-Americans today, and it surely deserves the admiration of those who have never had to cherish those virtues against what might have seemed insurmountable odds.

III

ROBERT ALLSTON'S
PLANTATIONS

11

The Capitalist as
Rice Planter

Such was the fame of Robert Allston's "Celebrated Georgetown [rice] seed" (grown on South Carolina's Pee Dee River seventy miles north of Charleston) that in 1858 the penny-pinching Charles Manigault had paid a 37 percent premium, and taken considerable trouble, to get his hands on a supply.[1] The times were good for Allston. In 1853 his rice alone sold for $43,500 (yielding a net revenue of perhaps $35,000).[2] At that time the most prosperous merchant in Charleston could hope for little more than $16,000 profits in a year, and the best-paid Charleston lawyer earned no more than about $9,000. Allston— keen to lure his son Benjamin into planting, and to consolidate his own operations—in 1859 bought (or assumed liability for the purchase of) some 192 slaves.[3] About this time he was also buying 450 additional acres of rice land for himself and Benjamin. He was a hardworking man who, unlike many of his rich neighbors, eschewed Charleston during the long summers, residing instead at Pawleys Island on the Atlantic, whence he could journey often to supervise personally the management of his estate. When Adele Petigru—a member of one of the liveliest families in Charleston—had married Allston in 1832, she knew she was exiling herself for most of the year from South Carolina's social capital, and her sisters had tried to dissuade her from doing so. Beginning in about 1855, however, Allston's daughters were sent to Charleston to Madame de Togno's finishing school (where all the boarders had to speak French); and in 1857 Allston bought what was reputed "the finest establishment in Charleston." The extravagant purchase of this "Mansion" (Allston's word), like his buying plantations and slaves in 1858 and 1859, seemed risky to his brother-in-law J. L. Petigru: Allston paid less than two thousand dollars cash for the imposing Nathaniel Russell house at 51 Meeting Street, Charleston, borrowing the other thirty-six thousand dollars.[4] His credit was so good that when he bought the slaves in 1859 he could issue his own personal notes for most of the purchase price. In 1860, master of his own 631 slaves (and the buyer of an additional 119 bondsmen and women for his son Benjamin, making altogether a total of 750 slaves), he was one of the grandees of the South (see genealogical table 21).[5]

He knew from his own experience that raising rice with slave labor was a splendid way of becoming rich. His prosperity depended wholly upon the preservation of slavery from any outside threat, and he was one of South Carolina's leading secessionists. President of South Carolina's most powerful political body—the state senate—from 1850 to 1856, Allston in 1851 was chairman of the eighty-five-member caucus of state legislators which, even after the Compromise of 1850, favored South Carolina's seceding unilaterally. Allston held state office continuously for thirty years after 1828: first in the legislature's lower house, then from 1832 (when he made his name as the most important nullifier in Georgetown District) in the state senate, and finally from 1856 to 1858 as South Carolina's governor. He bought the posh Charleston house not so much as a base from which to launch his daughters into Charleston society— Madame de Togno's school could have served that function—but as a stage upon which to play the role of governor during the many months each year when the legislature at Columbia was not in session. (He owned enough silver to serve forty-two, or even forty-eight, people at a grand dinner party.)[6] Allston probably could have been elected to Congress to represent the interests of the rice planters there, but he was a man of high temper (whose self-control doubtless fostered the digestive complaints that plagued him during his later years); and he could not abide having Northerners question the social system so vital to him. Occasionally he ventured to associate with proslavery Northern Democrats, and he also found solace in attending national conferences of the Episcopal Church, where (unlike the Methodists, Presbyterians, and Baptists) apologists for slavery remained in control. But Allston really felt at home only in the slave states, and in March 1861 he conversed eagerly with General Beauregard and the politicos gathered in Charleston: he was wildly impatient at Governor Pickens's delay in attacking Fort Sumter and—like the maddened Samson— pulling the pillars from under his own edifice. The collapse of slavery ruined the Allston fortunes: in 1869 his plantations were auctioned in bankruptcy proceedings which paid his creditors less than twenty-five cents on each dollar of his debts. When Allston had succumbed to pneumonia in April 1864 he died miserable, sensing already that his God did not love him. The tale of his ruin is a story of the destruction sometimes wrought by a man of probity, personal virtue, and inflexible conviction.

Allston had possessed three things conducing to success as a rice planter— substantial inherited wealth (encumbered though it was by debts); managerial

TABLE 21.   Robert Allston's Family

This simplified table omits, in the third and fourth generations, (1) Robert Allston's three elder sisters, (2) the five of
Robert's children who died young, and (3) his brother Joseph's
two sons.

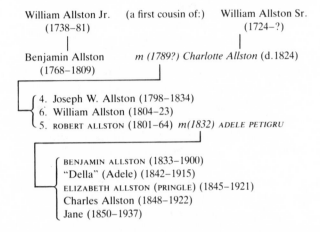

William Allston Jr.   (a first cousin of:)   William Allston Sr.
    (1738–81)   (1724–?)

Benjamin Allston   *m (1789?) Charlotte Allston* (d.1824)
    (1768–1809)

 4. Joseph W. Allston (1798–1834)
 6. William Allston (1804–23)
 5. ROBERT ALLSTON (1801–64) *m(1832)* ADELE PETIGRU

   BENJAMIN ALLSTON (1833–1900)
   "Della" (Adele) (1842–1915)
   ELIZABETH ALLSTON (PRINGLE) (1845–1921)
   Charles Allston (1848–1922)
   Jane (1850–1937)

skill; and a drive born in his case from the sense that he, surrounded by rich
relatives, was starting life comparatively poor: he must exert himself if he was
to establish his own place in the world. His clan was the most remarkable in
Georgetown District, with a claim to national fame. Robert's uncle Washington Allston (who had emigrated to Cambridge, Massachusetts) was perhaps
the most remarkable American painter of the early nineteenth century.[7] So
many Allstons proliferated in Georgetown that in 1791 the grandest of them,
"King Billy," who owned 300 slaves, began spelling his name Alston to distinguish himself from others of the same breed. King Billy's son Joseph (a
second cousin of Robert Allston's, but much older) became governor of
South Carolina in 1812; Joseph still appears regularly in historical novels
centered on his ill-fated marriage to Theodosia Burr, Aaron Burr's daughter.
Robert Allston's second cousins Charlotte and Rebecca Alston were married,
respectively, to South Carolina's Governor John Lide Wilson and to its Senator Robert Hayne, two of slavery's most vigorous defenders in the 1820s.
Before the American Revolution the Allstons had already been "the richest
family on Waccamaw River" (which ran parallel to the Pee Dee a few miles
across the Pee Dee–Waccamaw peninsula); and by 1790 five of them held a
total of 871 slaves—considerably more than any other Georgetown family.[8]
Seventy years later the Allstons, their cousins the Alstons, and their Pyatt
connections had increased their holdings to nearly 3,500 slaves[9]—almost one-
fifth of the district's total slave population.

Robert Allston, then, was well connected (his parents, second cousins of
each other's, were both born "Allston"), and by 1860 he had become rich; but

as a young man he was still relatively poor. He was only eight when his father died prematurely in 1809, leaving two plantations and 130 slaves (but a mass of encumbering debts) for the support of his widow and their six children. The estate was divided in 1819 when Robert's older brother, Joseph, gained his majority: "The poor Negroes appear[ed] in dread" before the division, wrote Robert's mother in the slave master's classic rationalization for the smashing of a slave community: "I feel for them, but it is evident they all cannot belong to me."[10] Robert inherited from his father, from Robert's younger brother (who died in 1823), and from his mother (who died in 1824) a total of 33 slaves; while from his father he also had a half share in "Chicora Wood,"[11] a Pee Dee rice plantation on most of whose 370 acres of potential rice land everything remained to be done—clearing, ditching, draining—before the rich soil would be fit for cultivation.[12] Although Robert's father had apportioned the slaves approximately equally among his wife, his three sons, and his three daughters, he had left all of the land to the boys. The death of Robert's younger brother from malaria in 1823 helped to reconcentrate the land.[13] Allston's older brother, Joseph, became seriously ill (probably from malaria) in 1819: so keen was Joseph to develop his newly inherited 370 acres of potential rice land at his "Waverly" plantation that he had resided near it during the autumn, before the malarial season was over; and he died young in 1834. Robert therefore—entrusted for years by Joseph's widow with running Waverly for Joseph's two young sons—found himself from 1834 managing all of his father's once-divided lands. Meanwhile, he cultivated the affection of a rich, childless aunt, Mrs. Elizabeth Allston Blyth, who came to stay summers with Robert's family at the seashore, bringing with her "her own barouche, horses, coachman and footman, and her own maid and laundress." In 1840, to the intense indignation of some of her other relatives and in-laws, she bequeathed to Robert a valuable Waccamaw rice plantation and 58 of her 157 slaves. Her will, furthermore, gave Robert the use of 39 of the other slaves, to be held in trust for Robert's sons and nephews.[14]

Inherited wealth was thus crucial to Robert Allston's rise to riches. But there was a marked difference between the 91 slaves he inherited (58 of them only in 1840, when he was already nearly forty years old) and the 631 Allston possessed by 1860. He was undoubtedly one of the most skillful managers in the rice kingdom. His mother had ardently advocated his learning a profession so that he would not depend on planting alone, while her sister (the aunt who later bequeathed her slaves to him) was keen that the high-tempered boy should be taught military obedience, so that he would become a good commander of slaves. The consequence was a four-year course at West Point, where, besides military discipline, Robert learned surveying. Leaving the army a year after his graduation, he served four years as South Carolina's surveyor general. Even during the five or six years after he took up the full-scale management of his plantation in 1827, his surveying skills were invaluable to him in supplying a substantial supplement to his income, and in helping him stake out his claims to the uncultivated wilds of his plantation, where his mother had already feared being sued by a covetous neighbor in a boundary dispute over 170 acres of prime rice land. Robert was orderly, methodical, and (before 1857) foresighted—the ideal capitalist entrepreneur. He gained a reputation for "forethought and discretion": "We have always looked up to you," his brother-in-law J. L. Petigru wrote in 1861, "as combining more than any one else, prudence with the other cardinal virtues."[15]

Drive, too, Robert had in abundance. Although the Allstons (together with their cousins the Alstons) were the leading clan in Georgetown District, Robert Allston's branch was down on its luck. Robert knew he must act energetically if the family fortunes were to be restored, for his patrimony was burdened with debt. His mother complained in 1823, "I have in the midst of Rich Friends and Possessions of Property been poor for years." She lamented that when Robert was in Columbia, South Carolina, as surveyor general, he was not even "able to keep a Horse or Servant." But thirty-one years later Allston could take satisfaction in his achievements: "I have improved my paternal estate," he wrote proudly to his wife in 1854, "adding field unto field"; and by 1856 he was so prosperous that he was looking to invest a spare hundred thousand dollars in more land and slaves. This reversal of fortune had been accomplished by hard work: "All the day light is consumed by me [in plantation administration and reading and writing connected with my business affairs] without the loss of a half hour after 8 O'clock," he wrote in 1852.[16]

Although the gentlemanly planter-capitalists on the Pee Dee had a different lifestyle from merchant or industrial capitalists in the North, Allston—even after his fortune was made by the 1850s—crowded more managerial labor into a week's activity than did some of his neighbors. At the height of Charleston's midwinter social season in 1852, he sailed from Charleston to Georgetown on a Friday, talked business with his Chicora Wood overseer that evening, overlooked his nephews' Waccamaw estate and rice-pounding mill on Saturday, and (after church on Sunday) spent all day Monday overlooking the nearly 370 acres of rice land at the "Nightingale Hall" plantation which he had bought in the 1840s. Georgetown's local male gentry tried to match in their own way the festivities of the Charleston social season: "Every one here is hunting or shooting today, tomorrow, and next day," Allston wrote Monday evening, after having spent the whole day at Nightingale Hall instead of hunting. "I will join them on Wednesday, if possible & meet the ["Planters" social] club on Thursday. Friday is my day for the Indigo Society [an educational and cultural institution in the town of Georgetown], and the same or day after for Mrs. Lance's Estate [for which he was the executor]." This was not a twentieth-century businessman's routine: Allston's hours were variable, and he guarded a gentleman's prerogatives of preserving ample leisure time and of mixing his business with social engagements; but a great deal of business got done. "I have [acquired] the reputation of a man of business," Allston wrote with satisfaction to his wife in 1854.[17]

Allston was born (and resided until he went to West Point) on the Waccamaw River, where his father's family had always planted. But after Robert's elder brother, Joseph, took over Waverly—the Allstons' Waccamaw plantation—in 1821, Robert's attention shifted seven miles westward to Chicora Wood on the Pee Dee. Most Waccamaw and Pee Dee rice fields were located on the peninsula between the two rivers; and most planters owned land on the peninsula as well as on the opposite side of one of the two rivers. Thus the "big house" at Waverly, and the slaves' dwellings, were on the east side of the Waccamaw, most slaves crossing the river each morning to work on the peninsula; while Allston and his slaves at Chicora Wood lived on the west side of the Pee Dee, and the slaves worked each day on the peninsula.

Before 1840 Robert confined his business to managing Chicora Wood and (after his brother Joseph's death) Waverly. He cleared, drained, and brought into cultivation Chicora Wood's 370 acres of rice land on the peninsula, and bought parcels of slaves every few years as he expanded his production. After 1834 he attacked, in a businesslike way, the problems of clearing the debts from Waverly—as will appear subsequently. His aunt's death in 1840 gave him the new responsibility of running the Waccamaw plantation he inherited from her. It was too far away for convenience, however, and he soon sold it, using the proceeds (and the profits of Chicora Wood) to buy a new plantation on the Pee Dee, only a few miles south of Chicora Wood. The 370 acres of Nightingale Hall's rice lands (including the "Waterford" lands which Allston bought at about the same time) were at the best "pitch" of the ocean tide; and their new owner soon established the reputation of its prizewinning crops so that he could sell the Nightingale Hall rice at a premium. So prosperous did Allston become that he greatly enlarged Chicora Wood by purchasing some 260 acres of adjacent rice lands early in the 1850s; and in 1858–59 he bought another 450 acres of nearby rice lands, both to consolidate his holdings at Chicora Wood[18] and to establish his twenty-five-year-old son Benjamin. This young man, after finishing West Point and serving several years in the army, was finally ready to be bribed into entering the same line of business as his father.[19]

The Pee Dee River was dominated by great planters, into the forefront of whose ranks Allston had pushed his way by 1857. Besides him there were just nine families who—when he was governor that year—occupied the whole twenty-five-mile strip along the Pee Dee from the Georgetown district line, in the north, to Keithfield in the southwest.[20] Of Governor Allston's neighbors the best known had been Joel Poinsett, secretary of war in President Martin Van Buren's cabinet, and a longtime diplomat in Latin America. (He was also a botanist, his name known to posterity in the poinsettia.) With only 103 slaves, however, Poinsett had been small fry as a Georgetown rice planter, and by 1860 his slaves had been absorbed into the estate of his stepson, J. J. I. Pringle. One of Allston's neighbors, by contrast, was among the richest slaveholders in the United States. This was J. H. Read II, with 510 bondsmen and women.[21] Other prominent neighbors were Ralph Stead Izard Jr., grandson of a U.S. senator, with 353 slaves; Francis Weston (whose cousin later became South Carolina's lieutenant governor), with 335 chattels; and J. H. Trapier—later a Confederate brigadier general—whose estate, added to that of his brother, W. H. Trapier, probably numbered at least 361 slaves.[22]

With one exception, Allston's neighbors all belonged to great planting families. The anomaly was Frederick Shaffer, the only Northerner in the group, who owned a mere 97 bondsmen and women. The three Tucker brothers had altogether about 171 slaves on the Pee Dee.[23] Dr. J. R. Sparkman with 166 slaves; J. J. I. Pringle (Poinsett's stepson) with 200; and Nathaniel Barnwell (whose brother had been a U.S. senator) with 230 slaves, completed the roster of Allston's neighbors.[24]

Allston himself owned some 500 slaves in 1857. He and the nine neighboring families probably owned, among them, over 2,900 slaves, an average of 292 per slaveholding family. George Washington, who with his 277 slaves[25] had been reckoned one of the richest men in the Virginia of his day, would have cut no great figure among the Pee Dee rice planters of the 1850s.

The stereotypical view of these grandees contrasts their leisurely pace of life with the hurry and bustle of the commercial North. The Connecticut novelist John De Forest—who had considerable acquaintance among lowcountry Carolinians just before the Civil War—offered a classic statement of this contrast. There certainly "was more suavity of manner at the South than at the North," De Forest averred.

> It is delightful to see two high-toned gentlemen of the old Virginian or Carolinian school greet each other. Such gracious bows and insinuating tones! Such mellifluous compliments, particular inquiries concerning health and welfare, animating congratulations as to future prospects!
> . . . If there were twenty-eight hours in a day the Northerner might possibly become thus urbane; as it is, he has barely opportunity to fill his pocket with the necessary greenbacks and his head with the necessary information to get on in the world; he is too much hurried by practicalities to make his manners. At the South there has hitherto been a leisurely caste which set the example to all the others.

But many years earlier Robert's cousin Joseph Alston had enunciated an important qualification to De Forest's generalizations, which illuminates the commercial success of Robert Allston and of such a grand Waccamaw rice planter as J. J. Ward (the owner in 1853 of more slaves, probably, than any other individual in the United States). Joseph believed that wealth and climate *tended* to sap the industriousness of Carolinians: "In steadiness and perseverance," Joseph alleged, the Carolinian "is naturally inferior to the native of the north; but this defect of climate is often overcome by his ambition or necessity; and, whenever this happens, he seldom fails to distinguish himself." Ambition and necessity produced in Robert Allston a remarkable exemplar of the masterful Carolinian gentleman capitalist.[26]

In some measure Allston's character was indeed that of a stereotypical oldfashioned gentleman: courteous, generous, fastidious in his conduct, pious, and somewhat aesthetic. Mary Chesnut—the usually acerbic South Carolina memoirist, who declared that scarcely anyone ever expressed gratitude to her husband for his assisting them to gain promotion during the Civil War—singled out Allston for his rare graciousness. When James Chesnut (an aide to

Confederate President Jefferson Davis) had secured for Allston's son-in-law a good job on General Whiting's staff, "Governor Allston spoke to J[ames] C[hesnut] and thanked him for his prompt action in the matter." As executor of Joseph Allston's estate, Robert appears to have acted openhandedly, paying certain legal fees out of his own pocket instead of his brother's funds. When considered for political office, Robert Allston acted scrupulously in conformity with the old-fashioned maxim that a gentleman should not seek office. His narrow defeat for South Carolina's governorship by James Hammond in 1842 probably arose from Allston's statement that he was not a candidate; and when he was elected president of the state senate in 1850 he proudly wrote to Adele from the state capital, "I have not stir'd out of my quarters except to go to Church and have not broach'd my own name to any individual." His letters breathe sincere religious conviction. "I miss'd you from my side," he once wrote to his wife after he had taken communion at the local Episcopal church: "There is a Holy beauty, most attractive to me in the spectacle of two persons so intimately connected, in one spirit of repentance & humble reliance on a Common Savior, bending the knee before this sacred feast." That spring Allston's valued overseer Jesse Belflowers—a bachelor who had run Chicora Wood for ten years—was gravely ill, and Robert visited him every evening, "reading for him a chapter [of the Bible] and a Psalm." On March 2 Belflowers almost died, and Robert was with him continuously, except for two hours, from 3:30 P.M. until 8:00 the next morning; and Dr. J. R. Sparkman was there the whole night too. This crisis presented Robert the opportunity to fulfill a religious duty: "It is now, if ever," he explained to Adele, that "an impression is to be made on poor Belflowers' untutor'd soul."[27]

One might at first be tempted to dismiss Allston's interest in the fine arts as the fondness of an indulgent father for the singing and piano playing of his genteel daughters, or as the offshoot of his family pride in being the nephew of Washington Allston. Robert's relation to the painter no doubt accounted for the Carolina Art Association's making the former governor its agent, in examining for possible acquisition some of Washington Allston's sketches. But only a genuine interest in the arts could have impelled Robert to urge upon the hardened politicos of South Carolina's secession convention that they pay occasional visits to the Carolina Art Association. And the contemplation of two Hiram Powers sculptures had the power to calm Allston's inner tensions: "I have come from a transient view of these masterpieces of Art," he wrote Adele (tempering his usual stiff style), "with a feeling of indescribable satisfaction. It would require a great deal to make me angry today." Allston's description of these sculptures shows that his interest in art was not perfunctory. "Power's Eve . . . is 5.6 feet high, the size of a rather tall woman," he reported,

and represents one just fully develop'd, standing on one foot, the leg of the other being slightly bent at the knee, barely enough to exhibit a variety of muscles in several functions. An apple, the forbidden fruit, is held in her right hand up to her right breast, two others, attach'd by a leaf from the tree are in the left hand, which depends naturally beside her. . . . The Tempter, after having wound himself partially around the broken trunk of a tree beside her, discovers the remainder of his scaly length along and around the top of the pedestal forming a border to it. . . . On the whole I deem it the most satisfactory statue I have ever seen.[28]

Allston's political duties and his interest in scientific agriculture led him to put some of his ideas into print. His *Report on the Free Schools* argued, with limited success, for an expansion of South Carolina's spindly public education system. Two long essays by Allston (his *Memoir of the Introduction and Planting of Rice in South Carolina* [1843] and his "Sea Coast Crops of the South" [1854]) have furnished twentieth-century historians with some of their best material on rice planting.[29] Yet despite his literary labors this Georgetown planter was never wholly at ease among men of letters. When Allston addressed the state agricultural society at Columbia in 1847, he was intimidated to find the novelist William Gilmore Simms and the cultivated Senator A. P. Butler among his auditors. "My audience was small," he wrote, "but very intellectual, the knowledge of which chill'd me somewhat." Allston's literary style was formal, reaching the apogee of stuffiness in one of his private letters to his rich aunt: "Your unmerited kindness towards me and mine together with the great and continued forbearance and indulgence which you have shown to me," he wrote two years before Elizabeth Blyth's death, "has, in a measure, unfitted me for mingling with the world."[30]

Aloof the stiff West Pointer certainly was. When asked at the last minute in 1842 to stand for governor against James Hammond—the election being by the state legislature, not by popular vote—Allston was thrown "among a number and kind of people [at Columbia] whom I never have been in the habit of meeting heretofore. New relations you know," he exclaimed proudly to Adele, "are what I am not apt to form." Two years later, a hostile Carolinian political opponent (associated, against the established families of the South Carolina hierarchy, with the upstart James Hammond, who had narrowly defeated Allston in 1842) claimed that as a young man the fatherless Allston had been effeminate, "a most superlative fop and ladies' man, dangling after his mother, carrying her fan or reticule bowing simpering and silly as any exquisite I ever met with." This is scarcely the imperious, self-controlled man of affairs staring from the Allston portrait probably painted when he was in his forties. Everything in Robert's later life suggests that his West Point training, his long drive for entrepreneurial expansion, and his ardent devotion to the political defense of slavery shaped him into a stern, imposing, unbending master of men, respected by some, liked by few except within the bosom of his family, and a source of some sorrow even within his own family. According to his daughter, he drove himself, and he believed people could achieve anything if they tried hard enough. He was a man of "stern silence," she declared, who "never found it possible to put his deeper feelings into words."[31]

Robert's cousin Joseph Alston might have been sketching the future character of Robert, when he wrote (just before Robert's birth) that "the possession of slaves renders [South Carolina planters] proud, impatient of restraint, and gives them a haughtiness of manner which, to those unaccustomed to them, is disagreeable." Some of Robert Allston's close acquaintances certainly found him disagreeable. He connected his summer house on Pawleys Island to the mainland by a private causeway across the salt marsh, and resisted his neighbors' wish to construct a road—parallel to the beach—which would go through his land. "You will be compelled in the course of time to let the road pass through your premises, as the others," Allston's son warned him in 1858, "or be esteemed very unaccommodating and unhospitable. Such is evidently the wish of many now." Allston's possessiveness, and his sense of duty, fueled disputes with his Waccamaw neighbors. One of these was John Izard Middleton—a grandee with 317 slaves in Georgetown and a one-sixth interest in 520 more slaves elsewhere in Carolina. Son of a former governor of South Carolina, Middleton had been Speaker of the South Carolina House, and he became a prominent member of the South Carolina secession convention. Like Allston, Middleton was an ardent secessionist—he even voted against ratifying the Confederate Constitution in 1861, probably because it banned the reopening of the African slave trade. Yet Middleton and Allston did not get on as neighbors. Middleton's slaves appear to have taken firewood from Allston's side of his Waterford plantation (on Waccamaw Neck), and Allston fumed that Middleton failed to control them. Middleton did not, in Allston's eyes, fulfill his neighborly duties: "A good neighbor will instruct his people. No one else has a right to do it." Allston thought that the slaves of another of his Waccamaw neighbors—Joshua Ward, scion of the great slave master J. J. Ward—were taking wood from the land of another rich slave owner, John LaBruce. In LaBruce's absence Allston felt impelled to intervene—not, of course, by giving orders to Ward's slaves, for that would have contravened Ward's prerogatives—but by writing to Ward. Ward, however, "does not seem to receive the notice kindly."[32]

"There are so few persons who understand and appreciate Mr. Allston," his wife once wrote, "that I was quite glad to find one who had." Adele herself seems to have trembled before her husband's captious spirit, and was relieved once to find that some arrangements she had made in his absence did not bring his wrath down upon her head. "I was very much afraid he would disapprove of the whole thing," she wrote to her grown son in 1862, "but the only thing he found fault with was that there was not supper enough [to feed some Confederate soldiers she had invited to a party]." Allston, aware that he was readily angered, kept this tendency well enough under control at home that his daughter claimed never to have seen him in a temper. His impatience expressed itself in chronic digestive complaints: thus in December 1843 he suffered "one of my periodical attacks" which lasted thirteen hours; and often he ate only a plate of milk and rice, or strained soup. He was unwilling to serve in Congress because of his seething indignation at antislavery spokesmen: "We are sorely press'd and boldly villified [sic] at Washington, in Massachusetts Vermont & N. York!" he cried out. "I could not contain myself in Congress, I would not therefore go there." Although he was considered for election as one of South Carolina's two senators in the Confederate Congress, his offers of service to the Confederacy during the first summer of the Civil War were fruitless: and while his aloofness was no doubt his decisive disqualification, his temper, peremptoriness, and martinet-like qualities may also have contributed to his being rebuffed.[33]

A stern sense of duty drove Allston, and he sought to implant it into his eldest son. Just before Robert was stricken with pneumonia in 1864, someone suggested that Ben—who was a colonel in the Confederate Army—should return home; but Robert would hear nothing of it. Slavery must be preserved and the war must be fought unremittingly: Allston "exclaimed with emotion, 'God forbid! [that Ben should return]. Ben's duty is there and I should regard him as a disgraced man were he to lose the situation he holds. He should devote his every faculty to the discharge of his duty there.' "[34]

Allston's strong sense of his own duties impelled him to the overwork which caused him to contract his fatal illness that year. He was responsible for more than one thousand slaves and for four estates—his own, his son Ben's, and those of his two nephews who were also away in the army. Besides supplying Confederate forces with rice, Robert organized a saltworks on Waccamaw Neck to manufacture that scarce and much-needed commodity. He disapproved the war profiteering conducted by the many private blockade-runners who sailed from Murrells Inlet, not far from his saltworks. The rights of a slave owner to unconstrained mastery of his slaves might be sacred, but, in this crisis of the whole slave system, individual merchants must sacrifice private to public interest. Blockade-running, Allston suggested unavailingly, should be run as a public, not a private, enterprise, so that the profits would accrue to the Confederacy, not to speculators. Harassed by his multiform duties—he had just shipped 160 barrels of his nephew's rice up the Pee Dee on a boat entrusted to an all-slave crew—Allston was already in 1863 working himself into that mood of self-reproach in which he died a year later. At the height of the malarial season he was at Plantersville—a planters' pineland summer place a few miles from Chicora Wood—whence he could supervise the plantations. (No thought now of sojourning at Pawleys Island, with Northern naval vessels patrolling the coast and occasionally making a raid.) He was to set off on business to Charleston soon, and return to Plantersville by August 1: "In moving about so," he confessed, "I am aware that I must neglect some things and overlook many things and perform my duty imperfectly. God grant me health and memory for my duties. . . . I am in dread of some accident [to his nephew's rice-laden boat]." When Allston was dying of pneumonia nine months later, sleepless from bad breathing, "He would repeat in a low voice, 'He giveth his beloved sleep'; then, 'I am not beloved!' " This unbending man of duty no doubt reproached himself for the hubris of 1857–59 which had caused him to load his plantations with debts that could never now be paid. But there is no evidence he ever regretted the political improvidence that impelled him impatiently to urge the attack on Fort Sumter; and surely he never wavered a moment from his conviction that mastery of his plantation enterprises and their enslaved labor force was his appointed destiny.[35]

Agricultural expertise was essential to Allston's commercial success. The knowledge acquired at West Point "of chemistry, electricity, mechanics, and engineering . . . has been," he averred, "of daily and extensive service to me in my [planter's] vocation." Practical experience and sound judgment were even more important than scientific training, and for a rice planter one of the most important requirements was to keep a sharp eye on the ocean tides. Rivalry between planters was keen, and the whole Allston family exulted in 1854 when Robert outguessed their neighbor, John Izard Middleton (who appears usually to have produced more rice per slave than anyone else in the neighborhood). The year 1854 was not a normal one, for the hurricane which wrought havoc at Gowrie in September struck Georgetown as well. The peninsula between the Waccamaw and the Pee Dee was wholly submerged: "On the 8th not one head of rice was to be seen above the water," Adele exclaimed:

> not a bank or any appearance of the land was to be seen. It was one rolling dashing Sea, and the water was Salt as the Sea. . . . Many persons had rice cut and stacked in the field, which was all swept away by the flood. Your papa had none exposed in that way for he apprehended high tides from the state of the moon, and prepared as far as possible for it. Mr J [I] Middleton had 40 acres of very superior rice swept away, a total loss, and many others suffered in the same way, tho' not to the same extent.[36]

Allston's produce won prizes as early as 1844. Crop rotation was an element in his success: thus his prizewinning rice in 1860 was raised on fifteen acres which had been "rested from rice in 1859 but grew a crop of oats and peas." This rice harvest—over eighty bushels an acre, measured by an outsider—was probably about 50 percent more per acre than the best Georgetown crops of the late 1830s. The overseer supplied businesslike records of its production: the land had been plowed late in January 1860 (so much for those planters who for years had claimed that rice lands were too waterlogged for plow animals, and that instead the slaves must be forced to break the soil, and their backs, by laboriously using hoes for this purpose); the land was planted on April 18, hoed on May 22 and June 1, and "flowed" (i.e., the field was flooded again) on June 9. The water was changed and the "grass" picked on July 5. The field was then flooded once more until the rice was cut on September 17; and because of rain, the harvest was not taken in until September 21.[37]

Robert Allston's pride in exercising his skilled and experienced judgment glowed from every line of a letter written to his wife in March 1859. His son Ben was away from the "Guendalos" plantation (where Robert had recently established him), and Robert himself directed the preparation of the fields for the coming season. "Ben's rested field was finish'd [preparing] today. It will be a Study for him to gain experience by when he comes up," Robert exulted with paternal satisfaction:

> remembering its condition, let him look at it now, tight as a jug and ready for the trenching hoe. [By contrast] I deemed it best to stop work on the [second] rested field . . . , the Season being too far advanced. If I could have procured the [newly purchased] hands . . . early in January, this now would be in as

fine condition as the other. But as it is, the surface is cover'd with the green of water weeds and there is too little space betwixt this and planting time to take the "sour" out of it, ¼th of the good seed would be lost in it, and the work can now be better bestow'd elsewhere. I will have 50 spades in the line-ditch on Monday, Tuesday and Wednesday. . . .

A planter was a general moving troops from one part of the battlefield to another; and the need for reinforcements kept the demand for slaves high, and subjected slave communities to constant threat of disruption. Robert had bought Guendalos without its labor force, and his exigent need of workers had impelled him to buy about 119 slaves early—but not quite early enough—in 1859.

Harvesting was so slow that it must be started early, and Allston spoke authoritatively as he continued training his son in planter's lore. "It would be a great mistake," he wrote Ben near the end of August 1860, for the overseers

to postpone the harvest until the 1st Septr. In 3 weeks thereafter much of their rice would be shelling in the field, and before the close of harvest still more. It is indispensable, when using water freely in the cultivation of the crop, to lose something in quantity in the first cutting, in order to save a great waste in the later bulk of the harvest. But the overseers do not realize this and are too apt to postpone the day of readiness.[38]

An experienced overseer might claim that Allston—while being a first-rate manager in the wider sense—was not really a "planter" in the narrow sense of being a skilled agriculturist: that was supposed to be an overseer's forte. But Allston's daughter—who herself managed the Chicora Wood plantation for many years after the war—realized that Allston had been a skilled "planter" too. He understood the agricultural operation thoroughly, and this was one reason he insisted on spending his summers at Pawleys Island. From there he journeyed early many mornings to the plantation,

seeing that the water was kept on the rice just at the right depth, that the fields which had been dried for hoeing were dry enough to begin on them with the hoe. There is a real science in rice-planting [Elizabeth Allston Pringle affirmed], and my father was thoroughly versed in it and most diligent in seeing after the treatment of each field.[39]

Yet the most important reason for Allston's long commercial success was his skill as a business manager. His spirit was that of Benjamin Franklin; indeed, he made that emigrant from Puritan Boston to bourgeois Philadelphia look an amateur at enunciating maxims calculated to promote one's worldly success. "Let the sun's first rays shine upon you in the morning," Allston enjoined his overseer, "and you will not lack a good hat to defend your head from the scorching rays at Noon. Earn your breakfast before you eat it, and the sheriff will not deprive you of your supper." The first of these adages might have suited a Philadelphian like Franklin; but Allston's "Maxims and Precepts" for his overseer made plain that, on a rice plantation, neither slave nor overseer could wait lazily in bed for the sun's first rays. "Be up in the morning," the rural Poor Richard insisted, "and have all up under your control as early as you can distinguish a sheep from a hog at a distance of thirty yards."

Though many of Allston's maxims conveyed farming lore, he did not hesitate to instruct his overseer in a wider sense, recognizable to any Puritan. "Educate your children," he urged, "and bring them up to habits of economy and industry. . . . If ever you make a business of your pleasures, they will most assuredly very soon make an end of your business." Business was indeed Allston's concern, and profits were the heart of the matter. The word thrice graced his admonitions to his overseer: "Cultivate the profits of your labor," he advised,

> and never do what does not pay.
> Never fear great labor or great expense, where fair calculation assures you of good profits. . . .
> True economy consists not so much in saving money as in spending it wholly, solely, and judiciously for purposes really useful. This normally increases your profits instead of diminishing them or keeping them stationary.[40]

Allston's talent for increasing his own profits was that of a masterful capitalist investor, as became evident when he restored the fortunes of Waverly plantation after his brother's death in 1834. At Waverly the investment (approximately forty-three thousand dollars) was overburdened with a debt of some fifty thousand dollars. Allston's eventual solution was to sell about fifty-nine people, more than half of all the slaves at Waverly.[41] This, of course, left the land short of labor. There was a way out, however, because Waverly's third principal capital investment—besides land and slaves—lay in a rice-pounding mill, whose use was less labor-intensive than land's, and which might earn a good return from milling the rice of neighboring planters. Allston's strategy for Waverly, therefore, was to raise rice in a less "labor-intensive" way—which (despite Allston's shifting a good deal of land from rice to other crops) doubtless meant *more* intensive labor from each slave in the depleted labor force—and to reconstruct the mill. The rebuilding could be done by hiring twenty carpenters on a monthly basis, some of whom were Allston's own slaves. Waverly's debts would be greatly reduced and its annual revenues could then, at first, be directed toward increasing the value of the rice mill, instead of being wasted on interest to creditors. Once the plantation was profitable again, its surplus could be used to buy new bondsmen and women from time to time, rebuilding the original capital investment in slaves. This strategy would, of course, destroy the old slave community, replacing over half the old faces gradually with new ones; but business was business.[42]

Allston's plan did not immediately gain the approbation of his brother's widow, who was upset at sundering the slaves' ties with each other. Fortunately for her peace of mind, her own brother (a Charleston factor who was the absentee owner of a cotton plantation) agreed to buy, in a single parcel, fifty-one slaves. Though these people would be deported so far away that they would never again see their friends and relatives at Waverly, at least the disruption of individual families would be minimized. The slaves' own peace of mind was less easily assured. When the sale was agreed, Allston gave only twenty-four hours' notice to the bondsmen and women he had selected for deportation. He knew the discontented slaves were likely, when they arrived in Charleston, to be hard for his agent to handle; when he loaded them on shipboard at the Waccamaw, therefore, he sent temporarily with them one of their drivers, Scotland—"to jolly the negroes and give them confidence, they are accustom'd to him and will give you less trouble," he assured the agent. Allston dispatched the slaves to Charleston even sooner than the agent expected them, so as "not to unsettle and harrass them any more." The slaves' mistress, Mary Allston, delayed a trip from Charleston to Waverly until she could be sure the deported people were gone: she did not want to face them, and was more concerned about her own discomfort than theirs: "I do not wish to be there [at Waverly] when the People leave," she wrote to her aunt; "the making up my mind to the sale, has been trial enough for me."[43]

Mary Allston vacillated to the end. The deported slaves included Sarah, the grown daughter of the trusted driver Scotland; but at the last minute Mrs. Allston changed her mind and sent orders that Sarah was to stay at Waverly. Scotland did not at first know this. He may have put into Allston's mind the idea of his accompanying the departing slaves as far as Charleston; and if so, he had his own motives. When Scotland reached Charleston he appears to have sought out Mary Allston and persuaded her to let not only Sarah return to Waverly but also Bob (presumably Sarah's lover), whom Mary Allston had *not* included in her earlier dispensation. Here was another instance (like Joe's successful protest at Butler Island) when a privileged slave was able—by a hairsbreadth—to prevent family heartbreak by cashing in on his special position.[44]

Clever businessman that he was, Allston succeeded in selling these slaves at the peak of the boom in January 1837, and their average sale price of $725 was much higher than normal before 1837 or for many years afterward. But a peril every businessman faces is that of being swindled by a defaulter. One of the three executors named in Joseph Allston's will—along with Robert Allston and Joseph's widow, Mary—was Alexander Campbell, a Charleston factor. Robert Allston entrusted him to continue handling Waverly's business after Joseph's death, even though Robert himself preferred doing his own business through the respected Charleston factor Alexander Robertson. As part of Robert's plan to reduce Waverly's debts, he had sold (via Campbell in Charleston) an especially valuable family of five slaves in early January 1837, but somehow Campbell failed to pay the net price of $4,000 into the estate's accounts; and he still had not paid it when the panic of 1837 struck. By August 1837 Campbell was overwhelmed with his own debts: "What a beautiful business?" exclaimed Robertson. In October Allston sacked Campbell as the factor for his brother's estate. The next month Campbell left Charleston secretly; and although he once wrote to Allston from Georgia (safe from the claws of his South Carolina creditors), he never paid the estate what he owed it. Here, as in so many other ways, running a rice plantation was a risky capitalist venture.[45]

Allston's whole entrepreneurial career followed the lines shown in his management of Waverly: he was a businessman with a sharp eye for maximizing the return upon his capital investment. When he bought a new plantation and fifty-one slaves in 1851, and yet another one in 1853, he was keen to pay off the new mortgage as rapidly as possible. Like a modern marketing expert seeking to choose the most attractive brand name for his product, Allston in 1853 changed the name of his enlarged home plantation from the prosaic "Matanzas" to the mellifluous "Chicora Wood." Reporting eagerly from the state capital, in December of that year, that the price of rice was at its highest in six years, Robert spurred on both his overseer and the engineer of the Waverly pounding mill. (Like a forward-looking New England factory owner, Robert had recently invested heavily in converting the mill from water to steam power. He was as fascinated as Charles Manigault by the technology of rice-pounding mills, and devoted no less than eight and a half pages of his 1846 article in *DeBows Review* to a detailed analysis of the efficiency of various types of mills.) "I hope [the overseer and the miller] will be able to keep up my brand 'Chicora,' " Robert nudged Adele, "which now has the opportunity to establish itself in the market. Nightingale Hall has establish'd itself fairly. I hope the two together will enable me to pay off, this winter, the mortgage to [my creditor] Moultrie." Six years later, Allston considered investing in a Charleston flour mill with a railway spur and a wharf but decided his profit would be greater if he confined his investments to agricultural land and slaves.[46]

Sometimes Allston tried to acknowledge frankly—even in public—that profit was his aim. "I have endeavored to profit by the principles of science, applying them to practical agriculture," he wrote in an autobiographical sketch for *DeBows Review;* but DeBow, preferring to distract attention from Allston's economic purposes, excised this sentence from the printed version of the sketch. Allston's private correspondence nevertheless showed that he thought of slaves as an investment like stocks or bonds. "I would give the revenue of any 10 negroes I own," he wrote Adele in 1844, "if your [lawyer] brother thought [politically] with me now." (Allston mistakenly expected to be elected governor that month and regretted that J. L. Petigru was a Unionist.) In order to profit most from his investment in slaves, Allston was eager to rent them out to help construct a railroad, even though everyone knew that such labor in the low country was likely, even more than in the rice fields, to undermine the slaves' health. "Men will do, generally, what it is their interest to do," he once wrote. And if philanthropy should occasionally lead someone else to sacrifice his own economic interest, this presented a sharp-eyed venture capitalist with an opportunity for a shrewd investment. "If you meet [in the Charleston slave market] with an orderly gang of some planter . . . who would sell you at [an average price of] *$500* rather than send away and separate his people at a higher figure," he advised his nephew (who was on the verge of buying some slaves), "then in such case you might adventure." Even a relatively tender-minded planter was likely, however, to select for separate sale some of the most valuable slaves, before selling the rest in a group. "I presume the [Heriot gang] has been culled . . . ," Allston continued. "I would not pay for them more than $500 and at a long credit."[47]

Planting was a "business"—"Pray tell [my nephew] to write and let me know what [his overseer] has to say about himself & the business," Allston wrote in 1855—and it brought the planter into contact with other sorts of capitalist investors. As a board member of the Bank of Georgetown in 1837, Allston corresponded with George Trenholm, who represented the Charleston stockholders. Allston wanted the bank to make relatively long-term loans (up to three years) to the planters, but Trenholm declared this would be too risky for the shareholders, because the bank's debts were callable almost upon demand. Planting was a business "Speculation" whose risks must be borne by the local planters, Trenholm insisted, not by the Charleston stockholders. The Bank of Georgetown soon failed, and in the absence of bank loans Allston financed some of his speculations by issuing his own bonds. These, according to the editor of his papers,

> passed from hand to hand [among Charleston businessmen] prior to final redemption. . . . Allston's creditors were inclined to treat plantation bonds in much the same way as other investors dealt in the securities of a corporation or a business partnership. In issuing these bonds, Allston himself probably did not feel very different from other businessmen who employed this means of augmenting their capital.

Allston's language was that of a capitalist investor; and when he wrote sympathetically in 1859 to the directors of the Blue Ridge Railroad, it was as one capitalist addressing another: "All that I am worth," he declared,

> lies in So. Carolina, and is invested in lands and negroes. . . . In projecting the Blue Ridge Railway . . . the suggestion [to extend tracks from Charleston westward via Tennessee, not Georgia, in order to circumvent obstructions from Georgians] made [by me] in Nashville in 1850 may have given some direction to the enterprising capitalists of the day.[48]

It was therefore ironic that (in reference to the Nashville Convention of 1850) Allston had accused Northern editors of a "plodding or a refined lust of gain," as though desire for gain did not motivate his own capitalist enterprises. The pot seemed to feel it must wrap itself in a flowing Roman toga before calling the kettle black. In a letter to James Hammond—congratulating Hammond on his "masterly" antiabolitionist *Letters to Thomas Clarkson* (1845)—Allston spoke language any businessman could understand: Allston, "as a planter . . . representing others who like himself, *have half their Capital invested in slaves* . . . , [sent to Hammond his] warm and grateful acknowledgements"; but having mentioned his capital investment in slaves, Allston felt impelled to wrap high-sounding rhetoric around his entrepreneurial vocation. "The life & pursuits of a Planter . . . ," he intoned,

> if view'd aright, regulated by the principles of Religion, that highest Philosophy, enlighten'd and aid'd by Science, affords both the means & opportunity to do as much good, and contributes to the true dignity of man, the elevation and just influence of his character, quite as much as any other avocation [*sic*] whatever.

Many a Boston merchant or industrialist would have felt his own capitalist calling no less honorable.[49]

12

Coercion

Robert Allston seemed in some respects a model slave master. He was remarkable among rice planters in personally supervising his properties during the long summer, instead of leaving his bondsmen and women to the uncontrolled dominion of overseers. He was far more successful than Charles Manigault, or most planters, in retaining the services of his overseers for years at a time, instead of subjecting his slaves to a constantly changing regime. The number of whippings his slaves endured was probably less than average, and the houses he furnished them were certainly less small than the norm. He granted six days of holiday at Christmas when a three-day break was usual in the rice kingdom, and he was assiduous in devising incentive plans which might seem to have attenuated the starkness of bondage.

Yet the slaves hated his regime. Allston was proud of imposing on them an overseer whom he knew they detested, and a famous Swedish visitor sensed that the slaves' detestation was not directed only at the overseer. The slaves' feelings became crystal clear during the turbulent early weeks of 1865, when the Northern army ended slavery on the Pee Dee. Allston was a strict disciplinarian, demanding implicit obedience from his chattels. As early as 1837 his backing a deeply unpopular overseer had almost caused a rupture between him and his sister-in-law—averted only by her capitulating to his furious ultimatum; and he never changed his ways. His overbearing manner toward even his wife disturbed her, and his peremptory conduct surely anguished his slaves as well. Velvet gloves there may sometimes have been, but Allston's grip was iron.

A businessman using enslaved labor needed fearsome punishments to discipline his workers, since the threat of sacking them was not available. The ultimate sanction was the power of the state to punish a recalcitrant slave, and Allston knew this power from helping to exercise it himself. In 1829 two Pee Dee slaves (one owned by Allston's brother-in-law John Coachman) were accused of conspiring to rebel. Allston, then twenty-eight, was chosen as one of the five local planters—along with two justices—who instead of a jury of peers were deputed to try one of the cases. Allston helped condemn the slave Charles to be hanged. The other slave was also executed, as was a third for assaulting (not killing) the black woman who had accused the two condemned slaves. "I am afraid you will hang half the country," Allston's future brother-in-law exclaimed.[1]

A different aspect of the state's police power came to Allston's attention in 1858. Fights among blacks at a Methodist camp meeting in Orangeburg led to the sentencing of six slaves to be lashed twenty-five to one hundred times each. General D. F. Jamison, a credible informant, complained to Allston that—according to Jamison's sources—the infliction of the punishment

> was cruelly severe. The constable employed was not the regular one, but he was gotten from an adjoining [county], for the occasion, as I have heard alleged, on account of his known severity in his treatment of negroes. The public indignation was aroused by the unmerciful manner in which the negroes were whipped.

One of the six slaves belonged to General Jamison, who was sure his slave had been falsely convicted ("an *alibi* was proved"). Yet such was the force of public backing for severe punishment of black men—even if the wrong slave were convicted, and even if some other Carolinians were shocked by the constable's severity—that General Jamison "was unwilling to interpose" to defend his own slave against an unjust, unmerciful, cruelly severe flogging.[2]

The state's repressive power was rolled out dramatically again in 1862, and this time in a way wholly palatable to genteel planters. For several months that year—until an effective Confederate battery was implanted near the town of Georgetown to discourage Northern naval vessels from intruding from Winyah Bay up the Waccamaw and Pee Dee Rivers—warships had occasionally darted up those two rivers, carrying off those slaves who "begged to be received on board." Among these were twenty-eight men owned by a Waccamaw planter of evil repute named Magill.[3] Three of these fugitives later returned to bring their wives with them. Many slaves had been escaping down the rivers by boat at night, to be picked up at sea by patrolling Union naval vessels: slaves "have been in numbers leaving different plantations," a Georgetown master complained, "and generally it has been by water." These three men and their wives hoped to join the stream of escapees but—disastrously for them—they were captured.[4]

The local authorities then had to decide what punishment was appropriate to men who loved their wives too dearly for their own good. The person in charge was Dr. Francis Parker, a rich Black River planter (only a few miles from Allston's Nightingale Hall) whose 220 slaves produced more rice than those of any other Black River planting family except the Trapiers. Like Allston, Parker was a keen secessionist: he was a delegate to the 1860 Secession Convention who, just before the attack on Fort Sumter, had got himself a commission in the army, and enthusiastically had gone "to Fort Moultrie to be in the thickest of the fight."[5] Parker and the court-martial he convened condemned the three men to death. Fearing that this draconian penalty for the crime of fleeing might be countermanded by the governor, Parker and his associates decreed that execution was to take place the next day. Like a lynch mob anxious to secure the hasty deaths of black men, the rich planters acted quickly—"that no executive clemency might intervene." The hangings took place at 1 P.M. on November 5. As H. A. Middleton, the master of 270 slaves, tersely reported: "It was in the gaol yard. Strong military drawn up. There was a crowd. The blacks were encouraged to be present. The effect will not soon be forgotten. As far as I can know [Middleton opined] Dr. P[arker] has acted with great decision and judgment." A very large capital investment (of Parker's, Middleton's, Allston's, and others) was at stake, and it must not be allowed to trickle away to sea on a pea green boat.[6]

Perhaps the execution also represented the Georgetown planters' response to the news of Lincoln's preliminary Emancipation Proclamation, which had been issued six weeks earlier. Many Northern newspapers defended that proclamation by claiming it would provoke slave insurrections all over the South, and would thus help the North to win the war.[7] The terrifying measures used by the Georgetown planters, to repress even flight, go far to explain why that prediction proved false, and why there was no substantial slave rebellion during the war. The slaves could see that the soldiers and civilians disciplining them were not engaged in some picturesque medieval pageantry devised— like *Gone with the Wind*—to beguile a later generation of compatriots. The attack upon slavery posed a revolutionary threat to the rice planters, and men like Robert Allston, Francis Parker, and H. A. Middleton had no intention that the slave regime should be overthrown.

Before the three Magill slaves were executed in November 1862, local military power had been vested in the hands of Major W. P. Emanuel, probably a Georgetown merchant, whose post in the militia was elective. His previously temporizing rule had not been to the taste of the rice planters; and their decreeing death for the three fugitives, through a provost martial's court, was part of a move to displace Emanuel. The major "is so feeble a man," H. A. Middleton had grumbled in October, "that—command going by election—he does not give an order." Ten days later Middleton, when expressing his gratification at the public execution of the three fugitives, reported that "efforts are in progress to get rid of our commanding officer Major Emanuel." Two months later Middleton could breathe a sigh of relief. By January 1863 Major Emanuel had been pushed aside, the rich planters had organized an efficient nighttime picket with their own boats across Winyah Bay, and Confederate forces had established a strong military presence which safeguarded the planters' investments. Slaves thinking of escape could now see—with chagrin—that, "within a month, from having none, deserving the name of soldiers, we now have 3000 men [Middleton exulted]. We have too piquets everywhere on the highland, and what is of more importance, boat piquets too." The power of the state was in full panoply, and remained so for as long as the Confederacy could spare the soldiers to guard directly the planters' interests.[8]

In peacetime the state's military force was organized in the militia, a principal function of which was to suppress any threat of insurrection or mass flight by the slaves. The ubiquity of military titles in the South was the product of a slave society, for these titles normally derived from the militia. Allston was always "Colonel Allston" (before he became "Governor Allston"), while his elder brother, Joseph, had been "General Allston" in the militia. The low-country planters had grounds for fearing that a seaborne enemy would tamper with their slaves, for in both 1780 and 1815 British invaders had done so. When Britain and France were at war in 1802 a panic—that a French invasion was imminent—had swept Georgetown District; and the alarmed local plant-ers had called out the militia posthaste to keep their slaves in order. The events of 1862 therefore fell into a pattern.[9]

Within this framework of state power Allston constructed his own system of plantation discipline. As befitted a man trained at West Point—and suffi-ciently satisfied with the result to send his son Ben there for training—Allston stringently demanded obedience from his slaves. When Ben was a colonel in the Confederate army, he gained a reputation for strictness with his soldiers; and there is reason to suppose his father even more of a martinet than Ben.[10] Robert Allston fulminated against rich neighbors who did not keep their house servants under firm control: the slaves of J. H. Tucker (owner of 335 bondsmen and women) were, according to Allston, "the most lawless set I have had to deal with [—] these and the Barnwell's." Like nearly every other Southern gentleman, Allston took for granted that selling a slave to New Orleans—and thus forever separating that person from her or his family—was fit punishment for any "ungovernable" slave. (For example, on the back of the bill of purchase of Alick, for whom Allston had paid the hefty sum of $820 in 1847, the dissatisfied Carolinian later inscribed, "Sold out of the State for gross and wicked misconduct.")[11]

Allston brooked no insubordination from his chattels, and his understand-ing of a slave's duties was broad: "Misconduct ought to be punished . . . ," he insisted; "I imperatively require of [slaves] honesty, truth, diligence and cheer-fulness in their work, wherever and whatever it is." He knew his strictness with the slaves would not be to the taste of a woman like his Aunt Elizabeth Blyth. When Mrs. Blyth's overseer was ill in 1838, her slaves complained frequently to her; but if she were to entrust Allston with full control over managing them, "I fear," Allston wrote with some pride, "the negroes would continue to trouble her with complaints." A gentleman like Allston normally deputed dirty work such as whippings to his overseers, and he might not like to impose such punishment with his own hands; but Allston did not hesitate to flog a slave himself if necessary. "I was happy," he wrote one beautiful spring day, "until I met with an ox which had been abused by John. . . . This quite upset me because of the poor animal, and because of the penalty which I had to impose."[12]

The gentleman's role was to find a firm overseer and get him to maintain discipline with the right amount of whipping. To discover and keep a satisfactory overseer was hard everywhere in the South because—unlike England—cheap land was abundant: an able farm manager would be sorely tempted to set up for himself, instead of remaining a lifelong employee (like the novelist George Eliot's father in Warwickshire). The problem was even more acute in the low country because an overseer needed resistance against malaria, which meant that most overseers there had to be recruited from the relatively small number of poorish whites born and bred in the low country, who thus had acquired—if they hadn't died first—some immunity against the dread "summer fever." Even so, malaria was a constant threat to the overseers. "I hope and trust Mr. Pitman [the overseer at Nightingale Hall and Guendalos] won't get sick," Allston wrote Ben at the height of the malaria season, as the 1860 harvest began.[13]

From the small number of eligible whites the master had to select an overseer who could impose himself upon the slaves. Not everyone had the required strength and personal force—as Robert's widowed mother had found when she employed the overseer Daniel Avant in 1823. A slave named Jerry "had a Horn which he Blew for his own amusement, which offended Mr. Avant." By trickery Avant got Jerry into a barn and locked him in; Avant then got his whip, and brought along his wife with a dog and flail sticks. "They Beat him a long time," Charlotte Allston reported, "he scuffleing all the while, he Bit and Avant choaked him twice till his streangth failed, and at last had to send for Geog [i.e., George, a slave], who tyed [him], and Avant then gave him 20 to 30 lashes, twice I understand." This long fight lends credibility to Frederick Douglass's famous account of his own struggle with the Maryland slave breaker Covey, and shows how vital to the whites it was to divide and conquer—to turn one slave (like George) against another. Avant obviously lacked what it took to make a successful overseer. Mrs. Allston disapproved his using the dog on Jerry, and of his enlisting his wife in the disciplinary proceedings; and Avant did not stay much longer in her employ.[14]

Tying down a slave before whipping him became part of the routine which Allston demanded of his overseers, and he defined precisely how floggings were to be administered. "The offender," he began,

> should be taken to the farm and tied within doors, and be well whipped on his [or her] buttocks [no doubt with the trousers down or the dress up, as at other plantations] with a leather thong which will not do him injury. He should receive a number of lashes according with [the] nature of the offence. Not less than one dozen [lashes] nor more than twenty-five to be executed by a driver.

You must be careful to always avoid either ordering or executing a punishment whilst you are angry.

The limit of twenty-five lashes applied only to the black driver, not to the overseer: for suboverseer F. A. Collins (in his only surviving report) mentioned in a routine way having punished Jacob "39 strips."[15]

As was clear from General Jamison's account of the "cruelly severe" whipping of six slaves by the unmerciful constable, the amount of pain endured by the slave depended not only on the number of lashes but on the force with which each one was inflicted. Years after the war, Ancrum—one of Allston's drivers deputed to whip other slaves—assured Allston's daughter that her father had not wished whippings to be too severe. Allston's purpose was more readily secured when a driver like Ancrum[16] administered the flogging than when the overseer did the whipping himself. Knowing how prone were overseers to abuse the slaves, Allston realized he could not depend simply upon exhorting them to confine the whip to the buttocks, and requesting them not to strike in anger. As the law offered an overseer irresponsible, virtually unlimited power over a slave's life, the master must try to stay the overseer's hand by instilling into him religious terror. Here, for the only time in Allston's seven closely packed pages of instructions to the overseer, a "negro" became suddenly a "person": "Regard all persons whose time and labor are wholly at your command," Allston warned, "as beings for whose health, comfort and good conduct in this life you will be held most fearfully responsible in the life to come."[17]

Allston was unusually particular in limiting the ferocity of whippings. Because he resided at Pawleys Island during the summer, and regularly visited Chicora Wood from there, he could control his overseers more than could most rice planters. And rather than depend on occasional, capricious, savage whippings, he tried to ensure that every "offence" would be punished one way or another, but often without a whipping. If order could thus be established, the severity of punishments might be relaxed. Hence Allston decreed a careful gradation of lesser penalties for minor offenses. If a private or public reprimand was ineffectual, the overseer might deprive a slave of some "desired priviledge"—such as a pass to visit a friend—or might deny a slave his rations for a period up to four weeks. (The slave would then have to eat the food of others in his family, or beg food from comrades.) The final sanction, short of whipping, was for the overseer to confine a slave in Allston's plantation jail, from the end of work on Saturday until the distribution of the Sunday allowance—and this penalty might be imposed for four successive weekends.[18] In directing that a whipped slave be tied indoors, Allston aimed to prevent escape, not to spare the slave's feelings; and in trying to ensure that the whipping be limited to the buttocks, he sought to prevent damage to valuable property, not to spare pain. Yet the consequence of Allston's precision in management (and of his success in retaining for twenty-four years at Chicora Wood the unusual overseer Jesse Belflowers) was surely to make his regime much less barbaric than that of, say, Solomon Northrop's drunken master Edwin Epps in Louisiana.

How frequently Allston's slaves were whipped remains uncertain. By the late 1850s a movement to reform slavery was well under way in the seaboard slave states—something like the movement in South Carolina late in the 1940s to improve the segregated (and woefully underfunded) black schools there, in order to forestall an attack upon segregation itself. The slavery reform movement made enough progress that plans were made to publish an up-to-date defense of slavery, buttressed by testimonials from rich planters about recent improvements in the conditions of the slaves. In Allston's projected contribution to this volume he asserted that his fostering religion among his slaves had served his own interest. "I have found the greatest advantage," he exclaimed, "from this [religious instruction], and I know many [slaves] who perform their services for me as a religious duty. . . . Thieving is much less common than it used to be." In this same self-assured memorandum Allston claimed that "on the plantation which I myself manage (containing 175 negroes) there are about three or four punishments annually."[19]

Can this statement be taken at face value? Virtually no overseers' reports (except for the untypical months just before emancipation) have survived, with which to test Allston's assertion. If one had to depend on Charles Manigault's justifications of his own regime, one's impression of the government of Gowrie would be very different from the picture formed from overseers' and other contemporary records. When Manigault declared that he had achieved among his slaves at Gowrie an annual increase of 4 percent he was not mistaken; but contemporary records showed that the 4 percent increase occurred in only one year. When Manigault stated that he had kept two or three slaves unproductively at Marshlands instead of sending them to Gowrie, he implied that concern for the slaves' attachments had governed his practice; yet contemporary records show that he had deported sixty-eight slaves from Silk Hope to Gowrie, sometimes sundering family ties.[20] Manigault's statement that he had granted some of his slaves, "particularly at Silk Hope," the privilege of raising pigs was not false, yet it was misleading: for contemporary sources show that not one Gowrie slave was ever granted the right to raise pigs.

When, therefore, Allston stated there were about three or four punishments annually (confining his statement to Chicora Wood), one wonders why he did not mention Nightingale Hall too. An overseer's weekly report for Nightingale Hall (in early May 1860, one of the handful before 1864 which survive) mentions matter-of-factly the flogging that week of eight women, twelve- lashes each, for "howing corn bad." Perhaps Allston would have counted this as "one punishment"; but it would be rash—in the absence of a positive statement by Allston—to infer that there were only three or four such punishments a year at Nightingale Hall. And even at Chicora Wood, doubt must remain, for only one fortnight's report has survived from the unusually candid suboverseer, F. A. Collins. Collins reported flogging three slaves within that one fortnight—thirty-nine lashes for Jacob, twenty-five for Jackson, and nineteen for a stranger on the plantation. Two punishments of Chicora Wood slaves in one fortnight, and only two during the other fifty weeks of the year?[21]

That whippings occurred much more than four times a year at carefully managed rice plantations like Chicora Wood and Nightingale Hall is suggested by a report of Frederick Olmsted's, which has the ring of authenticity. In 1853 Olmsted visited—in the Georgia low country—the Ogeechee River rice planter Richard Arnold, an exceptional master. (Arnold's slaves' houses, twenty-one feet square, were a bit larger than those which Allston furnished his own bondsmen and women; and Arnold banned his overseer from personally flogging a slave: such punishment must be administered by a driver.) Olmsted inquired of Arnold (whose two hundred slaves were nearly as numerous as those at Chicora Wood) how often his slaves were whipped. "Sometimes, perhaps, not once for two or three weeks," Arnold replied; "then it will seem as if the devil had got into them all and there is a good deal of it." The probability is that at Allston's plantations—as at Richard Arnold's and at nearly every other plantation in the South—whipping was a fairly regular, and indispensable, element in the regime.[22]

The principal officer for ensuring that slaves were whipped was the overseer, and planters made their distrust of overseers obvious. Allston's aunt Elizabeth Blyth felt obliged to write into her overseer's contract a ban on his beating a slave with an instrument that might break a bone: the overseer must agree "that he will in no instance strike a negro with a stick." The rich Georgetown planter H. A. Middleton, by asking Allston to report on an applicant's "temperance," showed his fear of getting a drunken overseer. Uncontrolled wrath was another common problem, for Allston knew many overseers abused slaves in anger: he praised Middleton's applicant by contrast as "a man of even temper." Allston remembered how his own slave Jack had suffered grievously at the hands of someone else's passionate overseer. When General Thomas Carr had been very sick in 1823 and unable to keep an eye on his overseer, Jack had been "most dreadfully beat . . . by Swinton, Genl. Carr's overseer, so much so that he had not been able to work [for at least a fortnight]. If the punishment was as severe as represented to me," Robert's brother had reported indignantly, "I think Swinton ought to be prosecuted as nothing could justify it."[23]

How low-country slaves were treated depended substantially on whether their masters abandoned them to the unsupervised control of overseers—whose temper might be like Swinton's—during the long malarial season. "It was almost impossible," according to Allston's daughter Elizabeth Pringle, "to get an overseer who would treat the negroes with gentleness and justice. . . . Their one idea [was] to get as much work from the hands as possible, and, consequently, make as much money." Pringle believed her great-aunt Blyth—whose rich fiancé had died, leaving his wealth to her—had finally married another man so that she could personally supervise her overseers. It would not have done for a young unmarried white woman to live alone on a plantation; but "after trying one [unsupervised] overseer after another, and finding them cruel and regardless in their treatment of her people," the aunt had married: so that she could live on the plantation—at least during the winter—to control her overseer.[24]

Pringle's conviction that most overseers were cruel and unjust was shared by many a genteel planter. Frederick Olmsted recorded that—according to the Georgia rice planter Richard Arnold—overseers "were almost universally drunken and dissolute, and constantly liable to neglect their duties." Olmsted realized that low-country planters had little choice among overseers, having to select mainly from among those "born and reared in the miasmatic district of the coast." Although overseers might "curry favor with [slaves], so they may not inform the proprietor of their own misconduct or neglect," Olmsted became convinced—through conversations all over the South, and his reading of Southern periodicals—that overseers' callousness and abuse of power was by far their more common failing. Often in the rice district no other white person would be present to testify against an overseer in court; and, of course, no court admitted a slave's testimony in a case where a white man had abused a slave.[25]

No doubt planters blamed overseers partly in order to pass the buck for their own responsibility. And some planters were certainly as cruel as many overseers. Olmsted learned of a Louisiana planter who castrated one of his slaves "under an impulse of jealousy"; and Bennet Barrow believed his neighbor Captain Howells to have been an even greater monster: Howells "has the name of being the most cruel Master I ever knew of—'tis said he has castrated 3 men of his." Richard Arnold told Olmsted of one neighbor who "sold an excellent man . . . , without having any fault to find with him, and without the slightest regard, apparently, to the strong ties of kindred which were ruptured in the transaction"; and of another who, when drunk, "attempted to shoot and stab" his own slaves. Yet doubtless on average overseers treated slaves worse than did owners. Olmsted concluded that "the slaves of the most humane rice-planters are exceedingly likely to be subject to the uncontrolled tyranny of men of the most heartless and reckless disposition."[26]

It is therefore worth trying to estimate what fraction of rice slaves were subject to an overseer's unconstrained dominion during the long "summer"— the malarial months each year from May until November. Olmsted (whose information was from coastal Georgia) believed that not 1 percent of the rice planters resided on their plantations during the summer. A few planters, however, who summered in Charleston or Beaufort, owned plantations near enough those towns that they could get to their estates and back between morning and evening. A few others ventured summer residence at pineland villages near their plantations, like Summerville or Plantersville. And others like Allston—though this practice was confined principally to the Georgetown District (and then only to Pee Dee and Waccamaw planters, not to those on the Santee, Sampit, and Black Rivers)—established summer homes on the breezy coast from which the master could make a quick trip to the plantation. On many a day Allston breakfasted at 6 A.M. in his Pawleys Island summer home; rode four miles horseback across the Waccamaw peninsula (perhaps shooting a deer or two for sport); was rowed by his slaves seven miles through the rivers and creeks of the Waccamaw–Pee Dee rice peninsula to reach his plantation; examined the crops' progress, accompanied by a slave trunk minder who would pick a few shoots of rice in each field for Allston's inspection; had a light snack at his big house west of the Pee Dee; and returned to Pawleys Island for dinner at 3 P.M.[27]

Allston, an unusually conscientious proprietor, regretted that not more planters followed his example of establishing summer residence near enough to supervise their plantations. But even he had had to spend years experimenting with various summer houses before finally hitting upon Pawleys Island as the least unhealthy. He and his family knew he was playing with fire, for death could strike early. Robert's father had died at 41, Robert's younger brother, William, died of malaria at 19, and his older brother, Joseph, was dead at 36. Of Robert's three sisters one died at 32, one at 41, and one at 54. If Robert happened to stay on his plantation into June while his family was at Charleston, they would implore him to leave: "The imminent danger attending such a course impressed me most painfully. . . . I cannot describe how unhappy I am," his wife cried,

> at the thought that you should be exposed to such a danger, and from no cause but the inconvenience of moving to the Beach. . . . To remain on the plantation and come down [to Charleston] on the 13th [of June] would be going against all experience. [Cousin Lynch] was shocked at the thought that you should remain on the plantation until [June] 13. Said she prayed you not to do so. . . . Oh my beloved do not expose your precious health or life.

Early in his marriage Robert's summer residence was at "Canaan," on Waccamaw Neck just across a salt marsh from Pawleys Island; but after several years the family concluded that it was too unhealthy. They then tried the pine woods eight miles northwest of Chicora Wood, but in September 1844 Robert nearly died of a summer fever which may have been malaria: his neighbor, Dr. J. R. Sparkman, was in attendance for thirty-six hours before concluding that the case was no longer desperate. This experience determined the Allstons upon Pawleys Island as their future place of summer residence, a spot already favored by certain other Georgetown planters.[28]

Allston, who deplored absenteeism, regretfully acknowledged that 11 percent of rice planters were wholly nonresident, and that another 43 percent (in an unrepresentative sample?) summered too far away from their plantations to supervise operations there for half the year.[29] But his figures certainly understate absenteeism; and they underestimate even more the impact of summer absenteeism upon the slaves. For the larger slaveholders were the more likely to be absentees—to spend their summers at Charleston, or in an Appalachian Mountain resort, or in some Northern town like Newport, or in Europe, leaving the overseer in charge. Allston's neighbors on the Pee Dee illustrate the point.

None would have considered summer residence in the town of Georgetown. Sixty miles north of Charleston, this settlement had once aspired to ape the South Carolina metropolis as a regional trading center, but in the summer it proved so malarial that it could never even rival Beaufort. During the winters, to be sure, Georgetown's eight hundred white inhabitants, eighty free blacks, and 850 slaves made the town a smallish commercial entrepôt,[30] and a good many Yankee vessels made their way to its quays; but in the summers well-to-do people deserted it like the plague. Allston owned two houses there but seems scarcely ever to have used them. The rich Pee Dee planters, several of whom spent their summers in Charleston, would no more have thought of passing a summer in the town of Georgetown than of making a voluntary sojourn in Hades.

As has been shown,[31] nine planting families besides Allston occupied the twenty-five-mile Pee Dee rice strip in 1857. Of the slaves owned by these other nine families, the great majority were subject to "summer" absenteeism. Four of Allston's neighbors are known to have spent the long "summer" far from their slaves, and these included the three largest owners. J. H. Read transferred his household to Charleston, as did Francis Weston; Ralph Stead Izard customarily traveled abroad; and J. J. Izard Pringle—whose name bore witness that his grandfather had been U.S. Senator Ralph Izard—spent his summers in Newport, France, or Rome (he died in Rome in 1864).[32] Probably the Northerner Frederick Shaffer and the genteel Yale graduate W. H. Trapier were also absentees at least during the summers. (Trapier was proud to have introduced the custom of mint julep drinking to New College, Oxford; but he does not appear to have been around to tell the 1860 census taker that summer how many houses his slaves had to live in.) Very likely, therefore, at least 76 percent of the slaves of Allston's Pee Dee neighbors experienced summer absenteeism; and the real proportion may have been much higher.[33]

No doubt summer absenteeism was even more common in other parts of the South Carolina low country than along the Pee Dee. Rice cultivation had been developed more recently in Georgetown District—which was booming in the 1850s—than it had been elsewhere in South Carolina. One's impression is that there was somewhat more assiduity among Georgetown planters, somewhat more willingness to cut themselves off from the comforts of Charleston's urban society, a greater willingness to experiment with summer residence at an outpost like Pawleys Island than was to be found closer to Charleston, or to its south.

For different reasons, an even higher proportion of slaves in the Georgia low country probably suffered from absenteeism than in South Carolina. The full development of rice cultivation in Georgia was an even more recent phenomenon than in Georgetown District; hence there had been even less time in Georgia to develop summer resorts like the one at Pawleys Island, where genteel planters could find enough congenial company to make summer residence tolerable to them. A Charlestonian like Charles Manigault thought Georgia uncivilized, and he kept his distance during the summer. It is clear that Allston's practice of living near his rice plantations during the summer was far from common, even in Georgetown District, and that the great majority of rice slaves were therefore subject to the virtually uncontrolled despotism of their overseers for about half of every year.

Allston, then, took more trouble than most rice planters to keep his overseers under his eye. But this did not mean that his slaves found life a bed of roses, for their master was a firm disciplinarian inclined to back an overseer until evidence of mismanagement was indisputable; and in any case Allston's desiderata in an overseer differed from his slaves'. That their complaints alone would not cause him to sack an otherwise satisfactory overseer became evident in Allston's administration of Waverly, his dead brother Joseph's plantation.

Joseph's widow did not like the way either of the first two of Robert's overseers at Waverly treated her slaves. Both of these supervisors—George Gotea and then, from 1838, Gabriel Ellis—have left a poor reputation. After Gotea departed from Waverly he was employed by Robert's second cousin Dr. William Allston, who soon sacked him for "his continued irregularities"; while Ellis earned from a later employer the characterization, a "Bad Man." Yet Robert Allston backed both overseers for a time. Early in 1837 Gotea wanted to buy a slave woman named Letty—probably in her midtwenties—owned by the estate of a dead sister of Robert's. Gotea was willing to pay twice as much as the woman's market value: one may therefore suppose he had a liaison with her and sought to continue it. Robert Allston did not at first accept Gotea's offer, and Letty was sold instead to someone in Charleston. The buyer, however, threatened to sue Allston on the grounds that Letty was "unsound": apparently she had been injured in a difficult childbirth some years before her sale. The illustrious Charleston lawyer J. L. Petigru (Allston's brother-in-law) predicted that a suit might be successful against Allston for selling unsound property. "As regards horseflesh," Petigru reported, deadpan, but not without a tinge of pleasure at comparing a black woman to a mare, "there is a vast contrariety of opinions, some judges holding that every sickness . . . almost is ground to rescind a sale, others that nothing short of some constitutional, radical infirmity will answer the purpose." To forestall a suit, Allston acted as Gotea's agent in repurchasing Letty from her Charleston buyer, and Gotea ended up possessing her as he had always wished.[34]

A few months later trouble overflowed between Robert and his sister-in-law Mary Allston, probably caused by complaints to her from the Waverly slaves about Gotea. Still upset that Robert had persuaded her to sell more than half of the Waverly slaves, Mary Allston let Robert feel her dissatisfaction with his management. He was unwilling, however, to abandon his methods of maintaining plantation discipline, and in October he served Mary Allston an ultimatum. "So far . . . from approving [my management of my brother's estate]," Allston wrote, formal politeness scarcely concealing his icy rage,

> I cannot doubt any longer, you are offended by it. . . .
> Therefore . . . I have determined to withdraw from the management as soon as the Court of Equity will release me. . . .
> I have overcome my reluctance to make the proposition by the following considerations. . . .
> 1st. As you were so dissatisfied with my management of the negroes. . . .
> [After I have withdrawn from the executorship,] you can employ such agent precisely as will suit you.[35]

This vehement language quickly brought Mary Allston to heel: Robert continued as executor of his brother's estate for the next twenty years, until his nephews were well past their majority. But Robert was not impervious to pressure. On Christmas Day 1837 the slaves at Waverly murdered one of their black drivers, Cudjo;[36] and Gotea's leaving Allston's employ at the end of 1837 was doubtless related to this clear expression of the slaves' discontent. Gotea was replaced by Gabriel Ellis, Allston's overseer at Chicora Wood since 1831, whose duties were now extended to encompass two trips each week to Waverly.

While the genteel lawyer Petigru was titillated to liken a female slave to a horse, Ellis thought automatically of blacks as comparable to animals, and talked of mares and black women in the same breath. "Do let me know," he wrote to Allston that summer "if you want the Mares at Waverly put to any Horse or not and if to any to what one. The bay Mare has a fine horse colt it is about 4 weeks old. Delier has a child at Waverly and Venes has one here [at Chicora Wood]."[37]

Within months the Waverly slaves were complaining to Mary Allston about their new overseer; Ellis then wrote to Robert Allston to try to get the tiresome white woman off his back. During the summer Mary Allston resided at the beach only a few miles from Waverly, where the slaves could easily reach her. In order to satisfy the South Carolina law that a white person must reside on each plantation—and since Ellis resided seven miles away at Chicora Wood—Allston had apparently hired Isaac Singleton as a "law screener" to live on the plantation, while the day-to-day management of the crop was probably left largely in the hands of the driver. In September Water, a Waverly slave, "Run away for nothing [Ellis alleged] not Even a cross word from Mr. Singleton nor the Driver." When Water returned he was put into stocks, and locked indoors. He broke "out of the Stocks and Barn" and fled to Mary Allston for protection. She took Water's part, sending him back—to Ellis's indignation—"with a virbel mesage by the same Negro to Mr Singleton for him to put it back in the stocks if he dares." Ellis appealed to Robert Allston: "Mrs [Mary] Allston has divested me of so much of my authority and the Negroes is aware of it that I can not Manage them as they aught to be. If one Runs away and goes to her [at the beach] she will not sufer me to punish it at tall."[38]

Mary Allston's hostility to Ellis would surely not in itself have turned Robert Allston against Ellis—Robert's confrontation with her a year earlier had proved this; but Robert received complaints against Ellis from at least two other sources during the same year. Allston's neighbor William Sparkman—a large planter who was the elder brother of Allston's esteemed medical adviser, Dr. J. R. Sparkman—fell into a serious dispute with Ellis, deeply imbued with class antagonism. Sparkman sent five of his slaves down the road, without a written pass, to get fence rails for him from a neighbor's land. Upon their return Ellis interposed. He whipped one of Sparkman's slaves "25 or 30 lashes," allegedly for forcing the wheel of a white person's gig off the road; and he may have threatened to lock up this slave. Sparkman accused the overseer of cruelty, but not to his face. Ellis reported threateningly: "I think [Sparkman] had beter Say as litl as posible. . . . I would rather convince Mr. S. of his Erer in a personal conversation." Sparkman haughtily distanced himself: "Mr Ellis," he pronounced, "is a man I would studiously avoid having any communication with."[39]

A slave who subsequently became a trusted driver of Allston's later claimed credit for having got Ellis sacked in 1838. Ancrum, then about twenty, had been Ellis's house servant for seven years. When Allston was in the North that summer, "Mr. Ellis treat me so mean I run' away," Ancrum told Elizabeth Pringle a half century later. In addition to cutting wood and doing all the other household chores, Ancrum was required at night to shoo the mosquitoes off Ellis's ill father. The overworked youth once fell asleep, and Ellis beat him. Slaves distinguished justifiable whippings from unjust ones: this one was unjust—it was not fair to expect a slave to work all day and then whip him for falling asleep at night—and Ancrum ran away: "I ben in de wood till I hear maussa cum home. Den maussa didn' keep Mr. Ellis anoder year."[40] Allston did indeed part from Ellis at the end of 1838; and although Ancrum doubtless told this story to feed Elizabeth Pringle's sense that her father was a just man who listened to the slaves' complaints against the despised overseers, the tale has the ring of authenticity. Allston's regime, stern though it was, was a despotism tempered by rays of humanity.

Yet Allston's slaves' dealings with supervisors resembled the experiences of other slaves with their own overseers. Among Allston's chattels were fifty-eight bondsmen and women he inherited from Elizabeth Blyth in 1840. Mrs. Blyth's overseer William Thompson (like so many others of his class) fathered a child by one of the slave women. This mulatto, Nelson, was favored by the Allstons, and he became a privileged house servant—their butler. Elizabeth Allston Pringle believed Robert Allston had sacked Thompson because of his siring a mulatto child, but this was not true of William Thompson. Thompson was Mrs. Blyth's overseer from 1822 "till the day of his death in . . . 1838," and there is no evidence that he was punished in any way for taking advantage of a slave woman. The fathering of mulatto slaves by overseers and other white men was commonplace, and was seldom commented upon in the records. Thus the ninety-eight slaves whom Robert Allston bought with Nightingale Hall in 1846 included two young mulatto women, the seventeen-year-old Seckey and fifteen-year-old Miley, both perhaps children of a former overseer.[41]

The overseer at Nightingale Hall who gave Allston greatest satisfaction was the highly paid Harman Pitman, who received a thousand-dollar salary already in his first year of service, and to whom Allston left a small legacy in his will. Yet Pitman appears to have neglected the slaves' health. Benjamin Allston, who was still rather new to the realities of rice planting in 1858, complained that summer to his father that Pitman "has lost another child on the plantation. He seems to be not very careful to the children when sick." Another case of medical neglect, reminiscent of those at Gowrie, occurred in the late summer of 1861. A male slave was taken sick on Sunday but Pitman did not call a doctor until Tuesday, by which time it was too late. Pitman's weak denial of responsibility echoed Skinner's and Venters's at Gowrie. "Robin . . . ," Pitman reported,

> was taken Sunday P.M. I saw him Monday A.M. & attended to him late that evening. He said he felt better as I told you. Tuesday morning he was walking about in the piazza said he had no pain but felt weak. about one O clock P.M. was calld to him sent for the Dr but he died between 2 & 3 oclock & before the Dr came. So many deaths trouble me greatly but I cant help or stop deaths.[42]

At Chicora Wood the Allstons managed to keep one overseer for over twenty-four years—and this in a region where Olmsted had never heard of any overseer's staying with an employer longer than eight years.[43] Allston had paid the twenty-seven-year-old Jesse Belflowers only three hundred dollars in 1842, but by increasing his pay rapidly and treating him well he kept him for the rest of Belflowers's life. This was, however, no boon to the Chicora Wood slaves. "The negroes," Allston delightedly informed his son, "dislike [Belflowers] mortally." Their hostility Allston attributed to Belflowers's practice of "always circulating [around the plantation] and no one knows where to find him." No doubt Belflowers's stealth—comparable to that of Frederick Douglass's master, Covey, who "always aimed at taking us [slaves] by surprise"—was a principal reason Allston held onto him so many years. "You must humor [Belflowers]," he instructed Ben, "he is a crooked stick."[44] Belflowers probably did not use the whip as much as was common, and the Allstons' only criticism of their cherished overseer was that he was not severe enough with the slaves. "He always required *backing* as [Robert] expressed it," Adele later murmured.[45]

For example, in 1858 the plowman Leander committed some offense which Benjamin Allston—just learning the ropes of plantation management—thought required a whipping. "I suppose," Benjamin addressed his father impatiently, "Belflowers has not punished Leander yet as he does not mention it—though I had thought he would have done so at once. You will see the pump has broken." Instead of whipping Leander, Belflowers probably briefly demoted him to field work, then quickly placed him again in his privileged job. "Leander has been restored to the plow," Benjamin reported six days later, with only a tinge of disapproval, "and seems to be giving satisfaction."[46]

Although Robert Allston's and Belflowers's recourse to lesser penalties probably enabled them to impose fewer whippings than was common, there is nevertheless reason to suppose that their regime was loathed by many of Allston's bondsmen and women. The slaves' conduct in 1865 is the strongest evidence of their discontent,[47] and corroboration seems to have come from the Swedish traveler Fredrika Bremer, who visited Chicora Wood in April 1850. Bremer's two-volume American travelogue, *Homes of the New World*, names those of her slaveholding hosts and hostesses about whom she could publish favorable reports—such as the agreeable former cabinet minister, Joel Poinsett, and his wife. During her delightful sojourn with the Poinsetts (eight miles down the Pee Dee River from the Allstons' house) Bremer attended two dinner parties with the Poinsetts' neighbors, and one of these was at Chicora

Wood. Adele Allston showed her foreign visitor "the condition of the ne-groes," but learned some weeks later from a Charleston friend that Bremer had not been pleased by what she saw. "In one slave village, near a great house," Bremer wrote, referring almost certainly to the Allston slaves, "I saw remarkably handsome people, and living in good houses. But I observed that the glances of the young men were gloomy and defiant, with no expression of kindness toward their owners. That did not look well."[48] These slaves' dislike of their overseer—to which Allston himself attested—evidently extended to the masters as well.

One would misunderstand slavery if one supposed that cruelty—as credibly described in Theodore Weld's abolitionist compilation *American Slavery as It Is* (1839), or in Solomon Northup's *Twelve Years a Slave* (1853)—was the only source of slaves' hating the regime. Nor were squalid living conditions neces-sary to provoke hostility, for the twenty-two-by-nineteen-foot dwellings which Robert Allston supplied his bondsmen and women were to Bremer's eyes—as compared to the cabins of most American slaves—"good houses." Allston's slaves may indeed have thought their master mean in his provision of food and clothing. Allston deliberately "only supplied [a slave] what I consider abso-lutely necessary for his health and endurance": any extra food or clothing was to be paid for by the slave with earnings from extra work. As the task system might give a slave respite from enforced labor before sundown, Allston was determined that the slave have "some occupation for his leisure time, and thus diminish the temptations towards robbery and plunder." The regime at Chicora Wood was to some degree based on principles of scientific management (over-seers being impressed by the "system and order which [Allston] enforces on all whom he controls"); and a slave—much more than an early-twentieth-century industrial worker exposed to the implementation of Frederick Taylor's manage-rial theories—might resent "system and order."[49]

Allston's exacting personality doubtless magnified the problem. How Allston sometimes addressed his slaves may be inferred from the peremptory tone he adopted even toward colleagues in the state legislature. Some of them had requested him, late in 1842, to let his name go forward as an opposition gubernatorial candidate against James Hammond. Allston had no use for Ham-mond as a politician, and a year earlier had tried unsuccessfully to organize against him. But by now Allston thought it was too late: proper notice ought to have been given to Hammond himself, and in any case some of Allston's friends had by now committed themselves to Hammond. Allston rejected the over-tures of Hammond's opponents with a priggish self-righteousness that alien-ated some of them. "No, gentlemen," Allston addressed them, "you have given timely notice of this opposition [against Hammond] neither to me, nor to the gentleman whom you would defeat. You have mistaken your man. Self-respect is more prized by me than any office. You have not my consent." While claiming that this language had been respectful to his interlocutors, even Allston ac-knowledged that he had "peremptorily refused to allow his name to be used in connection with the office of Governor, giving offence by his course to many personal and political friends, which was remembered afterwards."[50]

Yet Allston's wife believed him more genial at the state capital than at home. A few weeks before Fredrika Bremer's visit, Adele Allston confided to her journal her anxieties about Robert's probable mood when he got back from Columbia. "Will he return in good spirits?" she asked herself. "I scarce may hope he will. He always returns in a fretful peevish state. Many persons are happier from home." Adele did not keep her discontent to herself, as perforce the slaves must do. "[Last night I] offended Mr. Allston very seriously," she wrote a few days after his return, "by uttering the impression that past things and circumstances made on my mind." Nor did Adele bend easily to her husband's imperious ways. "Last night," she wrote five days later, "I offended Mr. A again by becoming impatient when he refused to tell me at once who he had in his eye for governess to the children." Even Allston's adoring daughter Elizabeth acknowledged that he was "considered a severe, stern man," and that he was capable of "almost cruel obstinacy" in imposing his will upon his wife; and Elizabeth wondered how her mother could stand Allston's stern silences. Adele Allston—Robert crossly complained—believed him "unjust, 'insincere & illiberal' ";[51] and his bondsmen and women are likely to have shared this belief. Certainly Belflowers's indefatigable surveillance of the slaves—and probably also Allston's exacting attention to detail, his punctiliousness in enforcing his rules, and his captious, peremptory spirit—made Allston's regime thoroughly disliked by his chattels. And this was true even though the master felt—as will be seen—that his rule was tempered by extensive grants of favor.

13

Privileged Slaves

There was more to managing his laborers, in Allston's view, than imposing firm discipline, hiring an overseer who had eyes at the back of his head, reducing the turnover among overseers, and giving an overseer "backing" if he threatened to be not quite severe enough. Order having been established, the next step was to temper despotism. This might be achieved by extending certain privileges to all of the slaves; by devising—in the absence of cash wages—alternative incentives for good work; and by trying to win over exceptional slaves by giving them special privileges. All such extensions of privilege offered the master substantial returns, and these returns were not solely economic. The pleasures of exercising dominion—of bestowing favor upon sycophantic menials—were intense. And the philanthropic sense of elevating the condition of deserving underlings was balm to a master's soul.

That a privileged underling did indeed deserve favor must be demonstrated by that slave's conspicuous display of "faithfulness"—by which the masters meant a willingness to place white people's interests above those of other bondsmen and women. Although white memoirists tended in retrospect to reduce all slaves to two simple caricatures—the "faithful servant" and the basely "ungrateful" schemer—no Allston slave fitted either stereotype. Among the seemingly faithful house servants was Stephen Gallant, whose intelligence and daring gleam forth from the dusty Allston records years after his most valorous deed. Stephen's mother-in-law, Mary Grice, at this time aroused Adele Allston's profound suspicions; and Adele then showed her own loyalty to her own class to be far deeper than any gender solidarity she may once have seemed to feel for a favored bondswoman.

Within the world of privileged slaves, male house servants played conspicu-ous roles. The shift which occurred in later years—when a black male domes-tic servant became a rarity—has obscured the route by which significant numbers of African-American men for generations managed to escape rou-tine field labor. Allston's cooks William Baron and Joe Washington, his butler Nelson, his coachman Aleck Parker, and especially his valet Stephen Gallant were among the most memorable of his bondsmen; and that four of these five were accorded a recognized surname suggests something of their distinctive position.

While one honors the intrepidity of a Stephen Gallant and the cunning of a Mary Grice, and while one may wish to believe that most privileged slaves lost little in return for the favors they accepted, the truth may be different. Robert Allston certainly intended that each privilege he granted should serve his own interest; and some slaves surely paid a substantial price for the compromises they inevitably made with the slave regime.[1]

An important source on Robert Allston's practices is the memoir of his life written by his intelligent and able daughter, Elizabeth Allston (Pringle), who tried to explain to herself how her revered father could have been involved in slaveholding, a position she thought she herself could not have abided.[2] Rob-ert Allston's motives, as has been seen, were those of a capitalist entrepre-neur, and the rational principles upon which he sought to govern his labor force must therefore be unpacked from the theory of paternalism which Eliza-beth Pringle many years later—her memoir was published in 1922—wove about them. Here, as with the Manigaults, "system of privilege," not "pater-nalism," is surely the preferable term with which to analyze Allston's conduct.

His views on privilege were doubtless affected by the usage of his aunt Elizabeth Allston Blyth, many of whose slaves he later inherited. Mrs. Blyth thought of herself as something like an aristocratic European woman, a "grande dame": a big fat woman whose feet in "black satin slippers without heels" never touched the earth except when she was stepping, "always as-sisted," into the barouche driven by her enslaved coachman Aleck Parker. She was also attended, in her royal progress through her estate, by the foot-man Frederick, "de boy [who] go behind de carriage, open gate an' ting." Mrs. Blyth was the woman who had persuaded her sister to send Robert Allston to West Point: there Robert must learn the habit of absolute obedi-ence which he could then instill into his bondsmen and women. Mrs. Blyth felt that the arbitrary exercise of regal power was best complemented, however, by an ostentatious display of royal favor. Her custom, when Aleck Parker drove her in the barouche around her Waccamaw River plantation, was to carry in a large silk bag a load of trifling gifts to distribute to her fawning dependents. "As they met darkies on the way," Elizabeth Pringle recounted, with relish at her great-aunt's display of patronage,

> Aunt Blyth would throw out to each one, *without stopping the carriage,* a handkerchief or apron, a paper of needles, or a paper of pins, or a spool of

thread . . . , or a spoon or fork—all things greatly prized, [or] a little pack-
age of tea or coffee or sugar. . . . Naturally, "Miss Betsey Bly" was looked
upon as a great personage, and her path in her daily drives was apt to be
crossed by many foot-passengers, who greeted her with profound courtesies,
and apron skilfully tucked over the arm, so that it could be extended in time
to receive anything.[3]

The rewards to the proprietors from the slavery version of capitalism were
complex, and Mrs. Blyth's exercise of power—this arbitrary dispensation of
favor—was not the smallest of those gratifications.

Abject servility was normally demanded of the slaves, but there was a
moment every year on Robert Allston's plantations when discipline was relaxed and the slaves' usual social alienation from the masters was suspended.
On Christmas Day, before the family prayers and breakfast, the house servants at Chicora Wood—eleven of them, including the gardener and his
assistant—momentarily dropped their usual "attitude of respectful and well-
trained servants" and went around the house to the bedroom door of each
white person, trying to say Merry Christmas before the white person did. "I
ketch you," was the cry of the successful slave, and a gift of two to twelve eggs
would be offered by the slave, whereupon the white people would offer the
slave in return gifts of "fruit and candy and dolls and nuts and handkerchiefs
and stockings and head-handkerchiefs." After breakfast a saturnalia atmosphere reigned, with ordinary field hands dancing on the piazza of the
Allstons' "big house"—except at the masters' mealtimes—until ten at night.
That evening there would be a fireworks display for all the slaves, organized
partly by the Allstons' privileged butler, the mulatto Nelson; and dancing on
the piazza would continue off and on for the next two days. Unlike Manigault,
Allston extended to his slaves three further days of holiday at the New Year,
beyond the three at Christmas. On January 2 and 3 there was a ceremonial
distribution of blankets and of material for the children's clothing: Mary
Grice, a favored slave woman who was cook and chief housekeeper at
Chicora Wood, would measure each child's material after Robert (or his wife,
or their eldest daughter) had read out the child's name to the assembled
multitude. A cow and several hogs were killed for the Christmas feast, and
there were for each slave "extra rations of sugar, coffee, molasses, and
flour."[4]

Although the motives of Elizabeth Pringle's generation were patent when
they conjured up, after the war, the tableau of faithful "darkies" thronging
gratefully around the "big house," receiving and enjoying the arbitrary largesse of their masters, one must not doubt the existence of this carefully
calculated extension of Yuletide privilege. The testimony of former slaves
confirms the impact of annual festivals upon the dull, impoverished, routinized lives of the bondsmen and women. Some miles inland from Chicora
Wood, on South Carolina's Congaree River, a black man named Charles
Ball had been enslaved early in the nineteenth century, and after escaping he
lived to tell his tale. On Ball's plantation the 260 slaves were annually

treated to a midsummer jamboree on the Sunday after the "laying by" of the cotton and corn—that is, at the moment the last hoeing was completed and the crop could be left to mature for a month before the harvest began. Ball was dispatched to the savanna to drive back a cow for the slaughter, and a big beef soup was served up on Saturday night. Peaches were distributed, and at the Sunday feast Ball gorged himself on a pound of beef—no stinting this day!—a small piece of bacon, and two pounds, he claimed, of cornmeal pudding. This feast fired the imagination of slaves accustomed to dull fare, week in and week out; and it filled their stomachs, too, after the singing and dancing that had lasted all of Saturday night until daybreak. Ball was candid about the rigors and severities of the slaves' daily lives; but this feast was received by the bondsmen and women with gratitude, he attested, and led temporarily to happiness, "universal hilarity and contentment."[5]

A similar report came from Louisiana, where from 1841 to 1853 a free Northern black named Solomon Northup was illegally enslaved. Northup's bitterness at his experiences was not edited out by his white amanuensis (as Ball's had been), and Northup covertly challenged Harriet Beecher Stowe—to whom his book was dedicated in 1853. "They are deceived," Northup declared in his most impassioned outburst,

> who imagine that [a whipped slave] arises from his knees, with back lacerated and bleeding, cherishing only a spirit of meekness and forgiveness [like Uncle Tom after Legree's whipping]. A day may come—it *will* come, if his prayer is heard—a terrible day of vengeance, when the master in his turn will cry in vain for mercy.

Yet Northup, like Ball, acknowledged the pacifying influence of the masters' extending to all the slaves the privilege of a grand annual blowout. Northup's three-day Christmas holiday was "the only time," he reported, "to which [the slaves] look forward with any interest or pleasure"; and even the slave woman Patsey whose spirits had been most thoroughly crushed—by a long, savage, and blatantly unjust whipping—could anticipate this moment. Some four hundred slaves from neighboring plantations were permitted to assemble for the Christmas supper, when the usual fare of corn and fatty "bacon" was banned. The long tables groaned instead under the weight of roast "chickens, ducks, turkeys, pigs, and not unfrequently [meat from] the entire body of a wild ox." There was also the rare treat of wheaten flour for the biscuits, and often peach or other fruit preserves with tarts and pies. The black men were seated on one side of the table and the women on the other: "Unalloyed and exulting happiness lights up the dark faces of them all." The dancing continued until "broad daylight" the next morning, with an ace woman dancer testing the stamina of her rival suitors; and after the violin ceased the dancing carried on, to the sounds of song, tapping feet, clapping, and hands striking knees. After Christmas the masters extended to slaves the general privilege of passes for traveling a limited distance from the home plantation. The slaves "may be seen at these times," Northup recalled, "hurrying in all directions, as happy looking mortals as can be found on the face of the earth."[6]

If Allston's Christmas fireworks were simply an elaborate version of a festival common wherever there were large, profitable plantations in the South, his 1859 experiment of allowing all his slaves to keep pigs was a rarer extension of privilege. Manigault let his bondsmen and women at Gowrie keep chickens but not pigs, and he tried to protect the former privilege from the overseer's incursions because he knew he allowed his slaves "no [other] perquisites." At Butler Island the favor of keeping pigs had been withdrawn, and Frances Kemble's companion Jack importuned her for a renewal of the privilege. Allston appears to have let his slaves keep chickens; some of them had dogs; and a handful of especially privileged slaves were allowed to keep a pig or even a cow. The slaves thereupon played an active role in converting pig owning from a special privilege, reserved for the few, to a general privilege extended to all. Allston had one hundred of his own swine; but during the years 1857 and 1858—when he was frequently away performing his gubernatorial duties—the slaves seem somehow to have appropriated many of these pigs. Putting a good face on this development, Allston wrote in 1859, "In as much as during my absence of two years, my negroes have taken possession of my stock of Hogs, the best breed in the [neighboring] country, and I have few to kill, I will try the experiment of letting them raise for me." Allston adapted to pig farming an incentive system comparable to those he had already devised elsewhere on the plantation. In return for "the privilege to keep one hog," presumed to be a sow, each head of family was required to supply Allston with two yearlings each autumn for him to buy. The slave had a motive to produce two hefty yearlings, for Allston paid for both according to the weight of the *smaller* of the two. All the other yearlings were the slave's own to consume, or (with the overseer's written permission) to sell. Unauthorized sale would lead to "chastisement for disobedience" and withdrawal of the privilege.[7]

The fine-tuning of his pig experiment proceeded from Allston's long experience at devising other incentives to motivate his unpaid labor force. The slave children learned early how things worked, because their scrubbing their faces, donning their best clothes, and sitting through Mrs. Allston's afternoon Sunday school culminated in their receiving a piece of cake baked especially for the occasion. The children were numerous, the cake huge, and the demeanor of the cook imposing: "After the lesson," Elizabeth Allston Pringle fondly recalled,

> a big cake was brought in a wheelbarrow by one of the house-boys, convoyed by Maum Mary [Grice, the cook and housekeeper who also superintended the New Year's distribution of cloth for the children] who cut it with much ceremony, and each went up to the barrow, dropped a courtesy and received a slice, then passed to my mother with another courtesy, filed out and scampered happily home as soon as safe from Maum Mary's paralyzing eye.

The quality of the cake was good, for the white children valued the pieces which Mary Grice was careful to save for them.[8]

When the slave children grew up, they found Allston had organized a network of incentives for good work. Every year he awarded prizes to the best plowman, the best sower, and the best harvest hand. For women the prize might be forks, spoons, or a calico frock, while men were rewarded with a good knife or some comparable item. And during the war, when the Northern blockade and the shortage of white supervisors forced Allston to depend on eight-man slave crews to pole boatloads of his rice up the Black River to the nearest railway junction, he offered a reward to the most successful crew.[9]

He also organized a barter system, whereby slaves could exchange eggs laid by their chickens, or allowance they did not wish to consume—tobacco, molasses, or grist—in return for luxuries like sugar, lard, potatoes, and grits. During the week (usually on Sunday, or on Saturday evening) most families at Nightingale Hall would engage in one of these tiny transactions. Occasionally cash would change hands; the overseer, acting on Allston's behalf, might pay thirteen cents for a (baker's?) dozen of eggs, or twenty-five cents for a hand-made basket. Eighty-two such baskets were sold by the slaves during one year: thus if there were thirty-three families, each family earned on average sixty-two cents per year by basket making—the equivalent of sixty-two eggs per year, a minuscule amelioration of the poverty of a six-person family. (And the slaves may have sold other baskets at Georgetown, six miles downstream from Nightingale Hall.) Although most cash purchases from the overseer were for only five or ten cents, a handful of slaves did rather better. Engineer Prince bought on credit molasses, soap, meat, and a handkerchief, while Richard bought a hog for four dollars, in return for delivering chickens, eggs, peas, and potatoes. And very occasionally a slave might lash out on the purchase of an "oven."[10]

As illness—and also the pretense of illness—was a major problem on every rice plantation (and as there was no way to dock the wages of a malingering slave, since wages were not paid), Allston devised a scheme to benefit those workers who finished a year without reporting ill. About 70 percent of his workers in 1859 lost working time because of illness, each ill worker averaging nearly eleven days off; but each of the eighty-two workers with perfect attendance was granted a special food ration. The half hands—young teenagers, or old or partially disabled workers—received a half bushel of "small rice" at the end of the year; the full hands one bushel; and each worker whose attendance had been perfect for three successive years gained one and a quarter bushels.[11] This "small rice"—so small that it fell through the sieves at the pounding mill—was somewhat less valuable commercially than rice of the normal size, and the incentive scheme probably cost Allston about $125 a year—about one-third of 1 percent of his net annual revenues. The reward to each favored slave was not munificent, its cash value per full hand being probably less than two dollars. Allston could earn that sum for himself from one day's rental of a skilled carpenter and his apprentice. A slave could gain a much larger sum—from seven to eleven dollars[12]—for selling a good-sized hog to Allston; and these figures help explain the slaves' strong desire for the pig-raising privilege. Yet slaves liked eating small rice better than their usual ration of corn, and the fact that Allston regarded a bushel of small rice as a substantial incentive was a measure of the slaves' poverty.

More significant than the bonuses open to all of his slaves were the special privileges Allston granted to selected bondsmen and women—artisans, trunk minders, drivers, and especially house servants. He seems to have divided a bonus for a successful crop between the trunk minder and the driver: thus, when the Nightingale Hall planting in 1858 was hurt (probably by "*too deep a flow in the 'sprout,'* "), Allston wrote, "I fear Trim [no doubt the trunk minder responsible for regulating the depth of water on the flooded fields] has forfeited his half." Toward the end of the Civil War a handful of privileged slaves, such as the drivers and the chief plowman, were the ones for whom the overseer made a special effort to obtain shoes. And the privilege of escaping the hard, boring, unhealthy routine of field labor in the wet fields was much valued. Ancrum, for example, who began life waiting on the overseer, working in the fields, and plowing, boasted that later Allston "make me captain of a gang in harvest, an' I was a regular arrand man, I nebber wuck in de field no mo'." Ancrum was charged with transporting rice from the Pee Dee to the pounding mill on the Waccamaw River; during the war he was made responsible for a gang of twenty-two Allston slaves deputed to work on the Confederate fortification of Charleston; and later he commanded one of the boats carrying rice up the Black River to the railway junction.[13]

Ancrum's duties illustrated one of Allston's fundamental practices: substantial managerial powers were deputed to certain slaves. In doing this, Allston merely extended a low-country custom born of the scarcity of white supervisors, especially during the long malarial summer. Even where there was a resident overseer, as at Butler Island, some five hundred slaves there were left under the sole direction of a slave—headman Frank—from dusk until after daybreak every day during the summer, when the white overseer retreated to his pineland summer house away from the mosquitoes. From 1837 through 1848 Charles Manigault usually depended, before the harvest, on a nonresident part-time overseer, and left his enslaved drivers to run the plantation with a minimum of white supervision.

When Allston was at West Point, his mother had sometimes deputed even more authority to her driver than the Butlers did to headman Frank. Thus in 1819, when Charlotte Allston's son Joseph attained his majority, she had a gang of only twenty-eight slaves at Chicora Wood, because most of its potential rice land was still uncleared. That summer, in Joseph's youthful ardor to develop his newly inherited Waverly plantation on the Waccamaw River, he stayed near his own plantation all "summer," and his mother had him visit Chicora Wood (on the Pee Dee) from time to time to see that the slaves, under their driver Scotland, were cultivating her rice satisfactorily. But Joseph got such a bad case of malaria in 1819 that Charlotte was unwilling to repeat the experiment the next year. Joseph "was so ill last fall," she wrote Robert in May 1820, that "if he stays [again near Waverly and Chicora Wood] he will expose himself, and to be so sick again this Fall would undermine his constitution very much if [indeed] he got over it." She therefore made an arrangement with the overseer of a plantation several miles down the Pee Dee. The overseer was to ride up to Chicora Wood two or three times a week to see how Scotland and his gang were getting on, and the overseer would be paid one dollar for every barrel more than one hundred that her slaves raised. Thus, in large measure Charlotte Allston deputed the raising and harvesting of her crop to the skill and discipline of her driver Scotland. Although she seems to have been dissatisfied with Scotland's management, and replaced him in 1821 by another slave as driver, she does not appear to have thought it worth the money to try to hire a resident full-time overseer for her relatively small gang of slaves.[14]

Robert Allston himself preferred to stay near Chicora Wood every summer, so that he could make frequent trips of inspection to the plantation. No doubt his remarkable commercial success arose from his own assiduous attention to detail. But this did not prevent him from entrusting slaves with greater authority than some of his neighbors could approve. A striking case occurred in 1838, when Robert was managing Waverly plantation and its pounding mill, after his brother Joseph's premature death. Robert insisted that, after rice had been pounded at Waverly, it must be carried the sixty miles by sea to the Charleston market on a local sailing ship, the *Waccamaw,* under Captain Tobey and an otherwise wholly slave crew. Captain Tobey, fearing malaria, habitually stayed at North Island at the entrance to Winyah Bay, and sent the vessel the last dozen miles up the river under wholly slave management. This was perfectly agreeable to Allston, even though there was no one who could give a legal receipt for the rice put on board. Allston trusted Captain Tobey's slaves, but one of Allston's neighbors did not. This was the Reverend Hugh Fraser (who seems to have neglected his Episcopalian vocation—once he had married an heiress—because there was more money to be made as a rice planter). Having sent his rice to Waverly to be pounded, Fraser complained about Allston's willingness to trust the ship's slave foreman. "The Sch[oo]n[er] Wacamaw is atending the Mill," Allston's overseer informed him in August 1838,

> and there is no white man in her when she comes up to the mill. Capt Tobey stays at the Island. [Your factor] has wrote to me to ship by her although I wrote to him that Capt T[obey] did not come up in the vesel and no one to give a receipt for the Rice put on board. He wrote to me that you told him to write me that you had Rather the Mill stop than for me to ship any Rice by any other vesel than the one he suggested. Mr. H. Frasier . . . is vext because I told him that the Mill arangements was that the vesel that atended [*sic*] the Mill was to carry all the Rice that she pounded.

Allston—whom Adele Petigru said she had married because he was "as obstinate as the devil"—was willing to risk losing one of the mill's good customers rather than give up his reliance on this ship, under slaves' direction.[15]

The Civil War—with its drain on Southern white manpower and its Northern raids upon the Carolina coast—increased Allston's willingness to depute

substantial authority to certain trusted slaves. The wartime salt shortage impelled him to set up a saltworks on Waccamaw Neck, close to the ocean's
supply of salt water, and this enterprise operated (apparently to his own
substantial profit) under black supervision. When the Northern blockade
forced planters to ship their rice inland up the Black River, a warehouse had
to be built at the junction with the railway, and Allston put his slave blacksmith, Sam Maham, in charge. Maham was permitted to travel about
unsupervised—once appearing unannounced, for example, at Charleston to
separate out thirty-seven damaged bags from the others and to take them
back to the warehouse for repair. Allston's son Charles testified that Maham
was a "very intelligent negro" who managed the storage of rice and its transfer
to the railway without complaint. As early as 1862 Allston was entrusting to
all-slave crews the shipment of rice to the interior, and when he decided in
1863 to send inland a carload of furniture from his Charleston house (whose
roof was subsequently damaged in the Northern bombardment), his butler
Nelson—the Christmas fireworks man—was in charge. In the summer of 1864
(after Allston's death) the 119 slaves of his son Benjamin carried on rice
production at Guendalos plantation under their driver Jacob, with a minimum
of white supervision. Benjamin, a colonel in the Confederate cavalry, was
away at war, and the Allstons' Nightingale Hall overseer (who was supposed
occasionally to travel several miles to overlook Guendalos) does not appear to
have made the trip often. "You Rote to mee that you would like mee to git
some whit[e] Pirson at [Guendalos]", the Nightingale Hall overseer reported
at the end of August. "I have Bin trying [but so far unsuccessfully] to get some
one to goe thare since June." In 1863, after the coast became insecure, about
100 of Robert Allston's slaves were sent far up the Pee Dee River to a North
Carolina farm under a white supervisor whom the Allstons did not wholly
trust. Here again considerable authority was deputed to a couple of black
drivers, who intervened sometimes to moderate the exactions of the white
overseer.[16]

It is important, however, not to exaggerate how far Allston deputed authority to slaves. He did not have a slave woman in charge of raising his
children, as many planters did; instead he employed for fifteen years an
Irishwoman, Mary O'Shea, to perform this function, and the slave nurses
worked under her direction. He even employed a white gardener with authority over the chief slave gardener, Moses Baron. He himself personally examined the growth of the rice in the flooded fields, accompanied by the trunk
minder Jacob (who later became the driver at Guendalos), and he knew that
assertion of an independent point of view was not in Jacob's character. "The
trunk minder . . . is full of information if you will take pains to develop it," he
advised his son Benjamin in 1858. But "if you give him too much of leading
questions, he will be apt to mislead you."[17] (This trait—deeply bred into
many bondsmen and women—survived into the 1930s, when leading questions from WPA interviewers sometimes elicited misleading information from
very old blacks about their experiences as slaves seventy-five years earlier.)

Although Allston was effusive in his praise of his head carpenter, Thomas, over whose grave in 1858 he erected a headstone, he never seems to have been quite so wholehearted in his praise of any driver. He confronted a dilemma: the enterprise and responsibility he felt an ideal driver should possess were incompatible with the tractability which he demanded as the indispensable quality in his subalterns. In the summer of 1860 Allston had rented out a gang of his slaves to help build a section of the Northeast Rail Road (some miles inland from the Pee Dee); and he was so keen for them to finish the job—so that they could return home in time for the harvest—that he tried to get their driver Tommy to make them work on Sundays. Tommy disobeyed his instructions on the first Sunday, and when he tried to impel the slaves to work on a later Sunday, they refused. Allston's vexation led him to contrast the qualities of Tommy with those of another driver, neither of whom seemed fully satisfactory. In disobeying his order on the first Sunday, Tommy, Allston complained,

> has given me reason to think less of his qualification as a Driver than I was disposed to.
>   The first element in the composit[i]on of one in authority is to obey orders [shades of Allston's West Point training!] and conform to instructions notwithstanding the privations necessary. Daniel [the Nightingale Hall driver] possesses that element and some few others, but he lacks energy, ready intelligence and satisfactory accountability which the other has.

Docility—which Allston demanded—destroyed in a driver like Daniel the independence of spirit that a person in authority needed.[18] The Manigaults had found the same thing: they were obliged to choose their drivers either from "determined" slaves like Robert and George (both of whom received at one time or another severe punishment for recalcitrance) or from "cunning" though obedient ones like Charles, who may have lacked the personal force to make an excellent driver. Seeking incompatible traits in his drivers, Allston— while better than many planters at delegating substantial power to a slave— could seldom unreservedly back a driver in a position of great authority. He was more likely to play off an overseer against a driver than to commit himself uncompromisingly to the one or the other.

The limits within which Allston confined his delegation of authority did not, however, hold him back from giving many of his slaves considerable vocational training. The essence of slavery may be powerlessness, but a slave with a skill has at least the potential for a certain command over his environment; and Allston attenuated powerlessness in this way. There were always several apprentice carpenters under the skilled workers at the carpenter shop, and several apprentice blacksmiths at the smithy. The chief housekeeper taught the slave girls to sew, knit, and spin, and some were also taught to weave. A slave boy like James (the first slave Robert Allston inherited, when Robert was nine) might be sent to Charleston to be apprenticed to a shoemaker, while the slave girl Mary was also dispatched to Charleston for training as a house servant: this may have been Mary Grice, who later became the Allstons' cook, and baked the cakes that rewarded the slave children for attending Sunday school.[19] Some twenty years after James had been sent to Charleston for his apprenticeship, a slave boy named Stephen Gallant—probably James's son—was sent to Charleston to be trained as a house servant. Stephen became Allston's trusted valet and "was in constant attendance [on Robert] and very efficient" during the master's last illness; and Stephen was one of the two slaves selected to lay out Robert's body after his death. Sam Gallant, apparently a much younger brother of Stephen's, was sent to a Mr. Dauer in Charleston for violin lessons, and he "played the violin very well" according to Allston's son Charles. The violin experiment was so successful that Robert Allston sent three other slave boys to Mr. Dauer for lessons, and he reported afterward with gratification, "They practice in the piazza every morning about breakfast time."[20]

To keep a substantial number of house servants as a conspicuous symbol of one's rank was perfectly consonant with a capitalist mentality. Charles Henry Fisher, for example—Pennsylvania's leading private banker in the 1850s, and heavily involved in financing capitalist enterprises like the Reading Railroad—employed no fewer than forty house servants at his elegant Philadelphia mansion. When Allston married in 1832, he had eleven house servants at Chicora Wood, including the gardener Moses Baron and a yard boy. Robert's bride, fresh from Charleston, would have liked to get rid of about five of them, for she felt it a burden to be obliged to direct the labors of such a large staff. The obstinate Robert overruled her. No doubt his principal motive was to maintain an establishment worthy of the Allstons' traditional status, and consonant with the renewed prosperity he was already beginning to experience. Yet in pursuing his own interest he was also protecting the special privileges of his domestic slaves, some of whom—unlike those at Gowrie—were a class rather distinct from the field hands. Many of Allston's house servants were unused to field labor, and they would have regarded as a severe deprivation their being translated from their "enjoyment of privileges and ease and comfort"[21] in the house to the exhausting, dull, unhealthy labor of the rice swamps. Those house servants who had always spent summers at Pawleys Island or Charleston were less likely than the other slaves to have acquired resistance against malaria, and their masters therefore shared with them an interest in keeping them away from the plantation during that season. In July 1858, for example (when Benjamin Allston and his parents were all going away from Carolina), Adele Allston favored putting Benjamin's house servant Margaret with someone in Charleston, rather than sending her to the Pee Dee. Adele's language suggested that financial considerations weighed more heavily with her than a concern for Margaret's welfare. "I do not think it well to send her to the plantation," Adele advised Benjamin: "It would be best to put her with a good washer, or seamstress here [in Charleston]. She might pay some wages I think. On the plantation she would have fever as she had last year, and do nothing."[22]

There were, however, gradations among the house slaves, and Robert Allston thought nothing of sending a relatively menial servant into the swamp. "Hagar and [a second house slave] must go in harvest," he directed coldly, at the same moment Margaret was being spared by Mrs. Allston. A very highly trained lady's maid like Lavinia—whom Adele Allston as a bride had brought with her from Charleston in 1832—was in a different class from Hagar. Among Lavinia's accomplishments, she was a first-class seamstress. "Lavinia's work is very well done," Adele assured Benjamin. "Beg her to go on as fast as she can—and give her a pound of sugar and a half pound of coffee occasionally." To Adele it would have been inconceivable to send such a slave into the rice fields, and such was Lavinia's privileged position that her mistress even tolerated the slave woman's expressing her terrible temper.[23]

Because none of Allston's domestic servants in 1832 had been so highly trained as Lavinia—even though some of them had also had Charleston instruction—Allston subsequently took trouble to improve the training and standard of his own retinue. The mulatto butler Nelson, for example, "was placed with Lee in Charleston [during the late 1840s] to learn to wait." After Nelson's return in 1850 he was useful in instilling into the Allston children a proper sense of their own place in the world. These children—alongside a relatively stringent academic routine, and along with learning to be fearless horse riders (both boys and girls)—must in Allston's view learn to be little gentlemen and ladies. When they were doing their schoolwork, with their English governess, in the two-room schoolhouse he built for them three hundred yards away from his summer house at Pawleys Island, they were accustomed to enjoy at their lunchtime "tea and bread-and-butter, handed by Nelson on the big silver waiter, and wine, handed by the footman on a smaller silver waiter, and a great deal of talk."[24]

When privileged slaves were thus allowed to natter with the white children, the slaves' usual social alienation from the master class was diminished. Allston's valet Stephen Gallant had a son named Brutus, who was an excellent horseman; and as a youth he, too, was granted the privilege of a certain intimacy with Allston's own son Charles. "Charley went to ride every morning [at Pawleys Island] with a negro boy a few years older than himself, to see that he was not too rash. [This youth, Brutus,] understood all about horses and was a good rider, teaching Charley a great deal, running races, and jumping ditches." And if a female slave were present when a white woman experienced a major emotional crisis, the intimacy between the two would become interwoven as a consoling element into the white woman's otherwise searing recollection of the event. When Sherman's army (after the destruction of Columbia early in 1865) reached the Allstons' inland refuge, at Society Hill ninety miles northeast of Columbia, the twenty-year-old Elizabeth Allston was distraught. For nearly four years she had been hearing of the deaths in battle, one after another, of cherished friends and relations; her father, Robert Allston, had recently died; and her two brothers were both away in the army. Fearing the worst as the Yankees approached, she sat up late at night with her elder sister, Adele, and with the old slave woman Phoebe, widow of the esteemed head carpenter, Thomas. "Twelve o'clock [midnight], and we still sit whispering over the fire," Elizabeth inscribed in her journal, "Phoebe on the floor nodding at the fire, Dell with her feet extended trying to rest and

I on a stool scribbling to while away the time until dawn. . . . A little after nine [the next morning] Phoebe ran in saying she heard *them* [the Yankees] coming." Elizabeth was terrified as the soldiers arrived, and although no physical assault ensued, a Union captain—proffered food on the piazza by the genteel young Allston women—boasted that he had often killed Confederate prisoners. He roused the defiant Elizabeth to a fever of hatred. The Southern white people, she exclaimed to her Yankee taunter, were fighting for their "Existence"—by which she meant the preservation of their very lives from domination by black "savages." Yet a key element in Elizabeth's memory of this traumatic encounter was the comforting presence of the "faithful" black Phoebe, who had seemed to the young white mistress to share her own piercing anxieties.[25]

The relative intimacy of house servants with the whites might not preclude malice. In 1852 Hagar, the fifteen-year-old daughter of one of the Pawleys Island seamstresses, was on good terms with Allston's seven-year-old daughter, Elizabeth; and when Allston's baby daughter died that year, Hagar thought it would be fun to creep through a window, with Elizabeth, into the room where the baby's corpse was still lying. Hagar encouraged Elizabeth to kiss the cold corpse, and Elizabeth's fright and terror at this horrific experience required much assuaging by her father. Nelson, too, probably had a good laugh with his fellow slaves two years later, after an episode on the river. He and another slave were rowing a small boat, with Robert Allston steering at the back, while Mrs. Allston, as a passenger, surveyed a field of ripe rice. "We came up to the bank broadside of the boat," Adele later recounted to her son, with some understatement;

> the tide was high, and the boat stood nicely for us to land. Papa call'd to Nelson to put out his oar to steady the boat, which he did, but just as I was in the act of stepping on the bank Nelson removed his oar and the boat swung round, [I fell into the river,] the water was deep, I was wet up to my waist, and a good deal agitated.

Although the Allstons contrasted Nelson's usual steadiness with the "folly and levity" of the older valet Stephen Gallant, Nelson after the river episode was doubtless as mirthful—in private—as Stephen might ever have been.[26]

The house servants' ambivalence toward their white masters did not lessen their awareness of their privileged position. What field hand could have been situated to tell so good a story to her peers as Hagar or Nelson could? And the story strengthened the servants' sense that, in associating closely with the masters, they raised themselves above the degradation common to the ordinary slaves. The laundress Milly (who also had the privilege of supplying the Allstons with butter, eggs, and chickens) was probably the sister of James Gallant, Allston's former valet; thus she was the aunt of both Stephen Gallant—his later valet—and of Sam Gallant the violinist. Milly, according to Adele Allston, "held herself and her family as vastly superior to the ordinary run of negroes, the aristocracy of the race."[27] No doubt it suited Adele to emphasize class distinctions among the slaves, for this seemed to her to help legitimize the caste differences imposed by whites upon the blacks. Yet class distinctions among the Allston slaves undoubtedly existed. Stephen Gallant, Allston's small, very black valet, modeled his demeanor upon that of his imposing, blond, blue-eyed master, and when Stephen returned from accompanying Governor Allston to Columbia, the other slaves satirically called him the "little guv'ner."

Stephen's privileges were substantial. He had been trained in Charleston and always traveled with Allston to Columbia—a tremendous widening of his world compared with that of the Pee Dee–bound field hand. The temper tantrums of Stephen's wife, Lizzie—even though exceedingly irritating to Adele Allston—were indulged by the mistress as they never would have been if Lizzie had been a field hand; and Lizzie retained her privileged exemption from field labor. "Stephen's wife Lizzie is getting worse and worse," Adele lamented in 1857:

> I do not know what is to be done with her; if some regular employment cannot be found *suitable to her* I think she will lose her senses from these tempers. I am very sure she *ought to leave this yard* where her example is unfavourable. If she was in a house next to old Thomas [the esteemed head carpenter] perhaps he would acquire some influence over her.

Lizzie (and Stephen, when he was not in Columbia or Charleston) evidently lived apart from the field hands, and near the "big house." Allston's overseer believed Lizzie was treated far too leniently and later cited her bad example, warning that if the wife of the new male cook "is favored to[o] much she will become another Lizzie." Such was the trust Allston extended to the privileged Stephen Gallant that, in 1860, he commissioned him to bring two horses from Lexington, Virginia, to Chicora Wood. Had Stephen elected to go northward from Lexington instead of returning to Lizzie and their children, he would have had some ten days' head start before the Allstons became suspicious. The privileges of a trusted slave extended further than status distinction.[28]

A favored slave, though subject like every other one to the possibility of sudden sale, might nevertheless be consulted about his or her future owner and job. For example, when Adele Allston's sister—who ran an unprofitable farm in western South Carolina—contemplated selling a valuable and trusted twenty-five-year-old house servant, she did at least discuss the matter with him (though she dishonored him by pretending he was not an adult). "I ask'd the boy if he is willing to be sold to you as coachman," she informed Adele; "he said quite willing." Similarly, in 1864 the Allstons' overseer asked a favored slave how she would feel about making the long journey to Adele's inland wartime refuge: Hannah, the overseer reported, "Says she is willing to go up to Society Hill & Spin." When Allston sent Ancrum to supervise a gang of twenty-two Allston slaves working on the Charleston fortification during the Civil War, he granted Ancrum's request that he be allowed to stay home one extra day before departure, so that he could finish hoeing his own corn. And about a year later, when Ancrum was sent to North Carolina to help supervise the hundred Allston bondsmen and women at Allston's slave refuge there, Ancrum secured permission to take with him his cow and calf to ensure their safety. The coachman Aleck Parker, who—after driving Elizabeth Blyth's barouche for years—had been bequeathed to Robert Allston, received in his privileged position special clothes and special food: for example, "sugar and coffee and tea and all the meat he wanted."[29]

Behind this network of privilege lay an attitude toward the privileged slaves less contemptuous than toward the ordinary slaves. When Allston used a switch on his three-year-old daughter, Elizabeth, because she had lied about stealing a peach (one of the only two times he ever punished her with this severity), he was protecting a house servant from being unjustly accused of the theft. Another sign of regard for a privileged slave appeared in 1861 when Daniel, the obedient driver at Nightingale Hall, was singled out for a special mark of favor. The Episcopal bishop, on a rare visit to the Pee Dee, preached at the local church, then "spoke a short while to the [Allston] people," and—no doubt in full regalia—confirmed Daniel before the assembled slaves: a distinction designed to make Daniel feel he was a cut above the others. And when Maum Phoebe—the chief nurse in the Allston slave children's house, the wife of their head carpenter, Thomas, and later Elizabeth's confidante when Sherman's army reached Society Hill—made gifts of eggs, potatoes, and figs to the Allston children, she knew she was buying from them an esteem such as they would seldom accord a field hand.[30]

Her very title, "Maum," bespoke her status difference from the field hands, as did the parallel titles the Allstons awarded other privileged slaves— they sometimes called her "Aunty" Phoebe, and one of the slave settlements became "Aunty Phibby Hill," while her husband was "Daddy" Thomas and the coachman was "Daddy" Aleck. South Carolina's was a society with strict gradations, and no black was ever, of course, "Mr."—that was a term reserved for white men, however poor they might be. The terms "Maum" and "Daddy" were not really terms of honor, as the white people pretended they were; but at least they mitigated the dishonor of slavery, as even the term "nigger" might do. To a modern ear it seems shocking that slaves referred to themselves as "niggers," but to them the term was less dishonorable than "slave," a word they almost never used about themselves. We may also cringe to hear a former slave like Ancrum denominating a fellow slave "Daddy," for we know that this term was part of the cotton wool which the masters tried— under the guise of respect—to wrap around those privileged slaves whom they hoped they had made innocuous by co-opting them into the system.[31] Yet from the slaves' point of view, a word like "Maum" or "Daddy," while not really a term of respect, was at least less dishonorable than the name alone without a family name. One of the central elements in slavery—along with powerlessness and social alienation—was dishonor; and one of the main elements in Allston's system of privileges was (for selected bondsmen and women) a diminution of this dishonor.[32]

In return for these privileges the Allstons reckoned to exact for themselves a number of rewards. Mere deference was not one of these, because all slaves were expected to be deferential: for example, slaves "begged" a favor—they did not "request" or even "ask" for it. Wallis, who had been so ill that the overseer sent for a doctor, "Begs that you will let his son come and see him if you soe Pleas." Lavinia, the highly trained lady's maid, "Begs Verry hard" that her daughter Anna not be sent to work with Bob at the Allstons' provision farm. Adele Allston even satirized the slaves' use of this word. All of Benjamin's slaves at Guendalos, she wrote to him in mid-1864, "begged to know when you would come home. . . . I begged them to let you find a good crop [when you return]."[33]

The boatmen who rowed the Allstons most of the way on their annual migration to the beach were in a good position to help the masters taste the gratifications of dominion which—along with monetary profit—were among the prime glories (to them) of slaveholding. The boatmen, ingratiating themselves for these few hours as house servants did constantly, sang "Roll, Jordan, Roll" and "Canaan's Happy Shore" (for the Allstons' house on Pawleys Island was named "Canaan"). "There is nothing like the rhythm and swing of those boat-songs," Elizabeth Allston Pringle exclaimed sixty years later. The whole Allston family was rowed each May by six singing boatmen "through Squirrel Creek, with vines tangled above them and water-lilies and flags and wild roses and scarlet lobelia all along the banks." The alligators in coves, turtles on floating logs, and snakes basking in the sun lent a frisson to the excursion: the trip in the rowboat, with the enslaved boatmen enacting their traditional role, was to Adele Allston "the most delightful revelation and sensation of her life almost."[34]

Yet the privileged slaves offered their masters something even more valuable—the sense that they were uplifting, not exploiting, their dependents. So long as the Allstons focused their attention on a dozen house servants and a handful of other privileged slaves, and ignored the other six hundred bondsmen and women, there was enough validity in this theory to make it credible to them. Surrounded as they were by the sea of lying, thievery, and deceit created by slavery itself, the Allstons sought hard for some slaves whom they could trust. Aunt Blyth claimed she had elevated her slaves "far above the average in every way," and she believed there were, by the time of her death in 1840, many trustworthy ones. It was a delicate matter to foster trust across the chasm of caste: "You must . . . seem to trust absolutely," she advised Adele Allston; "one trace of suspicion will kill it." Robert Allston set a high standard for honesty and truth among his house servants, and felt there was no sense in training an untruthful child to be a gentleman's body servant. He knew that truth was a rare quality among slaves. "There is not one of your boys or girls either but will lie," he admonished his son Benjamin, "and I would not take the pains or lose the time to train one who can not be depended on for the truth. I have assign'd to your service either Page (Pirce) or his brother Thomas as you shall choose, boys with both of whom it is worth while to take pains, truthful and honest, but high temper'd." Among the house servants as among the drivers—Allston had discovered—one often had to tolerate a certain independence of spirit if one wanted a subaltern worth putting into a position of responsibility.[35]

Having selected for privilege a few slaves whom he felt he could trust, Allston expected them to be "faithful" to him. His ideal was expressed on the headstone he erected at the grave of his head carpenter in 1858:

In
Memory of
My Servant Thomas
Carpenter,
Honest and true
He died as for 40 years
He had lived
My faithful friend

Thomas's wife, Phoebe—a "faithful" dependent like her husband—was expected as head of the children's house to report to the Allstons the slave mothers who did not keep their offspring in clean underwear. To another "faithful" slave, Abraham, Allston's son Charles turned late in 1864 to clear George, the head of the saltworks, from the suspicion that the latter planned to flee. Besides reporting on other bondsmen and women, privileged slaves were also supposed to influence the mass of slaves in the directions the masters approved.[36] This was a system of "divide and conquer": the favored slaves were expected to pay for their privileges by undermining the unity slaves might otherwise have shown vis-à-vis their masters.

Disunity doubtless existed. The rumors that George the salt maker was about to flee may well have been circulated by other slaves jealous of his privileges. And although some old ex-slaves optimistically testified to black WPA interviewers in 1937 that the slaves' thievery was directed only at the masters' property—not at possessions of other slaves—this was not the experience of the Allston bondsmen and women. Theft was directed against slaves among them who had managed to accumulate a bit of property—usually privileged slaves. Thus young Moses Baron, a house servant who had been rented to an acquaintance of the Allstons in Charleston, had two winter coats and his brother's hat stolen there, probably by another slave. In 1864 "Hannah lost 4 of her yong turkeys on chismas [Christmas] Eave Knigth," the overseer reported. "Some Pirson Broke open the house on the Back Part and taken them." Two weeks later "some pirson Kild the sow from [Minda's] pigs." Joe Washington—the driver of some Allston slaves rented in 1864 to labor at a Confederate navy yard up the Pee Dee—requested that his wife not be moved away from the plantation because "she is attending to what little property he has at home and if she is brought away it will all be stolen."[37]

The extent to which Allston's system of privilege secured for his family "faithfulness" from the favored bondsmen and women, and disunity within the slave community, came to a remarkable test in July 1864. The central figure was Allston's trusted valet, Stephen Gallant, who, as has been seen, was a member of one of the most privileged slave families at Chicora Wood. His father had for years been Allston's valet; his aunt Milly was the Allstons' laundress and butter maker; while his brother, Sam Gallant—a violinist who served Allston's son Charles as valet during the Civil War—was entrusted by Charles with getting two horses back from Virginia to South Carolina just before the Confederate surrender in 1865. Stephen's son Brutus had been Charles Allston's riding mentor at Pawleys Island. Stephen married the daughter of Mary Grice, the cook who, with intimidating demeanor, distributed cake after Sunday school. Mary Grice's brother Tom was a carpenter (possibly owned by Allston's niece Mrs. Francis Weston, who lived on the Pee Dee River a couple of miles north of Chicora Wood). Adele Allston was "much attached" to the family of Mary Grice, who "has been always a highly favoured servant," and whose children were given privileged jobs. Stephen's aunt Milly and his mother-in-law, Mary Grice, were the two house servants most punctilious about sending their "love and howdey" to the Confederate cavalry colonel Benjamin Allston when his mother wrote to him during the Civil War.[38]

They may have had a special motive in doing so on October 30, 1862, at the very moment Adele Allston was informing Benjamin of an unsettling event on the Pee Dee. For the last five months a Northern naval force had made its presence felt in the Pee Dee–Waccamaw area. On May 22, 1862, the *Albatross* sailed ten miles up the Waccamaw and received on board 80 fugitive slaves. In July another raid carried off 28 more Waccamaw fugitives, and in August two Northern vessels went up the Black River (an offshoot of the Pee Dee) and engaged in a duel with a Confederate battery. By November the Confederates succeeded in emplacing nine pieces of artillery to bar the entrance to the Pee Dee–Black River–Waccamaw estuary; but in October, when Adele wrote, this was not yet in operation. In May 1862 Francis Weston, the master of 335 bondsmen and women, had had his slaves hoist his big family boat up onto the piazza of his older house, for safekeeping from Northern raiders. The boat was "too large to be gotten into any lock up house, no door would admit it," Adele remarked, "and it required 20 men to move it." On October 27, 1862, the Westons went to a late party at a neighbor's plantation, and when they awakened the next morning they were astonished to learn that the big boat was no longer where it was supposed to be. Soon after dark the previous evening, "their head carpenter and 18 others of [Mr. Weston's] finest, most intelligent and trusted men had taken his family boat" and sailed down the Pee Dee and through Winyah Bay to meet the Northern naval vessels. The unwieldy enterprise of moving the boat from the piazza must have been known to hundreds of slaves, and they knew where the Westons were at the party; but not one informed their master of what was afoot. The Westons' head carpenter, who organized this mass escape, may have been Mary Grice's brother Tom: certainly her brother "Tom the carpenter" escaped sometime before July 1864 (apparently by sea), taking his whole family with him.[39]

By mid-1864 Mary Grice's sons Thomas (probably the "high temper'd" Thomas whom Allston had recommended in 1855 for training as a house servant) and Scotland had also escaped. The stakes were high. Nine days after the mass escape of Weston slaves in 1862, the local planters—as a deterrent to further flight—executed the three Waccamaw fugitives who had returned from freedom to bring their wives with them. The local planters also organized a nocturnal patrol across the inland end of Winyah Bay (to which Henry Middleton—the rich planter who reported with approbation the execution of the three fugitives—enthusiastically contributed "the best of my boats 22 feet long").[40] Seventy-five years later, the wartime activities of these patrol vessels were still part of the local blacks' folk memory. The patrollers, according to the former slave Sabe Rutledge, had not stopped at removing the captured males: the patrol vessel went "Up and down Pee Dee river. Meet flat[boat]! Bore hole in flat and women and chillun go down! Take men off." Perhaps several different events, including the taking of the three slave men to the Georgetown noose, were conflated in this version. In order to avoid offense to the Southern white woman who interviewed him, Rutledge blamed the drowning of the slave women and children on a *Northern* immigrant (this could have been Henry Buck, whose Waccamaw plantation was readily accessible to the Pee Dee); and Rutledge's interview did not mention the hangings of the three men, decreed as they were by Southern planters.[41] Rutledge's interview suggests that suppression of flight may have been even more heartless than Middleton's letter proves it to have been, with black women and children also victims of the planters' wrath. But whether or not Rutledge was correct on this point, the evidence of the Georgetown jail yard showed that the local planters—and they were rich planters, not the poor whites often blamed for ill treatment of blacks—were prepared to use draconian measures to stop the fugitives.

By the summer of 1864, even though the Confederate battery kept Northern vessels from renewing their sorties up the rivers, masters and slaves were highly suspicious of each other. Most of the Allston slaves remained at the Pee Dee plantations raising rice, but those particularly suspected of wishing to flee were transferred to the inland North Carolina farm Allston had purchased late in 1862 for the purpose; and any slave suddenly ordered to join Mrs. Allston at her inland refuge at Society Hill, South Carolina, might smell a rat: deportation to the North Carolina farm, only thirty miles from Society Hill, might impend. At the beginning of June 1864, overseer Belflowers reported a rumor that a party of Pee Dee slaves, including four or five of the Allstons', planned to escape. As June progressed, however, nothing seemed to come of it.[42]

Although Stephen Gallant apparently was not one of those suspected, Belflowers was nervous about Stephen's independence. There was a long tradition of autonomy in Stephen's family, and of rivalry with the white overseer. Stephen's elderly father, James Gallant, after being superseded as valet by Stephen, had been entrusted by Allston with work involving considerable supplies of lime. In 1858 James had twenty bushels of lime on hand, which he seems to have obtained in Georgetown. Some kilns were to be built, and the overseer Jesse Belflowers—to Allston's surprise—bypassed James and ordered a supply of lime through the Charleston factor. James Gallant's complaint to Benjamin Allston bespoke a man used to having his own way, and not submitting to dictation by a mere overseer. James "seemed to think his prerogatives very much encroached upon," Benjamin reported, "by [Belflowers's] sending to Charleston for lime. . . . James evidently does not like to be so much over looked by B[elflowers, and] says 'he never say any thing to me—minute lime comes he locks it up—locks it up—I have nothing to do with it Sir. I finds my own lime, etc.' "[43]

James's son Stephen Gallant carried on this tradition of prickly independence. Stephen's wife, Lizzie, now lived at "Brittons Neck," the main Allston provision farm, nearly twenty miles up the Pee Dee; and after Robert Allston's death in April, Stephen resided at Brittons Neck too when not carrying out commissions for Adele Allston at Society Hill. So much had the Allstons trusted Stephen that the white man loosely overseeing the provision farm did not require Stephen to carry a pass when he left Brittons Neck on an errand; but Belflowers disapproved this arrangement. On May 30, 1864, Stephen delivered a harness and sleigh to Belflowers from Society Hill. Belflowers was uncertain of his subsequent movements. "Stephen I think is Runing a bout a grate deal," he reported on June 1. "I think he has been a bout Planters Ville [a pineland summer settlement for the plantation owners, a few miles inland from Chicora Wood] the most of time Since he come down Withe the Harnas & Slay." A week later Belflowers wrote to the Brittons Neck supervisor, telling him "not to allow [Stephen] to Come down any more Without he was Sent for." Adele Allston wanted Stephen to come back to Society Hill, and therefore on Saturday, July 2, Belflowers did indeed send orders that Stephen was to come to Chicora Wood on Monday, July 4.

Unbeknownst to Belflowers, Stephen made a trip down the Pee Dee and back on Sunday, July 3, probably consulting friends at three plantations along the way; and at one of them he is likely to have met a slave who came over for the day from "Oatlands," the Waccamaw River estate of Allston's second cousin Mrs. Martha Allston Pyatt. Stephen probably borrowed from one of his Pee Dee friends a big dugout for the return journey to Brittons Neck on Sunday night. The next morning, when a slave sent by Belflowers came to accompany Stephen from Brittons Neck back to Chicora Wood, Stephen "Comp[l]aind of being sick." Giving Stephen a little while to recover, the other slave soon returned to find that "Stephen Was absant. Lizzie [Stephen's wife] told [the other slave] that Stephen said he Could go on [and] that he would take his Boat & Come on [separately]." By the time the other slave got to Chicora Wood and told Belflowers, it was too late in the day for the overseer to get in touch again with Brittons Neck.[44]

In the night of July 4 Stephen made his own declaration of independence. He and another slave named Toney put Stephen's wife, Lizzie, and Stephen's five children (Cotta, Morris, Stephen, Mary Anne, and Cecil) into a boat. Stephen took every one of his children except the eldest, Brutus, a young man of about twenty-one who was working at Society Hill. They seem to have stopped along the Pee Dee to pick up four other slaves—one from the Tucker plantation, one from Francis Weston's, and two from J. H. Read's—and they floated silently past Chicora Wood on their way to Squirrel Creek, which connected the Pee Dee to the Waccamaw. By daybreak they had secluded themselves in one of those delightful coves, bristling with alligators, turtles, and snakes, which had so charmed Adele Allston on her annual migrations from Chicora Wood to the beach; here they remained undetected all day Tuesday. That night, saying good-bye to the local alligators, they pressed on through Squirrel Creek to the Waccamaw. Crossing this wide river, they landed on the other side at Oatlands plantation, where they hid all day Wednesday, probably aided by four Oatlands slaves who joined the escaping party. The plan was to cross the Waccamaw peninsula by foot—some four miles; to creep through the Confederate picket line (which was thinly manned, as the Confederate general claimed to have only about three hundred soldiers to defend a seventy-mile coast); to steal a boat; and to row at night through the breakers and out to sea, where if neither storm nor wind drowned them, and if the moon shined through the clouds, they might hope to rendezvous with Northern naval vessels on the lookout for escaping slaves.[45]

Stephen's wish for freedom must have been overwhelming to impel him to embark, with his whole family, on this daring—if not foolhardy—enterprise. Northern officials referred to fugitive slaves like Stephen as "contrabands" (for the Confiscation Acts authorized seizing the contraband property of rebels), but the term should be avoided in historical writing. Stephen risked being eaten by alligators, shot by pickets, hanged by a stony-faced local court-martial if he were caught alive, or drowned if the sea were even normally treacherous. Gallant he was indeed, and the word "contraband" would undervalue the courage and intelligent planning that went into this desperate venture.

Desperate, surely: for on Wednesday night the overseer at Oatlands got wind of what was happening and managed to apprehend no less than eight of the fugitives. Only Stephen, Lizzie, their children, and Toney evaded capture. Toney became separated from the others. Stephen somehow got his family through the pickets; found near the sea (perhaps by prearrangement) a boat used by a slave of Dr. Andrew Hasell's for cutting salt marsh; and rowed his family out through the surf into the Atlantic Ocean. And they survived! They were picked up by a Northern naval ship, probably the sailing vessel *Williams,* which was patrolling the area early in July. The Union sailors along this coast had their eyes open for fugitives: one successfully escaped in this way from Charleston on July 4, and fifteen more on July 11 from Bull's Bay, thirty miles south of Georgetown.[46]

Toney, now on his own, knew that if he were captured he might be hanged, as had happened to the three Waccamaw fugitives in 1862. He decided, therefore, that his best course was to throw himself upon the mercy of the less hated of the two Allston overseers. Evading capture for forty-eight hours, he turned himself in on Friday night to W. Sweet, the Nightingale Hall overseer, and served up a whopper to explain his five-day absence. Stephen, he said, had "foold him," telling him at Brittons Neck that Belflowers had ordered Toney to help bring Stephen's whole family to Chicora Wood, whence Mrs. Allston had ordered the family to go to Society Hill. Once they were aboard Stephen's boat—Toney alleged—Stephen had coerced him: "Toney says he

Knew that Stephn was armd," Belflowers announced. This story, which contradicted at several points what Belflowers had heard from other sources, bore on its face the marks of Toney's anxiety to save his own skin; yet the two overseers chose to pretend to Mrs. Allston that they believed it. Knowing that if Toney were tried like the other eight captives he was likely to be executed, Sweet "Did not wish to Put him in the hands of the military Powe[r]."[47] Belflowers—who had encountered since Stephen's departure "a goodeal of obstanetry [obstinacy] in Some of the Peopl, mostly mongst the Woman, a goodeal of Quarling and disputeing & teling lies"—probably thought that a live harvest hand would be more serviceable to him than a slave dead as an example to others; and he probably calculated that he would have less trouble governing the Allston slaves if they did not hold him responsible for sending Toney to his death. Belflowers knew perfectly well that Toney was likely to disappear again if there were another Northern raid up the rivers: the overseers therefore kept Toney "watch[ed] Pretty clost" during the harvest, and he was sent inland to North Carolina for safekeeping soon after the harvest was finished.[48] Toney's long experience as a slave in telling lies[49] had enabled him to devise a tale which, though incredible, gave his overseers an excuse with which to save his life. Evidently the other eight captives were made to stand trial[50], but whether they were executed remains unknown. Belflowers's letter of July 27, which might have told, has been destroyed or mislaid. The chance that it has been deliberately destroyed is increased by the fact that it is one of the only two weekly reports unaccounted for between May 26 and the following January.[51]

With hindsight Allston's daughter Elizabeth sought to fit Stephen's character into a Procrustean bed of consistency. She had never liked her father's valet as much as she did Nelson the butler. This may have been partly because Stephen was (in her words) "very black," while Nelson was a mulatto; it may have arisen partly from the jealousy of a daughter—who adored her father—for the servant who had the privilege of accompanying Governor Allston on his journeys to Charleston, Columbia, Tennessee, and Virginia, and of staying with Allston at Chicora Wood during the war when Elizabeth was sent inland for safety; and it may have arisen from a sense that Stephen, for all his "folly and levity," was mentally more independent than the subservient Nelson. Allston had nearly always found that, if he wanted a subaltern with initiative, he must put up with some independence of spirit. Elizabeth could see in Stephen's brave escape nothing but base dereliction of duty, and she concluded that he must always have been dishonorable.

She tried to impugn Stephen's character by claiming that he might have been the person who stole two valuable jewels of her elder sister's in 1860, even though she acknowledged that no shadow of suspicion had then fallen upon him. So determined was Elizabeth to ruin his reputation that she even let her imagination gallop away with her, like an uncontrollable horse. Stephen might in 1860 have foreseen emancipation, she alleged most implausibly, and he might have calculated that jewels stolen then would be saleable by him once the slaves were freed! Elizabeth could scarcely conceal her satisfaction that, some years after gaining his freedom, Stephen—like Cato at Gowrie—had drowned while poling a flatboat up the river: Elizabeth seemed to feel that God's retributive justice had finally manifested itself. These were her ways of seeking to prove to herself that Stephen had always been "faithless."[52]

Far more believable is the view that Stephen was a man of remarkable character, true to himself and his master when the cards were heavily stacked against the slaves, as they were before 1864; and true to himself in a different sense when the military balance of power had shifted. Like Louis Manigault's confidant Hector at Gowrie, Stephen was neither an Uncle Tom nor a Nat Turner. He pursued his own interest, and that of his family, in his accepting the responsibility of bringing back the two Allston horses from Lexington, Virginia, in 1860; in his constantly and very efficiently attending his master on his deathbed; and in his masterminding his family's escape later in the year. The only difference among these acts was that Stephen calculated, rationally, that his interest and those of his family diverged from the Allstons' in mid-1864, as they had not previously done under the earlier military balance of power. A favored slave's resolute improvement of his or her own position in the antebellum world—by accepting privilege and trust and making the most of them—was not inconsistent with an equally resolute pursuit of self-interest in a different direction when opportunity struck.

This was not how Mrs. Robert Allston perceived things. Adele's mood was stormy when she learned of Stephen's astonishing bid for freedom. The unprotected heads of Stephen's mother-in-law, Mary Grice, and his father, James, coming into Adele's view, Jovian thunderbolts came crashing about them. Stephen's "wife is Mary [Grice]'s daughter," Mrs. Allston fulminated to the local military chief, Colonel Francis Heriot,

> and . . . she is the third of [Mary's] children who have gone off. Thomas and Scotland her sons were young men, and Tom the carpenter who went off with all of his family as Stephen has done, was her brother. It is too many instances in her family for me to suppose she is ignorant of their plans and designs. She has been always a highly favoured servant, and all her family have been placed in positions of confidence and trust. I think this last case should be visited in some degree on her. I do not think she should be allowed to retain her position in charge of the house with the keys etc unless she can prove her innocence.

Mrs. Allston wanted nothing rash, she protested—no executions of Stephen's relations—but the county police must act in order to "hold the near relations, parents etc, responsible for the ill conduct of the younger members of their families." Mrs. Allston goaded the overseer to get some soldiers or patrollers and

> have Mary's house surrounded and searched, and James['s] likewise at the same time. . . . He, Stephen, no doubt left what he could not carry, with them, to get at some future time. I think Mary and James should be taken up and sent to some secure jail in the interior and held as hostages for the conduct of their children. . . . The police of the country [should] require that

the older negroes should endeavour to influence the younger ones to order and subordination while this war lasts. . . . For this course to have the best effect it ought to be universal.[53]

The security measures of a totalitarian police state seemed to Mrs. Allston appropriate; and as the long-overdue history of American women is finally being written, her words (and those of her daughter Elizabeth) ought not be forgotten. Antebellum Southern white plantation women have occasionally been portrayed as soulmates of their oppressed black sisters, and even South Carolina's passionate supporter of a war to preserve white supremacy, Mary Chesnut, has sometimes been taken at her own self-appraisal as a proto-abolitionist. Mrs. Allston's outburst suggests that allegiance to class and to race may have been far more powerful motives for Southern plantation mistresses than loyalty to gender.[54]

Allston's policy of divide and conquer—of awarding substantial privilege to a handful of chosen dependents—therefore failed a major test in July 1864. But had it been ineffectual in earlier years, and with other slaves? The modern sensibility would wish to answer a resounding yes, for one wishes to affirm that most slaves, like Stephen, retained their manhood and womanhood, and that masters like Allston were building upon quicksand. The truth, however, may be less agreeable.

The most privileged of the Allston slaves was "Mulatto Joe," who may have been Robert Allston's uncle—that is, his mother's half brother. That there was some blood relation is suggested by the unusual terms of Allston's father's will, probated in 1809: Mulatto Joe and his wife were guaranteed an annuity of fifteen dollars "for services to be hereafter rendered" (the appended clause did not disguise the peculiarity of granting a cash annuity to a slave), plus the legacy of two cows and two calves, and the privilege of permanent residence at the Brittons Neck farm. Mulatto Joe was born about 1760—when Robert Allston's maternal grandfather, William Allston Sr., was thirty-six; and one surmises that William may have had a slave concubine (as occurred in the instances of W. E. B. Du Bois's great-grandfather; Thomas Jefferson's father-in-law; Angelina Grimké's brother in South Carolina; Mary Chesnut's father-in-law in the same state; South Carolina's Governor James Hammond; and in any number of other cases). Someone—perhaps William Allston himself—taught Mulatto Joe to read and write. An 1823 letter of Joe's to Robert Allston is extant, rather like an overseer's report but with only two misspellings, and with better grammar than the overseers usually commanded. "Malatto Joe," as he self-consciously signed himself, was given a headstone—the only other slave except carpenter Thomas to whom this privilege was extended—when Robert buried him in 1840. Besides driving sixty to one hundred hogs each year from Brittons Neck to the plantation, Mulatto Joe was in charge of one hundred cattle, including the milk cows which supplied the Allstons with butter; and he had a "fine Flock of sheep" of his own. Plums, apples, peaches, and walnuts were grown at Brittons Neck under Joe's supervision.[55]

In addition to his ownership of sheep, Joe's most remarkable distinction was his raising and apparently jockeying racehorses for his masters. Privileged slaves were expected to be especially loud in the expression of devotion to their masters, and Joe's riding skill and his accumulation of property—especially his numerous sheep—enabled him to be hyperbolic in his avowals. Mulatto Joe "talks a Deal of you," Robert learned from his mother during Robert's last year at West Point; and she seemed to take Joe's protestations at face value:

> He says the Philly must start on the Coarse next February, and he must Ride her himself and he will take the Prize for Master Robert. He will bet 20 sheep that he wins. . . . There is, if nothing happins, a fine set out for you to Gameing an Old Rider upwards of 60, so attached to you that he will run the Risque of his Life and Bones in your behalf.

Joe's status obviously was different from that of all the other Allston slaves, as was clear in the way Charlotte continued this letter. "Negro" meant slave—whether black or brown—but Joe's position was sui generis: "All these Negroes and Mulatto Joe send howdye to you," Robert's mother concluded.[56]

Joe, seeing which side his bread was buttered on, would have been foolish to risk privileges by rocking the boat. But within limits he used his special position to defend the interests of other slaves. He thought well of Ancrum, a young bondsman sent to help him at Brittons Neck, and he urged Robert Allston to give Ancrum special treatment: an intervention to which the younger slave partly attributed his eventually becoming one of Allston's drivers. And when Charlotte Allston learned in 1823 that one of her slaves had bitten the overseer, she turned to Mulatto Joe to find out what had happened. Joe's report of how the overseer had called in his wife and his dog to help subdue Jerry, whose horn he had impounded, led Charlotte to chastize the overseer.[57]

Another mulatto, the butler Nelson—a son of Mrs. Blyth's overseer—was Elizabeth Allston Pringle's favorite slave. "He was the best, most faithful, intelligent man possible," she effused, "and we were all devoted to him." Christmas Day was when most Allston slaves wed, and Nelson was married that day in 1851—by the Episcopal rector, as a mark of distinction—to Nelly, who became the Allstons' laundress. Nelly was probably a daughter of Milly, their previous laundress—now getting on in years; and if so, Nelly was a first cousin of Stephen Gallant in the close-knit community of Allston house servants.[58] Nelson, by contrast to Stephen, was in Elizabeth Pringle's eyes a paragon of all virtues. He had established his place in her affection when serving the Allston children at Pawleys Island with the big silver waiter, when his easy chat provided a welcome relief from their schoolwork. He was associated in Elizabeth's heart with the fireworks displays he managed for the slaves at Christmas. His intelligence appeared in the alacrity with which he learned to operate a mechanical piano—a sort of mid-nineteenth-century recording machine—which Robert Allston brought back from Paris in 1855. His faithfulness was evident a decade later when Sherman's army, marching northeast from Columbia, obtruded upon the privacy of the Allstons' inland retreat at

Society Hill. To forestall marauding soldiers, Nelson helped the Allstons bury their family silver and the Madeira which Robert—thinking it might be their most saleable possession after the war—had painstakingly shipped up from the plantation. The other slaves (except the coachman Aleck Parker) were not let into the Allstons' secret; and Nelson's loyalty at this moment engraved itself upon Elizabeth's memory. Nelson was a soft man who liked the comfortable life, and the Allstons' trust in him was fully repaid. Contrary to the racial stereotypes which Harriet Beecher Stowe endorsed by contrasting the faithful dark-skinned Uncle Tom with the determined (allegedly because partly Anglo-Saxon) mulatto fugitive slave George Harris, it was the dark-skinned Stephen Gallant who showed his determination in July 1864, while the mulatto Nelson was "faithful" to the Allstons' trust.[59]

Yet the picture of the "faithful" Nelson which glowed from Elizabeth Pringle's memoir through the flattering haze of time was not quite the real man. Nelson was, in fact, associated with one of Elizabeth's most unpleasant youthful experiences. On July 22, 1861, as the news reached Charleston that the Confederate army had won a great victory at the First Battle of Bull Run, Nelson—deeply disappointed at this news?—made himself thoroughly inebriated. Robert Allston was in Richmond, his son Benjamin was away in the army, and the Allston women were left to rattle around in their Meeting Street mansion with no white male to care for them. "Last night we had a dreadful time," the sixteen-year-old Elizabeth confided to her diary the next day.

> Nelson was quite drunk. [Uncle Henry Lesesne visited briefly in the evening "about bell ring" (the curfew time for all Charleston slaves since the Denmark Vesey conspiracy of 1822) and said he would go and see if there were any more news of the battle at the public bulletin board.] After he left Nelson came and locked the gate and door without heeding at all [Elizabeth's mother's summoning him by] the ringing of the bell. When he came upstairs I noticed that his clothes were all muddy just as tho he had fallen on his side into the street. Mamma told him not to put out the light in the entry, for Uncle H[enry] was coming back, but he put it out. About 11 o'clock Uncle H. came [and] rang at the bell but Mamma was obliged to go down and unlock the door and gate for him. . . . When Uncle H. left we rang and rang but no one came. Mamma went and locked the gate and bolted the door and then went into the pantry to look for Nelson. She found him fast asleep in the back door. She tried to wake him up, called, and at last took a stick and pushed him but all in vain. Then as there was no one to be seen Mamma wanted to put out the lights herself and leave him there.

The Allston house servants normally slept in slave quarters in the yard behind the Allstons' dwelling, and Elizabeth was terrified at what might happen if a drunk and ungovernable male slave were left in the house with her, her nineteen-year-old sister, Della, and their mother. "I was very much scared," Elizabeth continued,

> and so Della and I woke up Nannie and sent her to call Joe [Riley in the slave quarters]. She . . . had to wake him up and told him to shut up [the house

and, presumably, to remove Nelson] and so we went to bed. It was dreadful. I felt so miserable. This morning he did not seem yet to be quite sober. Mamma said she would send him to the work house [for a whipping] but he begged her pardon and seemed sorry.[60]

Below the surface of cordiality between the white women and even their most trusted male house slave lurked a deep anxiety, ready to leap forth in the dark like an ogre. Mary Chesnut realized that in 1861 Charleston house servants kept their thoughts to themselves: "Their faces are as unreadable as the sphinx."[61] Elizabeth Allston Pringle, however, thought it would not do to acknowledge publicly that Nelson had once loomed in her imagination like an ogre; and this story was never transferred from Elizabeth's journal into her memoir of her "best, most faithful" servant. Nelson, in fact—like Mulatto Joe—was a complex human being: a divided soul, not a pasteboard stereotype.

A different version of the "loyal house servant" appeared in the coachman Aleck Parker, whom Robert Allston had inherited from his Aunt Blyth in 1840. Aleck and Nelson "were never friends and distrusted each other," according to Elizabeth Pringle. Their personalities were contrasting: while Nelson was soft, Aleck was tough, brave, and combative. He "always sat as straight as if he had been trained at West Point," and he was not afraid to reprimand the young Elizabeth if he thought her conduct unbecoming. His independence may have been the source of his getting into trouble with young Benjamin Allston in 1859, and here again—as with Nelson—the picture of a loyal house servant drawn by Elizabeth Pringle many years later does not exactly accord with contemporary records. "I hope that Ma may find satisfaction in Aleck," Benjamin Allston wrote skeptically to his father after Aleck had delivered some horses to her in Charleston, "though I am afraid he will need some more discipline."[62]

Besides driving the coach, Aleck sometimes hauled manure or produce on a wagon, and during the Civil War "he felt he had risked his life" in carrying Allston's grain to a whiskey still; and he "openly grumbled" at the pouring away of this whiskey late in 1864 to keep it from Northern soldiers. In his different way, he was as faithful (or nearly so) to the Allstons as Nelson. As has been observed, Aleck was singled out for special clothing and food, and he repaid the Allstons many times over when Sherman's army approached. Entrusted to hide their riding horses and three women's sidesaddles in the swamplands, Aleck (and Stephen Gallant's younger brother, Sam Gallant) returned—after the Northerners had departed—with all the horses and two sidesaddles, though Aleck had "lost" the third. This slight failure, and the undercurrent of distrust evident in Benjamin's earlier warning that Aleck might need more discipline, probably contributed to Mrs. Allston's decision soon after emancipation to sack Aleck. He was indignant at this betrayal of his trust in his masters, and he even cried; but raising rice by tidal culture, without slave labor, was a risky and ultimately unprofitable venture, and Mrs. Allston thought she needed the proceeds from selling the 1864 rice crop to preserve the shreds of gentility for her own white family, not to pension off a loyal black servant. She felt that $2.50 and a half-pint of whiskey would compensate him adequately for a lifetime of service.[63]

Stephen Gallant's son Brutus, and Stephen's younger brother, Sam, were two other slaves whose service to the Allstons, as the Confederacy was collapsing, seemed to remain steady. Brutus had been young Charley Allston's riding mentor when the white boy was growing up, and when the eighteen-year-old Charley went to war, Brutus accompanied him as a body servant. Brutus once "marched six miles with [Charley] to carry his musket." And Sam Gallant, a hostler with Confederate General Wade Hampton's cavalry, brought two Allston horses safely home from Virginia to preserve them from capture by the Yankees, just before the surrender. Yet Brutus was the eldest son—and Sam the sibling—of Stephen Gallant, all the rest of whose family had daringly escaped to sea only a few months earlier.[64]

Among the other slaves who at one time or another held privileged house positions were Hynes, a predecessor of Stephen Gallant as Allston's valet; Moses Baron, a forerunner of Nelson as butler; and, in the next generation, the cook Joe Washington and William Baron (Moses Baron's son), who was Colonel Benjamin Allston's valet during the Civil War. One mark of the status of three of these men—like Stephen Gallant and Aleck Parker—was that the white people acknowledged their surnames, as they seldom did for any but a highly privileged slave, and almost never for a female slave (Mary Grice being a rare exception). Hynes, probably a son of old Phoebe (the slave children's head nurse), was a coachman who in about 1834 drove the Allstons with their first baby to the mountains for their summer holiday. Ten years later, when Robert Allston nearly died of a fever at the house where they then summered, only a few miles north of Chicora Wood, it was Hynes—now acting as valet, and "very faithful and intelligent"—who helped put Robert's legs up to the knees in hot water to induce sweating to calm his delirium so that he could sleep; and who then sat "by papa and fan[ned] him" during his drugged slumber before Dr. Sparkman finally arrived. Hynes, whose own health was not good, probably did not live for long after 1844.[65]

There was a certain amount of mobility, both upward and downward, among the house servants. While Hynes moved up from coachman to valet, Moses Baron—who at the time of Robert Allston's marriage was his butler— was eventually supplanted by the better-trained Nelson; Moses was demoted to being the head slave gardener, under a white gardener's supervision. Because the earlier generation of Allston's servants were not so well trained as, for example, Adele's lady's maid Lavinia, Allston took steps to improve the standard of his own house slaves. Joe Washington—perhaps a son of Philip Washington, an esteemed driver at nearby "Pipe Down" plantation to whom Adele Allston's brother granted freedom in his will—was sent to a fine Charleston restaurateur, Sam Lee, for two years of training; and Joe seems then to have supplanted Mary Grice as the Allstons' chief cook. Mary became the housekeeper and stayed during the long summer at Chicora Wood with the keys, commissioned to keep the house "fresh and clean" for Robert when he dropped in to drink a glass of buttermilk and to eat some fruit during his frequent summertime tours of the plantation. But Joe was with the Allstons doing the cooking.[66]

Joe Washington's responsibilities were not, during the war, confined to the kitchen. When Allston moved his household inland, Joe was put in charge of transporting the Madeira and Allston's collection of marble statues on flatboats which were oared and poled up the Pee Dee toward the inland refuge. Joe was also responsible for one of the boats carrying rice inland to the railway junction; but soon after Stephen Gallant's escape Adele Allston panicked that Joe Washington too might flee. Her son Charles tried to reassure her, and they decided to rent Joe, along with a group of their other slaves, to work at an inland Confederate navy yard not far from Marion, South Carolina. These slaves soon chose Joe as their spokesman to try to persuade Mrs. Allston to spend some money on clothing them: "Most of them are in a very destitute condition," the commandant of the navy yard attested, "needing both clothing and shoes." Early in December 1864 Joe was placed in charge of a boat which set out for a three-week journey up the Pee Dee, loaded with forty barrels of clean rice, nine hundred bushels of rough rice, and fourteen boxes of wine. Although these seem to have been safely delivered, a later boatload of rice fell into the hands of Northern soldiers. There is no way to determine whether Joe Washington deliberately facilitated the capture of his cargo. Perhaps he did, but it was harder to hide a big boat than to secrete the few horses which Aleck Parker led to a remote swamp, and Joe persuaded the Allstons that the loss of the cargo was unavoidable.[67]

William Baron, son of the former butler Moses Baron, served Colonel Benjamin Allston as valet during the whole war; and although Benjamin's subsequent praise was a shade grudging, he acknowledged that William had "been in the long run very faithful to me, through the War." When Benjamin dismissed William in October 1865 (because Benjamin "could not afford so luxurious a servant in these times"), he "wish[ed] him every success" and said—with rare warmth and real sincerity—that he would "be glad to learn that he is doing well." William's later career was striking. He converted his good reputation among the Charleston gentry into cash and substantial business success. He became one of the city's best-known caterers, responsible for providing food and drink at the St. Cecilia balls, where the acme of Charleston society had always gathered to exclude some of the more ordinary folk with whom they were forced to rub shoulders at the less discriminate Jockey Club balls. William Baron, very black and heavy, perfectly honest according to Elizabeth Pringle, and with "grand manners" (by which she signified cartloads of flattery), could scarcely have carved this particular niche for himself in the postwar world had he not been careful to establish his good name with Southern gentlemen before 1865.[68]

That males figured prominently in the Allstons' hierarchy of house servants is a notable fact. To be sure, Mary Grice was a figure of some authority; the laundress Milly was a proud woman; old Phoebe, the slave children's nurse, was careful to win the goodwill of the Allston children by her gifts to them; and a trained lady's maid like Mrs. Allston's Lavinia was something of a personage at Chicora Wood. But male servants such as the butler Nelson, the valets Hynes, Stephen Gallant, and William Baron, the coachman Aleck Parker, the cook Joe Washington, and the gardener Moses Baron figured even larger in Elizabeth Pringle's imagination than the females, and this may represent accurately their significance in the plantation's social economy. Here is the origin of another notable theme in African-American history: for, as late as the 1920s, three-quarters of the black waiters and waitresses in a city such as Chicago were male; and only more recently has the prominence of black males in service positions declined. The father of the first African-American on the Supreme Court, Thurgood Marshall, was a dining car waiter who became the chief steward of an elegant Maryland dining club, thus carrying on a tradition established by a man like William Baron at the St. Cecilia balls. Service jobs of this sort, growing out of the domestic service performed by black male slaves, were for years one of the few routes—except for artisan trades, and jobs like preaching and teaching that served a black clientele—by which a black man could escape agricultural toil. If Alice Walker's heroine in *The Third Life of Grange Copeland* is to be applauded when she gains a factory job and thus ends her bondage to the sharecropping system, is not William Baron to be applauded for escaping from agriculture into catering?

Not every house servant maintained Stephen Gallant's spiritual independence from the masters. Some—possibly Nelson or even Aleck Parker—may have feathered their own nests at the expense of their fellow slaves. Surely many others, however—perhaps Mary Grice, and Mulatto Joe, and Milly the laundress, and Joe Washington, and old Phoebe, and Moses and William Baron—steered an uneasy course between avidly sopping up every special privilege which was an offer, and maintaining their own integrity. What person who has not experienced their only alternative—doing hard, forced labor in the dank rice swamps—is to throw stones at these people because they willingly accepted privileges from their masters? Even Stephen Gallant compromised for years—and his flight in 1864 could not have succeeded except for his capitalizing on the relative freedom of movement he had been granted because of his "faithful" service to Robert Allston.

Almost every house servant who accepted the attendant privileges paid a price for doing so. The cost was substantial, for seeds of division were planted not simply between different members of the black community but within the souls of individual slaves. The concept of being "faithful" or "unfaithful"—the adjectives Elizabeth Pringle used most frequently to characterize the virtues or defects of house servants—implied a peeling off, from the community's core, of a layer of privileged slaves whose first loyalty was to the masters. The modern sensibility wishes to believe that the masters' policy failed: that the slaves' faithfulness was coerced, superficial, and feigned—that the slaves paid no price, or only a small one, for the privileges they accepted. This may, however, be a romantic view of the matter. Nelson did indeed help to bury the family silver, and Aleck Parker did indeed save the horses and most of the sidesaddles: hence his indignation when his genuine faithfulness was unrewarded. William Baron paid the price every flagrant flatterer pays for his hyperbole. It would not be fair to call these "bought men," for they often used their privileged position to benefit other slaves, as Mulatto Joe did when he reported on overseer Avant's conduct toward the horn-blowing Jerry. Yet the loyalties of these privileged slaves were divided. Perhaps they were richer human beings for feeling a certain trust in certain white people under certain circumstances; but their effectiveness in any potential united front of all slaves against their masters was diminished. To that extent the network of privilege which Allston constructed at Chicora Wood was more successful than our generation would like to believe.

That it was not wholly successful, however, became apparent during the extraordinary days of early 1865.

14

White Supremacy and Paternalist Theory

In October 1856, a few weeks before James Buchanan's election to the presidency, and less than two months before Allston's own election as governor, the Carolinian "sat some 2 hours" with Buchanan at the latter's Pennsylvania home. Allston's visit gratified him, for he discovered among Buchanan's Northern Democratic colleagues—such as Judge George Woodward (later the gubernatorial nominee of Pennsylvania's Democratic Party in the wartime year of 1863)—a more resolute proslavery stance than he had dared hope. The contest over slavery in Kansas, which he heard Buchanan's friends discussing "as fearlessly & fairly as it could be done in Carolina," had been causing Allston to reflect upon his own principles.[1]

Any Southerner conscious of the antipathy toward slavery which lay behind the program of the newly organized Republican Party—and aware that slavery had been abolished in British colonies during the 1830s and in French colonies in 1848—must acknowledge that emancipation was in the air. As a calculating entrepreneur, Allston might have been expected to couch his defense of slavery in terms of the inalienable property rights of capitalists. That he did not do so probably arose from his sense that in the mid–nineteenth century "property" rights to human beings could not command sufficiently widespread support to guarantee their safety. He turned, therefore, to the racial defense of slavery. Negroes were primitive savages, he declared— somehow forgetting the skills of his lifelong "faithful friend" carpenter Thomas; the ministrations of his valet Hynes when Allston was stricken in

1844, and of Stephen Gallant thereafter; the services of his butler Nelson, the enterprise of Mulatto Joe, the agricultural expertise of trunk minder Jacob, the leadership qualities of drivers Tommy and Daniel, the "How d'ye"s of the cook Mary Grice and the skilled laundress Milly, the responsibilities assumed by the children's nurse Phoebe. It would be intolerable, Allston thought, to free the Negroes without removing them from America; and "the computations of intricate calculation," he claimed, "have proved the impracticality of emancipation by deportation."[2] Deportation was certainly impractical for rice planters: for who would labor in the malarial rice swamps or dig out the ditches in the January winds, were enslaved blacks not compelled to do so?

There were only three choices, in Allston's view; and therefore if deportation were impractical, the status quo must continue, for the third "alternative cannot be contemplated, namely, the giving up of our beautiful country to the ravages of the black race & amalgamation with the savages."[3] Hence the preservation of slavery in the Carolina low country was not the selfish wish of a small group of profit-making rice grandees; it was instead a wider defense of the supremacy of the whole white race over the blacks.

Rationalization this may have been, but it was not the less deeply felt; and the Southern war for independence evidently was not just a defense of slavery, it was more generally a defense of white supremacy. There therefore was no inconsistency when South Carolina's Mary Chesnut called slavery "this hated institution" ("ours is a *monstrous* system & wrong & iniquity") yet passionately supported the war as a means of guaranteeing Southern white control of the Southern racial system. Just as Northern war aims shifted during the war (from a war for the Union to a war to destroy slavery), so to some extent did Southern war aims shift: from a defense of slavery to a defense of white supremacy in general. A sermon in September 1864 by a leading Carolina Presbyterian (Benjamin Palmer, a professor at the Columbia Theological Seminary) represented this shift, and it shook Mary Chesnut to the core. She wrote, "He is not for slavery, he says. . . . Every day shows that slavery is doomed the world over. For that he thanked God": yet the war must go on, for it was a battle to preserve Southern home rule—that is, to maintain the power of Southern whites to govern race relations with blacks, enslaved or free—without "foreign interference."[4] This battle for white supremacy continued, by other means, from the moment the Confederate armies surrendered in 1865. When Adele Allston (echoing her husband's view) had declared to a Northern friend at the beginning of the war, "All that we ask [is] to be allowed to govern our own Section in our own way," she was stating a formula which was as applicable in 1865 to the defense of white supremacy as it had been in 1861 to the defense of slavery.[5]

The political philosophy within which Allston's racial defense of slavery was embedded appeared to be old-school Federalism, though Allston was in his adult life a firm adherent to the extreme states' rights wing of the Democratic Party. As late as 1859 he subscribed to a patriarchal theory of government (founded "upon the principles of the Divine Law"), where those in authority were like a "Reverend Parent, rearing to efficient manhood and good citizenship a number of virtuous sons, who prove themselves . . . in the front ranks of Society."[6] Assiduous in rearing his own son Benjamin according to these principles, Robert Allston expressed the "republican" view that performance of public service was a duty incumbent upon members of the gentry; and gentlemen, unpolluted by personal interest, must of course defer strictly to their superiors in age and experience. In 1860 it appeared that twenty-seven-year-old Benjamin Allston—now retired from the army and recently launched upon his career as a Pee Dee rice planter—would be selected as a representative of Georgetown District in the state assembly. Benjamin was still too young for this distinction, his father advised him; yet if Benjamin were nevertheless chosen he "must submit to being advanced to the responsibility of a representative before you are ready for it." A gentleman must do his duty without consulting his own interest. Within three or four days, however, the name of Plowden Weston—master of 335 rice slaves, graduate of Harrow, a gentleman capitalist of more than local renown—was put forward for the same post; and Robert Allston immediately advised his son that he must withdraw his own name, instead of contesting the election against the older man. Politics in Georgetown District ought to be a stately quadrille in which one gentleman made way for another. Allston went so far as to pen for his son's use the exact words—formal, deferential, stuffy—with which Benjamin's withdrawal should be publicly announced. "The parish will be better served," Benjamin was to proclaim, "by [Weston], who has acquired already much experience in the House, who is a ripe Scholar and in whom I have every confidence, to whom therefore, I shall be gratified in being permitted to defer." There is no reason to doubt Robert Allston's sincerity, both in urging his son to accept the call of public duty, and then in urging him to defer to the other gentleman of similar political principles.[7]

This ethos of public service was associated in Robert Allston's mind with a thoroughgoing hostility to democracy. Unembarrassed by his own unrestrained mastery over the lives of his six hundred enslaved dependents, Allston declared that "the worst Tyranny which is known to mankind is that of king numbers weilding [sic] unrestrain'd power." The great rice planters of the low country were the most prominent beneficiaries in the 1850s of South Carolina's uniquely antidemocratic political system, which avoided a popular election either of national presidential electors or of the state's governor. Substantial property qualifications, moreover, were prescribed for membership in the state legislature; and the apportionment of seats in that legislature grossly overrepresented the rice grandees—especially in the state's most powerful body, its senate.[8] Allston, who was president of the state senate for the six years before he became governor, attempted to lift no finger from the low-country planters' grasp upon Carolina's body politic. This was not the opportunism of a man who had risen to political eminence in an undemocratic system; it was, rather, an honest expression of Allston's profoundly antidemocratic spirit. Allston's principles were consonant, nonetheless, with self-interest.

His mastery of politics in Prince George Parish was not quite so unchallenged as his mastery of his slaves. In 1832, as a principal leader of Georgetown's nullifiers against local Unionists, Allston had won election to the state senate after a hot contest involving two reruns and an investigation by the state legislature: he finally triumphed by a single vote. As late as 1842 the local Unionists mounted a substantial, but unsuccessful, challenge to Allston's reelection to the Senate. This contest seemed to align poorer whites from the interior of Georgetown District, allied with some townspeople from the village of Georgetown, against the rich coastal planters; but, as in the Roman republic, or the eighteenth-century South, the more popular party chose as its leader another rich planter—Peter Fraser, master of 133 slaves—to contest Allston's seat.[9]

Allston understood that in a system of popular elections gentlemen must act to assuage class rivalries between rich and poor whites. Four arenas where class divisions might be narrowed were the state militia, where Allston, a colonel, served together with poor whites of lesser military rank; the sport of hunting, which delighted rich and poor Carolinian whites alike; the state school system, where rich planters might offer certain educational crumbs to the poor; and the parish road system, which the gentry might maintain sufficiently to satisfy their lesser neighbors. Colonel Allston's own love of hunting was evident in the obituary he penned in 1860 for a poor white man who had probably served in his own militia unit. Allston's idealization of the independent life which could be attained by even impecunious white men in South Carolina—published in the local weekly newspaper—obviously was intended to lessen any resentment such people might feel toward the gentleman capitalists monopolizing the rich rice lands alongside the Waccamaw, Pee Dee, and Black Rivers. T. B. Hamlin, a retired overseer, had long—like any contented, dutiful, lowly participant in a hierarchical society—fulfilled his duties in his humble station. But Carolina offered the poor white male a reward. As Allston exulted in his paean to the virtues of the Carolina militiaman, Hamlin,

> exhibiting early in life a passionate fondness for hunting, lived a life of hardy exposure. For many years he devoted himself faithfully to the duties of an Overseer. But latterly he settled with his promising and thriving family in the pine lands of Georgetown District where, without anyone to say him nay, when disposed to roost a Turkey or trail the deer, he pass'd the remainder of his days. . . . (He loved the native forests in which he was wont to roam in pursuit of game. . . .) Possessing all the sagacious and generous qualities of the Forrester, there was no citizen-soldier more earnest, and efficient when on duty patiently enduring, perseveringly active, and intently watchful than he.[10]

However serviceable such rhetoric might be, Allston understood that something more than inspiration was needed to bind poor whites to the planting class. He seems to have thought the planters did not offer enough educational facilities to Carolina's poor whites, and he sought to fill the gap: partly by private charity to the deserving poor of Georgetown, partly by promoting less parsimonious provision of state funds for schooling. He was president of the Winyah Indigo Society, a Georgetown charity which disbursed several hundred dollars annually to help secure an education for twenty-five local boys. And although he loathed the abolitionist ideas emanating from Massachusetts, he was in 1838 so broad-minded as to study that state's common school system, of which (in Allston's words) he "became an admirer and thereafter sought to engraft some of its features" upon South Carolina. In 1852 Allston and his allies finally achieved a doubling of Carolina's minuscule free school fund.[11] Allston accepted, however, that well-to-do whites in the Carolina low country—unlike those in other parts of America—would not deign to send their own children to mix with the hoi polloi in state schools.[12] And if the rich were not to use the state schools for their own children, had they a duty to contribute substantially to schools for other whites, from which they themselves could expect no direct benefit? One suspects that this ambiguity at the center of rich Carolinians' thinking palsied Allston's considerable efforts as state senator to reform the state's educational system.

Allston was probably more successful in improving the local roads in Georgetown District than in bettering the state schools. The former lay within the power of a few active local planters, who by setting the example of sending a contingent of their own slaves twice a year to work on the local roads could do something for the public benefit at little financial cost, and with no infringement on their legal right to dispose of their slaves' time in whatever way suited their own will. Allston was assiduous in performing his own public duty in this way and in setting an example of noblesse oblige to his rich neighbors.[13]

Allston's long battle for Carolinian self-determination against the North may also, ultimately, have served the function of lessening class antagonisms between rich and poor Carolina whites (by subordinating those antagonisms to a perceived common interest in keeping down the blacks). As has already been suggested, however, the triumph of Allston's nullificationist and secessionist principles was not achieved, even in Georgetown District, without a contest. His actions here seem to have been determined almost exclusively by his self-interest as a capitalist planter. Everywhere in the South during the secession crisis (except in the sugar region, which depended on a high tariff wall against Caribbean sugar to protect its markets in the Northern United States, and in Mississippi, where nearly every white person was a secessionist) there was a close correlation between areas with slave majorities and those dominated by immediate secessionists.[14] The correlation was even stronger in the rice kingdom, and long predated 1860. For thirty years Allston was one of Carolina's most extreme advocates of state sovereignty as a means of protecting slavery. His intemperate pursuit of the big planters' self-interest made this passionate antidemocrat willing that people should die—if necessary by the hundreds of thousands—so that slavery might be preserved.

Allston did not pretend—as did his wife Adele—that South Carolina fought simply for an abstract political principle: "the cause of constitutional government," as Mrs. Allston said, "in opposition to the will of a mere majority, which sets at defiance all written law." Robert, by contrast, acknowledged as early as 1849 that a concrete social system, human bondage, was at the heart of the dispute. He was glad that in December 1849 Southerners were blocking the election of a Speaker of the House of Representatives at Washington: this was a means, he assured Adele, of notifying "our Northern friends of the feeling which pervades the Southern Country on the subject of slavery. . . . Unless the Northern people now come to be reasonable people, Revolution will be unavoidable." Allston's private purse backed his principles. In 1856 he contributed $430—no small sum then—to support the emigration of proslavery settlers to Kansas; and later he and his son Benjamin privately "raised and equipped a company of cavalry" to serve in the South's war for independence.[15]

The clearest expression of Allston's proslavery zeal came during the crisis of 1860–61. In early October 1860 he went out of his way to hear, with satisfaction, the Southern fire-eater William Yancey; and he already at that time favored "taking the Federal City and Treasury" when the South seceded, instead of leaving them to Northern control.[16] In late March 1861 he was one of the elder statesmen in Charleston advising General Beauregard and South Carolina's Governor Pickens during the Sumter crisis. His impatience to seize the fort knew no bounds. "I cannot leave the City until the harbor shall be restored to the State," he chafed to his son Benjamin three weeks after Lincoln's inauguration. Robert had no use for Governor Pickens's "shuffling with [the Union garrison at Sumter] in the hope that [Major] Anderson would evacuate of his own accord." Allston plainly preferred that the Confederates "commit ourselves by demanding and enforcing a surrender of [Anderson's] forces"; and doubtless this was his advice to General Beauregard when he dined with him on March 24. No believer in freedom of speech when slavery was at stake, Robert blamed Governor Pickens's "shuffling" partly on J. L. Petigru (Allston's brother-in-law), and he relished the thought that public pressure would drive Petigru out of Carolina into foreign exile, because of his Unionism.

Allston's determination to precipitate the crisis at Sumter led him to fabricate the flimsiest of arguments to support his case for immediate action. The families of the Carolina volunteers had already suffered three months of financial sacrifices; and in order to terminate these relatively small sacrifices, Allston advocated the quick attack on Sumter which would result in mowing down a generation of young Americans. No doubt he miscalculated the North's response to the bombardment of Sumter, but his eagerness to defend slavery was the source of his awesome misjudgment. If the Confederates would force Major Anderson to surrender, Allston argued, this would put an end to the "privation among families in town of the soldiers on duty whose revenues are materially diminish'd . . . by absence from their vocations these three months. I trust their relief is near at hand. Then what will J. L. P[etigru] do? I think he must go abroad."[17]

Three weeks later, Allston's son Benjamin was at Morris Island, on General Simons's staff, during the bombardment of Sumter. Benjamin considered the Northerners cowards; the failure (in obedience to President Lincoln's orders) of the Union naval vessels to come to Anderson's support was, in Benjamin's opinion, "dastardly conduct." Reporting the portentous happenings in Charleston harbor, Benjamin—blinded like his father by his eagerness to perpetuate Carolina's racial and labor system—grossly misjudged the events in which he was an avid participant. "Such a 'bloodless victory' has never yet," he crowed, "been recorded in the pages of history."[18] Yet Benjamin's vehement secessionism was by no means the product of overoptimism. Two weeks later he was already saying that Britain and France probably would not intervene: the war, he foresaw, was likely to last nearly four years, "until the next Presidential election comes around." Benjamin's commitment to a war to preserve slavery was not conditional upon the war's being brief and splendid; on the contrary, preserving the South's social structure was to him worth a long and deathly struggle.[19] Later generations of Americans have been curiously indulgent toward the authors of their country's most devastating and inglorious war—the war for Southern independence—and even toward the social system which fed the military zeal of these gentleman planters.

In later years Allston's daughter Elizabeth Allston Pringle tried to explain to herself and posterity how a man as personally honorable and virtuous as her father could have been so heavily implicated in the defense of a barbaric system of human coercion. Her solution to the problem, like that of many other descendants of rich slaveholders, was to seize on scraps of evidence from the antebellum period, and to elaborate them into a full-blown theory of paternalism that bore slight relation to the real nature of the slavery regime.

Elizabeth had begun in 1855 to taste the satisfactions of fulfilling a paternalist role when she was sent, at the age of ten, for a long stay with a Petigru aunt in up-country Carolina. One of the old slaves there was dying, and it was Elizabeth's pleasure to take to the old man each day a morsel of the white people's food, after they had finished their dinner. Any gratification this gesture may have given the slaves was crushed by the callousness of one of the big white boys (probably Elizabeth's cousin). As the old man neared his end, the slaves placed silver dollars in his eyes, in their preparation for his spirit to leave the body. The old man lay gasping for breath in his death struggle. The white boy decided this was an opportune moment to play a practical joke on his girly cousin, regardless of what the blacks might feel. He told Elizabeth, falsely, that old Joe wanted to see her; the young girl entered the room expectantly, was horrified by the old man's death struggle, and was so shocked it took a long time for her to recover.[20] In the white boy's eyes the old black man was a nearly useless old creature—fit still, however, to be used at this last moment as the instrument of a fine joke at the expense of the little white girl. The episode encapsulated the contrast between the theory of paternalism and the blacks' actual experience of slavery.

Elizabeth Allston, as a bookish, slightly rebellious teenage girl in wartime Charleston, had once toyed with antislavery ideas. These did not cause any wavering in her support of the Southern war for independence; and her reading of J. L. Motley's *Rise of the Dutch Republic* (she finished the 1,575-page work in three weeks) gave her added hope for Southern success in that war. Nor was Elizabeth Allston an abolitionist: to her, Yankee abolitionism meant "to kill the white and make the negro a murderer and theif [sic]." But colonization—a heresy in the eyes of Robert Allston and of nearly every other Carolinian—attracted Elizabeth. "I have often thought it would be much better to abolish" slavery, she wrote at the age of seventeen (in words which betrayed little paternalist benevolence toward blacks), if there "was any means by which they [the masters] could get rid of them [the slaves], form a colony of them or any thing else—certainly we [white people] would be much happier." An element in Elizabeth's quick retreat from this colonizationist impulse was her reading of two Charles Kingsley novels on the condition of poor people in England. "The reading of those two books," she wrote, with the relief of a believer in religion, after a brief bout of agnosticism,

> has done more to strengthen my faith in Slavery than anything else could have done. . . . I have come to the conclusion that it is a divine institution. We know that there must be two distinct classes, the Rich and the Poor. In whatever form of government, Democratic or otherwise, they will be distinctly and painfully marked—and from all I can read and know the condition of the negro slave here is much better than that of the poor working man in England.[21]

Slavery could be justified, Elizabeth had come to feel, only if it benefited the slaves. Thus her later exposition of a paternalist theory arose not from benevolence toward blacks but from her wish to justify slavery in the only way she believed that could be achieved.

Two wartime experiences probably intensified Elizabeth's attachment to paternalist theory. Although her teenage self-assertion had been directed mostly against her mother—to whom she often spoke disrespectfully, tauntingly, ironically, and with temper—sometimes she was also a trial to her father. "When I remember the *many many* times I have grieved the best and kindest of fathers by my wayward willful ways," Elizabeth mourned a few weeks after Robert Allston's death in 1864, "how remorse and unavailing regret overpower me." Her only remaining way to make amends to her father would prove to be by picturing his mastery of slaves as it must have been, in order to be justified: as a paternalist regime. And less than a year after her father died, another wrenching event affected Elizabeth's later memoir. As the culmination of the shattering succession of deaths of uncles, cousins, and friends during the war came the news that her beloved first cousin Hal Lesesne had been killed in battle on March 16, 1865. Elizabeth had been writing to him weekly for more than a year. "I loved my cousin dearly," she grieved, "and I doubt if any one but his Father and Mother will miss him as I will."[22] It was impossible for Elizabeth to accept that this dear man, and all the others, had died in vain. It was even more impossible for her to acknowledge that her own father bore any responsibility—through his vigorous secessionism—for Hal Lesesne's death. The war *must* have been right. And if the war was right, slavery *must* have been a paternalist institution.

Elizabeth Allston (Pringle)'s *Chronicles of "Chicora Wood"* was published in 1922, a year after her death at the age of seventy-six. Here Robert Allston's daughter articulated in classic form—for her own grandchildren's instruction— a vision of plantation slavery where the planter was a noble knight who, far from exploiting blacks to enrich himself, wore himself out in fulfilling paternalist duties to his dependents. The essence of slavery was, in fact, to free the masters from any meaningful legal obligations toward the slaves (i.e., to strip the slaves of any meaningful legal rights); hence the essence of paternalist theory had to be the claim that *moral* obligations toward the slaves—imposed by the masters upon themselves—served the interests of the slaves better than any legal obligation could have done. No wonder freedom from governmental constraint ranked so prominently in the vocabulary of secessionists like Robert Allston, for freedom from legal restraint was the central element in being a slave master. Because Carolinian slave masters were (in the words of Allston's second cousin Joseph Alston) "impatient of restraint,"[23] it was necessary, in any paternalist defense of slavery, to claim that the self-imposed moral constraints upon the slave masters were powerful and deeply felt. As Mary Chesnut alleged in her memoir—in words written long after slavery had been abolished—"Two-thirds of my religion consist[ed] in trying to be good to negroes because they [were] so in my power, and it would [have been] so easy"—in the absence of legal obligation—"to be the other thing."[24]

A remarkable illustration of paternalism appeared in a boast of Elizabeth Pringle's[25] first cousin Elizabeth Weston (wife of that Francis Weston, twenty of whose slaves in 1862 rowed down the Pee Dee to freedom in their master's big boat). Mrs. Weston claimed she was so tied by moral obligations to her slaves that she had to take fifty of them with her every May when her family moved to Charleston. This was, among other things, a not very subtle brag about how rich the Westons were. It would not do, Mrs. Weston asserted, to separate their privileged house servants—who were needed in Charleston—from their own families for six months every year; therefore, the families had to be moved too, useless though most of these slaves might be in Charleston.[26]

Pringle's clearest formulation of the paternalist theory appeared in a story her mother, Adele, told her about events a dozen years before Elizabeth herself was born. Once again a dying slave was involved. Adele Allston said that she—as a young bride, fresh from the lively society of Charleston and unused to low-country plantation life (for she had been born in up-country Carolina where slaves were less numerous)—had needed her husband's instruction in the moral obligations a plantation mistress owed the slaves. In Pringle's antifeminist narration, the wise male instructed the petulant female in her duty, and the female profited from this instruction. Adele's character was elevated by her submitting to her husband, and leading "a life full of service and responsibility" to the slaves—instead of devoting herself to reading and study as she (an intelligent woman who shared the mental power of her lawyer brother, J. L. Petigru) had originally intended. Pompey was dying in the sick house.[27] Allston's wife resisted his desire that she visit Pompey before he died, but Allston insisted. As Adele Allston told this story to Elizabeth years later, and as Elizabeth polished it for publication nearly ninety years after the event, Pompey opened his eyes when Allston and his bride appeared, "and a look of delight replaced the one of pain. 'My marster!' he exclaimed. 'You cum! O, I too glad! I tink I bin gwine, widout see you once more.' " For Pringle, this cherished recollection reinforced the message that the position of slave master was a hallowed one. As Robert and Adele drove away from the sick house in their buggy, Robert "was full of self-questioning and solemn thought: 'Had he been as faithful to every duty through life as Pompey in his humbler sphere had been?' " Adele, for her part, had learned a needed lesson in the moral obligations of a plantation mistress. "I beg you to forgive my petulance about coming," she murmured contritely.[28]

Pringle's message to her grandchildren was that Allston always—and his wife after accepting his instruction—had led lives of Christian service and responsibility. Slavery was a splendid institution, for it offered the masters and mistresses exalted opportunities for exercising Christian virtues. The plantation mistress's was a "very peculiar life, surrounded by hundreds of a different race," Pringle affirmed. "It is a very noble life," Allston's Aunt Blyth had believed, "if a woman does her full duty in it. It is the life of a missionary, really. . . . It is *our life*: the life of those who have the great responsibility of owning human beings." The satisfactions to the master class of exercising dominion over other human beings (as emphasized in Orlando Patterson's interpretation of slavery) are everywhere here evident.[29]

Although this pleasing picture of plantation life need not have made Pringle's grandchildren feel resentment toward the blacks, Pringle essayed to do so. She blamed the slaves for the bankruptcy of Allston's estate after the Civil War, and thus for the virtual disinheritance of those grandchildren. The problem, as Pringle presented it, was that her father was too much of a paternalist for the good of himself and his family. When his brother-in-law U.S. Navy Captain Tom Petigru died in 1858, leaving an estate of one hundred slaves who had to be sold, a black spokesman for the slaves approached Allston and begged him to buy them all. Allston, according to Pringle, did not need the slaves; but his paternalist wish to protect his brother-in-law's slaves from being sold out of the neighborhood, and to masters of unknown character, impelled him to buy them himself. To pay for them he signed the notes which—because of the war—he could never pay, and which led directly to the bankruptcy proceedings of 1869. The blacks who petitioned Allston to buy them were therefore the cause of Allston's bankruptcy; and any resentment Allston's grandchildren might feel at their disinheritance ought properly to be directed against the blacks (and perhaps against the Unionist lawyer J. L. Petigru, who played a part in persuading Allston to issue the personal bonds), but surely not against their grandfather, dutiful paternalist as he was.[30]

In blaming the blacks for taking advantage of Allston's paternalist benevolence, Pringle seriously misrepresented the events of the late 1850s. Allston's parlous financial position by the time of his death in 1864 arose from sources very different from the one Pringle specified. Allston had foolishly bought the most extravagant house in Charleston in 1857, almost entirely on credit. In 1858 and 1859 he incurred heavy financial obligations in buying Guendalos plantation and some 119 slaves in order to set up his son Benjamin as a planter—an object he had long had in view, but which the young West Pointer had resisted for several years until he had had a spell of army life first. Robert Allston's purchase of the Petigru slaves was motivated principally by his wish to consolidate his holdings near Chicora Wood, so that he could sell Nightingale Hall (seven miles distant from Chicora Wood) and have all of his lands directly under his own eye.[31] Insofar as paternalist motives entered the matter, Allston was affected mainly by his paternal wish to establish his own son in planting—he handed over about thirty-six of the Petigru slaves to Benjamin to work at Benjamin's new plantation—not by a paternalistic sense of moral obligation to the slaves themselves. This point was clear to J. H. Easterby, the editor of Allston's papers, as early as 1944.[32]

Allston's confidence, during the late 1850s, that a slave-based rice-planting business would continue to be as lucrative as it had been for the previous thirty years led him into grievous imprudence. Thinking himself worth perhaps half a million dollars in 1856, he incurred debts of nearly $200,000 during the next three years—$36,000 to buy the Charleston mansion; some $103,500 to establish his son Benjamin with about 119 slaves and 210 acres of rice land; and $57,500 for Mrs. Petigru's land and about 73 of her slaves.[33] Quite possibly these debts could have been paid—as all of Allston's previous obligations had been—if slavery had continued. Financial anxiety may therefore have contributed to Robert Allston's impatience that a blow against Fort Sumter be struck quickly in March 1861, so that the security of the slave system would be promptly and permanently established.

The ultimate reason for Allston's financial ruin was the war for Southern independence, which he himself had played a considerable part in inciting. That war led to the loss of all the capital he had invested in slaves, and to a precipitous decline in the value of the capital he had invested in land. Slave owners in Jamaica, by contrast, were substantially compensated by the British government in the 1830s for their acquiescence in the peaceful abolition of slavery. One of the principal uses of the paternalist theory, in the hands of Allston's daughter, was to direct the resentment of Allston's putative heirs against the blacks, instead of encouraging those heirs to look honestly at the terrible miscalculations—financial and especially political—which Robert Allston had made. Allston himself was probably conscious of some of these mistakes when, dying in 1864, he exclaimed miserably that he was not beloved by God; but Pringle, by falsely stressing a theory of paternalist obligation to slaves, led her readers away from a confrontation with the realities of her family's—and South Carolina's—history.

The major role of some Southern white women in promoting paternalist ideology becomes evident in the Allston family records. A male like Robert Allston, responsible for reestablishing his family's fortune, naturally turned his mind toward making a good profit from his capital investment in slaves; and as has been shown, his language reflected his capitalist motives. A white woman, by contrast—less responsible than a male for the economic support of her family, and belonging to a gender supposed more caring than were males—had more need than a man for the support of a theory which offered the mistress a significant moral function in the plantation world.

A woman like Mary Chesnut's mother-in-law—who, besides having two house slaves to sleep in her bedchamber, had two others just outside the bedroom door, ready to leap up in the middle of the night and iron her a fresh warm garment if the whim to change her nightdress should strike her—might have felt uncomfortable in her enjoyment of this extraordinary luxury, had she not felt she earned it by "paternalistic" service to those slaves. Mary Chesnut herself luxuriated in having a maidservant to light her bedroom fire in the morning, bring her breakfast in her third-floor bedroom if she chose to sleep late, and tidy the room for her while she was in the dressing room. The slaves' inefficiency, in her eyes, was more than compensated by their deference: "The Chesnut negroes . . . have such good manners, they are so polite you forget everything else. And they make you so comfortable if you can afford ten to do the work of one servant." Chesnut could justify to herself this life of ease only by enunciating a paternalist theory. Her mother, her grandmother, and her mother-in-law, Chesnut wrote long after the war (but as though she were writing in 1861), "strive to ameliorate the condition of these Africans in every particular. They set them the example of a perfect life—life of utter self-abnegation. . . . These women are more troubled by their duty to negroes, have less chance to live their own lives in peace than if they were African missionaries."[34] This was the language of Allston's Aunt Blyth: the life of a plantation mistress was that of a Christian missionary in darkest heathendom.

Robert Allston's wife, too, came to feel the pleasures of paternalist domination of her dependents. Having conquered her initial aversion, Adele, according to her daughter, "had come to love the plantation life, with its duties and its power to help the sick, to have the girls taught to sew and cut out simple garments, to supply proper and plentiful nourishment for the hospital—all this came to be a joy to her." Much of Adele's satisfaction arose from the deference the slave girls were taught to display, like that of courtiers before a king, or soldiers before their commanding general. When Adele inspected the slave girls' sewing, the children were "all lined up in rows . . . , dropp[ing] their courtesies as mamma passed, each one holding in her hand some piece of [sewing] work to exhibit."[35]

Having learned to savor her plantation role, Adele then passed paternalist lore on to her daughter, who, after countless retelling, had by 1920 perfected her account of an event that took place in 1824—nearly a century earlier, and twenty-one years before the narrator's own birth. As Pringle recounted this quintessentially paternalist story, her mother at the age of twelve had accosted an African-born slave woman with the idea that she must have been dreadfully sorry to have been taken away from Africa:

> Maum Maria stopped her work, rose to her full height—she was very tall and straight—clasped her hands and said, dropping a deep courtesy as she spoke: "My chile, ebery night on my knees I tank my Hebenly Father that he brought me here, for without that i wud neber hev known my Saviour!" She remained, hands clasped, and a look of ecstasy on her face, for some time before she sat down and resumed her work.

When Pringle's grandmother had died, three elderly Petigru slaves were offered their freedom; but only one of them, Pringle exulted, accepted the offer.

Daddy Prince and the aforementioned Maum Maria "said they were grateful to their beloved mistress, but they would rather remain just as they were [slaves]; they had all they needed and were happy and loved their white family, and they did not want to make any change."[36]

An indispensable witness in any paternalistic portrayal of slavery was the docile elderly black dependent, wholly reliant in old age on the goodwill of a white person for economic support and privileged treatment, who told the white people what they thirsted to hear. For Adele Allston this was "Maum" Maria; for Susan Dabney Smedes—author of the best-known example of this postwar genre of plantation reminiscences (*Memorials of a Southern Planter*)—it was the pathetic, eighty-year-old "Mammy" Harriet; and for Pringle herself it was an old man, "Daddy" Ancrum. Who can blame Maria for her words to Adele in 1824? Doubtless Adele's daughter exercised literary license here ("look of ecstasy . . . their beloved mistress"), but the kernel of her story was likely to be true. An old person might anticipate better life chances as a privileged slave than as an uprooted wanderer in a Carolinian environment hostile to free blacks. And Christian conversion might well have functioned for this woman to alienate her from African gods. Pringle's mistake lay not in her report of Maum Maria's words, but in her implying that these utterances of an elderly and privileged slave typified the feelings of the Petigru and Allston slaves. The events of 1864 and 1865 contradicted any such presumption.

Ancrum was Pringle's main black witness to the theory that paternalist motives primarily determined Robert Allston's conduct toward his slaves. "Daddy" Ancrum (as Pringle insisted upon calling him) was a man of some independence: he had shown this when he ran away—apparently for weeks— after what he thought an unjust whipping by the overseer Gabriel Ellis. During the Civil War Ancrum, when entrusted by his master with a driver's authority over other slaves, sometimes exercised this power to serve the interests of these slaves. He may have permitted the brother-in-law of the Allstons' privileged laundress, Fibby,[37] to escape in Charleston, when a gang was returning from work on the fortifications—"I couldn't stop him," Ancrum said, and Robert Allston accepted his word. Later, in North Carolina, Ancrum intervened to shorten a white overseer's whipping of a slave who finally confessed to stealing meat: Mr. Ballantine, in Ancrum's words, "give him a big licking, 'til he confess how he done it. Den I stop him, I hold 'e hand an' I say: 'Maussa only want de trut; he don't allow lick after dat, not another cut.' "[38] "Cut" was the right word for whippings which often broke the skin, and Allston, of course, authorized "cuts" and "big lickings." Whipping was for Allston the approved method for extorting a confession from a suspected slave. But in Allston's regime there often was a limit to the use of personal violence against a slave, and in this instance Ancrum helped enforce that limit.

After the war Ancrum worked for Allston's daughter, and by the time she wrote her *Chronicles* he was an old man probably almost wholly dependent upon her for his economic support. He continued even in his old age to give her a better day's work, she said, than any of the younger men. When she asked him for his plantation reminiscences, he naturally chose his words so as to put Elizabeth's father in the most favorable light. He flattered Elizabeth with how rich her father had been, how much land he had owned, how much agricultural produce he had sent inland during the war. Thinking back to his own youth, he claimed with false modesty to have derived his sense of self-worth solely through his master's esteem. His master's paternalist care was the only reason he had risen from field labor to posts of responsibility at Chicora Wood: "Maussa see someting in me I didn' see in myself, an' he hol' me back all 'e could [from menial labor]." When his master put Ancrum in charge of the twenty-two slaves whom Allston sent to work on the Charleston fortifications, the assignment was unwelcome. The work was the hardest and most unhealthy imaginable.[39] Every one of the slaves caught the fever, and one died of it. Allston knew he was likely to lose valuable slave property from disease or ill treatment, and he deputed Ancrum to try to protect the other slaves: "Boy, you see nobody hurt[s] my hands." When Allston finally drove up in a carriage to send his slaves home after their ordeal at the fortifications, they were of course delighted, and they cheered. Ancrum presented the matter in terms of transparent flattery: when Ancrum spoke to Pringle, he did not blame Allston, or even slavery in general, for the slaves' sufferings at the fortifications; instead, "him been a number one maussa dat. Him'll nebber back down from a man in trouble. He'll save you if you is to save!"[40]

A decisive clue—that Ancrum's real feelings about slavery diverged from those he reported to Elizabeth Pringle—lies in a detail which doubtless she noticed but to which she did not call attention. In February 1865 Ancrum, his wife, and their five children were at Allston's North Carolina farm, where Ancrum was the driver of one hundred Allston slaves sent there for fear they might otherwise run away. By this late date, however, security for slave property was not to be found even inland: a contingent of Northern soldiers under Sherman's cavalry commander (General H. Judson Kilpatrick) arrived in North Carolina, bringing with them the promise that Lincoln's Emancipation Proclamation would soon be enforced throughout the South. Several of the Allston slaves went off with Kilpatrick's forces when they departed, but of course Ancrum was in no position to do this with five young children and a wife more than eight months pregnant. The only thing he could do was to name his new child, when it was born a few days later, not "Lee," "Jefferson Davis," nor any other such designation, but "Kilpatrick."[41] The child bore until its dying day Ancrum's and his wife's memory of the Northern general who had brought to the whole family the promise of freedom.

The reason Pringle did not comment on this act of Ancrum's was that paternalist theory specified the blacks' true friends to be their Southern white masters, not the Northern interlopers. As part of this theory, Pringle blamed the bad treatment of low-country slaves upon overseers who "in those days [the early nineteenth century] were invariably from the North."

Roswell King Sr. (Pierce Butler's agent) was born in the North, to be sure, and no doubt there were a few others; but every historian knows that the great majority of low-country overseers were born in the low country, where they had a good chance of gaining some resistance against malaria. According to the South Carolina historian George Rogers, the overseers of Georgetown district "came from the poorer class of whites who inhabited the pine lands of the district. Most of the surnames of R[obert] Allston's overseers can be found in the Georgetown District census for 1790; his overseers, therefore, were generally natives." Elizabeth Pringle—prone to blame Northerners, however implausibly—was pleased to quote evidence that the Yankees were not the blacks' benefactors. The lady's maid of Elizabeth's older sister had somehow acquired jewelry which Northern soldiers stole from her, and Pringle recalled with satisfaction Margaret's disillusioned comment, "I always bin head dat de Yankees was gwine help de nigger!"[42] The view that Southern whites were the blacks' only true friends was not just a way of easing the minds of Southerners about their slave-owning ancestors; it also served the function of rationalizing Southern opposition during the late nineteenth and early twentieth centuries against Northern enforcement of the Reconstruction amendments.

Pringle went even further, however, for she thought slavery had benefited the blacks' character. Tears rolled down her cheeks as she lamented the fate of the descendants of her father's well-trained house servants: "In so many instances, to my great regret, they have fallen in character and good qualities instead of rising;—without training or discipline that is to be expected." Slavery, she felt, had been a means of instilling wholesome discipline into the savages. Historians have occasionally suggested that the adherents of a paternalist ideology were less racist than were nonpaternalists, but the Allston records do not support this view. The paternalist ideology elaborated by Elizabeth Pringle was clearly based upon, and intricately interwoven with, a profoundly racist stance toward blacks.[43] The two theories could be mutually reinforcing.

Beneath the paternalist surface of Pringle's *Chronicles* lay a far stronger and more genuine emotion: the sense that mastering slaves had created for the rulers a delightful existence. The Allstons led a life of luxury and ease, surrounded by house servants whose grand manners made the masters feel they were respected and even loved by their dependents. The ballroom of their splendid house at Charleston—the scene of Elizabeth's elder sister, Della's, wedding in May 1863, just a few weeks before the battle of Gettysburg shattered the dream that this way of life could go on indefinitely—bore witness to what the wealth produced by unpaid blacks could buy. (Thousands of present-day visitors to Charleston's famous Nathaniel Russell House, which Allston had bought in 1857, enjoy inspecting this room every year.) The "beautiful oval drawing-room or ballroom," Elizabeth recalled,

> had a very high ceiling and was papered in white with small sprigs of golden flowers scattered over it. There were four large windows on the south,

opening on the iron balcony which ran round on the outside, and, on the opposite side of the room, [were] two windows exactly like those opening on the balcony, running from the tall ceiling to the floor, but the panes of these were mirrors. It made you think you were looking into another crowded room. There was a high mantlepiece of white wood carved with exquisite figures of women dancing and holding aloft garlands of flowers, Adam's most beautiful designs; the cornice and the ceiling was also beautiful; the furniture was rosewood, covered with blue velvet with little pink rosebuds, and the carpet was velvet with bouquets of pink roses tied with blue ribbons.

Bouquets of roses were foremost among Elizabeth's hallowed recollections of the ancien régime. It was with "sensible" bouquets of flowers, picked by himself from his aunt's garden in Charleston, that young Pinckney Alston— Della's third cousin and an earlier, beloved suitor—had courted her before the ruinous war for Southern independence cut short his life. When the Allstons had summered only a few miles north of Chicora Wood, Adele Allston had loved to drive back to her plantation of an afternoon to "see after her flower-garden, which was beautiful and her delight." And it was at "White House," the most charming plantation on the Pee Dee, that Elizabeth herself was courted by her future husband, Julius Pringle, in 1865. "You entered on a lane bordered on each side with most luxuriant [white and pink] climbing roses," she remembered. Joel Poinsett (President Van Buren's secretary of war) had laid out the ornamental gardens, incorporating even a vegetable garden into his scheme. "The effect was delightful," Elizabeth continued:

> on the left the [Pee Dee] river, only a few feet away, on the right a green lawn, until you came to the vegetable garden. A picture garden! . . . I had never seen a vegetable-garden which was ornamental before. [Then] we entered the flower-garden, with a wilderness of roses, azaleas, camellias, and other beautiful shrubs and plants. . . .
>
> Oh, what a white day that stands out in my memory![44]

The color symbolism of these horticultural scenes was completed by the retinue of shining, devoted black faces by which the masters were normally surrounded. Clear expressions of devotion were expected from all the house servants, and if the demeanor of one of these servants did not come up to expectations, the Allstons' suspicions were aroused. Thus Little Andrew, a wartime dining room servant at Society Hill, had astoundingly been impassive— "he never expressed devotion or the contrary"—and this abnormal conduct led the Allstons to distrust him: they were surprised he did not flee in 1865 when Sherman's army was in the neighborhood. William Baron (the future caterer at the postwar St. Cecilia balls), like nearly all the other house servants, supplied what was expected: full of flattery, he was "an excellent servant, with very courteous manners."[45] The egos of the white people were wonderfully massaged by the displays of deference and devotion from every side (as was suggested in Pringle's fond recollections, familiar from previous pages):

[The black girls] dropped their courtesies as mamma passed. . . .

[The white children enjoyed] tea and bread-and-butter, handed by Nelson on the big silver waiter.

[Being rowed by six singing boatmen on the annual migration to the seaside was] the most delightful revelation and sensation of [Adele Allston's] life almost.[46]

Elizabeth Pringle's evocation of the charms (to the whites) of slavery was mingled with her passionate devotion to the memory of her stern, silent father. Robert Allston imposed a harsh switching on his daughter twice in her childhood, and she loved him for it. Allston would have been gratified if his slaves had responded to their whippings as his daughter did to her own switchings. "I used as a little child to thank and adore my father for his punishments," she recalled. "There were only these two that I have told of. Never afterward did my father have to give me even a stern look. It was my joy and pride to win his approval, generally only a smile, but it meant more to me than the most lavish praise from any one else." The blacks played a central role in Elizabeth's feelings about her father. Robert Allston was the stern, methodical, unbending governor of a hierarchical world where everyone knew his place and (except for a rare ingrate like Stephen Gallant) seemed to accept it gladly—a wonderful contrast, Pringle felt, to the anarchy when slavery no longer ordered human relations! The pageant of mourning black faces at Allston's funeral in April 1864 was for Elizabeth the last great display of the old order. Stephen Gallant (who had not yet revealed his secret thoughts) and another enslaved servant arranged, dressed, and laid out Allston's body. At the funeral the slaves "filled the large graveyard, standing at a little distance behind the family, according to their rank and station on the plantation. Those who dug the grave had been specially named by papa [in the instructions he prepared for his own funeral], and it was considered a great honor." Her father, Elizabeth believed, "carried the love and devotion of many people of all colors and classes."[47]

One of the few unpleasant sensations associated in Elizabeth's memory with the old regime was the exhalation from the stinking rice fields. "The cultivation of rice necessitated keeping the fields flooded with river water until it became stagnant," she acknowledged, "and the whole atmosphere was polluted by the dreadful smell."[48] Rich white people could escape the stench during most of the flooding season, for their six-month sojourn at the beach removed them from the swamps' "miasma": away from the smell, as well as from the mosquitoes. The paternalist theory was to the postwar generation of Southern whites something like a house at the beach: for a journey into the aromatic world evoked by this ideology removed one from the stench of slavery, just as a journey to Pawleys Island distanced one from the dreadful atmosphere near the stagnant fields. The recollection of the house servants' shining faces facilitated Elizabeth Pringle's giving credence to the paternalist theory; and the prominent position of domestic servants in her *Chronicles of*

"*Chicora Wood*"—as in Susan Smedes's *Memorials of a Southern Planter* and most other books of the genre—measured the value to the masters of the system of privileges Allston accorded this group of slaves. The fact that *Chronicles of "Chicora Wood"* said almost nothing about individual field hands—and not much about the plowmen, trunk minders, or even most of the drivers and artisans—suggested Pringle's failure to approach the whole truth about her father's regime.

Elizabeth Allston Pringle, then, was a beguiling paternalist ideologue: but were the Allstons themselves "paternalists" in the sense that benevolent motives principally guided their conduct? The answer on the whole must surely be no, even though benevolence did play a role in their regime. In 1860 Robert Allston enjoined his twelve-year-old son, Charles, "You must try to be a good boy, in order to treat [the slaves] judiciously and well, when Papa is gone." In the 1830s he had no doubt instructed his young bride in the paternalist duties of a plantation mistress, as Elizabeth Pringle vividly recounted. Allston showed a certain patience with the slaves, listening to their "long rigmaroles" in a manner impressive to his daughter. He did sometimes appear to assimilate house servants into the white "family," as paternalist theory adjured. Thus, in 1856, anxious for the safety of his eldest son, Benjamin (fighting Indians in the Oregon Territory), Allston in good paternalist fashion pictured slaves and his youngest white children—Charley and Jane—not only together, but using the same words, in order to make Benjamin feel he was loved by everyone at home. "All the negroes send how'dye for Mas Ben. [Charley] sends you howd'ye, so does Jane." Robert Allston served as intermediary in the exchange of goods between house servants and the master class, as paternalist theory prescribed. He once wrote from Chicora Wood to his wife in Charleston,

> Your note has been read to Mary [Grice, the cook], who, with a low curtsy "Do tell Miss heap a tanke for the frock, likewise for the letter Sir". . . . She will send six [turkey hens]. Mary reports tonight 10 dozen Eggs put up to go over [by ship to Charleston] Monday . . . , "6 last-fall chickens" and a small supply of butter.[49]

Allston, of course, disapproved sadistic treatment of slaves. He was upset in 1853 when, attending the state senate in Columbia, he read in the *Temperance Advocate* "a report of the most horrible cruelties & feindish [*sic*] brutality that ever disgraced the columns of a public journal. The catching by dogs and murderous killing of a runaway negroe by some men from this district. The case was tried in Walterborough before Judge O'Neal who has publish'd it." The disgrace lay in the event itself but perhaps also in its being reported in a public journal. Fearing that he was a subscriber to the *Temperance Advocate*, and that a copy might be delivered to Chicora Wood, Allston urged his wife to impound it. It might fall into the wrong hands. The white children, the Irish nursemaid, and the English governess ought not to learn about this aspect of slavery. "One of Miss Ayme's [the governess's] failings is to bruit such a thing."[50]

Although Allston sometimes purchased slaves "in the round"—that is, in a large group from a single plantation, and at an average price for the whole lot, rather than at different prices for different slaves—his principal motive appears to have been to save money, not to save the feelings of the slaves concerned.[51] No paternalist compunctions prevented Allston from selling Sango and his family when the master needed cash to buy the inland North Carolina farm in 1863; nor, of course, did paternalist scruples interfere with Allston's selling a slave like Brass—for disciplinary reasons—away from any family and friends he may have had. If Allston felt embarrassment in doing so, the matter was to be dealt with by doing the thing as secretly as possible. Impatient with Brass's intractability, Allston instructed his wife to "give Brass a new shirt and send him to Robertson Blacklock and Co. to be turn'd into money, forthwith. . . . There must be no fuss about it, no noise, or notice."[52]

A clear illustration of paternalism, and of its limits, appeared in January 1859. Dr. Frederick Rutledge was selling off both his mother's debt-ridden "Harrietta" plantation (on the Santee River) and its sixty-two slaves. He purchased the driver for himself, but with a degree of genuine paternalism he sought to sell the remaining slaves in a single group; and he offered them to Stephen Doar (the purchaser of her plantation), so that they need not be moved away from the neighborhood. Doar was willing to pay $34,100—that is, $550 per slave. This was not quite as much as Dr. Rutledge hoped for, and paternalism began to seep into the swamp. The bondsmen and women were instead sold away from Harrietta at $575 per slave. By this means Dr. Rutledge gained $1,525 for his mother's heirs, at the expense of separating the gang from their own local community. But Dr. Rutledge could feel that he had kept the sixty-one slaves together rather than ruthlessly selling them off in smaller parcels.[53]

The buyer of the Rutledge slaves was Robert Allston's nephew and longtime ward, Joseph B. Allston. Joseph was glad to take advantage of Dr. Rutledge's benevolent impulse by buying this gang of sixty-one slaves at a lower price than he would otherwise have had to pay. But he did not need sixty-one slaves, and could not afford them. He therefore determined to frustrate Dr. Rutledge's intention by keeping the more valuable slaves and selling the others in a parcel, for which, of course, he could not hope to receive as much as $575 per slave. In fact he received only $350 "in the round" for his group of culled slaves. Robert Allston's son Benjamin (who was associated with Joseph in some of their business dealings) wholly approved Joseph's selling some of the slaves, and was chagrined only because their sale price was lower than Benjamin had anticipated. Benjamin's language showed little paternalist concern for the welfare of the slaves who had just been sold. "I am sorry to inform you," he notified Robert, "that the blacks brought only $350. I do not know who bought them. . . . On the whole I think the blacks well gotten rid of, though I hoped they might have brought a higher price."[54]

These were the words and actions of profit-seeking businessmen, not paternalists. Evidently the Allstons used this kind of language in conversation, and indeed this was the very terminology employed by Benjamin's sister Elizabeth

Allston three years later, when she mused that colonization might be a good way to "get rid of" all the blacks. Neither Joseph nor Benjamin had compunctions about buying a group of slaves at a relatively low price "in the round," and then selling those surplus to their own requirements. Nor was Benjamin concerned about whether or not the surplus slaves were sold to a benevolent master. And indeed Joseph was acting wholly in accordance with Robert Allston's advice; for Robert had suggested (five days before Joseph bought the Harrietta slaves) that Joseph buy just such a gang—if he could get them from someone willing to sell cheap "rather than send away and separate his people at a higher figure."[55]

A similar contest between benevolence and financial self-interest transpired in the Petigru family. Adele Allston's sister Mary lived, not very prosperously, in the western part of the state. She owned eleven slaves, most of whom her brother James Petigru (Charleston's famous Unionist lawyer) thought she ought to sell to a relative, in order to improve her own financial position. Mary was keen to keep "little Charlotte," a young slave girl, for future domestic service, and was reluctant to separate this little girl from her mother, Peggy. Peggy, however, was "in the prime of life" and would make a good field hand on a cotton plantation. James Petigru—in order to overcome his sister's scruples about separating a young slave child from her mother—urged Adele Allston to use her influence on her sister, to persuade her to sell Peggy.[56] Petigru cared nothing for the family bond between Peggy and little Charlotte: his own sister's financial welfare was to him the important matter. His Unionism arose not from concern for the welfare of black people but from a hardheaded calculation that disunionism would ruin the slaveholders—as indeed it did.

If paternalist feelings were not to be discovered in James Petigru's letter, one might nevertheless expect to find them in the diary of his sister Adele Petigru Allston. But although Adele's surviving journal, from 1850 to 1852, tells something of her feelings for her husband Robert Allston and for their children, it is almost totally silent about the Allston slaves. Only twice during this period did Adele even bother to mention a slave by name—once when the head driver died, the other when the mulatto butler Nelson was married by the Episcopal rector. No field hand was ever named in this diary, and apparently even the most privileged house servants occupied only a small place in Adele's consciousness.[57]

Even when the Allstons went through the motions of paternalism, their motives were sometimes calculating, not benevolent. Thus toward the end of 1864 the young Charles Allston—visiting Chicora Wood, where the overseers feared many slaves would seek to escape if Union forces appeared in the neighborhood—urged his mother to come from Society Hill to try to secure the slaves's loyalty. "I think that you had better come down," Charles advised, "and give out clothes and any little thing you may have for them even if you do not stay. Some people think that we will have a raid here [in Georgetown District] this winter about Christmas."[58]

A different side of the paternalist coin had been evident four months earlier, at the time of Stephen Gallant's successful flight. Adele Allston's rage then had known no bounds. Part of the paternalist contract, in her eyes, was that special privilege granted by the master was to be repaid by special loyalty on the part of the slave. Stephen Gallant—but also inferentially his father, James, and especially his mother-in-law, Mary Grice—had viciously broken the compact, and those still under Adele's power must be made to feel her wrath. Mrs. Allston's passionate outbursts at this time[59] arose from her sense of betrayal: her previous grants of special privilege to Stephen, James, and Mary Grice seemed to her to justify an especially indignant response to insubordination.

Benevolent motives there were indeed at Chicora Wood, but they were not especially salient in comparison with the more exigent impulses guiding the Allstons' policy. The historian George Fredrickson, discussing Northern racial attitudes in the mid–nineteenth century, has called attention to "saliency" as a crucial element in his analysis. Both Northern Democrats and Republicans were racist at this time, Fredrickson shows; but racism was more salient in the motivation of Democrats than Republicans—and this was a difference with major implications for public policy.[60] Similarly, paternalist benevolence was one of the Allstons' motives, but a less salient one than the pursuit of a good return on capital invested, or than the preservation of order among their hundreds of bondsmen and women. Capitalists can be benevolent—as was no doubt true to some extent among the early mill owners at Lowell, Massachusetts—and Allston too was benevolent to a degree. Furthermore, he instituted (though not principally for benevolent reasons) a complex system of general and special privileges, and this system was a major component of the plantation's social economy. And paternalism was one element of his ideology, albeit small by comparison to the racist component. The true efflorescence of paternalist ideology at Chicora Wood came after 1865, when the postwar generation had to explain, in terms a more modern world might accept, the social system that had enriched its fathers before the incomplete revolution of 1865.

Harbingers of that revolution can be detected even in the Allstons' fragmentary surviving records. (Unfortunately, they contain, before 1864, practically none of those overseers' letters which make the Manigault records so illuminating.) These show that the Allstons often witnessed slave dissidence, of one sort or another, before 1864. Jerry's fight with the overseer Daniel Avant in 1823 has already been mentioned, as has Robert Allston's part in executing a suspected local insurrectionary in 1829, Ancrum's flight after being whipped by overseer Ellis in 1838, and the Allston slaves' refusal to do Sunday railway construction work in 1860. Allston was conscious of his bondsmen and women's capacity to pursue a divide-and-conquer policy of their own. They "will not fail to get up a disagreement and jealousy between [Belflowers, the overseer] and Collins [the suboverseer]," he cautioned in 1858.[61]

The ingenuity of privileged slaves in extending their privileges was evident. Thus in 1860 young Benjamin Allston was exasperated to discover that Toney—a hostler entrusted with putting a horse on a vessel at Georgetown for shipment to Charleston—had contrived to make the sixty-mile journey himself by land, and had presented himself to Robert Allston in Charleston with a cock-and-bull story; he had then managed to consume some three days more in making the return trip. "Toney has not yet made his appearance . . . ," Benjamin Allston fumed after learning from his father that the slave had showed up in Charleston: "How he could tell you that I sent him back for my saddle, is what I can scarsely [*sic*] understand, as he must know that I did not see him at all."[62] Similarly, in 1864, another slave, sent to search Waccamaw Neck for some of the Allstons' unfenced cattle roaming the woodlands, managed to prolong his absence for five days without his finding a single cow.[63]

When the barn of an old friend was consumed by fire in 1838, Robert Allston feared that vagrant slaves might have been responsible, though his warning to his wife was phrased in racially ambivalent terms so as not to alarm her. "Tell Mr. Ellis [the overseer] to keep a sharp look-out for stragglers at [Chicora Wood] and Waverly," he advised, "and send them to Jail unless they can give a reasonable account of themselves." Ellis, Allston continued, must speak with discretion—as when there was a fear of slave insurrection: "He must be watchful of every body who comes and goes without unnecessarily asking questions." The same discretion was exercised in 1856 when rumors of rebellion reached the Pee Dee. There had been talk in South Carolina, Adele wrote on New Year's Day 1857,

> of an effort at insurrection in Kaintucky and Tennessee. It . . . caused a good deal of anxiety, tho very little or no talk, as every one felt it should not be the subject of general talk. Belflowers and Oliver (the overseer at Waverly) brushed up their guns and amunition chests etc. and observed and listened, but held their tongues.[64]

In Charles Joyner's otherwise splendid study of rice slaves on the Waccamaw River (only a quick boat trip away from the Pee Dee) he has inferred that before 1862 the number of fugitive slaves there may have been small. This suggestion probably arises from the scarcity of extant letters written by overseers (and of candid private papers) for the Waccamaw plantations. By contrast, the Allston papers—even in the absence of many overseers reports—constantly throw up examples of antebellum Pee Dee slaves running away and otherwise dissenting from slavery; and surely more Waccamaw slaves would have been found engaged in similar dissidence, were similar records available. When Robert Allston purchased Nightingale Hall in 1846, he reckoned to buy ninety-eight slaves with the plantation, but two of them were absent. "January [a sixty-year-old driver] is in the woods," Allston noted soon after the purchase. "Having been ordered by Mr. L[igett, the previous owner] to take two fellows who were fighting to the Barn, [January] refused—and when the other Driver was order'd to take hold of *him* he drew on him his Knife, refused to be taken and walk'd deliberately out of the plantation." The other absentee was William, who "has been missing since the latter part of December, having been sent out on a very inclement day by Mr. L[igett] to shoot ducks for his table, and threatened to be whip'd in case he did not fetch them. He is represented . . . as having two guns when he disappeared." William, fearful of the threatened whipping, perhaps decided—like many of Charles Manigault's slaves—to hide in the swamp. But life there was precarious, and William (Allston icily noted) "drown'd before I took possession."[65]

History seemed about to repeat itself in 1851, when Robert Allston bought fifty-one slaves from the Reverend Hugh Fraser. London, nearly the most valuable of these slaves, was "now runaway" on the day the sale agreement was signed. In this instance, however, London returned during the next ten days, and his sale went ahead.[66]

That other forms of insubordination occurred regularly is evident from Benjamin Allston's correspondence during his brief stint as a planter. "Brister has been displaying a very violent temper," he reported in 1858, "—attempting to stab a [bonds]man—cutting him slightly and hurting him otherwise. He must be made to remember it or he will be as ungovernable as his father." In the same letter Benjamin alluded to his aunt's difficulty in controlling one of her Charleston house slaves. "She had better dismiss her man Peter and take some one else," young Allston advised; "—send him up to the plantation or some where else—do not keep him. It is not safe or prudent after what has happened." And this same letter mentioned a third case of insubordination—Leander's wrecking the pump—where again Benjamin felt punishment was needed.[67]

The young Allston might well feel paranoiac, for recently both of his horses had been mysteriously lamed. First, "I left my mare . . . in charge of Hannah. [The mare] some how cut herself in the rope—and . . . will not be [well] for some time." Then, only a few days later, Benjamin left his other horse at Waverly plantation on the Waccamaw, while he went by boat to supervise Chicora Wood. The horse "got injured . . . while I was at Chicora. He was left in the stable at Waverly, quite well—when I came back he was lame in the hip joint."[68]

Benjamin's letters in 1860 describe the flight of a group of no less than thirty slaves from a Waccamaw plantation.[69] These last examples of slaves' insubordination, or probable insubordination, are all taken from documents omitted from the published Allston papers. They suggest that the wartime dissidence of bondsmen and women in Georgetown District was not a new phenomenon; it was merely an ebullition of discontent which had long been simmering.

The normally overwhelming military balance of power against the local slaves began to change at the outbreak of the Civil War. Slaves near Georgetown were then discovered singing an old spiritual about the Lord's calling them soon to a better world: but could the masters now be sure their slaves were thinking about life after death?

We'll soon be free,
We'll soon be free,
We'll soon be free,
    When de Lord will call us home.

My brudder, how long,
My brudder, how long,
My brudder, how long,
    'Fore we done sufferin' here?

It won't be long,
It won't be long,
It won't be long,
    'Fore de Lord will call us home.

As a young black man later explained, the local whites feared "*de Lord* mean for say *de Yankees.*" The slaves singing this suddenly subversive song quickly found themselves incarcerated in the Georgetown jail.[70]

By 1864 the military balance of power had shifted dramatically, and the Allstons had real grounds for concern. Their plantations, Robert wrote in January 1864, were "within hearing of the Enemy's [naval] guns" across Waccamaw Neck. In addition to the numerous cases of wartime flight or attempted flight already mentioned—Magill's slaves from the Waccamaw in 1862, Francis Weston's boatload down the Pee Dee later the same year, Belflowers's locking up Elsey to prevent her fleeing, the many fugitives reported by Henry Middleton late in 1862, and Stephen Gallant's escape in July 1864 with his wife and five children—at least one more of Allston's associates had lost slaves in 1863. The possessions of these slaves washed up on the beach. Their master presumed they had drowned in the Atlantic, but Robert Allston was not equally sanguine that their flight had ended in disaster. "They were in an [illegible] life-boat which might fill and have things wash'd over board but would never sink," he wrote gloomily—illustrating how little he cared for the life of an insubordinate slave.[71] One of Allston's slaves succeeded in escaping in Charleston after working on the wartime fortifications; three of Mary Grice's children (including her daughter Lizzie, Stephen Gallant's wife) had also fled by mid-1864; William ran from Nightingale Hall at about the same time;[72] and in February 1865 at least three more Allston slaves, in North Carolina, departed with General Kilpatrick's army. When Allston had sought exemption of his Nightingale Hall overseer from conscription in summer 1863, he had played on the authorities' anxiety about unrest among the local slaves. Three times Allston iterated the noun "police" to describe the overseer's function:

I employ'd my own overseer J. M. Thompson to look after the police of my son's plantation. [Thompson] has been with my people since January, 1861, and I trust will ensure the police and government of Guendalos [Benjamin Allston's plantation] as well. If J. M. Thompson can be spared from the conscription . . . , it would contribute materially to the Police of the locality in which he resides.[73]

Everyone knew that the Confederacy's waning military fortunes might transform the slaves' conduct. Just before Allston's request for his overseer's exemption, black soldiers of the Union army had fought near Charleston (in the Battle of Fort Wagner), and they might return. A year later seventeen-year-old Charles Allston (his mother's deputy at Chicora Wood) was alarmed about the consequences of Stephen Gallant's escape to sea. "Stephen's going is the least part of it," Charles wrote to Adele Allston. "His coming *back* is what I fear more than any thing else, for he will not come alone." Driver Jack at Chicora Wood gave signs of breaking ranks with his white masters, and Charles Allston contemplated deporting Jack to the Allstons' North Carolina farm. Jesse Belflowers, however—the principal "police" officer on the Allston estates—restrained Charles, who then reported to his mother that "Jack's conduct has not been all that it should have been, but it was not so much as to need banishment."[74]

Yet by the autumn of 1864 even the cool Jesse Belflowers had become anxious. The slaves' usual petty insubordination, of course, persisted, in war as in peace. Thus in October Sammy the hog minder, a gamekeeper suspected of turning poacher, "killed one of the fatning hogs, for the hog was missing and . . . Samy had made no stir about it at all, whereas generally if any thing was missing he made a great stir, and then several of the people said that he had done it and that they had eaten some of the meat." More alarming, the driver once again aroused suspicion. "I can see in the last two weeks some change in the P[e]ople," Belflowers warned Adele in October 1864: "thay doant seem to care to obay orders & Jack the Drive[r] is not behaveing write. He doant talk write before the People. . . . I was told yeasterday that theare was some 7 or 8 [Northern naval] Vessels laying at the [Winyah Bay] Bar, some two or 3 inside." It was rumored that Georgetown would be attacked and that "the Negros will all Go to them or Pretty much all, for we have no force hear to prevent them." Though this fear soon subsided, the Nightingale Hall overseer W. Sweet was anxious that George the salt boiler, and Frank the hostler, were about to flee with their families, as Stephen Gallant had done; and plans were set afoot to separate these men from their wives and children, so as to deter them from flight.[75]

By March 1865 the Confederacy's end drew nigh. Sherman's army, marching northeast from Columbia, reached the Allstons' retreat at Society Hill early that month. Despite Elizabeth Allston's frightening encounter with the taunting Yankee captain, she acknowledged that "our experience of them was *mild*. They offered us no direct insult or injury." Matters were quite different at the Allstons' North Carolina farm, which Sherman's soldiers devastated on about March 10. All of the mules, cows, fowl, and corn were seized by the invaders, and "the gin house burnt with 18 tierces of salt and a good deal of cotton. On leaving," Elizabeth continued indignantly,

> they set fire to the house but the negroes put it out. They have destroyed *everything* in the house—furniture, pictures, glasses. The marble Mantle they took the marble off and broke it to atoms. Some beautiful old English oak

chairs they smashed and took the seats off them. Indeed there is nothing left on the place but a little rough rice. [Mamma] says [financial] ruin is inevitable. . . . We hear dreadful rumors of doings below [on the Pee Dee].[76]

In the low country, meanwhile, the Confederate commander had been obliged even before February 24 (by the troop shortage inland) to withdraw his garrison from the battery guarding the narrowest point of Winyah Bay, and to spike the guns. Marines from Northern vessels seized the battery, and on February 25 they occupied the town of Georgetown. The next day Admiral John Dahlgren, on his flagship in Georgetown harbor, proclaimed the end of slavery in this district. The local situation thereafter was fluid, depending partly on the political inclinations of the local Northern military chiefs. Both Dahlgren and his deputy—marine Lieutenant Stoddard, who as commander of six companies of marines became Georgetown's provost marshal—seem to have wished to protect the landed property of any planter who would take the oath contained in Lincoln's amnesty proclamation of December 1863. And, consonant with Dahlgren's proclamation, Lieutenant Stoddard promptly wrote a note assuring the local planters that those remaining on their plantations would not lose their land.

Within a few days, however, the climate changed. An army officer, Colonel P. P. Brown from New York State, arrived on March 1 to take command of Georgetown. Although the marines continued to be the principal Northern military instrument, Brown was in fact the commander of black troops, including elements of the 54th Massachusetts Volunteers and the 102d and 32d U.S. Coloured Troops, and he was doubtless more hostile to slavery and to the planters than were Admiral Dahlgren and Lieutenant Stoddard. The uncertainty of the planters' situation increased on March 1, when Dahlgren's flagship ran into a Confederate mine in Winyah Bay and sank. This humiliation was scarcely likely to improve the temper of the Northern occupation forces.[77]

A few weeks earlier the Northern Secretary of War, Edwin Stanton—whose political opinions had been radicalized by the war—had journeyed by sea to meet General William Sherman at Savannah, Georgia, where Sherman's army had recently arrived. The upshot of their meeting was General Sherman's famous "Field Order No. 15" (January 16, 1865), setting aside abandoned plantations in a thirty-mile strip of the low country, all the way from Charleston, South Carolina, to Florida, for the freedmen and women to cultivate as their own. Sherman was no antislavery radical, and the origin of his order has never been wholly explained. No doubt the general hoped his promise of forty-acre homesteads would persuade the thousands of blacks following his army to stay on the coast, instead of encumbering his troops on the march northward into Carolina. But one supposes that Stanton's principal motive was different: by getting Sherman to lend his own immense military prestige to a document upon whose formulation the influence of Stanton himself was certainly substantial, the secretary of war probably sought to influence Reconstruction policy. Were the freedmen and women to be merely a landless agricultural proletariat, or were they to have some of the land which generations of their unpaid ancestors had labored to convert from dank swamps into richly productive fields? More than thirty years earlier, William Lloyd Garrison had declared that the blacks had earned the right to land; and this opinion was shared by certain leading antislavery politicians like Pennsylvania's Thaddeus Stevens. Stanton appears to have sought to strike a preemptive blow for black land ownership.[78]

Since November 1861 a Northern contingent (including many antislavery radicals) had experimented on South Carolina's sea islands with free-labor plantations, and Sherman's order promised to extend the experiment thirty miles inland. The number thirty was not arbitrarily chosen, for this was the average distance from the sea that tidal culture of rice plantations was feasible, and rice was one of the two major crops of the low country. Sherman's order, although it encompassed most of the rice kingdom, did not reach north of Charleston; but the Freedmen's Bureau Act of March 3, 1865, did extend a similar principle north of that city, insofar as the great plantations had been abandoned by their owners. A revolutionary transformation was taking place, with planters struggling to prove to Northern authorities that they had not "abandoned" their land, while freedmen and women tested the limits of their new freedom.[79]

Soon after her husband's death in April 1864, Adele Allston had returned from the Pee Dee to Society Hill, and she did not venture again to her rice plantations until late in January 1865. The deteriorating military situation impelled her to leave again on February 24, the day before Georgetown was occupied. She was not present on Sunday, March 5, when Colonel Brown sent small detachments of marines out from Georgetown to proclaim freedom to the surrounding countryside. A handful of uniformed soldiers, as they approached the plantation, would be accompanied by blacks from Georgetown or from other plantations, and sometimes by a white imposter seeking to line his own pocket. The presence of uniformed whites encouraged the freedmen and women at many plantations to act out long-suppressed emotions. No white person was attacked, but the planters' property seemed to be up for grabs.

During the "orgy" on March 5 and 6, the houses and outbuilding of two Georgetown planters were burned. These were Dr. F. S. Parker, who had been largely responsible for the execution of the three Magill fugitives in 1862; and H. A. Middleton, who had contributed his boat to the wartime patrol of Winyah Bay (and who may have been confused by the Northerners with the notorious Georgetown secessionist J. I. Middleton). Even before March 5 a third slave master—George Ford, a Black River planter—was "burnt out . . . and lost almost every thing." But more common than arson was the former slaves' taking of furniture and livestock from the plantations, and their trying to seize the land. Robert Allston's niece Mrs. Francis Weston (she who had boasted of taking fifty slaves to Charleston each summer) reported that during the week after March 5 her freedmen and women

> divided out our land and wanted to root up our beautiful Wheat and Oats and Rye and pull[ed] down fences and would have no driver. Our Overseer went

off at once. . . . Large [clothing] presses too large to move were taken to pieces and every book carried off, many torn and strewed over the place. . . . Carpets were cut up into squares right off.[80]

Although the Allston slaves did not burn the "big house," their attacks upon property were even more systematic and thorough than elsewhere in the district. Belflowers reported from Chicora Wood on March 18, "No other Plantation of People have done what thease have done"; a year later Belflowers's successor confirmed to Adele that since his arrival in the district "the most want[on] scen[e] that my eyes has beheld . . . is the Destruction and depradations done to your house." The destruction began on Sunday, March 5, when, in Belflowers's words,

> two yankeys come up & turnd the People loose to distribet the house which they did, taking out every thing & then to the smoke hous and Store Room doing the same as in the house & took the Plough-oxen & Kild some of them. . . . The hogs in the Pen is Kild & all the Stock is taken a way. The horses is all taken a way. . . . The pore mules has been Road to death all most.

The saturnalia did not end with the seizure of furniture and animals. "After this," Belflowers continued, "the People have Puld down the mantle Pieces, Broke them to Piececes, taken of[f] all the doors & windows, Cut the Banisters & sawd out all such as wanted and have taken a way the fenceing a Round the yeard, brok down the old Stabel & the Carpenter Shop."[81]

Although, as a neighbor reported a few days later, "No outrage has been committed against the whites except in the matter of property," Belflowers—normally unflappable—did not trust the Allston slaves to refrain from assaulting whites. "The P[e]ople have behaved Verry badly," he warned Adele, "& I do think if you had been on the Plantation that you would have been hurt by the People. I have been Compeld by them on the Place to give up the Barn Key or to suffer from theare hands." Two days later, in Belflowers's view, things had gone from bad to worse, and the young Allston freedmen were enlisting in Colonel Brown's black regiment. Belflowers reported on March 20 that, since his earlier letter,

> the yankeys has bee[n] up and have taken all the Cotton [the Allstons having sold some of their rice for cotton]. [The people] tell the yankeys every thing. All the yonge men & boys have gone down to them to go in the army. . . . The Rest are doing nothing. I am not allowd to say any [thing] a bout Work and have not been to the Barn for the last five days. . . . Most all of them have arms.[82]

Chicora Wood was experiencing a social revolution of a sort never before or later seen on American soil. For a few weeks the scene bore a certain resemblance to an outburst of the peasantry during the Russian Revolution, but with Colonel Brown trying to impose a communal system upon the slaves' economic individualism. "The Peaple have divided the Cattle," Belflowers reported on

April 2. "But Col. Brown says thay [the cattle] must all go to geather and that [Horace] must mind them and Molley must milk them & Give the milk to the children." Brown did not stop the Allston freedmen and women from continuing their systematic destruction of property on or near the estate. "The negroes still go on in puling building[s] to Peicies," Belflowers continued.

> Thay have broke in to the Brick Church [the Prince Frederick Episcopal church, built with Robert Allston's substantial backing, whose vicar had dined with the Allstons every Sunday, and whose ruins can still be seen down the road from Chicora Wood] and taken out all the board that was left in it. Puld down the Club house [i.e., the Planters Club, where the Pee Dee grandees had been accustomed to gather weekly in the old days for a fine dinner] & the two little Barnes up Chapel Creek that belong to [Colonel] Ben [Allston, who was still away at the war], the houses . . . over Chapil Creek, the Pitman Summer house [the summer refuge of the former Nightingale Hall overseer] & the Summer house on the Exchange [another Allston property]. Have cut away the banisters in Ditchford house [yet another of Allston's big houses]. I hear that thay have made the attempt to Ripe up the floor in Chicora House.[83]

The Allstons' neighbor Jane Pringle (soon to become Elizabeth Allston's mother-in-law) confirmed Belflowers's account, and made plain that female slaves played a major role in the revolution. "Your negroes," she told Adele, "are I hear perfectly insubordinate; the men at "the upper plantation" [Chicora Wood] and the women at N[ightingale] Hall have behaved like devils. At N Hall the women turned in and killed the sheep and acted in a frenzied way Mr. S[weet, their overseer] told me." These were the same people who, as late as January 18, had assured Sweet they "all wishes to Be remembered to [Adele] and family." Even Lavinia, the highly trained lady's maid whom the young Adele Petigru Allston had brought with her in 1832 from Charleston, "claimed and took all the furniture in the [Allstons'] Plantersville house." With cold fury Adele Allston later summarized to Colonel Brown the events of March. After the soldiers and the freedmen and women had finished at Chicora Wood,

> not an article was left in the house, neither bed or sheet, table or chair. The banisters to the staircase broken down, every lock taken off, and the doors taken off their hinges. Then the meat house and store room were plundered in the same way, and I learn further that on a subsequent day you sent to the place and divided or caused to be divided among the negroes all the cattle and stock.[84]

A spirited woman, Adele Allston was determined to regain the upper hand. Her anger at Stephen Gallant's flight had been apparent in 1864, and now she was even more enraged. Her neighbor Jane Pringle—a Northern-born woman, deeply attached to slavery, who used her place of birth and her relative proximity to Georgetown to secure the protection of Northern soldiers for her own White House plantation—tried to deter Adele from doing anything rash until she could assess the situation from the security of White

House. Come and stay with us at our plantation for a few days, she implored Adele, before you venture to drive to your own estate: for you have no idea how turbulent the freedmen and women have become. An ambivalent message reached Adele (still at Society Hill) from her old and formerly trusted laundress Milly: things were unpredictable at Chicora Wood, Milly warned, and her mistress would do well to avoid the public road. This may have been the well-intentioned warning of an old house servant breaking ranks from the other former slaves, but Adele chose to interpret it as an attempt to frighten her from returning, and she would not be intimidated.[85]

These were times of duplicity and deceit, when the planters grasped at any straw to ingratiate themselves with their conquerors. Adele's brother Captain Tom Petigru of the U.S. Navy (who had died in 1858) had been esteemed by his fellow officers, and Adele's neighbors played on this fact to try to gain the Northern naval officers' protection for Pipe Down plantation (which Robert Allston had bought from Captain Petigru's widow). J. L. Petigru, another of Adele's brothers, in 1860 had been Charleston's best-known Unionist, and Adele's neighbors made much of this in trying to secure Northern protection of Chicora Wood—keeping quiet about the fact that Adele had been as passionate a secessionist as her husband, Governor Allston. When Adele herself petitioned Colonel Brown, she stated, "I acquiesce readily in the freeing of the negroes," a form of words which elicited Jane Pringle's scorn—Jane did not acquiesce at all—but which seems to have cut little ice with Colonel Brown.[86]

Soon it was May: the Confederate sympathizer John Wilkes Booth had killed Lincoln and had thus installed as president the Tennessee Negrophobe Andrew Johnson; the war was over; and a plantation mistress like Adele might hope the time was ripe for her to get into the saddle again. She went to Georgetown and requested Colonel Brown to send troops with her to force her insubordinate freedmen and women to return to her the keys to her houses and barns. The cononel supplied her with a written order to the blacks to restore her property but curtly refused to send any soldiers—the order itself would be enough, he said. Adele's "faithful" coach driver, Aleck Parker, then drove her and her twenty-year-old daughter, Elizabeth, to the Allston plantation closest to Georgetown: Nightingale Hall. Adele's eighteen-year-old son, Charles, just back from serving in Lee's army near Richmond, was ill and could not accompany his mother. This was just as well, for the Allstons met a hostile reception and the blacks might not have tolerated peremptory behavior from a Southern white male. As Elizabeth Pringle later wrote, a Southern white woman could compromise with insubordination: but "it was a very mortifying position for a [Southern white] man, whose impulse, under insolence or refusal to do the right thing, was naturally to resent it."[87]

"Insolence" was indeed rampant at Nightingale Hall, where the former slaves "had been specially turbulent": overseer Sweet had been kept in his house guarded by a freedman armed with a shotgun, and by now he had left the plantation. When Adele drove up, the atmosphere was far from welcoming. Although the driver Mack came to the carriage and dickered with her about the return of the barn keys, which were in his possession, a crowd of inhospitable freedmen and women accompanied him. Adele showed Mack the written order to return the key, whereupon "there rose a sullen murmur from the crowd, and a young man who had stood a little way off, balancing a sharp stone in his hand and aiming it at mamma from time to time, now came nearer and leaned on the wheel of the carriage." This did not intimidate Adele; she stepped out of the carriage into the midst of the crowd, showing "no sense that they could possibly be enemies," and asking after the black children by name. Her display of "friendly interest" won over the wavering crowd, and eventually Mack gave her the keys without interference from the others.[88]

Enough had been achieved by the mistress for a single day, and Adele did not go to Chicora Wood until the morrow. By then word of the events at Nightingale Hall had been discussed at Chicora Wood, and the freedmen and women there gave Adele and Elizabeth a seemingly warm welcome. The head carpenter, Primus, turned over the keys without question. The former slaves' apparent friendliness was belied by the evidence in front of Adele's eyes. Every piece of wood—such as the mahogany panels below the windows—had been ripped from the house; the zinc-lined water tank "had been torn to pieces"; the bathroom was all ripped apart; and Robert Allston's study "was almost waist-deep in torn letters and papers."[89]

The animosity which had accompanied these actions at Chicora Wood was still to be seen on the faces of the freedmen and women at Guendalos, the plantation upon which Robert Allston had established his son Benjamin in 1858. Benjamin, commanding his cavalry regiment, had never returned to his plantation during the war. The wartime shortage of white overseers had led the Allstons to place Guendalos, for the duration of hostilities, under the supervision of a slave headman, Jacob (probably the former trunk minder of whose plantation experience Robert Allston had urged Benjamin to avail himself). Although the white overseer at Nightingale Hall was expected to put in an appearance from time to time,[90] the blacks had thus had years—not just a few weeks as at Nightingale Hall and Chicora Wood—to run things largely on their own, and they were keen to keep the land for themselves. They did not intend the rich white people to return to give them orders and take the profits. "We heard the negroes were most turbulent and excited," Elizabeth recalled. As she and her mother neared Guendalos, driven by Aleck Parker, "the road was lined on either side by angry, sullen black faces; . . . not a sign of recognition or welcome, only an ominous silence." Jacob, the driver with the keys, was in a difficult middleman's position. If he felt any goodwill toward the Allstons, he was constrained by the angry mood around him to keep his feelings to himself. But when Mrs. Allston entered a corn barn, and a slave woman held out her arms to bar the white woman's exit, Jacob quietly pushed the black woman aside so that Mrs. Allston would not be trapped. The written order to return the keys convinced Jacob that he must reluctantly give them to Mrs. Allston, but the crowd refused to let him do so. A young freedman threatened bloodshed, "shaking his fist at Jacob. Then the crowd took up the shout, 'Yes, blood'll flow for true,' and a deafening clamor followed."

Adele ordered Aleck Parker to drive off to fetch her eighteen-year-old son, Charles, whose military experience might enable him to restore order. The two white women remained surrounded by the crowd—probably numbering over one hundred—in which "there was certainly not one friendly negro." The blacks' hostile song, in Gullah, was unintelligible to the Allstons except its chorus:

> I free. I free!
> I free as a frog!
> I free till I fool!
> Glory Alleluia!

The dance patterns of a still vital African heritage expressed the former slaves' economic demand, and women played a large role: the singing crowd

> revolved around us, holding out their skirts and dancing—now with slow, swinging movements, now with rapid jig-motions, but always with weird chant and wild gestures. . . . A little way off in the woods was a company of [black] men, drawn up in something like military order—guns held behind them—solemn, silent, gloomy, a contrast to the noisy mob around us.

The freedmen and women, accepting the authority of the Northern liberating army, were willing to submit this dispute to the arbitration of Northern soldiers; but they steeled themselves to prevent any Southern white man from imposing himself upon them before the Northern soldiers appeared. The many blacks who had no guns armed themselves with hoes, pitchforks, and sticks: " 'No, no, we won't let no white pusson een, we'll chop um down wid hoe—we'll chop em to pieces sho.' " This chant resounded in Adele's ears as she awaited her son's arrival. Elizabeth thought her brother would perish. "They wanted to kill some one," she believed, "but they couldn't make up their minds to kill two defenceless ladies."

Either Aleck Parker could not discover Charles Allston's whereabouts, or he thought it prudent not to do so. Nor could the Northern soldiers be found. Mrs. Allston and Elizabeth therefore left Guendalos, and the blacks agreed to send Jacob to Georgetown to hear from the mouths of the Northern soldiers whether the land was theirs. Distrusting Jacob, the crowd sent along with him a militant young man to listen with his own ears to what the Northern officer told Jacob. The land, they learned, must be returned to the Allstons. The young militant confirmed Jacob's report; no doubt the freedmen and women held a meeting at Guendalos later that night, where it was decided that further resistance was futile; and very early the next morning Jacob silently left the keys at the Allstons' house in Plantersville. He crept back to the plantation where one of freedom's dreams had been crushed.[91]

Fifty years later, Elizabeth Pringle understated the Northern army's role in restoring land to the returning planters. When her mother had first approached Colonel Brown at Georgetown and, requesting a military escort, had heard from him that a written order should be sufficient, Adele was livid.

"The negroes," Elizabeth lamented, "would look to the [Northern] officers for the tone they were expected to assume to their former owners. But it was evident these men [Colonel Brown and his staff] absolutely refused to back up the white people in any way." Yet Brown's backing of the Allstons quickly forced the former Guendalos slaves to submit to losing the land; and within a short time Brown had sent a corporal and three other soldiers to help Adele get back furniture which some of the freedmen and women would otherwise have refused to return.[92] Though reluctant to cooperate with someone like Mrs. Allston, Brown felt he had no alternative when this was his government's policy. General O. O. Howard, head of the Freedmen's Bureau, was in an even more unenviable position in October 1865 when he met sorrowful freedmen and women at Edisto Island, South Carolina, and told them the government was dishonoring the promise of General Sherman: even the land covered by Sherman's field order was to be returned to the planters.[93] The destruction of slavery was in itself a huge social revolution, and the Republican Party hesitated to go further. The bullet which killed Abraham Lincoln ended the last real chance that any substantial amount of the low-country plantation land might eventually have found its way into the possession of the newly freed blacks.[94]

One's first, modern, impulse might be to condemn Mack, Primus, and Jacob as betrayers of their people in returning the keys to Adele Allston. But had they any realistic alternative? The freedmen and women of 1865 were a very different generation from the Southern blacks who marched from Selma to Montgomery a century later. The whips, dogs, and guns of the masters, and the masters' power arbitrarily and at a moment's notice to tear apart the fabric of a slave's life by sale or deportation, had instilled fear into the very bones of most slaves. "The man quailed like a spaniel," Olmsted reported of a low-country slave threatened in 1853 by a twelve-year-old white girl who said she would have him whipped if he did not instantly obey her. The black clergyman Henry Turner declared in 1865 that the "old servile fear still . . . fills with terror the entire soul [of many freedmen and women] at a white man's frown. . . . This will be the case till they all die."[95]

The dissidence at Nightingale Hall and Guendalos, short-lived though it was, showed that Turner exaggerated the blacks' fear; but the quick collapse of that dissidence suggested that Turner did not fundamentally misunderstand his own people. How could it have been otherwise? Although the blacks had contributed substantially to their own liberation, their freedom had come essentially by the actions of Northern politicians and the Northern army,[96] and the former slaves had no chance in heaven of gaining land without the backing of their Northern white allies. For Mack, Primus, or Jacob to have tried to keep the keys would have been a mad adventurism, throwing away black lives to no purpose. For 1865 was not 1965; and even in 1965 the achievements of the black-led civil rights movement could never have been gained without black leaders' skillful nurturing of an alliance with significant elements in the white populace.

The saturnalia at the Allston plantation in March 1865, and the freedmen and women's hostile reception of Mrs. Allston in May, were therefore not precursors of a successful bid for land. They tell something important, however, about slavery on Robert Allston's estate. When Elizabeth Allston Pringle published her memoir a half century later, she vigorously attempted to assimilate the facts she reported to an image of faithful darkies loyal to their benevolent masters. The "poor things," she believed, were pathetic children misled by a few Northern white scoundrels—especially, a deserter from the U.S. Navy, seeking to fill his own pockets, who was said to have impersonated Lieutenant Stoddard on March 5.[97] Pringle's explanation of events does not wash. If this alleged Northern deserter ever existed, he certainly was not present during the four-week period when the Allston slaves were systematically tearing apart the masters' houses, church, and club building; the deserter did not impel the Nightingale Hall slaves to put a guard armed with a shotgun to confine overseer Sweet to his house; nor did the deserter provoke the Chicora Wood slaves to terrify overseer Belflowers. "They are just Ready to eat me up for it," Belflowers had reported anxiously on April 2, 1865, when a black messenger had opened one of his letters to Adele and told the other blacks what Belflowers was reporting to her about their conduct. Belflowers "is cowed by the violence of the negroes against him and is *afraid* to speak openly," Adele confirmed impatiently several months later.[98]

If Yankee instigation will not explain the freedmen and women's conduct in March 1865, neither will it account for the blacks' hostility toward Mrs. Allston when she returned in May. The slaves' feelings toward their masters had obviously been very different from what they were supposed to be, according to paternalist theory. So were the feelings of the masters. A wish for domination and profit, not benevolence, principally impelled Adele Allston in her dealings with the blacks. Toward the end of 1865 she had a flaming row with her son Benjamin about how the former slaves were to be governed, now that slavery was at an end. She addressed her son, a thirty-two-year-old West Point graduate who had served for four years as colonel in the Confederate cavalry, as though he were a babe in swaddling clothes. Benjamin had come to believe the freedmen and women must be treated in a conciliatory way, but this was far from Adele's wish. "They can ask nothing from you you are not prepared to grant," she raged at her son:

> You certainly take a very inadequate view of our [precarious financial] condition. But if we were ever so well off your conduct in rescinding your father's and my regulations with the precipitation of a child empowered for the first time to give orders, would fill me with dismay. . . . You ought to know how serious a matter it is to act as you have done. . . . I have no hope of making any impression on you. I spoke of the pain your conduct towards Antony gave me. It is all alike. You *consider* nothing. [Etc., etc.]

Adele's fury at her son's temporizing with the freedmen and women had not, however, prevented her from discovering something about her former slaves' mentality. She perceived that the blacks' thinking was influenced by the Bible; but it was not what it should have been according to paternalist theory. "The conduct of the negroes . . . shows you," she acknowledged indignantly, "they *think it right* to steal from us, to spoil us, as the Isrealites [*sic*] did the Egyptians."[99] Slavery on the Allston estate had not been essentially paternalist; and although Robert Allston believed his ingenious system of privileges provided the slaves ample compensation for their lack of freedom, this was not how the bondsmen and women saw it. Slavery in the American rice swamps was a hateful system of domination and exploitation, and one of its products, unsurprisingly, was hate.

IV

THE WIDER SCENE

15

The Rice Kingdom

Many causes have conspired to obscure from modern vision the doubly tragic role once played by rice on the American stage. Doubtless the principal factor has been the death of low-country rice planting itself. For years no person has lived at Gowrie. If occasionally a family of three raccoons can be perceived stirring the rank overgrowth of cane, not one among thousands of those motorists crossing the flat island on U.S. 17 is likely to reflect that human beings once lived in what is now a wildlife refuge; and that slaves like the persistently intractable house servant Jane, her cousin the compromising driver Robert, and the indomitable carpenter Jack Savage once aspired to a better life than was here afforded them. Sixty miles south, at Butler Island, a highway marker does indeed (though misleadingly) mention Frances Kemble; and the ruin of a steam pounding mill reminds one of a distant era. These are mementos, however, to the remarkable white mistress and to an abandoned plantation technology, not to the social system Kemble briefly experienced. One hundred and seventy miles north of Gowrie, at Chicora Wood, one can discover two gravestones commemorating bondsmen of Robert Allston's— Mulatto Joe and the "faithful" carpenter Thomas; and one can observe the beautifully restored house where each winter Governor Allston once resided, which his angry former slaves gutted in March 1865. "Captain Sandy's" riverboat still takes passengers on a fascinating journey among overgrown, uninhabited islands between the Pee Dee and the Waccamaw Rivers, where Allston's bondsmen and women labored. Yet on the Waccamaw peninsula— now almost wholly occupied by the comfortable dwellings of retired white people, and by thousands of pleasure seekers at the shimmering Atlantic beaches—how many will recall that in 1860, of the 4,595 inhabitants of the peninsula, blacks outnumbered whites by almost twenty-one to one? Among 4,383 African-Americans were scattered 212 white people; and every one of the black people was an enslaved rice worker. Today a spectacular display of outdoor sculpture amid groves of live oaks draws tens of thousands of visitors to South Carolina's premier tourist attraction, the Brookgreen Gardens, just four miles (as the duck flies) northeast of Chicora Wood; and only by pushing past the sculpture to the quiet riverside beyond can one imagine the lives of the 1,131 slaves who in 1860 toiled in the rice fields of J. J. Ward's "Brookgreen," then the greatest slave plantation in America.

Strangely, awareness of the rice kingdom has dimmed even among specialists. The mid-nineteenth-century cotton boom, and the naming of Frederick Olmsted's famous travelogue *The Cotton Kingdom,* drew attention away from the low country (even though Olmsted himself wrote with insight about this region). The figures in the 1850 census have often been misunderstood, while some of those in the manuscript 1860 census are ambiguous, and others printed in that year's census reports are downright mistaken. The statistical methods devised for the 1850 and 1860 censuses further minimized the role of the great rice planters. Even sophisticated modern studies have implied that rice was on its way out, at a moment in midcentury when, in fact, production was expanding, and profitably so.

As a glance will show, American rice production was indeed lower in the early 1820s than the peak reached thirty years earlier (see table 22). But by 1825 rice planters were recovering from Jefferson's embargo, the War of 1812, and the depression of the early 1820s. In the 1840s, rice production was higher than in the 1790s. And it continued to grow during the 1850s.

This expansion was obscured by the contemporaneous cotton boom, which led some Carolina planters south of Charleston to shift slaves from rice to sea-island cotton production. But at the same moment rice production was increasing north of Charleston, especially in Georgetown "County"[1] (where over one-quarter of all American rice was now grown); and on both sides of the Savannah River; and along the other rivers of low-country Georgia. The Carolina and Georgia low country's share of American rice production increased from 91 percent (1849) to 94 percent (1859).[2] Fortunes were still to be made—or squandered—from rice, as Robert Allston, Charles Manigault, Pierce Butler, and scores of other great planters were keenly aware; and with extraordinary unanimity they pursued the secessionist course which they reckoned best adapted to securing their massive capital investments in slaves and in embanked, richly developed, malarial swampland.

I

Two contrary streams flowed during the 1850s. On the one hand, the number of slaves working on tidal rice plantations did indeed decline that decade (by perhaps one-sixth); but on the other hand, the concentration of these slaves

TABLE 22.   American Rice
Production, 1767–1860 (est.)
(millions of pounds of "clean"
[i.e., milled] rice)

	Average Annual Production
1767–73	72
1790–95	82
1820–24	67
1825–29	90*
1830–34	91
1835–39	85
1840–44	94
1845–49	109
1850–55**	108
1856–60	114

Note: See appendix E for data and sources.

*The series from which the figures between 1820 and 1839 are calculated (estimates by Don Talmage's Sons, Co.) indicates an average of 83 million pounds, 1825–29. But as annual exports averaged 87 million pounds during these five years, I have substituted my own slightly higher estimate of annual production for this period.

**Omits the year 1854, when a September hurricane destroyed about 30 percent of the low country's crop.

into huge estates—comparable to those of the great Caribbean slave masters of an earlier era—proceeded apace.

In 1850 probably some fifty-eight thousand slaves lived on tidal rice plantations, while by 1860 the number had fallen to about forty-eight thousand.[3] (In addition, about two thousand domestic slaves were attached to the urban residences of rice planters in Charleston and Savannah.)[4] In two of the low country's best-known counties—Colleton and Beaufort—about thirteen thousand former rice workers were put during the 1850s to raising sea-island cotton, whose production in these counties increased two-thirds during the decade.[5] By the end of the 1850s, sea-island cotton had overtaken rice in the low-country economy. If the value of South Carolina's annual rice crop was then about $2,500,000, its sea-island cotton was worth some $3,000,000; and at a moment when Georgia's rice sold for $1,000,000, its sea-island cotton fetched $1,100,000.[6] More slaves—especially in Charleston, Colleton, and Beaufort Counties—worked on sea-island cotton than on rice plantations.

Yet rice production increased even in Charleston County; and elsewhere in the low country—in Georgetown County, along the Georgia coast, and along North Carolina's Cape Fear River—rice boomed during the 1850s (see table 23). The great planters of Georgetown added to the productivity of their slaves: by 1859 the same number of rural Georgetown slaves as in 1849 grew

TABLE 23.   Low-Country Rice Production, 1849 and 1859
(millions of pounds of "clean" rice)

	1849	1859	Change, 1849–59	Percent increase (or decrease) 1849–59
Low-country N.C. (New Hanover & Brunswick Counties)	2.5	5.6	3.1	124%
Georgetown County	28.9	34.4	5.5	19
Charleston, Colleton, and Beaufort Counties	66.8	44.8	−22.0	(−33)
Low-country Georgia (6 coastal counties)	22.9	31.9	9.0	39
TOTAL LOW COUNTRY	121.1	116.7	−4.4	(−4)
TOTAL U.S.	132.9	124.4	−8.5	(−6)

Note: Source for 1849: U.S. Bureau of the Census, *Statistical View of the United States, being a Compendium of the Seventh Census [1850]*, pp. 306, 210, 216; for 1859: appendix E (appendix table 7).

19 percent more rice. An extra three thousand slaves were set to growing rice in Georgia (and along the Cape Fear River), and productivity per slave also increased there. Georgia's rice production would have grown even faster than it did had not unhealthy conditions in the rice swamps impelled some planters to sell their slaves to the burgeoning West;[7] yet enough Georgia planters forced slaves into the rice swamps—at whatever cost to their health—that low-country Georgia's rice production increased by 39 percent during the 1850s.

In fact, these figures greatly exaggerate the decline of rice production in Colleton and Beaufort Counties: for 1849 was a year of extraordinarily high production—27 percent higher than the estimated annual average during the preceding five years—and the apparent decline after 1849 is therefore largely factitious. Even so, table 23 makes it perfectly clear that rice production was still increasing in many parts of the low country, and that some new rice lands were still being developed during the 1850s (though not so near Charleston and the town of Beaufort as in earlier days).[8]

Another reason that rice's continued development during the 1850s has been underemphasized is that specialists have focused on America's rice exports—which declined slightly after 1830—and have attended insufficiently to the growth of the American domestic market. For four years after 1828, and then steadily after 1846, the South Carolina low country (of all places!) came to depend on substantial tariff protection. Fixed at 20 percent from 1846 (when many other tariffs were reduced) to 1857—and at 15 percent from 1828 to 1832, and after 1857—"the duty upon foreign rice entering the United States . . . ," Louis Manigault recalled, was "so great as to have been simply a 'protective tariff,' in order to induce no foreign rice to be thrown upon our market."[9] Aided by this tariff barrier, production of low-country rice for American consumption nearly trebled between the 1830s and the 1850s (from 16 million to 45 million pounds of "clean" rice a year).[10]

As output shifted from older toward newer rice-growing areas, the number of producers declined, and their slaveholdings became increasingly concentrated in a small group of great planting families. To be master of two hundred slaves—which was thought a very large number by Georgetown rice planters as late as 1790,[11] and which was still a huge figure for most cotton planters—came to seem relatively small potatoes to certain rice grandees of 1860.

The Census Office reported then that only fourteen estates in the whole South numbered as many as five hundred slaves. No fewer than nine of these were rice plantations (see table below), and all but Butler Island were in South Carolina. They were scattered over the 250 miles from the Waccamaw River, in Georgetown, to the Altamaha River of Georgia.

The census figures, however, were incomplete, for two of these rice estates were larger than reported. Furthermore, there were actually twelve rice proprietors (not nine) whose estates numbered 500 slaves. The problem was that the Census Office counted as separate holdings the slaves owned by a planter in separate counties. In South Carolina this procedure was carried even further, for a planter's holdings in separate "parishes" of a single county were also counted separately. Thus the three holdings of W. H. Heyward—a grandson of old Nathaniel Heyward—were listed separately: 133 slaves in St. Bartholomew's Parish (Colleton County); 385 bondsmen and women in Prince William Parish (Beaufort County); and 133 slaves whom he jointly owned in St. Peter's Parish (also in Beaufort County). Heyward was the proprietor of 651 slaves, but instead he was misleadingly counted as the owner of three smaller plantations.

Similarly, the estate of Arthur Heyward (a son of old Nathaniel) comprised 352 slaves on Georgia's Ogeechee River and another 306 in St. Bartholomew's Parish (Colleton County, South Carolina). Heyward was, in fact,

	County	No. of Slaves
Estate of Lt. Gov. J. J. Ward	Georgetown	1131
Governor Robert Allston	Georgetown	631
John Harleston Read	Georgetown	510
Arthur Blake	Charleston	535
Governor William Aiken	Charleston[12]	700
Daniel Blake	Colleton	527
Walter Blake (proprietor of his father Joseph's estate)	Beaufort[13]	545
John Izard Middleton (and family)	Beaufort	520
Estate of John Butler (Pierce's brother, Pierce's slaves having been auctioned in 1859)	McIntosh, Ga.	505

master of 658 slaves, but the census listed his two plantations separately. And when the Waccamaw River planter W. A. Alston Sr. died in 1860, his 400 slaves went to his grandson W. A. Alston Jr., who already had 171 of his own. W. A. Alston Jr. was therefore, in 1860, the proprietor of 571 slaves.[14] His neighbor John Izard Middleton owned—besides the 520 slaves in Beaufort County of whom he was principal proprietor—210 bondsmen and women on the Waccamaw (Lower All Saints Parish) and another 107 across the Pee Dee River (Prince George Parish). Middleton's estate thus comprised 837 slaves, and this determined member of South Carolina's 1860 Secession Convention should thus have been listed as one of the handful of the South's truly great slaveholders. And Walter Blake, besides managing 545 slaves (Prince William's Parish, Beaufort County) still legally the property of his father—a resident of England—also owned 74 slaves of his own in St. Peter's Parish (Beaufort County). Walter Blake was therefore in fact proprietor of 619 bondsmen and women.

The Census Office's remarkable statistical technique had its most distorting effects on the proprietors of over 600 slaves. The 1860 census reported only three rice estates in this category (Lieutenant Governor J. J. Ward, Governor Aiken, and Governor Allston); but, in fact, there were seven—John Izard Middleton, Arthur Heyward, W. H. Heyward, and Walter Blake having been omitted. The same kind of error led to misleading figures for at least seventeen other large rice planters (and more cases will surely come to light when historians systematically analyze the manuscript census returns with this point in mind). The most egregious census errors—besides the cases already mentioned—are listed below:

	Actual no. of slaves	No. of slaves reported in census	Parish or river	County
Cheves, Langdon Jr.	ca.469	289	St. Peter's	Beaufort
		ca.180	Ogeechee R	Chatham
Alston, Charles Sr.	409	208	L. All Saints	Georgetown
		201	P. George	Georgetown
Heyward, Daniel	376	246	St. Peter's	Beaufort
		130	P. William	Beaufort
Doar, Stephen	342	235	Santee	Charleston
		107	P. George	Georgetown
Barnwell, Edward	337	245	St. Paul's	Colleton
		92	St. Peter's	Beaufort
Pringle, W. B.	284*	226	P. George	Georgetown
		58	St. Andrew's	Charleston
Trapier, W. H.	265	178	P. George	Georgetown
		87	L. All Saints	Georgetown
Middleton, Oliver	258**	121	S. Bartholomew's	Colleton
		137	Berkeley	Charleston
Bull, William	233***	138	P. George	Georgetown
		95	St. Andrew's	Charleston

	Actual no. of slaves	No. of slaves reported in census	Parish or river	County
Morris, Lewis	232	167	St. Paul's	Colleton
		65	S. Bartholomew's	Colleton
Read, B. H.	226	123	Berkeley	Charleston
		103	S. Thomas	Charleston
Dunkin, B. F.	224	128	L. All Saints	Georgetown
		96	P. George	Georgetown
Elliott, William	216****	114	St. Paul's	Colleton
		102	S. Helena	Beaufort

*226 of these were rice slaves.

**121 of these were rice slaves.

***138 of these were rice slaves.

****About 90 of these were rice slaves.

The fragmentary data presently available show that the Census Office's methods—as Superintendent of the Census J. D. B. DeBow himself vaguely acknowledged but sought to hide[15]—massively understate the slaveholdings of the great planters. Among the twenty-nine largest rice planters, the median holding (according to the misleading census figures) was 358 slaves. This figure does, to be sure, show a very high concentration of economic and social power in the hands of a few planters, but it underplays that concentration. In fact, all of the twenty-nine largest rice planters held more than 300 slaves, and among these planters the median holding was 453 bondsmen and women, not 358. Their median holding was nearly 27 percent larger than the census figures suggested. Slaveholding among these rice planters was on a scale scarcely known elsewhere in the United States.

Even these corrected figures, however, misrepresent South Carolina's social reality, for they treat separately planters who were, in fact, members of proud families. These planters normally had inherited fortunes in slaves, and they sought to pass on the slaves to their own children. The seven slaveholding sons and grandsons of old Nathaniel Heyward, listed individually in 1860, were members of a single clan—looking often to the old man's son Charles Heyward for guidance—and they are best considered as a single family group, exercising dominion over no less than 2,942 slaves. And the Blakes resembled one of those great families of Caribbean slave masters who resided in Britain early in the nineteenth century: for Joseph Blake did indeed live in England, and his son Walter and two other Blakes were born there. Two of these younger men had sought education at the University of Cambridge before setting off for Carolina to attend to their rice estates. The Blake family were masters of *more* than 1,682 slaves—for the figure of 1,682 does not include a group of less than 100 others of their bondsmen and women who still labored at the Blakes' ancestral "Newington" seat.

Nearly as rich were the members of the Middleton clan, whose holdings

included the 837 slaves for whom John Izard Middleton was principal proprietor, the 258 slaves of his brother Oliver, the 270 of their cousin Henry
Augustus, the 180 of James, and perhaps 70 owned by William. This total of
some 1,615 Middleton bondsmen and women is still a little too small, for it
does not include a group of slaves still working at the family's colonial seat,
"Middleton Place," on the Ashley River.

The other nineteen great rice-planting families—each of which owned at
least 500 slaves in 1860—contained names renowned in the political and
military annals of Carolina. Governors, U.S. senators and representatives, a
president of the Bank of the United States, a Speaker of Carolina's colonial
assembly, and ardent defenders of slavery galore flourished in the Alston,
Allston, Lowndes, Barnwell, Cheves, Aiken, Izard, Trapier, Elliott,
Manigault, and Butler families. In 1860 the twenty-two principal families
(i.e., the Heywards, the Blakes, the Middletons, and the other nineteen families) owned just over 20,000 slaves, nearly all on rice plantations (see table
24). This handful of families therefore held 40 percent of all the low-country
rice slaves.

These great families stood at the apex of a rice-planting hierarchy. A
dozen more families owned between 300 and 500 rice slaves.[16] And about 76
families owned 100 to 300 bondspeople, while perhaps another 140 families
owned 35 to 100 slaves. Thus virtually the whole low-country rice crop was
produced on about 320 plantations, owned by about 250 families.

Second only to rice in creating the low-country's social hierarchy was sea-
island cotton, and any social analysis of the region must disentangle cotton
producers from rice planters. This is easily done in Georgetown County,
where cotton production was negligible: everything depended on rice. But
south of the Santee River—and especially as one traveled southwestward
from Charleston to Savannah, and then along the Georgia coast, well into
Florida—sea-island cotton nourished another group of great slaveholders.
Alongside Carolina's twenty-one[17] great rice families were ranged nine sea-
island cotton families, each boasting possession of 500 or more slaves (see
table 25). Though only a few of these families were nationally famed—the
Legarés, the Pinckneys, and perhaps the Seabrooks and Porchers—all were
well known in the low country itself.

By contrast to the South Carolina low country's twenty-one great rice
families and its nine leading sea-island cotton families, all the rest of the state
(though its white population was nearly six times that of the low country)
could point to only a handful of families owning as many as 500 Carolina
slaves (see table 26). Governor Adams's family, Governor Gist's, and the
Palmers, Gourdins, and Witherspoons constituted the whole group; and not
one of them could rival the Heywards, Blakes, Middletons, Alstons, Wards,
Allstons, or Porchers as slaveholders.

If an up-country Carolinian sought the distinction which came with ownership of more than 600 slaves, the most promising avenue lay in absentee ownership of western slaves. Governor-to-be Wade Hampton III was reputed to
possess over 1,500 bondsmen and women in Mississippi, while South Carolina's

TABLE 24.   Number of Low-Country Rice-Planting Families, 1860 (est.)

Families owning	No. of planter families	No. of plantations* owned by these families	No. of rice-planting slaves held on these plantations
500 or more slaves	22	66	19,750
300–499 "	12	21	4,500
100–299 "	76	83	14,250
35–99 "	140	150	9,500
TOTAL	250	320	48,000

Note: see appendix G, p. 460 for sources.

*I.e., 35 or more slaves.

TABLE 25.   Carolina Sea-Island
Cotton Families, Holding Over 500
Slaves, 1860

Family	No. of Slaves
Porcher	1,130
Legaré	802
Seabrook	801
Fripp	733
Baynard	710
Whaley	692
Bailey	541
Jenkins	524
Pinckney	505

former governor John Manning was in 1860 master of 648 slaves, mainly in Louisiana.[18]

Surprisingly, white society in the low country was more heavily urbanized than anywhere else in the South. Of the South Carolina low country's 40,100 white inhabitants, almost exactly half—20,000—resided in Charleston in 1850; in 1860 the proportion was even higher.[19] This was the consequence of malaria, which deterred every rich rice planter from permanent residence on his estate, and of the economic domination of the region by huge rice and sea-island cotton plantations, which left few economic opportunities for the rural white population.

That the principal rice-planting families (and especially the thirty-four families which each owned more than three hundred slaves) dominated Charleston's economic and social scene was evident to every Carolinian. Thus at Charleston's premier boys' school (Mr. Coates's school) in the 1840s, as Dr. Gabriel Manigault later testified, most of the boys whose parents were conspicuous for wealth and social position were the sons of rice planters. That industry was very prosperous then, and as most of the large planters had inherited their wealth, or had developed it from small beginnings with their shares of the paternal estates, [there] had been education and refinement for several generations; and up to the civil war . . . the rice planters who had their residences in Charleston were, socially, the dominant class in that city.[20]

II

Dominant they may have been, socially; but according to Dr. Gabriel Manigault—who knew (from his elder brother Charles's experience) how inherited social position and the prospect of inherited wealth could sap a person's drive—many of them, mentally, were far from imposing. The best Charleston lawyers and doctors of the next generation, Gabriel thought, were the sons of relatively poor parents who could not afford Mr. Coates's tuition fees. Though many rich boys at Mr. Coates's school were bright, almost none later distinguished himself in any field requiring mental power: "This was evidently due," Manigault explained,

> to their being mainly the sons of planters, who expected to pursue agriculture as a vocation after graduating at College, and they therefore were indifferent to the ambitions that urge a boy onward, who has to depend upon the cultivation of his mind for his success in life. [The less well-to-do boys] had nothing beyond their education, and the training of their minds to start life with, and they easily distanced Mr Co[a]tes' boys, who, from their futures being more or less assured, did not have the same incentives to exertion.[21]

This lack of energy was not always confined to the mental sphere. Hugh Rose—the son of Charles Manigault's good friend James Rose, a Savannah River rice planter—was (in Gabriel Manigault's view) spoiled, selfish, and overbearing. He was

> typical of a class of young men from Charleston during the first half of this century, whose parents were more or less wealthy planters, who, after school

TABLE 26.   Up-country South Carolina Families
Holding Over 500 Carolina Slaves, 1860

Family	No. of Slaves
Adams	773
Palmer	760 (of whom at least 160 were on low-country rice plantations)
Gourdin	569 (of whom 105 were on a low-country rice plantation)
Gist	564
Witherspoon	519

or college . . . , spent many years before marriage in perfect idleness. Hugh made several visits to Europe . . . , was generally fashionably clothed, and altogether was conspicuous by his size . . . and his gentlemanly bearing. By degrees his habits became quite bad. . . .

Another corpulent young rice grandee was W. A. Alston Jr. (a great-grandson of the fabulously wealthy "King Billy" Alston of Clifton on the Waccamaw peninsula), who in 1861 excited Mary Chesnut's scorn: the thirty-one-year-old Willie Alston was one of "that set"—" 'the take-life-easys,' as they are called." Alston, a "gentleman of leisure" who lived mainly in New York City's Cherry Street, had by 1865 attained a three hundred-pound girth; he died two years later, a thirty-seven-year-old bachelor.[22]

Thus there was some substance to the stereotype that indolence, and too much drinking, often led to the ruin of scions of rice-planting families. Governor Robert Allston, reviewing troops near the Combahee River in 1858, was "fill'd with melancholy reflections at the decay of families, before which [had come] pride and vanity." Dining with Nathaniel Heyward III at the "Baronial [eighteenth-century] residence" of Judge Thomas Heyward (a signer of the Declaration of Independence, and the distinguished elder half brother of the great planter Nathaniel Heyward I), Allston was

> again oppress'd at the remnant of the evidences of former magnificence and luxury. . . . William Heyward died there not long ago, having taken to deep potations. . . . There are Oranges and Lemons, olives, and exotics cover'd up with weeds. . . .

> Here are the young Cuthberts who have run through everything that was left to them and are now loafers sponging on any body who will suffer them. . . .[23]

Yet dissipation obviously was not the principal story of the nineteenth-century rice kingdom. If one is to proceed beyond the stereotype of "the indolent Carolina gentleman," one must consider the roles both of ambitious men on the make, and of enterprising planters of inherited wealth and assured social position. A few new men did manage to break their way into the ranks of the rich planters. Roswell King Sr., for example, having come to Darien, Georgia, as an impecunious New England emigrant, found—as did his son Roswell King Jr.—that the management of the Pierce Butlers' estate was an avenue to wealth; and by 1854 the younger King was master of 179 slaves. The remarkable rise of four Scottish immigrants to the status of rich Savannah River rice planters impressed Louis Manigault. The eldest of these men, Archibald McLaren, was a mechanic and carpenter who early in the century built the three "splendidly constructed rice-pounding mills on Savannah River." In 1813 McLaren bought Gowrie (then a wilderness), cleared and ditched 220 acres, dug the canals, and constructed the floodgate; by 1832 his estate was probably worth at least thirty-five thousand dollars. Like McLaren, Norman Wallace, Henry Taylor, and Henry McAlpin all immigrated poor early in the nineteenth century. Wallace eventually owned East Hermitage, before Charles Manigault bought it in 1848. Taylor was first an overseer on a

Rutledge plantation on the Cooper River, then on the Rutledges' Savannah River estate, and finally the owner of 600 valuable rice acres and 104 slaves just across the river from Gowrie. Wallace, Taylor, and McAlpin, Louis Manigault exclaimed, "each commenced life as Overseers on Savannah River. . . . McAlpin was [also] a Carpenter and Bricklayer on an extended scale. McAlpin commenced life poor and died worth about $400,000."[24]

More common, however, than these Horatio Algers were those rice planters who, like Robert Allston, inherited enough to get started, and who then devoted themselves assiduously to enlarging their fortunes. Thus Allston's brother-in-law John Hyrne Tucker was the son of a Georgetown merchant who had bought a Waccamaw plantation before 1797. By 1850 Tucker had parlayed this inheritance into an estate of three rice plantations—the fifth most valuable holding in the county—and 201 rice slaves. He also possessed a twenty-three-thousand-dollar Charleston house (the ninth most valuable such house owned by a Georgetown rice planter), staffed with 22 other house slaves. Tucker was cut from very different agricultural cloth from either the scholarly Dr. Gabriel Manigault or the corpulent, "take-life-easy" Willie Alston. Of course, Tucker enjoyed wine; and no doubt he, like Nathaniel Heyward, also relished establishing his daughters comfortably in Charleston society. As for Tucker himself, however, "rice planting was [according to an acquaintance] his sole delight. He lived for and in rice. It was the first and the last thought of his mind."[25]

Carolina planters—known in the eighteenth century for building their houses near rice swamps or indigo dams—were then "more careful to acquire splendid Fortunes than to preserve their Healths." Although the shift to tidal rice culture (with its attendant worsening of the malarial "miasma") altered these residential habits, it did not kill the planters' devotion to rice. The price of "rice fell badly," Robert Allston's mother had written to him from Georgetown in 1820, "and that depresses the spirits of the Majority of the People here, whose chief object is to make Rice to buy Negroes and Buy Negroes to make Rice." The passionate interest of two premier Georgetown planters in their crops—and the wish of one to convey grateful news to the other about the latter's newly cleared field—appeared in September 1838 in J. J. Ward's communication to the temporarily absent Robert Allston. Ward began with a complaint of

> very bad harvest weather; rain nearly every day [for a week] and Oh my fine big rice at Long Wood has been in all of it; and such a litter left in the field you never saw; however today the sun shines. . . . When I took [Oliver, the overseer of Allston's nephew's plantation] around my Main fields which is fine Rice, the best I have, he said . . . it was the best Rice he had seen this year excepting Col. Robert Allstons' reclaimed fields.[26]

The career of J. Motte Alston may illustrate how the gentlemanly, sports-loving son of an illustrious Carolina family could turn energetically to rice planting in order to secure his fortune. Motte was born to the purple in 1821—or rather, to the dark green, for this was the favorite color of his resplendent grandfather, "King Billy" Alston, with whom Motte spent much of his child-hood. When, in 1791, King Billy had entertained President George Washing-ton at his "Clifton" seat (on Waccamaw peninsula), the king's three hundred slaves had merely matched those of the president; but the Carolinian later far outdid the Virginian, raising his slaveholding by 1839 to well above five hundred—indeed, Motte Alston supposed one thousand the actual number. King Billy's royal progress each summer from Clifton to Charleston took place in a "large dark green and red coach with the coat of arms on the panel of the door," and the horses of two outriders matched the four horses drawing the carriage. King Billy's servants—in Charleston's most famous residence, the Miles Brewton house—ostentatiously "wore dark green broadcloth coats and vests trimmed in silver braid and red facings with trousers of green plush."[27]

King Billy's son Joseph became governor of South Carolina in 1812; and because King Billy's fortune had attracted well-placed suitors for his daughters' hands, Motte Alston's uncles included not only Governor Joseph Alston but also Governor John Lide Wilson, Senator Robert Hayne, and Arthur Hayne (who was also briefly a U.S. senator). The political career of Motte's father, T. Pinckney Alston, was not so eminent as those of Motte's uncles, though Pinckney Alston, like many another gentlemanly rice planter, "had a fancy for politics . . . to quite a degree." A stalwart nullificationist, Pinckney did a stint in the Carolina state senate from 1832 to 1838, supporting (like his relatives) that "state sovereignty" doctrine which promised to secure the planters' inter-ests. Pinckney was himself no businessman; but every rice planter hoped to raise at least one businesslike son, who could carry on the family planting concern; and not long after Pinckney inherited some three hundred slaves from King Billy in 1839, he turned to his own son Motte to superintend "True Blue" and "Weehawka" plantations (on the Waccamaw) during Pinckney's long sum-mer absences.[28]

Many years later Motte recalled with pride his first real testing, in 1845, when he was only twenty-four years old. A very dry summer had lowered the Waccamaw River, causing salt water to come much farther upstream than normal and threatening to kill the rice if saline water should be allowed to enter the fields. In this crisis—and against the advice of the overseer—Motte ordered the fields to be flooded for the "harvest flow" much earlier in the summer than was customary (and he ensured that water would be let in only during those brief intervals when the river was at half tide, and therefore not yet saline). While plantations above and below him did badly, Motte rejoiced in raising for his father a crop worth some thirty-five thousand dollars![29]

By this time Motte had already embarked upon making his own fortune. Like Robert Allston eighteen years earlier, the young man depended on help from his family to launch his own rice-planting enterprise. His father gave him an overgrown morass—five hundred acres of uncleared swampland, twenty miles farther upriver, worth perhaps five thousand dollars as potential rice land—where great cypress trees of seven-foot diameter reared themselves above the rich alluvial soil. The cane was fifteen to twenty feet high, and the "enormous cypress, gum, ash [trees were] matted together with huge grape vines." Motte borrowed some of his father's hundreds of slaves to commence the backbreaking toil of digging and carrying mud from the dank swamp—in order to erect miles of river embankments—and then of clearing the land. Most of the trees and thick vines must be axed down, while the largest ones were girdled (and months later burned). "The [slaves'] work is slow and arduous," Motte acknowledged, "week by week, month by month, year by year. . . . Through fire and water, through felling and burning the work goes on, and when the sun goes down, it alone brings rest." As the new plantation lay on a peninsula between the Waccamaw and Bull Creek, "the river banks now are nearly four miles in length. . . ." Motte's father gave him a driver and sold him a skilled carpenter; but Motte, in order to buy his own gang of eighty slaves, must borrow $45,000—and here again his family's backing was indispensable. The key factor was that, some years earlier, King Billy Alston had forced the Charleston rice factor Charles Kershaw to make Kershaw's able clerk, Alexander Robertson, a partner in Kershaw's firm; and now Robertson, out of gratitude, was willing to lend King Billy's grandson $45,000 without security, and with no prospect of the early repayment which creditors for slave purchases normally demanded. For two years Motte Alston's slaves were employed in embanking the plantation and clearing the first 75 acres for planting; and then in the third year—in August 1847—a freshet swept over the half-built embankment and destroyed the whole first crop.[30]

Yet by 1858 Motte Alston had made his fortune. By then 450 acres of prime rice land had been cleared, and Alston sold for $45,000 a plantation that had been worth only $5000 when his father gave it him. From the sale of a decade's fine rice Motte Alston had earned enough to pay off the $45,000 debt to Robertson; to support comfortably himself, his wife, and their children; to buy an expensive $6,000 house at Columbia, South Carolina; and (when he had sold the plantation, and most of his slaves, and his fine new house at Murrells Inlet) to put $135,000 into other investments. No doubt he reckoned that these—which included investments in a Mississippi cotton-planting business (Wade Hampton III's?)—would yield him a splendid income of at least $10,000 a year. Not bad for an initial investment of about $6,000 supplemented only by borrowed capital![31]

Motte had learned the business by running his father's plantations in the early 1840s. Rice planting, he declared with some hyperbole, was a science: "Nothing is left to chance. The field must be flowed or dried and worked according to a regular system, learned only by long experience, or instruction. The cultivation is an expensive one, and therefore mistakes are very serious. The fields are kept in garden order, no grass is allowed to grow. . . ." A duck-shooting gentleman Motte Alston might be; yet when he married Wade Hampton III's first cousin in February 1848—Alston's first successful crop not yet sown—the young planter was resolutely businesslike. During the nonmalarial months he forced his bride (accustomed as she was to a lively social life in Augusta, Georgia) to live in isolation (albeit in a twelve-room house) at the wild new plantation. As Alston explained in impeccably capitalist terms,

If this was to be a business success, there was nothing else to do. A large amount of money was invested here before my marriage, and so it was either this or long months of separation.

[After a few years] I was making headway in my business and could not well trust the same into the hands of agents. In order to render matters pleasanter, and yet not to sacrifice, in any way, my planting interests, [I bought at Murrells Inlet, two miles from the plantation, 100 acres, and built a fine house there where my wife and children could enjoy the society of other planting families]. . . . Every day I could look after my planting interest and return to dinner [with my family].

"Business," "A large amount of money was invested," "planting interests"— these words speak for themselves in defining Alston's purposes. This gentleman capitalist had made himself so rich with his business that he was able, at the age of thirty-seven, to retire from entrepreneurial activity.[32]

Like farmers the world over, successful rice planters were obsessed with agricultural lore. Georgetown's Winyah and All Saints Agricultural Society disseminated information about the latest experimental methods in rice culture and awarded prizes for rice, corn, and the use of manures. Years later the grandson of Charles Heyward (old Nathaniel's capable son) boasted that Charles had for five successive years, on twelve hundred acres, averaged forty-five bushels of rice per acre—the low-country average being closer to thirty-five bushels; while in 1860 Robert Allston could experience the joy of having secured just over eighty bushels per acre in one fifteen-acre field, a record perhaps never equaled by any other planter. As late as 1869 Pierce Butler's daughter—herself no mean planter—grumbled that "night after night" (when she was visiting a pinewoods retreat that summer, probably at Plantersville in Georgetown County),

gentlemen met at one house or another, and talked and discussed one, and only one subject, and that was rice, rice, rice.

Farmers are supposed never to exhaust the two subjects of weather and the crops, and we certainly never did, until one evening the [thirty-year-old] daughter of the lady with whom I was staying burst out with, "Do—do talk of something else; I am so tired of rice, rice, from morning till night, and day after day."[33]

That their own prosperity and comfort, more than those of their slaves, filled the imaginations of antebellum planters becomes evident from scattered information about their sale of slaves. The low country ought theoretically to have been the most stable area of the whole South, where slaves would experience the least chance of being sold away from their native community. In Virginia thousands of bondsmen and women were sold every year to the booming Southwest, never to see home again; and in Mississippi thousands of new slaves were imported each year to begin the slow process of establishing new communities. But the slave population of Georgetown County—the low country's premier rice county—seemed to remain virtually static. Historians have supposed that some slaves were sold westward, from the putative natural increase of the slave population; but on the whole stability is thought to have reigned.

The correspondence of Georgetown planters, however, belies this impression of rural stability. Of the approximately 5,000[34] Waccamaw rice slaves, 10 or 12 percent—probably at least 476 bondsmen and women, and perhaps as many as 636—appear to have been sold during the brief period from December 1857 through December 1859. Four separate transactions occurred. The scholarly Plowden Weston, one of the two or three richest Waccamaw planters—whose instructions to his overseers have been much quoted to illustrate a planter's kindly intentions—decided in 1856 to get rid of "Laurel Hill," his northernmost Waccamaw rice plantation, in order to concentrate his holdings near his princely "Hagley" seat. He finally sold Laurel Hill in 1859 to a prominent Horry County resident, Daniel Jordan, who sought to break into the ranks of the great rice planters.[35] By 1860 Jordan had acquired 261 slaves, yet none was Weston's. And although Weston may have balked at entrusting the welfare of his slaves to Jordan, perhaps Weston also thought the latter did not offer him enough cash for them.[36] (This was why Henry McAlpin had refused Charles Manigault's offer for his East Hermitage slaves, when he sold him the plantation in 1848; and it was also the reason the heirs of Mrs. H. P. Rutledge refused Stephen Doar's offer for 61 of her slaves when, in 1859, they sold him her South Santee plantation.) Rather than accept Jordan's offer, Plowden Weston preferred to sell many of his Laurel Hill slaves West, and he deported them—numbering perhaps 100 of his Laurel Hill slaves, and possibly as many as 180[37]—forever from their Waccamaw friends and relations. "Those left here assembled on the wharf," Mrs. Emily Weston at Hagley plantation wrote during the Yuletide, touched by the slaves' anguish, "and the vessel [bearing those deported from Laurel Hill] steamed along for a little while very slowly. Tears filled my eyes as I *looked* and *listened* to the wail from those on shore echoed by those on board."[38]

By this time Motte Alston's father, T. Pinckney Alston, who was sixty-three, had retired from rice planting. As neither Motte nor Motte's younger brother wished to carry on the concern, Pinckney sold to Plowden Weston both True Blue and Weehawka plantations, which were adjacent to Hagley: and Weston's plan to consolidate his holdings now reached fruition.[39] But Pinckney Alston was not able to sell the bulk of the True Blue and Weehawka slaves to Weston, so that they could remain at home, laboring for the reputedly kind master of Hagley.[40] Instead, the slaves were to be auctioned—albeit in families—at the best attainable price. "Families" were narrowly defined: thus Pinckney Alston could profit by selling "prime hands" in their twenties (like Katy, Josey, Peter and Simon) separately from any elderly encumbrances. Meanwhile, relatively old women like those numbered 3, 9, 31, 137, and 168 on the slave sale list—Nancy, Liddy, Nancy, Sary, and Suckey—were in danger of being separated from most of their grown children.[41] Across the Pee Dee River, Robert Allston was then setting up his son Benjamin as a rice planter and, by private sale before the auction, he bought about 42 of Alston's slaves for Ben.[42] This may have had the effect of keeping one or two of these mothers together with their grown children. At the auction Robert Allston also bought a thirty-five-year-old bricklayer and his wife. The other 133 of Pinckney Alston's slaves were scattered to the wind. Pinckney Alston, by selling his slaves in this way, realized $112,350—probably over $9,000 more than he would have received had he sold the gang in two or three large groups.[43]

Meanwhile, Pinckney Alston's son Motte—having made his fortune by developing "Woodbourne," the northernmost rice plantation on the Waccamaw River—was retiring from business and moving to Columbia, South Carolina. He sold his posh new Murrells Inlet house to a brother for some slaves; he then sold these slaves and most of his others (perhaps 90 altogether) to Governor John Manning, who removed them from Georgetown County.[44]

The fourth big Waccamaw sale during this brief period involved the 109 slaves of Mary Ann LaBruce Petigru, a sister-in-law of Robert Allston's. When Mary Ann's husband—Captain Tom Petigru of the U.S. Navy—died in 1858, his widow wished to turn her Sandy Island rice plantation (Pipe Down) and its bondsmen and women into cash. Robert Allston bought the whole Pipe Down concern in 1859, immediately deporting about 36 of its relatively "prime" slaves to help stock his son Benjamin's new Guendalos plantation on the Pee Dee. Among the 109 Pipe Down slaves whom Robert purchased (at only five hundred dollars in the round, as a number of them were elderly) was Conky—an old man married, as it turned out, to a slave woman owned on the Waccamaw by Mary Ann's nephew. Mary Ann Petigru pocketed the five hundred dollars for Conky, knowing that the sale would permanently separate Conky from his wife. When Robert Allston learned the facts, he sent Conky to stay permanently with Conky's wife on Mary Ann's nephew's plantation; and the nephew grudgingly agreed to accept him. But Mary Ann declined to return to Robert Allston the five hundred dollars, or any part of it. A business contract was a contract, in her view. Mary Ann—"a real LaBruce, meek and unbending" (according to J. L. Petigru)—refused to concede a penny of the five hundred dollars which she, by arranging that Conky was to be sold away from his wife, had obtained for herself.[45]

Thus, of some 500 or 600 Waccamaw slaves exchanged in these four transactions, 400 or 500 were removed from their old community and required to start life anew, elsewhere. Meanwhile, a host of new slaves were imported into these (and other) Waccamaw plantations. By 1860 Daniel Jordan had accumulated 261 bondsmen and women at Laurel Hill, nearly all apparently bought at slave auctions.[46] Henry Buck (the buyer of Motte Alston's newly developed Woodbourne plantation) owned 311 slaves in 1860; and although the majority of them worked in Buck's big sawmill business, probably Buck had purchased a good number to replace those Motte Alston had removed from Woodbourne in 1858.[47] And Robert Allston's nephew J. B. Allston—twenty-four years old when he married in November 1857—bought 61 slaves a year later (from the Rutledge heirs, as explained above) in order to expand his operations at Waverly. The Waccamaw, far from being a stagnant rural retreat, was a bustling commercial area where substantial numbers of slaves were bought and sold during the winter: when some planters (like Pinckney and Motte Alston) retired, others (like Plowden Weston) shifted their field of operations, and others (like Daniel Jordan and J. B. Allston) entered or expanded their entrepreneurial ventures.

Similar transactions took place all over the rice kingdom. Although no slave on E. T. Heriot's Sandy Island plantation appears to have been sold when his three-plantation estate of 369 bondsmen and women was settled in 1859, buyers were sought for some of the slaves from Heriot's two other Georgetown rice plantations. And the death of Robert Allston's neighbor Frederick Shaffer in 1859 led to the sale of his rice slaves; Shaffer's were surely the 102 Pee Dee chattels auctioned in Charleston on January 5, 1860.[48] The perpetual buying and selling of rice slaves was one reason that, according to Frederick Bancroft, "before the end of the 'fifties Charleston had perhaps outstripped Richmond as a [slave-] selling market." Bancroft (whose statistical inferences have in some other respects proved remarkably accurate) estimated that, in the exceptionally busy year beginning October 1859, rather more than 5,000 slaves were sold in Charleston—reaping for the vendors some four million dollars.[49] Many of those auctioned were cotton slaves from up-country South Carolina, intended for the western market; but the sale of rice slaves for a vigorous local market played a larger role in this commerce than Bancroft realized. The coastal vessels destined for Charleston were sometimes laden with human beings unlikely ever to set eyes on home again. And Charles Manigault was not unique among rice planters in his wish to "make a dash" at the Charleston slave market.

III

Does it make sense to call these great planter-entrepreneurs "capitalists"? Not perhaps if one is shackled by the classical economists' conception of a capitalist: one who seeks to maximize his return from an investment in a factor of production—"capital"—which is logically distinct from either of the other two factors of production: (wage) "labor" and "land." But the classical economists understood little about slavery, and devised an intellectual framework for analyzing their own society, not that of an alien plantation world. Obviously J. J. Ward, John Hyrne Tucker, and those other planters whose chief object was "to make Rice to buy Negroes and Buy Negroes to make Rice" were interested, like other capitalists, in securing a good return upon their capital investments.

A planter's investments were not, however, those of a merchant capitalist—in a ship, a cargo, and a counting house. Nor were they those of an industrial capitalist—in a factory building, machinery, and raw materials. On the contrary, only $2,500 of J. J. Ward's $1,100,000 capital was investment in implements and tools. This was a tiny sum—only about one-tenth of even Ward's investment in livestock: and livestock, in turn, formed but a small proportion of Ward's total investment. He did not own a rice mill; and the huge majority of his investment was in cultivated land, and in slaves.[50] His swampland, once practically valueless, had been splendidly improved: for Ward and his predecessors had made a massive investment (of other people's labor) in embanking, clearing, and ditching the swamp, so as to enhance the productivity of future laborers.

This is what capitalist development is all about—the increase of labor productivity by combining an ever-increasing proportion of capital with the labor of an individual worker, so that that laborer's product becomes much larger than it could otherwise have been. What observer of the twentieth-century Midwest and Southwest can deny that a capitalist agricultural revolution— tractors, combine harvesters, huge irrigation schemes—has magnified a farmworker's productivity almost beyond imagination? A similar development of the rice kingdom was well under way by 1800. Great irrigation schemes (i.e., the creation of tidal rice plantations) quadrupled the productivity of the individual laborer. The erection of tidal rice-pounding mills—followed by steam-powered pounding mills—meant that J. J. Ward's slaves no longer had to waste their time hand pounding the product; Ward instead could ship his rough rice to a pounding mill elsewhere on the Waccamaw, or in Charleston itself. And, beginning in 1830, the gradual introduction of threshing mills started to increase even further the slaves' productivity.

The slaves hated the exhausting labor of hand threshing, especially if some of it had to be postponed until June, after the new year's crop had been planted. Early in the nineteenth century, threshing in June seems to have been common at Butler Island; but Roswell King Jr.—by working the slaves hard—claimed to have improved matters by January 1833. "Every negro trembles at the Idea of Thrashing Rice in June, so do I," he expostulated. "Each are [therefore] feeling the necessity of exertion [now]." That year a new steam-powered pounding mill was installed on Butler Island (the one whose ruined chimney can still be seen by passersby). King's ardor—and his willingness to drive his enslaved laborers to their limit—resembled that of a profit-seeking industrial entrepreneur. He knew that the owners wanted a good return on the capital investment: "The New Mill . . . performs well," he reported enthusiastically:

> If I do not make this Mill a source of profit, I am deceived. Have never gone over 12 or 13 hours daily. By pushing I can get out 150 [barrels of clean rice] weekly. . . . We get Steam on about 7 A.M. and blow off at 7 or 8 P.M. without any interruption unless throwing in or out of Gear the mill stones, which takes about three minutes.

Three weeks later King declared that, if enough rice had been threshed, he "could [have] run [the new mill] 14 hours daily." And if the price of rice were high at Charleston, the mill could produce even more rice per day, by lengthening the hours; but as he could not make the gang work more than fourteen hours a day, that would require a "double Gang at the mill." Working twelve to thirteen hours a day, the gang (he alleged) was less fatigued than it had been at the old water mill. However that may be, the new steam pounding mill worked faster than the old water mill, and this increased the pressure on the hand threshers. "We have *thrashed* [rice]," King disingenuously boasted to his employer ten days later. "Some of our hands almost sick, and had to break off for a week and go to other work to give them a respite after getting 150 [barrels] ahead."[51]

The parallel between this form of agricultural development and the birth pangs of industrial capitalism was made even clearer by an incident a few years later on another rice plantation. William Daniell was a Savannah doctor who in 1826 had published his medical *Observations on the Autumnal Fevers [i.e. Malaria] of Savannah.* He later became editor of the *Savannah Republican,* mayor of the Georgia seaport, and—probably through his marriage into the Screven clan—a prominent Savannah River rice planter: master of some 120 slaves. He equipped his plantation—located almost directly across the river from Savannah—with a modern steam mill. "Dr. Daniell's Mill Boiler exploded yesterday," the Savannah rice factor Robert Habersham reported in January 1852,

> killing one negro [the engineer] and numbing several others [five were injured], and burning 13,000 bushels of rice in the Ricks. We sent a [fire] Engine etc. [via Screvens ferry]. The explosion was seen and heard for miles, and from the boiler, parts of it, being hurled 80 yards all the ricks, 20 or more, were instantly fired so that they could not stop the fire before it got well ahead.

The *Savannah News* considered the death of the slave engineer in property terms, along with the destruction of rice and damage to the mill: "The loss to Dr. Daniell," the newspaper opined, "will probably amount to between 5 and 10 thousand dollars."[52]

The valuation of a human being as property reminds one of the major difference between slave-based agricultural capitalism and free-labor industrial capitalism: in the former, about half of the capital investment might be in slaves. This was immensely beneficial to the rice planter. The principal advantage was that slaves could be coerced to do work which free laborers would not perform—especially clearing the swampland in the first place and then cleaning out the ditches and canals each winter. Furthermore, the annual cost of a slave's labor was substantially less than a free laborer's would have been, even if one could have been secured to do that work. And—despite the perennial recurrence of temporary flight from the plantation—the slaveholder could be confident (as he could not with free laborers) that nearly all of the workers would be present to gather the harvest.

Nor were the disadvantages (to the planters) of slave labor so great as has sometimes been thought. To be sure, a slave could not be sacked so quickly as a wage laborer; but neither was the master's stake in a slave so permanent as that in a feudal serf: for the slave had no tie to the land, and could be sold virtually at the drop of a hat. The principal limitation on the master's getting rid of a slave was that the Charleston and Savannah slave markets were active only during the winter, when the rice harvest had been gathered, and before the new crop had been sown. A planter wishing to sell a slave at a good price might therefore have to wait for six months, as Louis Manigault did with the insubordinate house servant Jane. But a planter's capital investment in a slave was not so "fixed" and unchangeable as that in a steam mill.

A substantial economic disadvantage to the planter was that his slaves, though highly "productive," were simultaneously "inefficient."[53] The principal economic liability of slave-based capitalism accrued, however, not to the individual planter but to the low-country economy as a whole. In a wage-labor system any new capital investment increased the ratio of the nonlabor factors of production (especially machinery) to labor, and thus enhanced the productivity of each laborer: hence the economic dynamism of free-labor capitalism. And to the degree that the rice planter's capital investment was in massive irrigation schemes (i.e., in creating tidal plantations) and in pounding and threshing mills, this form of capitalism was also economically dynamic, enhancing the productivity of each laborer. But insofar as the planter's investment was in slaves themselves, this could increase the laborer's productivity only to the extent that a slave could be forced to do dreadful work which free laborers would not readily consent to do. Beyond this point, there was no further increase of a laborer's productivity to be gained for the economy as a whole—though, of course, the individual capitalist profited through spending a relatively low annual sum to secure his laborer's work.

Slave-based rice planting was therefore a peculiar form of agricultural capitalism—not, in the long run, so economically dynamic as the wage-labor variant of capitalism; yet far from economically stagnant either, as the complex development of tidal irrigation works, rice-pounding mills, and, eventually, steam threshing made abundantly clear. Slaveholding capitalists were even more jealous to preserve their "property" rights against any form of government regulation than wage-labor industrial capitalists proved to be during the nineteenth and twentieth centuries. The main disadvantage of slave-based capitalism was not so much that it formed an impediment to economic development as that it came at an immense cost to the enslaved workers. And it cost the American people a bloodletting unparalleled in their history, when the slaveholders went to war rather than countenance either diminution of their power to control their laborers or a challenge to the security of their massive investment in slaves.

The response of Henry Augustus Middleton (1793–1887) to the Civil War throws light upon these matters. Middleton—master in 1850 of 270 Georgetown rice slaves, as well as of bondsmen and women elsewhere in the state—was (in the words of the South Carolina historian George Rogers) "one of the truly rich men of the [Georgetown] district." Grandson of a president of the Continental Congress and nephew to a signer of the Declaration of Independence, Henry Middleton was at midcentury (along with his cousin John Izard Middleton) one of the two most prominent members of a famous clan. His marriage to an inheriting only child established him in 1823 (when his bride's father died) as master of two plantations just north of the town of George-town: part of the way from that enclave toward the Nightingale Hall planta-tion subsequently acquired by Robert Allston. Middleton was, through a female Manigault, a cousin of Charles Manigault's; and Middleton's claim that his branch of the family should be buriable in the Manigault vault at Charleston led for a time to frigidity between these two haughty gentlemen. Charles Manigault—immensely full of family pride—believed some of the Middletons tainted with insanity, and he urged the rights of the line of *male* Manigaults as the ground for excluding these interlopers from the sanctuary. One of Henry Middleton's sons was indeed in a private mental asylum, and his next son (according to Robert Allston's daughter Elizabeth) was "very near it." Middleton's hopes therefore became centered upon his only other son, Henry A. Middleton Jr., who assumed management of his father's Georgetown plantations in 1855.[54]

The young man was a systematic, methodical entrepreneur, and he kept careful records of the number of bushels of rice produced each year, and the quantity of clean rice. "The only test of a crop is the number of barrels sold of 600 [pound] weight," he wrote once after being deceived by a lying overseer; "little reliance can be placed on the bushel measurements, particularly those of J. K. Munnerlyn." Young Henry Middleton also neatly recorded the re-ceipts from sales each year (e.g., net receipts of $25,300 in 1858).[55] And he took for granted that slavery would continue into the far distant future: for in the plantation book left to posterity when the young man died in 1861 were inscribed the years "1861," "1862," "1863," and so forth, right up until the year "1879," with blank spaces to be filled in with the receipts for each of those years.

Like almost every other rice planter, young Middleton was an ardent supporter of secession. "Lincoln says in his inaugural that he will enforce laws, collect duties, etc.," he exclaimed on March 5, 1861: "So hurrah for war!" Middleton eagerly helped to recruit soldiers, and himself quickly "went forth in such [high] spirits as a private" to fight in Virginia. A Northern bullet pierced his lungs at the First Battle of Bull Run. The slightly misleading telegram announced a neck wound, and the young soldier's father (now sixty-eight years old) hastened to the bedside of his afflicted son in Virginia. The father "had much better have stayed at home," Elizabeth Allston confided to her diary, "they do not agree at all." Henry Jr. soon succumbed to this mortal wound: his grief-stricken mother was nearly unhinged, his father's hopes were blasted, and the sixteen-year-old Elizabeth Allston thus experienced the first of a never-ending series of deaths of beloved friends and relations, which for four years trailed the ghastly comet of military carnage through the Southern skies. The white people of Carolina paid a fearful price for their attempt to hold the blacks in thrall.[56]

Old Henry Middleton—bereaved but apparently indomitable—now re-sumed management of the two plantations. He dispatched his wife and their daughter to the mountainous inland retreat of Flat Rock, North Carolina, while he remained near his plantations in order to oversee their management;

and the family conducted an impassioned correspondence about how best to secure its massive stake in slaves. Having managed to invest a great deal of his money—some three hundred thousand dollars—in property in Newport, Rhode Island (where his family had customarily summered before the war), Henry Middleton was one of the few rice planters who had been lukewarm about secession. Recalling that the two Georgetown plantations acquired from his Tory father-in-law had nearly been confiscated from that gentleman in 1782, Henry Middleton feared that his own Newport properties would be seized by federal authority after the passage of the Confiscation Act of 1862. He now felt the more urgency in securing his Southern investments.[57]

Insecurity had appeared on the Waccamaw River on May 22, 1862, in the form of a Northern naval expedition, which proceeded ten miles up the river and took on board eighty fugitive slaves. On June 24 a similar expedition up the Santee River enabled four hundred more slaves to escape. And on August 14 Northern naval vessels passed within a few yards of Middleton's plantations, on a raid up the Black River.[58] When three of J. D. Magill's Waccamaw slaves returned to take their wives to freedom, and were captured, Middleton heartily approved the men's public execution in the Georgetown jail yard, just a little way down the road from his own plantation house. He was pleased when a Confederate battery was erected southeast of Georgetown to scare off the Union war vessels; and he was delighted when by 1863 the local Confederate garrison had been increased from twelve hundred to three thousand soldiers. He then hoped that planters might once again sleep quietly, assured that their slaves would no longer be tempted to flee to the Yankees, and thus despoil their masters of the capital they had painstakingly invested in human property.[59]

In order to secure this investment and to forestall flight, many low-country planters spent large sums on buying otherwise-valueless land in upland Carolina, to which they could evacuate their costly slaves. Middleton's friends and neighbors the Fords spent $27,000 for this purpose, and Judge B. F. Dunkin $22,500.[60] But Middleton prided himself on staying near enough his bondsmen and women that his presence might deter them from flight. When his family urged him to seek his own personal safety from the Northern raids, he repulsed them: "I cannot sacrifice the future, to the comforts of the present . . . ," he declaimed. "My whole energies are employed, to save to the family, as much of the property as is possible." Here was a paternalist indeed: but it was the economic security of his own family, not the welfare of the blacks, which filled his mind: "As to the removal of the negroes" to some western haven, he continued the next day to his daughter, "you had better throw it off your minds. If *I* can do nothing, who am constantly racking my invention to do the best, how can it be expected, that you should do more, who are hundreds of miles distant? . . . Eat more, and you will think less, of raids which are to deprive us of our people."[61]

There were still big profits to be made from growing rice, and by staying near the plantation Middleton reaped an 1862 crop of 475 barrels of rice, netting him no less than $30,000. For a few months—with the execution of the three Magill slaves on November 5, the stationing of thousands of Confederate troops nearby, and the news of the Northern defeat at Fredericksburg (which Middleton believed "had a noticeable effect . . . among the negroes")—his spirits temporarily rose. By mid-1863, however, the Yankees' advance along coastal islands northward from Port Royal toward Charleston caused the Midd-letons to panic again, lest they lose their slave property. "The negroes [of our friends the Rutledges] have all been taken by the enemy . . . ," Middleton reported gloomily on July 19: "nearly 200 negroes are lost to them." The patriarch then spelled out, in words of one syllable, that the one thing on his mind was to defend his own family's investment in their enslaved property:

> You all urge me as to my negroes [he continued testily]. Should Charleston be taken, my effort will be to leave the seaboard [taking the slaves with me], immediately. This may not be in my power. Should I lose them, let me impress it upon my family to bear well, that evil, which will be felt by thousands. If the country is conquered, the *property* of all will be lost.[62]

No honeyed utterance here of paternalist duty to childlike dependents! On the contrary, this was evidently the language of a desperate property owner, seeking to hang onto his enslaved bondsmen and women in order to preserve the luxurious lifestyle of his own immediate family. Middleton's frankness about his own motives throws light upon those of his acquaintance Plowden Weston—educated at England's famous Harrow school, the most scholarly of the Georgetown rice planters,[63] and South Carolina's lieutenant governor from 1862 until his death in 1864. Foreseeing war, the wealthy Weston (master of 335 slaves) had sent late in 1860 to his native England for a shipment of 120 Enfield rifles, to be purchased at his own private expense.[64] If Yankees must be killed to protect a gentleman's investment in slaves, so be it.

IV

While the creation of great fortunes based on slave labor was one remarkable feature of the rice kingdom, another was the dismal health of those slaves. The facts of the matter are hard to come by, for the census reports on low-country mortality were of limited value. It was "difficult to obtain correct returns of mortality," a candid census taker acknowledged in St. Peter's Parish (South Carolina), "few records of same being kept, and in many instances changes of overseers and agents the first of the year. Consequently many deaths unreturned."[65] The census taker was supposed to record, soon after June 1, 1860, every death during the twelve months preceding that date; but most of those overseers who had begun a new job in January had no idea how many slaves might have died during the seven months from June 1 to December 31, 1859. Nor had the overseers usually made written notes even of those deaths since their arrival at the plantation. On the large estates (which predominated), most overseers would scarcely remember—without a written record—the brief life of an infant who had died within a few weeks of birth from "puniness," malaria, or lockjaw. The problem was exacerbated in the low country, because few planters were present during the summer to jog the overseers' memory.

The best starting point may therefore be the list (mentioned earlier in this chapter) of "One hundred and seventy-seven remarkably PRIME NEGROES" whom Pinckney Alston sold in 1859.[66] Probably this was a reasonably typical group of rice field workers and artisans (though Alston evidently kept most of his house servants). The relative absence of large families is striking: one woman had six living children, but no one else had more than four. Most women, indeed, had three or less. And the total number of children on the plantation was comparatively small. While children under fifteen constituted 45 percent of all American slaves, they made up only 32 percent of the population of this rice plantation.[67] Everything suggests that here—as at Butler Island and at Gowrie—a dreadful mortality mowed down enslaved children in the rice kingdom at an even higher rate than in the cotton and tobacco regions.

The clearest way to measure this mortality is to compare the number of living children with the number of slave women of childbearing age. Pinckney Alston listed 19 women in their thirties, all of whom had husbands (17), or children, or both. No more than 1 or 2 children are likely to have been separated from *these* women, because the women were relatively young (only 4 being listed as thirty-five to thirty-nine years old, and the others all as thirty to thirty-four years old). Yet these 19 women were sold with only 24 living children: clear evidence of devastating child mortality. The situation was not quite so bad as at Gowrie, for an Alston woman was more likely to have a living child than not—but only barely so. Of these women, only Silvy and Maria had more than 3 living offspring; nearly half of the women had no surviving children at all. Clearly (as at Butler Island and Gowrie), miscarriages, stillbirths, infant mortality, and child mortality had wrought a fearful toll:

Alston Slave Women in Their Thirties

No. of women	No. of children sold with each woman	Total no. of children sold with these women
1	6	6
1	4	4
2	3	6
2	2	4
4	1	4
9	0	0
TOTAL 19	—	24

In the whole South, the number of slave children living in 1860 was much larger than the number of slave women aged twenty to forty-nine. The ratio was 2.52 (i.e., 1,770,400 slave children under fifteen years old, compared with

702,500 slave women aged twenty to forty-nine). Yet on Alston's plantation the ratio was scarcely over half as great: 1.30 (i.e., 57 slave children under fifteen years old, compared to 44 slave women aged twenty to forty-nine). The effect of a dreadful child mortality was especially noticeable among children aged ten to fourteen, when childhood diseases (malaria and enteric diseases were probably the most prominent killers) had had at least a decade to take their childhood toll. For slave children in the whole South the ratio (of slave children aged ten to fourteen to slave women aged twenty to forty-nine) was 0.77; but on Alston's plantation it was not even half as great—just 0.34.[68]

Thus, at each rice plantation which one examines—Gowrie, Butler Island, Pinckney Alston's estate—the evidence is clear that slave child mortality was even worse than elsewhere in the South. Yet one needs proof that this was true in the rest of the rice kingdom. At first sight the intermixture, almost everywhere in the low country, of rice plantations with sea-island cotton estates seems to defeat one's purpose: for the sea-island cotton plantations were less unhealthy (as Roswell King Jr.'s records illustrated); and there seems no way of distinguishing the two types of plantation within the census statistics. Georgetown County, however, proves almost ideal for the purpose, for this was the only low-country county which produced virtually no commercial crop except rice; and as Georgetown by 1860 produced nearly 30 percent of the whole low-country rice crop, its experience cannot have been insignificant. The facts about Georgetown appear below. Although Pinckney Alston's plantation turns out to have been even more unhealthy than most other Georgetown rice plantations, the figures show starkly that rice plantations—even when the slaves' settlements were in mainland woods, not out on an island subject to freshets like Gowrie—were dreadful places to raise children (see table 27).

Thus a slave child on a Georgetown rice plantation was only about five-eighths as likely to survive to maturity as a slave child elsewhere in the South. (This conclusion follows from contrasting the low ratio of children, aged ten to fourteen, to adult women in Georgetown [0.483] with the much higher ratio [0.770] in the whole South.)

TABLE 27.   Comparison of the Number of Surviving Slave Children to the Number of Slave Women Aged 20–49, 1860*

	Whole South	Georgetown County, S.C.
(1) Number of slave children aged 0–14	1,770,400	6,572
(2) Number of slave children aged 10–14	541,200	1,910
(3) Number of slave women aged 20–49	702,500	3,956
(4) Ratio (1):(3)	2.520	1.661
(5) Ratio (2):(3)	.770	.483

*Computed from figures in 1860 printed U.S. census.

If further proof were required of the rice kingdom's melancholy health record, it glares forth from the rest of the Carolina low country. Charleston, Colleton, and Beaufort Counties (where both rice and sea-island cotton were raised) were all afflicted by high child mortality rates—albeit not so bad as in Georgetown, since rice did not monopolize these counties as it did Georgetown. By contrast, up-country South Carolina (where tidal rice was *not* grown) was substantially healthier for slave children than the Southern average: up-country South Carolina resembled Virginia in rearing relatively large numbers of slave children to maturity (see table 28).

Although the ratios shown here point toward high child mortality on rice plantations, a second factor seems also to have caused the low country to stand out from other regions: probably slave women there were not quite so fertile as elsewhere. Chronic malaria among women in the tidal-rice counties probably resulted in an unusually large number of miscarriages.[69] And the low-country fertility rate may have been further reduced by higher mortality among female rice workers than among slave women elsewhere in the South.[70]

TABLE 28.   Further Comparison of the Number of Surviving Slave Children to the Number of Slave Women Aged 20–49, 1860*

	Ratio of slave children (aged 0–14) to slave women aged 20–49	Ratio of slave children (aged 10–14) to slave women aged 20–49
WHOLE SOUTH:	2.520	.770
SELECTED NONRICE AREAS:		
Up-country South Carolina (i.e., all of South Carolina except the four low-country counties)	2.74	.85
Virginia	2.69	.85
CAROLINA TIDAL-RICE COUNTIES:		
Beaufort	1.95	.58
Colleton**	1.87	.57
Charleston***	1.78	.56
Georgetown	1.66	.48

*Computed from figures in 1860 printed U.S. census.

**The 1860 census figures for "Colleton County" (upon which this table necessarily is based) mistakenly include St. John's Colleton Parish of Charleston county, in addition to all of the parishes in Colleton County. This parish primarily produced sea-island cotton, and therefore the error probably causes my figures for "Colleton County" to be slightly higher than they should be.

***The 1860 census figures for Charleston County mistakenly omit St. John's Colleton Parish. This error probably causes my figures for the county to be slightly lower than they should be. And the ratios in Charleston County are influenced by the fact that 37 percent of the slaves whom the census attributed to this county lived in the city of Charleston, where demographic conditions were much different from those on the rice plantations.

Yet other census figures (though maddeningly unreliable) suggest rather certainly that high child mortality was the principal cause for the relative shortage of surviving children in the rice kingdom. In the whole South, some 16 percent of young slave children (under five years old) in 1840 appear to have died during the following decade; but in Georgetown County the figure was about 41 percent. Child mortality stands bleakly forth as far worse in Georgetown than elsewhere in the South.[71]

The 1840s were the only decade between 1830 and 1860 when Georgetown's slave population increased; and one might incautiously suppose that this growth (from 15,990 slaves in 1840 to 18,250 ten years later) arose from a great excess of births over deaths. This was far from the case. The slaves' age distribution in 1850 makes plain that the slave population scarcely increased naturally at all. A tremendous bulge in the age profile of young adult male slaves, and an even larger one for females, showed that nearly two thousand slaves (aged by 1850 between fifteen and thirty-nine)—and perhaps several hundred other ones as well, accompanying these "prime hands"—had been imported during the decade.[72]

These considerations help one to interpret the decade of the 1850s, when Georgetown's slave population remained virtually static (declining by 144). Historians have long supposed that South Carolina frantically exported slaves to the West during the cotton boom which immediately preceded the Civil War. This idea is surely correct for up-country South Carolina; but the rice kingdom was a different kettle of fish. Probably Georgetown's net exports of slaves that decade were no more than about nine hundred, and quite possibly fewer.[73] For each Plowden Weston sending slaves West was a Daniel Jordan, importing fresh slaves into the county; and for each Pinckney Alston, selling slaves "accustomed to the culture of tide swamp rice lands" to other parts of the rice kingdom, was a Joseph B. Allston, importing slaves from other rice plantations. The child mortality rate was so high that there were few surplus slaves to ship West.

So varied were the experiences at different rice plantations that it is difficult to generalize about rates of slave population growth. That the number of slaves did often increase on South Carolina plantations is suggested by Carolinian rice planters' taking notice of negative growth rates on the Savannah River— as though population decline was the not the Carolina norm. Some planters achieved (or thought they had once achieved) a growth rate on a rice plantation comparable to that in the rest of the South. Thus Robert Allston claimed that before 1852 he had often achieved a 2 to 3 percent growth per year. But this was not the norm, for the relatively high growth of a plantation's population during one period was often offset by later disasters. Allston acknowledged that 28 of his slaves—"22 of whom were *task hands*"—had perished in one such calamitous year. Some years later the number of Allston's slaves appears to have declined from 631 (in 1860) to only 590 (by 1864); and although perhaps nine of those lost were fugitives to the patrolling Yankee naval forces, most must have died. At Butler Island the decennial growth rate from 1824 to 1859 was about 10.5 percent—far below the 26.6 percent rate of the whole South.[74] Yet conditions at Butler Island were probably less bad than the low-country norm. At "Weehaw"—Henry Middleton's plantation in Georgetown County—there was often a large excess of births over deaths; yet two of those epidemics which from time to time attacked every rice plantation mowed down terrific numbers of Weehaw's bondsmen and women. Of the 324 slaves there in 1855, 18 percent—59 people—perished in that one year, largely because whooping cough and measles epidemics added their ravages to the usual toll of child mortality. Two years later 40 more slaves—another 13 percent of the slaves then there—succumbed, principally to a dysentery epidemic. The death toll during these two ghastly years reduced what would otherwise have been a substantial population increase to a decennial growth rate of just 5.5 percent.[75]

Yet against plantations with moderate growth like these must be set others like Gowrie—with its 39 percent decennial decrease of slave population.[76] And the record of America's largest plantation in 1860—the J. J. Ward rice estate on the Waccamaw—was not brilliant. In 1850 Ward had owned 1,193 slaves, while in 1860 there were 1,131: a decline (if the number of slaves imported cancelled any exported) of 5 percent during the decade.[77] In the Manigault, Butler, and Grimball Papers are references to many other rice estates where the death rate was regularly larger than the number of births. Planters with negative growth rates were less likely to preserve careful records of their failures than were planters like Roswell King Jr. and Henry Middleton, who believed their records of 10.5 percent and 5.5 percent (at Weehaw) decennial population growth to be exemplary for the rice kingdom. The population profiles of Georgetown County suggest that its population growth in both the 1820s and 1840s resulted mainly from the importation of fresh slaves, and that there was little or no excess of births over deaths in the county during these decades. One's impression from this mixed collection of evidence is that the slave population of the whole rice kingdom—setting off the Chicora Woods and the Butler Islands against the Savannah River plantations, and negative-growth estates in Georgetown—probably did increase a little, but not quickly. Perhaps a decennial growth rate of 4 percent was average during the mid–nineteenth century—far below the slave norm (in the whole South) of 26.6 percent.

A 4 percent decennial growth rate would be consonant with the following estimates (for the mid–nineteenth century) of rice kingdom fertility and mortality:

> Fertility rate (for all slave women who survived to age 15): 6.6 live births per woman.[78]
> Mortality rate (to age 15, of all slave children born alive): 66 percent.[79]
> [This estimate is somewhat higher than Butler Island's rate (to age 15) of 60.4 percent, but much lower than Gowrie's rate (to age 16) of 90 percent.]

If these estimates are correct, 66 percent of a woman's 6.6 children died—that is, on average 4.36 children died; and this left 2.24 children who survived to age fifteen. With about thirty years separating a mother from her median surviving child, the decennial growth rate would be just below 4 percent.[80]

Clearly, slave child mortality in the rice kingdom was ghastly, even by the standards of the mid–nineteenth century. While some 28 percent of American free children then died by age fifteen,[81] about 66 percent of slave children on rice plantations perished by the same age. This was an even worse record than the Southern norm for slave children, which was perhaps 46 percent by age fifteen.[82] The fertility of American slave women was so high (even on rice plantations) as to offset the deaths—and probably even to produce a small decennial growth rate—despite horrific child mortality on rice plantations. Masters subjected slaves to these appalling conditions because rice plantations promised them large fortunes.

16

Retrospect

In 1937–38—over seventy-two years after emancipation—the WPA worker Genevieve Chandler (a Southern white woman seemingly related to one of the antebellum Waccamaw planters) interviewed elderly Waccamaw blacks about slavery times on the Waccamaw rice plantations. These interviews are a rich mine of information, yet they—like every other source on slavery—have serious shortcomings and must be used carefully. Chandler (like Frances Kemble a century earlier) encountered in the blacks a vein of coarse flattery of the powerful whites; but Chandler—unlike Kemble—appeared to accept it at face value. She was convinced that "most old ex-slaves in the South Carolina lowcountry . . . love and revere the names and memories of their old masters";[1] and few of the Waccamaw blacks sought to undeceive her.

Chandler's was an unrepresentative sample, for more than one reason. To begin with, all of her interviewees were very old, and their recollections of slavery were largely based on stories their parents had told them. (Kemble, by contrast, had spoken mainly with young or middle-aged slaves, as yet untainted by old people's natural appreciation of the time when they were not yet physically infirm; and Kemble's interlocutors spoke from their own fresh tears and blood, not from those of an earlier generation and a bygone age.) Chandler's sample was unrepresentative in another way, for nearly every black person whom she interviewed in 1937–38 was a member of the small, atypical group of black landowners, mainly descended from privileged drivers, artisans, or house servants. And Chandler biased her sample by recording a long conversation with Sabe Rutledge (who alleged of his master, "Sho treat his colored folks good"), yet not bothering to interview Sabe's sister Jane.

Jane's "quite acid" interventions into Sabe's interview suggested a very different view of slavery (derived, like Sabe's, from their parents) from the one Sabe found politic to express.[2] If a black person like Gabe Lance, after suitably polite remarks, began to criticize slavery, Chandler appears sometimes to have interjected a leading question—Did you have a good master?—which turned the flow of conversation into less critical channels.[3]

Yet despite these faults the Chandler interviews are a most valuable source on slavery, and especially on the African-Americans' stance toward that institution. The interviews indicate that the blacks' attitudes were very different from the ones Chandler believed she had discovered.

Chandler viewed slavery through paternalist spectacles, and the interviews might initially suggest that some of her interlocutors shared her vision. The kindly white interviewer wished there was a paternalist white master—as she believed there had been in the old days—to protect old Ben Horry in 1938 from having his land stolen from him by an unscrupulous white lawyer.[4] Yet Chandler did not make the observation that in the old days—when the masters denied slaves title to land—Ben Horry would not have been able to become possessor of fifteen acres of land in the first place. The idea—that blacks needed a white paternalist protector—was indeed shared by some blacks, and adapted by them to serve their own interests. Thus word had spread throughout the land by 1938 that government old-age pensions (created by the 1935 Social Security Act) were on their way—but not for the old freedmen and women. Gabe Lance's bitterness welled up as he considered the injustice of white people's driving his parents into the field, for their whole lives, without pay, and then leaving him without support in his old age. Lance's hyperbolic depiction of his parents' lives as slaves might be seen as corroboration of Eugene Genovese's paternalist thesis; yet the mood is scarcely elegiac: "Beat my Pa and Ma to death," Lance complained "and turn me loose! Ought to take care o' me! I send off my 35 ct. fust (first) time, next time twenty-five cents. . . . Take what little I have and don't send me nothing TALL! I tired with that now! . . . (Referring to 'old age compensation.')" A bitter sense of continuing injustice, not a hankering for a restoration of the old system, lay at the center of the old man's recollections.[5]

The most striking feature of the Chandler interviews is the profound bitterness of the blacks which constantly bursts through the interviews' sometimes placid surface. Thus Ben Horry—a man in his eighties, who after emancipation had been foreman at the Wards' Brookgreen, and whose father had at one time during slavery been head driver there—would not in 1938 have dreamed of overtly criticizing the Wards to a Southern white woman, who might have been a blood relation of his old master. In slavery, he hastened to assure Chandler, "most o' people treated right by owner." Yet Ben's flattery of his own master, Joshua Ward, contained—by implication—a criticism of neighbors whose conduct fell below a bearable standard. "Our Master didn't want to see us patchety up—nor naked!" Horry obliquely reported of Joshua Ward's actions just after emancipation: "They ain't treat you like a beast.

Ain't take no advance [advantage] o' you." In slavery times Joshua Ward (like Charles Manigault at Gowrie) had supplied his bondsmen and women with small rice, instead of confining them to corn; and he had gone further than Manigault by keeping "three nets running" to supply the slaves fish, and by allotting them vegetable gardens.[6]

Chandler knew that Ward's neighbor J. D. Magill had a bad reputation as a slave master, and her inquiries to Ben Horry about Magill's "Oregon" plantation stimulated him to talk more candidly. Although Horry had not had much contact with Oregon "in them dark days," he now alluded instead to the darker side of his own experience. He had told Chandler how some white people were absolutely determined to govern their slaves: "Some these white people that day something! They either manage you or kill you." Now he continued: if a young male slave traveled without a pass to visit his girl friend on another plantation, and was caught by the patrol, "Dem patroller put you cross a log! Beat you to death. I see them beat Ben Sharp. Beat 'em till Ben kin hardly git cross fence."[7]

Horry's recollection of his own mother's whipping was engraved in his memory. Once—before Horry's father had been appointed driver—the then driver sought sex with Horry's mother; when she refused, the driver set her an excessive task, and at the end of the day whipped her for not fulfilling it. He put her in the "Bull Pen," over a "thing called the Pony. Hands spread like this and strapped to the floor and all two both she feet been tie like this. And she been give 25 to 50 lashes till the blood flow. And my father and me stand right there and look and ain't able to lift a hand!" The boy witnessed his mother's wound: "I see gash so LONG (measuring on fore-finger) in my Mama—my own Mama! . . . If one them driver want you . . . they give you task you CAN'T DO. You getting this beating not for you task—for you flesh!"[8]

Horry reckoned that these stories need cause no offense to Genevieve Chandler, because he was making no accusation against the master class: those using the whip were either poor whites (the patrollers) or a black driver. Mrs. Chandler's black maid, however, was present at Horry's interview, and she understood him to be talking about a white man trying to force sex upon a black woman. " 'That why nation get mix up so' (Races)," the maid responded to Horry's narration of his mother's whipping.[9] Horry replied, in effect, that masters, too, forced sex on their slave women. He gave as an example Susan, a house servant to a "buckra woman": "To my knowing . . . had three white chillun. Not WANT 'em. HAB 'em. Boy . . . near bout clean [white] as them boy of Missus! Tief [thief, i.e, through stolen sex] chillun show up so! Women over-power[ed]!" It was a violent world; and the black man who had tried to force Horry's mother was later shot down by the local white people "because he led Yankees to where [the Wards'] silver, etc. was buried." "Thousand of them things happen," Horry murmured, "but I try to forget 'em."[10]

Horry never explicitly criticized his own master, but he expressed satisfaction at that man's comeuppance. Joshua Ward—the eldest son of the great J. J. Ward, and manager of the estate after his father died in 1853—commanded a local Confederate detachment which helped police the Waccamaw region during the Civil War. Eventually he escaped to England. Horry did not seem grieved when, in their master's absence, the black driver—whom Horry had no cause to love—had proved unfaithful to the Wards. Drivers were often entrusted with the keys to the stores, and according to Horry this driver was "the man control all the Buckra ting. And, by God, he go and show Yankee all dem ting!" Upon Joshua Ward's return from England, Ward (in Horry's words) "take into big drinkin'," and wasted his money. Horry betrayed no sorrow that, by the time Joshua Ward died in 1869, he was relatively impoverished: "He been fell tru wid his money (lost his property). Didn't bury so destent (decent)."[11]

To criticize slavery without seeming to criticize the masters was the delicate problem presented to every WPA respondent interviewed by a Southern white interviewer. The standard response was to deflect the blame onto the shoulders of the black drivers, or of the poorer whites. Yet Horry's praise of the masters was equivocal: "Dem white people didn't treat you *so* brutish! Dem obersheer!"[12] Horry professed to give great weight to the masters' good intentions, while his comments about what actually happened during the masters' long "summer" absences remained parenthetical. Circumlocution warred with truth telling: "Fore freedom we were treated by our former owners [and here no doubt Horry inwardly paused] I will say good—cording to situation of time. Every year when Massa and Missus gone mountains," the old man continued, with apparent loyalty to those figures, "they call up obersheer (overseer) and say, 'Don't treat them anyway severe. Don't beat them. Don't maul them.' (Mr. Hemingway been severe.)"[13] Horry seemed publicly to maintain that all would have been well had Massa and Missus only been able to learn what went on at the plantation. The driver could not have got away with whipping Horry's mother if Marse Josh had known: but "everybody can't go to boss folks! . . . Just the house servant get Marse Josh' and Miss Bess' ear." Why Joshua Ward did not institute a better system for learning the truth, Horry did not inquire.[14]

If Ben Horry's report—reeking with stories of injustice as it was—was that of a man who claimed that "most o' people treated right by owner," one wonders what a less diplomatic interviewee might have said. One such person was Hagar Brown, whose mother had been one of the two hundred slaves on "The Oaks" plantation (on the Waccamaw), owned by Joseph Alston Jr. Brown was bitter that in slavery a woman who was not well might be set a task beyond her strength, and whipped when she did not complete it. This happened to Brown's Aunt Henrietta, even though Brown's mother tried to help her sister finish the task: "My Ma," Hagar complained (using Gullah pronouns), "have to work he self to death to help Henrietta. . . . Some obersheer mean." Hagar had been born in about 1860, too late to have direct experience of the whippings imposed on workers for failure to complete an unreasonable task. "I too glad my chillun aint been here Rebs time!" Hagar's mother Sally exulted. "Gin [give] you task you rather drown than not done that task!" If a slave didn't complete her task satisfactorily, Sally had continued, "Driver wave that whip, put you over the barrel, beat you so blood run down!" Similarly, the patrollers brutally punished slaves caught trying without permission to attend a nighttime religious meeting. And in slavery, Hagar Brown complained angrily, "Massa sell you all about." Hagar knew this from her mother's experience: Sally apparently was sold to Columbia, South Carolina, and would never (except for emancipation) have been able to return to her home and dear ones at The Oaks.[15]

The Oaks may have been home to Sally Brown, but the plantation had produced a long history of discontent among its bondsmen and women. When the master caught some of his slaves planning to flee, he "lay 'em cross barrel. Beat dem till they wash in blood." (Though the language Chandler reports here may appear flat and stereotypical, one might err in underestimating the strength of feeling that lay behind these simple words. The blood repeatedly drawn by the lash evidently filled the former slaves' imagination.) Whippings did not cow these slaves, for in June 1860 no less than thirty Oaks slaves— about half of the male workforce—took to the woods, apparently because of a dispute about work. When, several days later, they still had not returned, Joshua Ward's younger brother Mayham (then twenty-three) called out his militia company, composed of posh young Waccamaw planters, to scour the woods for twenty-four hours: unsuccessfully. After a night's sleep the young planters went out again, but three days later the fugitives still had not been caught. "They have been pillaging the country," young Benjamin Allston had reported to his father, "and to some extent carrying their operations [from the Waccamaw] on to Peedee in some instances. Doubtless your Waterford cattle have been troubled by them." To his fiancée, Benjamin adopted a jocose tone: "Few things happen to create excitement with us," he began,

> but just now we have had some little out of the ordinary way. Some negroes, about 20 odd [he minimized the number so as not to alarm his fiancée] from the plantation of that bright youth Joseph Alston have taken to the woods, and some of the neighbors were quite scandalised that they should remain unmolested so long. Consequently they went out in a body some days ago to overtake them but after being out for two days they returned bootless home. What have become of the negroes mean time I have not heard.

Benjamin Allston, a West Point man who had spent several years fighting Indians in the West before embarking on a rice planter's career, evidently regarded the body of fugitives as relatively harmless, except to the cattle roaming in the unfenced woods. He seems also to have been unimpressed by the military efficiency of the young planters' posse. He refused to join it, and felt confident the fugitives would quietly return to The Oaks in due course. This confidence had been fed by the report to Benjamin from his father's then-trusted valet Stephen Gallant that Stephen had run into fifteen of the fugitives in the woods, and they—Stephen claimed—had told him they were all returning home.[16]

In the absence of fugitive slave advertisements (except J. D. Magill's), or of many sheriff's notices of fugitives held in the Georgetown jail, one might be tempted to infer that before the Civil War few Waccamaw slaves ran away from home;[17] but this private report of Benjamin Allston's implies that public advertisements were misleading. Contrary to what the *Pee Dee Times* and the *Winyah Observer* might suggest, the Waccamaw woods and swamps were probably as well populated with temporary fugitives as those of the Savannah River, and every other densely populated plantation area in the slave South.[18] These low-country fugitives could be expected to return home in good time, once they had had a few days or weeks to cool off, and to experience the local reptilian fauna. "On Rutledge Plantation [the Santee River estate from which J. B. Allston had purchased sixty-one slaves for his Waccamaw plantation in 1859] a man wouldn't take no beating," Ben Horry recalled. "Found a large hollow cypress tree. . . . Gone in. Lie down sleep. Fore day wake up! Feel something crawl over him. Nother one crow like game chicken! (Negroes all say rattlers crow! [Chandler commented].) Smell him. Crawl over him. Crawl out. Get out."[19] With such natural deterrents to prolonged flight, what planter (except the notorious Magill) need advertise in the local press for his fugitives? Only the unusual flight of thirty slaves in one group—and their staying out for several days—stirred the planters into a temporary spasm of excitement.

Although individual fugitives might regularly snatch brief moments of freedom in the woods and swamps, normally the slaves were virtually powerless. Their sense of helplessness was symbolized in the African-American folk memory by a story Hagar Brown passed on from her mother. "Dey put 'em [slaves] in the grave [in a wooden coffin] live!" Hagar exclaimed. "And you holler under the dirt till you weary and hafter dead. . . . Beat! Beat! Beat the box. . . . I [Hagar] say, 'Good thing I aint been here!' Ma say, 'No, dater, you couldn't do nothing—not a thing.' " This story may have been adapted from a real event generations earlier in South Carolina. In 1712 the Anglican clergyman Dr. Francis LeJau reported that a slave—for letting a parcel of rice fall into the river—had recently been chained, flogged twice a day for several days, starved, and put "at Night . . . into a hellish Machine contrived by [the overseer] into the Shape of a Coffin where [the slave] could not Stirr."[20] That some such event recurred during the lifetime of Hagar's mother is not impossible: Ben Horry was on the point of naming to Chandler a Waccamaw white man supposed to have been buried a slave alive, but he thought better of doing so.[21] Yet even if no such event was repeated in the nineteenth century, the living folk memory of the earlier torture perfectly symbolized the real sense among the slaves of their powerlessness. Although the dread of being whipped lay principally in the accompanying physical agony, horror came also from the feeling—the essence of slavery—that one was powerless.

As the weak are always prey to exploitation, one old former slave after another burned with a sense of slavery's unfairness. "Any slave run way or didn't done task," Gabe Lance murmured, "put 'em in barn and least cut they give 'em (with lash) been twenty-five to fifty. Simply cause them weak and couldn't done task—couldn't done task! Give 'em less rations to boot!" J. D. Magill—sixty-five years old in 1860, and master then of 189 slaves—was the most hated of the seventeen great planters on Waccamaw peninsula. Three times within eighteen months the local sheriff advertised for Magill to come to collect fugitives lodged in the Georgetown jail; Magill himself advertised for six months for another runaway. One reason these slaves fled was that their master did not feed them enough: "McGill people have to steal for something to eat," the most servile of Genevieve Chandler's interlocutors nevertheless complained. Chandler could not delude herself into imagining that the memory of Dr. Magill was revered by his bondsmen and women: Magill's "Oregon" plantation, Chandler admitted, "from all accounts, had a cruel master." Magill was no uncouth Simon Legree; on the contrary, he was a graduate of the newly founded College of South Carolina (later University of South Carolina) in 1815, and obtained his medical degree from the University of Pennsylvania in 1818; and he had married the daughter of a Georgetown rice planter so rich and well regarded that he had been selected to give a dinner to the touring President George Washington in 1791. Magill's cruelty was no bar to his being fully accepted by the other Waccamaw grandees: he was a vestryman of the local Episcopal church, a member of the charitable Winyah Indigo Society, a trustee of All Saints Academy, and a founding member (in 1845) of the local gentlemen's club, the Hot and Hot Fish Club—a name which presumably reminded the assembled gentry of their distinction from the menial "Hottentots" whose unpaid labors made possible the gentlemen's elegant dinners.[22]

The failed escape of some of Dr. Magill's slaves in 1862 was still vivid in the recollection of Chandler's interviewees in 1938, and illustrated the nearly helpless plight of the bondsmen and women. Maria Heywood's mother told Maria that her own sister, Tilla Kinloch, had been one of the three women who tried to escape, when their husbands returned from the Yankee vessels to fetch them. Tilla had brought her baby, Marsh, with her in the boat which stealthily essayed the twenty-five-mile nocturnal journey downriver from Magill's plantation into Winyah Bay. Marsh cried. "Mother say [that Tilla Kinloch] take her apron," Heywood recounted, "and stuff the child mouth. Blockade (patrollers) wuz hiding. Shot in range of that sound. [Tilla's eye was shot out by the patrollers.] Row! Row! Row! Put everything in Jail! All in jail!" Sabe Rutledge confirmed that, in one of the many Civil War escape attempts, a woman's eye had been shot out; and he said that in one case women and children were killed too.[23]

None of Chandler's interlocutors told her that the three Magill men had been hanged (or else Chandler or her editor failed to record a story so discreditable to the image of the kindly paternalist masters); and as the story of the hanging was not printed in the local newspaper, one would still be ignorant of what actually happened at the Georgetown jail yard if H. A. Middleton's letter describing the public execution had not been preserved. Chandler did, however, record a different version of the fate of one of Magill's men— perhaps because it was so implausible that no reader would have taken the story seriously. Mack McCusky, a Confederate officer locally responsible for requisitioning supplies for the Confederate army,[24] probably witnessed the hanging of the three Magill men. In 1873, during the tense Reconstruction period, McCusky sought to terrify local blacks by concocting a different version of Nemo Ralston's public execution. Apparently Maria Heywood accepted his version of Ralston's death, and thus increased her sense of the blacks' helplessness in the face of white power. "Mr. McCuskey told us Nemo Ralston was one [who tried to escape]," Heywood recalled. "Say he never see a fatter man. . . . (They running way from Oregon—Dr. McGill place.) Say they put four horses to him—one to every limb. Stretch 'em. And cut horses [loose] and each horse carry a piece! Mr. McCuskey was one help lynch Nemo."[25]

The massacre of black prisoners of war—commonplace after almost every Civil War battle in which black soldiers participated[26]—was but an extension of the execution of fugitives who dared to return to challenge white power. Ben Horry mentioned one such local event, when a Northern white soldier associated with a returning fugitive was also executed. Some Yankee raiders had come inland on Waccamaw peninsula, were cut off from the ocean by Confederate forces, and were captured: "Hang one colored man and one white man to Oaks Seashore." This, to Horry, was a "murdering."[27] Although Horry's recollection three-quarters of a century later cannot be wholly conclusive evidence that the two men were executed, the story—taken in conjunction with the hangings of the Magill men, which are fully authenticated—has the ring of truth. The old people's stories of the execution of captured fugitives suggest that the planters' purpose in these hangings—to confirm the blacks' sense of powerlessness in a hostile world—had been substantially achieved.

Another element in the blacks' perception of slavery was their sense of being dishonored. In slavery times, Sabe Rutledge said with a stutter (stuttering sometimes being associated with suppressed anger), planters did not have even horses or mules: "Didn't have nothing but ox. And the colored folks—they came next to the ox." No doubt Rutledge's remark was born of experiences like the one Kemble reported, of cattle freely grazing among the wooden markers of the slaves' dishonored graves, while the graves of white artisans were protected from the cattle by a fence. So little did the rice planters value the labor of a slave, Ben Horry complained, that the slaves were obliged to "mash" the earth with their hoes, harrowing machines (pulled by draft animals) being introduced only after emancipation. And so little were slave women valued that they were assigned tasks sometimes beyond their strength, leading to a Saturday whipping known to the other slaves from the women's screams. "Mausser gin (give) the women a task," the Reverend Albert Carolina recalled in 1937. "Didn't done it. Next day didn't done it. Saturday come, task time out! Driver! . . . You could hear those people, 'Murder! Murder!' "[28]

To Margaret Bryant the dishonored position of the bondsmen and women appeared in the planters' disrespect for the slaves' family ties. When she and her mother were sent to "Wachesaw" plantation (whence her mother had been temporarily removed), Margaret Bryant "ain't meet aunty, uncle—none. . . . I ain't meet none when I come here. All been sell." Dishonor was also evident in the long hours of labor forced on the slaves. Margaret's mother's work as a weaver seemed never-ending: "Have to weave day and night to make up that cloth to please obersheer." And the punishments were degrading. "Put duh switch," Bryant expostulated. "Put you 'Bull pen.' Hab 'um (have them) a place can't see you hand before you. Can't turn round good in there. Left you in there till morning. Give you fifty lash and send you to work. You ain't done that task, man and woman lick!"[29]

Yet the slaves' response to their degradation was often assertive, and the old blacks' pleasure at the discomfiture of their white oppressors was transparent. When a naval expedition came by Wachesaw plantation (twenty miles up the Waccamaw) in 1862, these first raiders were not yet interested in the slaves, Margaret Bryant remembered: "Been after the buckra!" Could Louisa Brown's favored plantation song have masked anything except hostility to the tricky whites?

> Wish I had a hundred dog
> and half was hound!
> Take it in my fadder field
> and we run the rabbit down!

When Ben Horry was asked to distinguish plantations where slaves were decently treated from those which were "cruel to the colored," he managed to name only his master's brother's estate, two of the planters' summertime beach houses, and Plowden Weston's estate.[30] Yet even at Weston's Hagley plantation an overseer was said to have been murdered by slaves at the end of the Civil War.[31]

Solidarity within the slave community, and exultation at the end of slavery, were clearly evident. Against the case of Ben Horry's cruel black driver may be set that of Albert Carolina's driver, who at nighttime illegally taught favored slave children to read. Illegal wartime religious gatherings (when, under cover of darkness, the bondsmen and women prayed for freedom) continued the antebellum tradition of the slaves' secret prayer meetings where—contrary to law—no white person was present. The blacks' joy at freedom—even among those who spoke most fawningly of their white masters—was unfeigned. Some old slaves in the 1860s had associated freedom with the Second Coming of Jesus: thus, according to Maria Heywood (as transcribed by Chandler), elderly slaves like Maria's grandmother Harriet said " 'Tank God! Massa, HE COMING!' (Referring to 'Freedom')." Maria identified freedom with the Yankees' naval artillery, which during the war sporadically bombarded the Confederate saltworks on Georgetown peninsula, or the blockade-runners' exit at Murrells Inlet. "I know when Lincoln shoot the chain of slavery off my neck," Heywood exulted. "I know when the big gun shooting to free me! Yankee come and free Waccamaw! No slave hold."[32] Freedom was to Ellen Godfrey intoxicating; so great was her delight as to make her silly: "I glad for Freedom till I fool!"[33] A song still remembered in the 1930s bore the marks of Republican Party election-eering during Reconstruction, adapted to the Civil War memories of the role reversal when Confederate soldiers fled to the swamps to avoid the Northern naval bombardment:

> Freedom forever!
> Freedom everymore!
> Want to see the Debbil run
> Let the Yankee fling a [cannon] ball
> The Democrack will take the swamp![34]

This welcoming of freedom drew on the deep tradition of black dissidence against slavery. One interviewee after another recounted stories of slaves fleeing the plantation—and especially so when the presence of Yankee naval vessels opened for the first time the opportunity for permanent escape. Even slave children combated the master class. Thus Maria Heywood presented a more realistic version than Harriet Beecher Stowe's of Topsy's response to Little Eva's admonition, "What does make you so bad, Topsy? . . . I wish you would try to be good." Since 1832 the religious indoctrination of Waccamaw slaves had been entrusted by the local planters—Episcopalian almost to a man—to the English-born Anglican clergyman Alexander Glennie. "Parson Glennie come once a month to [our plantation]," Maria Heywood said curtly. "Tell us obey Miss Minna [Alston]." Although Mary Alston, the daughter of this Miss Minna Alston, had been born in the same year as Maria Heywood (1855), she was not as tall as the slave girl. The white child Mary Alston understood—already at the age of eight—how religious sanction might be invoked to try to control a slave girl, but the latter took no notice of this brand of white Christianity. "We'd fight," Maria Heywood recalled. "She [Miss Mary] knock me. I knock back! Wouldn't take a knock! She say 'I tell Parson Glennie! Lord won't bless you! You bad.' I say, 'You knock me, I knock you!' "[35]

The stakes were higher when an adult slave woman defied an overseer. Margaret Bryant's father being the number one carpenter at Dr. Allard Flagg's Sandy Island rice plantation, the carpenter took "One" as a surname for himself and for his wife Mary. "Couldn't manage my ma," Margaret proudly attested. "Obersheer (overseer) want to lick ma, Mary One say, 'Going drownded meself! I done my work! Fore I take a lick, rather drownded meself.' " Tied to a long rope held by another slave, Mary One managed to jump into the river while the overseer was seeking Dr. Flagg; but (perhaps because Flagg was at hand) the outcome was different from when, under similar circumstances, Louis Manigault's servant London jumped into the Savannah River. Mary's resolution caused her master to make a concession, which he expressed in financial terms: "Doctor say, 'You too good labor for drown. Take dem (them) to Watsaw [Wachesaw, Flagg's plantation on the Waccamaw, opposite Sandy Island]. Bring her to weave."[36]

Some slaves bequeathed to their descendants pride in their capacity for hard work. Ben Horry—referring to the digging of a canal by hand labor—declared glowingly to Chandler, "Missus, slavery time people done something."[37] Horry's black visitor Gabe Lance immediately elaborated, and with equal pride: "Yes sir. All them rice field been nothing but swamp. Slavery people cut kennel (canal) and dig ditch through the raw swamp. All these fields been thick woods."[38] "Slavery-time people," or "slavery people"—but not "slaves": the choice of words shows that subjection to the condition of slavery had not, in these men's eyes, transformed "people" into contemptible "slaves."

Ben Horry's passionate loyalty to his father suggested how little slavery might undermine family ties. Ben's father was a privileged bondsman: trained to play the violin for "the white folks to dance," esteemed by his master, Joshua Ward, and entrusted by Ward with a key to the rice barn. Like Stephen Gallant and many another favored slave, Ben's father used his privileges to serve his own interests. "My father love he liquor," Ben lucidly explained. "That take money. He ain't have money but he have the rice barn key and *rice* been money! So my father gone in woods (he have a head, my father!), take a old stump, have 'em holler out." Then he ground the stolen rough rice, using the stump as mortar, with two purloined pestles. This was the Wards' famous golden rice, which set the standard for high-quality grain as far away as Louisiana. "I been old enough," Ben proudly related fourscore years later, "to go in the woods with my father and hold a . . . torch for him to see to pestle off that golden rice he been tote out the barn and hide." Ben's fidelity was to his father, not to the master; and this demanded of the young child total reliability as a liar. "When that pestle been miss (missed)," said Ben radiantly, "I wuzn't know nothing!"[39]

It is a heartwarming story of a child's devotion to his intrepid, quick-witted parent—"he have a head, my father!" Yet this may also be a melancholy tale. Ben's father had the agricultural expertise, and the capacity for leadership, to be a head driver (for this was the position to which the Wards eventually promoted him). Yet he was impelled to squander his ingenuity on stealing rice, laboriously grinding it by torchlight, illicitly trading it for whiskey, and teaching his son to lie in order to cover his tracks. What a waste! One thinks of Gowrie's most talented craftsman—Jack Savage—moldering for eighteen months in the fetid swamp in order to taste a breath of freedom.

Thus Genevieve Chandler's interviews exhibit a very different tableau from the one she believed she was painting. To be sure, her interlocutors did sometimes express sentiments which might seem to corroborate a paternalist view of slavery. Chandler was delighted that Ben Horry appeared to regard his white mistress, Miss Bess Ward, as a kind of divine protector who would have set everything right—if only the house servants had permitted her to learn what was actually happening on the plantation! Doubtless Chandler was also gratified when Ben spoke of his happiest day during slavery times: the joyful annual distribution of new clothes to the children, followed by a children's footrace before the benevolent gaze of "Marse Josh . . . and Miss Bess."[40] But these bits of evidence must not be isolated from their context; and the Chandler interviews, taken as a whole, present a grim picture. Patrollers mercilessly flogged night travelers. Black drivers and white masters alike raped slave women. Masters failed to curb their overseers' severity. Callous sale of slaves ruptured the closest of family ties. The combination of rattle-snakes in the woods and venomous white people rendered slaves virtually powerless. Arbitrary punishments fed a raging sense of injustice. The blacks exulted at their release in 1865: for they had perceived slavery as a brutally harsh system, over which was daubed only a paper-thin veneer of paternalism. Ben Horry spoke truly of "them dark days": pernicious alike—though in different ways—to oppressors and oppressed.

17

Slavery

Self-esteem once beclouded Americans' vision of human bondage, and to some extent it still does. More than 125 years after the end of slavery, the Georgetown (South Carolina) Rice Museum's valuable display of plantation technology yet testifies to white people's unquenchable thirst to think well of their ancestors. The museum's model of a slave settlement features a little building labeled "School"—as though the typical rice planter thus ostentatiously defied Carolina's law of 1834 which banned any free person from teaching a slave to read and write.[1] The labels on the museum's exhibition say that oxen or mules plowed the rice fields, ignoring the fact that some planters like Nathaniel Heyward never used a plow to lessen the arduousness of his slaves' labor in breaking the soil. These labels imply that only seed rice was hand threshed, failing to acknowledge that the exhausting toil of hand threshing the whole rice crop lasted almost universally in the low country until 1830, and usually later than that date.[2] The word "malaria" is never named on the museum's displays, despite the profound effect of this disease upon both the lives of the slaves and the social structure of the white community; nor is the appalling rate of slave child mortality mentioned. Indeed the word "slavery" never appears in the Rice Museum's exhibition, even though slavery was central to the history of tidal rice culture.

Some Northern white people have been similarly keen to think well of their ancestors. They have remembered the North as a hotbed of abolitionist fervor, at a moment when abolitionists were in fact a despised minority in most parts of the North, and when antipathy to blacks—and even indifference to their bondage—characterized most of the Democratic Party and a substantial portion of the Republican Party. Some African-Americans, too, have been tempted to accept a romanticized view of their own ancestors' lives: the claim that slavery (while forging the character of masters) left the slaves spiritually unscathed.

Three radically different interpretations of slavery have shaped Americans' perception of the institution. In the view of Ulrich Phillips—which dominated high school textbooks until the 1950s, and which appears still partially to inform the Georgetown Rice Museum's exhibition—American slavery was a mild "school" for civilizing and Christianizing savage Africans; and the paternalist benevolence of the slaves' kindly masters lay, on the whole, beyond reproach. But as the civil rights movement girded its loins in the 1950s, Kenneth Stampp's *Peculiar Institution* mounted a vigorous onslaught upon this self-congratulatory formula. Slaveholders principally sought profit, Stampp alleged; and they governed primarily by fear, not by winning the slaves' affection. The slaves resisted their bondage by every means at their disposal; and if lying, thievery, and sabotage were endemic among slaves, these forms of dissidence were the natural—indeed admirable—products of a vicious system of exploitation. Slavery, Stampp believed, wrecked the bondsmen and women's family institutions and (by cutting them rudely from their African heritage) plunged them into a cultural void.[3]

The reflorescence of black nationalism in the 1960s soon shaped a third way of seeing slavery, profoundly different from either Phillips's or Stampp's. The most significant versions of this new view—though one of its formulations has been repudiated by many black scholars—have been expounded by John Blassingame, Eugene Genovese, Herbert Gutman, Charles Joyner, and Deborah White. These historians all celebrate the strength of the slaves' cultural defenses against their oppressors. In this interpretation, African-Americans creatively shaped strong family institutions, a magnificent folk religion, and a vital folk culture. Solidarity, not division, characterized the slave community; and privileged bondsmen and women—even drivers and house servants—normally threw in their lot with their fellows of the field. The vibrant community life of the slave quarters put the lie to any claim that slavery had demoralized its putative victims.[4]

The adherents of this view differ among themselves about the sources of the slaves' culture. The most influential—and most controversial—formulation has been Eugene Genovese's. He asserts that nineteenth-century American slavery—though dependent on the world markets provided by Europe's and the North's capitalist development—was a noncapitalist institution whose American form (unlike that in the Caribbean) was essentially paternalist. While Genovese constantly declares that slavery was a vicious form of labor exploitation, he also presents evidence that slaveholders were "paternalistic": not only in their ideology, and in their system of allowances and privileges to their dependents, but even in the benevolence of many planters' actions. The shrewdness with which Genovese discusses the slaves's accommodation to this paternalist regime, the originality of his analysis, the breadth of his erudition, and the depth of his research: these have marked Genovese as the leading interpreter of American slavery during his generation. Not only is this author a great historian, but he has helped shape a past in which almost everyone can take pride: African-Americans in their ancestors' heroic cultural resistance, and Southern whites in their ancestors' paternalism.

Only the spiritual descendants of Northern white abolitionists might take pause; for according to one influential school of modern historians, the abolitionists—their substantial achievements notwithstanding—were in many respects conservative Victorian moralists: racist and deeply implicated in the "self-help" philosophy of burgeoning Northern capitalism. The abolitionists were partly responsible, in this view, for forging the ideological and political chains which quickly after 1865 bound the "freed" African-Americans into a new form of labor exploitation little different from—and in some respects even worse than—the exploitation inherent in a paternalist, noncapitalist form of human bondage.[5] If slavery was simply one among many different forms of labor exploitation, one might incautiously wonder, were the designers of the Georgetown Rice Museum perhaps right to omit the word "slavery" from their exhibition of the antebellum rice industry?

It may be useful to outline a fourth way of looking at American slavery, novel (if at all) only in its conjunction of the most convincing elements of the second and third interpretations just sketched. Surely, as the preceding pages have shown, neither Stampp's nor Genovese's views—taken separately—wholly illuminate the rice kingdom; and they probably do not fully illumine the cotton kingdom or the tobacco kingdom either. The rice industry, to be sure, affords an unaccustomed angle of vision upon slavery. The planters' massive capital investments, their long "summer" absenteeism, the huge preponderance of slaves in the low country's population, the heavy dependence of planters upon privileged slaves to make the system function, and the task system—these all gave a special character to the low country. Yet slavery was slavery, despite local modifications. The rich documentation for certain rice plantations may suggest ways of viewing slavery applicable (with suitable amendments) to other regions of the South.

One must begin with the glaring fact that slavery proved, for the masters, a splendid way of making money. The fortunes built upon the backs of black bondsmen and women—while only moderate when compared with those of the greatest landowners of Europe—were huge by American standards. In the United States most land could scarcely be monopolized, as in Europe; consequently, the acquisition of large numbers of slaves was the surest American agricultural route to wealth. The slave-based agricultural capitalism of the Carolina and Georgia low country nurtured the growth of a proud "aristocracy" (in Disraeli's sense) whose impact on American history was spectacular.

Callousness toward the slaves' welfare was the hallmark of this system. The masters knew that slave infants died like flies in the malarial swamps; yet no planter discovered a financial interest in calculating the death rate (e.g., from the records carefully tabulated at Butler Island by Roswell King Jr.), and in making an appropriately humane inference. Neither did it seem in the financial interest of Charles and Louis Manigault to calculate the mortality rate at Gowrie. If an inconvenient number of "negroes" persisted in dying at that swampy island, others could always be purchased in the Charleston slave market, or deported from Silk Hope. The governance of slaves rested on despotism—where the master's word could scarcely be challenged, where the overseer's whip and the Charleston "dark hole" were intended to terrify every slave into subordination, and where slaves like Jack Savage and cooper George's sister Jane would (without compunction) be sold forever away from spouse, family, and friends, if this was deemed necessary to preserve plantation discipline. The callous indifference of Elizabeth Allston's youthful cousin to the feelings of the family of a dying slave (when as a joke the cousin lyingly told Elizabeth that the slave, then in his death throes, had summoned her) may symbolize the heartless arrogance of the masters, which regularly afflicted the slaves. Only the anguished pleas of a privileged bondsman like Joe, and the passionate intervention of Joe's peculiar English mistress, prevented Pierce Butler and Roswell King Jr. from permanently separating Joe from his wife, Phoebe, and their young children. To denominate a system like this as "paternalism"—no matter how carefully the word's meaning is redefined— cannot clarify one's understanding of low-country slavery. When in February 1865 Charles Manigault's Silk Hope slaves contemptuously stood the Manigault family portraits in the rain, then parceled them out to grace the walls of their cabins—or when, some weeks later, the Allstons' sullen freedmen and women angrily swarmed about their mistress's carriage, upon her return to the low country to reclaim her plantations—these African-Americans would have been outraged at any suggestion that "paternalism" was an essential characteristic of the system from which they joyfully found themselves free.

But they did not kill Adele Allston, when it might seem that they could have done so; nor were other Georgetown planters assaulted during the blacks' turbulent transition to freedom. And during the antebellum period, insurrections were scarcely on the cards—even in a low country where slaves vastly outnumbered the whites. Some rice planters routinely put muskets into the hands of their bird minders, knowing that nothing untoward would happen. And each evening, for six months at a stretch every year, thousands of rice slaves were left the whole night unsupervised by a white man: their masters were in Charleston or farther abroad, and the overseers often took nightly refuge in pinelands away from the plantations' malarial "miasma." How could this have happened, if masters and overseers had actually lived in constant danger of insurrection?

Part of the answer lies, no doubt, in the elaborate system of general and special privilege which formed an essential ingredient in the whole unholy brew. Charles Manigault prided himself upon furnishing adult males with made-up trousers and jackets, of relatively good quality, instead of requiring the slave women to make every stitch of plantation clothing. And in the absence of pigs or vegetable gardens for his slaves, Manigault banned his overseer from raising chickens, so that the slaves' one prerogative of this sort would not be infringed by the overseer's family. Of a spring evening Louis Manigault enjoyed playing his guitar for some of the slave children; and one Christmas, after a disastrous "cholera" epidemic, he went so far as to try (unsuccessfully) to hire a fiddler to jolly things up for a plantation dance. Pierce Butler in 1839 permitted his slaves, and his own wife, to talk him into the daring experiment of using mules instead of human labor to plow the rice fields; and the Butler brothers were delighted to discover that this remarkable innovation was good for the quality of their rice crop, as well as for the relief of their slaves.[6] Robert Allston, besides special rewards for slaves in key positions, paid a bonus to any slave who managed to avoid illness the whole year. And in 1859 (acceding to practices already instituted by his slaves during his absence as governor) he devised a complex set of regulations whereby each slave family could raise pigs. Although such grants of privilege won these masters little goodwill, they undoubtedly helped to turn many slaves' minds from their more profound grievances.

And often discipline on these plantations was relatively lax. A privileged slave like John Izard or Stephen Gallant might be entrusted to travel alone for days at a time, unaccompanied by any white man. Everyone knew that, at harvesttime, many of James Potter's bondsmen and women stayed overnight at Gowrie—against plantation rules—without the drivers interfering. Many of Charles Manigault's slaves, too, left Gowrie at night without permission, as suggested by the accidental drownings of Big Sampson (a former Silk Hope driver, subsequently deported to Gowrie) and later of Bob (the vendor of stolen rice) after unauthorized nocturnal expeditions. Even when a slave fled to the swamp for an extended stay, this was not the signal for a concerted, massive effort by the masters to recapture the fugitive. After all, slaves ran away regularly, and they were unlikely to escape permanently. (Dolly appears to have been the only Gowrie slave to do so, and her success occurred in unsettled wartime conditions, when Louis Manigault was residing in the unfamiliar town of Augusta, far from the plantation.) If the masters simply bided their time when a slave ran away, the fugitive was likely to be caught by some white person; or to return voluntarily when rattlesnakes, or hunger, or cold, or a subsidence of rage impelled her or him to forsake the swampland hideaway. Only once—when five slaves were out simultaneously—did the Manigaults threaten to go hunting fugitives with dogs, and the threat alone was sufficient to achieve its purpose. If recalcitrant slaves could be "fixed" as easily as Charles Manigault believed—by whippings, trips to the Savannah jail for "correction," threats of sale, or milder measures like withdrawing the privilege of eating "small rice"—why make a fuss about an occasional runaway?

Accommodation undoubtedly occurred on both sides of that ditch which divided masters from slaves. Masters carefully apportioned little rewards to privileged slaves—an overcoat to protect a driver from the rain, or the privilege (to captain Hector, the boatman) of a confidential "plantation talk" with Louis Manigault about what the overseer and the other slaves had been up to in Louis's absence—and the slaves in turn adapted their conduct to their masters' whims. If the high-tempered Carolina house servant Robert was sent away from his wife and infant child to toil in Gowrie's muddy fields, prudence suggested to Robert the reining of his temper, and his conforming to the demands of Gowrie's overseer; and before too many years Robert—his wife, Hester, restored to his embrace until she succumbed to one of the "cholera" epidemics—had accepted the key position as Gowrie's head driver. Stephen Gallant, too—derisively called the "little guv'ner" for his imitation of his master's ways—accommodated for years to the system, until the moment when Stephen's extraordinary license to roam the countryside enabled him to organize the complex, daring, and successful escape of almost his whole family in 1864.

Accommodation might be a mere pose, then, masking an insubordinate spirit. Yet can anyone doubt that the effects of subordination etched themselves deeply into the character of many slaves—as deeply as the effects of domination shaped the character of many masters? Slavery did not, of course, turn most slaves into "Sambos": the canard has been repeatedly, and convincingly, refuted. But since striking a white man was virtually beyond the pale, and since running to the swamp was very dangerous (and almost certain eventually to be followed by terrible retribution), "day-to-day dissidence" was by far the most common outlet for the slaves' insubordination. "There were . . . under my observation," Frederick Olmsted reported from Richard Arnold's Ogeechee River rice plantation in 1853,

> gates left open and bars left down, against standing orders; rails removed from fences by the negroes, as was conjectured, to kindle their fires with; mules lamed and implements broken, by careless usage; a flatboat, carelessly secured, going adrift on the river; men ordered to cart rails for a new fence, depositing them so that a double expense of labor would be required to lay them . . . ; men, ordered to fill up holes made by alligators or craw-fish in an important embankment, discovered to have merely patched over the outside, having taken pains only to make it *appear* that they had executed their task— not having been overlooked while doing it, by a driver . . . ;—all going to show habitual carelessness, indolence, and mere eye-service.[7]

To shirk one's work in every way one successfully could, to lie and deceive the master, to steal from him—these were the accustomed and well-filled sluices which regularly helped drain the slaves' overflowing rivers of resentment and hostility.

Circumstances change morality; and no white person can conscientiously condemn a slave for stealing back, from the masters, portions of what the masters stole every day from the slaves. Yet condemn the slaves for lying, stealing, and shirking work was exactly what cooper London, and some other religious leaders of their people, did; for they apprehended the damage which this servile conduct could do to a slave's self-respect. That the morale of many of Pierce Butler's slaves had been battered stands forth from every page of Kemble's *Journal*: "Missis, what for me learn to read?" Israel had asked his mistress. "Me have no prospect!"[8] And well into the twentieth century—

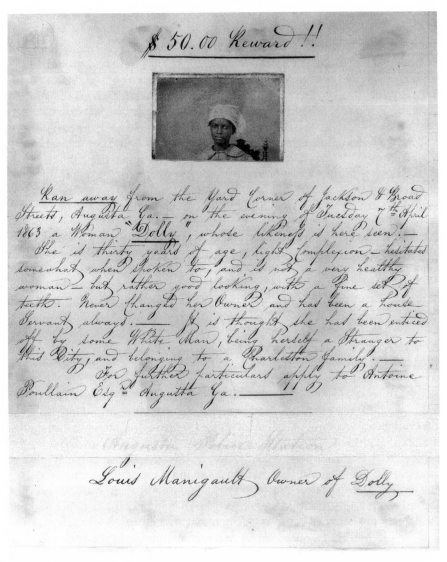

Fugitive slave "Dolly"

according to the credible testimony of the Alabama sharecropper Nate Shaw—the "back yonder 'ism' " bred by slavery into Nate's father, Hayes Shaw, impelled Hayes to an improvidence disastrous to his own advancement.[9] While the character of many courageous slaves was ennobled by their response to adversity—Stephen Gallant springs quickly to mind—slavery also sapped the morale of many other bondsmen and women. One would do no service to the African-Americans of the mid-nineteenth-century low country if one supposed they could all withstand slavery's relentless assault upon their self-regard.

Modern studies of African-Americans' cultural defenses against slavery—
for rice plantations one thinks of Charles Joyner's *Down by the Riverside,* and,
for the nearby sea-island cotton plantations, of Margaret Creel's book *"A
Peculiar People"*—need therefore to be set against the dark background of the
circumstances of the slaves' lives.[10] The masters were profit-seeking agricultural capitalists, not paternalists; and callousness toward their slaves marked
their rule. The regime, almost incredibly harsh in some ways, was nevertheless lax in others; and masters seldom gave a thought to the possibility of
insurrection. A complex system of general and special privilege was an essential element in the governance of slaves. Few bondsmen and women, however, felt they had any substantial "prospect," and constant lying, thievery,
and shirking were the most important outlets for the slaves' chronic discontent. At every turn the system was designed to undermine the slaves' morale.
Against the regime's assault upon their dignity, the slaves' defense—in building families, religious institutions, and their own folk culture—was formida-
ble. Yet despite this vigorous cultural dissent, morale may nevertheless have
been undermined depressingly often.

If individual slaves are to be cited for their gallantry in combating the
harsh effects of their condition, perhaps not all the awards should go to the
cultural separatists, or to those persistently unaccommodating, like carpenter
Jack Savage and Louis Manigault's house servant "Sister Jane." Those
African-American workingmen and women may also deserve honor whose
"bourgeois" sobriety helped them to maintain self-esteem when every circumstance impelled them in a different direction. Headman Frank and his wife,
Betty, built a strong family, despite Roswell King Jr.'s early rape of Betty; and
in Frank and Betty's tidy house were raised children who carried into the next
generation an artisanal tradition of skilled carpentry. Cooper London, the
discreet religious leader and educator of his people (with his requests for
Bibles from Philadelphia); Mary Grice, a housekeeper apparently always
"faithful" to the Allstons, yet whose brother and three of whose children, with
mysterious and disconcerting regularity, made good their wartime escapes
from slavery; Dolly, Louis Manigault's favored laundress (prior to her flight in
1863)—no doubt all of these bondsmen and women deceived their masters
deeply, and more than once; yet all had accommodated to the system during
most of their lives. And each one of them cherished—against all odds—that
self-respect which the system, too often successfully, was designed to destroy.

Appendix A

Gowrie's Profits, 1833–60

N.B.: Abbreviations are listed and explained at head of notes section.

This appendix explains tables 1–3 (see chapter 1), where Gowrie's profits, capital account, and cash balance are estimated for each year for the period 1833–60. Much approximation is contained within the figures presented with seeming confidence in those tables. The following comments refer to the named column in each table.

Under the *"Year of crop"* designation (tables 1–3), revenue from a year's crop is included, even when the crop was sold—as was usually the case—in the next calendar year. Only those recurrent expenses properly attributable to the current year's crop are included for that year. But from 1848 the "year" includes capital expenses incurred between April of one year and April of the following year, because at that time the Manigaults' annual slave lists (from which additions and losses of slave "capital" are computed) were nearly always compiled in April.

Table 1

Column a: Risk capital. Manigault's initial risk capital was $32,000 ($20,000 cash, plus the $12,000 imputed value of the twenty-two Silk Hope slaves he deported to Gowrie). The additional $20,000 which he borrowed, in order to complete his payment for Gowrie and its slaves, was not risk capital: it was a liability upon which he paid a fixed rate of interest. Each installment subsequently paid by him—to reduce that liability—increased the amount of his own money at stake as risk capital. These installments, and other cash capital payments (principally to buy new slaves) are listed in table 2, column b. Other capital additions and deductions during the year are listed in columns c, d, and e. The total amount of Manigault's risk capital at the end of each year is shown in column f; this number is then entered into the *next* year's column a, both in table 2 and in table 1.

Column b: Gross revenues. A starting point is LM's "Statement of Sales," 1855–60, IV (SHC), which carefully itemizes gross revenues, recurrent expenses, and net revenues for those six years. Gross revenues for the crops of 1833–34, 1837, 1839–41, 1844–46, 1848, and 1851 are stated in the yearly accounts of Manigault's Savannah factor, Robert Habersham (SCHS). For 1838 I have reduced Manigault's figure (Clifton, p. 3), because he estimated rice's average price a little too high, and he included small rice and peas not actually sold. For the other years I have estimated gross revenues according to the following formula: Gross Revenues = Barrels produced × 600 × 85% × Price per pound. This formula fits reasonably well all known years before 1854. (After the 1854 crop the Manigaults sent their "rough rice" to be milled in Charleston; and their gross revenues were therefore smaller during those years than the formula would suggest, because milling charges had to be deducted.)

"Barrels produced" is listed each year in Manigault MS, II (inside cover), (SHC). This list contains the figures for 1845 (644 bbl) and 1846 (573 bbl), in addition to those printed in Clifton, p. 1. The figures for 1833–38 include the toll charged by Manigault for milling some of his neighbors' rice.

"Price per pound" is derived from figures in Arthur Cole, *Wholesale Commodity Prices in the United States, 1700–1861* (Cambridge, Mass., 1938), 1:154. I employ a formula that the price the Manigaults received in Year A = 1/4 Cole's average price for year A + 3/4 Cole's average price for year (A + 1). The reason for devising this formula is that most of year A's crop was sold between November of Year A and April of year (A + 1): and perhaps 3/4 of it was sold in the year following the harvest.

"Eighty-five percent" is inserted into the formula above, because evidently the Manigaults received—on average—only about 85 percent of the "price per pound" as calculated from Cole's figures. One cause was that factor's charges, drayage, and so forth, had to be deducted. A second reason was that a proportion of the Manigaults' rice—like that of any other planter—was below the prime quality to which Cole's figures refer. A third cause was that sometimes the Manigaults—like other planters— got their rice to market at a time when prices were lower than average for the year.

Column c: Recurrent Expenses. From LM's "Statement of Sales," 1855–60 (SHC) one can calculate that expenses averaged $3,600 during those six years. This average does not include the unusual purchase of seed rice in the crisis year of 1857 (which boosted that year's recurrent expenses); nor does it include money spent on buying new slaves—which is separately listed in my accounts (table 2, column b2)—nor money spent on capital improvements to the thresher and in the purchase of a pineland camp (I include these also in table 2, column b2). As LM included some of his personal expenses under "plantation expenses" (and these increased after he married in 1857), but as the average number of slaves in 1855–60 was 18 percent less than during the preceding six years, it is reasonable to estimate that average annual recurrent plantation expenses in 1849–50 and 1852–54 were $3,500 or $3,600; and that before 1849 (when the plantation was only about half as big) they averaged perhaps $1,800 (plus interest on the original debt). This last figure can be regarded as consonant with CM's rough rule in 1838 (Clifton, p. 1) that his recurrent expenses had been about $2,000 per year. For I presume that Manigault had in mind (and meant to include in his figure), some of the interest he had had to pay during the early years, but that—in his characteristically sanguine way— he underestimated the sums required for interest payments. For the years 1834–48, therefore, I have estimated annual recurrent expenses at $1,800, plus interest at 7 percent on the amount of the original $20,000 debt which was still outstanding in any given year. The actual expenses for 1833, and LM's calculations of the actual expenses in 1851, are in the Habersham accounts for those years (SCHS).

Column d: Undistributed capital gains. I estimate that the average value of the Gowrie slaves on Nov. 30, 1848, was $450 per slave, taking infants and the superannu- ated along with "prime hands." But slave prices rose so much during the 1850s that I conservatively estimate the value of the 94 slaves at the end of 1860 at $700 per slave. This inflation of slave prices produced an increase in their capital value of $23,000, which I have spread over the twelve years from 1849, in rough proportion to the increasing slave prices indicated in Ulrich Phillips's *Life and Labor in the Old South* (Boston, 1929), p. 177.

I have *not* tried to adjust for the changing values of slaves before 1849, because higher prices late in the 1830s were canceled by falling prices in the early 1840s.

Seventy-eight acres of land were cleared and ditched in 1839–41, increasing the value of the land by about $3,000: a capital gain which I have distributed equally over the three years.

Column e: Capital loss of slaves. This is my estimate of the capital loss Manigault experienced during those years when more slaves died than were born. The annual figures for deaths and births appear in table 6 (chapter 3). I have not listed here every instance of an excess of deaths over births, but only those years where the figure was large enough to affect profits substantially.

Table 2

Column a: Risk capital. See the explanation above in this appendix, under table 1, column a.

Column b1: Repayment of debt. Presumably Manigault paid off the $20,000 debt he had incurred in 1833 as soon as he had the cash to do so. The amount of cash available for this purpose, after each year's crop was sold, is taken from table 3 ("Cash Balance"), column e.

Column b2: Other cash invested during year. In the 1848 fiscal year Manigault spent $28,000 to buy the East Hermitage tract, including its steam thresher (LM, "Negroes Purchased 1849" [DU]). (That the purchase price was $28,000—not $25,000 as stated in Clifton, p. xx—is confirmed in the Habersham accounts for 1851 [SCHS]). I estimate that the cost of Manigault's buying the 148-acre Legaré tract in 1853 was $11,100 (at $75 per acre).

Almost all of his other cash investments were for buying new slaves. The Manigault records give the exact prices for his purchases in 1837 (3 slaves), 1839 (16 slaves), 1848 (52 slaves), 1853 (19 slaves), and 1856 (21 slaves). The figures for four years are my estimates of the slaves' prices (based on the ages and skills of each slave): 1842 (8 slaves), 1852 (19 slaves), 1859 (1 slave), 1860, (1 slave, more than offset by the sale of two slaves, leading to a negative investment of $500 that year).

In addition, Manigault spent about $1000 to build a house for himself in 1833. Included also in this column are $1,000 spent on thresher improvements in 1851, $700 on thresher improvements in 1855, and $2,300 for buying a 750-acre pineland camp in 1856. Otherwise I have *not* included small capital expenses, assuming that they (e.g., the building of some new houses for the slaves—in 1853 and 1860—and the improvements to LM's house and grounds) were approximately offset by the depreciation of the pounding mill.

Column c: Value of Silk Hope slaves deported to Gowrie. I have estimated these values according to the number of slaves and their ages. The ages are nearly always specified in the annual list which records their arrival at Gowrie. In addition to the 22 slaves deported from Silk Hope in 1833 (whose estimated value of $12,000, is included in Manigault's 1833 total initial investment of $32,000 [column a]), the net number of Silk Hope slaves deported, between 1837 and 1858, was 38. (Six were sent to stock East Hermitage in 1849; 40 were deported to Gowrie in other years; while 8 [not including the man who was returned to Gowrie in 1849] were exported from Gowrie to Manigault's Carolina properties. (See table 8 and accompanying notes in chapter 3.)

Column d: Undistributed capital gains. See notes in this appendix under table 1, column d.

Column e: Capital loss. See notes in this appendix under table 1, column e.

Table 3

Column a: Debt at beginning of year. Manigault started with a cash balance of −$20,000. This was the sum he borrowed in order to buy Gowrie and its slaves. He borrowed $10,000 of this total at 7 percent interest, with the slaves (and probably the signatures of a couple of financial backers) as collateral. He borrowed the other $10,000 with the land as collateral, presumably also at 7 percent.

I assume that Manigault at first plowed back all of his profits into Gowrie, paying off his original debt and making new capital investments there (mainly to buy new slaves in 1837 and 1839). Once he had built up a positive cash balance (at the end of 1839), this balance was always large enough to cover his later capital investments—especially his purchase of East Hermitage in the 1848 fiscal year, the Legaré tract in 1853, and new slaves in 1842, 1848, 1852, 1853, 1856, 1859, and 1860. There was enough cash left over for him to use it for outside investments. These are discussed in paragraph h below.

The debt at the beginning of a year = the previous year's column a plus its column e.

Column b: Interest on debt. 7% × column a. This interest payment is always counted as part of the same year's "Recurrent Expenses," in table 1, column c. The figure is always placed within parentheses, to remind one that (since it is included in "Recurrent Expenses") it has already been taken into account when table 3's column c ("Cash Return") has been calculated (see next paragraph).

Column c: Cash return. Table 1, column b minus table 1, column c. "Cash return" is *not* the same as "profit." To calculate a year's "profit," one must add to "cash return" any "undistributed capital gains," and subtract any "capital loss of slaves." This is done in table 1, where the year's "profit" is stated in column f.

Column d: Cash earmarked for immediate reinvestment. Table 2, column b2.

The cash to be reinvested in one year is always earmarked for this purpose, in table 3, column d, at the end of the *previous* year (except, of course, in 1833).

Column e: Repayment of debt. I assume that, until Manigault's original $20,000 debt was completely paid off, he used all of his cash profit for this purpose, except for the sums he earmarked for immediate reinvestment. Therefore, until the original debt was discharged, column e = column c − column d.

Column f: Annual cash balance. Column c − column d − column e.

Column g: Accumulated cash balance. Until the original debt was repaid, g = a + e + f.

Thereafter, a year's g = the sum of the items in column f (up to and including that year's f), plus that year's h.

Column h: Earnings on previous year's accumulated cash balance. When Manigault invested his accumulated cash balance elsewhere—e.g., in the stock of Charleston banks and insurance companies—his average rate of return (taking account of losses arising from risky investments) may have been about 3 percent. (The size of this rate of return is discussed on pages 17–20 and their notes 35 and 38.) I have used this figure of 3 percent to estimate these earnings in column h. Were a higher rate of return assumed, Manigault's total profit would, of course, be even higher than I have calculated.

Appendix B

Gowrie's Slave Population, 1833–61

This appendix explains the population estimates in table 6 (see chapter 3).

Table 6

Column b: "Births (estimated)". Although no complete register of births is extant, the annual lists of slaves living at Gowrie permit reasonably accurate estimates. Those lists specify 89 babies born at Gowrie, 1833 to Apr. 1861, who survived long enough to be recorded when the subsequent list was compiled. I estimate that another 59 babies were born at Gowrie during this period but died before the subsequent list was compiled (bringing the total number of births to 148).

The estimate of 59 unrecorded births comprises four classes of babies.

1. *2 infants* born between Jan. 1835 and Apr. 1837. (Manigault was in Europe most of this time, and there is a twenty-seven-month gap in the records.) I estimate that, if annual lists had been kept during this period, an average of 2.2 births would have been listed each year (2.2 was the average rate of births listed from each year from 1837 to 1842, by those women who were alive on Jan. 1, 1835). This rate would have produced 5 listed births from Jan. 1835 to April 1837. Only 3 of these were actually listed, and I therefore estimate that 2 more would have been listed if annual lists had been kept.

2. *7 infants* born between Dec. 1845 and Apr. 1849. (Manigault was in Europe most of this time, and there is a 40-month gap in the records.) I conservatively estimate that, if annual records had been kept during this period, an average of 3.3 births would have been listed each year (3.3 was the average rate of births listed from 1840 to 1845 inclusive, when there were slightly fewer women of childbearing age than by Dec. 1845). This rate would have produced 11 listed births from Dec. 1845 to April 1849. Only 4 of these were actually listed, and I therefore estimate that 7 more would have been listed if annual lists had been kept.

3. *46 other infants* born between 1833 and 1861 (excluding 1834 and 1854, which are discussed separately in paragraph 4 below), who died before the subsequent annual list was compiled. This estimate is derived from my inference, based on the Pierce Butler birth and death records, 1819–34 (see next paragraph), that some 32.6 percent of Gowrie's babies died during the first six months after their births, and did not therefore live long enough to be recorded in the annual lists of living slaves. Excluding 1834 and 1854, 87 births were recorded in the annual lists (and about 2 more would

have been recorded in 1835–37, and about 7 more in 1845–49, if Manigault had not been in Europe during those periods). About 46 unrecorded births must therefore have taken place during these years (because 46 unrecorded births + the 96 births previously mentioned [87 listed + the 9 births when Manigault was in Europe] = 142, minus 32.6 percent death rate in first six months = the 96 births listed or which occurred when Manigault was in Europe). I have distributed these 46 unrecorded births over the periods 1833–41, 1842–54, and 1855–61 in proportion to the number of listed births in those periods, and randomly within each of these periods. These figures are shown, each year, in appendix table 1 (column d).

My inference that 32.6 percent of Gowrie's babies died during their first six months depends on an assumption that infant mortality at Gowrie (to age six months) was identical to that at Butler Island—Pierce Butler's Georgia rice plantation. This is a conservative assumption, for at every other age child mortality was even worse at Gowrie than at Butler Island; but I have nevertheless assumed that it was identical during the first six months, because I do not wish to exaggerate Gowrie's child mortality rate. At Butler Island exact birth and death dates were recorded from 1819 through 1834. Of 331 live births there (1819–June 30, 1834), 108 infants—i.e., 32.6 percent of them—died during their first six months. See appendix table 4 in appendix D.

4. *4 infants* born during the cholera years of 1834 and 1854. As can be seen from appendix table 1 (column c), 1834 is the only year when no births were listed; and the number listed in 1854 is unnaturally low, considering that the number of women of childbearing age was then virtually at its peak. I guess that in 1834 two children, and in 1854 two more children, died before the annual list was compiled, in consequence of the serious illness or death of mothers afflicted by cholera. This procedure still leaves my estimate of the total number of births in each of these two years as low as, or lower than, during every nearby year.

The 89 recorded births, and the estimated 59 unrecorded ones, are listed by year in appendix table 1 (columns c and d). The total for each year (appendix table 1, column e) is reproduced on p. 52 in table 6, column b.

Column c: "Deaths (estimated)". Although no complete register of deaths is extant, the annual lists of slaves living at Gowrie permit reasonably accurate estimates. Those lists specify 254 slaves, who lived at Gowrie, whose names are omitted from subsequent lists (usually scratched out). Of these about 10 were sold (before April 1861), and 9 others were exported from Gowrie to CM's South Carolina properties. [See the section on "Exports" (column e), which discusses these figures.] The other 235 died. In addition, I estimate (as explained in the preceding paragraphs) that 59 infants born at Gowrie died before their names were recorded in the annual lists.

The 235 deaths of named slaves, and the 59 unrecorded ones, are listed each year in appendix table 1 (columns f and g). The total for each year (appendix table 1, column h) is reproduced on p. 52 in table 6, column c.

Column d: "Imports". Manigault stocked Gowrie with 72 slaves in 1833 and 58 more in 1848–49. In addition to this total stock of 130 bondsmen and women (which included 28 taken away from Silk Hope), he imported another 129 slaves between 1836 and 1860 (88 bought at auctions and 41 more moved from Silk Hope: see table 8, chapter 3). The names of all the imported slaves appear in the annual lists; no estimates are involved.

Column e: "Exports". The nineteen slaves exported from Gowrie include ten whom Manigault sold, 1833–60, for insubordination: Friday (1833); Minda (1834);

APPENDIX TABLE 1.   Slave Population at Gowrie, 1833–61 (with details of estimates)

Year*	(a) No. of slaves at start of year	(b) Imports	Births (c) Listed	Births (d) Not listed (est.)	Births (e) Total (est.)	Deaths (f) Listed	Deaths (g) Not listed (est.)	Deaths (h) Total (est.)	(j) Exports
1833	72	0	3	2	5	7	2	9	1
1834	67	0	0	2	2	25	2	27	1
1835–36	41	8	3	2	5	3	2	5	1
1837	48	10	1	1	2	2	1	3	0
1838	57	0	7	2	9	7	2	9	0
1839	57	17	1	2	3	6	2	8	0
1840	69	0	4	2	6	6	2	8	0
1841	67	1	2	2	4	5	2	7	0
1842	65	9	3	1	4	5	1	6	0
1843	72	0	2	2	4	1	2	3	0
1844	73	5	4	2	6	7	2	9	1
1845	74	5	5	2	7	2	2	4	0
1846–48	82	0	4	7	11	24	7	31	1
1849	119**	1	5	3	8	7	3	10	0
1850	118	4	4	3	7	18	3	21	2
1851	106	7	4	3	7	8	3	11	2
1852	107	19	6	3	9	18	3	21	0
1853	114	19	3	3	6	16	3	19	4
1854	116	0	2	2	4	29	2	31	1
1855	88	0	2	2	4	10	2	12	3
1856	77	21	7	2	9	8	2	10	0
1857	97	0	5	2	7	4	2	6	0
1858	98	1	4	3	7	7	3	10	0
1859	96	1	4	2	6	3	2	5	0
1860	98	1	4	2	6	7	2	9	2
April 1861	94								
TOTAL 1833–61		129	89	59	148	235	59	294	19

*Beginning in 1849, the "Year" normally begins in April and ends in April of the next calendar year. Before 1849 the "Year" normally runs from December to December (Thus "1841" = Dec. 1840 to Dec. 1841.) (There are some exceptions to these rules: thus "1833" = Jan.–Nov. 1833; "1834" = Nov. 1833–Jan. 1835, etc.)

**Includes 61 still alive at end of 1848, plus 58 slaves brought in to stock the new East Hermitage section of the plantation.

Charlotte (1837); probably Quash (1844); Posh (1851–52); Prince, William, Frederick, and Jane (1853–54); and Fortune (1860). The other nine exported were John Izard (1846–48: imported again in 1849); Jacob (1850); Tom (1850); Willy (1851); Adam Hunt (1854); Little Betsey (1855); King (1855); Fanny (1855); and Martha (1860).

The number of slaves exported from Gowrie is not absolutely certain: (1) In addition to the ten slaves listed, Manigault may have sold one or two others between 1837 and 1844; and (2) he may also have sent a handful of slaves to his South Carolina properties besides the nine named here. If either happened, I have slightly exaggerated the number of deaths at Gowrie. But any such exaggeration is likely to be insignificant for the following reasons:

1. The "several" (Manigault's word) slaves he sold between 1833 and 1845 can scarcely have included more than one or two others in addition to the four I have specified during that period.

2. Manigault is unlikely to have sent other slaves to South Carolina in addition to the nine specified above, because Gowrie suffered from a perpetual labor shortage. He was constantly sending slaves from Silk Hope to Gowrie, and would not have wished to counteract this flow by sending slaves in the wrong direction.

3. Any possible exaggeration of Gowrie's death rate, arising from either the first or second points, is probably more than offset by my underestimating the rate at which infants died during the first six months after birth. I have assumed that they died at the same rate as on Butler Island; but as—at all other ages—Gowrie's slaves died even faster than Butler Island's, they probably did so, too, during their first six months.

Appendix C

Child Mortality at Gowrie

This appendix explains the estimates of child mortality (to age sixteen) of children born before April 1855. (These estimates appear in table 7 [chapter 3]).

Table 7 shows that an estimated 128 infants (under three years old) lived at Gowrie between 1833 and 1855. Of these, 6 were already there when Manigault bought Gowrie in January 1833; 13 more were imported by April 1855; and an estimated 109 others were born at Gowrie from 1833 to April 1855. As may be calculated from appendix table 1 (columns c and d) in appendix B, these 109 included 63 recorded in the annual lists, and an estimated 46 babies unrecorded because they died before the subsequent list was compiled. The estimating methods are explained in appendix B (Column b, paragraphs 1–4).

Of the estimated total of 128 infants, the annual lists show that no more than 13 reached their sixteenth birthday: a child mortality rate of 90 percent. The 115 children who died are listed below in appendix table 2.

APPENDIX TABLE 2. Child Mortality (individual children) at Gowrie

	Infants at Gowrie (born before April 1855)	
	Died before age 16	Still alive at age 16
Infants (under 3 years old) at Gowrie, Jan., 1833. *Total: 6*	Jane (1830–33) John (ca. 1832–33) Louisa (1830–34) Maria (Juna's), (ca. 1832–33) Molly (1831–34) Sandy (1830–33)	None
Infants (under 3 years old) imported into Gowrie, 1833 through Apr. 1855. *Total: 13*:	of whom 12 died: Patty (1836–38) Chloe (ca. 1838–39)	and of whom one lived to age 16: Ben (1836–58)

APPENDIX TABLE 2. *(continued)*

	Infants at Gowrie (born before April 1855)	
	Died before age 16	*Still alive at age 16*
	Nelly (Hester's) (ca. 1844–45)	
	Charles (ca. 1852–54)	
	Daniel (ca. 1852–53)	
	Dolly (1849–52)	
	Elsey 1853–55)	
	Jane (1852–54)	
	Joe (ca. 1852–53)	
	Lizzie (ca. 1851–53)	
	Moses (1849–50)	
	Sue (1851–53)	
Infants born at Gowrie, 1833 through Apr. 1855 *Total: 109:*	of whom 97 died:	and of whom 12 lived to age 16 (or until record ceases in 1864):
	Jane (Binah Currie's), (1833–38)	Nat (1836–62)
	Lena (1833–37)	London (1838–60)
	Robert (1833–37)	Scotland (1838–
	Jack (1835–38)	Polly (1838–
	Matilda (1836–37)	Fortune (1840– sold 1860)
	Jenny (1837–49)	Tirah (1842–
	Nat (Elsey's), (1838–39)	Captain (1844–
	Ned (1837–40)	King (1848–
	Nelly (1838–39)	Betsey (1851–
	Anonymous (Charlotte's) (1838–38)	Martha (1852–
	Paul (1839–39)	Cato (1853–
	March (1840–42)	Mendoza (1853–
	Maria (1840–44)	
	Anonymous (Phillis's), (1840–40)	
	Chattum (1841–41)	
	Charles (1841–44)	
	Maleciah (1842–42)	
	Job (1842–44)	
	Peter (1843–ca. 1847)	
	Isaac (1843–ca. 1847)	
	Mary (1844–56)	
	Patty (1844–44)	
	Tecumsee (1844–ca. 1847)	
	Amos (1845–ca. 1847)	
	Bella (1845–54)	
	Harry (Amey's)(1845–58)	
	Harry (Juna's) (1845–ca. 1847)	
	Solomon (1845–52)	
	Cosum (1848–52)	
	Nelly (ca.1847–49)	
	Will (ca.1847–50)	
	Chloe (1849–50)	
	Elizabeth (1849–52)	

Infants at Gowrie (born before April 1855)	
Died before age 16	*Still alive at age 16*
Minda (1849–ca.1863)	
Sawny (1849–50)	
Tommy (1849–50)	
Affy (1850–51)	
Anonymous (Phillis's) (1850–50)	
Lazarus (1850–55)	
Sary (1850–50)	
Matty (1851–52)	
Minna (1851–53)	
Sarey (1851–53)	
Edward (1852–56)	
Frances (1852–54)	
Isaac (1852–55)	
Liza (1852–53)	
Mary (1852–55)	
Anonymous (Die's) (1853–53)	
Brister (1854–54)	
Lucy (1854–55)	
AND an estimated 46 others who died before the subsequent list was compiled	

Appendix D

Child Mortality, Butler Estate

This appendix presents the figures from which the mortality rates in tables 17 and 18 (chapter 8) are calculated. Of 331 babies born on the Butler Island rice plantation (from 1819 to 1834), fifty-four died in their first fortnight and another fifty-four during the remainder of their first six months. From figures like these one can compute (see appendix table 3) "age-specific" mortality rates to age 6. These can then be contrasted, in the same table, with the rates at the Butlers' sea-island cotton plantation on St. Simons Island.

These data indicate that 38 percent of the Butler Island infants died during their first year, and just over 50 percent by age 6. The calculations leading to these results are set out in appendix table 4. This table also contains, for comparison, the figures for the Butlers' sea-island cotton plantation.

The child mortality rates, to ages 16 and 21, printed on the last two lines of appendix table 4 are estimates based on the 105 children born to a sample of twenty-four Butler Island mothers. These children's experiences are detailed in appendix table 5.

APPENDIX TABLE 3. Child Mortality Rates (to age 6), 1819–34 (Butler Estate)

The underlined percentages are those which appear (rounded off) in table 17 (chapter 8).

	Sea-island Cotton (St. Simons Island) (%)			Rice (Butler Island) (%)		
CHILDREN BORN ALIVE, 1819– JUNE 30, 1834						
Total number:	158			331		
Of whom, died in weeks 1–2	18	(<u>11.39</u>)		54	(<u>16.31</u>)	
" " died in remainder of first month	3	(1.90)	(<u>6.33</u>)	9	(2.72)	(<u>16.32</u>)
" " died in months 2–6	7	(4.43)		45	(13.60)	
CHILDREN BORN, 1819–33, AND STILL ALIVE AT THE END OF 6 MONTHS						
Number:	128			210		
Of whom, died in months 7–12	6	(<u>4.69</u>)		17	(<u>8.10</u>)	
CHILDREN BORN, 1819–31, AND STILL ALIVE ON FIRST BIRTH-DAY						
Number:	106			166		
Of whom, died in years 2–3	11	(<u>10.38</u>)		21	(<u>12.65</u>)	
CHILDREN BORN, 1819–28, AND STILL ALIVE ON THIRD BIRTH-DAY						
Number:	68			100		
Of whom, died in years 4–6	4	(<u>5.88</u>)		8	(<u>8.00</u>)	

Source: Birth and Death Lists, 1819–34, Butler Papers (HSP).

APPENDIX TABLE 4. Cumulative Child Mortality Rates (to age 21) (of children born 1819–34, Butler Estate)

The underlined percentages are those which appear (rounded off) in table 18 (chapter 8).

	Sea-island Cotton (St. Simons Island) (%) (%)		Rice (Butler Island) (%) (%)	
(a) Children born alive, 1819–June 30, 1834	(158)		(331)	
(b) Number who died in first 6 months	(28)		(108)	
(c) *Proportion of original group who died in first six months* (b/a)		<u>17.72</u>		<u>32.63</u>

APPENDIX TABLE 4.   (*continued*)

	Sea-island Cotton (St. Simons Island) (%)	(%)	Rice (Butler Island) (%)	(%)
(d) Proportion of original group still alive at age 6 months (100% − c)	82.28		67.37	
(e) Mortality rate, months 7–12 (from appendix table 3)	4.69		8.10	
(f) Proportion of original group who died in months 7–12 (d × e)	3.86		5.46	
(g) *Proportion of original group who died before first birthday* (c + f)		21.58		38.09
(h) Proportion of original group still alive at first birthday (100% − g)	78.42		61.91	
(j) Mortality rate, years 2–3 (from appendix table 3)	10.38		12.65	
(k) Proportion of original group who died in years 2–3 (h × j)	8.14		7.83	
(l) *Proportion of original group who died before third birthday* (g + k)		29.72		45.92
(m) Proportion of original group still alive at third birthday (100% − l)	70.28		54.08	
(n) Mortality rate, years 4–6 (from appendix table 3)	5.88		8.00	
(p) Proportion of original group who died in years 4–6 (m × n)	4.13		4.33	
(q) *Proportion of original group who died* before sixth birthday (l + p)		33.85		50.25
(r) *Estimated proportion of original group who*: died before 16th birthday (See note below)		—		61.0
(s) died before 21st birthday (See note below)		—		63.8

Note: In appendix table 4 the estimates in Lines r and s that 61.0 percent of Butler Island slaves died before their sixteenth birthday, and 63.8 percent before their twenty-first birthday, are based upon the 105 children born alive (1819–34) to the 24 youngest Butler Island women named on the 1821 list of field hands. These 24 women should comprise a representative sample of Butler Island women, because they include every woman on that list between certain ages (14 to 21 inclusive). Of the 105 children whom these twenty-four women bore (1819–34), 66 had died by the time the 1849 slave list was compiled. I estimate that one more child died after 1849 but before reaching age 21 (from among the 39 children still alive in 1849), bringing the total number of deaths, before age 21, to 67.

The deaths of 47 of these 67 children are recorded as having occurred before their sixth birthday. Of the other 19 children who died before 1849 (and the one estimated as dying after 1849), I estimate their ages at death in columns b and c in appendix table 5.

My estimates in columns b and c of appendix table 5 are based on the ages (on Jan. 1, 1835) of the 19 children known to have died by 1849. (Eight of these children were in 1835 under 3 years old; five were aged 3 to 5; five were aged 6 to 10; and one was aged 11.) The proportions of children placed, according to my estimates, in the three age-groups between 6 and 20 are roughly consonant with Richard Steckel's findings about the proportion of all those American slaves dying between 6 and 20 who fell into each of the three 5-year age-groups.

My estimates for Butler Island in lines r and s of appendix table 4 are unlikely to be mistaken by more than about 1 percent, because the ages at death of 47 of the children are exactly known; and because it is also known that 66 children (of the original 105 live births) had died by 1849; and because the birth dates of all of these 105 live births are known.

APPENDIX TABLE 5. Estimated Mortality Rate of the 105 Children Born Alive, 1819–34 (to a sample of 24 mothers)

	(a) Died before 1835	(b) Died 1835–49*	(c) Died after 1849*	(d) Total deaths	(e) Mortality rate (% of live births)
Total deaths before age 21	47	19	1	67	63.8
Deaths before age 6	47	6	—	53	50.5
Deaths at ages 6–10	—	7	—	7	6.7
Deaths at ages 11–15	—	4	—	4	3.8
Deaths at ages 16–20	—	2	1	3	2.8

Sources: Birth and death lists, 1819–34; 1821 list of Butler Island workers, in RK Jr. to Major Pierce Butler, Feb. 18, 1821; 1849 list of all Butler Estate slaves, in "Inventory . . . of the estate of Capt. John Butler," Feb. 13, 1849, Butler MS (HSP). Richard Steckel, "A Dreadful Childhood: The Excess Mortality of American Slaves," *Social Science History* 10 (1986): 428.

Note: *Ages at death are estimated.

Appendix E

American Rice Production

This appendix explains the figures for American rice production in tables 22 and 23 (chapter 15).

My estimates of annual American production of "clean" rice, 1839–60, appear in appendix table 6. Those from 1839 through 1848 are identical to the ones printed in previous scholarly works, but all of those from 1849 through 1860 are different. In particular, those for 1849 and 1859 are very different from the ones printed in Lewis Gray's standard *History of Agriculture in the Southern United States to 1860* (Washington, D.C., 1933), p. 723:

APPENDIX TABLE 6.   American Rice Production, 1839–60 (est.)
(millions of pounds of "clean" rice)

1839	80.8
1840	84.3
1841	89.0
1842	94.0
1843	89.9
1844	111.8
1845	89.8
1846	97.7
1847	103.0
1848	119.2
1849	132.9
1850	107.8
1851	110.9
1852	107.5
1853	106.4
1854	74.4
1855	108.7
1856	104.5
1857	113.5
1858	122.0
1859	124.4
1860	106.6

Sources (for appendix table 6, and for tables 22 and 23 [chapter 15]): The basic source is George K. Holmes, *Rice Crop of the United States, 1712–1911* (U.S. Department of Agriculture, Bureau of Statistics, Circular 34 [Washington, D.C., 1912]); but I have substantially adjusted some of Holmes's figures (see below).

1767–73. Annual exports averaged 69.7 million pounds. I estimate domestic consumption at about 2.3 million pounds.
1790–95. Annual exports averaged 78.6 million pounds. I estimate domestic consumption at about 3.4 million pounds.
1820–38, 1840, and 1850–58. Holmes used estimates (of marketed production in the Carolinas and Georgia) made by Dan Talmage's Sons Co. I assume that nonmarketed production was negligible. Big planters sold virtually their whole output; and (as George Rogers's and Dale Swan's figures suggest) small rice farmers—those producing less than 100,000 pounds per year—accounted by the mid–nineteenth century for only 2 to 4 percent of the total low-country production (Rogers, *History of Georgetown County,* p. 253; Swan, "The Structure and Profitability of the Antebellum Rice Industry: 1859" [Ph.D. diss., University of North Carolina, 1972], p. 107).
For 1850–58 I have increased each of Talmage's figures by 4.9 percent, because the 1850 and 1860 censuses indicate that by this time Louisiana and other states were contributing this much to American rice production, in addition to the rice which Talmage attributed to the Carolinas and Georgia.
1839. Holmes took his figure from the 1840 census, and (unlike the 1850 and 1860 census figures) this one is consistent with Talmage's estimates, and with those for 1841–48.
1841–48. Holmes took his estimates of total U.S. rice production from the U.S. Commissioner of Patents, and I have reprinted his figures.
1849 and 1859. Holmes's figures for these two years must be discarded, for he incautiously took them from the censuses of 1850 and 1860, failing to observe that the census figures referred to (threshed, but not milled) "rough rice," not to (milled) "clean rice." These census figures for 1849 and 1859 are totally out of line with the commissioner of patents' figures for "clean" rice (1840–48), and the Talmage figures for "clean" rice (1850–58), until one converts the census figures for "rough" rice into "clean" rice (162 pounds of rough rice = 100 pounds of clean rice). Lewis Gray's figures for 1849 and 1859 are also mistaken, as Gray simply reprinted the census figures (Gray, *History of Agriculture,* p. 723). But the words of Superintendent of the Census J. D. B. DeBow make it certain that the 1850 census measured rough rice: "Rough rice is returned for 1850, and clean rice for 1840" (*Statistical View of the United States* [1854], p. 170. See also pp. 173 and 178 of the same work, on both of which pages DeBow refers to "rough rice"). Robert Gallman alerted Peter Coclanis to this feature of the 1850 census, and Coclanis correctly converted "rough rice" to "clean" rice for 1849 (Coclanis, *Shadow of a Dream,* pp. 117 n, 142).
The same procedure needs to be adopted for 1859. This inference is strongly supported by Louis Manigault's estimates of rice production for 1859 in Chatham and Bryan Counties, Georgia. Manigault was very well informed about rice production on the Savannah and Ogeechee Rivers, yet his estimates would have been wildly mistaken if the census figures referred to clean rice; but Manigault's estimates fell within 5 percent of the figures reported by the Census Office if one assumes that the census was reporting rough rice, as it had done in the 1850 census. (The census reported 27.5 million pounds of rice produced in those two counties; Manigault estimated 584,000 bushels which—at 45 pounds of rough rice per bushel—would total 26.3 million

pounds of *rough* rice.) James Clifton, a leading expert on the economics of rice plantations, is also aware that the census figures for 1859 refer to rough rice. (Clifton
converts bushels to pounds of [rough] rice at the ratio of 1:45. The ratio for conversion
to "clean" rice would have been about 1:27⅞: Clifton, "Golden Grains of White: Rice
Planting on the Lower Cape Fear," *North Carolina Historical Review* 50 [1973]: 381 n.)

(If further corroboration were required that the census figures for 1859 refer to
rough rice, it might be found in the figures for rice imports into the Northern United
States in 1861 and 1862, when the low-country supply had been cut off. Annual
imports during those two years were about 52 million pounds, a figure comparable to
America's domestic consumption in 1859 and 1860 if the census's 1859 figures refer to
rough rice—but highly deviant if the 1859 figure were presumed to measure clean
rice.)

Four further corrections must be made to production figures for 1859. These are
shown in the four notes to appendix table 7. Subsequent paragraphs explain those
adjustments.

James Clifton has proved that the census mistakenly omitted 2,176,000 pounds of
rough rice produced in New Hanover County, North Carolina. Even more important,
the Beaufort County (S.C.) manuscript census returns suggest that the printed census
mistakenly omitted some 12,100,000 pounds of rough rice produced in that county.
These two errors mean that the actual production of rice in the United States in 1859
was about 7.5 percent larger than reported in the official census (i.e., about 14,300,000
pounds of rough rice more than officially reported). In both cases the error arose
because census takers mistakenly recorded *bushels* of rice instead of *pounds,* and the
census officials failed to convert bushels to pounds (1 bushel = 45 pounds of rough
rice) before doing their sums.

The situation in St. Peter's Parish (in Beaufort County) is complicated by the further
fact that one (or more?) plantations reported *pounds* of rice, while all the rest reported
bushels; but the census taker did not indicate which was which. The overseer G. W.
Brunson's report of "560,000" is surely pounds, for no American rice plantation produced anything remotely as large as 560,000 bushels. It is equally certain that most of the
other figues for this parish are in bushels—e.g. Langdon Cheves's "56,000" and Walter
Blake's "20,000." But as a handful of other informants besides Brunson appear to have
reported pounds rather than bushels, I have sought to avoid this kind of ambiguity
(which led Dale Swan to discard all of the Beaufort County manuscript figures) by
accepting the estimates of St. Peter's Parish production prepared by Lawrence Rowland
(Rowland, "Alone on the River: The Rise and Fall of the Savannah River Rice Plantations of St. Peter's Parish, South Carolina," *South Carolina Historical Magazine*
88(1987):148). These depend, in turn, upon estimates made by Louis Manigault in 1860.
Manigault's estimates for Chatham and Bryan Counties (Ga.) are very near the official
census figures, and it is therefore reasonable to presume that Manigault's estimates for
St. Peter's Parish are equally reliable. Confidence in his estimates grows when one
observes that his estimate of the total rice acreage in St. Peter's Parish (11,800 acres) is
virtually identical to that indicated in the manuscript census returns (11,887 acres).

Accepting Rowland's basic methodology, I estimate that 13.1 million pounds of
clean rice were grown in St. Peter's Parish in 1859. This figure differs from Rowland's
in only one respect: I assume (as Holmes did) that 162 pounds of rough rice = 100
pounds of clean rice; therefore (at 1 bushel = 45 pounds of rough rice) I calculate that
1 bushel = 27⅞ pounds of clean rice. (Louis Manigault in 1860 used a slightly higher
ratio: 1 bushel = 28.57 pounds of clean rice [i.e., 21 bushels = a 600-pound barrel].)
The actual turnout at Weehaw plantation, 1856–59, was 1 bushel = 26.6 pounds

APPENDIX TABLE 7. American Rice Production, 1859 (corrected)
(millions of pounds)

	"Rough" rice		"Clean" rice
	1860 census figures (mistaken)	Corrected figures (see notes below)	Corrected figures (162 rough = 100 clean)
Low country (12 counties, arranged north to south):			
N.C. (New Hanover & Brunswick Counties)	6.8	9.0*	5.6
S.C.			
Georgetown	55.8	55.8	34.4
Charleston	18.9	20.4**	12.6
Colleton	22.8	21.3***	13.1
Beaufort	18.8	30.9****	19.1
Ga.			
Chatham	25.9	25.9	16.0
Bryan	1.6	1.6	1.0
Liberty	2.5	2.5	1.5
McIntosh	6.4	6.4	4.0
Glynn	4.8	4.8	3.0
Camden	10.3	10.3	6.4
Total low country	174.8	189.1	116.7
Up-country S.C.	2.8	2.8	1.7
Louisiana	6.3	6.3	3.9
Rest of U.S.	3.3	3.3	2.0
TOTAL U.S.	187.2	201.5	124.4

Note: Totals are not always exactly the sum of individual counties, because of rounding errors.

*Includes 2.2 million pounds omitted by the census in New Hanover County: James Clifton, "Golden Grains of White: Rice Planting on the Lower Cape Fear," *N. C. Hist. Review* 50 (1973): 381 n.

**Includes 1.5 million pounds omitted by census when it mistakenly omitted St. Johns Colleton Parish from Charleston County.

***Omits 1.5 million pounds included by census when it mistakenly included St. Johns Colleton Parish in Colleton County.

****Includes 12.1 million pounds omitted by census (through confusion of bushels with pounds on most St. Peter's Parish plantations).

(H. A. Middleton Jr., plantation journal, pp. 78–79, Middleton MS, [SCHS]). Rowland prefers a more cautious and lower ratio: viz., 1 bushel = 24 pounds of clean rice.

And Rowland, while accepting Louis Manigault's estimate of 40 bushels of rice per acre, feels anxious that Manigault's figure may be too high. I feel confident, however, that Manigault's estimate was accurate, because when Manigault assumed 40 bushels per acre for Chatham County's Savannah River estates, and 50 bushels per acre for Ogeechee River plantations, those figures proved correct there (i.e., consonant with the census returns for Chatham and Bryan Counties). Yields of over 50 bushels per acre were sometimes reported on fertile land in Georgia. Productivity on the Savannah and

Ogeechee Rivers was higher per acre than on older South Carolina rice lands, and the St. Peter's plantations were all on the Savannah River (Julia Smith, *Slavery and Rice Culture,* p. 9; Gray, *History of Agriculture,* pp. 730–31). And Manigault's estimates are consonant with the manuscript census returns for St. Peter's Parish, insofar as the ambiguities of those returns can be deciphered (Louis Manigault, "Rice Lands Planted on the Savannah & Ogeechee Rivers, [June](1860)," Manigault MS, IV [SHC]).

These estimates indicate that nearly 4,700 pounds of clean rice were being raised per slave in St. Peter's Parish—considerably more than in most parts of the low country. The figure is not, however, unbelievable: for the slaves at Gowrie raised 4,700 to 4,800 pounds of clean rice per slave regularly during the 1850s, and the Manigaults (attributing their bad luck to incompetent overseers) frequently complained that even this was not as much as they expected. Gowrie—like the St. Peter's Parish plantations—was on fertile Savannah River rice land. And at Gowrie the proportion of workers to the total slave population was high, because so many children died. If this was also true on the St. Peter's plantations, the high productivity per slave there would be easily explicable.

In Prince William Parish (also, like St. Peter's Parish, in Beaufort County) the manuscript census taker recorded unambiguously that 214,350 *bushels* of rice were produced. At 1 bushel = 27⅛ pounds, this was 5,950,000 pounds of clean rice. As rice production in the other two parishes of Beaufort County was negligible, I estimate Beaufort County's total production at 19,050,000 pounds of *clean* rice. The Census Office reported 18,800,000 pound of (rough) rice in Beaufort County, thus understating the county' production by 64 percent. (Possibly the Census Office mistakenly added figures for clean rice in Beaufort County to those for rough rice in every other county!)

1860. Talmage's estimate for this year includes Louisiana. To determine total American production, I have increased Talmage's estimate by 1.3 percent, in proportion to the share of U.S. production (as indicated in the corrected 1859 census figures) contributed by those states not included in Talmage's figures.

Appendix F

Low-Country Rice Slaves, 1860 (and 1850)

This appendix explains my estimate (p. 389) that there were about 48,000 low-country rice slaves in 1860. (And note 3 to that page explains my estimate that there had been about 58,000 low-country rice slaves in 1850. That figure is further discussed at the end of this appendix.)

APPENDIX TABLE 8. Low-Country Rice Slaves, 1860, by Parish

Parishes, in 12 counties (arranged north to south)	No. of slaves (est.)		
	In parish	In county	In state
NORTH CAROLINA (NEW HANOVER & BRUNSWICK COUNTIES)			1,600
SOUTH CAROLINA			33,800
Georgetown		16,100	
Lower All Saints	4,400		
Prince George Winyah	11,700		
Charleston		6,100	
St. James Santee	2,000		
St. Stephen	—		
Christ Church	100		
St. Thomas and St. Denis	800		
St. John's Berkeley	1,900		
St. James Goosecreek	500		
St. Andrew's	100		
St. John's Colleton	700		
Colleton		6,600	
St. George	100		
St. Paul's	2,000		
St. Bartholomew's	4,500		

APPENDIX TABLE 8.   *(continued)*

Parishes, in 12 counties (arranged north to south)	No. of slaves (est.)		
	In parish	*In county*	*In state*
Beaufort		5,000	
Prince William	2,200		
St. Helena	—		
St. Luke's	—		
St. Peter's	2,800		
GEORGIA			12,600
Chatham		5,300	
Bryan		1,200	
Liberty		700	
McIntosh		1,800	
Glynn		1,300	
Camden		2,300	
TOTAL			48,000

Sources:

North Carolina: Clifton, ". . . Rice Planting on the Lower Cape Fear," *North Carolina Historical Review* 50 (1973): 381.

South Carolina:

Lower All Saints: Joyner, *Down by the Riverside,* p. 19.

Prince George Winyah: Excluding the town of Georgetown, there were 12,900 slaves in this parish. Although virtually no cotton was grown in Georgetown County, I estimate that perhaps 1,200 of these slaves did other agricultural work than raising rice.

All other South Carolina parishes (except St. Peter's): My estimates are based on the 1860 Manuscript Census returns for agriculture, and on Davidson, *The Last Foray.* The manuscript returns enable one to list each substantial producer of rice (over 20,000 pounds)—except where a plantation such as Charles Manigault's "Silk Hope" was omitted by the census taker. From the same returns one can list each substantial producer of cotton (principally sea-island cotton). With this information one can usually determine which of South Carolina's large slaveholders (as enumerated by Davidson) were rice planters, and which grew cotton. Occasionally a large slaveholder planted both of these crops, and from the plantation's production figures one can then estimate how many of his slaves raised rice, and how many cotton.

Holders of less than 100 slaves are seldom listed in Davidson. And the production figures even for some of the big slave owners are unknown, for the census taker sometimes named the overseer rather than the plantation's owner. In both cases I have estimated—parish by parish—the number of slaves required to raise the quantity of rice produced in that parish by other plantations than the ones whose slaveholders can be identified in Davidson. On these—usually smaller—plantations I have assumed a somewhat lower productivity ratio (i.e., the quantity of rice produced, divided by the number of slaves) than on the nearby plantations of identified large slaveholders. No doubt when other scholars analyze the manuscript slave returns, they will find errors in my estimates. But I hope these estimates will nevertheless suggest more or less correctly the number of rice slaves in each parish, and thus begin the complex task of distinguishing rice planters from sea-island cotton planters in the low country.

In St. Peter's Parish I have used Davidson's figures to supplement those of Lawrence Rowland (" 'Alone on the River,' " *South Carolina Historical Magazine* 88 [1987]: 148). This results in a slight revision from Rowland's total (2,600 slaves) upwards to 2,800 rice slaves in that parish. The revision arises principally from my using the 1860 figure for Mrs. Mary (Taylor) Wilkins instead of the 1850 figure for the Taylor Estate; the 1860 figure for Mrs. Ann (Chisolm) Bee instead of the 1850 figure for the Chisolm Estate; Davidson's figure for Dr. J. A. Huger, in addition to his figure for the Huger family's "Trinity"; Davidson's figure for Dr. J. P. Screven (which appears to be consonant with data on Screven's rice slaves in Julia Smith, *Slavery,* p. 221); and Davidson's figure for Dr. W. C. Daniell.

Georgia: I depend—for data on the slaveholdings of individual rice planters—on Julia Smith, *Slavery and Rice Culture,* pp. 219–26; and on the printed census figures for rice production in each county. Here again, as with the Carolina parishes, I have first listed the slaveholdings of the largest planters in each county and then estimated the number of additional slaves required to produce the remaining quantity of rice in that county.

The number of rice slaves in 1850. I estimate that during the 1850s the number of rice slaves increased by 3,000 in Georgia and North Carolina; remained stable in Georgetown and Charleston Counties; and fell by 13,000 in Colleton and Beaufort Counties. These estimates are based on figures for rice production, and for the slave population, in each county.

Essential to making a sensible estimate was the discovery that, in the printed 1860 census, St. John's Colleton Parish had mistakenly been included within Colleton County: it should have been subsumed under Charleston County, as was correctly done in 1850. Thus the printed 1860 census counted Governor William Aiken—the only important rice planter in St. John's Colleton Parish—as though he resided in Colleton County; therefore, the printed census reported too small a quantity of rice produced in Charleston County. (The manuscript returns showed 19,922,000 pounds of rough rice produced by producers of over 20,000 pounds each [and no doubt another 478,000 pounds by the smallest producers], yet in the printed report only 18,900,000 pounds were recorded; this happened because the compilers had omitted the 1,500,000 pounds of rough rice produced by Aiken's 700 slaves. And they mislocated not only Aiken's rice slaves but also the approximately 10,000 nonrice slaves—mostly raising sea-island cotton—who also lived in St. John's Colleton Parish. [The total number of slaves reported by the 1840 census for St. John's Colleton Parish was 10,745.])

This gross error in the printed 1860 census was spotted by Alfred G. Smith Jr., "Economic Readjustment of an Old Cotton State: South Carolina, 1820–1860" (Ph.D. diss., Columbia University, 1954), pp. 103–4. If one accepts the census figures for 1850, but substitutes the South Carolina comptroller's figures for 1860 (as reported by Alfred G. Smith Jr. in place of the mistaken census figures for that year), the actual number of slaves was as follows (in thousands):

	Rural Charleston County	*Colleton County*
1850	35.3	21.4
1860	35.9	21.6

Thus—quite contrary to what the census suggested—the slave populations of both Colleton and rural Charleston remained virtually static during the 1850s. The number of rice slaves in rural Charleston was probably stable, and the county's rice production actually increased by about 20 percent. Rice production in both Colleton and Beaufort Counties fell, but less than the mistaken census figures seemed to imply (see appendix table 7 in appendix E, and table 23 in chapter 15). I estimate the decline in rice slaves during the 1850s at some 6,000 in Colleton County, and about 7,000 in Beaufort County.

Appendix G

Number of Low-Country Rice Plantations, 1860

This appendix explains table 24 (p. 395). Appendix Table 9 locates the 170 largest rice plantations (those with over 100 slaves) specified in the middle column of table 24. The rest of this appendix gives the sources for the estimates in these two tables.

APPENDIX TABLE 9. 170 Largest Rice Plantations (those with over 100 slaves), 1860, by Parish (est.)

| | No. of large rice plantations | | |
	In parish	In county	In state
NORTH CAROLINA (NEW HANOVER & BRUNSWICK COUNTIES)			3
SOUTH CAROLINA			137
Georgetown		54	
Lower All Saints	13		
Prince George Winyah	41		
Charleston		28	
St. James Santee	9		
St. Stephen	0		
Christ Church	0		
St. Thomas and St. Denis	4		
St. John's Berkeley	11		
St. James Goosecreek	3		
St. Andrew's	0		
St. John's Colleton	1		
Colleton		35	
St. George	0		
St. Paul's	9		
St. Bartholomew's	26		

	No. of large rice plantations		
	In parish	*In county*	*In state*
Beaufort		20	
Prince William	8		
St. Helena	0		
St. Luke's	0		
St. Peter's	12		
GEORGIA			30
Chatham		13	
Bryan		6	
Liberty		1	
McIntosh		3	
Glynn		3	
Camden		4	
TOTAL			170

Sources for appendix table 9 and table 24 (chapter 15):

Plantations with over 100 slaves:

North Carolina: Clifton, ". . . Rice Planting on the Lower Cape Fear," *N.C. Hist. Rev.* 50 (1973): 381–82.

South Carolina: Chalmers Davidson, *Last Foray,* pp. 170–267; 1860 Manuscript Census of Agriculture for Charleston, Colleton, and Beaufort Counties.

Georgia: Julia Smith, *Slavery and Rice Culture,* pp. 219–26.

My estimates differ from the figures in the printed census, and in Clifton, ed., *Life and Labor on Argyle Island,* p. xiv, for three reasons:

1. I define a "rice planter" as one who owned at least 35 slaves (and who therefore produced more than about 100,000 pounds of rough rice). Dale Swan has shown that farmers smaller than this produced almost negligible quantities of rice—only 4 percent of the low-country rice crop. I estimate the number of individual "rice planters" (with more than 35 slaves) at 320. This figure is consonant with Swan's calculations: his sample suggests that there must have been about 344 plantations which produced over 100,000 pounds of rice; and when double counting of plantations owned by an individual planter is eliminated, his figure is virtually identical to mine (Swan, "Structure and Profitability of the the the Antebellum Rice Industry: 1859 [Ph.D. diss., University of North Carolina, 1972], pp. 107, 15).

By contrast to my procedure, the printed census includes among rice "estates" not only those producing more than 100,000 pounds but also those where production was between 20,000 and 100,000 pounds. According to James Clifton's calculation, there were altogether 579 such estates.

2. As explained in chapter 15, I have eliminated the double counting of 22 plantations (i.e., the 18 mentioned in the text, and 4 others owned by planters with less than 200 slaves) owned by those planters who held property in more than one parish.

3. In table 24 (though not in appendix table 9) I have placed the plantations into family groupings.

Plantations with 35–99 slaves (table 24, chapter 15):

My estimates are projections derived initially from figures in Rogers, *Georgetown,* pp. 524–27. Rogers shows that the 77 Georgetown "rice planters" (with more than 35 slaves) listed in the 1850 manuscript census were distributed as follows:

Size of slaveholding	*Number of planters*
100 or more slaves	45
50–99 "	27
35–49 "	5
TOTAL	77

If slaveholdings elsewhere in the low country were distributed in the same proportions as in Georgetown, the 170 low-country planters with over 100 slaves would be matched by 121 planters with smaller holdings:

Size of slaveholding	Number of planters
100 or more slaves	170
50–99 "	102
35–49 "	19

But as relatively small rice planters appear to have been more common in North Carolina, Georgia, and the rest of South Carolina than in Georgetown County, I have estimated in table 24 that the number of planters with fewer than 100 slaves was almost one-quarter larger than would be suggested by the Georgetown figures.

In Georgetown the average holding on those plantations with 35 to 99 slaves was almost exactly 70 slaves; and rice plantations with 70 to 99 slaves were more common than those with only 35 to 69 slaves. These facts support my estimates of the number of slaves on the smaller plantations.

In due course my estimates are likely to be superseded by exact figures for the holders of fewer than 100 slaves. My estimates of the number of such planter families may well prove to be too large; if so, this will show that slaveholding was even more heavily concentrated among a small number of rice-planting families than I have suggested.

Notes

Abbreviations

AA	Adele Allston (Robert Allston's wife)
BA	Benjamin Allston (Robert Allston's elder son)
Bell	Malcolm Bell Jr., *Major Butler's Legacy* (Athens, Ga., 1987)
Clifton	James Clifton, ed., *Life and Labor on Argyle Island: Letters and Documents of a Savannah River Rice Plantation, 1833–1867* (Charlottesville: University Press of Virginia [For the Beehive Press], 1978)
CM	Charles Manigault
Davidson	Chalmers Davidson, *The Last Foray: The South Carolina Planters of 1860* (Columbia, S.C., 1971)
DU	Special Collections Library, Duke University
Easterby	J. H. Easterby, ed., *The South Carolina Rice Plantation, as Revealed in the Papers of Robert F. W. Allston* (Chicago: University of Chicago Press, 1945)
FK	Frances Kemble
GM	Dr. Gabriel Manigault (Charles Manigault's third son)
HSP	Historical Society of Pennsylvania (Philadelphia)
Journal	Frances Anne Kemble, *Journal of a Residence on a Georgian Plantation* (1863; rpt. [ed. John A. Scott] New York, 1961)
Joyner	Charles Joyner, *Down by the Riverside: A South Carolina Slave Community* (Urbana, Ill., 1984)
LM	Louis Manigault (Charles Manigault's second son)
PB	Pierce (Mease) Butler (Frances Kemble's husband)

Pringle	Elizabeth W. Allston Pringle, *Chronicles of "Chicora Wood"* (1922; rpt. Atlanta, Ga., 1976)
RA	Robert Allston
RK	Roswell King (Butler estate agent before 1819)
RK Jr.	Roswell King Jr. (Butler estate agent after 1819)
Rogers	George C. Rogers, Jr., *History of Georgetown County, South Carolina* (Columbia, S.C., 1970)
SCHS	South Carolina Historical Society (Charleston)
SCL	South Caroliniana Library, University of South Carolina
SHC	Southern Historical Collection, Library of the University of North Carolina at Chapel Hill

Chapter 1

1. The records are printed in Clifton's book. Its "Introduction" (esp. pp. xvii–xxi, xxviii–xlvi) is a valuable source of information on the Manigaults. The account of the mill's destruction is in LM, journal, March 22, 1867 (Clifton, p. 362).

2. References to the Manigaults' correspondence and records are always (except where otherwise specified) to the Manigault Family Papers. These are divided among four research libraries (SCHS; SCL; SHC, where the references are to the Manigault Family Papers, No. 484; and DU, where the references are to the Louis Manigault Papers) and are identified simply by the library's abbreviation: LM, family records, pp. 109–14 (SCL). GM, notes on family, p. 4, 11/278A/13 (SCHS). I here follow these two sources, not the figure of 301 slaves suggested in Maurice Crouse, "Gabriel Manigault: Charleston Merchant," *South Carolina Historical Magazine,* 68 (1967): 221. I infer that Gabriel Manigault I had already given 190 slaves to his two grandsons (both of whom were of age) before he died in 1781, and that these therefore were omitted from the inventory of his estate, which mentioned 301 slaves.

3. CM to LM, Dec. 30, 1857 (DU). So successful a student of French did Louis's bride prove—especially during their long wedding trip to France—that "she never spoke a word of English to [her eldest child]" from his birth in Paris in 1858 until her death nearly ten years later (LM, notebooks, II, 134 [Charleston Museum]).

4. The second largest was probably Samuel Hairston of Virginia, who, according to Clement Eaton, owned (in 1850?) "nearly two thousand Negroes and controll[ed] another thousand owned by his mother-in-law" (Clement Eaton, *The Growth of Southern Civilization* [London, 1961], p. 316).

5. Only about 187 acres were cleared when Manigault bought Gowrie in 1833. He cleared the other 78 in 1839–41. CM, memo, Dec. 1842; LM, notebook, 1852 (DU).

6. The plantation bought in 1848 was "East Hermitage," while that purchased in 1854 was the Legaré plantation. These two were merged into a single tract, with a settlement of slave houses at East Hermitage, and usually with its own East Hermitage "driver" (a slave who acted as foreman). Because the original Gowrie and the new East Hermitage tracts were operated together as a single agricultural unit, under a single white overseer, I use "Gowrie" (for simplicity) to refer to the whole combined unit after 1848.

The acreage of rice lands on these tracts (not including the two slave settlements, nor the mills, barnyards, and embankments) was:

original Gowrie	265	acres
East Hermitage	228	"
Legaré tract	ca. 148	"
Total "Gowrie":	ca. 641	acres

The figures for "original Gowrie" and East Hermitage are from LM, notebook, 1852 (DU). These are more trustworthy for "original Gowrie" than the rounded numbers in CM's 1839 journal (Clifton, p. 2), which (because it included the vendor's original exaggeration, and lands used for the pounding mill, the barnyard, the slave settlement, the master's house, and the canals) overstated by perhaps twenty-seven acres the amount of land actually available for planting rice. By 1852 about eight more acres had been lost through the contraction of embankments (after the river had broken through and undermined the margins) and through extending the canals. See CM, memo, Dec. 1842 (DU).

The size of Legaré's fields is from CM, memo, Dec. 12, 1843 (DU). For their date of purchase, CM to LM, Jan. 12, 1854 (Clifton, p. 169).

7. LM to CM, Dec. 26, 1854 (Clifton, p. 190).

8. The figure was Louis Manigault's.

9. Some of the richest rice planters also gained part of their wealth from long-staple sea-island cotton.

10. When in 1833 Manigault paid seventy dollars per acre for Gowrie's cleared rice land, and thirty-seven dollars per acre for its uncleared rice land (while nearby pineland, unfit for rice, was worth only three dollars per acre), the premium on uncleared rice land over pineland had two sources: the embankments had already been built, and the previous owners had already set the price of potential rice land well above three dollars. They and potential buyers calculated that—so long as slave labor was available—the productivity of the land could be raised by ditching and clearing it. Thus the market value of "land" depended not only on how much labor had already been invested in improving it but also on a calculation of what could be achieved by investing future labor into its improvement. CM, journal, Apr. 11, [1845] (Clifton, pp. 22–23).

11. Cf. Peter H. Wood, *Black Majority: Negroes in Colonial South Carolina from 1670 Through the Stono Rebellion* (New York, 1974), pp. 83–90.

12. CM, journal, Apr. 1850 (Clifton, p. 75).

13. CM to Jesse Cooper, July 12, 1848 (Clifton, p. 63).

14. The sixteen rivers are listed in Clifton, p. xiv.

15. E.g., Jesse Cooper to CM, Aug. 24, 1849 (Clifton, p. 72).

16. CM, journal, Apr. 1850 (Clifton, pp. 75–76).

17. CM to James Haynes, Jan. 1, 1847 (Clifton, pp. 44–45).

18. Elizabeth Manigault to LM, Aug. 28, 1856 (DU).

19. K. W. Skinner to CM, Oct. 11, Nov. 13, 1851 (DU).

20. The list of fourteen overseers in Clifton, pp. 1–2, omits an overseer (Gibbons) employed in 1836 but sacked before the year's end, and one (Heargroves) who died early in 1840. On the other hand, the list includes the name of one man (Darby) who was only a suboverseer. (Crum was the overseer in 1835.)

21. CM to LM, Nov. 1, 1853 (Clifton, p. 162).

22. CM to LM, Mar. 11, 1858 (Clifton, p. 259).

23. CM to LM, Mar. 18, 1858 (Clifton, pp. 260–61).

24. CM to Alfred Huger, Apr. 1, 1847 (Clifton, p. 52). CM to Tom Middleton, Sept. 15, 1846; to R. Habersham & Son, Nov. 1, 1846 (copy), (SCL).

25. CM to Alfred Huger, Apr. 1, 1847 (Clifton, p. 53).

26. About one-third of Gowrie's profits during this seven-year period were capital gains arising from the increased value of Manigault's slaves, as the southwestern cotton boom caused the price of slaves to rise.

27. LM, journal, Feb. 1, 1857 (Clifton, p. 215).

28. Over $45,000 in 1848–49 for the new land and fifty-two slaves to work it; some $11,000 for the Legaré land in the 1853 financial year; about $34,000 on fifty-nine slaves shipped to Gowrie from 1852 to 1857, nearly $2,000 on improvements to his thresher, and over $2,000 on purchasing in 1856 a five-hundred-acre pineland retreat for his slaves. The $8,000 worth of Silk Hope slaves whom Manigault deported to Gowrie during these years did not cost him cash, and therefore are not included in the figure of $94,000.

29 CM to LM, Jan. 17, 1860 (Clifton, p. 291).

30. The figure for 1862 was $20,000. 1861 and 1863 crops: LM, plantation journal (Clifton, pp. 322, 341; 344, 347 [mistakenly inscribed "Crop of 1864"]). 1862 crop: R. Habersham & Sons, accounts, Feb. 28, 1863 (SCHS).

31. He had launched his enterprise in 1833 with $20,000 of his own money and $12,000 worth of his father-in-law's Silk Hope slaves. Between 1836 and 1858 he deported another $17,500 worth of Silk Hope slaves to Gowrie, bringing his total investment there to $49,500.

32. The plantation and its slaves were by then worth about $138,000; the accumulated profits since 1833—after covering every expense, including the repayment of the original mortgage, the purchase of East Hermitage (1848) and the Legaré land (1854), and the acquisition of dozens of slaves at auctions in Charleston and Savannah—were about $93,000; and the accumulated earnings from placing these profits into outside investments were perhaps another $35,000.

Charles Manigault had always taken his own family's living expenses out of the income from Silk Hope and his other properties. In 1861 he reckoned his wealth at nearly half a million dollars (a substantial sum at a moment when few Northern capitalists were worth more than $1 million); and half of his fortune was derived from Gowrie.

33. LM, notebooks, II, 131 (Charleston Museum). I include this $10,000 wedding gift within the $266,000 value of the estate. Charles Manigault probably considered this supplement to Louis's $17,000 income for managerial services as comparable to the $50 tip with which he had sometimes rewarded an inexperienced young overseer at the completion of a successful year's work.

34. Gray was the victim of census figures which were variously unrepresentative, downright mistaken, and muddled. The 1850 census measured the atypical crop of 1849, a freak year when production was much higher than in the rest of the 1840s. The size of the 1859 rice crop was 7.7 percent larger than the next census mistakenly reported. And Gray failed to detect a confusing shift in the census reports, from "clean" rice in 1839 to "rough" rice in 1849 and 1859 (162 pounds of "rough" [unmilled] rice were equivalent to about 100 pounds of "clean" [milled] rice). See appendix E (Lewis C. Gray, *History of Agriculture in the Southern United States to 1860* [Washington, D.C., 1933], p. 723).

35. The hypothetical return which might have been received from a fixed-rate loan is called "imputed interest." Economic historians have sometimes measured "imputed interest" by the legal rate of interest (which in antebellum South Carolina was 7 percent), but this procedure takes no account of bad debts. One thus runs the danger of comparing the *actual* profits received by entrepreneurs with the *fictional* returns which

fixed-rate lenders might have received had none of their investments turned sour. In important studies of the profitability of the antebellum rice industry, Peter Coclanis assumes a 7 percent imputed interest rate, while Dale Swan follows Conrad and Meyer's estimate of a 6 percent Southern bank rate of interest (Peter A. Coclanis, *The Shadow of a Dream: Economic Life and Death in the South Carolina Low Country, 1670–1920* [New York, 1989], pp. 105, 140–41; Dale E. Swan, "The Structure and Profitability of the Antebellum Rice Industry" [Ph.D. diss., University of North Carolina, 1972], p. 62).

36. The plantation's value grew from $49,500 (i.e., an initial investment of $32,000 in 1833 [table 2, column a, top line], plus $17,500 worth of Silk Hope slaves imported between 1836 and 1858 [table 2, column c, bottom line]), to $138,500 in 1861 [table 2, column a, bottom line].

37. See the preceding note.

38. I estimate that in certain years Manigault might have earned 7 percent or more on this hypothetical alternative investment—say in a Charleston bank or insurance company; but that fluctuations in dividends, or occasional capital losses, would have reduced the average annual return, taking the bad years with the good, to perhaps 3 percent.

39. On the original $32,000 investment, I have calculated the 3 percent return from 1833; on the additional $17,500 worth of Silk Hope slaves, the calculation is from the subsequent dates (1836 to 1858) when he deported the several groups of slaves.

40. The four overseers who died were Crum (1835), Heargroves (1840), Clark (1855), and Capers (1864). The overseers' salaries are listed in Clifton, pp. 1–2.

41. Skinner to CM, Oct. 13, 1852; Cooper to CM, July 24, 1849 (Clifton, pp. 122, 68 [emphasis added]).

42. CM to LM, Dec. 1, 1856; to Anthony Barclay, Apr. 15, 1847; to LM, Dec. 4, 1856 (Clifton, pp. 236, 54, 237).

43. CM to LM, Nov. 28, Feb. 28, 1856; Dec. 28, 1858 (Clifton, pp. 235, 211, 267).

44. CM to LM, Apr. 17, 1859; Jan. 17, 1860; Oct. 11, 1856; Dec. 1, 1857 (Clifton, pp. 287, 291, 228, 254).

45. CM to LM, Jan. 3, Feb. 20, 1859 (Clifton, pp. 269, 281).

46. CM, "Description of Paintings" (typescript), p. 24 (SCL).

47. LM to CM, Feb. 27, 1853; Nov. 22, 1852 (Clifton, pp. 140, 128).

48. Sidney Fisher, diary, Jan. 17, 1841, in Nicholas B. Wainwright, ed., *A Philadelphia Perspective* (Philadelphia, 1967), pp. 111–12.

49. Robert Blake, *Disraeli* (London, 1966), pp. 278–83.

50. This argument follows Orlando Patterson, "On Slavery and Slave Formations," *New Left Review* 117 (1979): 40, 52–55.

Chapter 2

1. I.e., 1771–83. She was born in 1768 (Wylma Wates, "Precursor to the Victorian Age: The Concept of Marriage and Family as Revealed in the Correspondence of the Izard Family of South Carolina," in Carol Bleser, ed., *In Joy and In Sorrow: Women, Family, and Marriage in the Victorian South, 1830–1900* [New York, 1991], p. 5).

2. Joshua F. Fisher, *Recollections* [written 1864–67, printed 1929], pp. 277–87, (HSP).

3. LM, family records, p. 287, SCHS. LM, family records, p. 179, SCL. LM and GM, "The Manigault Family," *Transactions of the Huguenot Society of South Carolina* 4 (1897): 82.

4. CM to Tom Middleton, Aug. 1, 1847; to Alfred Huger, Apr. 1, 1847, letterbook, SCHS.

5. LM, memoir of CM, pp. 287–88, SCHS.

6. I follow here CM, "N. Heyward's Will as last signed by him in 1846" (legal-sized file), (SCL); CM had the figure of about two hundred from Nathaniel himself. This source contradicts GM's much later figure of seventy slaves, in GM, autobiography, p. 74, SCHS. Nathaniel Heyward's great-grandson J. B. Heyward II, in his *Heyward* (n.p., n.d. [1931, 1968]), (SCL), supports CM's figure.

7. I infer from Phillips, *American Negro Slavery* (New York, 1918), pp. 134, 136, 368, and chart opposite p. 370, that a group of slaves in Charleston in the late 1780s would not have cost more than $250 in the round.

8. GM, autobiography, p. 76 (SCHS). Heyward, *Heyward,* pp. 23, 69.

9. GM, autobiography, pp. 72–73.

10. Ibid., p. 73. LM, family records, p. 281 (SCHS). GM, notes on family, pp. 6–8, 11/278A/13 (SCHS). Duncan C. Heyward, *Seed from Madagascar* (Chapel Hill, N.C., 1937), pp. 14, 54, 62, 64–65.

11. I follow here GM, whose analysis, though no doubt inaccurate in detail, plausibly accounts for the massive shift from inland to tidal rice culture (GM, "Notes on Family," p. 7, 11/278A/13 [SCHS]). Modern accounts are Joyce Chaplin, "Tidal Rice Cultivation and the Problem of Slavery in South Carolina and Georgia, 1760–1815," *William and Mary Quarterly,* 3d ser., 49 (1992): 29–61; and David O. Whitten, "American Rice Cultivation, 1680–1980," *Southern Studies* 21 (1982): esp. 8–18.

12. The year 1855 was the third of the nineteenth-century peaks. Arthur Cole, *Wholesale Commodity Prices in the United States, 1700–1861* (Cambridge, Mass., 1938), 1:154.

13. GM, autobiography, pp. 74–75. Heyward, *Seed from Madagascar,* p. 90.

14. The 2,340 slaves acquired by Nathaniel Heyward include about 475 to whom by the time of his death in 1851 he no longer had legal title, having previously presented them as outright gifts to certain of his children. Among these were about 100 given his daughter Ann; about 100 for whose purchase he had given his son Arthur the cash, in order for Arthur to stock his wife's plantation Valambrosa; about 135 he had given his son Nathaniel Heyward II, which by 1851 were owned by the old man's grandson Nathaniel Heyward III; and perhaps 140 whom I infer that he had previously given to his son Charles Heyward. (These last 140 slaves would substantially account for the difference between the 563 slaves listed by J. B. Heyward as Charles Heyward's inheritance in 1851 and the 704 slaves whom Charles Heyward himself acknowledged in 1851 as the total number he had been given by his father.)

In addition to these 475 bondsmen and women previously given away, Nathaniel Heyward bequeathed another 1865 slaves at his death in 1851. These comprised:

1851 Bequest	Previous gifts	Total gifts
ca. 564 to his son Charles	ca. 140	ca. 704
200 " " " Arthur	100	300
100 " " grandson Nathaniel III	135	235
433 " " " W. H. Heyward	—	433
394 " " " J. B. Heyward	—	394
168 " " daughter Elizabeth		168
— " " " Ann	100	100
6 other house servants	—	6
___ (legatees unknown)		
1,865	475	2,340

The best source for these calculations is CM, "List of Mr. Nathl Heywards Negroes, June 1851" (11/278A/13, SCHS), which was recorded by Charles Manigault on May 24, 1851, from his conversation that day with Charles Heyward. The total in the "List" is 2,334 slaves "not counting Several House Servants, given" (whom I have estimated as 6, making a grand total of 2,340 slaves).

In CM's separate notes on "N. Heyward's Will as last signed by him in 1846," SCL, I infer that the 100 slaves previously given to Ann Heyward have been omitted from the total, specified there as 2,234 slaves (or else that Manigault erred in copying the second digit of this total), and that the "Several House Servants" have also been omitted. I believe the total in CM's 1851 "List" is the correct one because it (unlike CM's notes on the 1846 will) specifies the number of slaves given to each legatee, and the total of these items is 2,334 slaves (not counting the "Several House Servants").

The numbers indicated in CM's "List" for each legatee are more or less consistent with those specified many years later in J. B. Heyward, *Heyward,* pp. 66–69, 91, 93. The only substantial difference between these two records is the previously mentioned disagreement about how many slaves Charles Heyward received. I accept CM's figure of 704, as he recorded it on May 24, 1851, the day he heard it from Charles Heyward's lips.

The names of Nathaniel Heyward's plantations, with the number of slaves at each, appear in J. B. Heyward, *Heyward;* this is my source for the number of rice plantations Nathaniel Heyward owned. The number of his Charleston house servants is from U.S. Manuscript Census, 1840, Charleston, p. 39. The quotation is from Heyward, *Seed from Madagascar,* p. 81.

15. CM, memoir [1873], VII (SHC). CM to LM, Mar. 19, 1864, scrapbook, p. 213 (SCL). C. Drie, "Bird's Eye View of . . . Charleston . . . 1872," Catalog Room (SCHS).

16. CM, "Nathaniel Heyward's Will as last signed by him in 1846" (SCL).

17. Heyward, *Heyward,* pp. 64, 93.

18. GM, autobiography, pp. 75–77 (SCHS).

19. The custom of marrying first cousins persisted in the next generation of Heywards, for Nathaniel's grandson W. H. Heyward wed his first cousin Esther Heyward, and another grandson, J. B. Heyward, espoused his first cousin Maria Heyward. This tradition served the function of counteracting, to some degree, the dissipation of a large fortune in a society which did not practice primogeniture (William H. Heyward, "Table of Descents," June 27, 1853 [copy], Manigault MS, 11/278A/13 [SCHS]).

20. CM, souvenirs (SCL). Fisher, *Recollections,* pp. 276, 280 (HSP).

21. CM, note Nov. 1850 on CM to Nathaniel Heyward, Sept. 19, 1843 (misfiled 1845); LM, family records, p. 239 (SCL).

22. GM, notes on family, pp. 4–5, 11/278A/13, SCHS. LM, family records, p. 270, 45/40, SCHS. CM, souvenirs, p. 8, SCL. CM to Alfred Huger, Apr. 1, 1847; to Tom Middleton, Sept. 15, 1846, letterbook (SCHS).

23. Fisher, *Recollections,* p. 227 (HSP). CM, souvenirs, p. 55 (SCL).

24. Dumas Malone, *Jefferson and His Time* (Boston, 1981), 6:176.

25. LM, family records, p. 56 (SCL). CM, "Description of Paintings," SCL. LM, family records, pp. 267–68, 270, 45/40 (SCHS).

26. Heyward, *Heyward,* p. 91. Harry's full name was Gabriel Henry Manigault.

27. Gabriel and Margaret I. Manigault estate matters, 1817–27, 11/278A/3 (SCHS).

28. The remaining one-quarter went to her daughters. LM, family records, pp. 60–61 (SCL).

29. Eight thousand dollars plus interest since 1818. CM, souvenirs, p. 8 (SCL). Decree of equity court, May 1826 (copy), Gabriel and Margaret I. Manigault estate matters, 1817–27, 11/278A/3; settlement by J. L. Petigru between CM and G. H. Manigault, 11/278A/5 (SCHS).

30. CM, "List of Mr. Nath'l Heywards Negroes, June 1851," 11/278A/13 (SCHS).

31. Anthony Barclay to CM, Feb. 13, 1846 (SCHS).

32. Margaret I. Manigault to CM, Apr. 2, 1824, in LM, family records, p. 275, 45/40 (SCHS).

33. CM to his mother, Apr. 14, 1824, in LM, memoir of CM, p. 277 (SCHS).

34. LM, memoir of CM, p. 286 (SCHS). CM, souvenirs, p. 42 (SCL).

35. GM, autobiography, p. 22 (SCHS).

36. Heyward, *Heyward,* p. 96.

37. Elizabeth Manigault to CM, Jan. 1, 1845 (SCHS).

38. Heyward, *Heyward,* p. 96.

39. On the deportation of the Silk Hope slaves, see table 8, including its first two notes (chapter 3).

40. This son, Charles Heyward Manigault, was not strictly a "Jr.," but I so denominate him to distinguish him from his father, Charles Izard Manigault.

41. CM to William N. Habersham [1847?] (SCL).

42. GM, autobiography, pp. 68–69 (SCHS).

43. LM, family records, p. 299 (SCHS).

44. CM to LM, Feb. 21, Mar. 6, 1856 (Clifton, pp. 210, 213).

45. GM to CM, Apr. 10, 1856 (SCHS).

46. LM, family records, p. 287 (SCHS); LM, scrapbook (SCL).

47. LM, "Visit to Charleston, Dec. 2, 1863" (SHC). Jane G. Mahler, ". . . Two Manigaults in China," *Transactions of the Huguenot Society* 76 (1971): 5. CM to LM, Aug. 4, 1853 (SCHS). LM, note on CM to LM, Aug. 31, 1864, LM scrapbook, p. 46 (SCL).

48. LM, notebooks, II, 131 (Charleston Museum).

49. LM, notes, Dec. 1, Nov. 28, 1863, scrapbook, pp. 63, 58 (SCL).

50. CM to GM, Apr. 10, 1865; LM, memo, Feb. 1866, in LM, "Book, 1861–1866" (SHC).

51. CM to Alfred Huger, Apr. 1, 1847, letterbook (SCHS).

52. LM, family records, pp. 54–55, 3 (SCHS).

53. CM to Alfred Huger, Apr. 1, 1847, letterbook (SCHS).

54. LM, family records, pp. 266–69, 45/40 (SCHS).

55. LM, memoir of CM, p. 280 (SCHS).

56. CM to James Rose, Sept. 28, 1847, letterbook (SCHS).

57. CM to R. Habersham & Son, Feb. 1, 1847, letterbook (SCHS).

58. CM to Alfred Huger, Apr. 1, 1847, letterbook (SCHS).

59. Ibid.

60. CM to R. Habersham, Jan. 10, 1848, letterbook (SCHS).

61. CM to LM, Sept. 18, 1853 (SCHS).

62. Anthony Barclay to CM, Sept. 14, 21, 30, 1841 (SCHS).

63. In 1837 Manigault expected to pay $88 for the lumber and construction of each two-room slave house. I estimate that the brick pillars and the central brick chimney cost another $20, bringing the total cost of such a house to $108 (CM, memo [1837], II [SHC]). On Marshlands: Samuel G. Stoney, *Plantations of the Carolina Low Country* (Charleston, S.C., 1938), pp. 8, 77; CM to J. C. H. Claussen, Aug. 1, 1872 (typescript, "Papers, 1776–1872," p. 35), (SCL).

64. Middleton's [the Charleston factor's] statement, Oct. 1859–Oct. 1860, IV (SHC). Capers's spending on tobacco and molasses in 1859 ($1.45 per slave) was less than half of what the relatively openhanded overseer Washington Skinner had spent on these two items ($3.03 per slave) in 1851. LM, memo on expenses, May 1851–May 1852 (filed 1851), (SCHS).

65. CM, "The Close of the War—The Negro" [1870], pp. 12, 4, 10, VII (SHC).

Chapter 3

1. Solomon Northup, *Twelve Years a Slave* (1853; rpt. [ed. Sue Eakin and Joseph Logsdon] Baton Rouge, 1968), pp. 194–99. E. A. Davis, ed., *Plantation Life in the Florida Parishes of Louisiana, 1836–1846 as Reflected in the Diary of Bennet H. Barrow* (1943; rpt. New York, 1967), Nov. 11, 1845.

2. James Oakes, *The Ruling Race* (New York, 1982), pp. 196–98.

3. Lyell introduced these sentences by acknowledging that up-country slaves "are healthier than those in rice plantations, and multiply [even] faster" (Charles Lyell, *Second Visit to the United States,* 2 vols. [London, 1849], 1:334).

4. The annual lists are the most important source for the following discussion of the slaves' health. Births often, and deaths sometimes, were recorded on these lists; but one can also infer a birth or death from the sudden appearance or disappearance of a name on the next annual list. The names of a baby's mother and her husband are nearly always evident, for the slaves were listed in nuclear family groups, with the husband's name before the wife's. (The Dec. 1837 and the 1850 lists even designate the family groups with brackets.) One or two unspecified names may have disappeared before 1849 because the slaves were sold for disobedience, but after 1849 such persons were identified. A few other names were removed from the lists because the slaves had been sent from Gowrie to Silk Hope for their health or for training as house servants, such individuals often being specified. Since many slaves are identified as having been sold, or sent to Silk Hope, one can reasonably infer that names simply disappearing from the lists indicate deaths; and overseers' letters often confirm the inference.

The lists were compiled yearly with two exceptions: there is none between January 1835 and April 1837, nor between December 1845 and April 1849, the Manigaults being in Europe during both of these intervals. The age of every Gowrie slave was recorded in 1833; and the age of nearly every slave imported into Gowrie was recorded on the list where the slave's name first appears.

Sixteen of the twenty-six annual lists are printed in Clifton. The other ten are in the Manigault MS at SHC; I have also used the manuscript lists at SHC to make slight corrections to those printed in Clifton. William Capers's list of Gowrie's slaves on Mar. 8, 1864 (SHC)—and other Civil War correspondence and later records—enables one to trace survivors almost to the end of the war, and sometimes beyond.

5. On Friday and Minda: CM, notes on Gowrie slave lists, Jan. 1, Nov. 14, 1833 (SHC).

6. CM to Alfred Huger, Apr. 1, 1847 (Clifton, pp. 52–53).

7. Deaths exceeded births by about nine during the three years after Sumter.

8. The figure reported for Gowrie in the 1860 manuscript census is misleading. That the number of Manigault's slaves there on April 22, 1860, was 98 is clear from the complete list compiled that day by Louis Manigault and printed in Clifton, pp. 295–96. Yet the overseer William Capers reported 116 slaves to the 1860 census taker (U.S. Manuscript Census: Georgia, Cherokee Hill, Frames 413–413A). Capers, whom Charles Manigault later came to believe a habitual liar, was involved in a South

Carolina lawsuit, and he may have counted slaves of his own as part of Gowrie, in order to disclaim his own possession of any attachable property. And some Silk Hope slaves had probably been sent temporarily to help with Gowrie's harvest in the summer of 1860 (and enumerated there when the census was compiled).

9. My calculation that 90 percent of all Gowrie children died before age sixteen is based, in part, on the inference that 32.6 percent of them died during their first six months. (This was the figure at Pierce Butler's rice plantation, 1819–34, and there is no reason to suppose conditions were better at Gowrie. See table 18 [chapter 8].) But my 90 percent figure does *not* depend heavily upon this inference about the infants' first six months. Had I assumed instead that only 15 percent of Gowrie's babies died during those first six months (an unbelievably low assumption, as 15 percent would be only a bit higher than the national average for all Americans in the mid–nineteenth century), Gowrie's child mortality rate to age sixteen would still have been 88 percent. Its very high child mortality rate, in other words, derived principally from the deaths of children *after* they were six months old.

10. The figure was 5.1 percent at Pierce Butler's rice plantation from 1819 to 1834 (see chapter 8). There is no reason to presume a smaller figure at Gowrie. Indeed, Richard Steckel believes that for all American slaves the rate of stillbirths was over 11 percent (Steckel, "Birth Weights and Infant Mortality Among American Slaves," *Explorations in Economic History* 23 [1986]: 193).

11. Kemble spoke to these nine women at her husband's sea-island cotton plantation, whose child mortality rate was *lower* than at his Butler Island rice plantation (see table 17, chapter 8). (*Journal,* pp. 229–30.)

12. Ibid., p. 130.

13. The figure of 3 percent for lockjaw is taken from Pierce Butler's rice plantation, 1819–34. See table 19 (chapter 8).

14. See chapter 8.

15. The emphasis is Manigault's: plantation journal, Apr. 7, 1845, IV (SHC).

16. A. R. Bagshaw to CM, Apr. 28, 1843 (SCL).

17. Peter Wood, *Black Majority* (New York, 1974), pp. 88–90.

18. K. W. Skinner to CM, July 31, 1852 (Clifton, p. 114).

19. T. R. Heargroves to CM, Oct. 13, 1835 (SCHS). Betsey's family appears prominently in chapter 4.

20. Bell, p. 402. F. L. Olmsted, *A Journey in the Seaboard Slave States* (New York, 1856), p. 418 (emphasis added). Duncan C. Heyward, *Seed from Madagascar* (Chapel Hill, N.C., 1937), pp. 76, 80.

21. Lawrence Rowland, " 'Alone on the River': The Rise and Fall of the Savannah River Rice Plantations of St. Peter's Parish, South Carolina," *South Carolina Historical Magazine* 88 (1987): 143. For further discussion of malaria among adult slaves, see pp. 74–75.

22. Enteric diseases, in both adults and children, are discussed later in this chapter.

23. Emphasis added. LM, journal, Mar. 22, 1867 (Clifton, p. 363).

24. See chapter 5.

25. A. R. Bagshaw to CM, May 19, 1843 (SCHS).

26. The camp Manigault finally succeeded in renting in 1852 was nearly destroyed two months later by a fire—set by a hostile neighbor? LM to CM, Mar. 6, 1853 (Clifton, p. 144).

27. See chapter 5.

28. See Roger Ransom and Richard Sutch, *One Kind of Freedom* (New York, 1977), pp. 6, 44–47, 55.

29. Venters to CM, Oct. 23, 1857 (Clifton, p. 253).

30. The one possible exception to this statement was a different "Old Hannah," who had cost Manigault nothing when acquired (age unspecified) with her son two years earlier. I have counted Fortune as fifty-seven years old (Clifton, p. 5), not fifty-five as Louis stated (Clifton, p. 193).

31. Again, the "Old Hannah" acquired in 1853 (whose age cannot be determined) is a possible exception to this statement.

32. By 1863 three of Gowrie's longtime slaves (Betsey, Phillis, and Clary) had actually attained the ages of sixty-one, fifty-nine, and fifty-nine. In addition, Manigault acquired during the 1850s three other slaves (Daniel, Eve, and Old Hannah—so elderly that he got all of them free) who still survived in 1863; but these three had reached old age before they reached Gowrie.

Gowrie's 1863 Confederate tax return (Clifton, p. 344), which reported ten slaves over fifty-five, is mistaken: only seven slaves had, in fact, reached that age (the six listed above and Binah Currie, who was fifty-five). I have based my calculations on the ages listed at the time of acquisition, *not* on approximations made many years later.

33. Clifton, pp. xli, xvi; CM, plantation journal, [Jan. 1, 1845], [Dec. 5, 1844] (Clifton, pp. 22, 11–12).

34. Jesse Cooper to R. Habersham & Son, June 20, 30, 1848 (copies), (SCHS). CM to Cooper, July 12, 1848 (Clifton, p. 63).

35. Cooper to CM, Sept. 4, June 17, Sept. 4, 1850 (SCHS).

36. LM to CM, Dec. 24, 26, 1854 (Clifton, pp. 187, 190).

37. LM, note on 1854 Gowrie slave list (Clifton, p. 185).

38. Although LM recorded "Mr. Hunt's" residence as the Santee River, I infer that the slaves actually came from B. F. Hunt's Pee Dee estate, because Hunt sold his Pee Dee plantation ("Richland") virtually at the same moment that CM bought the "Hunt" slaves (Rogers, pp. 255, 273, 277, 525; Clifton, p. 185).

39. LM to CM, Dec. 24, 1854 (Clifton, p. 187).

40. Jesse Cooper to CM, Aug. 24, 1849 (Clifton, p. 72). Cooper's letter was probably written later than the Pringle Smith letter cited in Joseph Waring, "Asiatic Cholera in South Carolina," *Bulletin of the History of Medicine* 40 (1966): 464, which mentions the first forty-five of these fifty deaths. The two stricken Smith plantations had 241 slaves in 1860 (Lawrence Rowland, " 'Alone on the River' . . . ," *S.C. Hist. Mag.* 88 [1987]: 148). Therefore, presuming that those slaves who died in 1849 had been replaced (by 1860) with others purchased in Charleston, the 1849 cholera had killed some 21 percent of the slaves on these two plantations.

41. "As the cold increases all danger [from cholera] will cease," he had written to his wife late in September 1835, in reference to a trip they projected to Italy (CM to his wife, Sept. 20, 1835 [SCHS]).

42. K. W. Skinner to CM, Nov. 4, 19, 1852 (Clifton, pp. 126–27).

43. Mrs. M. M. Clark to LM, Dec. 18, 1854 (SCHS). The figure here for deaths in the 1854 epidemic is one higher than that given in Clifton, p. xxxiv. I have included Phoebe (who did not die until Feb. 1855) as well as Ben's Nancy and the eleven slaves listed in LM to CM, Dec. 26, 1854 (Clifton, pp. 184, 190).

44. LM to CM, Dec. 24, 26, 1854 (Clifton, pp. 187–88, 191).

45. LM to CM, Dec. 24, 1854 (Clifton, p. 187).

46. James Haynes to CM, July 1, 1846; Nov. 24, 1847; Stephen Clark to LM, Sept. 18, 1853 (Clifton, pp. 36, 61, 159).

47. Jesse Cooper to CM, Sept. 5, 1849 (Clifton, p. 73).

48. Skinner to CM, July 26, 1851 (DU).

49. LM to CM, Mar. 10, 12, 1854 (Clifton, pp. 181–82).

50. Skinner to CM, July 26, 1851 (DU). CM, plantation journal, 1844–45 (Clifton, p. 9).

51. LM to CM, Dec. 26, 1854; CM, plantation journal, Apr. 17, 1845 (Clifton, pp. 190–91, 25).

52. Postwar rice production in the low country never approached the 1859 level; by 1899 it had fallen even further, and soon thereafter it was derisory compared with the rice boom—no longer dependent on tidal irrigation—then taking place in Louisiana and Texas (Peter Coclanis, *Shadow of a Dream* [New York, 1989], p. 142).

53. Skinner to CM, Jan. 21, 1852, DU. See chapter 6.

54. LM, "Visit to Charleston [late 1863]," in LM, "Book, 1861–1866" (SHC). LM's sketch of the seven triangular log tents which housed the 1852 refugees is in his "Notebook 1852" (DU).

55. GM to LM, Oct. 1, 1854, SCL. Bill of lading (New York), Nov. 16, 1854; LM to R. Habersham & Son, Sept. 13, 1855 (draft); CM to LM, Feb. 24, 1859 (DU).

56. LM, note on 1854 slave list; Dr. J. M. Gregorie's bill, Mar. 8, 1855; LM to CM, Christmas 1854 (Clifton, pp. 183, 186, 189).

57. GM to LM, Dec. 11, 1860 (Clifton, p. 311).

58. F. L. Olmsted, *A Journey in the Back Country* (London, 1860), pp. 29–30.

59. Dr. Ogier's 1858 bill for the eight slaves, including medicines, was $164 (bill, Jan. 19, 1859 [filed 1858], [SCHS]).

60. Dr. William Bullock to CM, Dec. 12, 1857, DU. Betty traveled to Charleston on a sailing vessel which had delivered seed rice to Gowrie; thus no steamboat fare had to be paid. CM to LM, Mar. 26, 1858, DU.

61. CM, journal, [spring 1844, Apr. 15, 1845], (Clifton, pp. 10, 23). Profits are stated in table 1 (chapter 1).

62. Financial accounts, Jan., Dec. 1846; Jan. 12, 1849 (SCHS).

63. Doctors at Gowrie from 1857 through 1859 averaged charges of $148.00 for ninety-seven slaves (and the total included the $41.00 payment for Hector's eye). In 1855 the doctor's bill was $72.00 for eighty-eight slaves. These figures exclude the cost of medicines, which in these four years averaged $0.68 per slave (medical bills, IV [SHC]).

64. James Haynes to CM, June 1, 1846; Jesse Cooper to CM, Aug. 14, 1849 (Clifton, pp. 35, 71).

65. Cooper to CM, Mar. 1, June 17, 1850 (SCHS).

66. K. W. Skinner to CM, Sept. 7–9, 1851 (Clifton, pp. 85–86).

67. Skinner to CM, May 15, 23, 1852 (Clifton, pp. 97–98).

68. Skinner to CM, Oct. 31, Nov. 4, 1852 (Clifton, pp. 125–26).

69. Skinner to CM, May 15, Nov. 19, 1852 (Clifton, pp. 97, 126–27).

70. The $8,700 profit includes (because the price of slaves was rising during the 1850s) a $1,700 "undistributed capital gain" resulting from the increased value of those slaves still alive.

71. R. Habersham & Son to CM, Sept. 16, 1852 (SCHS).

72. Overseer contract, 1853 (Clifton, p. 136).

73. LM to CM, Mar. 20, 1853 (Clifton, p. 149).

74. LM, note on 1854 slave list, (Clifton, p. 185).

75. LM to CM, Christmas 1854 (Clifton, p. 189).

76. LM to CM, Dec. 26, 28, 1854 (Clifton, pp. 190–92).

77. Stephen Clark to LM, July 15, Aug. 10, 1855 (Clifton, pp. 195–96).

78. Venters to CM, Oct. 23, 1857 (DU).

79. CM, memo, Apr. 21, 1844 (DU). James Haynes to CM, Nov. 2, 1846, Mar. 23, 1847; CM, plantation journal, Apr. 14, 1845; CM to LM, Mar. 12, 1859 (Clifton, pp. 422, 51, 23, 282).

80. CM, essay on "Rice Culture, by Open-Planting" (July 1852), (Clifton, p. 102). Skinner to CM, Feb. 8, 1852 (Clifton, p. 91). Jesse Cooper to CM, Feb. 14, Mar. 1, 1850 (SCHS).

81. LM, "Season of 1876" (IV, SHC). CM, Memo, Dec. 1839 (II, SHC).

82. Skinner to CM, Nov. 13, 1851 (DU). The larger flatboat which had to fit into this canal was four feet deep, twelve feet wide, and forty-five feet long. Skinner to Robert Habersham & Son, Dec. 21, 1851 (Clifton, p. 86).

83. Skinner to CM, Jan. 21, 1852 (DU), and Jan. 24, 1852 (Clifton, p. 89).

84. The tidal-powered threshing mill—on which Manigault relied at the original Gowrie tract from 1846 until even after he started using his new steam thresher at East Hermitage in 1849—was incapacitated for a month while broken floodgates for the millpond were being repaired.

85. Jesse Cooper to CM, Nov. 22 [misprinted "Nov. 23"], 1849; LM to CM, Mar. 1, 1853 (Clifton, pp. 75, 142).

86. Newspaper clipping [n.d.], pasted in LM, journal [ca. June 1865] (IV, SHC). Eleven years after the Civil War, Louis Manigault once hired Irish workers to do the winter's ditching, but their expense helped impel him quickly to abandon the unprofitable experiment of managing the free-labor plantation himself (James M. Clifton, "A Half-Century of a Georgia Rice Plantation," *North Carolina Historical Review* 47 [1970]: 414–15). By 1890 low-country rice plantations were on their way to extinction, being rapidly replaced by new, mechanized, labor-efficient plantations west of the Mississippi which did not rely on tidal irrigation.

87. Emphasis added. CM to LM, Dec. 28, 1858; Jan. 4, 1859 (Clifton, pp. 267, 270). See pp. 198–99.

88. James Coward to CM, Mar. 17, 1845 (SCHS).

89. Similarly, Charles presumed the overseer likely to force the aforementioned Nanny to work outdoors in bad weather. CM to LM, Jan. 4, 1859; Feb. 20, 1853; 1853 overseer contract (Clifton, pp. 270, 139, 136).

90. CM to LM, Feb. 20, 1853; Jan. 29, 19, 22, 1857; Jan. 20, 1859; LM, notes on 1858 slave list (Clifton, pp. 138–39; 244, 241, 243; 274; 265).

91. Wood, *Black Majority,* pp. 83–84, 86–90. Although Wood's introduction of modern medical evidence into a historians' debate has proved very valuable, he incautiously quoted a claim that in eighteenth-century Jamaica one doctor had *never* met among blacks "a pure tertium intermittent." Thus, while correctly suggesting that whites died even faster than blacks of malaria, Wood may inadvertently have led some readers to underestimate the debilitating or fatal impact of that disease upon thousands of low-country slaves. A more recent, more complex discussion of blacks' defenses against malaria is in Kenneth Kiple and Virginia King, *Another Dimension to the Black Diaspora: Diet, Disease, and Racism* (Cambridge, England, 1981), pp. 15–22, 50–57.

92. Skinner to CM, July 12, Sept. [9], 1851, July 31, Aug. 14, 1852, Clifton, pp. 83, 86, 114. A former South Carolina bondsman testified that a slave with ague and accompanying fever might well be forced to continue field work until the illness became acute (Charles Ball, *Fifty Years a Slave* [1836; rpt. (ed. Philip Foner) New York, 1970], p. 207). The previously quoted letter of Jesse Cooper's makes plain that a

Gowrie overseer, knowing that slaves were not fully recovered from an illness, might nevertheless send them to work in the harvest (Cooper to CM, Sept. 4, 1850 (SCHS), quoted on p. 58.)

93. Skinner to CM, Sept. 4, 1852, Clifton, p. 117. Olmsted, *Journey in the Seaboard Slave States,* p. 418; cf. Olmsted's further comments on the blacks' susceptibility to malaria, quoted on p. 54.

94. *Journal,* p. 145. In this passage Olmsted called malaria "intermittent fever" (*Journey in the Seaboard Slave States,* p. 474).

95. John Butler to Pierce Butler, Jan. 31, 1841, Wister MS (HSP).

96. The phrase is the Scottish naval captain Basil Hall's (Hall, *Travels in North America* [Edinburgh, 1829], 3:188).

97. Olmsted, *Journey in the Back Country,* p. 78.

98. I have omitted the years 1846 through 1848, when the Manigaults were in Europe, as data on births and on the year of women's deaths are too fragmentary for analysis during this period. One further instance, however, certainly occurred during these years: in 1848 a woman still in the house after a very recent confinement contracted and died of dysentery. This (ninth) case is not included in the statistics given in the text (Jesse Cooper to R. Habersham & Son, June 20, 1848 [copy], [SCHS]).

99. Elsey, who had been made pregnant by the Silk Hope overseer, died at Gowrie in 1838 soon after bearing his child. Renty's wife, Charlotte, died in 1840 soon after the birth of Fortune (the perennial runaway). John Izard's wife, Matty, died in 1844 soon after the birth of their baby, and so did Short Jack's wife, Susey, in the same year. Sibby died soon after her infant Sary was born in 1850; Crecie (Ishmael's wife) soon after her baby Cato was born in 1854; Phillis soon after the birth of a short-lived infant in 1855; and Joaney (boat captain Hector's wife) soon after the birth of an anonymous child in 1862. Childbirth was not, of course, the immediate cause of every one of these deaths: Matty, for example, contracted pleurisy six days after her baby's birth and was dead four days later. Similarly, Phillis died of a bowel complaint shortly after her confinement, and one presumes that her exhaustion from childbirth—like Matty's—undermined her resistance against an illness which need not otherwise have been fatal. The annual lists usually do not permit this degree of accuracy in dating the connection between childbirth and the mother's subsequent death; yet the number of such deaths is so striking as to make it probable that childbearing was the greatest direct hazard to the health of young and middle-aged slave women. (And as about 40 percent of Gowrie's births were never recorded in the annual lists [because the infants died too soon], the discussion here probably understates the actual deleterious effects of childbirth on the health of the slave women.)

100. A. R. Bagshaw to CM, June 15, 1844; James Haynes to CM, Nov. 2, 1846; May 24, 1847 (Clifton, pp. 14, 42, 57). Gynecologic illnesses are further discussed in chapter 8.

101. James Haynes to CM, Apr. 21, 1846; Oct. 25, 1847 (Clifton, pp. 34, 59).

102. Skinner to CM, July 12, 1851 (Clifton, p. 83).

103. Max Farrand, ed., *Records of the Federal Convention of 1787,* 4 vols. (New Haven, Conn., 1937), 2:371.

104. But cf. pp. 371–72, 421–22.

105. My calculations, based on figures in Richard Steckel, "Slave Mortality," *Social Science History* 3 (1979): 90, 92, 106.

106. See chapter 15.

107. Steckel, "Slave Mortality," p. 90.

108. Hall, *Travels in North America,* 3:188, 196, 205. For another illustration of

the low-country rice swamps' contemporary ill repute see E. S. Abdy, *Tour in the United States* (London, 1835), 2:230.

109. The destination of Bryan's newly acquired Maryland slaves was no doubt his Broughton Island, Georgia, rice plantation, visible one-third of a mile across the Altamaha estuary from Butler Island (the plantation discussed in chapters 8–10). Broughton's first rice planter, William Brailsford, gave up the island because so many of his slaves there died in the hurricane of 1804. Rice planting nevertheless continued on the island under its later owner, Thomas Bryan, the "careless desolation" of whose plantation in 1839—its "ruinous, rackrent, tumble-down house," and "the untidy, slatternly, all but beggarly appearance" of Bryan's wife (daughter of a former governor of Georgia)—is recorded in Frances Kemble's *Journal,* pp. 278–79; 388, 403, xl, 57. Sidney Fisher, diary, May 13, 1846, in Nicholas B. Wainwright, ed., *A Philadelphia Perspective* (Philadelphia, 1967), pp. 188, 181–82.

110. LM, "Visit to Charleston," Dec. 2, 1863, in LM, "Book, 1861–1866" (SHC).

111. The term was Oliver Ellsworth's, in his previously quoted speech at the Constitutional Convention of 1787.

Chapter 4

1. Any otherwise undocumented statements in this chapter are based on Gowrie's annual slave lists and on overseers' letters. The annual lists are described in chapter 3 (note 4). My way of inferring the birth year for each slave is explained in this chapter's note 4.

I focus on the sixty-one slaves resident at Gowrie on Nov. 30, 1848, because records are much fuller for them than for the fifty-eight bondsmen and women Manigault sent from Dec. 1848 to Feb. 1849 to work his newly acquired property at "East Hermitage." (Nearly all of the new slaves lived on the new tract nearly half a mile from the sixty-one established residents at "Gowrie." It should therefore be noted that—while for convenience I customarily use "Gowrie" to refer to both plantations— the term usually refers in this chapter only to the older tract.)

2. This statement is based on all the women of childbearing age, resident at Gowrie on Nov. 30, 1848, for whom firm information is available. As the early lives of Binkey and Hannah are uncertain, and as Peggy and Crecie died before reaching age twenty-eight, the group comprises fifteen women. Seven probably had only one marriage (Amey, Betty, Joaney, Louisa, Nancy, and probably Binah Currie and Hester). Eight had more than one marriage:

2 marriages :	4 women		(Juna, Big Lucy, Pender, Sary)
3 "	: 1		(Julia)
4 "	: 2	"	(Catherine, Minty)
5 "	: 1		(Rhina)

Details on these marriages appear in the latter half of this chapter.

3. The probable number of unlisted births was about 66 percent higher than the number of listed births, because in addition to the eighty-nine babies born at Gowrie (1833–61) who appear in the slave lists, an estimated fifty-nine others were born during this period who died before the subsequent list was compiled. (59/89 = 66%; this estimate is printed in the bottom line of appendix table 1 in appendix B; the reasoning behind the estimate is explained in appendix B).

4. Throughout this chapter it should be understood that many seemingly confident assertions about dates and ages of slaves are really only approximations. Ned was listed as "50" on Jan. 1, 1833, but in fact he probably was older. Though tempting, it would be a mistake to use the ages recorded by Charles Manigault on the 1849 list (Clifton, pp. 64–66) because they obviously are very approximate and inaccurate—usually being recorded in multiples of five. And Charles Manigault (and later Louis) made a few demonstrably large errors in registering or calculating the ages of certain slaves. For date of birth I have therefore relied, wherever possible, on the age of the slave when first recorded at Gowrie. This is usually the one specified in 1833 (Clifton, pp. 3–6), or the one shown on manuscript lists from 1833 to 1845, or (for slaves bought in 1849) the one on Clifton, pp. 67–68. This procedure appears to be reasonably satisfactory for slaves imported from Silk Hope; but the ages of those whom Manigault purchased are sure to be less accurate, because vendors had strong incentives to understate the ages of adult slaves, and (in view of the high child mortality rate) to overstate the ages of children. Consequently, I have sometimes adjusted the alleged age of a purchased slave in light of later evidence.

The most frequent uncertainty about year of birth arises when a slave was born between April of one year and April of the next. In these cases, unless there is strong evidence to do otherwise, I have assumed the latter year as the time of birth of slaves imported from Silk Hope, and for purchased child slaves; and the former year as the time of birth of purchased adults—i.e., slaves age sixteen or older. To insert "probably" or "approximately" in every such case would make the text unreadable.

Many of the dates, however, are exact; thus the severe attack of dysentery which ended Harry's being driver was reported in James Haynes to CM, July 1, 1846; and Binah's date of death was added onto the 1852 slave list.

5. John died in infancy; Bina (not to be mistaken for either Binah the nurse or Binah Currie), Matilda, and Becky died in the Asiatic cholera of 1834; and Peggy died at twenty-two in 1850.

6. CM, 1833 slave list (Clifton, p. 5).

7. CM to James Haynes, Mar. 1, 1847; to LM, Jan. 20, 1862 (Clifton, pp. 49, 337); 1850 slave List (SHC).

8. That rice plantations' irrigation systems presented a common hazard to poorly supervised slave children is suggested by a notation in the Butler Papers: Hannibal, aged one, "drowned in a ditch" at Pierce Butler's low-country Georgia estate in June 1816. Frances Kemble was struck by the neglect of young slave children at this same rice plantation. The voluntary movement by freedwomen away from full-time field labor toward caring for their children is regarded by Roger Ransom and Richard Sutch as one of the most far-reaching economic consequences of emancipation ("Births and deaths, 1816," Butler Papers [HSP]; Kemble, *Journal,* pp. 156–57; Roger Ransom and Richard Sutch, *One Kind of Freedom* [New York, 1977], pp. 6, 44–47, 55).

9. CM, note on inventory, Jan. 13, 1857, IV (SHC); James Haynes to CM, Sept. 15, 1845 (Clifton, p. 29).

10. Ned remarried about 1835, espousing a daughter of Old Fortune named Julia (Howard), by whom he had two short-lived children.

11. LM, journal, Mar. 22, 1867; CM to LM, Aug. 25, 1856 (Clifton, pp. 361, 225).

12. LM, journal, Mar. 22, 1867; K. W. Skinner to CM, Oct. 9, 1852 (Clifton, pp. 361, 122).

13. LM, 1856 slave list (Clifton, p. 220).

14. LM, journal, Mar. 22, 1867; A. R. Bagshaw to CM, Oct. 20, 1844; LM to CM, Dec. 28, 1852 (Clifton, pp. 363, 19, 133).

15. The age given by LM in Clifton, p. 317, is incorrect; cf. Clifton, p. 78.

16. See chapter 5.

17. Stephen Clark to CM, Sept. 25, 1855 (Clifton, p. 198).

18. LM to CM, Dec. 5, 1861 (Clifton, p. 331).

19. CM to LM, undated [ca. Apr. 20, 1858], file 11/277/52 (SCHS); cf. Clifton, p. 264.

20. LM, journal, Mar. 22, 1867, Clifton (p. 357).

21. Lucy had been imported from Silk Hope in 1837 with her previous husband and their baby. The baby, of course, had soon died, and so did her husband at the age of twenty-eight; after about a year's interval, Lucy tried her luck again with Primus.

22. James Haynes to CM, Nov. 24, 1847 (Clifton, p. 60).

23. K. W. Skinner to CM, Aug. 20, 1852; CM to LM, Oct. 18, 1856 (Clifton, pp. 115, 230).

24. See chapter 5.

25. T. R. Heargroves to CM, Nov. 19, 1835 (SCHS).

26. Although it is not certain that John and Matty were married before 1842, they probably were living together before then whenever John was sent from Silk Hope to work at Gowrie, which seems to have occurred for several months in each of a number of years after 1835. In 1840, for example, he was sent off from Charleston to walk to the Savannah River; and when he came permanently to Gowrie in 1842, he and Matty were housed together (Habersham accounts, Sept. 2, 1835, May 2, 1836 [SCHS]; on the 1840 trip, II [SHC]).

27. A. R. Bagshaw to CM, July 20, 1844 (Clifton, p. 14).

28. The overseer's words about her. Jesse Cooper to CM, July 30, 1849 (Clifton, p. 69).

29. E.g., LM to CM, Mar. 1, 6, 1853 (Clifton, pp. 141, 145).

30. Skinner to CM, Jan. 21, 1852; Stephen Clark to CM, Oct. 8, 1853 (Clifton, pp. 88, 160). Margaret's family circumstances are delineated later in this chapter.

31. I.e., Judy's eldest child.

32. See pp. 115–16.

33. Jane's complex tale is recounted at the end of chapter 5.

34. LM to CM, Nov. 24, 1861 (Clifton, p. 328).

35. A. R. Bagshaw to CM, Aug. 14, 24, Sept. 14, Oct. 20, 1844; LM to CM, Dec. 28, 1852 (Clifton, pp. 15–17, 19, 133).

36. Bishop Andrew was expansive in his remarks about certain other plantations he visited on this tour, but very reserved about Gowrie (*Annals of Southern Methodism,* III, 306, [DU]. CM to LM, Apr. 9, 1857 [Clifton, p. 247]).

37. LM to CM, Nov. 24, 1861; CM to William Capers, Jan. 26, 1862; LM, journal, Mar. 22, 1867 (Clifton, pp. 328, 339, 363).

38. LM, journal, Apr. 1858; 1859 slave List (Clifton, pp. 250, 289).

39. LM, journal, Mar. 22, 1867 (Clifton, p. 359).

40. See chapter 5. LM to CM, Apr. 9, 1853; Stephen Clark to LM, July 23, 1853 (Clifton, pp. 151, 157). LM, "New Hands [1853]," (DU).

41. Tommy, like Catherine, had had three previous marriages. By the age of twenty he was married to Matty (a different Matty, not Betsey's daughter), but their child died quickly and Matty did too a few years later. At twenty-eight he married Minty, thirteen years his senior. She died after two years. He then married nineteen-year-old Phiby, but she was dead in two years, this time from "cholera."

42. 1858 allowance list; William Capers to LM, Mar. 8, 1864, IV, (SHC).

43. LM, journal, Mar. 22, 1867 (Clifton, p. 363).

44. I include among the sixteen children of this generation: (1) fourteen grandchildren of Old Mary's; (2) an infant of Charles's wife, Juna, fathered by a Silk Hope slave, from whom Charles Manigault separated Juna when he deported her to Gowrie; and (3) a foster child of Charles and Juna's.

45. See p. 108.

46. Bob's character is discussed near the end of chapter 5.

47. LM, 1860 slave list (Clifton), p. 295.

48. A. R. Bagshaw to CM, Aug. 14, 1844 (Clifton, p. 15). The foregoing enumeration of families at Gowrie in Nov. 1848 omits two unattached people: the superannuated ratcatcher Abram, and an "Old Betsey" (not to be confused with cooper George's mother) who died in 1853 at the age of forty-seven.

49. Here, as throughout this chapter, I speak of the sixty-one slaves who lived at Gowrie on Nov. 30, 1848. My statements about the families usually refer to births, deaths, marriages, and other events between 1833 and 1864, though sometimes information is available earlier or later. The number of surviving children is calculated as of March 1864.

50. The nineteen women include every female born between 1807 and 1832 who resided at Gowrie on Nov. 30, 1848. Their ages then ranged from sixteen to forty-one.

51. Jane, Betsey's unmarried daughter, was not shiped from Silk Hope to Gowrie until after Nov. 1848; her name therefore is not included in these calculations.

52. In one instance, however, the apparent absence of births may simply result from insufficient data: Binkey was already twenty-four when she first appears in the records, and she may well have had children (who did not survive) before 1833.

53. Although these women's average number of recorded births was 3.0, their actual fertility rate was probably at least 5.0, because the number of births at Gowrie was at least 66 percent higher than the number of infants surviving long enough to be recorded in the annual lists (see p. 85 and its note 3). Yet on other American rice plantations the slave women's fertility was about 6.6 (see p. 415; and see final paragraph of this note). Two possible explanations—both probably correct—would account for Gowrie's peculiar record: (1) slave women at Gowrie apparently died even younger (and therefore lived only long enough to produce fewer children) than at most rice plantations; and (2) Gowrie's infant mortality (during the first six months) was probably even higher than the 32.6 percent rate at the Butler Island rice plantation. Therefore, its child mortality rate (to age fifteen) was probably even higher than I have estimated.

At Gowrie a fertility rate of 5.0, combined with a child mortality rate (to age *fifteen*) of 89 percent would have resulted (if the average slave woman was thirty years old at the birth of her median child) in a decennial population decrease of 35 percent. This is below the 39 percent decennial decrease actually recorded at Gowrie (see p. 415 and its note). The discrepancy suggests that I have underestimated Gowrie's infant mortality, and that child mortality there (to age *fifteen*) may in fact have been 91 percent.

(To contrast the fertility rate of these Gowrie women (ca. 5.0) with that of slave women on other rice plantations (ca. 6.6) is legitimate, because: (1) In 1864, when Gowrie's record ceases, the eldest of these nineteen women was fifty-seven, and even the youngest—at thirty-two—had not very many childbearing years still to come; but (2) the fertility rate on other plantations was that of *all* rice slave women who had survived to age fifteen, while the Gowrie group was older, comprising all women of childbearing age who were at the plantation in November 1848. Thus (1) the fertility of the Gowrie women would have been a little *higher* than 5.0 by the time all these women reached the end of their childbearing years; but (2) the fertility of those women on other rice plantations *who survived to the same ages as the Gowrie women had attained by Nov. 1848* would have been *higher* than 6.6. Therefore, the contrast between Gowrie and other plantations would have remained as great as (or greater than) the contrast between 5.0 and 6.6.)

54. This paragraph is based on the usual group of the sixty-one slaves who lived at Gowrie on Nov. 30, 1848, *plus* all other women known to have married men in this group. Altogether thirty-seven such women lived to the age of twenty or more. The age at which eight of these first married is totally unknown: these are usually "old" women like Hannah and Maria, whose marriages probably occurred before the Gowrie records begin. For four other women something is known about the date of marriage, but so little that the information could be very misleading. Thus one knows that Bess was no more than twenty-one when her child Charles was conceived, but she may have been much younger when she married. Instead of engaging in baseless speculations about when such women married, one obviously must constrict the discussion to the twenty-five women about whom relatively firm dates are available.

55. When I speak of "marriage," I refer to a man and woman's living together regularly so that they appear together in the annual lists—the man always listed just before the woman. In the 1850 list Manigault placed a mark (⌐) at the upper left of the man's name, and a mark (∟) at the lower left of the couple's last child, to demarcate all nuclear families; and in the Dec. 1837 list a bracket ({) at the left of the nuclear family was inscribed for the same purpose. Brackets on the Jan. 1833 list demarcate extended families (1837 and 1850 lists [SHC]. 1833 list [Clifton, pp. 3–6]).

My inference as to the date of marriage is always based on the first time a man's name is relocated on an annual list to place him just before a particular woman, or the first time the woman's name is relocated to put her just after that man. Often other evidence—such as the (subsequent) penciled-in insertion of an infant's name alongside the mother's inked name—confirms the inference, and indicates the year when the child was born.

I usually cannot prove that these were formal marriages (though occasionally an overseer's letter makes it plain—e.g., the previously cited announcement that "Carpenter John [Izard] has got his wife [Matty] up at last" [Bagshaw to CM, July 20, 1844 (Clifton, p. 14)]). But family customs of other American slaves, and the longevity of many of the Gowrie connections (like that of driver Charles and Juna) make it probable that "marriage" is a proper term for most of these unions.

56. Amey was either twenty or twenty-one when she married, and Julia nineteen to twenty-one. The other twenty-one of these twenty-three women were all certainly no more than twenty when they married or conceived their first child. Several of the ages in the table are probably too high, for I have sometimes had to use the date of conception of the first child when there may well have been a substantially earlier marriage date. On the other hand, I have accepted the vendor's statements about the ages of Mary and Phillis (he said Phillis was thirty-five and had a nineteen-year-old child); and this may have led to two small errors in the opposite direction. On the whole, I believe my assertions in this paragraph probably overstate the actual ages of the women at marriage or first conception, but I have wished to err on the side of caution.

57. E.g., Herbert Gutman and Richard Sutch, "Victorians All?" in Paul David, ed., *Reckoning with Slavery* (New York, 1976), pp. 141–46.

58. The group is the same as for the preceding paragraph: the sixty-one slaves at Gowrie on Nov. 30, 1848, plus all other women married by men in this group. Ages of couples are often known (later in the marriage) even when the date of marriage is unknown, and the statements in the text are based upon the forty-seven marriages for

which the age gap can confidently be determined. In a few cases two marriages involve the same person—e.g., Betsey's marriages to carpenter Tony and, subsequently, to driver Harry.

59. The group in table 14 is that specified in note 58.

60. CM, undated MS [1833], 11/277/52, (SCHS).

61. "I allow no strange Negro to take a wife on my place" (CM to Jesse Cooper [a new overseer], Jan. 10, 1848 [Clifton, p. 62]).

62. See p. 107.

63. That large age gaps may also have been common on other plantations—for the same reasons as at Gowrie—is suggested by the examples just cited of Joe and Die, and of Daniel and Miley, both of which couples Manigault bought in South Carolina.

64. T. R. Heargroves to CM, Nov. 19, 1835 (SCHS); Clifton, p. 5.

65. This was Juna's infant, probably still breast-feeding, who could not well be separated from her eighteen-year-old mother.

66. Silk Hope slave list, Nov. 5, 1833, II (SHC); "Negroes at Gowrie, Dec. 3, 1848" (DU); GM to LM, Jan. 11, 1863 (SCHS).

67. In 1846 Manigault acknowledged that the Silk Hope "gang has not yet recovered the 30 young & prime [hands] which I *picked out* of it for Gowrie 12 years ago" (CM to James Haynes, Aug. 15, 1846 (emphasis added), [Clifton, p. 37]).

68. On the terms of McAlpin's original offer: James Haynes to CM, June 1, 1846; cf. CM, journal, Dec. 1848 (Clifton, pp. 35, 32).

69. The most likely residence of Hannah's husband was East Hermitage, because it was almost the only plantation readily accessible to Gowrie, and because McAlpin owned both Gowrie and East Hermitage before 1833 (by which time the twenty-five-year-old Hannah was probably already married). Another reason for believing Hannah's husband an East Hermitage slave of McAlpin's was that she bore no child after McAlpin removed his slaves late in 1848, except the one with which she was then pregnant. Although she was by then forty-one, this would still seem a slightly surprising coincidence unless her husband had been at East Hermitage.

70. These are, again, the nineteen women of childbearing age living there on Nov. 30, 1848.

71. The percentages in these paragraphs, and in table 15, add up to more than 100 percent because several women fall into more than one category. Thus Amey's marriage was broken by deportation, but it had by then survived long enough to count as a "long" marriage.

72. 1835 and 1844 lists; Apr. 1837 list (SHC).

73. CM, notes on inventory of slaves, Jan. 13, 1857, IV (SHC). 1857 slave list, Clifton, pp. 249, 296, 340. (I have taken Will's age from LM's slave list, not from the vendor's apparently mendacious inventory.)

74. Manigault had special difficulty in preventing newly purchased slaves from running away. See chapter 5.

75. CM to Jesse Cooper, July 12, 1848 (Clifton, p. 64).

76. 1853 overseer contract (Clifton, p. 136).

77. Slave lists, Apr. 1837, Nov. 1838 (SHC).

78. Jesse Cooper to CM, July 30, 1849; LM to CM, Mar. 6, 1853 (Clifton, pp. 69, 145).

79. LM to Joseph Dench, Apr. 15, 1854 (DU). Leonard Venters to CM, Oct. 9, 30, Nov. 7, 1857 (Clifton, pp. 252–53).

80. CM to LM, Apr. 17, 1859; William Capers to LM, July 22, 1860; LM, note on 1861 slave list (Clifton, pp. 287, 303, 317).

81. C. Vann Woodward and Elisabeth Muhlenfeld, eds., *The Private Mary Chesnut: The Unpublished Civil War Diaries* (New York, 1984), Mar. 18, 1861, p. 42.

82. C. Vann Woodward, (ed., *Mary Chesnut's Civil War* (New Haven, Conn., 1981), pp. 243, 20. Although the words "those beastly negress beauties" were penned by Chesnut in the 1880s, they accurately represent her original emotion on Nov. 26, 1861, when her diary entry, "These beastly negroes," referred particularly to a mulatto slave woman, Martha Adamson (Woodward and Muhlenfeld, *The Private Mary Chesnut*, p. 207).

83. CM, "Respecting Slavery," p. 16; CM, souvenirs, p. 10 (SCL).

84. CM to Charles H. Manigault (CM's eldest son), Oct. 1, 1846 (typescript), (SCL).

85. CM to LM, Jan. 30, 1864 (SCHS). CM's reference to "true Izard blood" implies that John Izard—born in 1815—was a grandson (or great-grandson) either of Charles Manigault's grandfather Senator Ralph Izard or of Senator Izard's brother.

86. Ibid. GM, "Plantation Memo book, 1868–79," Nov.–Dec. 1871; Apr. 4, 1877 (SCHS).

87. See chapter 5.

88. 1850, 1851 lists (SHC); LM, "Notebook, 1852," "New Hands at East Hermitage [and Gowrie]", [1853, misdated "ca. 1860"], (DU).

89. LM to CM, Jan. 8, 1854, Clifton, p. 167. Julia Smith, *Slavery and Rice Culture in Low Country Georgia* (Knoxville, Tenn., 1985), pp. 67, 54 n.

90. E. L. Ladurie, *The French Peasantry, 1450–1660* (trans. Alan Sheridan; Aldershot, England, 1987), pp. 279–80, 283–84.

91. Theodore Rosengarten, ed., *All God's Dangers* (New York, 1974).

92. LM, 1861 slave List, Clifton, p. 319.

93. The figures here and in ensuing paragraphs are based as usual upon the nineteen women, born between 1807 and 1832, who lived at Gowrie on Nov. 30, 1848, before Manigault imported additional slaves to work the newly purchased East Hermitage tract.

94. Binah Currie's husband was the miller, Betty's was the cooper, Amey's was carpenter Jack Savage, and Hester's was driver Robert. Thus of these seven women in this group (including Joaney), only Big Lucy and Louisa were married to field hands.

95. Herbert Gutman, *The Black Family in Slavery and Freedom, 1750–1925* (New York, 1976), e.g., p. 65.

96. In addition to the twelve survivors, a thirteenth child—Hannah's Nat—had lived to age twenty-six but then died in 1862 without surviving issue.

97. Skinner to CM, May 30, 1851 (Clifton, p. 80).

98. LM to CM, Feb. 27, 1853 (Clifton, p. 140).

99. Deborah White's *Ar'n't I a Woman* (New York, 1985) points toward a more realistic assessment of the slaves' family institutions than prevailed during the 1970s.

100. One thinks, for example, of the stimulating hypotheses of Richard Steckel, "Birth Weights and Infant Mortality Among American Slaves," *Explorations in Economic History* 23 (1986): 173–98.

Chapter 5

1. Jesse Cooper to CM, Aug. 14, 1849; CM to LM, Feb. 21, 1856; Mar. 16, 1860 (Clifton, pp. 71, 210, 293).

Alfred Huger expected a "prime hand" to cultivate only about two acres of rice land; at Gowrie in 1833 the ratio was closer to five, and in the late 1850s it approached eleven acres per hand. In 1857 Gowrie's fifty-five prime hands (not including drivers, artisans, and house servants) cultivated over six hundred acres of rice land. Clifton, p. 210 for Huger and pp. 2–6, 248–49 for Gowrie.

2. Here, as elsewhere in this work, I use "master" wherever convenient in preference to "owner." The word "owner" is a euphemism, developed in Roman law to throw a veil of legitimation—through the concept of "property"—over what is essentially domination of one human being over another. The term "master" conveys nakedly the power relation at the heart of slavery. See Orlando Patterson, *Slavery and Social Death* (Cambridge, Mass., 1982), esp. pp. 18, 21, 28–32.

3. CM to LM, Mar. 6, 10, 1854 (Clifton, pp. 177–79).

4. CM to James Haynes, Mar. 1, 1847 (Clifton, pp. 49–50).

5. Stephen Clark to LM, Jan. 21, 1854; 1853 slave list; LM to CM, Jan. 6, 1854 (Clifton, pp. 171, 152, 164).

6. LM, journal, Sept. 20, 1862; CM to LM, Apr. 5, 1859 (Clifton, pp. 342, 285). Bagshaw to CM, June 15, 1842 (SCL).

7. CM to LM, Apr. 7, 1859 (Clifton, p. 286).

8. Skinner to CM, Oct. 9, 1852 (Clifton, pp. 121–22).

9. Capers to LM, Sept. 5, 1859 (emphasis in the original); Aug. 8, 1859 (DU).

10. Capers to CM, Nov. 14, 1861 (Clifton, p. 325); to LM, June 17, July 2, 9, Aug. 14, 1863 (DU).

11. Cf. the reference to the Charleston workhouse in Michael Hindus's otherwise excellent *Prison and Plantation* (Chapel Hill, N.C., 1980), pp. 147–49. CM to LM, Jan. 26, 1860, to William Capers, Jan. 26, 1862 (Clifton, pp. 292, 339). Thomas R. Heargroves to CM, Oct. 13, 1835 (SCHS).

12. CM to LM, Jan. 20, 1862 (Clifton, p. 337).

13. LM, journal, June 12, 1862; LM to CM, Dec. 5, 1861 (Clifton, pp. 319, 331).

14. LM to CM, Nov. 24, 1861 (Clifton, p. 328). Chatham County Jail receipt, Jan. 31, 1860 (DU).

15. Capers to LM, Aug. 8, 1859; CM to LM, Mar. 6, 1861 (DU). CM hadn't visited Gowrie for several years, and in this 1861 letter he confused Little George Hunt with Jack Savage's son Harry, who also had been trained as a carpenter boy under his father but had died in 1858. When, in 1861, CM wrote "the Carpenter Boy Harry," he could only have meant the carpenter boy George.

16. Skinner to CM, Jan. 21, 1852 (Clifton, p. 88).

17. CM to LM, Dec. 6, 1855 (Clifton, p. 201). Overseer Clark complained that year of Gowrie's labor shortage: Clark to LM, Aug. 10, 1855 (Clifton, p. 196).

18. Capers to CM, Sept. 21, 1863; CM to Anthony Barclay, Apr. 15, 1847 (Clifton, pp. 345, 54). Thomas Clay to Richard Arnold, Sept. 29, 1837, in Charles Hoffmann and Tess Hoffmann, *North by South: The Two Lives of Richard Arnold* (Athens, Ga., 1988), p. 31.

19. These include ten sold before Apr. 1861 (and counted as "Exports" in chapter 3's table 6) and two thereafter. They were Friday (1833); Minda (1834); Charlotte (Friday's sister, 1837); probably Quash (1844); Posh (1852); Prince, William, Frederick, and Jane (1854); Fortune (1860); Martha (late 1861); and Jack Savage (1863). There may have been others, unspecified in the sparse records between 1837 and 1844.

20. LM to CM, Jan. 6, 1854; CM to LM, Jan. 12, 1854 (Clifton, pp. 164, 168).

21. Skinner to CM, Jan. 27, 1852 (Clifton, p. 90). C. E. Waldhauer to [Stephen Clark], Nov. 30, 1853; Capers to CM, July 5, 1860; Middleton & Co. to LM, Dec. 14, 1853; R. Habersham & Son to CM, Dec. 27, 1854 (DU). LM to CM, Mar. 7, 1852 (Clifton, p. 94).

22. After the death in 1855 of Gowrie's overseer Stephen Clark, the captain of the local patrol—the overseer of a neighboring plantation—tried to bully Louis Manigault into serving on the patrol. Louis did not think his plantation needed the patrol's services, and he tried to avoid serving on it by requesting the patrol to cease visiting Gowrie. His father thought this poor policy: "It is a very good plan to have a Patroll agreement with ones neighbours for the Overseers to ride." But, of course, a gentleman should not have to participate in patrol duties. Charles advised trying to buy off the persistent captain by offering the free services of some Gowrie slaves to help strengthen an embankment on the neighbor's plantation. If this did not work, "it wont be very killing to pay" the statutory fine for failure to serve on the patrol. Louis made the offer, but the captain declined it civilly and persisted with his summonses to patrol duty. Apparently Louis then devised a more efficacious means of buying off the patrol captain: he hired him temporarily to oversee Gowrie during a brief period when Louis was attending the midwinter balls at Charleston, and before the new overseer Leonard Venters had been installed.

This is a nice instance of a relatively poor white man's exercising his democratic powers, as patrol captain, to harass a rich planter. (The patrol captain, rejecting Louis's letters, thrice within thirty-two days sent him summonses for the fortnightly patrol duty.) It also illustrates a gentleman's capacity to evade his democratic duties. CM to LM, Dec. 27, 1855; Jan. 10, 4, 1856; C. W. Jones to LM, Dec. 17, 1855 (Clifton, pp. 204, 206, 202). C. W. Jones to LM, Jan. 1, 14, 17, Feb. 8, 1856; George A. Pullen et al. to LM, Jan. 10, 1856 (DU).

23. CM to LM, Mar. 6, 1861 (DU). Thomas Clay to Richard Arnold, Sept. 29, 1837, in Hoffmann and Hoffmann, *North by South,* p. 31.

24. GM to LM, Jan. 21, 1861 (Clifton, p. 314).

25. Ibid.

26. E.g., E. A. Davis, ed., *Plantation Life in the Florida Parishes of Louisiana, 1836–1846 as Reflected in the Diary of Bennet H. Barrow* (1943; rpt. New York, 1967), Nov. 11, 1845; Solomon Northup, *Twelve Years a Slave* (1853; rpt. [ed. Sue Eakin and Joseph Logsdon] Baton Rouge, 1968), p. 186.

27. A fifth fugitive had returned before the others did, after only a week's absence, and he was spared the whipping.

28. LM to CM, Apr. 9, 1853 (Clifton, p. 150).

29. R. Habersham & Son accounts, Apr. 2, 1849; Sept. 28, 1846; Nov. 24, 1851 (SCHS).

30. CM to LM, Mar. 3, 1854; LM to CM, Dec. 28, 1854; Nov. 24, 1861 (Clifton, pp. 176, 193, 328).

31. Robert Fogel and Stanley Engerman, *Time on the Cross* (London, 1974), 1:174–75, 222.

32. For example, Olmsted attributed the supposed mental characteristics of blacks to the way Southern whites treated them: he referred to "the proverbial stupidity and dogged prejudice of the negro (but peculiar to him only as he is more carefully poisoned with ignorance than the laborer of other countries)" *A Journey in the Seaboard Slave States* [New York, 1856], p. 481).

33. Ibid., p. 388.

34. Olmsted, *A Journey in the Back Country* (London, 1860), p. 106. Cf. Eugene Genovese, *Roll, Jordan, Roll* (New York, 1974), esp. pp. 289–92, 311–12; and Fogel and Engerman, *Time on the Cross,* 1:180.

35. Although Dale Swan exaggerates low-country rice profits (by greatly overestimating the number of children who survived to an age when they might be sold West to

enhance a planter's profits), his conclusion is convincing, that big planters—in whose hands practically all American rice production was concentrated—were still making large profits in the late 1850s. These matters are discussed in my chapter 15 (Dale Swan, "The Structure and Profitability of the Antebellum Rice Industry: 1859" [Ph.D. diss., University of North Carolina, 1972]).

36. Olmsted, *Journey in the Seaboard Slave States,* pp. 480–81.

37. E.g., Raymond and Alice Bauer, "Day to Day Resistance to Slavery," *Journal of Negro History* 27 (1942): 388–419; Kenneth Stampp, *The Peculiar Institution* (London; rpt. 1964), pp. 101–12, 125–29.

38. Gavin Wright, *The Political Economy of the Cotton South* (New York, 1978), pp. 7, 90–94, 91 n.

39. Claims by blacks to land ownership were promoted in parts of coastal South Carolina by federal wartime policy, and by the postwar taxation and land policies of the state's Reconstruction governments.

40. CM, "Instructions for Sub-Overseer," 1845 (Clifton, p. 23).

41. LM, plantation journal, Apr. 24, 1860; CM to LM, Jan. 12, 1854 (the enumeration in brackets is added), (Clifton, pp. 289, 168). Eugene Genovese, *The Political Economy of Slavery* (New York, 1965), pp. 113, 112.

42. LM to CM, Jan. 6, 1854 (Clifton, p. 166).

43. CM, journal, 1844 (Clifton, pp. 8–9).

44. CM to James Haynes, Aug. 15, 1846 (Clifton, p. 37).

45. CM to LM, Oct. 18, 1856; to James Haynes, Mar. 1, 1847 (Clifton, pp. 230, 50). Other examples of the slaves' probably deliberate inefficiency in operating the threshing machinery are in James Haynes to CM, Apr. 22, 1847; and Leonard Venters to CM, Nov. 7, 1856 (Clifton, pp. 55, 232).

46. This was the trunk admired by a Carolinian neighbor of Manigault's (see chapter 4). LM to CM, Mar. 1, 1853; CM to LM, Aug. 25, 1856 (Clifton, pp. 141, 225).

47. E.g., Bagshaw to CM, July 20, 1844 (Clifton, p. 14).

48. Jesse Cooper to CM, July 30, 1849 (Clifton, p. 69). Jane's character is discussed at the end of this chapter.

49. LM to CM, Apr. 19, 23, 1853; CM to LM, Apr. 20, 1853 (Clifton, pp. 155–56).

50. Venters to CM, Sept. 19, 1856 (Clifton, p. 226). Bagshaw to CM, June 15, 1842 (SCL). Slave lists, 1841, 1842 (SHC).

51. Skinner to CM, Oct. 13, 1852; Venters to CM, Oct. 30, 1857 (Clifton, pp. 123, 253).

52. Charles Manigault believed Mrs. Clark was trying to cheat him, and claimed she was attempting the same thing in regard to some horses. There is no way now to assess the balance between the rival cupidities of the overseer's wife and of the Gowrie slaves (J. L. Courtney to CM, Feb. 18, 1856 [DU]. CM to LM, Feb. 28, 1856 [Clifton, p. 211]; Mar. 30, 1856 [DU]).

53. Emphasis added. Bagshaw to CM, June 15, 1842 (SCL).

54. CM to LM, Mar. 21, 1861 (DU). Bagshaw to CM, July 10, 1842 (SCL). CM to LM, Feb. 28, 1856 (Clifton, p. 211). K. W. Skinner to CM, Jan. 27, 1852 (Clifton, pp. 89–90), also alludes to the slaves' theft of food.

55. CM to Jesse Cooper, Jan. 10, 1848; James Haynes to CM, Nov. 24, 1847 (Clifton, pp. 62, 60). Ten percent was less improbable than the figure of 25 percent of his own rice crop which General C. C. Pinckney claimed was annually lost to thieves (William Freehling, *Prelude to Civil War* [New York, 1966], p. 63).

56. Skinner to CM, May 30, 1851; June 6, 1852 (Clifton, pp. 80, 99). 1853 slave list (SHC). See pp. 174–75.

57. Cf., e.g., Dusinberre, *Civil War Issues in Philadelphia, 1856–1865* (Philadelphia, 1965), pp. 53–54. There were about four million slaves in 1860.

58. Although Jack's anxiety no doubt arose largely from his fear of condign punishment if any mischance should befall Kemble, it still suggests that danger from rattlesnakes was strongly apprehended (Kemble, *Journal,* p. 241).

59. Louis's words were in Spanish, a language to which he resorted when in a jocular mood, or to cover up embarrassment: "El es un Carajo! Se ha muerto." Dr. Tony McFarlane kindly advised upon, but is not responsible for, the translation (Clark to LM, July 23, 1853 [Clifton, p. 157]. LM, "Notebook, 1852" [DU]).

60. LM, 1854 slave list (Clifton, p. 185).

61. Capers to LM, May 7, 1860 (Clifton, p. 298).

62. I omit the five members of Jupiter's family who in 1854 ran away from Silk Hope to their old mistress, desperately but unsuccessfully seeking to avoid deportation to Gowrie. The twenty-four do, however, include William, sold in 1854, who pretty surely had been a fugitive; Frederick (sold at the same time), who Louis thought "should be punished for 'kicking up the devil' here"; and one unnamed fugitive in the summer of 1860. Probably there were others, but I have confined the enumeration to those about whom little question can arise.

63. There is no double counting between the seven fugitives after Nov. 1861 and their twenty-four predecessors: thus a total of at least thirty-one individuals fled Gowrie between 1851 and late 1864. The total number of flights was well over thirty-one, as some of these fugitives fled more than once: Fortune four times; Posh, Little George Hunt, Will, and Jack Savage at least twice each; and perhaps several others as well.

64. Three of these ten are not known ever to have fled, and are not therefore included in the total of thirty-one fugitives previously mentioned. These three were Ralph (the driver who was broken in 1860), Isaac, and Tommy (LM, "List of Negroes sent from Gowrie to Silk Hope" [SHC]).

65. By "adult" I mean aged sixteen or more.

66. The gender of one fugitive is unknown.

67. Judge J. M. Berrien—recently attorney general in President Andrew Jackson's administration—also served some fifteen years as a U.S. senator from Georgia (*Dictionary of American Biography* [London, 1929], 2:225–26).

68. CM, undated MS [1833], 11/277/52 (SCHS). Manigault's suspicion of his driver's complicity in the escapes is clear: in the last sentence he began the clause about Harry, "when he winks at the," then struck out these last three words and continued "knows that he is going to run away."

69. R. Habersham & Son accounts, June 10, July 2, 1834; Mar. 28, 1835 [re Aug. 1834]; James Coward to CM, Mar. 24, 1844 (SCHS).

70. Charles Manigault wrote in 1847 that during his proprietorship of Gowrie he had sold "several" runaways to New Orleans. He had dispatched Friday, Minda, and Charlotte in this manner between 1833 and 1837; and if there were four, Quash was probably the fourth. Quash's name appeared on the Dec. 1844 allowance list, yet he had been deported from Gowrie before the annual slave list was compiled later that year (A. R. Bagshaw to CM, July 20, 1844; CM to Anthony Barclay, Apr. 15, 1847 [Clifton, pp. 14, 54]. Slave lists, Jan., Nov. 1833; 1835; 1844, II, [SHC]. Allowance list, Dec. 1844 [DU]).

71. Habersham accounts, June 19, 1834, July 29, 1835 (SCHS). For 1846, 1849, and 1851, see p. 133.

72. Skinner to CM, Jan. 21, 27, 1852 (Clifton, pp. 88, 90). For Jane, see pp. 175–76.

73. Cicero's sister was Phoebe. On the 1851 list Louis Manigault's penciled addition that Phoebe was "taken" is repeated beside the name of "Phillis": this was not Stafford's wife, Phillis (whom Manigault separately identified by another penciled addition), and must therefore have been "Little Phillis," who by the time of her flight was fifteen (1851 list, II, [SHC]. Slaves lists, 1849, 1853; LM to CM, Mar. 7, 1852 [Clifton, pp. 67, 152–53, 94]).

74. Joe wanted Louis Manigault to give a message to his cousins at Bennets Mill, William had communications for his mother in Charleston, and Frederick had messages for a brother in Charleston and a sister in St. Thomas Parish (LM, "Notebook, 1852," [DU]).

75. C. W. Jones to Clark, Dec. 14, 1853 (DU). LM to CM, Jan. 6, 1854 (Clifton, p. 164).

76. Judy fled before Sept. 25. Although Louis Manigault later noted that she had been away "one month," this was probably true only of Julia. Charles Manigault's letter implies that the two runaways had been jailed only a few days earlier (LM, "New Hands" [1853], [DU]. Clark to CM, Sept. 25, 1855; LM, 1855 slave list; CM to LM, Dec. 6, 1855 [Clifton, pp. 198, 193–94, 201]).

77. These included three in 1832–33 (Betsey, Maria, and Minda) and seven between 1851 and 1864 (Phoebe, Little Phillis, Jane, Judy, Julia, Martha, and Dolly). I infer that Maria was the thirty-two-year-old field hand who later became the plantation cook, and not the twenty-three-year-old woman of the same name (who had a young child).

Of the twenty-five male fugitives, two fled in 1832–33 and twenty-three between 1851 and 1864. (In addition, there was a thirty-sixth fugitive—in the summer of 1860—of unknown name and gender.)

78. The second woman, Betsey, was twenty-three years younger than Toney, the man with whom she lived; I infer she was Toney's wife, not his daughter.

79. The flight of the once-favored house servant Jane—which occurred in 1854—is discussed later in this chapter. Another fugitive was Short Jack, who fled for a few days during the 1855 harvest (Stephen Clark to CM, Sept. 25, 1855 [Clifton, p. 198]).

80. LM, 1860 slave list (Clifton, p. 295).

81. Louis's houseboy was still in Charleston as late as Christmas Day after the summer of 1854 (LM to CM, Dec. 28, 1852; Christmas 1854 [Clifton, pp. 133, 189]).

82. London's assistant houseboy at Gowrie was Fortune's sixteen-year-old step-cousin, Captain; Captain's elder sister, Polly, was the new Mrs. Louis Manigault's maid; Polly's husband, Simon, was Louis's cook; and Polly's elder brother, Nat, was the field hand in whose company London got into trouble on the fatal morning of June 11, 1860.

83. In the case of Fortune, it was the family in which he had been raised—that of his stepmother, Minty—which had been at Gowrie since before 1833.

84. During the summer of 1858 Bryan had spent more time with his family at their pineland malaria refuge than he was authorized to do. Collusion between slaves and certain overseers—at the expense of the proprietor—sometimes occurred in the rice kingdom, as Bryan's tenure may illustrate. Cf. Olmsted, *Journey in the Seaboard Slave States*, p. 438.

85. LM, plantation journal, May 3, 1859 (Clifton, p. 266).

86. Ibid. Gowrie's total production in 1856 and 1857 was 1,690 barrels; in 1859 and

1860, 1,617 barrels. Annual gross revenues under Venters were $12,850, while in Capers's first two years they averaged $12,100. Under Venters the average annual profit rate was 8.6 percent, while Capers in 1859 and 1860 averaged 7.3 percent. Gowrie was lucrative under both overseers, though less so than in the 1840s. The number of acres cultivated, and the total capital investment, were more than double what they had been in the 1840s, while these crops were only about 40 percent larger than those averaged in the 1840s. One important cause for lower production per acre in the 1850s was that the high death rate led Charles Manigault to keep fewer slaves at Gowrie than he had intended, and to require each slave to cultivate more acres than in the 1840s.

87. LM, crop ledger, 1833–67; journal, 1864 (Clifton, pp. 1, 347).

88. "You cant believe him [Capers] in any thing of importance," Charles expostulated in 1863. CM to LM, Dec. 28, 1863, in LM, "Book, 1861–1866" (SHC).

89. Capers to CM, June 13, 1860; LM to CM, Nov. 24, 1861 (Clifton, pp. 300, 328).

90. A Manigault rarely spent six out of any twelve months at the plantation. "I leave Gowrie this day having been here since November last—longer than I have ever been before," wrote Louis Manigault on May 3, 1856. (And, in fact, he had attended the Charleston balls for about a fortnight during this period, early in 1856; LM, planting schedule, May 3, 1856 [Clifton, p. 216]).

91. Capers to CM, June 13, 1860 (Clifton, p. 300).

92. CM to LM, Feb. 28, May 2, 1856; Mar. 26, 1859 (Clifton, pp. 211, 221, 283).

93. Capers to CM, July 1, 1860 (DU). Capers to CM, July 11, 1860; to LM, July 22, 27, 1860 (Clifton, pp. 302–3).

94. Capers to CM, Aug. 19, 5, 11, 1860; LM, 1860 slave list; LM to CM, Nov. 24, 1861 (Clifton, pp. 304–5, 296, 328).

95. LM, 1860 slave list; Capers to LM, Aug. 19, 27, Oct. 3, 1860; LM, journal, 1867 (Clifton, pp. 296, 305, 307, 363).

96. Capers to LM, Oct. 31, 1860; LM, journal, 1867 (Clifton, pp. 309, 363).

97. Nancy appears to have been regarded by the Manigaults as a superior woman like Jane, and she may have regarded herself as such; she had succeeded Jane for spells as plantation nurse and as the overseer's cook. This may explain why she, like Jane, had held out against the nearly universal pattern of a woman's marrying by, at most, age twenty. She was twenty-three or twenty-four when she married driver John, twenty years her senior.

98. LM to CM, Nov. 22, 1852; Nov. 24, Dec. 5, 1861; CM to LM, Jan. 20, 1862; LM, journal, 1867 (Clifton, pp. 128, 328, 331, 337, 363–64). The fifth foreman was a postwar newcomer to Gowrie.

99. LM, 1860 slave list; Capers to LM, Nov. 3, 10, 1860 (Clifton, pp. 295–96, 310). CM to LM, Dec. 28, 1863 (SHC).

100. G. W. Wylly, "Receipt [for Will]," Apr. 17, 1860 (DU); LM, slave lists, 1860, 1861; LM, plantation journal, 1867; CM to LM, Jan. 20, 1862 (Clifton, pp. 295–96, 318, 363, 337).

101. LM, 1860 slave list; LM to CM, Dec. 28, 1852 (Clifton, pp. 296, 133).

102. CM to LM, Jan. 19, 1861 (Clifton, p. 313). Although secessionists exaggerated the extent of slave unrest to serve their own political purposes (and Charles Manigault himself proceeded immediately from the problem of runaways to expressing his enthusiasm for secession), his claim that Lincoln's election prompted slaves to flee may deserve consideration. A year later, in Nov. 1861, unrest among Gowrie's slaves certainly increased once Northern military force made its presence felt in the low country, and in 1860 news of Lincoln's election—magnified by the secessionists' alarms

and panics—may also have heartened the slaves. But insubordination at Gowrie late in 1860 obviously had other roots, aggravated by Capers's arrival in Apr. 1859. The most that can be said is that news of Lincoln's impending victory (after the Pennsylvania gubernatorial election of mid-October) and of his actual victory in November may have given further courage to fugitives whose discontent was fired primarily by local circumstance. The same may have been true elsewhere in the South.

103. Ibid.; LM, 1860 slave list (Clifton, pp. 313, 295–96). A shed near the Gowrie thresher's boiler was on fire in Mar. 1861; this may have been arson, but there can be no proof (CM to LM, Mar. 6, 1861 [DU]).

104. After writing "more ideas" in his draft, Louis thought better of making this observation to his father and omitted it in the final version (LM, 1860 slave list [Clifton, p. 296]. LM to Capt. Thomas M. Newell [draft], Mar. 22, 1860; to CM [draft], Mar. 13, 1860 [DU]).

105. CM to LM, Jan. 17, 26, 1860 (Clifton, pp. 291–92).

106. CM to LM, Jan. 26, 1860 (Clifton, p. 292).

107. CM to LM, Mar. 16, 1860 (Clifton, p. 293). LM to CM (draft), Mar. 13, 1860; to Capt. Newell (draft), Mar. 22, 1860 (DU).

108. Fannie Manigault to LM, Nov. 26, 1860 (DU).

109. I infer sale from Louis's words "no longer with me," a euphemism like the "sent away" with which he denominated the sale of Frederick and of Quash's William in 1854 (LM, note on 1860 slave list [Clifton, p. 296]).

110. If—as is likely—the payment of ten dollars to the Williamson's driver in 1851 was for help in capturing a group of Gowrie runaways, the total number of fugitives was probably well over twenty-four.

111. E.g., the statement of plantation expenses from Oct. 1860 to Aug. 1861 includes $4.50 for "1 pr. Ankle Irons," but nothing for advertising the five slaves who fled between October and January (LM, "Financial Statement," 1860–61 [Clifton, p. 308]). The Manigaults' only known fugitive slave advertisements (for Dolly in 1863) were posted in the Augusta and Charleston police stations, not printed in a newspaper (fugitive slave notice, Apr. 7, 1863, IV [SHC]).

112. CM to James Haynes, Mar. 1, 1847; crop ledger, 1833–67 (Clifton, pp. 49, 1).

113. See pp. 125–26.

114. Late in 1844 Charles Manigault, as usual, had been trying to shave his costs, and this had led to Bagshaw's leaving him. Bagshaw, normally very successful in raising a large crop—though less skilled at keeping slaves alive—wanted to achieve the American dream of "independence" for his family. He drove a hard bargain with his employers. In 1844 he received one thousand dollars a year for overseeing Henry McAlpin's sixty-five East Hermitage slaves (McAlpin had had ninety-five slaves in 1838 but the others had since then "died off," as so often happened on Savannah River plantations). In addition, Bagshaw received from McAlpin the house where he lived on McAlpin's plantation, and the use of some of McAlpin's slaves as his servants in that house. Besides all of this, Bagshaw garnered from Manigault six hundred dollars for his part-time services, plus some rice flour which may have been worth two hundred dollars (though Bagshaw denied that it had much value); and he appears also to have received a salary from one of the Legarés for the part-time overseeing of thirty-five of their slaves. Bagshaw knew that the services of a "successful"—by the criteria of the rice kingdom—overseer were in great demand, because thousands or even tens of thousands of dollars were at stake in a plantation's annual harvest, and he sought from Manigault a rise from six to eight hundred dollars. Manigault refused, and Gowrie ended up with a new overseer; for Bagshaw was able to secure satisfactory terms from

another Savannah River planter. This was the former governor James Hamilton, one of South Carolina's leading nullifiers (Clifton, pp. 1, 11, 16–18, 20–21).

115. CM to Anthony Barclay, Apr. 15, 1847 (Clifton, p. 54). Frederick Douglass, *Narrative of the Life of Frederick Douglass, an American Slave* (1845; rpt. [ed. Benjamin Quarles] Cambridge, Mass., 1960), pp. 106–9. James Haynes to CM, Jan. 6, 1847 (Clifton, p. 46).

116. Anthony Barclay to CM, Aug. 23, 1847 (SCHS). Haynes to CM, Jan. 6, Apr. 22, 1847 (Clifton, pp. 46, 54).

117. CM to Haynes, Mar. 1, 1847; Haynes to CM, Dec. 7, 1846 (Clifton, pp. 49, 44).

118. CM to Anthony Barclay, Apr. 15, 1847 (Clifton, pp. 53–54).

119. I share George Fredrickson and Christopher Lasch's uneasiness about the current usage of "resistance," although their solution to the problem differs from mine. Fredrickson and Lasch, "Resistance to Slavery," *Civil War History* 13 (1967): 315–29.

120. GM to LM, Jan. 21, 1861, Clifton, p. 314.

121. Olmsted, *Journey in the Seaboard Slave States,* p. 485. Fisher, diary, Dec. 26, 1852, in Nicholas B. Wainwright, ed., *A Philadelphia Perspective* (Philadelphia, 1967), p. 244. Henry Bibb, *Narrative of the Life and Adventures of Henry Bibb, an American Slave* (1849; rpt. in Gilbert Osofsky, ed., *Puttin' on Ole Massa* [New York, 1969], p. 66).

122. *Savannah Journal and Courier* [Sept. 1855], in Olmsted, *Journey in the Seaboard Slave States,* pp. 441–42. LM to CM, Dec. 2, 1861 (Clifton, p. 329).

123. Cf. the planters' panic in Georgetown District, South Carolina, in 1802 at the rumor of a French landing on the coast: Howard A. Ohline, "Georgetown, South Carolina: Racial Anxieties and Militant Behavior, 1802," *South Carolina Historical Magazine* 73 (1972): 130–40.

124. CM to Capers, Jan. 26, 1862 (Clifton, p. 339).

125. LM, journal, 1867 (Clifton, p. 363).

126. T. W. Higginson, *Army Life in a Black Regiment* (1870; rpt. East Lansing, Mich., 1960), pp. 9–10.

127. I infer that "Dov Jack" (Clifton, p. 325) is a mistranscription of "Car[penter] Jack": this is the only way to make sense of subsequent events.

128. LM to Fannie Manigault, Nov. 12, 1861; Capers to CM, Nov. 14, 1861; Skinner to CM, Oct. 9, 1852; LM, journal, May 1862 (Clifton, pp. 324–25, 122, 320).

129. CM to Capers, Jan. 26, 1862 (Clifton, p. 339).

130. LM, plantation journal, 1863 (Clifton, p. 342). Jack Savage's long, and well-authenticated, absence lends support to the claim of former slaves (many years after the event) that inland fugitives had been known to survive for three years, sheltered in caves or in holes dug in the ground. Cf., e.g., Jennie Kendricks to Edwin Driskell, in George Rawick, ed., *The American Slave* (1941; rpt. Westport, Conn., 1972), XIII, part iii, 6.

131. Capers to LM, Aug. 10, 1863 (DU). LM, journal, 1862–63; 1861 slave list (Clifton, pp. 342, 317–18). Regarding maroons near Savannah, see Higginson, *Army Life in a Black Regiment,* p. 193.

132. CM to LM, Dec. 28, 1863 (in LM, "Book, 1861–1866"), (SHC).

133. He was sold for eighteen hundred dollars of the inflated Confederate currency, even though he was a skilled (albeit middle-aged) carpenter. Ordinary "prime hands" appear to have been fetching three thousand dollars as early as June 1863 (LM, plantation journal, 1863; Capers to CM, Sept. 15, 1863 [Clifton, pp. 341–42, 345]).

134. Capers to CM, Sept. 28, 1863; LM, journal, 1863 (Clifton, pp. 345, 342). Capers to LM, Aug. 16, 1863 (DU). CM to LM, Dec. 28, 1863 (SHC).

135. Fugitive slave notice, Apr. 7, 1863, IV (SHC). Capers to LM, Feb. 25, 1863 (DU). LM to Charles W. Henry, Apr. 10, 1863 (SCL).

136. John B. Habersham to LM, Apr. 13, 1863 (emphasis in the original); Capers to LM, Apr. 12, 1863 (DU).

137. LM, note which he later added to Capers to LM, Apr. 9, 1863; Capers to LM, Apr. 9, July 2, 1863 (DU). Susan Smedes, *Memorials of a Southern Planter* (1889; rpt. [ed. Fletcher Green] Jackson, Miss., 1981), p. 71.

138. Capers to LM, June 17, Aug. 13, Sept. 5, 1863 (DU). Cf. Capers's list of slaves remaining at Gowrie, Mar. 8, 1864, IV (SHC).

139. Capers to LM, Sept. 5, 1863 (DU). Leon Litwack, *Been in the Storm So Long* (New York, 1979), pp. 87–93.

140. CM to LM, Dec. 1, 1860 (DU). CM to LM, Jan. 11, 1864 (scrapbook, p. 1215), (SCL). CM to James Haynes, Mar. 1, 1847 (emphasis added), (Clifton, p. 50).

141. LM, journal, 1867, 1864 (Clifton, pp. 363, 347).

142. LM, journal, 1864 (Clifton, p. 348).

143. LM, journal, 1867 (Clifton, pp. 360–61, 357).

144. Smedes, *Memorials of a Southern Planter,* pp. 60, 71. Genovese, *Roll, Jordan, Roll,* pp. 327–98.

145. Patterson, *Slavery and Social Death,* pp. 11–13.

146. Thomas Jefferson, *Notes on the State of Virginia* (rpt. [ed. T. P. Abernethy] New York, 1964), p. 155 (chap. 18).

147. CM to LM, Feb. 28, 1856 (Clifton, p. 211).

148. See pp. 98–99.

149. Haynes to CM, Apr. 21, 1846; CM to Capers, Jan. 26, 1862 (Clifton, pp. 34, 339).

150. LM, journal, 1867 (Clifton, p. 361).

151. LM to CM, Nov. 24, 1861 (Clifton, p. 328).

152. Cf. Patterson, *Slavery and Social Death,* pp. 77–101.

153. LM, journal, 1867; LM to CM, Mar. 3, 1852 (Clifton, pp. 360, 92–93).

154. LM, journal, May 1862, 1867; CM to LM, Oct. 18, 1856 (Clifton, pp. 321, 363, 360, 230). Another "cunning" slave was Charles the trunk minder, whose career is detailed in chapter 6.

155. Skinner to CM, Aug. 20, 1852 (Clifton, p. 115). John Izard, the most versatile and reliable artisan at Gowrie, appeared to have been another "upright conformist" until he finally tried, unsuccessfully, to flee in 1863. His career is discussed in chapter 6.

156. CM, 1833 slave list (Clifton, p. 6).

157. Skinner to CM, June 6, 1852 (Clifton, p. 99). LM, notes on 1853 slave list, II (SHC). (Bob's death is mistakenly printed as having occurred on "Saturday" night in Clifton, p. 151, and Crecie's name is misprinted "Cretia.")

158. See pp. 112–13.

159. CM to James Coward, Mar. 1, 1847 (SCL).

160. Jesse Cooper to CM, July 30, 1849 (SCL). ("Severity" is misprinted in Clifton [p. 69] as "scarcity.")

161. Ibid. Cooper to CM, Aug. 14, 1849 (Clifton, p. 71).

162. LM to CM, Nov. 22, 1852; Mar. 6, 1853; Mar. 17, 1854; 1853 slave list (Clifton, pp. 128, 145, 183, 152).

163. In particular, it is glaringly evident that slave women will have developed numerous types different from the six here sketched; but Gowrie's records on female slaves are inadequate to specify with confidence these other types.

164. Kenneth Stampp expressed years ago his disbelief that the personalities of most slaves could be fitted into either "Sambo" or "rebel" categories. Stampp, "Rebels and Sambos: The Search for the Negro's Personality in Slavery," *Journal of Southern History* 37 (1971): esp. pp. 385–92.

165. The "cunning" trunk minder Charles certainly told tales on Jack Savage (see p. 165).

166. Religion, folklore, and the formation of a distinctive Gullah language were some of the low-country slaves' tools in this combat, splendidly analyzed in chapters 5–7 of Charles Joyner, *Down by the Riverside: A South Carolina Slave Community* (Urbana, Ill., 1984), and in chapters 8–10 of Margaret Creel, *"A Peculiar People": Slave Religion and Community-Culture Among the Gullahs* (New York, 1988).

Chapter 6

1. From 1846 to 1864, when Harry's eight successors held the office of driver, Gowrie had eight overseers. The comparison is not exact, however, because from 1849 to 1860 there were two drivers (one at the Gowrie and one at the East Hermitage tract) but only one overseer.

The rapid turnover of both overseers and drivers illustrates the general principle that there was often much more flux on a plantation than might appear in a traveler's report (or even in the fragmentary recollection of an aged former slave). The traveler fixes a moment in time and makes it appear to be almost changeless.

2. Philip Morgan, "Task and Gang Systems: The Organization of Labor on New World Plantations," in Stephen Innes, ed., *Work and Labor in Early America* (Chapel Hill, N.C., 1988), pp. 202–6.

3. See chapters 11–14.

4. Occasionally, when Manigault's Silk Hope plantation was unusually productive, he shipped surplus corn or a couple of barrels of pork from there to Gowrie, but normally Gowrie's supplies of corn and pork were purchased.

5. CM, journal, 1845 (Clifton, p. 21). A. R. Bagshaw to CM, "June 20," on June 15, 1842 (SCL). Julia Rush, in George Rawick, ed., *The American Slave* (1941; rpt. Westport, Conn., 1972), XIII. part iii, 229; (cf. *Brunswick [Ga.] Advocate,* Dec. 6, 1838, in Kemble, *Journal,* p. 326 n). The scarcity of meat rations occurred on both sea-island cotton plantations like DuBignon's and rice plantations like Manigault's.

6. CM to LM, Mar. 6, 1853; Stephen Clark to LM, Oct. 8, 1853 (Clifton, pp. 142, 160).

7. CM to Jesse Cooper, Jan. 10, 1848 (Clifton, p. 62).

8. Small rice was not always more costly than corn. In 1859 Charles Manigault sent to Gowrie "14 Blbs. Small Rice, because at the price it brings now It is Cheaper than Corn, & there is no necessity to give of Small Rice more than 6 Quarts per week, to each full hand [compared with 8 quarts of corn]. At that they will snatch at it, in preference. It is all eatable, whereas Corn has much waste in grinding & winnowing, &c. & it keeps for a long time when Corn would heat & spoil" (CM to LM, Feb. 15, 1859 [Clifton, p. 279]).

9. CM to James Haynes, Jan. 1, 1847 (Clifton, p. 45). See pp. 204–5.

10. CM to Haynes, Mar. 1, 1847 (Clifton, p. 49). I have altered the punctuation for clarity.

11. Philip Morgan has demonstrated—from the records of the Southern Claims Commission—the possession by some low-country slaves of pigs, a few cows, and even

a rare horse. One suspects (though Morgan denies this) that ownership of these animals occurred only on a relatively small number of plantations, and was confined principally to slaves in privileged jobs. At Silk Hope, for example, Manigault acknowledged (even in a romanticized postwar memoir) that he permitted ownership of only a "hog or two for some of [the slaves]." Where a master let a privileged slave own pigs or a cow, he was extending the principle of "divide and conquer" which was at the heart of the whole system of selective privilege, discussed in the next section (CM, "Memoir [1870]," p. 12 [SHC]. Philip Morgan, "The Ownership of Property by Slaves in the Mid-Nineteenth-Century Low Country," *Journal of Southern History* 49 [1983]: 399–420).

12. Robert Habersham & Son accounts, Nov. 5, 1835; Jan. 18, 1837; Oct. 1851 (SCHS). Skinner to CM, Oct. 9, 1852; LM to CM, Feb. 27, 1853; Venters to CM, Sept. 27, 1856 (Clifton, pp. 121, 140, 226).

13. Manigault did spend twelve dollars to supply beef at Christmas after the disastrous measles and dysentery epidemic of 1848 (Cooper to CM, July 24, 1849 [Clifton, p. 69; also pp. 128, 132]. LM, notes on 1852 slave list [SHC]. Habersham accounts, 1848 [SCHS]).

14. CM to Cooper, Jan. 10, 1848; 1849 slave list; LM to CM, Christmas 1852 (Clifton, pp. 62, 64, 3; 241, 289, 297; 132).

15. The much-cited record of Manigault's clothing expenses in 1839 as $7.00 per year per grown hand (printed by Ulrich Phillips in John Commons's *Documentary History of American Industrial Society* [Cleveland, Ohio, 1910], 1:135) is therefore misleading. Although Manigault spent about $7.00 per year for clothing adult males, he shaved the cost of cloth for each adult female to about $1.85 per year by making the women sew all of their own clothes [CM, notes on 1844 slave list [Clifton, p. 21]).

16. CM to LM, Mar. 29, 1857 (Clifton, p. 246).

17. Clifton, pp. 7, 20, 31, 78, 153. LM to CM, Nov. 22, Christmas 1852 (Clifton, pp. 127, 132).

18. CM to Cooper, Jan. 10, 1848; Leonard Venters to CM, Aug. 15, 1856 (Clifton, pp. 62, 224).

19. The pigs which the Manigaults started raising at Gowrie during the war were not reared for the slaves' consumption. This fact may throw light on the mysterious disappearance of eight Gowrie pigs in 1862.

20. LM, journal, May 1863 (CLifton, p. 343; see also p. 319).

21. K. W. Skinner to CM, Oct. 25, 1851 (DU).

22. Skinner to CM, Oct. 13, 1852; CM to LM, Oct. 24, 1856 (Clifton, pp. 123, 231).

23. Cf. Julia Smith, *Slavery and Rice Culture in Low Country Georgia, 1750–1860* (Knoxville, Tenn., 1985), pp. 126, 130.

24. Gowrie's houses may have been subdivided into two or three rooms, as was the case at Richard Arnold's rice plantation on the Ogeechee River. The houses of Arnold's slaves had 36 percent more floor space than those at Gowrie and were divided into three rooms—one common room and two small sleeping rooms, each half the size of the common room. But Arnold's was one of the two plantations visited by Olmsted in the whole South whose conditions the latter thought most favorable for the slaves: and it seems a little unlikely that Manigault undertook the extra expense of subdividing his slaves' (smaller) houses (CM, note [1837] on 1832 [Judge Wayne to A. Barclay] house-building bill, II [SHC]. F. L. Olmsted, *The Cotton Kingdom* [1861; rpt. (ed. A. M. Schlesinger) New York, 1953], pp. 184–85, 445. Cf. Paul David et al., *Reckoning with Slavery* [New York, 1976], pp. 293–94).

25. Two Gowrie dwellings are sketched on "Plan" for "Kitchen" (Jan. 1855), IV (SHC). LM, "New Hands at East Hermitage [and Gowrie]" [1853, filed 1860], (DU).

26. LM, "Notebook 1852" (DU). LM, journal, 1867 (CLifton, p. 360). The "Hermitage" slave houses pictured in Mills Lane, *The People of Georgia* (Savannah, Ga., 1975), p. 147, are *not* those of Manigault's "East Hermitage" tract, but rather of another of Henry McAlpin's plantations, on the Georgia side of the river three miles above Savannah (Mary Granger, ed., *Savannah River Plantations* [Savannah, Ga., 1947]).

27. LM, journal, 1867 (Clifton, pp. 358–59; see also p. 316). CM, "Description of Paintings" (typed copy, emphasis in the original), p. 14 (SCL).

28. LM to CM, Dec. 28, 1852; Dec. 5, 1861 (Clifton, pp. 133, 331).

29. E.g., Cooper to CM, Mar. 1, 1850 (SCHS).

30. LM, journal, Apr. 21, 1861 (Clifton, p. 297); LM, family records, pp. 235–36 (SCL). Overseer Capers alleged that at least once in July 1860 he took the slaves out of the heat—the greatest he had ever experienced—"after 10 Ocl." (Capers to LM, July 5, 1860 [DU]).

31. Cf. Susan Smedes, *Memorials of a Southern Planter* (1889; rpt. [ed. Fletcher Green] Jackson, Miss., 1981), p. 70.

32. Skinner to CM, Jan. 28, 1851; Jan. 21, 1852 (DU). Skinner to CM, Jan. 27, May 15, 1852; LM, journal, Apr. 24, 1860 (Clifton, pp. 89, 97, 290). LM, "Season of 1876," IV (SHC).

33. Skinner to CM, May 30, 1851 (Clifton, p. 80). Skinner no doubt had learned his skill at overseeing from his father, who, among other employers, served Manigault's neighbor James Potter for three years. Charles Manigault's parting ways with K. W. Skinner after 1852, and his failure to secure equally competent successors, contributed greatly to Gowrie's being relatively less prosperous later in the 1850s than when it was under Skinner's management. The Savannah factor Robert Habersham tried to persuade Manigault that Skinner had deceived him about the extent of damage to Manigault's crop done by the 1852 freshet. It is likely, however, that Skinner took the initiative in ending his employment at Gowrie. Like Bagshaw earlier, he may have been unwilling to submit to Manigault's penny-pinching. Probably, however, Skinner—like many other overseers—lost his health in the swamps and felt obliged to withdraw from Gowrie, even though he was still quite a young man. He certainly had malaria in the summer of 1851, and his father reported in 1853 that his health was bad. After studying medicine in Savannah under Dr. Bullock, he emigrated to Texas and became a medical doctor (R. Habersham & Son to CM, Sept, 16, 1852 [SCHS]; S. Skinner to CM, Jan. 27, 29, 1853; June 22, 1857; K. W. Skinner to CM, Oct. 29, 1853 [DU]).

34. CM, "On Milling of Rice," June 1852; CM to Haynes, Mar. 1, 1847 (Clifton, pp. 111, 50).

35. GM to LM, Dec. 11, 1860 (Clifton, p. 311). Betsey's mother, Crecie, had died when Betsey was three. After the 1854 "cholera" Betsey had been sent to Silk Hope—separating her from her father, Ishmael, and from Crecie's mother, Betsey—and she was still living there in 1860.

36. CM to LM, Feb. 28, 1856 (Clifton, p. 211). Skinner to CM, Aug. 29, 1851 (DU).

37. LM, notes on 1861 slave list; LM, journal, 1867 (Clifton, pp. 318, 363; see also p. 323). Capers to LM, July 11, 1863 (DU). LM, notebooks, II, 134 (Charleston Museum).

38. CM to LM, Nov. 18, 1856; LM to CM, Nov. 24, 1861 (Clifton, pp. 233, 328).

39. Silk Hope allowances, Nov. 5, 1833, I (SHC). Habersham accounts, Sept. 23, 1836; 1835–36; Dec. 17, 1835; Dec 20, 1845 (SCHS). CM to LM, Mar. 29, 1857 (Clifton, p. 246).

40. Dr. W. G. Bullock to CM, Oct. 13, Dec. 12, 1857; CM to LM, Mar. 20, 1858 (DU). CM to LM, Mar. 26, Apr. 15, 1858 (Clifton, p. 264).

41. CM to LM, Feb. 10, 1859; Skinner to CM, Sept. 7, 1851; LM to CM, Apr. 17, 1853 (Clifton, pp. 278, 86, 154). Clear evidence of the high value some privileged slaves lay upon winning the esteem of a master or even an overseer appears in Solomon Northup, *Twelve Years a Slave* (1853; rpt. [ed. Sue Eakin and Joseph Logsdon] Baton Rouge, La., 1968), p. 70; and in Charles Ball, *Fifty Years in Chains* (1836; rpt. [ed. P. Foner] New York, 1970), p. 217.

42. See p. 165.

43. CM to Cooper, July 12, 1848; Skinner to CM, Jan. 24, 1852; LM to CM, Mar. 10, 1854; 1854 slave list (Clifton, pp. 63–64, 89, 180, 184).

44. CM to LM, Jan. 3, Mar. 27, 1859 (Clifton, pp. 269, 284). Manigault did not execute his plan of leaving Gowrie under slave management, for a few days later he unexpectedly discovered he could hire William Capers as overseer.

45. CM to Anthony Barclay, Apr. 15, 1847 (Clifton, pp. 53–54).

46. CM, instructions for suboverseer, 1845; overseer contract, 1853 (Clifton, pp. 23, 136).

47. The change was occasioned by Manigault's purchase of East Hermitage: he decided then that his larger estate required closer supervision than during the previous dozen years. Only thrice during that period—in 1840, 1845, and 1847—had he employed a resident overseer or suboverseer—and in 1847 this was in consequence of Mrs. Barclay's unexpected sacking of James Haynes. After buying East Hermitage, Manigault in 1849 and 1850 hired an inexperienced suboverseer to reside permanently at Gowrie under the supervision of the nonresident overseer Jesse Cooper. Thereafter Manigault's overseer was expected to reside at Gowrie (although, of course, he left the plantation every evening during the long summer to sleep at the pineland retreat). On Cooper's nonresidence, and the resident suboverseer during 1849 and 1850: CM to Cooper, Jan. 10, 1848; Cooper to CM, Nov. 22 [misprinted 23], 1849 (Clifton, pp. 61, 75); CM draft letter of recommendation for Thomas Waldhauer, Dec. 30, 1850 (DU).

48. LM to CM, Dec. 28, 1854; CM to LM, Nov. 22, 1856; LM, journal, Feb. 1, 1857 (Clifton, pp. 192, 233–34, 215).

49. Eugene Genovese, *Roll, Jordan, Roll* (New York, 1974), pp. 359–61.

50. T. R. Heargroves to CM, Nov. 19, 1835 (SCHS). Skinner to R. Habersham & Son, Dec. 21, 1851) (Clifton, pp. 86–87).

51. Cooper to CM, Oct. 19, 1849 (Clifton, p. 74). Cooper to CM, June 17, 1850 (SCHS). Skinner to CM, Oct. 31, 29, 1852 (Clifton, pp. 125, 124).

52. Stephen had been restored to his old office of miller after Cato drowned earlier in 1852.

53. Schadenfreude, and respect for the slaves' skills at day-to-day dissidence, tempt one to suppose that—in the cases of both repairing the pumps and aligning the millstones—Gowrie's artisans deliberately feigned incapacity in order to sabotage production. But John Izard was not a trained engineer, nor was Stephen a trained millwright; and in these two instances lack of training appears to me the more plausible explanation for their failures to get the machines into working order (Skinner to CM, Oct. 31, 1852 [Clifton, p. 125]).

54. A new boiler was being installed by a Charleston machinist firm.

55. CM to LM, May 2, Apr. 30, 1856 (Clifton, pp. 221, 219).

56. The experiment ended in one year, soon after the suboverseer's wife had died—presumably of malaria. The suboverseer by then wanted the pay and responsibility of a full overseership.

57. CM, journal, Apr. 17, 1845 (Clifton, p. 25).

58. CM to LM, Dec. 1, 1860 (DU). CM, notes on 1844 slave list, II (SHC). J. W. Bandy to LM, June 18, 1865 (copy), IV (SHC).

59. CM to Cooper, Jan. 10, 1848; Haynes to CM, Sept. 1, 1845 (Clifton, pp. 62, 28).

60. 1833 slave list (Clifton, p. 3).

61. So was the brief stint of Nancy Hunt as plantation nurse in 1855.

62. CM to LM, Dec. 28, 1858; Jan. 4, 1859 (Clifton, pp. 267, 270).

63. 1852 slave list (Clifton, pp. 95–96).

64. I believe these comments about Gowrie's social structure are also true, in the main, for rice plantations where the master—unlike Gowrie's Charles Manigault—had his "big house" on the estate. But the presence of a "big house," with house servants who sometimes spent their whole lives in domestic service, fostered a somewhat greater social differentiation among the slaves than existed at Gowrie. See the discussion in chapter 13 of Robert Allston's plantations. Cf. John Blassingame, "Status and Social Structure in the Slave Community," in Harry P. Owens, ed., *Perspectives and Irony in American Slavery* (Jackson, Miss., 1976), pp. 137–51.

65. This number includes Charles's foster child, Nat; and Charles's wife, Juna, had of course lost her earlier child Maria too, making ten dead children in all. See chapter 4.

66. Elizabeth Manigault to LM, Aug. 28, 1856 (DU).

67. Genovese, *Roll, Jordan, Roll,* e.g., pp. 64–70, 75–86, 123–33, 452–58.

68. An explanation for Genovese's usage lies in his conviction that "the slaveholders' [paternalist] ideology . . . developed in accordance with the reality of social relations" (ibid., p. 86). Were this true, there might be more reason for using the same word to designate both ideology and the system of social relations. But whether the statement is true has to be decided by evidence; and until the matter is settled, clarity suggests the use of two different terms for ideology and social relations.

69. Pp. 46–47.

70. CM to LM, Mar. 10, 1854 (Clifton, pp. 178–79).

71. Skinner to CM, Aug. 20, 1852 (Clifton, p. 115).

72. GM to LM, Jan. 21, 1861 (Clifton, p. 314); Helen Catterall, ed., *Judicial Cases on Slavery,* 2:311, in Frederick Bancroft, *Slave-Trading in the Old South* (Baltimore, 1931), p. 173 n.

73. LM, journal, 1864; Capers to LM, July 27, 1860 (Clifton, pp. 347–48, 303).

74. As is well known to specialists, even the South's preeminent propounder of paternalist theory, George Fitzhugh, fell back ultimately upon a racialist defense of slavery. Cf. his *Cannibals All!* (1857; rpt. [ed. C. Vann Woodward] Cambridge, Mass., 1960), p. 201, with his earlier *Sociology for the South* (1854).

75. The thought, in a different 1862 context, is Henry Adams's: *The Education of Henry Adams* (Boston, 1918), p. 131. LM, journal, June 12, 1862 (Clifton, p. 320).

76. She went to Savannah that year for Louis's wedding, and may have made a trip upriver to the plantation.

77. CM, souvenirs (SCL).

78. When Mrs. Barclay sacked Haynes from her employ a year later, Manigault concluded that Barclay's slaves had had good cause for their complaint against Haynes; and so probably had Manigault's slaves a year earlier (CM to Anthony Barclay, Apr. 15, 1847 [Clifton, p. 53]).

79. CM to Haynes, Jan. 1, 1847 (Clifton, p. 45).

80. See pp. 173–74. Skinner to CM, Aug. 20, 1852 (Clifton, p. 115).

81. LM, notes on 1854 slave list; LM, journal, May 1, 1856 (Clifton, pp. 184, 194–95).

82. Kenneth Stampp, *The Peculiar Institution* (1956; rpt. London, 1964), p. 86, quoting *Southern Cultivator* 7 (1849): 69. CM to LM, Nov. 22, 1856 (emphasis added), Clifton, p. 234. The five Gowrie slaves who died from pneumonia between Jan. 1857 and Dec. 1859 were Dinah (aged 35), Sam (22), William (32), Rhina (39), and Mathias (34).

83. LM, journal, 1865, 1867; J. W. Bandy to LM, June 18, 1865 (Clifton, pp. 349, 357, 361, 353–54).

84. LM, journal, 1867; J. W. Bandy to LM, June 18, 1865 (Clifton, pp. 362, 358–60; 353–54).

85. CM to LM, Apr. 30, 1865 (Clifton, p. 353). CM, Souvenirs, pp. 16–17; LM, scrapbook, pp. 64, 73 (SCL).

86. CM, souvenirs, pp. 20–21, 18, 22, 19, 21 (SCL). CM to GM, Apr. 10, 1865, in LM, "Book, 1861–1866" (SHC).

87. CM to GM, Apr. 10, 1865, in LM, "Book, 1861–1866" (SHC). CM, souvenirs, pp. 26–27; CM, "Description of Paintings" (typescript), p. 14 (SCL).

88. CM, souvenirs, pp. 20, 22, 19, 24–25 (SCL). CM to GM, Apr. 10, 1865, in LM, "Book, 1861–1866" (SHC).

89. CM, Memoir, VII (SHC).

Chapter 7

1. The connection between the Manigaults and Gabriella Butler was close: Charles Manigault "was throughout his life most devotedly attached" to his niece, according to Louis Manigault. Gabriella visited the Manigaults in South Carolina whenever she went South, and was hostess in Philadelphia to Louis Manigault when he was a Yale student. "Get Mr. [John] Butler to go with you immediately on your arrival . . . to the best Tailor," Charles Manigault admonished the eighteen-year-old Louis in 1846. When the Manigaults in 1866 could no longer afford the French lady's maid who had served them for thirty years, she became Gabriella's maid in Philadelphia. LM, family records, p. 148, Manigault MS (SCHS). CM to LM, Nov. 15, 1846, Manigault MS (SCL). Gabriel Manigault, autobiography, p. 7 (SCHS).

2. Fisher later became the brother-in-law of Harry Ingersoll, owner of a big Louisiana sugar plantation; his cousin Joshua Fisher (married to South Carolina's Eliza Middleton) augmented his personal fortune with income from his wife's share of the Middleton rice plantations; and two of Sidney Fisher's other brothers-in-law were leaders during the Civil War of the vehemently pro-Southern faction of Philadelphia's Democratic Party. Dusinberre, *Civil War Issues in Philadelphia, 1856–1865* (Philadelphia, 1965), pp. 135, 142 and n, 154, 157–58, 164 n, 174.

3. Sidney George Fisher, diary, Sept. 22, 1844; Jan. 24, 15, 24, 1841, in Nicholas B. Wainwright, ed., *A Philadelphia Perspective* (Philadelphia, 1967). [Hereafter: Fisher, *Diary.*]

4. Bell, pp. 320, 327, 329. Fisher, *Diary,* June 3, Nov. 29, Dec. 13, 1856.

5. Her mother, Elizabeth Manigault, was Charles Manigault's eldest sister.

6. 1848 crop report, Butler Papers 1447 (Box 7, Folder 8), (HSP).

7. Bell, pp. 75–76; 2, 4–7, 15, 24–25, 229–34, 239–42, 601; quotation at p. 229. Joshua Francis Fisher, *Recollections* [written 1864–67, printed 1929], (HSP), p. 262.

8. Bell, pp. 159–60. R. M. Myers, ed., *The Children of Pride* (New Haven, Conn., 1972), p. 23.

9. This was the title of Jones's second book published for the purpose (Savannah,

Ga., 1842). The Jones family correspondence is printed in Myers, *The Children of Pride.* Bell, p. 316. *Journal,* p. 134.

10. Bell, p. 240.

11. *Journal,* p. 144.

12. Fisher, *Diary,* Sept. 30, 1867; Nov. 2, 1836; Aug. 26, 1862. Bell, pp. 245; 609, 294. Constance Wright, *Fanny Kemble and the Lovely Land* (New York, 1972), p. 153. John A. Scott, "Introduction," *Journal,* p. lvi.

13. Bell, pp. 290, 312. Fanny Kemble Wister, ed., *Fanny* (Tallahassee, Fla., 1972), p. 205. Bell, p. 292.

14. Dusinberre, *Civil War Issues in Philadelphia,* pp. 102, 117, 117 n, 128. Fisher, *Diary,* Dec. 26, 1860; Aug. 20, Sept. 23, 1861; Apr. 17, May 5, 1865.

15. Dorothy Marshall, *Fanny Kemble* (London, 1977), pp. 14–15, 24–27, 96, 103. FK, *Records of Later Life,* 3 vols. (London, 1882), 1:79–80. Henry James, "Frances Anne Kemble," *Essays in London and Elsewhere* (London, 1893), pp. 86–127.

16. Fisher, *Diary,* Nov. 2, 1836. Wright, *Fanny Kemble and the Lovely Land,* p. 28. FK to Kate Sedgwick, [June 20, 1840], in Wister, *Fanny,* p. 170.

17. Ellen Terry, *The Story of My Life* (Woodbridge, England, 1982), p. 113. Fisher, *Diary,* Apr. 19, 1840; Feb. 28, 1844. FK to Harriet St. Leger, Mar. 25, [1841], in FK, *Records,* 2:47. Marshall, *Fanny Kemble,* pp. 22–23. *Journal,* pp. 209–10, 58–59, 218.

18. William Macready, *Journal,* in Wright, *Fanny Kemble and the Lovely Land,* p. 109.

19. Philip Hone, *Diary,* in Marshall, *Fanny Kemble,* p. 84. Terry, *Story of My Life,* p. 113. James, *Essays in London,* p. 104.

20. Marshall, *Fanny Kemble,* p. 108. *Journal,* p. 218. Fisher, *Diary,* Aug. 27, 1860; Sept. 30, 1867.

21. FK to George Combe, Jan. 6, 1837, in Wister, *Fanny,* p. 156. FK to H[arriet St. Leger], Nov. 14, 1837, in FK, *Records,* 1:117; also 7–8, 10–11, 51. Kemble's first play, *Francis I* (written before she was eighteen), had been performed and published in London in 1832; and her *Star of Seville* was published in 1837 (Marshall, *Fanny Kemble,* pp. 28, 54). *An English Tragedy* was published in Kemble, *Plays* (London, 1863).

22. FK, *Records,* 1:48–49, 51–52; also, 66–67.

23. FK to Emily [Fitzhugh], Jan. 30, 1839, *Ibid.,* 228.

24. *Journal,* pp. 67, 154, 159–61; see also pp. 72–74, 85–86.

25. Ibid., p. 210.

26. FK to Harriet St. Leger, Dec. 14, 1839, in FK, *Records,* 1:278.

27. FK to Harriet St. Leger, June 24, Aug. 9, 1839; Oct. 26, [1839, misattributed by Kemble to 1840], in FK, *Records,* 1:246, 258; 2:39–40, 42 (quotations at 2:39–40).

28. Presumably this comprised chapters 1–3 of the 1961 edition of the *Journal.*

29. FK, *Records,* 1:259–61; 2:216. FK to [Lydia Maria Child (or Elizabeth Sedgwick, for Child)], Nov. 2, 1841, in Wister, *Fanny,* p. 178. Child was editor of the *Standard* from May 1841 to May 1843. In 1841 she urged Kemble to publish her "Journal" in the *Standard* (Milton Meltzer et al., eds., *Lydia Maria Child, Selected Letters, 1817–1880* [Amherst, Mass., 1982], p. 340). Upon publication of Kemble's *Journal* in 1863, Child—who obviously believed it had been ready for publication in 1841—reminisced that "Mrs. [Elizabeth] Sedgwick told me about it, years ago, and wished to have it inserted in *The Anti-Slavery Standard,* which I then edited; but this was prevented by the peculiar state of Mrs. Kemble's domestic affairs. I was disappointed at the time" (Child to Oliver Johnson [before Aug. 22, 1863], in Meltzer, *Lydia Maria Child,* p. 435. See also FK to Harriet St. Leger, June 29, 1842, in FK, *Records,* 2:235).

30. FK to Katherine Sedgwick Minot, Mar. 2, 1842, in Wister, *Fanny,* p. 180.

31. Marshall, *Fanny Kemble,* p. 183.

32. Fisher, *Diary,* May 28, 1848. Rebecca Gratz to Miriam Cohen, Sept. 13, 1845 (Bell, p. 299).

33. Fisher, *Diary,* Feb. 18, 1862; Oct. 19, 1867; Aug. 27, 1860.

34. Ibid., Oct. 19, 1867.

35. FK, *Records,* 2:42–43. Fisher, *Diary,* Aug. 20, 1863.

36. *Journal,* pp. 90, 343–44.

37. Corroboration of certain details can also be found in Kemble's letters written from the Butler estate—e.g., FK to Mrs. Henry Cleveland [Jan. 15, 1839], in Wister, *Fanny,* pp. 164–65. Even John Butler acknowledged in 1841 the previous "disorder and want of attention" of the Hampton plantation (John Butler to PB, Jan. 31, 1841 [Wister MS, HSP]).

38. Frank was valued at one thousand dollars. With three exceptions, no other slave was assigned a worth of more than eight hundred dollars. The three other slaves also valued at one thousand dollars—two subdrivers and a blacksmith—were all much younger than Frank ("Inventory and Appraisement of the estate of Capt. John Butler dec'd," Feb. 13, 1849 [Butler MS, HSP]).

39. See pp. 249–50 nn. 2, 3.

40. The photographs are in Bell, pp. 454–55, 457. The heartrending story of the appeal against the trumped-up rape charge is in Bell, pp. 452, 456, 458.

41. PB to RK Jr., Feb. 17, 1839 (copy), (Wister MS, HSP). This letter refers to "your woman Sac and her children whom I have purchased from Mr. Oden [the overseer]"; and as Kemble explains in the *Journal,* Psyche was known as "Sack" (*Journal,* pp. 132, 134–40).

42. See pp. 235–37.

43. RK Jr. to PB, Mar. 23, 1839 (Wister MS, HSP). Bell, p. 281. *Journal,* pp. 238, 269, 362. That the white father of Sophy's child Sally was named Walker is confirmed in RK Jr. to PB, Apr. 18, 1845 (Butler MS [Box 5], HSP).

44. *Journal,* pp. 317, 317 n; 190–91; 136–38. Bell, pp. 180, 182, 235–36, 601; 254, 316, 532.

45. FK to Emily [Fitzhugh], Jan. 30, 1839, in FK, *Records,* 1:230. *Journal,* pp. 147–48.

46. John A. Scott, "Introduction," *Journal,* pp. lv–lvii; 292, 319, 325–27, 332, 343. Margaret Davis Cate, first draft of her "Mistakes in Fanny Kemble's Journal" (Cate MS, Georgia Historical Society). On the *Journal'*s being ready for publication in 1841, see sources in note 29 esp. FK to [Lydia Maria Child, via Elizabeth Sedgwick], Nov. 2, 1841, in Wister, *Fanny,* p. 178; and Meltzer, *Lydia Maria Child,* pp. 340, 435.

Probably the idea of altering the dates had first entered Kemble's mind as a (clumsy) means of protecting the anonymity of the participants in the duel—just as she tried to protect the anonymity of Roswell King Jr. by deliberately mislocating his Georgia plantation.

47. Couper's own account of the rescue states that a slave woman was transferred to a second lifeboat; but Kemble (perhaps relying on conversation with Couper's father) says the woman remained in Couper's lifeboat and was rescued at his order (*Journal,* pp. 338–40).

48. *Journal,* pp. 224, 94–95, 344. Kemble's choosing to conclude her *Journal* in this way is evidence of her own motives for turning back from her flight to Darien in Feb. 1839. She felt a parallel between her own (contracted) duty to her husband and

the (uncontracted) obligations laid upon slave women not to flee; in both cases she knew the attachment to children could be decisive in halting a mother's flight.

49. Phillips was so blinded by racialist doctrine that he could not perceive the doctrinaire biases vitiating the apology for slavery published many years later by Kemble's second daughter, Frances Butler Leigh, in her *Ten Years on a Georgia Plantation* (1883; rpt. New York, 1969), pp. 230–40 (Ulrich Phillips, *Life and Labor in the Old South* [Boston, 1929], pp. 262, 261–67).

50. *Journal,* pp. 270, 215–16, 146. Genovese refers to the first, but not to the second or third, of these pieces of evidence (*Roll, Jordan, Roll* [New York, 1974], p. 371).

51. Ibid., p. 380. Cf. *Journal,* p. 124. See pp. 270–71.

52. The only European traveler whose egalitarianism matched Kemble's was the Cambridge don E. S. Abdy; but he never visited the Deep South, and his contact with slavery, even in the border states, was more superficial than Kemble's (E. S. Abdy, *Journal of a Residence and Tour in the United States of North America,* 3 vols. [London, 1835]).

53. *Journal,* pp. 17–18, 100–101, 127–28; see also p. 260.

54. Margaret Davis Cate to John A. Scott, Aug. 1, 1959; Apr. 2, 1960; Mary B——to Margaret Cate, Aug. 28, 1959; E. M. Coulter to Margaret Cate, Oct. 7, 29, 1959 (Cate MS, Georgia Historical Society).

55. *Journal,* pp. 129, 177, 80.

56. Ibid., pp. 77–79, 234.

57. Ibid., pp. 177, 145. FK to Emily [Fitzhugh], Mar. 10, 1839, in FK, *Records,* 1:238. Cf. *Journal,* p. 161.

58. *Journal,* pp. 213, 212, 216–17; James, *Essays in London,* p. 125; *Journal,* p. 69; Fisher, *Diary,* July 7, 1863.

59. *Journal,* p. 308.

60. Ibid., pp. 100, 298–99, 211.

Chapter 8

1. Although the Butler estate is treated here as a unit whose characteristics resulted primarily from rice production, one must remember that cotton production at the Butler's St. Simons Island tracts partially shaped the experiences of a considerable number of Butler slaves, and that before 1830 substantial quantities of cotton and some sugar were grown even at Butler Island, to supplement its rice crop. Butler Island was always more valuable during the nineteenth century than the cotton lands at St. Simons. A substantial majority of the estate's "prime" male and female hands were early concentrated at Butler Island: by 1821 three-fifths of the field workers lived at Butler Island, and about three-fifths of the revenue was derived from there. And by 1830 Butler Island was dedicated almost entirely to raising rice. In purchasing new slaves, Major Butler had made it plain as early as 1807 that he wanted slaves inured to the hardships of rice cultivation—"I want no Cotton Negroes. I want people that can go in the ditch" (Bell, p. 140).

The two plantations were operated as a unit. Strong young men and women were culled from St. Simons to work at Butler Island, while some ailing children, some recuperating "prime" slaves, and some of the superannuated were sent to St. Simons because it was less unhealthy than Butler Island (*Journal,* pp. 202, 146). The cotton lands becoming less profitable than the rice tract, many slave huts at St. Simons were allowed to fall into disrepair, and the St. Simons sick house with its dirt floor was more noisome than the wooden-floored infirmary on Butler Island.

The slaves complained even more to Kemble at St. Simons than at Butler Island, but this is not to be explained simply by the neglect of their living accommodation. The slaves at "Hampton" (Butler's principal St. Simons tract) were somewhat older, more decrepit, and therefore more conscious of their ills. Furthermore, they could finish their tasks earlier at this season than on Butler Island, and consequently had more time and energy to talk to Kemble; and the slaves began to feel more confidence in the strange Englishwoman than when she had first arrived at Butler Island. A crucial reason for the St. Simons slaves' talking more openly to Kemble was their belief that their overseer, Mr. Gowen, was less likely to whip them for complaining to Kemble than the Butler Island overseer, Thomas Oden, had been. And Pierce Butler was absent from St. Simons—supervising the rice planting at Butler Island—during much of Kemble's stay at St. Simons. The slaves felt less constrained when Butler was fifteen miles away and so did Kemble, for this was when she instituted her Sunday morning Bible readings and even began to teach Aleck to read.

Yet much of what Kemble learned at St. Simons was the product of conditions at Butler Island, for many of the St. Simons slaves to whom she talked had worked at Butler Island during some substantial part of their lives. This was true of four among the nine women about whose experiences of pregnancy she inquired on Mar. 2, 1839 (see pp. 235–37). These women's physical and mental afflictions probably arose from the estate's being essentially a rice plantation. That the experience of raising rice penetrated the whole Butler estate becomes clear when one considers the later lives of those female Butler Island field hands who were young in 1821: by 1849 half of those still alive had been moved away from the rice plantation to St. Simons Island. (The group comprises every such field worker listed in 1821 who was then under twenty-two years old. Of eighteen such women still alive in 1849, nine had been moved to St. Simons. See pp. 242–44.) Similarly, an old woman at St. Simons named Scylla "was extremely lame, which she accounted for by an accident she had met with while carrying a heavy weight of rice on her head; she had fallen on a sharp stake . . . and had never recovered the injury she had received" (*Journal*, p. 255).

2. References in my chapters 8–10 to Butler records are always to the Butler MS, HSP, unless otherwise specified. These records contain—among other things—a list of field hands in 1821, with their ages; a list of all slaves in 1849, in family groups, with their ages; and complete birth and death lists (with dates and the names of the babies' parents) for 1816, and for 1819 through 1834 (RK Jr. to Major Pierce Butler, Feb. 18, 1821 [Box 3, File 17]; "Inventory and Appraisement of the estate of Capt. John Butler dec'd," Feb. 13, 1849; birth and death lists [Box 10, Files 13–15]).

The conversations occurred on the evening of Mar. 2, 1839, at St. Simons Island. Four of the nine women had worked most of their lives at Butler Island, including Molly, whom Pierce Butler had temporarily transferred to St. Simons on Feb. 6 (*Journal*, pp. 229–30. PB to Mr. Gowen, Feb. 9, 1839 [copy; Wister MS, HSP]).

Molly was the wife of Quamina (not Quambo, as Kemble misunderstood the name). She was no. 282 on the 1849 list. *Sophy* (no. 17, on column 3 of the 1821 list) was born in 1790. She had stillborn children on Apr. 16, 1825, and Sept. 26, 1828. Her William (b. 1819), Clary (b. 1822), and Mimba (b. 1825) may have still been alive in 1839. Her other five children must have been born before 1819. *Sukey* (no. 784 on the 1849 list), probably born before 1806, was married to Rentee the shoemaker (perhaps the name "Bush," which Kemble reported to be her husband's appellation, was Rentee's nickname). Her dead children include one stillborn (1824) and Emanuel

(Aug. 24, 1832–Jan. 10, 1833). Her living children included Betty (b. 1830), Peter (b. Jan. 12, 1834), and Dicey (b. 1838/39). Her other children included Amos (b. 1825) and Rentee (b. 1828); and if her account was correct, four (including twins?) must have been born during the period 1835/38, or before 1819.

3. *Journal*, p. 229. *Leah* (no. 729 on the 1849 list), born in 1812, had her first child Amey (b. 1829) before she was married to Caesar. Their child Adam was born in 1831. These were her only children still alive in 1849. The third of her children still alive in 1839, and the three dead ones, must have been born 1835/39. *Nanny* (no. 189 on the 1849 list) had borne her living child Frank in 1835. One of her two dead children was Daphne (Aug. 13, 1831–Nov. 22, 1833), and the other was probably born in 1837/38. *Charlotte* (no. 14 on column 7 of the 1821 list; and no. 738 on the 1849 list), the wife of cooper Rentee, was born about 1791. She had no recorded children 1819/34 (nor in 1816). This is consistent with her assertion that she had had two miscarriages but no children. She was pregnant again when she spoke to Kemble in 1839, and this probably resulted in her third miscarriage; certainly she had no living child in 1849. *Sally* (no. 817 on the 1849 list) was married to Castile (a name which Kemble thought was "Scipio"). She was born in 1814. Her living children were John (b. July 15, 1834) and Noble (b. 1835/36). Her anonymous infant died of lockjaw on May 5, 1833, nine days after birth. *Fanny* (no. 12 on column 8 of the 1821 list; and no. 761 on the 1849 list) had a living child, Wallace (b. 1836). Her dead children included an earlier Wallace (Dec. 3–Dec. 16, 1819), two stillbirths (1827 and 1831), and probably Bina (b. 1832) and another infant born either 1817/18 or 1835/38.

4. *Journal*, p. 230. *Sarah* (no. 19 on column 6 on the 1821 list; and no. 625 on the 1849 list), born about 1799, married Stephen after her first husband's death. In 1839 her two living children were Joan (b. 1828) and Simon (b. 1830). Her children dead by 1839 were Matty (Oct. 3, 1819–June 12, 1821), Hagar (May 17–Aug. 18, 1827), Anonymous (Dec. 1–Dec. 3, 1832), and probably Richard (b. Oct. 18, 1833 and surely dead before 1849) and a child born 1835/38.

5. Charles Lyell, *A Second Visit to the United States* (London, 1849), 1:334.

6. The numbers were:

May	1824	572
Aug.	1830	615
Dec.	1845	780
Feb.	1849	840
Feb.	1859	919

Any of this increase which may have resulted from the purchase of a handful of new slaves was probably offset by a small decrease through the sale of a few slaves for disciplinary reasons (Box 11, Folder 9, Butler MS; Bell, p. 327).

7. Calculated from U.S. Bureau of the Census, *Historical Statistics of the United States* (Washington, D.C., 1975), p. 18.

8. *Journal*, p. 146. From 1819 to June 30, 1834, 67.7 percent of the Butler estate's babies were born to mothers at Butler Island (birth lists, Butler MS). The movement of slaves back and forth between Butler Island and St. Simons prevents one's making a more accurate estimate of the growth of population at the two different types of plantation than that suggested here. But children certainly died much faster at Butler Island than at St. Simons, as is shown subsequently. And the estimate that Butler

Island slaves increased at about a 10.5 percent decennial rate is consistent with the experiences of the sample of twenty-four Butler Island women discussed later in this chapter.

9. Although other crops were sometimes grown there, Butler Island was essentially a rice plantation. From 1819 to 1829, rice occupied on average 58 percent of its acreage; thereafter, rice was virtually its only crop. The island's malarial disease environment was always that of its rice swamps. And the health of the mothers—which, as will be seen, had a strong influence upon that of their newborn babies—was shaped by the likelihood that all of the women at Butler Island worked in the rice swamps at least during those parts of the year when demand for their labor was most exigent (crop reports, Box 7, Files 7–8).

10. The proportion of stillbirths is calculated from the figures in the following table:

Butler Estate, 1819–June 30, 1834

	Cotton (St. Simons)	Rice (Butler Island)
Live births	158	331
Stillbirths	9 (5.7% of live births)	17 (5.1% of live births)

Sources: Birth and death lists, 1819–34, Butler MS.

11. Indeed, a figure near 20 percent may be valid for slave women in the whole South. This has important implications for studies of the slaves' family and sexual customs, because these studies depend partly on estimating the median age at which a slave woman's first child was conceived. In view of the number of miscarriages and stillbirths, this median must have been rather lower than the median age at which a woman's first live-born child was conceived. The age at which her first *live-born* child was conceived would therefore be misleading.

By "miscarriages" I mean not all cases of "early fetal wastage" but only those where the fetus was sufficiently developed that the woman would report its loss as a miscarriage. Total "early fetal wastage" was doubtless even higher, for "in the 1980s," Angus McLaren reports, "still something like a third of all conceptions [were] spontaneously terminated" (Angus McLaren, *Reproductive Rituals* [London, 1984], citing Edward Shorter, *A History of Women's Bodies* [New York, 1982], p. 193).

I base my Butler Island estimate on the following reasoning. (1) Stillbirths at Butler Island numbered 5.1 percent of all live births (see the preceding note). If the fertility rate of all those slave women who survived to about age eighteen was some 7.2 (as it was for the sample of twenty-four Butler Island women discussed later), the number of stillbirths would have been 0.37 per woman (i.e., 5.1 × 7.2). (2) Miscarriages among Kemble's nine interlocutors numbered 1⅓ per mother; but these women had not yet finished their childbearing careers, and therefore they no doubt later experienced more miscarriages. Furthermore, the other childbearing experiences of these nine mothers—as will soon be shown—were *less* harsh than was common at the rice plantation. And the effect of chronic malaria on the mothers' health probably made the number of miscarriages at the rice plantation even larger than in Kemble's sample (only four of Kemble's nine interlocutors having worked on Butler Island). Taking all these factors into account, one may infer that Butler Island mothers experienced an average of perhaps 1⅔ miscarriages per mother. (3) On this presumption, the average number of pregnancies at Butler Island would have been 9.24 (i.e., 7.2 + 0.37 + 1.67), and the proportion of these pregnancies culminating in miscarriage or still-birth would have been 22 percent.

A figure of this magnitude is made plausible by data on miscarriages and stillbirths among working-class English mothers during the generation before World War I: probably at least 17.7 percent of such women's pregnancies terminated in stillbirth (4.9 percent) or miscarriage (12.8 percent) (I calculate these figures from Margaret Llewelyn Davies, *Maternity: Letters from Working Women* [1915; rpt. London, 1978], pp. 294–95).

12. Richard Steckel, *The Economics of U.S. Slave and Southern White Fertility* (New York, 1985), pp. 95, 90–92. Steckel, "Slave Mortality: Analysis of Evidence From Plantation Records," *Social Science History* 3 (1979): 92, 106. Similarly, Steckel may have underestimated the extent to which mortality of slave children aged five through fourteen on rice plantations exceeded that on nonrice plantations. See chapter 15, note 82.

13. RK Jr. to Thomas Butler, Jan. 12, 1834.

14. Infant mortality was probably about 27.5 percent in the slave South as a whole, while it was 21.6 percent on the Butlers' sea-island cotton plantation. Similarly, infant mortality on the typical rice plantation may well have been about 43 percent, as compared with the rate of 38.1 percent at Butler Island. See chapter 15, note 82.

15. As eighteen women bore children in 1822, the six mentioned in the text constitute one-third of that year's mothers. One or two of them may have experienced miscarriages, followed soon by a successful pregnancy. But miscarriages cannot have accounted for many of these instances of lengthy "breeding," unless the proportion of miscarriages among these women was far higher than those reported to Kemble in 1839. Nor is there reason to suppose King was enough interested in miscarriages to record them (and for this year alone) in what would have been a very oblique manner.

That, beginning in 1823, King may have demanded visual proof that a slave woman was really pregnant is suggested by his annual birth lists from 1823 to 1834, which never again mentioned an alleged pregnancy of over nine months. Perhaps King had controlled this form of malingering simply by punishing any woman whose pregnancy turned out not to have started as soon as she claimed. If King demanded visual proof after 1822, the younger Pierce Butler—when he first visited Butler Island in 1836–37, and required King to diminish the tasks of all slave women—evidently insisted on reverting to earlier practice. By 1839 Kemble reported that "every woman who is pregnant, as soon as she chooses to make the fact known to the overseer, is relieved of a certain portion of her work in the field." If a pseudopregnant woman failed to produce a child she was then whipped, as happened to Markie in 1839 (RK Jr., "On the Management of the Butler Estate," *Southern Agriculturalist* 1 [Dec. 1828]: 527. 1822 birth list [HSP]. *Journal*, p. 95; see also pp. 66, 277).

16. RK Jr. to Thomas Butler, Jan. 6, 1833, Jan. 12, 1834.

17. Richard Steckel, "A Dreadful Childhood: The Excess Mortality of American Slaves," *Social Science History* 10 (1986): 441–42. *Journal*, p. 293.

18. The Butler records illuminate yet another aspect of rice plantations' dreadful health record. Robert Fogel reports that in most high-risk societies about 60 percent of infant mortality occurs during the first month, and this has proved true of the Butler's sea-island cotton plantation. But the statement is not true for the Butler Island rice plantation, where the correct figure is 50 percent. The explanation is that infant mortality at the rice plantation—though much higher during the first month than at the cotton plantation—was *immensely* higher than at the cotton plantation during the

second through twelfth months. (During these months, this so-called postneonatal infant mortality rate was well over twice as high on the rice plantation—19.1 percent as contrasted with 8.3 percent):

Infant Mortality Rates (to age 1), 1819–34
(dead/all children born alive)

	Cotton *St. Simons Island (%)*	Rice *Butler Island (%)*
(a) Died during first month	13.3	19.0
(b) Died during months 2–12	8.3	19.1
(c) Total died during Year 1	21.6	38.1
Proportion of infant mortality which occurred during first month: (a)/(c)	61.6%	50.0%

Note: Data from appendix D, appendix tables 3 and 4 (calculated as indicated in appendix table 4). Cf. Robert Fogel, *Without Consent or Contract* (New York, 1989), p. 147.

19. The sample should contain a representative group of Butler Island women, for it comprises every woman on the Feb. 1821 list of Butler Island workers who was twenty-one years old or less. The youngest women on the list were fourteen years old. That the lives of Butler Island women were harsher than those of the nine women to whom Kemble spoke on Mar. 2, 1839, is evident from the following table:

	Average Butler Island woman (based on sample of 24 women)	*Average of nine women interviewed by Kemble*
Average number of live births per woman	7.2	5.6 (as of Mar. 1839)
Average number of surviving children per woman	2.6 (survived to age 21)	2.9 (survived to Mar. 1839)
Average number of live-born children who died	4.6 (died before age 21)	2.7 (died before Mar. 1839)

The main reason Kemble's sample understates the women's hardship is that she interviewed women at St. Simons, and only four of her nine interviewees had spent their working lives at the Butler Island rice plantation, where conditions were harsher than on the sea-island cotton plantations. My data include virtually the whole child-bearing history of the twenty-four women in the sample, whereas most of the women to whom Kemble spoke would have borne other children after their conversations with her in 1839; and some of their children who survived until 1839 would have died before reaching age twenty-one.

Kemble's women experienced five pregnancies which led to stillbirths: I have subtracted these both from the births Kemble reported and from the number of children she reported as having died (*Journal,* pp. 229–30).

20. Death lists, 1823, 1831, 1832. Of Butler Island's approximately 425 slaves in 1832, 10 died in the epidemic that year, including three infants, two very old people, Esther (who had just delivered a child), Dido, one able-bodied man, and two other youngish women.

21. Birth and dead lists, 1819–34. Sinder (no. 1 on column 11 of the 1821 list of

field workers) was no. 511 on the 1849 inventory. Tina (no. 5 on column 7 of the 1821 list) was no. 231 on the 1849 inventory.

22. The calculation is more complex than the text might suggest. The simplest way to begin is to estimate the fertility rate of all slave women who survived to age fifteen, and to multiply this by the mortality rate of all children to age fifteen; at Butler Island I estimate these figures to have been, respectively, 6.8 live births and 60.4 percent. Thus, of a woman's 6.8 children, 4.1 are likely to have died, and 2.7 to have survived. With an average of thirty years separating a mother from her median surviving child, the 2.7 surviving children would ensure a decennial growth rate of 10.5 percent.

(The reason I estimate the fertility rate at 6.8—not 7.2 as in the sample of twenty-four women—is that these twenty-four women were nearly all older than fifteen in 1821 [eleven of them being by then about twenty years old]. At least one of their contemporaries (Mirah) had survived until age fifteen but died before 1821, and is therefore not included in my sample. If one had been able to record the name of every woman like Mirah—born between 1799 and 1806, and who survived to age fifteen— the total number of women in the sample would have been not twenty-four but at least twenty-five, probably more; and the fertility rate of this larger group would have been correspondingly lower than 7.2).

(My estimate that the mortality rate [to age fifteen] was 60.4% is an interpolation into column e of appendix table 5, in appendix D.)

23. *Journal,* pp. 245, 240–41.

24. Ibid., p. 130.

25. Ibid., pp. 293, 222–23.

26. Ibid., p. 214. I have substituted in this quotation the words in brackets, "three weeks" (which are consistent with Kemble's report elsewhere in the book), in place of her words "in the third week."

27. Ibid., pp. 235, 236, 274, 229–30.

28. Ibid., pp. 77, 67, 50, 67.

29. Ibid., pp. 293–94, 114; 210.

30. Ibid., pp. 303, 241–42.

Chapter 9

1. *Journal,* pp. 238, 362. See also *Journal,* pp. 201, 269. PB to RK Jr., Mar. 17, 1839 (copy); RK Jr. to PB, Mar. 23, 1839, Wister MS (HSP). Bell, pp. 217, 280–81.

Both Bell and the indexer of John Scott's edition of Kemble's *Journal* have mistakenly supposed Roswell King Jr. the father of Judy's and Sinder's children. This would be inconsistent with Kemble's assertion (*Journal,* p. 362) that these two children's father was a different overseer from Renty's father (who was Roswell King Jr.). Nor could Mrs. King Jr. have been the Mrs. King who ordered the flogging of Judy and Sinder in 1814, for she did not marry until 1825.

That Roswell King Sr. was Bram's father was supposed by Pierce Butler (*Journal,* p. 201). The elder King's siring children by Judy and Sinder was asserted by Judy and Sophy (*Journal,* pp. 238, 269). Roswell King Jr. confirmed in his 1839 letter to Pierce Butler that Sophy, Judy, and Sinder had all produced mulatto children in about Aug. 1814, but he avoided discussing the paternity of their children except to deny that he himself was the father. He did not deny that his own father was the father of Judy's child but confined himself instead to remarks about the mendacity of slaves, the profitability of the estate, and the good treatment of the slaves by his father and himself, to which he believed the increase of the Butlers' slave population attested. Kemble slightly misspelled Bram's, Jim's, and Sinder's names. Her later memory slip about the paternity of Sophy's child is mentioned at p. 227.

2. *Journal,* p. 250. Betty and Frank's previous child was born on Jan. 28, 1816, and was still alive in 1849 (1816 birth list; 1849 inventory [HSP]). See note 3 for further documentation.

3. *Journal,* pp. 276 (quotation), 201, 249–50, 273–74, 282, 176 n. I have inferred the slaves' ages from the 1849 list (no. 1: Frank; no. 2: Betty; no. 810: Rentee); and Daphne's and Ben's birthdate is recorded on the 1824 birth list (HSP). Bell, pp. 280, 243, 455 (photo of Daphne), 531, 224.

4. RK Jr., "On the Management of the Butler Estate," *Southern Agriculturalist* 1 (1828): 524.

5. Ibid., 524. Charles Spalding Wylly, *The Seed That Was Sown in the Colony of Georgia: the Harvest and the Aftermath, 1740–1870* (New York, 1910), p. 48.

6. RK, "Narrative," Feb. 14, 1815 (Bell, p. 182).

7. RK to Major Pierce Butler, Feb. 26, Mar. 4, 1815 (Bell, pp. 178, 180; see also pp. 235–36, 601).

8. RK to Major Butler, Aug. 13, 1815 (Bell, p. 185; see also pp. 179–87).

9. Death list, 1816, Box 10, File 13; RK to Major Butler, Dec. 22, 1816, Butler MS (HSP).

10. RK Jr., "On the Management of the Butler Estate," 525. *Journal,* pp. 175, 241, 309.

11. RK Jr. to Frances Butler, Feb. 8, 1824; to Thomas Butler, Mar. 8, 1829 (Bell, pp. 238, 244–45). Death list, 1829 (Butler MS). Frederick Douglass, *Narrative of the Life of Frederick Douglass, an American Slave* (1845; rpt. [ed. Benjamin Quarles] Cambridge, Mass., 1960), pp. xxiii, 47–48. Dickson Preston, *The Young Frederick Douglass* (Baltimore, 1980), pp. 222, 73.

12. *Journal,* pp. 109, 136–40. See my pp. 279–81.

13. *Journal,* p. 66. Wylly, *Seed That Was Sown,* p. 49.

14. Bell, pp. 366, 451–58. Frances Butler Leigh, *Ten Years on a Georgia Plantation* (1883; rpt., New York, 1969), pp. 33–35, 55, 60–62, 71–72, 77–78.

15. *Journal,* pp. 132, 70, 364, 79. The younger Pierce Butler led his wife to believe that these rules of Major Butler's limited the overseer to fifty lashes without the owner's permission; but RK to Major Butler, May 26, 1816 (Bell, p. 219), makes plain that the latter expected the infliction of at least one hundred lashes as punishment for flight. And Roswell King Jr. took for granted that the younger Pierce Butler would approve "a cool 100 lashes" to penalize serious theft (RK Jr. to PB, Apr. 18, 1845 [Butler MS, Box 5]).

16. Bell, p. 315.

17. Wylly, *Seed That Was Sown,* p. 50.

18. Major Pierce Butler to RK Jr., Nov. 10, 1821; RK to Major Butler, July 2, 1806; July 23, 1808 (Bell, pp. 226, 166).

19. RK to Major Butler, May 26, 1816; June 24, 1817 (Bell, pp. 219, 218).

20. Emphasis in the original. RK to Major Butler, Dec. 31, 1808 (Butler MS). Bell, p. 167.

21. Major Butler to William Page, Apr. 25, 1798 (Bell, p. 156).

22. *Journal,* pp. 246, 238.

23. RK Jr. to Frances Butler, Aug. 9, 1835 (Bell, p. 247).

24. *Journal,* p. 267.

25. Ibid., p. 315.

26. Ibid., pp. 110, 154, 160–61. I infer that the driver's whip, whose description is quoted, was the same one used to flog Teresa.

27. Ibid., pp. 72–73, 85–86.

28. Ibid., p. 189.

29. Ibid., pp. 174, 215–16, 175.

30. Ibid., pp. 207, 92–93, 310, 186; 285–86, 166; 125, 120. RK to Major Butler, Mar. 30, 1804 (Bell, pp. 151–52).

31. *Journal*, p. 275.

32. Wylly, *Seed That Was Sown*, pp. 50, 49.

33. *Journal*, pp. 307–8.

34. RK Jr. to Frances Butler, May 17, 1835 (Bell, p. 247); *Journal*, p. 254.

35. *Journal*, p. 268.

36. Ibid., pp. 358–59, 288.

37. Ibid., pp. 359, 156, 359–60.

38. PB to RK Jr., Feb. 17, 1839, Wister MS (HSP). *Journal*, pp. 69–70. I infer that "ground" in this passage is a synonym for (boarded) "floor," by contrast to the "earth" at the Hampton infirmary, whose floor "was not boarded" (*Journal*, p. 255).

39. *Journal*, pp. 255–56, 71–72.

40. Dr. James Holmes to PB, June 22, 1841 (Butler MS).

41. John Butler to PB, Jan. 31, 1841, Wister MS (HSP).

42. "Inventory and Appraisement of the estate of Capt. John Butler, dec'd," Feb. 13, 1849.

Chapter 10

1. *Journal*, p. 78. Theodore Rosengarten, ed., *All God's Dangers* (New York, 1974), pp. 26–27. Leon Litwack, *Been in the Storm So Long* (New York, 1979), p. 451.

2. Stanley Elkins, *Slavery* (Chicago, 1959). The best rebuttal was John Blassingame's study *The Slave Community* (New York, 1972).

3. *Journal*, p. 377. "The world the slaves made" is the subtitle of the most influential study of the slaves' culture, Eugene Genovese's *Roll, Jordan, Roll* (New York, 1974).

4. *Journal*, pp. 49–50, 66, 91, 94. Emphasis in the original.

5. *Journal*, pp. 356–57; FK, *Records of Later Life*, 1:218; *Journal*, p. 127.

6. *Journal*, pp. 336, 314, 236–37, 93.

7. Ibid., pp. 71; 297; 336, 334, 336. The parallel between old Rose's conduct at the infirmary and that of Kemble's slaves at Little St. Simons suggests a somewhat different view of Rose's motivation from that proposed by Eugene Genovese. The men who offered to lie in the salt marsh, to be trod on by Kemble, demonstrated not so much pride in fulfilling a duty as a (calculating) gratification in abasing themselves for their mistress's supposed satisfaction; and so perhaps did Rose. Cf. Genovese, *Roll, Jordan, Roll*, pp. 140–41.

8. *Journal*, pp. 95–96. F. L. Olmsted, *The Cotton Kingdom* (1861; rpt. [ed. A. M. Schlesinger] New York, 1953), pp. 320, 263–64.

9: *Journal*, pp. 229, 203. Frederick Douglass, *Narrative of the Life of Frederick Douglass, an American Slave* (1845; rpt. [ed. Benjamin Quarles] Cambridge, Mass., 1960), p. 44. Douglass erroneously identifies the neighbor as Jacob Jepson (Dickson Preston, *Young Frederick Douglass* [Baltimore, 1980], p. 221).

10. *Journal*, pp. 174–75, 251. I have changed the punctuation of this passage, which otherwise would not make grammatical sense.

11. Ibid., pp. 233–34; 249; 260–61.

12. Ibid., p. 124. Solomon Northup, *Twelve Years a Slave* (1853; rpt. [ed. Sue Eakin and Joseph Logsdon] Baton Rouge, La., 1968), p. 172. *Journal*, pp. 270, 215–16, 146. Cf. Genovese, *Roll, Jordan, Roll*, pp. 371, 380.

13. *Journal*, pp. 305, 281. That Kemble referred in this last quotation to ordinary slaves, not to drivers armed with whips, is shown by her saying in the same paragraph that this "unbounded insolence and tyranny" was only "of manner, of course it can go no farther." Cf. Genovese, *Roll, Jordan, Roll*, p. 380.

14. *Journal*, p. 314.

15. Ibid., pp. 67–68. When Sir Charles Lyell paused momentarily at Butler Island in 1846, en route from James Hamilton Couper's Hopeton plantation to his summer residence at St. Simons Island, he formed a superficial impression of neat tidiness at the Butler Island slave settlement. Probably the houses had been given a coat of whitewash subsequent to Kemble's visit. Evidently Lyell did not learn that two families shared the houses he described, and very probably he was shown into only one of them—the dwelling of headman Frank—whose tidiness Kemble too admired, contrasting it with the state of most of the other dwellings on the island (Lyell, *Second Visit to the United States* [London, 1849], 1:332–33).

16. *Journal*, pp. 68, 98, 271, 302.

17. Ibid., pp. 60–62.

18. Ibid., pp. 61, 156, 62.

19. Map in Bell, pp. 118–19. The map in *Journal* (ed. John Scott), p. 57, mislocates the tidal rice mill.

20. 1849 inventory, Butler MS (HSP).

21. Major Butler to R. P. Saunders, Sept. 5, 1791; Philip Morgan, "Black Society in the Lowcountry, 1760–1810," in Ira Berlin and Ronald Hoffman, eds., *Slavery and Freedom in the Age of the American Revolution* (Charlottesville, Va., 1983), p. 118. Bell, pp. 111, 146.

22. RK to Major Butler, Aug. 24, 1806 (Bell, p. 146). *Journal*, pp. 317 n, 84. RK Jr. to Major Butler, Feb. 18, 1821, Butler MS (HSP).

23. *Journal*, pp. 270; 201, 215. Bram (misspelled by Kemble) was no. 635 in the 1849 inventory.

24. *Journal*, pp. 113, 81; see also pp. 176 n, 250.

25. 1849 inventory (no. 1: Frank; no. 2: Betty, no. 3: their son Quash; no. 5: their daughter Philada; no. 7: their daughter Phoebe; no. 212: their son carpenter London; no. 810: Betty's mulatto son, carpenter Rentee; no. 800: Betty's probable father, Driver Morris (of St. Anne's plantation). On the 1821 list, "Morrison" was the driver of "Experiment" plantation, and Betty's name appears directly below those of "Morrison" and his wife, Dorcas. ("Morrison," the driver at Experiment, was called "Morris" by 1829, as is proved by "Morrison" being specified as the father of the child named March [born Mar. 26, 1824] who died on Apr. 28, 1829, then described as "Morris child.") Kemble's conversation with this Morris (about Morris's father's silver cup) is in *Journal*, pp. 317–18. A photograph of the cup is printed in Bell, p. 145. Betty's husband, carpenter Frank, does not appear on the 1821 list, which names only workers in the field, not artisans.

That Betty's probable father, driver Morris, raped the slave woman Sophy, at about the same time that Roswell King Jr. raped Betty, may remind one that despotic power could corrupt slaves as well as masters. It would be tempting to suggest that Morris's action was an outraged reaction when he learned how King had dishonored the driver's own married daughter; but quite apart from the other imponderables in these two cases, there is no way to be sure in which chronological order the two events took place.

26. *Journal,* pp. 81, 176 n; see also pp. 250, 133. Dr. James Holmes to PB, June 22, 1841; cf. John Butler to PB, Jan. 31, 1841, Wister MS (HSP).

27. *Journal,* pp. 187–88, 168. Perhaps Kemble's intervention led Pierce Butler to lessen Eve's task, for she was still alive ten years later (no. 114, 1849 inventory; birth and death lists, 1819–34; RK Jr. to Thomas Butler, Jan. 12, 1834 [Butler MS]). Kemble mistakenly implied that Ned had never done any other work except as an engineer.

28. *Journal,* pp. 165, 193–94. Douglass, *Narrative,* pp. 113–15.

29. *Journal,* pp. 147–49. *King Lear,* 4.7.58–59; 5.3.10–11.

30. Bell, pp. 238, 549. *Journal,* p. 94.

31. *Journal,* pp. 154, 255, 133. On John and Abraham: ibid., pp. 320, 328.

32. Ibid., pp. 136, 249, 138. PB to RK Jr., Feb. 17, 1839 [not long after Joe's protest] (copy; Wister MS, HSP), confirms that Butler had recently bought King's slave Psyche and her children from Thomas Oden, partly "because they wished me very much to buy them."

Chapter 11

1. See chapter 1. LM, plantation expenses, Manigault MS, IV (SHC); LM, plantation journal, Apr. 1858 (Clifton, p. 250); but cf. CM to LM, Feb. 10, 1861 (Clifton, p. 315).

2. References to Allston records are always, in chapters 11 through 14, to the Allston MS at SCHS or SCL (identified simply by these latter abbreviations), unless otherwise specified. A selection of these documents is printed in Easterby. Gross revenues for Chicora Wood and Nightingale Hall are in plantation journals, file 12-4-13, SCHS. I probably exaggerate Allston's expenses in estimating them at eighty-five hundred dollars (nearly two and a half times as large as those at Gowrie in 1853, when Allston's gross revenues were two and a half times those at Gowrie). For Allston, unlike Manigault, paid little to feed his slaves: he raised their food on his own provision farms, especially at Brittons Neck. If one included in Allston's profits the increased value of his slaves (as slave prices were rising during the 1850s), his profits for 1853 were probably about forty thousand dollars. To this should be added the thousands of dollars worth of a rich planter's annual "perquisites": the use of a posh house and gardens, staffed by many house servants and supplied with much food from the plantation, all at no additional expense.

3. Of these slaves, RA bought 41 in January 1859 (RA to AA, Jan. 25, 1859 [typescript; SCL]) and 109 (not 116 as stated in the original bill of sale [Easterby, p. 353]) in May 1859 when he acquired for himself Pipe Down plantation (slave list, file 12-6-24 [SCHS]). In addition, in Jan. 1859 RA signed the bond for $29,000 with which about 42 slaves were bought from T. P. Alston for RA's son Benjamin. RA was held liable for this purchase, the $29,000 bond forming an important element in the $197,000 debt with which he was saddled at the time of his death. Of these 192 slaves, RA kept about 73 (and two free blacks) to work his own Pipe Down plantation, while about 119 slaves were for Benjamin at his new Guendalos plantation (J. B. Allston to RA, Jan. 11, 1859 [typescript]; AA, journal, Apr. 25, 1865 [SCL]; 1860 U.S. Manuscript Census of Benjamin's slaves).

4. Easterby, pp. 23, 45. Inventory, Apr. 1864, file 12-6-25 (SCHS).

5. Easterby, p. 43. 1860 U.S. Manuscript Census. Davidson understates by one the slaveholdings of RA, and of BA.

6. Inventory, Apr. 1864, file 12-6-25 (SCHS).

7. William Freehling, *The Road to Disunion* (New York, 1990), 1:232–36. A brief nineteenth-century appreciation of Washington Allston appears in Henry Adams's *History of the United States* (New York, 1889–90), 9:213–17, which may throw as much light on Adams's own artistic ideals as on the South Carolinian's.

8. Rogers, pp. 159, 166, 188, 197, 523.

9. The 3,458 slaves enumerated in the 1860 census fell into three groupings:

1,085: *the family of Robert Allston,* including:

631	Robert Allston
119	Robert's son Benjamin
185	Robert's nephew Joseph
150	Robert's nephew William

1,180: *the family of W. A. Alston Sr. (Robert's second cousin)* (including W. A. Alston Sr., his brother, and his two grandsons)

1,193: *the family of Mrs. Martha Allston [Pyatt] (Robert's second cousin)*
(including Mrs. Martha Allston [Pyatt], her two sons, and her son-in-law)

TOTAL: 3,458

These figures (except for RA's and BA's slaves [which are from the Manuscript Census] and the 90 slaves at Mrs. Pyatt's son-in-law's "Turkey Hill" plantation [which are from Joyner, p. 19]) are all based on Davidson's list of South Carolina planters who had at least 100 slaves in one parish. By omitting holdings of less than 100 slaves these figures probably understate the number of slaves actually accumulated by members of the Allston, Alston, and Pyatt clans.

10. Charlotte Allston to RA, Feb. 21, 1819 (Easterby, p. 51).

11. For clarity I refer always to this plantation as "Chicora Wood"; in fact the Allstons did not substitute this romantic appellation for the original, less glorified term "Matanzas" until 1853 (Easterby, pp. 19–20).

12. Of Chicora Wood's 920 acres, 370 were eventually cultivated in rice (the remainder being high land on the west bank of the Pee Dee); but only 100 acres of this rice land had been cleared when Robert Allston took over their management in the mid-1820s (Easterby, pp. 20–21).

13. The deceased brother's half share of Chicora Wood was divided equally between the two surviving brothers. Robert gained full possession of this plantation by buying his brother Joseph's share in 1832 (Easterby, p. 20).

14. Pringle, pp. 73, 75. Frame A10, file 12-21-1 (SCHS). Easterby, p. 28 n. The bequest to Robert also included a second, less valuable estate, which supplied food for the slaves at the aunt's rice plantation.

15. Pringle, p. 78. RA to J. D. B. DeBow, Feb. 28, 1852, file 12-4-8 (SCHS). Charlotte Allston to RA, Sept. 27, 1818; Aug. 12, 1819; J. L. Petigru to RA, Dec. 1861 (Easterby, pp. 50, 53, 185).

16. Charlotte Allston to RA, June 8, 1823; RA to BA, [Mar. 1856]; to AA, Mar. 7, 1852 (Easterby, pp. 60, 133, 114). RA to AA, May 7, 1854, in Michael Johnson, "Planters and Patriarchy: Charleston, 1800–1860," *Journal of Southern History* 46 (1980): 56.

17. RA to AA, Feb. 2, 1852, Easterby, p. 113. RA to AA, May 7, 1854, in Johnson, "Planters and Patriarchy," p. 56.

18. He hoped to sell Nightingale Hall (which was seven miles south of Chicora Wood), and to concentrate all of his holdings near Chicora Wood, where, even with advancing years, he could keep everything under his own eye (Philip Porcher to RA, Dec. 7, 1859; RA to Porcher [Dec. 1859], [typescripts], [SCL]).

19. In this paragraph "acreage" always refers to rice lands, *not* the total acreage of the plantations. The latter was much larger:

		Rice land	Other improved land	Total acreage
Chicora Wood:	before 1851	370	550	920
	extensions, 1851–53	260 ⎫	25	960
	extension, 1858	100 ⎭		[100?]
Pipe Down, 1859		140		645
Nightingale Hall (including Waterford)		370	185	1580
Robert Allston's TOTAL (n.i. his 3,700-acre Brittons Neck provision farm, nor his 1,425-acre inland swampland at Carvers Bay, nor 120 acres of residential land on Waccamaw Neck and Pawleys Island, nor the 500 acres mentioned in note [a])		1240	760	ca. 4200.
Guendalos (Benjamin Allston's share, n.i. RA's Chicora extension), 1858		210	104	714.

Sources:

(a) *Total acreage:* 1860 U.S. Manuscript Census; AA, journal, Jan. 25, 1865 (SCL); Easterby, pp. 20–22. Nightingale Hall's Waterford also comprised 500 acres of seashore, on the east side of Waccamaw Neck, *not* included in its "total acreage" above.

(b) *Total improved acreage:* 1860 U.S. Manuscript Census.

(c) *Rice land:* (1) Chicora before 1851: Easterby, p. 20.

(2) Nightingale: RA, diary, 1859, in Easterby, p. 452.

(3) Chicora extensions, 1851–53: Estimated from the fact that the enlarged Chicora Wood produced 54 percent more rice than Nightingale Hall in 1853; and assuming that, because Chicora Wood was at a less good pitch of tide than Nightingale Hall, it produced only about forty bushels per acre in contrast to the forty-eight bushels per acre at Nightingale Hall.

(4) Guendalos and Pipe Down: The estimate that about 210 acres of Guendalos and 140 acres of Pipe Down were rice lands was based on the ratio of the number of Benjamin Allston's slaves (119) to Robert's (631) in 1860, and on the number of blacks (75) whom Robert Allston kept at Pipe Down to work its land.

20. I have included in this twenty-five-mile strip the first three plantations on the northeast side of the Black River, whose location on the peninsula south of Pringle's Ferry made them virtually adjacent to several of the Pee Dee plantations. I follow here Elizabeth Pringle and George Rogers in including these three Black River plantations as part of the Pee Dee social unit (Pringle, pp. 156–59; Rogers, pp. 273–80).

21. The figures in this and the following paragraph are from the nearest census (1860, as reported in Davidson) except for Poinsett and Shaffer (1850: Rogers, pp. 525–56). As Barnwell died in 1857 and Izard in 1858, the figures for them refer to the holdings in 1860 of Barnwell's widow and of Izard's estate (Davidson, pp. 176, 213).

Poinsett had died in 1851, and his widow (the former Mrs. Mary [Izard] Pringle) seems also to have died by 1860, leaving their estate to J. J. I. Pringle, Mrs. Pringle's son by her first marriage (*Dictionary of American Biography* [London, 1935], 15:30–32).

22. W. H. Trapier held 265 slaves in 1860, most of them at "Ingleside" plantation on the Pee Dee. In 1853 his brother, J. H. Trapier—soon after marrying Elizabeth Heyward—purchased "Keithfield" plantation, virtually adjacent to Ingleside. Keithfield had been the center of an enterprise which in 1850, with 384 slaves, was probably the second-largest rice producer on the Pee Dee and Black Rivers. If J. H. Trapier acquired even one-quarter of those slaves to work the plantation he bought in 1853, his and his brother's holdings would together have numbered 361 slaves (Davidson, pp. 256–57; Rogers, pp. 279, 284, 301).

23. Their father's 335 slaves had been left in 1854 to four heirs, and those slaves not on the Pee Dee worked a Waccamaw plantation. I have estimated the number of Tucker slaves on the latter plantation in accordance with the production figures in Joyner, p. 20, attributing the remaining slaves to the Pee Dee.

24. I have presumed that by 1857 the Pee Dee farm of Robert Collins, a mulatto who owned nineteen slaves in 1850, had been absorbed by a neighbor. Collins died in 1856 (Rogers, p. 278).

25. This figure (probably for 1796) comprises George Washington's own 124 slaves and Martha Washington's 153 dower slaves but not, of course, the 40 slaves Washington hired from Mrs. French (J. C. Fitzpatrick, ed., *Writings of George Washington* [Washington, D.C., 1940], 37:268; on the probable date of this inventory: 34:448).

26. John W. De Forest, *A Union Officer in the Reconstruction* (ed. James Croushore and David Potter: New Haven, Conn., 1948), p. 186. Joseph Alston to Theodosia Alston (Rogers, p. 189). Ward, who died in 1853, owned 1,193 slaves in 1850 (see p. 415 and note 77). Although the Wade Hampton estate in Mississippi was said in 1862 to have held 1,500 slaves, ownership was probably divided among several Hamptons (C. Vann Woodward, ed., *Mary Chesnut's Civil War* [New Haven, Conn., 1981], p. 334).

27. Woodward, *Mary Chesnut's Civil War*, p. 685. RA to Alexander Campbell, Feb. 3, 1837; *Charleston Courier*, Dec. 10, 1842; RA to AA, Nov. 25, 1850; Feb. 2, Mar. 7, 1852 (Easterby, pp. 385; 90 n; 106, 114).

28. Pringle, pp. 126, 23. A. Sachtleben to RA, Mar. 15, 1859; RA to AA, Dec. 10, Nov. 27, 1851 (Easterby, pp. 155, 112, 108).

29. Easterby, p. 97 n. The *Memoir* was reprinted under the title "Rice" in *DeBow's Review* 1 (1846): 320–57; "Sea Coast Crops" is in *DeBow's Review* 16 (1854): 589–615.

30. RA to AA, Nov. 25, 1847; to Elizabeth Blyth, July 11, 1838 (Easterby, pp. 98, 76).

31. RA to AA, Dec. 10, 1842 (Easterby, p. 90). Benjamin Whitner to James Hammond, Dec. 20, 1844, in Bertram Wyatt-Brown, *Southern Honor* (New York, 1982), p. 277. Easterby, frontispiece. Pringle, pp. 200–201, 66, 96. On sorrow in Allston's own family, see the end of chapter 12.

32. Joseph Alston to Theodosia Burr, Dec. 28, 1800, in Matthew L. Davis, *Memoirs of Aaron Burr*, 1:431 (Rogers, p. 189). BA to RA, June 4, 1858; RA, diary, July–Aug. 1859 (Easterby, pp. 142, 451).

33. Easterby, p. 17. AA to BA, Oct. 30, 1862; RA to AA, Dec. 10, 1851 (Easterby, pp. 190, 112). RA to AA, Dec. 3, 1843 (typescript), (SCL). Pringle, pp. 210, 200. RA to BA [Mar. 1856] (Easterby, p. 132).

34. AA to BA, May 31, 1864 (Easterby, p. 199).

35. RA to AA, July 18, 1863 (Easterby, p. 195). Pringle, p. 204.

36. RA, page proofs for *DeBow's Review,* autobiographical sketch, 1852 [p. 574], file 12-4-8 (SCHS). AA to BA, Sept. 20, 1854 (Easterby, p. 120).

37. Harman Pitman to RA, Apr. 25, 1861 (Easterby, pp. 265–66, 36).

38. RA to AA, Mar. [1859]; to BA, Aug. 29, 1860 (Easterby, pp. 153, 164).

39. Pringle, pp. 36, 72.

40. RA, instructions to overseer, Nightingale Hall plantation journal [1846], pp. 2–6, file 12-6A-6 (SCHS).

41. Waverly had 106 slaves in 1834 (Easterby, p. 28). Easterby states (p. 29) that 51 of them were sold in 1837 in "the largest transaction of this kind" recorded in Allston's papers. Five Waverly slaves had been sold earlier in 1837 (p. 384), and several (3?) had been sold in the previous year (p. 48). The buyers apparently paid the following sums:

	$36,975	for 51 slaves × $725	(p. 67)
	4,100	" 5 "	(p. 384)
	1,564	" [3?] "	(p. 48)
TOTAL:	$42,639	" [59?] slaves	

This estimate of 59 slaves accords with Easterby's statement (p. 44) that the value of Waverly slaves sold was $43,000.

42. Easterby, pp. 44, 341, 46–47, 74.

43. This interpretation of Mary Allston's feelings is not invalidated, I think, by her expressing uneasiness at becoming financially involved with her own brother (RA to Alexander Campbell, Feb. 2, 1837; Mary Allston to Elizabeth Blyth, Jan. 30, 1837 [Easterby, pp. 384–85, 67–68]).

44. Mary Allston further eased her conscience by letting Sibba (an old slave) return to Waverly on the same boat with Scotland, Sarah, and Bob. By including Sibba in the original lot of fifty-three slaves, sold "in round" at $725 each (i.e., at an average price, regardless of the value of each individual slave), Mary Allston had pocketed $725 for Sibba, and had the added satisfaction then of returning Sibba to spend her dying days among her own people. The purchaser was willing to let Sibba go because feeding her would have been a financial burden to him. He did not, of course, pay for Sarah or Bob; in the end, therefore, the estate received payment for fifty-one slaves in this transaction (RA to Alexander Campbell, Feb. 3, 1837; Campbell to RA, Feb. 11, 1837 [Easterby, pp. 385–86; 331]).

45. Alexander Robertson to RA, Aug. 8, 1837 (Easterby, p. 396; see also pp. 384, 75, 393, 402, 403 n).

46. RA to AA, Dec. 4, 1853 (Easterby, p. 118; see also pp. 19–20, 28, 341, 415–16). RA, "Rice," *DeBow's Review,* I, 342–50.

47. RA to J. D. B. DeBow, Feb. 28, 1852 (file 12-4-8, SCHS). RA to AA, Dec. 6, 1844; to BA, Aug. 18, 29, Sept. 6, 1860 (Easterby, pp. 94, 164–66). RA, notes for a speech, plantation journal, ca. Oct. 1848, file 12-4-11 (SCHS). RA to J. B. Allston, Jan. 13, 1859 (Easterby, p. 151). Immediate profit was not Allston's only motive in renting his slaves to build the railway; he sought also to speed the construction of a work which would have military value if South Carolina seceded (RA to BA, Aug. 18, 1860 [Easterby, p. 164]).

48. RA to AA, Dec. 4, 1855; George Trenholm to RA, Apr. 18, 1837; J. H. Easterby, "Plantation Finance"; RA to Blue Ridge Railroad Committee, Aug. 11, 1859 (Easterby, pp. 124–25, 72, 43–44, 162).

49. RA, "Remarks by Robert F. W. Allston Concerning the Nashville Convention of 1850"; to James H. Hammond, July 24, 1846 (emphasis added), (Easterby, pp. 445, 95).

Chapter 12

1. "You" meant RA's brother Joseph (a member of the court which hanged the slave named Wood), and Joseph's associates in the hanging business: J. L. Petigru to Joseph W. Allston (Easterby, p. 35; Rogers, p. 236). The alleged conspiracy may have been an extensive one: William Freehling, *Prelude to Civil War* (New York, 1966), pp. 62–63; Norrece T. Jones Jr., *Born a Child of Freedom, Yet a Slave: Mechanisms of Control and Strategies of Resistance in Antebellum South Carolina* (Hanover, N.H., 1990), pp. 182–83.

2. This incident is accurately recounted in Bertram Wyatt-Brown, *Southern Honor* (New York, 1982), p. 379, where, however, Allston is mistakenly said to have been the master of the innocent slave (General D. F. Jamison to RA [typescript], Dec. 24, 1858 [SCL]).

3. *Official Records of the Union and Confederate Navies in the War of the Rebellion*, 1st ser. (Washington, D.C., 1894–1914), 13:214; Joyner, pp. 27–28.

4. [H. A. Middleton to Harriott Middleton, Nov. 5, 1862], Cheves-Middleton MS (SCHS).

5. Davidson, p. 236. Rogers, p. 301. Alexander Robertson to RA, Apr. 11, 1861 (Easterby, p. 418 [where "Dr F J Parker" is evidently a mistranscription of "Dr F S Parker"]).

6. [H. A. Middleton to Harriott Middleton, Nov. 5, 1862], Cheves-Middleton MS (SCHS). George Rogers deserves the credit for first calling attention to Middleton's letter (Rogers, p. 407; see also pp. 285, 524). Cf. Davidson, p. 229.

7. Dusinberre, *Civil War Issues in Philadelphia* (Philadelphia, 1965), pp. 147–48.

8. H. A. Middleton to Harriott Middleton, Oct. 26 [Nov. 5,] 1862; Jan. 5 [1863, mistakenly written 1862], Cheves-Middleton MS (SCHS).

9. Easterby, p. 84. Rogers, p. 241. On 1780: Sylvia Frey, *Water from the Rock: Black Resistance in a Revolutionary Age* (Princeton, N.J., 1991), esp. pp. 108–42. For 1815 at Butler Island, see chapter 9. Howard A. Ohline, "Georgetown, South Carolina: Racial Anxieties and Militant Behavior, 1802," *South Carolina Historical Magazine,* 73 (1972): 130–40.

10. J. L. Petigru to RA, Dec. 1861 (Easterby, p. 186). One doubts that Robert Allston—had he survived the Civil War—would have been willing to take the somewhat compromising role in politics that Ben did in 1867, after the blacks had been granted voting rights.

11. Joyner, p. 19. RA to AA, Mar. 11, 1859 (Easterby, p. 154). RA, note on bill of sale, Apr. 19, 1847 (SCHS). Another example of Allston's selling a slave for disciplinary reasons appears on p. 368.

12. RA to Sarah Carr (copy), Jan. 17, 1859; to AA, Dec. 9, 1838; Mar. [1859], (Easterby, pp. 152, 85, 153).

13. Rogers, p. 325. RA to BA, Aug. 29, 1860 (Easterby, p. 165).

14. Joseph Allston complained that Avant was also incompetent at raising a crop and at the medical care of ill slaves (Charlotte Allston to RA, June 8, 1823; Joseph Allston to RA, July 6, 1823 [Easterby, pp. 60–61]). Frederick Douglass, *Narrative of the Life of Frederick Douglass an American Slave* (1845; rpt. [ed. Benjamin Quarles], Cambridge, Mass., 1960), pp. 103–4.

15. To Allston's unpunctuated instructions I have added punctuation consonant with the suboverseer's laying on thirty-nine "strips," as reported on July 18, 1858 (Easterby, p. 262). RA, instructions to overseer, Nightingale Hall plantation journal [1846], p. 1, file 12-6A-6 (SCHS).

16. Pringle, p. 362. On Ancrum, see esp. chapter 14.

17. RA, Nightingale Hall plantation journal, p. 3 (SCHS).

18. Ibid., p. 1.

19. [RA], memo, n.d. [1858?], fiche 12-16-10 (SCL).

20. Table 8, including its first two notes (chapter 3).

21. Harman Pitman to RA, May 6, 1860; suboverseer's reports, July 18–31, 1858 (Easterby, pp. 262–63). At the moment Allston wrote of "the plantation which I myself manage (containing 175 negroes)," the Chicora Wood unit actually had about 284 slaves. Evidently, in stating the annual number of punishments, Allston was not only excluding his Nightingale Hall plantation but was also for some reason excluding the whippings at his "Ditchford," "Exchange," and "Breakwater" plantations (which he had bought in 1851–53, and whose production and demographic statistics he usually counted as part of a single Chicora Wood unit [Easterby, p. 21]). His reason for omitting these other plantations may have been that many of their slaves—being relatively recently purchased—were flogged more often than those whom Allston had governed for many years.

My estimate that about 284 slaves lived at the whole Chicora Wood unit is composed of the following elements:

236	slaves lived at Chicora Wood in Apr. 1864.
ca.37	Chicora Wood slaves were probably in Apr. 1864 at Morven, N.C., or Croly Hill, S.C. (I estimate that 45 percent of the 83 Morven and Croly Hill slaves had been sent there from Chicora Wood.)
ca.11	slaves comprised the net decline of Chicora Wood's slave population, 1858–64. (The number of RA's slaves declined by 41 from 1860 to 1864. I estimate that it rose by about 20 from 1858 to 1860. Of the net decline of about 21 slaves from 1858 to 1864, I estimate that half were Chicora Wood slaves. 1860 U.S. Manuscript Census. RA's estate inventory, Apr. 1864, file 12-6-25 [SCHS].)

TOTAL: ca. 284 slaves

22. F. L. Olmsted, *A Journey in the Seaboard Slave States* (New York, 1856), p. 439. But see the discussion of the Chicora Wood overseer Jesse Belflowers later in this chapter.

23. Overseer's contract, 1822; H. A. Middleton to RA, Apr. 15, 1858; RA to H. A. Middleton, Apr. 16, 1858; Joseph W. Allston to RA, Sept. 25, 1823 (Easterby, pp. 245, 261, 63).

24. Pringle, pp. 74–75.

25. Olmsted, *Journey in the Seaboard Slave States,* pp. 486–87, 438. Olmsted, *A Journey in the Back Country* (London, 1860), pp. 56–62.

26. Olmsted, *Journey in the Seaboard Slave States,* p. 619. Bennet Barrow, diary, Dec. 11, 1839; also July 4, 1840, in Edwin A. Davis, ed., *Plantation Life in the Florida Parishes of Louisiana, 1836–1846 as Reflected in the Diary of Bennet H. Barrow* (1943; rpt. New York, 1967). Olmsted, *Journey in the Seaboard Slave States,* pp. 485, 487. See p. 161.

27. Olmsted, *Journey in the Seaboard Slave States,* p. 485. Pringle, pp. 37, 67, 72–

73. The reason nearby summertime coastal residence was feasible for Pee Dee and Waccamaw planters was that those two rivers—unlike others where rice was grown—ran parallel to the ocean instead of at an angle; this meant that a coastal residence could be built close enough to the rice fields for the master to make a round trip between morning and evening.

28. AA to RA, June 3, 1861 (Easterby, pp. 176–77). Pringle, pp. 85, 96–99.

29. *North Carolina Farmer* 3 (1848): 193–94 (Clifton, p. xxviii).

30. 1860 U.S. census.

31. Pp. 290–91.

32. Joel Poinsett (the former owner of half of J. J. I. Pringle's slaves) had also spent summers in Newport; and as he spent most winters in Washington, his slaves had experienced absenteeism most of the year.

33. Pringle, pp. 157–59. Shaffer: Rogers, pp. 277, 321. J. J. I. Pringle: Davidson, pp. 34–36. The slaveholdings of these planters are stated on pp. 290–91 above. I have omitted the (estimated 96) slaves of J. H. Trapier (W. H. Trapier's brother) from this calculation, as I have no evidence whether or not he was a summer absentee. Of the remaining 2,324 slaves, the masters of at least 1,760 were probably summer absentees.

This estimate that at least 76 percent of the slaves of Allston's Pee Dee neighbors experienced summer absenteeism is a conservative one, depending on an inference from Elizabeth Pringle's memoir that Nathaniel Barnwell spent his summers close enough to the Pee Dee to be able to supervise his 230 slaves. If my inference is mistaken, summer absenteeism was probably 86 percent.

I have omitted Robert Allston's slaves from this calculation. He was an unusually conscientious proprietor, and I believe that including his slaves would give a substantially distorted picture of common practice in Georgetown District—and an even more distorted picture of common practice elsewhere in the South Carolina and Georgia low country.

34. William Allston to RA, June 19, 1838; Carroll and Porter to RA, Mar. 22, 1837; J. L. Petigru to RA, Apr. 15, 1837 (Easterby, pp. 250, 25, 68–69, 73, 387, 389).

35. RA to Mary Allston, Oct. 1, 1837 (Easterby, pp. 74–75).

36. Robert Nesbit to RA, Dec. 26, 1837 (Easterby, p. 76).

37. Gabriel Ellis to RA, June 20, 1838 (Easterby, p. 252).

38. Ellis to RA, Sept. 16, 1838 (Easterby, p. 255).

39. Ellis to RA, Mar. 3, 1838; William Sparkman to RA, Mar. 4, 1838 (Easterby, p. 249). Rogers, pp. 281, 277, 256.

40. Pringle, p. 354.

41. Ibid., p. 169. Pringle's knowledge of the matter was secondhand, as she was born seven years after Thompson's death. RA, "A Card," 1842 (Easterby, pp. 257, 245–47). Slave list, Jan. [1846] (filed January 1850), (SCHS).

42. BA to RA, July 7, 1858; Harman Pitman to RA, Oct. 3, 1861 (Easterby, pp. 262, 27; 145; 268).

43. Olmsted, *Journey in the Seaboard Slave States,* p. 486. Roswell King Jr.'s long tenure at Butler Island was not comparable, for as resident agent for a nearly permanent absentee owner King held a status—and a salary—quite different from that of a mere overseer.

44. 1850 U.S. Manuscript Census. RA to BA, June 8, 1858 (Easterby, pp. 27, 144). Douglass, *Narrative,* p. 92.

45. AA to BA, Sept. 10, 1865 (Easterby, p. 213). Like Charles Manigault's overseers, Belflowers seems usually to have mentioned only the whipping of a privileged slave, where the punishment required explanation (e.g., Belflowers to AA, June 8,

1864, reporting the switching of the privileged Charley, whom Belflowers advised reducing to field labor [Easterby, p. 284]). In the eleven surviving weekly reports from the summer of 1862 (Easterby, pp. 269–75) Belflowers did not once mention discipline, except to say (Aug. 23) that he had locked up Elsey two nights—probably to prevent her from fleeing when Northern naval vessels were raiding the Black River (Rogers, p. 404). (To be sure, the nine reports from the same period which have been destroyed—or were never written—might have told a different story.) Belflowers's reticence, and the absence of any other series of his letters except those written during the extraordinary months just before emancipation, make guesswork about his disciplinary practices hazardous. Yet Allston's boast about the small number of floggings on his home plantation, the infrequency of Belflowers's mentioning whippings, and the Allstons' complaint that Belflowers was not firm enough suggest to me that Belflowers depended heavily on penalties less severe than whipping.

46. BA to RA, June 23, 29, 1858 (fiche), (SCL).

47. See chapter 14.

48. AA, journal, May 26, 1850 (fiche 12-16-3), (SCL); Fredrika Bremer, *Homes of the New World* (1853; rpt. New York, 1968), 1:295. During her stay with the Poinsetts, Bremer went to only two "great dinners with planters some miles from here" (1:294). Surely it was during one of these two excursions that she visited the village "near a great house"; and it would be a remarkable coincidence if Bremer's displeasure at her visit to the Allstons—reported by Adele Allston—were not the source for her passage about the defiant-looking young men.

49. [RA], memo, n.d. [1858?] (fiche 12-16-11), (SCL). Joseph B. Allston, [memoir] (Pringle, p. 36).

50. RA to J. D. B. DeBow, Feb. 28, 1852; RA, autobiography (unpublished page proofs for *DeBow's Review*), p. 575, file 12-4-8, (SCHS).

51. AA, journal, Feb. 28, Mar. 12, 17, 1850 (fiche), (SCL). Pringle, pp. 60, 87, 66. RA to AA, [May 7, 1854?], in Jane Pease and William Pease, *Ladies, Women and Wenches* (Chapel Hill, N.C., 1990), p. 31.

Chapter 13

1. The imbalance between this longer chapter on privilege and the briefer previous chapter (on coercion) misrepresents the relative significance of the two phenomena. In governing slaves, coercion was, of course, nearly always more important than grants of privilege. But the absence of many surviving letters from Allston's overseers, and the publication of his daughter's memoir (where privileged slaves predominate) conduce to a somewhat misleading emphasis here. The splendid collection of letters from Charles Manigault's overseers made it easier to avoid this imbalance in discussing Gowrie.

2. For simplicity I often refer to this daughter as "Elizabeth Pringle," even though her marriage was subsequent to the Civil War. Pringle, p. 8.

3. Pringle, pp. 73, 79, 353, 78, 79 (emphasis added). Here, as in many other passages of her memoir, Elizabeth Pringle—born five years after Mrs. Blyth's death—is reporting her mother's treasured recollections of the ancien régime.

4. Ibid., pp. 150–54.

5. Charles Ball, *Fifty Years in Chains* (1836; rpt. [ed. Philip Foner] New York, 1970), pp. 197–203; quotation, p. 203.

6. Solomon Northup, *Twelve Years a Slave* (1853; rpt. [ed. Sue Eakin and Joseph Logsdon] Baton Rouge, La., 1968), pp. 191, 163, 164–65, 167, 169.

7. Pringle, p. 359. Jesse Belflowers to AA, June 16, 1864; Jan. 4, 1865; to RA, Aug. 25, 1862; William Faulk to RA, May 27, 1854; RA, agreement, 1859 (Easterby, pp. 285, 325, 274; 260; 350). U.S. MS census of agriculture, 1850, 1860 (RA reported one hundred swine in each year).

8. Pringle, p. 93.

9. Ibid., pp. 15, 30.

10. Forty-one transactions took place on March 7 through 13, 1859, of which twenty-three were on Sunday and seven on Saturday. As there were 106 "hands" at Nightingale Hall in 1860, the plantation's total population must have been about 200. Nightingale Hall plantation book, Mar. 5–13, 1859, Mar. 26, 1853; H. Pitman to RA, Mar. 9, 1861 (fiche 12-6-24), (SCHS).

11. Allston's figures for number of days of illness lost by sickness (706 in 1858) refer only to Nightingale Hall, while the list of slaves rewarded for perfect attendance includes both Nightingale Hall and Chicora Wood but not Pipe Down. He probably had nearly 500 slaves at the two former plantations in 1859. I guess that his workforce there, excluding young children and the superannuated, may have been about 265 (170 at Chicora Wood and 95 at Nightingale Hall). This estimate is in proportion to the rice production that year at each plantation—some 33,500 bushels at Chicora Wood and about 20,000 at Nightingale Hall—slightly adjusted because productivity per worker was probably a little higher at Nightingale Hall, since it was at the best "pitch of the tide." The 82 workers who did not lose a day included 53 at Chicora Wood and 29 at Nightingale Hall. (Forty-nine of these workers were full hands, of whom 12 received the extra bonus for three years of perfect attendance; Robert Allston, diary, 1859–60, [Easterby, pp. 452, 454–55]).

12. Ibid., p. 456.

13. RA to BA, June 3, 1858; W. Sweet to AA, Dec. 14, 1864 (Easterby, pp. 141, 320). Pringle, pp. 354, 356, 358.

14. Charlotte Allston to RA, May 8, 1820; Apr. 2, 1821 (Easterby, pp. 55, 57).

15. Gabriel Ellis to RA, Aug. 4, 1838 (Easterby, p. 253). Rogers, pp. 195, 268, 271–72, 276, 279. Pringle, p. 59.

16. Pringle, pp. 27–29, 269, 240, 214–15, 361, 363. Robertson, Blacklock & Co. to RA, Sept. 9, 1862; Aug. 31, 1863; W. Sweet to AA, Aug. 31, 1864 (Easterby, pp. 423, 426, 298).

17. Pringle, pp. 24–25, 108, 170, 72. RA to BA, June 8, 1858 (Easterby, p. 144).

18. RA, inscription, 1858; RA to BA, Aug. 29, 1860 (Easterby, pp. 356, 164–65).

19. Pringle, pp. 12–13, 91. Charles Kershaw to Charlotte Allston, Dec. 24, 30, 1817 (Easterby, pp. 28, 365–66).

20. Lewis and Robertson to RA, Apr. 24, 1837; RA to Charles Allston, Nov. 8, 1860 (Easterby, pp. 387–88, 169). Pringle, pp. 276–77, 203, 207.

21. AA's words, referring to Mary Grice's and James's families, AA to Jesse Belflowers, July 16, 1864 (Easterby, p. 293). Sidney G. Fisher, diary (HSP). Pringle, pp. 61–62.

22. AA to BA, July 5, 1858 (fiche), (SCL).

23. RA to BA, July 9, 1858 (typescript); AA to BA, June 28, 1858 (fiche), (SCL). Pringle, pp. 61, 72.

24. Pringle, pp. 62, 82, 119, 123–24. Easterby, p. 33.

25. Pringle, pp. 172, 121–22. Elizabeth Allston, diary, [ca. Mar. 3, 1865], Allston-Pringle-Hill MS, (SCHS). The term "savages" was Robert Allston's: emancipation, he alleged, would inevitably lead to "amalgamation with the savages": RA to BA, [Mar. 1856] (Easterby, p. 132).

26. Pringle, pp. 114–15. AA to BA, Oct. 3, 1854 (Easterby, pp. 121, 33).

27. Pringle, pp. 351–52, 61, 253 (quotation). Easterby, pp. 221, 285, 193.

28. Pringle, pp. 171–72, 60. AA to RA, May 17, 1857 (emphasis added); Jesse Belflowers to AA, Dec. 14, 1864; RA to BA, Oct. 6, 1860; to Charles Allston, Nov. 8, 1860 (Easterby, pp. 137, 321, 168, 169).

29. Mary Petigru to AA, Dec. 27, 1860; Jesse Belflowers to AA, Dec. 27, 1864 (Easterby, pp. 171, 323). Pringle, pp. 356, 359, 283–84.

30. Pringle, pp. 110; 13, 90. BA to RA, Mar. 31, 1861 (Easterby, p. 173).

31. Pringle, pp. 90, 63; 13; 168; 355.

32. I seek to develop here—by relating them to Allston's network of privileges—the three elements of slavery specified in Orlando Patterson, *Slavery and Social Death* (Cambridge, Mass., 1982) pp. 1–101.

33. W. Sweet to AA, Jan. 4, 1865; Belflowers to AA, Sept. 7, 1864; AA to BA, May 31, 1864 (Easterby, pp. 324, 300, 198–99).

34. Pringle, pp. 68–70.

35. Pringle, pp. 76–78. RA to BA, May 25, 1855 (Easterby, p. 123).

36. RA, inscription, 1858 (Easterby, p. 356). Pringle, p. 91. Charles Allston to AA, Nov. 16, 1864; Elizabeth [Weston] to AA, Mar. 17, 1865, P.S. (Easterby, pp. 202, 207).

37. Rebecca Bryan to AA, Aug. 17, 1863 (typescript), (SCL). Sweet to AA, Jan. 18, 11, 1865; E. J. Means to AA, Dec. 19, 1864 (Easterby, pp. 326, 325, 204–5).

38. AA to BA, Apr. 16, 1868; to Col. Francis Heriot, [July 1864]; to BA, Oct. 30, 1862 (Easterby, pp. 242, 200, 190).

39. Rogers, pp. 399–406. AA to BA, Oct. 30, 1862; to Col. Francis Heriot, [July 1864] (Easterby, pp. 190, 200). As Mrs. Francis Weston was the daughter of Robert Allston's sister, the Westons could have come into possession of Mary Grice's brother Tom through a division of family property (Rogers, pp. 262, 274).

40. AA to Col. Francis Heriot, [July 1864] (Easterby, p. 200). [H. A. Middleton to Harriott Middleton, Nov. 5, 1862], Cheves-Middleton MS (SCHS).

41. Sabe Rutledge, interviewed by Genevieve Chandler, in George Rawick, ed., *The American Slave* (1941; rpt. Westport, Conn., 1972), III, part iv, 63. The absence from Rutledge's printed interview of any mention of the three executions (beyond the cryptic remark "Take men off") may possibly have resulted from editing by white WPA staff, such as has been proved to have taken place with WPA interviews with former slaves in Virginia and Georgia. John Blassingame, ed., *Slave Testimony* [Baton Rouge, La., 1977], pp. xlviii–l. On Henry Buck: Joyner, pp. 29–30.

42. AA to BA, Oct. 30, 1862; Belflowers to AA, June 1, 8, 9, 1864 (Easterby, pp. 189, 281, 284).

43. RA to BA, June 3, [1858]; BA to RA, June 9, 1858 (typescripts), (SCL).

44. Belflowers to AA, May 30, June 1, 9, July 6, 1864 (Easterby, pp. 281, 284, 289–90).

45. Slaves no. 253–54, 256–60, inventory of RA's estate, Apr. 1864 (fiche 12-6-25), (SCHS). Belflowers to AA, July 6, 13, 1864 (Easterby, pp. 290–91).

46. Belflowers to AA, July 13, 20, 1864; W. Sweet to AA, July 13, 1864 (Easterby, pp. 290–92, 294). Pringle, p. 172. *Official Records of the Union and Confederate Navies in the War of the Rebellion,* 1st ser. (Washington, D.C., 1894–1914), 15:550, 570; Capt. J. F. Green to Adm. Dahlgren, July 9, 14, 1864, Ibid., 568.

47. Belflowers to AA, July 13, 1864; Sweet to AA, July 13, 1864 (Easterby, pp. 290–92).

48. Belflowers to AA, July 13, Oct. 26, 1864; Sweet to AA, Oct. 5, Dec. 7, 1864 (Easterby, pp. 291, 312, 306, 319).

49. See p. 371.

50. The eight captives under military arrest were all "in jail" (Sweet to AA, July 13, 1864). "Some thinks that [Toney] ought to stand his triall [too]" (Belflowers to AA, July 13, 1864 [Easterby, pp. 290, 292]).

51. The other missing report was that of Aug. 17. Neither is in Easterby (pp. 281–325), or on the microfiche at SCL.

52. Pringle, pp. 171–72.

53. AA to Col. Francis Heriot, [July 1864]; to Belflowers, July 16, 1864 (Easterby, pp. 200, 292).

54. Elizabeth Fox-Genovese's splendid *Within the Plantation Household: Black and White Women of the Old South* (Chapel Hill, N.C., 1988) develops this theme. C. Vann Woodward, ed., *Mary Chesnut's Civil War* (New Haven, Conn. 1981), pp. xlix, lii, 246, 255.

55. Charlotte Allston to RA, Apr. 2, 1821 (Easterby, pp. 53 n, 56, 337, 356). Rogers, p. 521. Pringle, p. 351.

56. Charlotte Allston to RA, Apr. 2, 1821 (Easterby, pp. 56–57).

57. Pringle, p. 351. Charlotte Allston to RA, June 8, 1823 (Easterby, p. 60).

58. Pringle, pp. 169–70. AA, journal, Dec. 25, 1851 (fiche), (SCL). I infer Nelly's relation to the older woman from the fact that Nelly left Mrs. Allston's service just after the war and went to live with Milly on a neighboring plantation—to Mrs. Allston's great annoyance (AA to Jane Allston, Aug. 1, 1865 [Easterby, p. 212]).

59. Pringle, pp. 124, 152, 142, 221–22, 238.

60. Elizabeth Allston, diary, July 23, 1861, Allston-Pringle-Hill MS (SCHS).

61. Woodward, *Mary Chesnut's Civil War,* p. 233. Although this sentence was added to her memoir by Chesnut many years later, it probably represents correctly her perception in Nov. 1861.

62. Pringle, pp. 238, 168. BA to RA, Mar. 6, 1859 (SCHS).

63. Pringle, pp. 227, 238, 288, 283–84. AA, journal, Apr. 25, July 22, Aug. 8, 1865 (file 11-17-1), Allston-Pringle-Hill MS (SCHS).

64. Elizabeth Allston, diary, Mar. 12, 1865, Allston-Pringle-Hill MS (SCHS). Pringle, pp. 121–22, 250, 276–77, 240.

65. Easterby, p. 332. Pringle, pp. 351–52, 97 (quotations).

66. Pringle, pp. 352, 62, 170, 61, 352, 72 (quotation). AA to BA, Apr. 22, 1866 (Easterby, p. 218). On Philip Washington: Joyner, pp. 31–32.

67. Pringle, pp. 216, 358. Charles Allston to AA, Aug. 15, 1864; E. J. Means to AA, Nov. 15, 1864 (typescripts), (SCL). Belflowers to AA, Dec. 14, 1864; AA to BA, Apr. 22, 1866 (Easterby, pp. 321, 218). AA, journal, Apr. 25, 1865, Allston-Pringle-Hill MS (SCHS).

68. BA to AA, Oct. 10, 1865 (typescript), (SCL). Pringle, pp. 194, 169–70.

Chapter 14

1. RA to AA, Oct. 19, 1856 (Easterby, p. 135).

2. RA to BA, [Mar. 1856] (Easterby, p. 132).

3. Ibid.

4. C. Vann Woodward and Elisabeth Muhlenfeld, eds., *The Private Mary Chesnut: The Unpublished Civil War Diaries* (New York, 1984), p. 42 (Mar. 18, 1861); Woodward, ed., *Mary Chesnut's Civil War* (New Haven, Conn., 1981), p. 644 (Sept. 21, 1864).

5. AA to Mrs. [John] Hunter, May 15, 1861 (Easterby, p. 175). Cf. Rogers, p. 279 (on Hunter's name).

6. RA to Thomas Y. Simons, July 4, 1859 (typescript), (SCL).

7. RA to BA, Sept. 6, 10, 1860 (Easterby, pp. 165, 167).

8. RA to BA, [Mar. 1856] (Easterby, p. 132). William Freehling, *Prelude to Civil War* (New York, 1966), pp. 89–91.

9. Rogers, pp. 238–44, 276, 525; Easterby, p. 257 n.

10. RA, obituary of T. B. Hamlin (Easterby, p. 264).

11. Pringle, p. 19. RA to J. D. B. DeBow, Feb. 28, 1852; RA, page proofs of "Autobiography" for *DeBow's Review* (1852), p. 575 (file 12-4-8); RA, notes for an autobiography, 1853 (file 12-4-13), (SCHS).

12. His remarks (undated, but after 1847) on the free school system acknowledged that "the people" (i.e., the planter elite) of South Carolina would not submit to the principle, agreed in other states, that "all the children in the State were included in them" (Easterby, p. 443).

13. Pringle, p. 20.

14. David Potter, *The Impending Crisis* (New York, 1976), p. 504; Ralph Wooster, *The Secession Conventions of the South* (Princeton, N.J., 1962), pp. 264–66, 115–17, 45–46.

15. AA to Mrs. [John] Hunter, May 15, 1861; RA to AA, Dec. 16, 1849 (Easterby, pp. 176, 98–99, 131). Pringle, p. 175.

16. RA to BA, Oct. 6, 1860 (Easterby, p. 168). Although Stephen Channing believes this letter shows Allston to have been uneasy at this time about the precipitancy of South Carolina's secessionist movement, the language suggests a different view. The Carolinian was determined that his state secede in the event Lincoln was elected president, and he very much hoped Virginia (and Maryland) would seize Washington before Inauguration Day, so that the new Southern Confederacy would possess "the Treasury, the Archives and Offices, . . . the prestige of office." Allston's expression, "not to secede from the Union, but to *take the Union along* [emphasis added] by taking the Federal City and Treasury" was the wordplay of an ardent secessionist. His wish that Washington be seized before March 4 was consistent with his later desire that Fort Sumter be occupied immediately. Cf. Stephen Channing, *Crisis of Fear* (New York, 1970), pp. 243–44.

17. RA to BA, Mar. 24, 1861 (Easterby, pp. 172–73).

18. BA to RA, Apr. 14, 1861 (Easterby, pp. 175, 174).

19. BA to AA, Apr. 29, 1861; also BA to RA, May 2, 1861 (typescripts), (SCL).

20. Pringle, p. 141.

21. Elizabeth Allston, journal, Mar. 27, 1862; also (on Motley) Feb. 18, Mar. 10, 1862, Allston-Pringle-Hill MS (SCHS).

22. Ibid., May 20, 1864 (emphasis in the original); Apr. 11, 1865 (SCHS). Easterby, p. 17.

23. Joseph Alston to Theodosia Burr, Dec. 28, 1800, in Matthew L. Davis, *Memoirs of Aaron Burr,* 1:431 (Rogers, p. 189).

24. In *Mary Chesnut's Civil War* these words are printed in the present tense; but as they are not in her original diary but were added by Chesnut many years later, they are most appropriately recorded here in the past tense (Woodward, *Mary Chesnut's Civil War,* p. 199 [Sept. 24, 1861]; Woodward and Muhlenfeld, *The Private Mary Chesnut,* p. 164 [Sept. 27, 1861]).

25. I usually call Robert Allston's daughter "Pringle," though she did not marry until after the Civil War.

26. Pringle, pp. 158–59. That Francis Weston seems to have kept thirty-seven domestics in Charleston all year round—more than any other Georgetown rice planter—suggests that only thirteen slaves actually accompanied the Westons on their annual migration to Charleston (Charleston Taxpayers List, 1859 [Rogers, p. 525]).

27. In her romanticized account of this event, Pringle calls it the "hospital," claiming that "sick-house" was the term used "by the darkies"; but Gabriel Ellis's employment of the word "Sickhouse" in a letter to Robert Allston shows that the term was then in general use (Ellis to RA, Sept. 16, 1838 [Easterby, p. 254]).

28. Ibid., pp. 64–66.

29. Ibid., pp. 76–77; Orlando Patterson, *Slavery and Social Death* (Cambridge, Mass., 1982), pp. 78–79, 94–96.

30. Pringle, pp. 9–10.

31. He put Nightingale Hall (and the "Waterford" tract) up for sale late in 1859, but his withholding an important right-of-way from the latter tract lessened the attractiveness of this offer. Allston's "retention of the sea shore and particularly of a right of way is *most injurious* to the sale"—and would greatly lower the attainable price— Plowden Weston warned Allston's brother-in-law. Although Allston partially backed down on this point, no acceptable offers were made (P. C. J. Weston to Philip Porcher, Dec. 3, 1859; Philip Porcher to RA, Dec. 7, 1859; RA to Porcher, [Dec. 1859]: typescripts [SCL].

32. Easterby, p. 22. The labor shortage at Benjamin Allston's new "Guendalos" plantation, and Benjamin's consequent need for more slaves—the approximately thirty-six Petigru bondsmen and women whom Robert Allston soon deported from "Pipe Down" plantation—was clearly expressed in Robert's plaint of Mar. 1859. "If I could have procured the hands from Pipedown early in January," he wrote to Adele, "this ["rested field" at Guendalos] would be in as fine condition [for planting] as the other. But as it is, the surface is cover'd with the green of water weeds" (RA to AA, Mar. [1859], Easterby, p. 153).

33. *Estimated cost of Benjamin's "Guendalos" plantation* and its slaves:

$28,000: "Guendalos" (This is the declared value of the plantation land, machinery and implements, and livestock in the 1860 Manuscript Census;

$29,000: the cost of ca. 42 slaves bought from T. P. Alston (J. B. Allston to RA, Jan. 11, 1859 [typescript], [SCL]);

ca. $26,000: the cost of 41 slaves bought from Mrs. Withers (RA to AA, Jan. 25, 1859 [typescript], [SCL]);

$20,500: the cost of ca. 36 slaves bought at Pipe Down and deported to Guendalos (file 12-6-24), (SCHS); Easterby, pp. 353–54);

TOTAL: ca. $103,500

Estimated cost of RA's new "Pipe Down" plantation and its slaves:

$20,000: "Pipe Down" (AA, journal, Jan. 19, 1865 [fiche], [SCL]);

ca. $37,500: the cost of the ca. 73 slaves retained there (the total cost of Pipe Down's 109 slaves—including the ca. 36 sent to Guendalos—was $58,000: AA, journal, Jan. 19, 1865 [fiche], [SCL]; a list of these 109 slaves is in file 12-6-24, [SCHS]);

TOTAL: ca. $57,500

---

34. Woodward, *Mary Chesnut's Civil War,* pp. 235, 245; also (on the Chesnuts' luxurious life) pp. 202–3, 251.

35. Pringle, pp. 90–91.

36. Ibid., pp. 54–55. For simplicity I use Adele's later, Huguenot-sounding spelling of the family name, though at the time of this incident they still spelled it in the Scots-Irish manner, "Pettigrew."

37. Fibby was the daughter of Allston's esteemed carpenter Thomas.

38. Pringle, pp. 357, 362.

39. "Hiring out Negroes (and particularly to Government) is a Business we have been obliged to give up . . . ," Allston's Charleston factor warned him early in 1864. "The writer . . . cannot well attend to negroes when abused, which is always happening" (Robertson, Blacklock & Co. to RA, Jan. 21, 1864 [Easterby, p. 428]).

40. Ibid., pp. 354, 356–57.

41. Ibid., pp. 365, 239. Cf. inventory of RA's slaves (nos. 141–47), Apr. 1864 (file 12-6-25), (SCHS).

42. Ibid., pp. 74, 233; Rogers, p. 325.

43. Pringle, p. 61. Cf. Potter, *The Impending Crisis,* p. 458.

44. Pringle, pp. 187–88, 146–47, 85, 256–58.

45. Ibid., pp. 236, 169.

46. Ibid., pp. 91, 124, 70.

47. Ibid., pp. 119, 209.

48. Ibid., p. 67.

49. Most of the poultry, eggs, and butter were the Allstons', though some may have been Mary Grice's own property. RA to Charles Allston, Nov. 8, 1860 (Easterby, p. 169). Pringle, p. 214. RA to BA, Feb. 1, 1856; RA to AA, Mar. [1859], (Easterby, pp. 129, 153).

50. RA to AA, Nov. 27, 1853 (Easterby, p. 117).

51. Cf. his letter of advice to his nephew J. B. Allston, Jan. 13, 1859 (Easterby, p. 151).

52. J. C. Yates to RA, Jan. 11, 1863; RA to AA, Apr. 10, 1863 (Easterby, pp. 276, 194).

53. Robertson, Blacklock & Co. to RA, Jan. 13, 18, 1859; J. B. Allston to RA, Jan. 18, 1859 (Easterby, pp. 414, 152). Rogers, pp. 299, 295; Davidson, p. 246.

54. BA to RA, Feb. 1, 1859 (SCHS). In 1863 Joseph sold the remaining Rutledge slaves, thus thoroughly smashing this slave community (Robertson, Blacklock & Co. to RA, May 9, 1863 [Easterby, p. 426]).

55. RA to J. B. Allston, Jan. 13, 1859 (Easterby, p. 151).

56. J. L. Petigru to AA, Apr. 17, 1858 (typescript), (SCL).

57. AA, journal, Feb. 26, 1850; Dec. 25, 1851 (fiches 12-16-3, 4), SCL.

58. Charles Allston to AA, Nov. 9, 1864 (Easterby, p. 202).

59. See chapter 13.

60. George Fredrickson, *White Supremacy: A Comparative Study in American and South African History* (New York, 1981), pp. 151–52, 160–62, 197–98.

61. RA to BA, June 8, 1858 (Easterby, p. 144).

62. This was doubtless the same Toney who in 1864 tried to escape with Stephen Gallant and then lied imaginatively to save his skin (BA to RA, June 18, 1860 [Easterby, p. 163]).

63. W. Sweet to AA, Aug. 31, 1864 (Easterby, p. 298).

64. RA to AA, Dec. 9, 1838; AA to BA, Jan. 1, 1857 (Easterby, pp. 85, 136).

65. Joyner, p. 27. RA, notes on two copies of advertisement, Jan. 16, 1846 (filed Jan. 1850), (file 12-6-21), (SCHS).

66. RA, slave papers, Mar. 14, 1851 (SCHS).

67. BA to RA, June 23, 1858 (SCL).

68. BA to RA, June 9, 1858 (typescript), (SCL).

69. See chapter 16. BA to RA, June 17; to Henrietta, June 20[?], 1860, Allston MS, (SCHS).

70. T. W. Higginson, *Army Life in a Black Regiment* (1870; rpt. East Lansing, Mich., 1960), pp. 168–69.

71. RA to Confederate secretary of war, Jan. 5, 1864; RA to AA, Mar. 26, 1863 (Easterby, pp. 278, 193).

72. Later note on RA, inventory (slave no. 531), Apr. 1864 (file 12-6-25, SCHS).

73. Pringle, pp. 357, 246; AA to Col. Francis Heriot, [July 1864]; RA, affadavit, Aug. 26, 1863 (Easterby, pp. 200, 277).

74. Charles P. Allston to AA, Aug. 15, 30, Oct. 30, 1864 (typescripts), (SCL).

75. Charles Allston to AA, Oct. 30, 1864 (typescript), (SCL); Jesse Belflowers to AA, Oct. 19, 1864 (Easterby, p. 310). Also, Belflowers to AA, Oct. 26, Nov. 3, Nov. 16, 1864; W. Sweet to AA, Oct. 19, Nov. 16, 30, Dec. 7, 14, 1864; Charles Allston to AA, Nov. 9, 16, 1864 (Easterby, pp. 309–20, 201–3).

76. Elizabeth Allston, diary, [ca. Mar. 6], Mar. 12, 1865, Allston-Pringle-Hill MS (SCHS).

77. Rogers, pp. 417–19.

78. It was Stanton who suggested to Sherman that the latter issue his famous field order; and during the meeting when the two men considered the general's original draft, Stanton (Sherman acknowledged) made "many changes." General Rufus Saxton—commandant of the Port Royal experiment and an antislavery radical who wanted freedmen and women to become landowners—had already proposed settling blacks on abandoned coastal plantations. Just before the field order was drafted, Saxton had twice consulted with Stanton, bringing with him (at Stanton's request) Saxton's annual report upon the Port Royal experiment, where he had officially recorded "a note of his unhappiness" that few blacks there had become landowners. Stanton impelled Sherman to collect twenty black clergymen (nine of them recent freedmen) whose opinions he wished to canvass. Stanton's questions to these clergymen elicited their desire that the freedmen and women "have land" for their own cultivation. The field order, issued four days later, authorized granting freedmen "possessory title" to forty-acre plots. Stanton took an advance copy of this field order to General Saxton, who was forthwith appointed administrator of the plan, and whose authority was almost immediately increased by his promotion to be major general of the volunteers.

Everything points toward collaboration between Stanton and Saxton to achieve a purpose different from Sherman's own aim. Sherman declared in Feb. 1866 that he had intended only to place the blacks in temporary possession of the land. Stanton, by contrast, seems to have sought—like General Saxton—to grant the blacks a land "title" which, though ambiguous, might be transformed by later congressional legislation into permanent possession. Stanton and Saxton both acted, after Lincoln's assassination, to obstruct President Andrew Johnson's policy of dispossessing the blacks and returning the Sherman land grants to the former plantation owners (Howard C. Westwood, "Sherman Marched—and Proclaimed 'Land for the Landless,' *South Carolina Historical Magazine,* 85 (1984): 33–50 (quotations on pp. 39, 41, 39); William T. Sherman, *Memoirs* [London, 1875], 2:244–52 (quotation on p. 251); Claude Oubre,

Forty Acres and a Mule: The Freedmen's Bureau and Black Land Ownership [Baton Rouge, La., 1978], pp. 18–19, 52, 80; Willie Lee Rose, *Rehearsal for Reconstruction: The Port Royal Experiment* [New York, 1964], p. 153; Eric Foner, *Reconstruction: America's Unfinished Revolution, 1863–1877* [New York, 1988], pp. 70–71; Benjamin Thomas and Harold Hyman, *Stanton* [New York, 1962], pp. 343–45).

79. Foner, *Reconstruction,* pp. 69–70; Rogers, p. 423.

80. Elizabeth [Weston] to AA, Mar. 17, 1865; also Jane Pringle to AA, Apr. 1, 1865 (Easterby, pp. 206–11); Rogers, pp. 419–22.

81. Jesse Belflowers to AA, Mar. 18, 1865; W. J. Westbury to AA, June 8, 1866 (Easterby, pp. 328, 330).

82. Jane Pringle to AA, Apr. 1, 1865; Belflowers to AA, Mar. 18, 20, 1865 (Easterby, pp. 211, 328–29).

83. Belflowers to AA, Apr. 2, 1865 (Easterby, p. 329).

84. Jane Pringle to AA, Apr. 1, 1865; W. Sweet to AA, Jan. 18, 1865; AA to Colonel Brown, [Mar. (?) 1865] (Easterby, pp. 211, 210, 326, 208).

85. Jane Pringle to AA, Apr. 1, 1865 (Easterby, pp. 209–11); Pringle, p. 252.

86. Jane Pringle to AA, Apr. 1, 1865; AA to Colonel Brown, [Mar. (?) 1865] (Easterby, pp. 211, 210, 208). Pringle, pp. 257, 298. In view of the hostility later shown Adele at Guendalos by former Pipe Down slaves, I am skeptical of the rumor which circulated among the planters that it was a Pipe Down slave woman who wrote to the U.S. naval officers to obtain their protection of Adele's Pipe Down plantation (Easterby, p. 211).

87. Pringle, pp. 260–61, 267.

88. Ibid., pp. 264–67. AA, journal, May 10 [or 18], 1865 (fiche 12-16-7), (SCL) indicates that she was in possession of Nightingale Hall by that date.

89. Pringle, pp. 268–69.

90. RA, affadavit, Aug. 26, 1863 (Easterby, p. 277); Pringle, pp. 269–70.

91. Pringle, pp. 269–74.

92. Ibid., pp. 261, 279.

93. Foner, *Reconstruction,* pp. 159–61.

94. The inference that Lincoln's death altered the course of events regarding the land issue is based on the view that Lincoln's attitudes to blacks, his feelings about slavery, his relation to the moderate and the radical factions within the Republican Party, his stance toward "states' rights," and his humanitarian idealism all distinguished him from Andrew Johnson. Lincoln was also, unlike Johnson, a politician who grew in office. His policy toward slavery in Sept. 1862 could scarcely have been predicted from his utterances in Mar. 1861; his attitude toward blacks' voting rights was different in 1864 from what it had been in 1858; and his stands toward the issues of Reconstruction would surely have changed as the depth of Southern white opposition revealed itself in 1865 and 1866. Lincoln would not have sacked antislavery radicals like General Rufus Saxton from the Freedmen's Bureau, and it is inconceivable that he would have vetoed the original Freedmen's Bureau bill of 1866, with its provisions for getting certain lands into the hands of the freedmen and women. Johnson, by doing so, killed these provisions.

95. F. L. Olmsted, *A Journey in the Back Country* (London, 1860), pp. 444–45; Leon Litwack, *Been in the Storm So Long* (New York, 1979), p. 451. See p. 265.

96. This assertion runs contrary to the spirit of the introductory essay, "The Destruction of Slavery," in the excellent collection *Freedom: A Documentary History of Emancipation,* 1st ser. (ed. Ira Berlin, Barbara Fields et. al., Cambridge, Eng., 1985), 1:1–56, and of Leon Litwack's valuable *Been in the Storm So Long.*

97. Pringle, pp. 264, 254, 277–78; Elizabeth [Weston] to AA, Mar. 17, 1865; Jane Pringle to AA, Apr. 1, 1865 (Easterby, pp. 207, 211). Belflowers to AA, Mar. 18, 1865, does not mention any such deserter at Chicora Wood, nor does AA to Colonel Brown, [Mar. (?), 1865] (Easterby, pp. 328, 208).

98. Belflowers to AA, Apr. 2, 1865; AA to BA, Sept. 10, 1865 (Easterby, pp. 329, 213).

99. AA to BA, Sept. 9, 1865 (Easterby, p. 213).

Chapter 15

1. For simplicity I use throughout this chapter the anachronistic term "county"—instead of the technically correct but confusing word "district"—to refer to each of the four political jurisdictions (Georgetown, Charleston, Colleton, and Beaufort Counties) into which low-country South Carolina was divided. Each of these "counties" was, in turn, subdivided into several "parishes," whose colonial names were as bemusing to some nineteenth-century census officials as they are to a modern eye. The Census Office managed to distinguish "St. Johns Berkeley" Parish from "St. Johns Colleton"; but in 1860 it failed to comprehend the ultimate refinement in this nomenclature: "St. Johns Colleton" Parish was actually in Charleston County, not in Colleton County. This error made hash of the 1860 census report. I have attempted below to distinguish the beef from the potatoes in this tasty but upsetting concoction.

2. By "low country" I mean the twelve coastal counties—two in North Carolina, four in South Carolina, and six in Georgia—which extend from North Carolina's Cape Fear River to the St. Mary's River, dividing Georgia from Florida. 1850 and 1860 census figures, as revised in appendix E.

3. Estimates of the number of rice slaves in 1860, in each low-country parish, appear in appendix F.

Historians have long believed that 125,000 slaves grew rice in 1850. This figure was suggested in 1854 by the superintendent of the census, J. D. B. DeBow, who estimated that 2,500,000 slaves worked directly in agriculture, and who guessed that 5 percent of them grew rice. He appears to have chosen a conveniently round figure without much thought.

But as about 16,000 rice-growing slaves in Georgetown County produced nearly 24 percent of the low-country rice in 1850, one can easily see that the number of low-country rice slaves was unlikely to have been more than about 65,000. And as the newer rice lands along the Savannah River (and along the Ogeechee, Altamaha, Satilla, and St. Mary's Rivers of Georgia) were more productive than those of the longer-cultivated fields of Georgetown County, I have estimated the total number of low-country rice slaves in 1850 at about 58,000. At that time they grew 91 percent of the American rice crop (U.S. Bureau of the Census, *Statistical View of the United States, being a Compendium of the Seventh Census [1850]* [1854; rpt. Washington, D.C., 1970], pp. 94, 306, 210, 216).

4. Georgetown planters paid taxes on 423 domestic slaves in Charleston in 1859. As Georgetown then accounted for 29.5 percent of low-country rice production, one might suppose that the number of Charleston and Savannah domestic slaves owned by all low-country rice planters would be about 1,430. But because planters filling in tax returns may have underreported the number of their domestic slaves, I estimate the total number of such slaves at 2,000 (Rogers, pp. 524–27).

5. I estimate that during the 1850s the number of rice slaves fell by about six

thousand in Colleton County and seven thousand in Beaufort County. See the last section of appendix F.

Cotton production in these two counties was 15,700 bales in 1849 and about 26,200 bales in 1859. (The census mistakenly reported 28,800 bales in the latter year, because it attributed to Colleton County about 2,600 bales raised in St. Johns Colleton Parish, which actually lies in Charleston County. See the last section of appendix F.) As the census figures do not distinguish "sea-island" from other types of cotton, I have been obliged to assume that the increase in sea-island production was at the same rate as that of all cotton in these two counties; in so doing, I may have underestimated sea-island cotton's rate of increase (1850 and 1860 printed census figures; the estimate that 2,600 bales were raised in St. Johns Colleton Parish is my own, based on the manuscript census returns, which report 2,300 bales raised by those producers who each produced at least 50 bales: I have estimated that 300 additional bales were raised by smaller producers).

6. Although Dale Swan asserts that rice production in 1859 was more than four times as valuable as cotton production in the ten South Carolina and Georgia low-country counties, the source for this estimate is not clear. It appears to depend upon an assumption that the cotton sold at between $.10 and $.13 per pound. But sea-island cotton was far more valuable than ordinary cotton, selling in 1857 for $.38 a pound, and in 1858 for $.29. (cf. Dale Swan, "The Structure and Profitability of the Antebellum Rice Industry: 1859" [Ph.D. diss., University of North Carolina, 1972], p. 15).

My estimates are based on the following reasoning: South Carolina's "sea-island" cotton crop (Sept. 1857–Aug. 1858) was 26,700 bags. Most—though not quite all—of this crop was raised in the three low-country counties of Charleston, Colleton, and Beaufort. (Practically none was grown in Georgetown.) A bag contained 300 to 400 pounds. If we assume an average of 350 pounds per bag (which may be too high), the crop weighed 9,345,000 pounds. I assume that one-third of this crop was sold at the 1857 average price for "sea-island" cotton ($.381 per pound) and two-thirds at the 1858 average price ($.293 per pound): an average price for the year's crop of $.322 per pound. This would yield a revenue of $3,009,000. (The average price, from 1850 to 1859, was $.343 per pound.)

Low-country South Carolina's 1859 rice crop was 79,200,000 pounds of clean rice. If this rice sold at $.032 per pound, the revenue was $2,534,000—about 16 percent less than the proceeds of the sea-island cotton.

By similar reasoning, Georgia's sea-island cotton crop (10,000 bags in 1857) would have sold for $1,127,000. Low-country Georgia's 1859 rice crop (31,900,000 pounds of clean rice) would have brought $1,021,000—about 9 percent less than Georgia's revenue for sea-island cotton (Swan, "Antebellum Rice Industry," pp. 15–16; Lewis Gray, *History of Agriculture in the Southern United States to 1860* [Washington, D.C., 1933], pp. 734, 1030–31; my table 23).

J. D. B. DeBow estimated the value of the total U.S. rice crop in 1849 at $4 million, only about two-thirds of which was exported (U.S. Bureau of the Census, *Statistical View*, pp. 176, 188).

7. Gray, *History of Agriculture*, p. 724.

8. Peter Coclanis's somewhat contrary picture of the mid-nineteenth-century low country—stressing incipient decline in the rice industry—arises partly because his focus upon the South Carolina low country excludes Georgia and the Cape Fear River: exactly the regions where the number of rice slaves was growing. Furthermore, he includes within his "low country" three South Carolina counties—Horry, Marion, and Williamsburg—where tidal rice culture was never practiced. Inland rice

may once have grown there, but in the mid–nineteenth century tidal plantations virtually monopolized the production of rice; and the economic situation of these three counties no longer threw light upon the fortunes of the rice industry. And Coclanis, like other historians, became an unwitting victim of the Census Office's spectacular error—12.1 million pounds of rough rice—in underreporting Beaufort County's 1859 production (see appendix E; Peter A. Coclanis, *The Shadow of a Dream: Economic Life and Death in the South Carolina Low Country, 1670–1920* [New York, 1984]).

9. LM, "Season of 1876," Manigault MS, IV (SHC); Gray, *History of Agriculture*, p. 724.

10. American rice production (millions of pounds of clean rice):

	1830s	*1840s*	*1850s (omitting the hurricane year of 1854)*
Annual total produce	88	101	111
Annual exports	72	72	66
Domestic consumption	16	29	45

Note: Exports: see Gray, *History of Agriculture*, p. 1030, for sources. Total produce: see table 22.

11. Rogers, p. 166.

12. The 1860 census mistakenly counted Aiken's Edisto Island plantation as though it were in Colleton County.

13. The census mistakenly counted this Combahee River plantation as though it were in Colleton County.

14. Davidson, pp. 172–73; Joyner, p. 16; Rogers, p. 523.

15. "Where the [planter] owns slaves in different counties or in different states," DeBow conceded, "he will be entered more than once [in the Census Office's figures on the size of a planter's slave holdings]. This will disturb the calculation very little," he alleged, "being only the case among the larger properties, and it will account for the fact that a smaller number of such properties are reported in some of the States than are known to exist, particularly in South Carolina, Virginia and Louisiana" (U.S. Bureau of the Census, *Statistical View*, p. 95).

Compilation of the 1850 and 1860 censuses was principally directed by a Pennsylvania Whig, Joseph Kennedy (superintendent of the census, 1849–53 and 1858–65), who no doubt believed it would be too complicated for his hard-pressed clerks to search out and add together the slaveholdings of a planter in more than one county or parish. DeBow, who was superintendent of the census only from Mar. 1853 until Nov. 1855—but who was responsible in 1854 for the widely circulated *Statistical View of the United States* (a compendium of the 1850 census)—was a proslavery propagandist anxious to persuade Southern nonslaveholders that they had as much interest in defending slavery as did the great slaveholders. Thus DeBow had no ideological impulse to unscramble Kennedy's work: DeBow did not seek to emphasize (more than was unavoidable) the extremely unequal distribution of slaves among the slaveholders (Margo Anderson, *The American Census: A Social History* [New Haven, Conn., 1988], pp. 35–72. J. D. B. DeBow, *The Interest in Slavery of the Southern Non-Slaveholder* [1860], in Eric McKitrick, ed., *Slavery Defended* [Englewood Cliffs, N.J., 1963], pp. 169–77).

16. These dozen families were:

Family	No. of slaves	County
Corbin	470	Glynn (Ga.)
Potter	440	Chatham (Ga.)
Mazyck	ca. 423	Charleston, Georgetown
Rutledge	419	Georgetown, Charleston, Beaufort
Habersham	394	Chatham (Ga.)
Ball	373	Charleston
Doar	342	Charleston, Georgetown
King, Stephen	311	Camden (Ga.)
Screven	310	Beaufort
Johnstone	304	Georgetown
Gibbon	over 300	Chatham (Ga.)
Guerrard	ca. 300	Georgetown, Beaufort, Camden (Ga.)

Note: See Davidson; Julia Smith, *Slavery and Rice Culture in Low Country Georgia, 1750–1860* (Knoxville, Tenn., 1985), pp. 219–26, 54 n for sources.

17. The Butlers of Philadelphia were the twenty-second great rice-planting family.

18. C. Vann Woodward, ed., *Mary Chesnut's Civil War* (New Haven, Conn., 1981), pp. 334, 9 n.

19. U.S. Bureau of the Census, *Statistical View,* p. 302; Richard Wade, *Slavery in the Cities* (New York, 1964), p. 326.

20. Dr. Gabriel Manigault, autobiography, pp. 13–14, Manigault MS (SCHS). Cf. Rogers, pp. 307–9.

21. Dr. Gabriel Manigault, autobiography, pp. 14–15, Manigault MS (SCHS).

22. Ibid., p. 81. C. Vann Woodward and Elisabeth Muhlenfeld, eds., *The Private Mary Chesnut* (New York, 1984), p. 57; Woodward, *Mary Chesnut's Civil War,* p. 44; Davidson, pp. 12, 80, 172–73.

23. RA to AA, Apr. 24–25, 1858 (typescript), Allston MS (SCL).

24. LM, ". . . Notes upon Gowrie," pp. 4–5; also, pp. 13, 6, Manigault MS, IV (SHC).

25. Rogers, pp. 262–63, 524.

26. Peter Wood, *Black Majority* (New York, 1974), pp. 74–75. Charlotte Allston to RA, Mar. 17, 1820; J. J. Ward to RA, Sept. 28, 1838 (Easterby, pp. 54, 83–84).

27. J. Motte Alston, *Rice Planter and Sportsman: The Recollections of J. Motte Alston* (ed. Arney R. Childs: Columbia, S.C., 1953), p. 12; see also pp. 6, xii. Rogers, pp. 188, 173, 166, 522–23.

28. Alston, *Rice Planter and Sportsman,* pp. 107, 71. Rogers, pp. 522–23, 240, 250.

29. Alston, *Rice Planter and Sportsman,* pp. 62–64.

30. Ibid., pp. 51, 119, 67–69, 71.

31. Six thousand dollars was the approximate value of the initial land and the driver, which his father had given him (ibid., pp. 51, 126–27, 101).

32. Ibid., pp. 44, 120, 123–24.

33. Rogers, pp. 339–41. Duncan Heyward, *Seed from Madagascar* (Chapel Hill, N.C., 1937), p. 86. Easterby, p. 266 n. Frances Butler Leigh, *Ten Years on a Georgia Plantation Since the War* (1883; rpt. New York, 1969), p. 153.

34. These comprised 4,383 in Lower All Saints Parish; perhaps 110 at J. Motte Alston's "Woodbourne" (the only important rice plantation in Upper All Saints Parish, except for J. D. Magill's "Oregon" plantation, whose slaves are included with Magill's "Richmond Hill" plantation within the Lower All Saints figure); and possibly 530 on Sandy Island (Joyner, p. 19; Rogers, pp. 253, 256, 527; Easterby, p. 353).

35. Ulrich Phillips, ed., *A Documentary History of American Industrial Society* (Cleveland, Ohio, 1910), 1:115–22. Joyner, pp. 256, 24, 82.

36. "[I] would be obliged to ask a fair price," Weston had insisted, when offering to sell two hundred Laurel Hill slaves to his cousin in 1858 (Joyner, pp. 256, 24, 82).

37. The Weston holdings were 392 slaves in 1850. (The 1850 manuscript census recorded 380 slaves under the name of Plowden Weston's father, F. M. Weston [not 196 slaves as stated in Rogers, p. 524], in addition to Plowden Weston's 12; and Plowden inherited his father's whole estate in 1854 [Rogers, p. 258]). As Plowden Weston was said to be a relatively good master, I guess he achieved the same rate of natural population growth as at Butler Island—10.5 percent in a decade—bringing his holdings to 433 by 1860. As he reported only 334 slaves in the 1860 census, I infer that he sold about 100. (But the number sold may have been closer to 180: see note 40.)

38. Emily Weston, diary, Dec. 24–27, 1859 (Joyner, pp. 24–25, 256).

39. Rogers, pp. 258–59.

40. Pinckney Alston *may* have sold a parcel of as many as 80 slaves to Plowden Weston, along with True Blue and Weehawka, in Dec. 1858. (The reason for this surmise is that Alston held 274 slaves in 1850; he kept some house slaves for his own use—and may have made a gift of a few more to his younger son—and he auctioned 177 in Jan. 1859.)

But if Alston did sell a parcel of slaves to Plowden Weston, then Weston must have sold even more than 100 of his own Laurel Hill slaves in Dec. 1859. For Weston surely owned well over 400 of his own slaves in Dec. 1858 (see note 37); and if he bought 80 more then (in order to keep True Blue and Weehawka at high production, while he continued during 1859 to try to get rid of Laurel Hill), he would have had to sell many more than 100 in Dec. 1859 to reduce his holdings to the 334 slaves whom he reported to the census in 1860.

Thus an estimate that 476 Waccamaw slaves were sold between Dec. 1857 and Dec. 1859 would be a conservative one. If, in fact, Alston sold 80 to Weston in Dec. 1858, and if Weston then sold about 180 Laurel Hill slaves in Dec. 1859, a total of about 636 Waccamaw slaves were sold during this two-year period.

41. Advertisement, Jan. 13, 1859, Allston MS (SCHS); Easterby, p. 414.

42. Benjamin theoretically bought these slaves in his own name. But Pinckney Alston required Robert Allston to sign the bonds for them; and as Benjamin—because of the Southern war for independence—could never pay for them, Robert Allston's debt to Pinckney Alston for these slaves was one of the financial encumbrances which led to the bankruptcy sale of Robert Allston's estate in 1869 (J. B. Allston to RA, Jan. 11, 1859 [typescript]; AA, journal, Apr. 25, 1865, [SCL]).

43. I presume Alston might have sold the gang in large parcels for some $580 in the round, since a week later the Rutledge heirs sold a gang of sixty-one slaves at $575 "round," even though they had removed the valuable driver from the parcel (Frederic Bancroft, *Slave-Trading in the Old South* [Baltimore, 1931], p. 177). J. B. Allston to RA, Jan. 18, 1859; Robertson, Blacklock & Co. to RA, Jan. 13, 1859 (Easterby, pp. 152, 414).

44. Alston, *Rice Planter, and Sportsman*, p. 126. Joyner, p. 29.

45. J. L. Petigru to RA, Apr. 1, 1859 (Easterby, p. 157; see also pp. 148–49, 153, 157, 352–54).

46. Joyner, pp. 24–25.

47. Davidson, p. 181.

48. Rogers, pp. 256, 277. Joyner, p. 25 and its note 46. Bancroft, *Slave-Trading in the Old South,* p. 177.

49. Bancroft, *Slave-Trading in the Old South,* pp. 175, 177.

50. 1850 U.S. Manuscript Census.

51. RK Jr. to Thomas Butler, Jan. 20, 1833, Jan. 5, 12, Feb. 3, 13, 1834, Butler MS (HSP).

52. Lawrence Rowland, " 'Alone on the River': The Rise and Fall of the Savannah River Rice Plantations of St. Peter's Parish, South Carolina," *South Carolina Historical Magazine* 88 (1987): 124, 141–43. Davidson, pp. 188–89. Robert Habersham & Son to CM, Jan. 30, 1852, Manigault MS (SCHS).

53. See chapter 5.

54. Rogers, p. 285. CM to Tom Middleton (draft, never sent), Sept. 15, 1846, CM letterbook, Manigault MS (SCHS); Elizabeth Allston, diary, July 25, 1861, Allston-Pringle-Hill MS (SCHS).

55. H. A. Middleton Jr., plantation journal, pp. 79, 81, Middleton MS (SCHS).

56. Ibid., pp. 131, 137. Elizabeth Allston, diary, July 24, 26, 31, 1861 (SCHS).

57. H. A. Middleton to his wife, [July] 24, [1862]; Mar. 4, 1864, Cheves-Middleton MS (SCHS). Rogers, pp. 317, 374, 427, 427 n.

58. Rogers, pp. 399–404.

59. H. A. Middleton to his wife, Nov. 5, 1862; [July] 24, [1862]; to Harriott Middleton, [July 25, 1862]; Jan. 5, [1863], Cheves-Middleton MS (SCHS).

60. H. A. Middleton to Harriott Middleton, Jan. 5, [1863] (SCHS).

61. H. A. Middleton to his wife, [July] 24, [1862]; to Harriott Middleton, [July 25, 1862] (SCHS).

62. H. A. Middleton to Harriott Middleton, Jan. 12, July 19, 1863 (emphasis added), (SCHS).

63. Weston's *Documents Connected with the History of South Carolina* (London, 1856) is one of the few nineteenth-century works on colonial Carolina still regularly consulted by modern scholars.

64. Woodward, *Mary Chesnut's Civil War,* p. 331 (Apr. 29, 1862); Elizabeth Collins, *Memories of the Southern States* (Taunton, England, 1865), p. 11.

65. 1860 U.S. Manuscript Census, Beaufort District, St. Peters Parish, p. 2. In J. D. B. DeBow's compendium of the 1850 census, he acknowledged that in some areas the census takers had recorded only "a very small . . . part of the whole" number of deaths (U.S. Bureau of the Census, *Statistical View,* p. 58).

66. See p. 402.

67. Whole U.S.: 1,770,400 (slave children) / 3,953,700 (total slave population) [1860 printed U.S. census]. Alston slave sale: 57 (children) / 177 (total number of slaves).

68. Whole U.S.: 541,200 (slave children aged 10–14) / 702,500 (slave women aged 20–49) [1860 printed U.S. census]. Alston slave sale: 15 (slave children aged 10–14) / 44 (slave women aged 20–49).

69. Richard Steckel reports that twentieth-century "African women infected with *Plasmodium falciparum* malaria . . . had newborn weights that were 263 grams below those born to non-infected mothers." And mothers whose infants' birth weights are

low tend to have unusually large numbers of fetal losses (Richard Steckel, "A Dreadful Childhood: The Excess Mortality of American Slaves," *Social Science History* 10 [1986]: 441–42. Steckel, "Birth Weights and Infant Mortality Among American Slaves," *Explorations in Economic History* 23 [1986]: 193).

70. I estimate a fertility rate of 6.6 among all slave women in the rice kingdom who were alive on their fifteenth birthday (see p. 415 and its note 78). The corresponding rate for slave women in the whole South was probably about 7.5—a figure consonant with the growth rate of the South's slave population (see p. 416, note 82).

71. Census figures misleadingly imply that in the whole South, of all slave children under age five in 1840, about 9 percent died during the next ten years. In Georgetown, by contrast, the same misleading figures imply that some 35 percent of the children in this age-group perished. But when statisticians suitably adjust these figures for census errors, the numbers suggested in the text are likely to be fairly accurate, as explained in the following paragraphs:

Georgetown County. The 1840 census reported 4,408 slave children aged zero to nine. I assume that 58 percent of them were aged zero to four (because in Georgetown this ratio was 59.9 percent in 1850 and 57.4 percent in 1860). Thus about 2,557 slave children were aged zero to four in 1840. The number of Georgetown's slave children still alive in 1850 (i.e., aged ten to fourteen then) was 1,650. This implies that about 907 of this cohort of children died during the 1840s—a mortality rate of 35 percent.

The disappearance of these children from the census returns cannot be explained by emigration because—as shown in the next paragraph of the text—the 1840s were a period of large importation of slaves into Georgetown, not of exportation.

The whole South. The 1840 census reported 844,100 slave children aged zero to nine. In 1850 there were 793,300 slave children aged ten to nineteen. Thus 50,800 of this cohort of children died during the 1840s (the number of manumissions and of permanent fugitives of this age being negligible)—a mortality rate of 6 percent. As slave child mortality rates were always much higher for the cohort aged zero to four than for that aged five to nine, the census figures imply that the rate for the former cohort was about 9 percent.

But these figures (both for the whole South, and for Georgetown) are surely too low. The census takers—who often rounded off the ages of slaves—seem to have reported many eight- or nine-year-old slaves as "10." Thus the reported number of children aged zero to nine was too small, while the reported number of children aged ten was too large. Similar census errors seem to have occurred in every age cohort. By careful comparison of the figures from the 1850 and 1860 censuses, I estimate that the South's actual mortality rate for the 1850 cohort of children aged zero to four was about 16 percent by 1860. The rate was probably the same during the 1840s.

And by similar analysis of Georgetown's figures in the 1850 and 1860 printed censuses, I estimate that Georgetown's mortality rate for the same age cohort during the 1850s was about 41 percent—a rate probably true also in the 1840s.

72. In 1850 the number of Georgetown's slaves aged ten to fourteen was 1,650, while those aged forty to forty-four totaled only 714. If each five-year group between these two had simply reflected the natural diminution of a stable population, one might have expected slave numbers approximately as projected in column a below. But the number of slaves actually recorded in the 1850 census (column b) shows that the number of slaves (aged fifteen to thirty-nine by 1850) imported into Georgetown during the decade must have approximated 1,959—in addition perhaps to several hundred younger and older slaves accompanying these ones in family groups. These

imported slaves principally (or perhaps fully) accounted for the growth of slave population (by 2,260 slaves) during the 1840s:

Age	(a) Expected no. of slaves	(b) Actual no. of slaves*	(c) Approximate no. of slaves imported
10–14	1,650	1,650	
15–19	1,600	2,624	1,024
20–24	1,550	1,671	121
25–29	1,450	1,804	354
30–34	1,289	1,364	75
35–39	1,039	1,424	385
40–44	714	714	
TOTAL			1,959

*For sources: see Sherman L. Ricards and George M. Blackburn, "A Demographic History of Slavery: Georgetown County, South Carolina, 1850," *South Carolina Historical Magazine* 76 (1975): 218.

A similar growth of Georgetown's slave population had occurred during the 1820s, and again the bulge of youngish slaves was a sure sign that importation of "prime hands"—not a big natural population growth—fueled the development of the tidal rice plantations. Thus in 1830 Georgetown had 4,316 slaves aged twenty-four to thirty-five, but only 3,629 aged ten to twenty-three; yet the latter group undoubtedly included a good number of young slaves recently imported. These figures suggest that in the 1820s, as in the 1840s, the growth of the enslaved population arose almost wholly (or perhaps entirely) from the importation of prime hands—not from a great excess of births over deaths (printed U.S. census, 1830).

73. In the next three paragraphs of the text I explain the reasons for estimating the decennial growth rate of slaves on rice plantations at 4 percent. This would imply during the 1850s a natural growth of 730 in Georgetown's slave population. As this population actually declined by 144, the number of slaves exported may have been about 874.

74. [RA], memo, n.d. [probably 1858], fiche 12-16-11, Allston MS, (SCL). RA to J. B. Allston, Jan. 13, 1859 (Easterby, p. 151). 1860 Manuscript Census; inventory, Apr. 1864 file 12-6-25, Allston MS (SCHS).

For Butler Island, see p. 237.

75. In Jan. 1845 Weehaw had about 263 slaves. During the next seventeen years there were 402 births and 378 deaths. (Two of these deaths—in 1861—were not listed, because the record was "negligently kept" after young Middleton entered the Confederate army.) The 324 slaves in 1855 included the initial population of 299, and 25 born during the year. The 301 slaves in 1857 included an initial population of 279, and 22 born during the year (H. A. Middleton Jr., Weehaw plantation journal, opposite p. 1, Cheves-Middleton MS [SCHS]).

76. *1833 through 1848.* Gowrie's decennial rate of decrease was *36 percent.* (The population was 122: i.e., the 72 who lived at Gowrie in Jan. 1833, plus net imports of 50 slaves. The excess of deaths over births was 61, which decreased the population 50 percent during sixteen years—equivalent to a 36 percent decennial decrease.)

1849 through 1860. Gowrie's decennial rate of decrease was *42.5 percent.* (The population was 179: i..e, the 61 still alive at the end of 1848, plus 58 slaves brought in to stock the new East Hermitage tract, plus net imports of 60 more slaves after Jan. 1849. The excess of deaths over births was 85, which decreased the population 47.5 percent during these twelve years—equivalent to a 42.5 percent decennial decrease.)

Averaging the *36 percent* decennial decrease during the first sixteen years with the *42.5 percent* decennial decrease during the last twelve years results in about a *39 percent* rate of decennial decrease over the whole twenty-eight years. (Annual figures for Gowrie are from chapter 3 [table 6].)

77. 1850 and 1860 U.S. Manuscript Censuses. This figure for 1850 is 101 slaves more than those reported in Rogers (p. 524); evidently Rogers, while recording 1,092 slaves (listed on frames 1025–50), omitted the other 101 male slaves of Ward's who—confusingly—are listed on frames 88–90 of the microfilm at the South Carolina Department of Archives and History.

78. This is slightly lower than my estimate for Butler Island (I infer a fertility rate there—for all slave women who survived to age 15—of 6.8), because I believe Butler Island—with its decennial growth rate of some 10.5 percent—to have been a little less unhealthy than the average rice plantation. Probably slave women there lived a little longer than elsewhere in the rice kingdom, and therefore bore slightly more children. My estimate of Butler Island's fertility rate is explained in chapter 8, note 22.

Robert Fogel estimates the fertility of all U.S. slave women who survived *until age forty-nine* at 9.2. As explained in note 82, I estimate the fertility of all U.S. slave women who survived *until age fifteen* at 7.5 (a figure substantially higher than that for the rice kingdom). Because many slave women died between the ages of fifteen and forty-nine (and because the fertility of those who died was smaller than of those who survived to age forty-nine), my estimate of 7.5 is likely to be consonant with Fogel's estimate of 9.2 (Robert Fogel, *Without Consent or Contract* [New York, 1989], p. 149).

79. This estimate depends on figures presented earlier in this section (p. 412). They show that a slave child on a Georgetown rice plantation was only about five-eights as likely to survive to age fifteen as a slave child elsewhere in the South. Since about 54 percent of Southern slave children survived to age fifteen (see note 82), only about 34 percent of slave children on rice plantations survived to age fifteen (⅝ × 54% = 33.8%). Thus the child mortality rate on rice plantations (to age fifteen) must have been about 66 percent. This estimate is consonant with the age-specific mortality rates suggested in note 82.

80. The presumption that about thirty years separated a mother from her median surviving child appears consonant with the data in Richard Steckel, "Children and Choice: A Comparative Analysis of Slave and White Fertility in the Antebellum South," in Robert Fogel et al., eds. *Without Consent or Contract, Conditions of Slave Life and the Transition to Freedom: Technical Papers* (New York, 1992), 2:375–76, 379.

81. The child mortality rate for the entire United States was about 29 percent. As the slaves' rate was substantially higher, the rate for the free population must have been a little lower than 29 percent. Richard Steckel, "Work, Disease, and Diet in the Health and Mortality of American Slaves," in Fogel et al., *Without Consent, Technical Papers,* 2:490. Steckel's figures here are based on Michael Haines and Roger Avery, "The American Life Table of 1830–1860: An Evaluation," *Journal of Interdisciplinary History* 11 (1980): 88.

82. This figure of 46 percent is consonant with the known rate of growth of the Southern slave population. For if slave child mortality (to age fifteen) was 46 percent, and if the average fertility of all Southern slave women who survived until age fifteen

was 7.5 (somewhat higher than Butler Island's figure of about 6.8), then on average 4.05 of a woman's children survived. With about thirty years separating a mother from her median surviving child, the South's decennial growth rate would be 26.6 percent— which, in fact, it was. My estimate of a 46 percent child mortality rate for all Southern slaves is based on the age-specific rates suggested in the following table, and explained in the notes to that table.

The estimate of a 66 percent child mortality rate on rice plantations is explained in note 79. It is consonant with the estimates of age-specific rates in the following table:

Age-Specific Child Mortality Rates (to age 15, estimated)

	Slaves in whole south (%)	Rice slaves (%)
Mortality rate, first year (Dead/children born alive)	$27.5^{a/}$	$43^{d/}$
Mortality rate, Ages 1–4 inclusive (Dead/those alive at first birthday)	$18.9^{b/}$	$23.4^{e/}$
Mortality rate, Ages 5–14 inclusive (Dead/those alive at fifth birthday)	$8.5^{c/}$	$22^{f/}$

Cumulative Child Mortality Rates (to age 15, estimated)

	Slaves in whole South (%)	Rice slaves (%)
Died before first birthday	27.5	43
Died before fifth birthday	41.9	56.3
Died before fifteenth birthday	46.2	65.9

Notes:

a. This estimate of infant mortality comprises two components—the "neonatal" and the "postneonatal" mortality rates:

(I) *"Neonatal mortality rate," i.e., during the first month of the infant's life:*

I accept Richard Steckel's figure of 15.2 percent (Steckel, "Birth Weights and Infant Mortality Among American Slaves," *Explorations in Economic History* 23 [1986]: 192). Steckel convincingly argues that previous estimates have been much too low, because incomplete plantation records frequently omitted the births and deaths of infants who died soon after birth. The accurate Butler Island records fully support Steckel's surmise, for they show a 13.3 percent "neonatal" mortality rate on the sea-island cotton plantation, and a 19.0 percent rate on the rice plantation (appendix D, appendix Table 3).

But I have not accepted the addition of 7.5 percent to this rate—for neonatal tetanus—which Steckel has suggested (Steckel, "A Dreadful Childhood: The Excess Mortality of American Slaves," *Social Science History* 10 [1986]: 456), because (1) the Butler records indicate that the mortality rate for neonatal tetanus was about 2.5 percent or 3.0 percent ("Lockjaw": table 19), not 7.5 percent; and (2) as Robert Fogel seems to imply (Robert Fogel, et al., eds., *Without Consent or Contract, Evidence and Methods* [New York, 1992], p. 286) mortality from neonatal tetanus may already be included within the chain of reasoning which led to Steckel's neonatal estimate of 15.2 percent.

(II) *"Postneonatal mortality rate," i.e., during months 2–12 of the infant's life:*

I start with Steckel's figure of a 16.2 percent mortality rate on the eleven plantations he studied (in Fogel et al., *Without Consent, Technical Papers*, 2:495). But this figure is substantially affected by the presence of three rice plantations in the group. Steckel has discovered that their infant mortality rates were much higher than those on the nonrice plantations: "Compared with other crops," he explains, "the expected probability of death in rice cultivation was 41 percent higher among infants." As about 35 percent of all the infants he studied were on these three rice plantations, I have broken down Steckel's figure of 16.2 percent into two components: mortality rates of about 14.2 percent on nonrice plantations and about 20.0 percent on the three rice plantations. This would imply that in the whole South (where the proportion of slaves working on rice plantations was much smaller than in Steckel's sample) the "postneonatal" rate would be about 14.5 percent. Combining this with the "neonatal" rate of 15.2 percent results in a cumulative rate (for the whole first year of the infant's life) of 27.5 percent $[1 - (.855 \times 84.8\%) = 27.5\%]$.

b. For slave children of ages one to four inclusive, Steckel reports a 20.1 percent mortality rate on his eleven plantations; again, he finds a higher rate on rice plantations than elsewhere—"26 percent higher" (in Fogel et al., *Without Consent, Technical Papers,* 2:397, 407). Again, I have broken his figure into two components: mortality rates of about 18.6 percent on nonrice plantations and about 23.4 percent on his rice plantations. It follows that in the whole South the rate would be about 18.9 percent.

c. For slave children of ages five to fourteen inclusive, Steckel's figures imply a 9.0 percent mortality rate on his eleven plantations; and once more he finds a higher rate on rice plantations than elsewhere—"28.7 percent higher" (ibid.). By breaking his figure into two components, one discovers a mortality rate of about 8.3 percent on nonrice plantations and 10.7 percent on his rice plantations. This implies in the whole South a rate of about 8.5 percent.

d. I estimate the rice kingdom's infant mortality rate as a little higher than the Butler Island rate (38.1 percent), because Butler Island—with its 10.5 percent decennial population increase—was probably not quite so unhealthy for young children as the average rice plantation: certainly it was less unhealthy than Gowrie and many other Savannah River rice plantations. My estimate is also higher than the figure Richard Steckel reports for the Ball family's three rice plantations. Probably two of those three plantations underreported neonatal deaths; and by presuming that neonatal deaths accounted for 50 percent of infant mortality on these two plantations (as they did at Butler Island), one may estimate a total of thirty-three unrecorded neonatal deaths, which would bring the infant mortality rate on these three plantations to about 35 percent—a figure comparable to that at Butler Island. But here again, I suspect that the Ball plantations were less unhealthy than the rice kingdom norm. Masters who cared enough about their plantations to keep accurate records were likely, in other respects too, to be less uncaring than the average rice planter.

e. This estimate for rice kingdom children of ages one to four inclusive is derived from Steckel's figures, as explained in note b.

f. This is my estimate of Butler Island's mortality rate for children of ages five to fourteen inclusive, derived from the figures in appendix D, appendix Table 4 (and explained in the "Note" to that table). Mortality among children over five was lower at Butler Island than at Gowrie, but higher than that reported by Steckel on the Ball plantations. I suspect the Ball plantations were very untypical of other rice plantations for this age cohort. Certainly the 1860 census indicates that child mortality rates for this age-group on Georgetown rice plantations were much higher than those elsewhere in the slave South. Of all Georgetown slave children aged zero to four in 1850 (and even allowing for the exportation of a few of these very young children during the 1850s), about 41 percent had perished by 1860.

When demographers adjust the 1860 census for its probable reporting of many slave children as older than they actually were (e.g., census takers' reporting four-year-old slave children as though they were five; eight- and nine-year-old children as though they were ten; and eighteen- and nineteen-year-olds as though they were twenty), I believe they will find that about 16 percent of all Southern slaves aged zero to four in 1850 died before 1860. The comparable figure for Georgetown—perhaps 41 percent—indicates that slave children in this age cohort died more than twice as fast on rice plantations as elsewhere in the South: a difference even greater than Steckel's pathbreaking research has suggested (see note 71). I believe demographers will find that their adjusted figures for Georgetown will be consonant with my estimate of about a 22 percent mortality rate between the fifth and fifteenth birthdays.

Chapter 16

1. George Rawick, ed., *The American Slave* (1941; rpt. Westport, Conn., 1971–72), II, part ii, 157, 298 (quotation); First Supplement (Westport, Conn., 1977) (hereafter "S1"), XI, 105, 290.

2. Rawick, III, part iv, 61.

3. Ibid., III, part iii, 92.

4. Ibid., S1, XI, 201.

5. Ibid. III, iii, 92.

6. Rawick, S1, XI, 197–99.

7. Rawick, II, ii, 303–4.

8. Ibid. II, ii, 305, 311, 304.

9. "(Races)" is Chandler's insertion, to explain her maid's meaning. Ibid. II, ii, 304.

10. Ibid. II, ii, 305, 304, 307–8.

11. Rogers, pp. 392, 406–8, 414, 260. Rawick, S1, XI, 199.

12. Emphasis added. Rawick, II, ii, 319.

13. Ibid., II, ii, 317. That Hemingway was an overseer of the Wards was confirmed by Ellen Godfrey. Ibid., II, ii, 158.

14. Ibid. II, ii, 305, 311.

15. Davidson, pp. 80, 172. Rawick, II, i, 110, 112–13.

16. Rawick, II, i, 110. BA to RA, June 17, to Henrietta, June 20 [?], 1860, Allston MS (SCHS). Rogers, p. 261.

17. Joyner, pp. 27–28, 257.

18. Cf. F. L. Olmsted, *The Cotton Kingdom* (1861; rpt. New York, 1953), e.g., pp. 387–90, 418–19, 431–32, 437, 456–57.

19. Rawick, II, ii, 301.

20. Rawick, S1, XI, 83. Peter Wood, *Black Majority* (New York, 1974), p. 136.

21. Rawick, II, ii, 303.

22. Ibid. III, iii, 92; II, ii, 159, 303. Davidson, p. 226. Joyner, pp. 19, 27–28, 257.

23. Rawick, II, ii, 287; III, iv, 63. Rutledge is quoted on p. 337.

24. Rawick II, ii, 323. McCusky was sufficiently accepted in polite Georgetown society that in 1866 he was thought a suitable tenant for Benjamin Allston's comfortable Pawleys Island residence. J. B. Allston to BA, June 3, 1866 (Easterby, p. 221).

25. Rawick, II, ii, 287–88. To intimidate blacks by fictions as well as by actual brutality was a long-established custom. For example, Frederick Olmsted heard a Tennessee white man in 1854 tell a group of black children that "when a nigger do n't behave," Olmsted's dog would, at command, "snap a nigger's head right off, just as easy as you'd take a chicken's head off with an ax" (Olmsted, *A Journey in the Back Country* [London, 1860], p. 247).

26. Leon Litwack, *Been in the Storm So Long* (New York, 1979), pp. 87–93.

27. Rawick, S1, XI, 200; II, ii, 318.

28. Ibid., III, iv, 60; II, ii, 302; II, i, 197. Kemble, *Journal,* pp. 307–8.

29. Rawick, II, i, 146–47.

30. Ibid., 146, 115; II, ii, 317–18. Rogers, pp. 261, 256, 256 n, 314.

31. Frances Butler Leigh, *Ten Years on a Georgia Plantation Since the War* (1883; rpt. New York, 1969), p. 149. Leigh's informant in 1869 evidently was the wife of Francis Weston, who was Plowden Weston's first cousin. The narrative centers on Plowden Weston's English wife, Emily Esdaile Weston, and on her ally Alexander Glennie, the English-born Episcopal clergyman at Waccamaw peninsula. By the time of the overseer's alleged killing, Plowden Weston had died and his wife was back in England. Although the details of Leigh's story are garbled (as she later came to realize), the Hagley slaves may indeed have "murdered the overseer," as Leigh in 1869 reported Mrs. Francis Weston to have stated.

32. Rawick, II, i, 198, 197; II, ii, 284–85; S1, XI, 188; II, ii, 288.

33. Ibid., II, ii, 156. A similar wording, sung by freedmen and women at Benjamin Allston's plantation, is quoted on p. 381.

34. Rawick, II, ii, 157.

35. H. B. Stowe, *Uncle Tom's Cabin* (1852; rpt. [ed. Kenneth Lynn] Cambridge, Mass., 1962), p. 288 (chap. 25). Rawick, II, ii, 284–85. Rogers, pp. 356–58.

36. Rawick, II, i, 146–47.

37. Horry in this instance was referring to a postwar achievement of the former slaves.

38. Rawick, II, ii, 311–12.

39. Ibid., 309.

40. Ibid., 310.

Chapter 17

1. William Freehling, *Prelude to Civil War: The Nullification Controversy in South Carolina, 1816–1836* (New York, 1968), p. 335.

2. Robert Allston, "Rice," *DeBow's Review* 1 (1846): 340.

3. Ulrich Phillips, *American Negro Slavery* (New York, 1918), and *Life and Labor in the Old South* (Boston, 1929). Kenneth Stampp, *The Peculiar Institution* (New York, 1956).

4. John Blassingame, *The Slave Community* (New York, 1972). Eugene Genovese, *Roll, Jordan, Roll: The World the Slaves Made* (New York, 1974). Herbert Gutman, *The Black Family in Slavery and Freedom, 1750–1925* (New York, 1976). Charles Joyner, *Down by the Riverside: A South Carolina Slave Community* (Urbana, Ill., 1984). Deborah Gray White, *Ar'n't I a Woman: Female Slaves in the Plantation South* (New York, 1985).

5. Ronald Walters, *The Antislavery Appeal* (Baltimore, 1976). David Brion Davis, *The Problem of Slavery in the Age of Revolution, 1770–1823* (Ithaca, N.Y., 1975). Leon Litwack, *Been in the Storm So Long* (New York, 1979).

6. "Our experiments in ploughing [have been] of the most striking and apparent advantage. . . . Some of the finest rice was made from the [plowed] land." John Butler to PB, Jan. 13, 1841, Butler MS (HSP).

7. Olmsted, *A Journey in the Seaboard Slave States* (New York, 1856), pp. 480–81.

8. Kemble, *Journal*, p. 314.

9. Theodore Rosengarten, ed., *All God's Dangers* (New York, 1974), pp. 26–27.

10. Joyner. Margaret Creel, *"A Peculiar People": Slave Religion and Community-Culture Among the Gullahs* (New York, 1988).

Index

Numbers in *italics* refer to main discussions. Slaves are alphabetized by first name (e.g., "Jack, Short") unless they had a surname known before 1865. (A) indicates an Allston slave, (B) a Butler slave, and (C) a former slave reported in Chandler's interviews. All other slaves (unless specifically identified) were Manigault's.